# SOFTWARE DESIGN: FROM PROGRAMMING TO ARCHITECTURE

**ERIC J. BRAUDE**
*Boston University*

JOHN WILEY & SONS, INC.

ACQUISITIONS EDITOR    Paul Crockett
MARKETING MANAGER    Katherine Hepburn
SENIOR EDITORIAL ASSISTANT    Jovan Yglecias
EDITORIAL ASSISTANT    Simon Durkin
SENIOR PRODUCTION EDITOR    Christine Cervoni
ILLUSTRATION EDITOR    Sandra Rigby
SENIOR DESIGNER    Karin Kincheloe

This book was set in 10/12 Times Roman by Publication Services, Inc. and printed and bound by Malloy Lithographing, Inc. The cover was printed by Phoenix Color Corp.

This book is printed on acid free paper.

*Library of Congress Cataloging-in-Publication Data*
Braude, Eric J.
    Software design : from programming to architecture / Eric Braude.
        p. cm.
    Includes bibliographical references and index.
    ISBN 0–471–20459–5 (cloth)
        1. Computer software—Development.  I. Title.

QA76.76.D47 B73 2003
005.1—dc21

2002190816

WIE ISBN: 0–471–42920–1

Printed in the United States of America

10 9 8 7 6 5 4 3 2 1

*To Judy*

# *PREFACE*

This book is written for students who have taken courses in Java programming and data structures, and who now need to learn software design methods. It assumes the technical maturity that results from studying topics such as sorting and searching algorithms. The book begins where data structures courses end—close to the code level—then graduates step by step in abstraction and scope. In particular, it leaves software architectures and frameworks to the last chapters. This is because experience has convinced the author that generalities, architectures and abstractions interest students only after they have worked with and implemented software designs at a lower level.

## CHOICE OF TOPICS

To appreciate the context of software design, students need to understand the basics of software process. The book therefore includes a prologue on the development process that can be covered and reviewed at any time during a software design course.

Because design patterns have proven so useful as a set of techniques and as a language among software engineers, they occupy an important place in this book (Chapters 6–9). It is challenge enough for students to learn the classic patterns introduced by "The Gang of Four" (Gamma et al. [Ga]), and thus no special attempt has been made to include other design patterns except for the occasional one such as *Null*.

Before approaching design patterns, students need to understand the very goals and motivations of software design, and for that reason the book begins by discussing these issues and their manifestations in programs (Chapters 1-3).

Understanding Object Orientation itself is essential (Chapter 4), and so is a habit of creating UML for expressing designs (Chapter 5).

Chapters 10–12 cover Component technology, using Java Beans and .NET as examples. Component thinking has already established its usefulness, and since Web Services are components, it is growing in importance.

The last Chapters (13 and 14) cover Object-Oriented Analysis and Design, including Software Architectures and Frameworks. By the time students reach this part of the book, the author has found them motivated to "put it all together."

## ORGANIZATION

This text begins with programming issues such as method specification, moves on to midlevel techniques such as design patterns and components, and ends with architectures and frameworks. This order is the reverse of the Waterfall software development process, of course. Its relationship with the Waterfall development process is illustrated in Figure P.1.

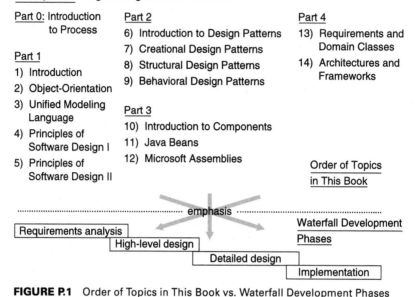

Prerequisites: Programming and Data Structures

**Part 0: Introduction to Process**

**Part 1**
1) Introduction
2) Object-Orientation
3) Unified Modeling Language
4) Principles of Software Design I
5) Principles of Software Design II

**Part 2**
6) Introduction to Design Patterns
7) Creational Design Patterns
8) Structural Design Patterns
9) Behavioral Design Patterns

**Part 3**
10) Introduction to Components
11) Java Beans
12) Microsoft Assemblies

**Part 4**
13) Requirements and Domain Classes
14) Architectures and Frameworks

Order of Topics in This Book

emphasis

Waterfall Development Phases

Requirements analysis

High-level design

Detailed design

Implementation

**FIGURE P.1**  Order of Topics in This Book vs. Waterfall Development Phases

# APPROACHES TO TEACHING SOFTWARE DESIGN WITH THIS BOOK

A straightforward approach to using this book is to simply cover the Prologue and then Chapters 1 through 14 in sequence. However, this book is organized to accommodate several teaching strategies.

Next, we describe two basic approaches to teaching software design, and an account of how this book accommodates them. Whichever approach is taken, Chapter 12 on Microsoft Assemblies can be omitted without prejudicing the flow of learning. This chapter is included because Microsoft's .NET architecture is a good illustration of components, and because it complements the Java Beans material.

## Approach 1: Teaching design separately from the other aspects of software engineering

Instructors following this approach will teach Chapters 1 through 12 in sequence if they want students to progress from where they typically are when the course begins—at the programmer level—to dealing with design at the highest levels. Variations on this approach depend on whether the instructor wants to include software engineering principles (Prologue), de-emphasize design patterns (Chapters 6 through 9), de-emphasize components (Chapters 10 through 12), or include architectures and frameworks (Chapters 13 and 14).

### Approach 2: Teaching software engineering as a software design course, or software design as a software engineering course

Instructors following this approach will cover the Prologue (on process), Chapters 1 through 5 (on design principles and notation), Chapter 13 (requirements and OO analysis), and Chapter 14 (architectures and frameworks). With the remaining time, the instructor will choose from the chapters on design patterns (6 through 9) or components (10 through 12).

## DEPENDENCIES AMONG THE CHAPTERS

The dependencies of chapters on each other are shown in Figure P.2. A solid line means that one cannot really understand the chapter at the beginning of the arrow unless one understands the chapter at its end. A light dotted arrow also denotes dependency, but a weak one: One can learn most of the dependent chapter without having to cover the other one. Note that all of the chapters following Chapter 3 (on UML) depend strongly upon it.

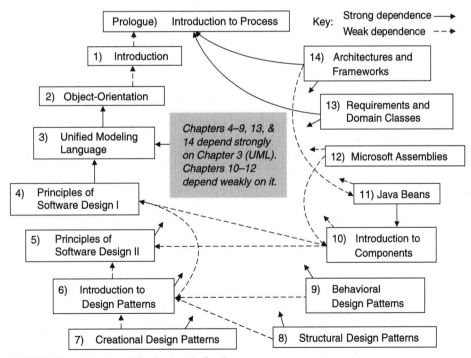

**FIGURE P.2**   Relation of Topics in this Book

This book is written to provide students with a window into the satisfactions and challenges of software design, present and future. Its practical rewards are maintainable, flexible, and clear applications. Its ultimate reward is an aesthetic sense of harmony.

## WEB SITE

The web site for this book can be found at `www.Wiley.com/college/braude`. Students will find the complete source code for all of the examples there, together with code associated with exercises. Instructors will find solutions to many of the exercises there as well.

All of the figures occurring in this book are available to faculty and students as fully editable PowerPoint slides at the web site. A web site is a living thing, and it is expected that the site will adapt to accommodate the ongoing needs of students and faculty.

# *ACKNOWLEDGMENTS*

I want first to acknowledge the many fruitful discussions about design I have enjoyed with my students at Boston University's Metropolitan College. Although these students range from the totally uninitiated to the experienced software engineer, every one has provided insight, whether it be technical or as a prod to me to improve my teaching and writing. Tanya Zlateva, Chairman of the Metropolitan College Computer Science Department and Jay Halfond, Dean of the Metropolitan College have encouraged me at every step. I am grateful to my faculty colleagues at the University for their feedback, and to the reviewers for their splendid and helpful comments: Jorge L. Diaz-Herrera, Southern Polytechnic State University, Computing and Software Engineering; David C. Kung, University of Texas at Arlington, Computer Science Engineering; David L. Levine, Washington University in St. Louis, Computer Science; Ethan V. Munson, University of Wisconsin, Milwaukee, Computer Science; Allen Parish, University of Alabama, Computer Science; David C. Rine, George Mason University, Computer Science; and Shengru Tu, University of New Orleans, Computer Science Dept.

Paul Crockett, Computer Science Editor at John Wiley & Sons, has shown invaluable persistence, faith, and insight, without which this project would not have succeeded. In this, he has been vigorously assisted by Jovan Yglesias. I am grateful to Christine Cervoni for her unfailing patience in shepherding the production process.

My dear son Michael, a Computer Science major and budding software engineer, has helped me enormously by providing me with smiles, frowns, or comments as I have discussed this book's topics with him. Thanks for being such an affectionate guinea pig, Mike.

Finally, I want to record my appreciation and love for my dear wife, Judy, whose constant affection, encouragement and support have enabled me to contribute this book.

# SUMMARY TABLE OF CONTENTS

# CONTENTS

## PART III. *COMPONENTS*

# THE SOFTWARE PROCESS

The principal challenges in developing useful software are the complexity of code and the tendency for project goals to shift while projects are under way. This book explains how to create designs that meet these challenges. The present chapter reviews the process by which software is produced, enabling the reader to understand the context of complexity and shifting project goals.

## 0.1 INTRODUCTION TO SOFTWARE PROCESS

A software project passes through identifiable phases before a usable application emerges. There are several ways to progress through these phases, and each way is called a "Software process."

### 0.1.1 The Phases of Software Process

The main phases of a software process are listed in Figure 0.1.

1. *Requirements Analysis* (answers "WHAT?")
   Specifying what the application must do

2. *Design* (answers "HOW?")
   Specifying what the parts will be, and how they will fit together

3. *Implementation* (a.k.a. "CODING")
   Writing the code

4. *Testing*
   Executing the application with test data for input

5. *Maintenance*
   Repairing defects and adding capability

**FIGURE 0.1**  Main Phases of Software Process

Figure 0.2 shows examples of what these phases produce for a personal finance application.

The requirements phase causes difficulty for many technically minded students. Requirements are often confused with design. As will be seen, requirements answer the question "what?" rather than "how?" One litmus test for requirements is that they should be clear to the layman—a person who knows nothing about technical concepts such as programming and object orientation. On the other hand, the *design* deals with technical issues such as the classes that the application is to be built from and how they relate via inheritance, etc. The layman is not expected to understand these aspects.

- *Requirements Analysis:* Text
  e.g., "... The application shall display the balance in the user's bank account. ..."
- *Design:* Diagrams and text
  e.g., "... The design will consist of the classes *CheckingAccount*, *SavingsAccount*, ..."
- *Implementation*: Source and object code
  e.g., `...class CheckingAccount{double balance;...}...`
- *Testing:* Test cases and test results
  e.g., "... With test case: *deposit $44.92/deposit $32.00/withdraw $101.45/*...the balance was $2938.22, which is correct. ..."
- *Maintenance:* Modified design, code, and text
  e.g., Defect repair: "Application crashes when balance is $0 and attempt is made to withdraw funds. ..."
  e.g., Enhancement: "Allow operation with Pesos."

**FIGURE 0.2**   Software Process Phases: Personal Finance Example

**KEY CONCEPT**   *Software Process*

A procedure followed by the development team to produce an application.

## 0.1.2   Styles of Software Process

Project personnel perform the software process phases in various orders, depending on many factors. The sequence shown in Figure 0.3 is sequential, with a degree of overlap between the phases. For example, some personnel will be performing the last part of requirements analysis while others will have already started the design phase. This software process is referred to as the *waterfall*. The waterfall process is logical, easy to understand,

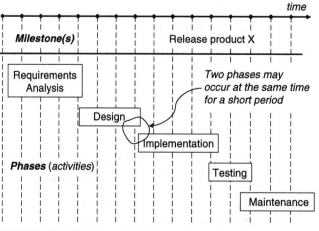

**FIGURE 0.3**   The Waterfall Software Process

and relatively easy to manage. However, it is more of an ideal or baseline than a realistic process. Some reasons for this are listed in Figure 0.4.

- *Don't know up front everything wanted and needed*
  - · Usually hard to visualize every detail in advance
- *We can only* estimate *the costs of implementing requirements*
  - · To gain confidence in an estimate, we need to design and actually implement parts, especially the riskiest ones
  - · We will probably need to modify requirements as a result
- *We often need to execute intermediate builds*
  - · Stakeholders need to gain confidence
  - · Designers and developers need confirmation they're building what's needed and wanted
- *Team members shouldn't be idle while the requirements are being completed*
  - · Typically put people to work on several phases at once

**FIGURE 0.4**   Why a Pure Waterfall Process is Usually Not Practical

A software process usually progresses through the waterfall phases in one of many possible ways. The *spiral process,* in which the waterfall is traversed several times, is commonly used in many forms. Each pass (or "iteration") through the waterfall produces an intermediate product more capable than the previous one, until the deliverable product is produced (see Figure 0.5).

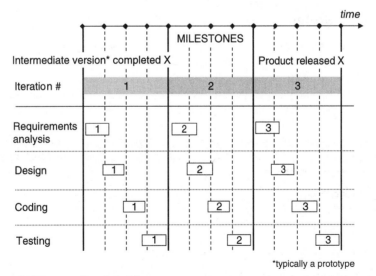

**FIGURE 0.5**   The Spiral Process

**KEY CONCEPT**   *Waterfall Process*

A basic software process in which requirements analysis, design, coding, testing and maintenance are performed in sequence, but with some overlap.

### 0.1.3 Common Procedures for Software Process: Writing Against Prior Phases; Inspection

During every software process, we keep our goals clearly before us. In particular, we aim always to *design only from requirements*. Similarly, we do not program in a vacuum: We keep before us the design that the code is intended to support. In other words, we aim to *code only from design*. These practices reflect common engineering precepts: After all, we don't build machines such as motorcycles without plans.

There are two issues that we need to consider. The first is *how* to express designs on paper: The book is designed to teach this. The second issue is more subtle and somewhat particular to software process. Because there are many ways in which a software application can accomplish given objectives, it is frequently advisable to program parts of an application *before* they are fully specified in the requirements and even in the design. It's not that we do not believe that requirements and design should be completed before coding; it's just that our poor human brains often can't envision every detail ahead of time. In any case, we continually *strive* to design only from requirements and code only from designs.

---

**KEY CONCEPT**     *Work Against the Product of Prior Phase*

In each phase of the software process, we strive to design and code within the specifications produced by the prior phase.

---

An *artifact* is a document or code. An *inspection* of an artifact is the process of reading through the artifact in a complete and entirely thorough manner. This process is performed at various points in a software process by the author of the artifact and by other engineers. The purpose is to assure the artifact's correctness by seeking defects. A meeting of inspectors is normally held during which defects are confirmed. The repair of defects is the author's responsibility.

---

**KEY CONCEPT**     *Inspections*

The process of reading meticulously through an artifact. Authors inspect their code before compiling it. Teams inspect when the author is done.

---

## 0.2 REQUIREMENTS ANALYSIS

Requirements analysis is the process of understanding, and putting in writing, a statement of what the application is intended to do once it has been built. This process may sound simple but it is not. An application can carry out functionality in many ways. For example, consider the requirements for an application that allows users to enter their bank check data. One can enter bank check data in one graphic text box per check; or in a table-like structure listing multiple checks; or in one table per checking account; or on a physical picture of a check; or in a text-like line. It is often difficult for the customer to decide which alternative requirement to select, or even to envision the alternatives in the first place: And when he does picture his requirements, expressing them may be a rather wordy process. In addition, the customer is likely to change his mind when he sees a result! Software engineers are tempted to throw up their hands and exclaim that there is no point in putting requirements in writing at all: The code itself "will express the requirements," he is tempted to exclaim. This is a mistake, however, for the following reasons.

It is a feature of civilization that we write down agreed-upon conditions in advance. Your cell-phone company, for example, makes sure that you sign a specific, detailed contract before it supplies you with service. A "see what you get when you get it" approach is a recipe for failure. In addition, the maintenance of an unspecified application is an expensive quagmire. (See Section 0.6.)

---

**KEY CONCEPT** *Requirements Analysis*

The process of understanding what's needed or wanted, and expressing the results in writing.

---

## 0.2.1 Styles of Requirements Analysis

The difficulties in creating a requirements document are: using appropriate ways to express the requirements, organizing them, and managing them over time (see Figure 0.6 for a summary).

- *Express requirements in ordinary, clear English*
  - Nontechnical
  - From the user's perspective
- *Organize the requirements into logical groupings*
  - Make easy to access and change

  *Arrange for the management of requirements*
- · A procedure must be developed in advance for
    keeping the requirements documents up to date
    - · Who, how, and when

**FIGURE 0.6** The Challenges of Requirements Analysis

This chapter will use the following example to illustrate software process. It is deliberately simple for illustration purposes. We start with a statement of the job's requirements, as specified in Figures 0.7, 0.8, and 0.9. The requirements are organized by input and output sections.

### 1. Overview

*CustomFootnoter* generates e-mail footers to promote customer relationships. Initial versions will produce simple courtesy statements. Later versions will contain helpful tips and offerings tailored to the recipient's interests.

This requirements specification is for a prototype which accepts command-line input and generated console output.

**FIGURE 0.7** Requirements for *CustomFootnoter,* 1 of 3

## 2. Detailed Requirements

### 2.1 Input

1) *CustomFootnoter* will accept the first 10
   characters of the recipient's first name as follows.
   Please type in the sender's first name:
   Abcd

2) The application will accept a single middle initial
   with the following format.
   Please type in the sender's middle initial:
   M

3) The application will accept the first 10 characters
   of the recipient's last name as follows.
   Please type in the sender's last name:
   Xyz

4) The application will accept the sender's name in the same
   manner as 1), 2), and 3) above

**FIGURE 0.8** Requirements for *CustomFootnoter*, 2 of 3

### 2.2 Output

5) *CustomFootnoter* outputs the following text to the console if it
   is less than or equal to 60 characters long
   -- To Abcd M. Xyz from Eric J. Braude. --
   (the number and position of blanks is indicated by the example)
   Otherwise the three initials may be used, as in
   --To A.M.X. from E.J.B.--

### 2.3 User Interface

The requirements in sections 2.1 and 2.2 will conform to the I/O
   format in Figure 0.10.

**FIGURE 0.9** Requirements for *CustomFootnoter*, 3 of 3

```
Please type in the sender's first name:
Eric
Please type in the sender's middle initial:
J
Please type in the sender's last name:
Braude
        The sender's name will he taken as 'Eric J. Braude'
Please type in the recipient's first name:
Joe
Please type in the recipient's middle initial:
Q
Please type in the recipient's last name:
Doe
        The Recipient's name will be taken as 'Joe Q. Doe'
        ---- To  J o e  Q.  D o e  from  E r i c  J.  B r a u d e ----
```

**FIGURE 0.10** Input/Output Format for Requirement Specifications

Notice that requirement 5 uses the word "may," and thus allows flexibility in the way it can be interpreted. Although we try to write requirements in a completely specific manner, we may want some ambiguity like this, usually because we are unable to be more specific until we have viewed some possibilities.

### 0.2.2  Tips on Analyzing and Specifying Requirements

A good attitude to take when specifying requirements is to think about your own experiences with the specification provided by others. In other words, put yourself in the shoes of the customer. The closest that many students come to this situation is in solving exercises assigned by their professor. For example, suppose that your instructor asks you to implement a program that "accepts names and addresses, and is able to produce the details of a person on request." You duly slave away at this exercise, and are proud to produce an application that behaves as illustrated by the following.

```
E)nter or R)etrieve Q)uit: E
First name: John
Middle initial: Q
Last name: Doe
Date of Birth (YY/MM/DD): 75/11/14

E)nter or R)etrieve Q)uit: E
First name: Jayne
Middle initial: V
Last name: Doyle
Date of Birth (YY/MM/DD): 85/01/11

E)nter or R)etrieve Q)uit: R
Last name: Doe
John Q. Doe, born November 14, 1975

E)nter or R)etrieve Q)uit: Q
Application ends
```

Your instructor gives you a "D" grade for your solution. Barely containing your anger, you try to ask politely where the mistake is. Your instructor ticks off the problems. *You were supposed to provide a graphical interface: You were supposed to allow for people with no middle initial. You were supposed to be able to enter the date from a list box of months. You should have allowed for the entry of a paragraph of text for each name. You failed to store the records so that they could be retrieved in future executions.*

You reply that you did not know these were required: Your instructor replies that he announced them to the class when he assigned the exercise. In the true manner of an aggrieved customer, you reply that *the requirements should have been written down completely and clearly.* You would be quite right: Just remember to practice this principle yourself.

## 0.3  DESIGN (WHAT THIS BOOK COVERS!)

We restrict this section to distinguishing design from requirements and implementation. The rest of this book deals with specific issues and techniques of software design.

### 0.3.1 The Meaning of "Software Design"

The "design" of an application expresses how the application is to be constructed. It describes the parts involved and how they are to be assembled. A design consists of a set of documents: Typically, these are diagrams, together with explanations of what the diagrams mean. The student may already be familiar with flowcharts, which are a form of design.

A design is produced from requirements. It excludes code. An extremely useful notation for design documentation is the *Unified Modeling Language,* which is explained in Chapter 3 on page 61. You can think of design documents as a blueprint for the application. Figure 0.11 shows a (simple) design for our (simple) *CustomFootnoter* application whose requirements were specified in Section 0.2.1 on page 5. The design in this case consists simply of a single class, its attributes, and its methods.

| CustomFootnoter |
|---|
| senderFirstName: String |
| senderMidInitial: char |
| senderFirstName: String |
| recipientMidInitial: char |
| recipientLastName: String |
| recipientLastName: String |
| CustomerFootnoter() |
| main() |
| getSenderName() |
| getRecipientName() |
| createExpandedRecipientName() |
| createFootnote(): String |

**FIGURE 0.11** Design for *CustomFootnoter*

The figure shows Unified Modeling Language notation for a class. It includes the type of each attribute after the attribute name. We won't *justify* this design except to point out that it allows for some limited expandability. (Otherwise, we would collapse some of the methods.) Note that the design does not take advantage of object-orientation: Although it uses a class, it could just as well be a C program.

### 0.3.2 The Manner in Which this Book Teaches Design

Recall that the classical sequence of phases for producing an application is: *Specify requirements* → *Create design* → *Write code,* etc. (waterfall process), usually repeated. The principal purpose of this book is to explain how to carry out the design phase. Because students reading this book are already familiar with programming, the book begins the learning process by asking, "What should design documents provide so that we can create programs from them?" We then move into learning about the design of *parts*. The book ends with how to think about software architectures and frameworks—the highest design levels. Note that this order was chosen to facilitate *learning*: We do not advocate starting actual software projects by coding!

# 0.4 CODING

By "coding" we mean typing commented source code, reading it thoroughly before compilation to convince ourselves that it does what it is supposed to, compiling it, and then executing it with other code against informal test cases. The words "implementation" and "programming" are also used for "coding." The word "development" is sometimes used as well, although this can also apply to phases besides coding. *Formal* testing is described in Section 0.5 on page 15. This section discusses implementation in the context of software process: It is not intended to teach programming *per se*.

## 0.4.1 When Does Design Stop and Coding Begin?

As mentioned in Section 0.1.2, on page 2, the waterfall process is a baseline, or reference, process: We don't usually develop applications by progressing just once through the waterfall phases. In particular, we usually can't fully complete designs before we begin coding. This is not because we don't want to do so; doing so would be ideal, in fact. Figure 0.4 outlined some of the reasons it is usually impossible to complete a phase once and for all before beginning the next one. In any case, we try to specify the design of the *portions* that we intend to code, and then we write the code for those portions. This is reflected in the spiral process shown in Figure 0.5.

Sometimes we push ahead with a small piece of coding even though we have not completed a design for that piece, but we do this for very focused reasons. An example is the development of a graphical user interface. Instead of specifying every detail up front, we may code it—possibly using a visual tool—and only then complete the design document. This process of going backwards is called *reverse engineering*. Its very name indicates that it goes backwards (i.e., relative to a normative process). In any case, we continually return to the waterfall process, striving to code only from designs.

## 0.4.2 Basic Coding Tips

This section discusses programming in the context of software process.

A step that bears reiteration is what we will call *author inspection*: "Read the code you have typed, and edit it if necessary until you are totally satisfied it's correct." This advice sounds rather obvious but, although it is profound, it is rarely followed! Instead, programmers frequently skip this step, compiling the code to "see if it works."

Let's take an apparently simple example. Suppose that we are tasked with writing a word processor having *cut* and *paste* commands etc., and we want the ability to undo commands. A common way to do this is to capture command as *Command* objects, and push each command onto a stack of past commands, as in the statement

```
CommandStack.push( currentCommand ); // 'push' statement
```

"Undo" executes the opposite of the command at the top of the stack and then pops the stack. (This is an application of the *Command* design pattern described in Section 9.8 on page 314.)

We could compile the 'push' statement together with others in the same block of code: We can run informal tests with it, and find that it "works fine." A week before critical release, in the midst of testing, however, we might well find that the entire application crashes mysteriously. The development team enters a state of panic and despair. At this point, the 'push' statement cited is just one of hundreds or thousands of other statements that could be at fault.

The problem with skipping the author-inspection step is that code containing defects may compile cleanly, and pass all tests we give it. As emphasized in the next section, however, testing establishes the *presence* of defects, *never their absence*: So what procedure *does* prove that there are no defects in a block of code? Only we humans can prove that a block of code does what it is supposed to do. We accomplish this proof process by looking at the code, thinking it through meticulously, and editing it until we become convinced of its correctness. "Author-inspect" is a good term for this process. Whereas it is true in theory that we could author-inspect after compilation, programmers rarely do. Syntactical correctness (i.e., the code compiles) masks semantic incorrectness (it does not do what it's supposed to in all cases). For that reason it is far better discipline to look at our code *before* we submit it to a compiler. Watts Humphry [Hu] suggests maintaining statistics on how many defects you find per thousand lines of code during author inspections.

Returning to the 'push' statement example, what difference would it have made if we had reflected on the source lines before submitting it to compilation and self testing? We are much more likely to ask searching and *focused* questions about this line of code at the time. There is no guarantee that we would catch defects, but we might well ask questions such as: "Will there always be enough memory to push another command?" On the other hand, the likelihood gets smaller and smaller that we would ask this particular question while grappling with an additional 100, 1,000, 100,000, or 1,000,000 lines of code. A major reason for this is the increasing difficulty of reconstructing the reasons that we coded lines the way we did. We capture many of our reasons in comments, but it is not practical to explain every decision (why we chose "capsule" for a variable name rather than "pill," for example). Figure 0.12 summarizes coding tips.

- *Code only against a design*
    This book explains how to express designs
- *Specify precisely what each method accomplishes*
    Chapter 1 on page 25 explains how to do this in comment sections
- *Before compiling, satisfy yourself that the code you have typed is correct. Read it meticulously.*
    · "correct" means that it accomplishes what's required of it
    · This is "author-inspection"
- *Build-a-little-test-a-little*
    1. Add a relatively small amount of code ("build-a-little")
    2. (Again): Read what you have typed and correct it if necessary until you are totally satisfied it's correct
    3. Compile
    4. Test the new functionality ("test-a-little")

**FIGURE 0.12** Tips on Coding

Here is another example, taken from an early version of code intended to implement the *FootnoteCustomizer* application already specified.

```
/*******************************************************************************
 * Returns: A footnote in accordance with requirement 5 in section 0.2.1 of the
 * Software Requirements Specification, based on the sender's name and the recipient's name.
 */
public static String createFootnote()
/******************************************************************************/
{
   StringBuffer footnote = new StringBuffer( "" );
   footnote.append( "\t---- To " );
   footnote.append( createExpandedVersionOf( recipientFirstName ) );
   footnote.append( " " + recipientMiddleInitial + ". " );
   footnote.append( createExpandedVersionOf( recipientLastName ) );
   footnote.append( " from " );
   footnote.append( createExpandedVersionOf( senderFirstName ) );
   footnote.append( " " + senderMiddleInitial + ". " );
   footnote.append( createExpandedVersionOf( senderLastName ) );
   footnote.append( ". ----" );

   return footnote.toString();
}
```

This looks simple enough, but a sustained focus on the text itself may well induce us to ask questions such as "could *createExpandedVersionOf()* return a *null String*?" and if so, does this code produce the output we intend?

There are informal ways to establish the correctness of code, as well as formal ones, which use mathematical logic.

**KEY CONCEPT**  *Author-Inspect Before Compiling*

Inspect and edit the block of code you have just written until you are convinced it does exactly what it is meant to do. Only then compile it.

In the code sample below we precede each substantive method with *Precondition / Parameters / Postconditions / Returns* descriptions, as applicable. *Postconditions* describe the state of the application upon conclusion of the method, thereby expressing what the method is for. Actually, the "state of the application" is confined to the status of variables and outputs that the method's execution could potentially change. This book will cover the use of *Preconditions / Postconditions / Returns* descriptions in detail in Section 1.2 on page 22.

Here is (faulty!) code written to implement the *CustomFootnoter* class: We will use this in Section 0.5 on testing.

```
import java.io.*;

/**
 * Customized e-mail footers.                    Note: Known faulty
 */
class CustomFootnoter
{
   // Sender name
   private static String senderFirstName = "senderFirstName not assigned yet";
```

```
    private static char senderMiddleInitial = 'X';
    private static String senderLastName = "senderLastName not assigned yet";

    // Recipient name
    private static String recipientFirstName = "recipientFirstName not assigned yet";
    private static char recipientMiddleInitial = 'Z';
    private static String recipientLastName = "recipientLastName not assigned yet";

    // Constants
    private static final int MAX_FOOTNOTE_LENGTH = 70;
    private static final String SPACING_BETWEEN_EXPANDED_NAMES = " ";

/*************************************************************************************
 */
public CustomFootnoter()
/*************************************************************************************/
{  super(); // (in case a base class is introduced in the future)
}


/*************************************************************************************
 * Returns: "A B C ..... X" for aName == "ABC....X"
 */
public static String createExpandedVersionOf( String aName )
/*************************************************************************************/
{
    StringBuffer returnBuffer = new StringBuffer( "" ); // in which we build the string to return

    // Insert a space after each character except the last
    for( int nameIndex = 0; nameIndex < aName.length() - 1; ++ nameIndex )
    {
        returnBuffer.append( aName.charAt( nameIndex ) );
        returnBuffer.append( ' ' );
    }
    returnBuffer.append( aName.charAt( aName.length() - 1 ) ); // last character of 'aName'
    return returnBuffer.toString();
                                                      ┌─────────────────────┐
                                                      │ Note: Known faulty  │
                                                      └─────────────────────┘
}  // end createExpandedVersionOf()
/*************************************************************************************
 * Note to the student: At least one defect has been deliberately left in this method.
 *
 * Returns: A footnote in accordance with requirement 5 in section 2.2
 * of the Software Requirements Specification, based on the sender's name and the recipient's name.
 */
public static String createFootnote()
/*************************************************************************************/
{
    StringBuffer returnFootnote = new StringBuffer( "" ); // returned String obtained from this

    // The parts that make up the full version of the custom footnote
    String toPadding = "\t---- To" + SPACING_BETWEEN_EXPANDED_NAMES;
    String expandedRecipientFirstName = createExpandedVersionOf( recipientFirstName );
    String paddedRecipientMiddleInitial = SPACING_BETWEEN_EXPANDED_NAMES +
      recipientMiddleInitial + "." + SPACING_BETWEEN_EXPANDED_NAMES;
    String expandedRecipientLastName = createExpandedVersionOf( recipientLastName );
    String fromPadding = SPACING_BETWEEN_EXPANDED_NAMES + "from" +
      SPACING_BETWEEN_EXPANDED_NAMES;
    String expandedSenderFirstName = createExpandedVersionOf( senderFirstName );
    String paddedSenderMiddleInitial = SPACING_BETWEEN_EXPANDED_NAMES +
      senderMiddleInitial + "."+ SPACING_BETWEEN_EXPANDED_NAMES;
    String expandedSenderLastName = createExpandedVersionOf( senderLastName );
    String endPadding = " ----";

    // --------- CASE 1. Message with full names and middle initial

    StringBuffer footnoteInFull = new StringBuffer( "" ); // to build a full version

    // Build footnote with full names
    footnoteInFull.append( toPadding );
```

```
    footnoteInFull.append( expandedRecipientFirstName );
    footnoteInFull.append( paddedRecipientMiddleInitial );
    footnoteInFull.append( expandedRecipientLastName );
    footnoteInFull.append( fromPadding );
    footnoteInFull.append( expandedSenderFirstName );
    footnoteInFull.append( paddedSenderMiddleInitial );
    footnoteInFull.append( expandedSenderLastName );
    footnoteInFull.append( endPadding );

    if( footnoteInFull.length() <= MAX_FOOTNOTE_LENGTH ) // length acceptable: Leave as constructed
    {       returnFootnote = footnoteInFull;
    }

    // --------- CASE 2. Message without middle initials; full first and second names
    else // too long for full expansion                    ┌─────────────────────┐
    {                                                       │ Note: Known faulty  │
        // Build footnote without middle initials           └─────────────────────┘
        StringBuffer footnoteWithoutMIs = new StringBuffer( "" );
        footnoteWithoutMIs.append( toPadding );
        footnoteWithoutMIs.append( expandedRecipientFirstName );
        footnoteWithoutMIs.append( expandedRecipientLastName );
        footnoteWithoutMIs.append( fromPadding );
        footnoteWithoutMIs.append( expandedSenderFirstName );
        footnoteWithoutMIs.append( expandedSenderLastName );
        footnoteWithoutMIs.append( endPadding );

        if( footnoteWithoutMIs.length() <= MAX_FOOTNOTE_LENGTH ) // acceptable: Leave as constructed
        {           returnFootnote = footnoteWithoutMIs;
        }
        else // still too long (omitting middle initials)

    // --------- CASE 3. Message with initials only
        {
            // Footnote with initials only
            StringBuffer footnoteWithInitials = new StringBuffer( "" );
            footnoteWithInitials.append( toPadding );
            footnoteWithInitials.append( recipientFirstName.charAt( 0 ) + "." );
            footnoteWithInitials.append( paddedRecipientMiddleInitial );
            footnoteWithInitials.append( recipientLastName.charAt( 0 ) + "." );
            footnoteWithInitials.append( fromPadding );
            footnoteWithInitials.append( senderFirstName.charAt( 0 ) + "." );
            footnoteWithInitials.append( paddedSenderMiddleInitial );
            footnoteWithInitials.append( senderLastName.charAt( 0 ) + "." );
            footnoteWithInitials.append( endPadding );

            returnFootnote = footnoteWithInitials;
        }
    }
    return returnFootnote.toString();

} // end createFootnote()

/**********************************************************************************************
 * Postcondition: Application has prompted user with 'aPrompt'
 *
 * Returns: Line of text typed by user.
 */
public static String getInputFromUser( String aPrompt )
/*********************************************************************************************/
{
    String returnString = "not yet assigned";

    System.out.println( aPrompt + ":" );

    try
    {
        BufferedReader bufReader = new BufferedReader( new InputStreamReader( System.in ) );
        returnString = bufReader.readLine();
```

```
    }
    catch( IOException e )
    {    System.out.println( e ); }

    return returnString;

} // end getInputFromUser()

/******************************************************************************
 * Postconditions:
 * (1) 'RecipientFirstName', 'RecipientMiddleInitial', and 'RecipientLastName'
 *     have been obtained from the user via command-line interface prompts.
 * (2) The Recipient's full name has been echoed to the monitor.
 */
public static void getRecipientName()
/******************************************************************************/
{
    recipientFirstName = getInputFromUser( "Please type in the recipient's first name" );
    recipientMiddleInitial =
      ( getInputFromUser( "Please type in the recipient's middle initial" ) ).charAt( 0 );
    recipientLastName = getInputFromUser( "Please type in the recipient's last name" );

    System.out.println // echo to console
      ( "\n\tThe Recipient's name will be taken as '" +
      recipientFirstName + " " + recipientMiddleInitial + ". " + recipientLastName + "'\n");

} // end getRecipientName()

/******************************************************************************
 * Postconditions:
 * (1) 'senderFirstName', 'senderMiddleInitial', and 'senderLastName'
 *     have been obtained from the user via command-line interface prompts
 * (2) The sender's full name has been echoed to the monitor.
 */
public static void getSenderName()
/******************************************************************************/
{

    senderFirstName = getInputFromUser( "Please type in the sender's first name" );
    senderMiddleInitial =
      ( getInputFromUser( "Please type in the sender's middle initial" ) ).charAt( 0 );
    senderLastName = getInputFromUser( "Please type in the sender's last name" );

    System.out.println // echo to console
      ( "\n\tThe sender's name will be taken as '" +
      senderFirstName + " " + senderMiddleInitial + ". " + senderLastName + "'\n");

} // end getSenderName()

/******************************************************************************
 * Postconditions:
 * An e-mail footnote has been generated as specified in the Software Requirement Specification
 * for "Custom Footnoter".
 */
public static void main( String[] args )
/******************************************************************************/
{
    getSenderName();
    getRecipientName();
    System.out.println( createFootnote() );
}

}
```

> Note: Known faulty

In addition to encouraging author inspections, good software development organizations conduct *code inspections,* structured meetings attended by a group of software engineers who have read the code in detail. Code inspections have benefits not available at author-inspection time, including the minds of engineers who are much more independent than the code writer, and the advantage of perspective. An inspection would probably uncover the lack of precondition "*aName != null*" for *createExpandedVersionOf(),* for example.

# 0.5  TESTING

The testing phase consists of supplying input to the application and comparing the output with that mandated by the Software Requirements Specification. Tests on parts of an application (individual methods, classes, etc.) are called *unit* tests: Tests of an entire application are *system* tests.

## 0.5.1  Testing and Correctness

Testing is indispensable because it helps to uncover defects. Testing proves the *presence* of bugs, but *never their absence*. Even the most comprehensive test plan covers only a tiny fraction of the set of all possible input combinations. For this reason, testing is a kind of detective work in which we use the sample of test cases to uncover as many defects as possible. Although we feel more confident about an application after it has passed a rigorous set of tests, we can never be entirely confident based only on testing: Bugs are still generally present in thoroughly tested, substantial applications.

## 0.5.2  Types of Testing

Figure 0.13 shows on the left side the principal kinds of testing. For each of these, there are two ways to go about designing the test cases (the inputs): *White box* and *black box*.

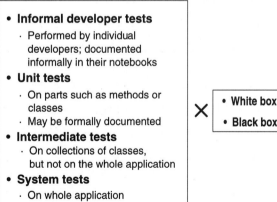

**FIGURE 0.13**  Types of Testing

*Black-box* testing compares the output obtained with the output specified by the requirements document. The selection of black-box test cases does not take into account the manner in which the application is designed. An example report for black-box testing of the *CustomFootnoter* example follows.

**TABLE 0.1**

| Test # | Test case input | Required output | Actual output |
|---|---|---|---|
| 1 | sender: Jay R. Cox receiver: John Q. Doe | `---- To Jay R. Cox from John Q. Doe ----` | `---- To Jay R. Cox from John Q. Doe ----` |
| 2 | sender: Jay Cox receiver: John Q. Doe | `---- To Jay Cox from John Q. Doe ----` | Application crashes when no input is given for middle initial (just return key) |
| 3 ... | .... | .... | .... |

*White-box* testing, on the other hand, is based on the design. White-box test cases are selected to exercise specific design features such as branching, loops, interfaces between modules, limits on storage, etc.

An example of a white-box test for *CustomFootnoter* is constructed around the logic used in the design. The method *main()* calls *createFootNote()*, which covers three cases. We would design test cases that specifically exercise each of these branches in the code. We can exercise the second case with sender name *Eric J. Braude* and recipient *John Q. Doe,* for example. When we do, the output in Figure 0.14 appears. Since the defect evident in the last line shows up only for names with particular length combinations, it is quite possible that black-box testing would miss it entirely.

```
Please type in the sender's first name:
Eric
Please type in the sender's middle initial:
J
Please type in the sender's last name:
Braude

    The sender's name will be taken as 'Eric J. Braude'

Please type in the recipient's first name:
Johannes
Please type in the recipient's middle initial:
P
Please type in the recipient's last name:
Brahms

    The sender's name will be taken as 'Johannes P. Brahms'

    ----To JohannesBrahms  from  EricBraude----
```

**FIGURE 0.14**   Output of a White Box Test

## 0.5.3  Tips on Testing

Figure 0.15 lists some basic testing do's and don't.

- Test early and often
- Test with extreme values
  - Very small, very big, etc.
  - Borderline
  - "Illegal" values
- Vary test cases
  - Don't repeat tests with same test data except when specifically intended

**FIGURE 0.15**   Tips on Testing

**KEY CONCEPT**   *Testing*

Test early and often: Note that "passed all tests" doesn't equate to "bug free."

## 0.6   MAINTENANCE

### 0.6.1   The Meaning of "Maintenance"

"Maintenance" refers to the work performed on an application that occurs after it has been delivered. These are of two general types, as defined in Figure 0.16. *Defect removal* consists of bringing the application into compliance with its requirements. *Enhancement* means introducing and satisfying new requirements.

- Defect Removal
  - Finding and fixing all inconsistencies with the requirements document
- Enhancement
  - Introducing new or improved capability

**FIGURE 0.16**   Types of Maintenance

### 0.6.2   How Maintenance Considerations Affect Process

This book is about design. In this connection, however, it is important to understand maintenance because maintenance is very expensive when requirements analysis and design are not performed properly. For example, if there is no up-to-date requirements document, maintenance can be farcical: We cannot know what an application is supposed to do if the requirements are not written down and if many of the people who may once have had a mental image of what it was supposed to do are no longer available. We can guess at requirements, but guesswork can hardly be considered responsible engineering.

An application with an inflexible design is relatively difficult to repair or enhance. An example is a web-page generator that creates pages for the *shopper-browsing-catalog* state and the *shopper-checking-out* state. When more states are introduced (e.g., *credit-card-being-checked*), it can be very expensive to untangle the first two states and develop a clean design involving all of the states. The *State* design pattern (see Section 9.6 on page 306), if used from the start, makes the addition of new states straightforward.

# SUMMARY OF SOFTWARE PROCESS

A software process is a way of going about the creation and upkeep of a software product. The basis for most processes is the waterfall. In the waterfall process, design progresses almost sequentially through the specification of requirements, the creation of a design, the coding of the design, its testing, and finally its maintenance.

- *A way of going about the creation and upkeep of a software product*
- *Commonly based on the waterfall process*
  1. Specify requirements ⎫
  2. Create design ⎪ In sequence
  3. Write code ⎬ with some
  4. Test ⎪ overlap
  5. Maintain ⎭

**FIGURE 0.17** Summary of *Software Process*

# EXERCISES

**Exercise 0.1**  **(Part 0.1.1)** Name at least four phases of the software development process.

**(Part 0.1.2)** Explain the waterfall process.

**(Part 0.1.3)** Give three potential advantages of the waterfall process, and three potential disadvantages.

**(Part 0.1.4)** Would you use the waterfall process for the following project? Explain your reasoning. You are tasked to build a system for designing skyscrapers. The application supports collaboration among team members.

**(Part 0.1.5)** Would you conceivably use the waterfall process for the following project? Explain your reasoning.

You are tasked to build a system that provides information about loans. It takes as input the amount borrowed, the length of the loan, and the payment frequency. It provides as output the payment amounts. The interface to be used is as follows. . .

Points to watch for:
*Serious*:
1. Use of the waterfall process alone for a large application.

*Less than serious, more than trivial*:
1. Use of a complex process when the problem is simple enough for a pure waterfall process

**Exercise 0.2**  **(Part 0.2.1)** What does "Requirements analysis" mean?

**(Part 0.2.2)** In 3 to 20 sentences plus figures, give possible precise requirements for an application that takes up to seven recipes as input, and generates a shopping list as output.

Evaluation criteria:
- ▨ Clarity of your response          A = completely clear organization and prose
- ▨ Specificity                       A = precise and complete statement of requirements

The following are errors that you should watch for in this question:

*Serious*:
1. Mixing design with the requirements statement
2. Outright ambiguous specifications
3. Poor organization of the requirements

*Less than serious, but more than minor*:
1. Somewhat ambiguous specifications
2. Unsatisfactory organization of the requirements

**Exercise 0.3**   **(Part 0.3.1)** Before writing code, what condition(s) do you need to ensure? (Besides obvious issues such as whether your computer has booted!)

**(Part 0.3.2)** What should you do as soon as you have written a block of code, before compiling it?

**Exercise 0.4**   **(Part 0.4.1)** In two to six sentences, describe and contrast *code inspection* and *testing*.

**(Part 0.4.2)** Provide an advantage of inspection that testing does not possess.

**(Part 0.4.3)** Provide an advantage of testing that inspection does not possess.

**Exercise 0.5**   Name the two principal types of maintenance actions and give examples not found in this chapter.

# PROGRAMMING REVIEW
# AND INTRODUCTION
# TO SOFTWARE DESIGN

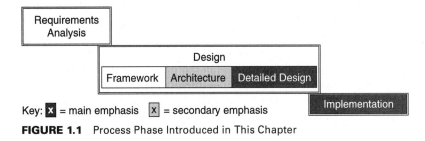

**FIGURE 1.1**   Process Phase Introduced in This Chapter

## 1.1 "SOFTWARE DESIGN:" ITS MEANING AND HOW THIS BOOK INTRODUCES IT

A "software design" is a set of documents on whose basis a software application can be fully programmed. In other words, a complete software design should be so explicit that a programmer could code the application from it without the need for any other documents. Software designs are like the blueprints of a building, which are sufficient for a contractor to build the required building.

This book is about software design, but it starts by discussing programming because the reader is assumed to be already comfortable with that activity. From there, the text moves up, level by level, into design and finally into architecture and even higher, into frameworks. When this learning process is completed, students can boast that they program only from designs. Note that the sequence of topics in this book is tailored to *learning,* and is the opposite order from that used in *developing* applications. When performing actual software development, we start by considering architecture, not programming.

The core of this chapter is Section 1.4 (page 27), which sets out the specific goals of software design. Since code is used throughout the book to illustrate principles, we begin by describing the standards used in our code.

> **KEY CONCEPT**   *Where We're Headed*
>
> In development, we start by thinking about architecture and end with programming. For learning purposes, this book begins by discussing programming and ends by explaining architecture.

### 1.1.1 Part I of this Book: Design Principles, the Unified Modeling Language, and Code-Level Design

In Chapters 1 through 5 we discuss the kinds of design drawings and documents that programmers need in order to do their job. We use the Unified Modeling Language (Chapter 3, page 61) to specify designs. We also need to comment individual methods in a way that clearly expresses their intentions. For this we use terms such as "preconditions" and "post-conditions:" ways of organizing what we need to say. This chapter describes these terms.

We need to keep clearly in mind what the goals of design are. In this regard, we discuss principles of *correctness, robustness, flexibility, reusability,* and *efficiency* (see Chapters 4 and 5 on pages 82 and 104 respectively).

### 1.1.2 Part II of this Book: Design Patterns

We move on to a set of extensively developed design techniques known as "design patterns." These were divided into three types by Gamma et al [Ga]. Creational patterns (Chapter 7, page 147) handle ways to flexibly create complex objects at runtime; structural patterns (Chapter 8, page 205) handle ways to represent complex structures of objects; and behavioral patterns (Chapter 9, page 276) handle ways to capture the manner in which objects exhibit behavior at runtime.

### 1.1.3 Part III of this Book: Components

It has long been the goal of software development to use ready-made parts in a fluid manner, customizing the parts as we assemble them into applications. Employing object-orientation goes a long way toward this goal; using components takes us even further. We show how this is done in the Sun Java Bean environment (Chapter 11, page 404) as well as the Microsoft .NET environment (Chapter 12, page 428).

### 1.1.4 Part IV of this Book: Object-Oriented Analysis and Design

The final part of this book reviews the selection of the highest level of design—architecture—and how it is arrived at (Chapter 13, page 458). It also looks at an even higher level: Frameworks (Chapter 14, page 479). A framework is software that can be used as a basis for many applications. The Java API is an example of a general-purpose framework.

That's the story of how this book progresses from the code level to the architecture level. Now we go back to the beginning for a bit and look at functions.

## 1.2 DOCUMENTING FUNCTIONS

Although this book is about software *design,* it includes Java implementations of designs to make designs more understandable and to illustrate the consequences of choices in concrete terms. Since functions are the building blocks of software implementations, we first cover some of the basics of documenting and writing functions. This includes a brief discussion of documentation standards, coding standards, ways to specify functions, and ways to handle errors.

## 1.2.1 Java Coding Standards Used in this Book

To assist the reader in understanding the origin of variables encountered, we use the coding standards shown in the following figure. The principles of object-orientation will be covered in Chapter 2, page 44: However, we use object-oriented languages (mostly Java and a little C#) throughout this book, and so our coding standards necessarily refer to classes.

- Instance variables may be referred to with "this."
  - · Example: class Car {int milesDriven;...}
    May use **this.milesDriven** within methods of Car to clarify
- Static variables may be referred to with class name.
  - · Example: class Car {static int numCarsSold;...}
    May use **Car.numCarsSold** within methods of Car to clarify
- Parameters are given prefix "a" or "an"
  - · Example: public...getVolume(int **aLength**) {...}

**FIGURE 1.2**  Coding Practices Used in this Book

## 1.2.2 Specifying What a Function Does

Besides in-line documentation, nontrivial functions are usually documented within the comments at the beginning using the categories *precondition, postcondition, return, invariant,* and *known issues,* as explained in Figures 1.3 and 1.4.

- *Preconditions:* conditions on nonlocal variables that the method's code assumes
  - · Includes parameters
  - · Verification of these conditions not promised in method itself
- *Postconditions:* value of nonlocal variables after execution
  - · Includes parameters
  - · Notation: $x'$ denotes the value of variable $x$ after execution
- *Invariants*: relationships among nonlocal variables that the function's execution does not change (The values of the individual variables may change, however.)
  - · Equivalent to inclusion in both pre- and postconditions
  - · There may also be invariants among local variables

**FIGURE 1.3**  Programming Conventions: Method Documentation, 1 of 2

- *Return:*
  - · What the method returns
- *Known issues:*
  - · Honest statement of what has to be done, defects that have not been repaired, etc.
  - · (Obviously) limited to what's known!

**FIGURE 1.4**  Programming Conventions: Method Documentation, 2 of 2

Preconditions define the assumptions that the method makes about the value of variables external to the method, including the parameters, but excluding local variables of the method. Postconditions are similarly defined. For example, if we define a method

```
int weirdSum( int addend1, int addend2 )
```

in which *addend2* is assigned the sum of *addend1* and *addend2*, then calling *weirdSum (x, y )* changes the variable bound to *y*, and so *addend2* is mentioned in the postconditions as follows.

Postcondition: *addend2' = addend1 + addend2*

We have used the notation $x'$, that is, the value of a variable $x$ at the conclusion of a method.

An *invariant* is a statement that must be true at the beginning and also at the end of a method invocation. For example, we may be writing a method that manipulates the dimensions of a rectangle made from a fixed length of string, in which case the invariant is something like 2*( *length* + *width* ) == *STRING_LENGTH*. An invariant is equivalent to including the statement with both the preconditions and the postconditions. Invariants can also apply to blocks of code that are not separate functions.

A method is *purely functional* if it has a return, no postconditions, and if its preconditions refer only to parameters. In this case, *return* describes the entire reason for the method's existence. We make methods purely functional unless we want them to participate in an object-oriented design (which is very often). When a class has objects, which we want in most cases, we need methods that depend on the variables of the objects, and are thus *not* purely functional. Take, for example, the method *area( ... )* in the class *Rectangle*. We could define *area()* purely functionally as in

```
class Rectangle { . . .
    //Preconditions: a Length>10, a width >10
    //Returns: a Length X a Breadth . . .
    public double area( double aLength, double aBreadth ) . . . . }
```

This has the property of being independent of the class to which it belongs. We would almost certainly make it *static* and would *use* this version of *area()* as in

```
. . . Rectangle.area( l, b ) . . . .
```

Alternatively, we could define *area( )* with preconditions on the instance variables *length* and *breadth* of *Rectangle*, as in

```
class Rectangle { . . .
    //Preconditions: length >-0, breadth >- 0
    //Returns: length X breadth . . .
    public double area() . . . . }
```

This leverages the object-oriented nature of *Rectangle*. We would use this version of *area()* as in

```
. . . rectangle.area() . . .
```

When a method depends on another method from which preconditions or postconditions are to be repeated, it is preferable not to literally repeat the preconditions, but merely to reference the methods on which it depends. The benefit of this is that if the preconditions in the called method change, it is not necessary to then update the preconditions in every method using them.

**KEY CONCEPT**   *Specifying Methods*

We specify each method in its comment section with preconditions, postconditions, returns, invariants and known issues.

In addition to these specifications, the programmer will want to help the reader with an "Intent" section that informally summarizes the goal of the method.

### 1.2.3  Describing *How* a Function Satisfies Its Specification

***1.2.3.1  Activity Diagrams***   Flowcharts are among the oldest graphical methods for depicting algorithms. Figure 1.5, for example, contains a flowchart for a *setName()* method, and shows two of the most commonly used flowchart constructs: Decisions

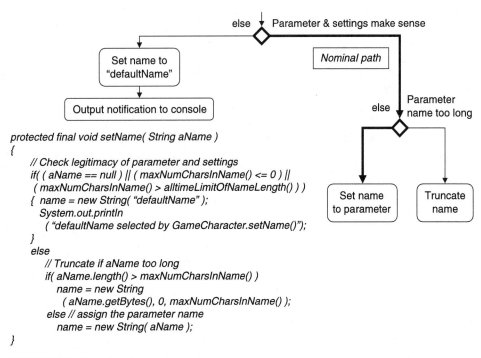

```
protected final void setName( String aName )
{
    // Check legitimacy of parameter and settings
    if( ( aName == null ) || ( maxNumCharsInName() <= 0 ) ||
    ( maxNumCharsInName() > alltimeLimitOfNameLength() ) )
    { name = new String( "defaultName" );
        System.out.println
          ( "defaultName selected by GameCharacter.setName()");
    }
    else
        // Truncate if aName too long
        if( aName.length() > maxNumCharsInName() )
            name = new String
              ( aName.getBytes(), 0, maxNumCharsInName() );
        else // assign the parameter name
            name = new String( aName );
}
```

**FIGURE 1.5**  Flowchart Example

(diamonds) and processes (ovals). The flowchart notation in the diagram is actually a part of the Unified Modeling Language (UML), which uses an extended form of flowcharts called *Activity Diagrams*. We will return to activity diagrams in Chapter 4.

Flowcharts are not necessary for all methods in an application, but they do help to clarify the more complex ones.

**1.2.3.2 Pseudocode** Pseudocode is a means of expressing algorithms without getting bogged down in the details of programming languages. It enables us to inspect algorithms alone, thereby making it more likely that the end result is correct. Suppose, for example, that you are responsible for programming the controlling mechanism for an X ray that could seriously injure a patient if functioning improperly. You would surely want to verify the algorithm alone, and then verify its implementation in the target programming language. Example pseudocode for the hypothetical automated X-ray controller is shown in the following figure.

```
FOR number of microseconds supplied by operator
    IF number of microseconds exceeds critical value
        Try to get supervisor's approval
        IF no supervisor's approval
            abort with "no supervisor approval for unusual duration" message
        ENDIF
    ENDIF
    IF power level exceeds critical value
        abort with "power level exceeded" message
    ENDIF
    IF (patient properly aligned & shield properly placed & machine self-test passed)
        Apply X ray at power level p
    ENDIF
ENDFOR
```

**FIGURE 1.6** Pseuodocode Example For an X-ray Controller

**1.2.3.3 When to Use Flowcharts or Pseudocode** We don't always use flowcharts and pseudocode: It depends on whether the advantages outweigh the drawbacks. The figures list some of both.

- Clarify algorithms in many cases
- Impose increased discipline on the process of documenting detailed design
- Provide additional level at which inspection can be performed
  - Help to trap defects before they become code
  - Increase product reliability
- May decrease overall costs

**FIGURE 1.7** Advantages of Pseudocode and Flowcharts

- Create an additional level of documentation to maintain
- Introduce error possibilities in translating to code
- May require tool to extract pseudocode and facilitate drawing flowcharts

**FIGURE 1.8**   Disadvantages of Pseudocode and Flowcharts

The decision whether or not to use pseudocode and/or flowcharts depends on factors particular to the application. Some developers shun flowcharts as old fashioned, but drawing flowcharts and pseudocode can be worth the trouble for selected parts of applications, helping to produce better quality products.

> **KEY CONCEPT**   *The* What *vs. the* How *of Methods*
>
> Preconditions, etc., specify *what* a method accomplishes. Activity charts, etc., describe *how* the method accomplishes these.

### 1.2.4   Error Processing

A large proportion of the code in real applications is dedicated to processing exceptional or unusual circumstances (e.g., absent files or erroneous user input). Some estimate that 90% of the code written is for this purpose (see, for example, Jon Bently [Be1]). The prevalence of exceptional behavior informs this book throughout. However, we more frequently omit serious error processing from the examples so as not to obscure the design issue under discussion.

## 1.3   REVIEW OF GOOD PROGRAMMING HABITS FOR WRITING FUNCTIONS

Although this is not a book about implementation *per se*, it does introduce a significant amount of source code as concrete illustrations of design principles. Figures 1.9–1.11 summarize some good habits for writing individual functions.

## 1.4   GOALS OF SOFTWARE DESIGN

When designing software, we are faced with challenges peculiar to the software engineering field. One of the biggest is the tendency of requirements to change while the application is being built: The very goals of a typical application shift after the decision has been made to build it. A good project manager tries hard to pin down the customer's requirements as early as possible—certainly by the time the design begins—but this is frequently not possible. In practice, we may have a good idea of the nature of an application, but we do not know exactly what is wanted until a preliminary version or a prototype has been produced. For this reason, we design with *flexibility*, enabling the designer and the programmer to more easily change what has already been done. Other goals of software design include *correctness* and *robustness*. These goals are explained here and also in Chapters 4 and 5. This section begins with an example used to illustrate how these goals are met or not met. It also demonstrates the manner in which we will document functions in this book.

- *Use expressive naming*: the names of the function, the parameters, and the variables should indicate their purpose
    - *… manipulate (float aFloat, int anInt)*            ←*poor*
    - *… getBaseRaisedToExponent(float aBase, int anExponent)*
- *Avoid global variables*: consider passing parameters instead
    - *… extract(int anEntry) {… … table = …}*            ←*replace?*
    - *… extract(int anEntry, Employee Table anEmployee Table)*
    *But not when the number of parameters exceeds   7*
- *Defend against bad data*
    - Check parameter and other input values
        - Use exceptions  −or−
        - Use defaults      −or−
        - Return special values (less desirable)

**FIGURE 1.9**   Good Habits for Writing Functions, 1 of 3

- *Don't use parameters as method variables*
- *Give names to numbers*
    for(i= 0;i < 8927; ++i) ←*poor: why 8927?*
    · Instead:
    int NUM_CELLS = 8927;
    for(cellCounter = 0; cellCounter<NUM_CELLS; ++cellCounter)
- *Limit number of parameters to 6 or 7*
- *Introduce variables near their first usage*

**FIGURE 1.10**   Good Habits for Writing Functions, 2 of 3

- *Initialize all variables*
    - reinitialize where necessary to "reset"
- *Check loop counters, especially for range correctness*
- *Avoid nesting loops more than 3 levels*
    - introduce auxiliary methods to avoid
- *Ensure loop termination*
    - a proof is ideal — in any case, be convinced
- *Inspect before compiling*

**FIGURE 1.11**   Good Habits for Writing Functions, 3 of 3

## 1.4.1   An Example

A good example to start with is a simple command-line addition application that establishes any number of "accounts" at runtime. We will call it *CommandLineCalculator*, and it has the requirements shown in the figure.

1. *CommandLineCalculator* begins by asking the user how many accounts he wants to open. It then establishes the desired number, each with zero balance.

2. *CommandLineCalculator* asks the user which of these accounts he wants to deal with.

3. When the user selected an account, *CommandLineCalculator* allows the user to add whole numbers of dollars to, or subtract them from, the account for as long as he requires.

4. When the user is done with an account, he is permitted to quit, or to pick another account to process.

**FIGURE 1.12** Informal Requirements for *CommandLineCalculator* Example

*CommandLineCalculator* produces output such as that shown.

```
================== How many accounts do you want to open: ==================
11
The application will deal with 11 accounts

---------- Please enter account number between 1 and 11 or type 'Quit application': ----------
2
    The balance in this account is 0

    Please enter the amount you want added, or type 'stop' to stop adding for now:
33
    Added 33, getting total of 33
    Please enter the amount you want added, or type 'stop' to stop adding for now:
44
    Added 44, getting total of 77
    Please enter the amount you want added, or type 'stop' to stop adding for now:
stop
    Addition ends.

---------- Please enter account number between 1 and 11 or type 'Quit application': ----------
5
    The balance in this account is 0

    Please enter the amount you want added, or type 'stop' to stop adding for now:
66
    Added 66, getting total of 66
    Please enter the amount you want added, or type 'stop' to stop adding for now:
stop
    Addition ends.

---------- Please enter account number between 1 and 11 or type 'Quit application': ----------
2
    The balance in this account is 77

    Please enter the amount you want added, or type 'stop' to stop adding for now:
88
    Added 88, getting total of 165
    Please enter the amount you want added, or type 'stop' to stop adding for now:
stop
    Addition ends.
---------- Please enter account number between 1 and 11 or type 'Quit application': ----------
Quit application
        ================== Application ends ==================
```

**FIGURE 1.13** Typical I/O For *CommandLineCalculator*

One implementation of *CommandLineCalculator* is listed in the appendix for this chapter (page 41). This particular one does a *poor* job of implementing the requirements. Some of the problems with this particular implementation are as follows.

- How can we tell from the code that all required functionality has been handled? (*correctness*)
- If the user makes a mistake the system crashes or performs unpredictably (*robustness*)
  The following cause crashes
  · Invalid number of accounts
  · Invalid account
  · Invalid amount to add (not an integer)
  · Invalid string (not "stop" or "Quit application")
- Not clear what some of the methods are meant to do (*documentation*)

**FIGURE 1.14** Problems with *CommandLineCalculator* Implementation\*, 1 of 2
\*See appendix to this chapter

An example of the last point—on inadequate method documentation—is the method *interactWithUser()*. The name gives us a general idea of course, but does not tell us what the interaction is intended to accomplish. As mentioned above, it is a poor substitute for "just read the code" to find out: After all, the code is there for a purpose, and reading the code cannot tell us what the purpose should be. Reading the code to divine its purpose is circular reasoning as in "the purpose of the code is any purpose that matches the code." There is no proper alternative to stating the method's purpose in plain natural language.

- Hard to modify, add or remove parts. (*flexibility*)
- Executes fast enough? (*speed efficiency*)
- Satisfies memory requirements? (*space efficiency*)
- Class usable for other applications? (*reusability*)

**FIGURE 1.15** Problems with *CommandLineCalculator* Implementation\*, 2 of 2
\*See appendix to this chapter

*CommandLineCalculator* is hard to modify: For example, if accounts were to comprise additional data such as the number, the transactions made against them, etc., this implementation would be entirely inappropriate. (We will not see a good remedy for this deficiency until we utilize object-orientation, discussed in the next chapter.)

The *CommandLineCalculator* class is tailored too much to the requirements of this particular problem to be reusable as a whole. Trying to reuse parts of the application in this case means reusing the methods because there is only one class. Reusing methods can be useful (e.g., the method *getInputFromUser()*), but methods are often too small in scale to keep track of, when compared to classes or groups of classes.

The requirements stated at the beginning of this section do not refer to efficiency, and we may be tempted to conclude that there are no such requirements. However, applications are executed on real computers, and are used by real people. Computers do not have unlimited memory (can we really introduce $10^{10}$ accounts?) nor are users willing to wait forever for applications to complete their operations.

The class *CommandLineCalculator* seems completely special to this application, but can it be redesigned to be usable in future applications built by this development organization?

## 1.4.2 Correctness, Sufficiency, Modularity, and Readability

The first goal of a software design is to satisfy the requirements for the application. For example, suppose that the requirement is to compute a bank balance based on the user entering a series of check numbers and amounts. We can ask whether a design consisting of a single class *Account* with method *getCheckData()*, etc. is sufficient. Our question is thus about the sufficiency of a design. Instead of the term *sufficiency,* we sometimes use the term *correctness*, although it is frequently reserved for design at a detailed level. There are informal and formal approaches to sufficiency / correctness. These are expained in Section 4.1 on page 82.

---

**KEY CONCEPT** *Ensure Correctness*

We are primarily responsible for ensuring that our code does what it's intended to.

---

## 1.4.3 Robustness

A design or implementation is *robust* if it is able to handle miscellaneous and unusual conditions such as bad data, user error, programmer error, and environmental conditions. Let's make the code in the class *CommandLineCalculator* in the appendix more robust. One way to do this is to allow it to continue to function when the user enters an illegitimate integer or even a string that is not an integer. The figures show a more robust interaction with these qualities. If the user's input is not a true integer, the application prompts the user to try again.

In the implementation, the *main()* method of the *CommandLineCalculator* calls *solicitNumberOfAccount()*, then *interactWithUser()*.

> The method *solicitNumberOfAccount()* invites the user to specify the number of accounts desired. It then sets the value of the *Vector* variable calculators by creating a separate *CommandLineCalculator* object for every account.
>
> The method *interactWithUser()* is essentially a loop that solicits an account number from the user and calls *executeAdditions()* on the account selected. The method *executeAdditions()* solicits the amount that the user wants to add to (or subtract from) the account.

This version of *interactWithUser()* is much more robust than the version in the appendix. Figure 1.17 is its activity diagram. The term "nominal path" refers to the path

```
================== How many accounts do you want to open: ==================
xyz
Sorry, not an integer: Try again.
================== How many accounts do you want to open: ==================
11
The application will deal with 11 accounts.

--------- Please enter account number between 1 and 11 or type 'Quit application': -----------
22
Please enter a legal account number

--------- Please enter account number between 1 and 11 or type 'Quit application': -----------
3
    The balance in this account is 0

    Please enter the amount you want added, or type 'stop' to stop adding for now:
abc
    Sorry -- incorrect entry: Try again
    Please enter the amount you want added, or type 'stop' to stop adding for now:
44
    Added 44, getting total of 44
    Please enter the amount you want added, or type 'stop' to stop adding for now:
55
    Added 55, getting total of 99
    Please enter the amount you want added, or type 'stop' to stop adding for now:
stop
    Addition ends.

---------- Please enter account number between 1 and 11 or type 'Quit application': ----------
6
    The balance in this account is 0
    Please enter the amount you want added, or type 'stop' to stop adding for now:
77
    Added 77, getting total of 77
    Please enter the amount you want added, or type 'stop' to stop adding for now:
stop
    Addition ends.

---------- Please enter account number between 1 and 11 or type 'Quit application': ----------
Quit application
        ================== Application ends. ==================
```

**FIGURE 1.16**   I/O for Robust *CommandLineCalculator*

where everything progresses "normally." This is a rather informal concept, but it does help the reader of the design to understand it.

Although the code for *CommandLineCalculator,* below, is much more robust than the code in the appendix, it still has many shortcomings, which we'll discuss. In addition, it does not attempt to leverage the benefits of object-oriented design. Such benefits are explored in Chapter 2, page 44.

---

**KEY CONCEPT**   *Good Code Is Not Necessarily Good Design*

The code here is more robust, but it does not exploit object-orientation or exhibit a clear design. Consequently, it's inflexible, not easy to verify, and unlikely to be reused.

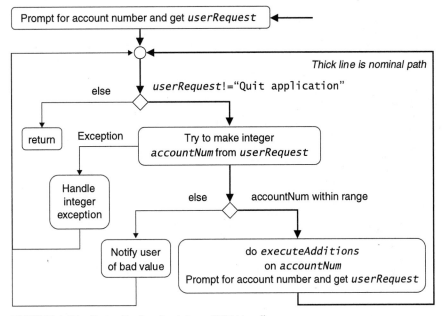

**FIGURE 1.17** Better Design for *interactWithUser()*

```
// MOST ROBUST IMPLEMENTATION IN THIS CHAPTER


import java.io.*;
import java.util.*;

/**
 * Performs addition from the command line on multiple accounts.
 *
 * Known issue: See known issues for indivudual methods
 */

class CommandLineCalculator
{
    private int accumulatedValue = 0;    // affected by arithmetic operation(s) on this

    // The accounts active in this session: Each object will be a 'CommandLineCalculator' instance
    private static Vector calculators = new Vector();

/***********************************************************************
 */
public CommandLineCalculator()
/***********************************************************************/
{  super();
}

/***********************************************************************
 * Intent: Performs addition of amounts enterd by the user to 'this'
 *
 * Precondition: 'CommandLineCalculator.calculators' != null
 *
 * Postconditions:
 * (1) The user has been prompted to add a sequence of integers or "stop" to quit this function
 * (2) The console displays each integer added as requested and the accumulating total
 * (3) The application has ended after the user has entered "stop"
 * (4) 'accumulatedValue' contains the total of all integers entered since the application began
```

```
 * (5) The console displays "Please enter an integer only." whenever the user has
 *     entered a non-integer, and allowed re-entry.
 *
 * Known issue: No provision for overflow
 */
protected void executeAdditions()
/**************************************************************************/
{
    // Get amount to add
    System.out.println
     ( "\tPlease enter the amount you want added, or type 'stop' to stop adding for now: " );
    String userRequest = getAnInputFromUser();

    // Add the amount if valid until "stop" entered
    int amountAdded = 0;
    while( !userRequest.equals( "stop" ) )
    {
        try   // -- to add the amount entered
        {
            amountAdded = ( new Integer( userRequest ) ).intValue();   // exception if not an integer
            this.accumulatedValue += amountAdded;
            System.out.println
             ( "\tAdded " + amountAdded + ", getting total of " + this.accumulatedValue );
        }
        catch( Exception e )   // non-integer entered
        {System.out.println( "\tSorry -- incorrect entry: Try again." );
        }

        System.out.println
         ( "\tPlease enter the amount you want added, or type 'stop' to stop adding for now: " );
        userRequest = getAnInputFromUser();
    }

    System.out.println( "\tAddition ends." );

}   // end executeAdditions()

/**************************************************************************
 * Postcondition: the user has been prompted at the console for a string
 *
 * Return: String input by user if the user provides one, otherwise one blank
 */
private static String getAnInputFromUser()
/**************************************************************************/
{
    try
    { BufferedReader b = new BufferedReader( new InputStreamReader( System.in ) );
      return ( b.readLine() );
    }
    catch( IOException e )
    { System.out.println( e + " Input taken to be a single blank." );
      return " ";
    }

}   // end getAnInputFromUser()

/**************************************************************************
 * Intent: Get account from user and allow additions to and subtractions from it.
 *
 * Precondition: 'CommandLineCalculator.calculators' != null
 *
 * Postconditions:
 * (1) Application has prompted user repeatedly for an account in 'calculators' until
 * an existing account number is entered, and reported the balance on the account
 * (2) Application has ignored all inputs that make no sense and output explanation
 * (3) For each account chosen, the postconditions of 'executeAdditions()' apply
 * (4) User has entered "Quit application" and this method has terminated
 *
```

```
   * Known issue: The name of this method should be more precise.
   */
public static void interactWithUser()
/*************************************************************************/
{
   System.out.println
     ( "\n---------- Please enter account number between 1 and " + calculators.size() +
       " or type 'Quit application': ----------" );
   String userRequest = getAnInputFromUser();

   int accountNum = 0;   // account currently requested
   while( !userRequest.equals( "Quit application" ) )   // return if "Quit ...."
   {
      try
      { // This should be an integer -- if not, handle exception below
         accountNum = ( new Integer( userRequest ) ).intValue() - 1;

         if( accountNum >= 0 && accountNum < calculators.size() )   // account number within range
         {
            CommandLineCalculator cLC =   // get the account
              (CommandLineCalculator)( CommandLineCalculator.calculators.get( accountNum ) );
            // Report on balance
            System.out.println
              ( "\tThe balance in this account is " + cLC.accumulatedValue + "\n");
            cLC.executeAdditions();   // make the additions
         }
         else   // account number out of range
            System.out.println( "Please enter a legal account number." );
      }
      catch( Exception e )
      { System.out.println( "Please enter an integer for an account number: Try again." );
      }

      // Repeat solicitation for account number
      System.out.println
        ( "\n---------- Please enter account number between 1 and " + calculators.size() +
          " or type 'Quit application': ----------" );
      userRequest = getAnInputFromUser();
   }

}   // end interactWithUser()

/*************************************************************************
 *
 * Postconditions: As specified in the requirements document for "Command Line Calculator"
 */
public static void main( String[] args )
/*************************************************************************/
{
   solicitNumberAccounts();
   interactWithUser();
   System.out.println( "\n\t\t================ Application ends. ================" );

}   // end main()

/*************************************************************************
 * Precondition: 'CommandLineCalculator.calculators' not null, and has no elements.
 *
 * Postconditions:
 * (1) The application has prompted the user for the number of required accounts until the user has
 * complied properly.
 * (2) 'CommandLineCalculator.calculators' contains one 'CommandLineCalculator' object
 *      for each desired account, each initialized to zero.
 *
 * Known issue: No check on numer of accounts less than 0 or greater than overflow
 */
private static void solicitNumberAccounts()
/*************************************************************************/
```

```
{
   int numAccounts = 0;

   // Get the number of accounts
   System.out.println
      ( "\n================== How many accounts do you want to open: ==================" );
   try
   {
      numAccounts = ( new Integer( getAnInputFromUser() ) ).intValue();   // repeat if not integer

      if( numAccounts > 0 )   // legitimate number of accounts
      {
         System.out.println( "The application will deal with " + numAccounts + " accounts.\n" );

         // Establish the accounts
         for( int accountIndex = 0; accountIndex < numAccounts; ++accountIndex )
         { CommandLineCalculator.calculators.addElement( new CommandLineCalculator() );
         }
      }
      else   // not legitimate number of accounts
      {
         System.out.println( "Please type a positive integer" );
         CommandLineCalculator.solicitNumberAccounts();   // try again
      }
   }
   catch( NumberFormatException e )
   {
      System.out.println( "Sorry, not an integer: Try again." );
      solicitNumberAccounts();   // repeat solicitation
   }

}   // end solicitNumberAccounts()

}
```

Various ways in which robustness can be attained are provided throughout this book, including Section 4.2, page 94.

**KEY CONCEPT**   *Write Robust Code*

Good designs withstand anomalous conditions.

### 1.4.4 Flexibility

The requirements of an application can change in many ways. Some of these are listed in the figure.

- *Obtaining more or less of what's already present*
  - · Example: handle more kinds of accounts without needing to change the existing design or code
- *Adding new kinds of functionality*
  - · Example: add *withdraw* to existing *deposit* function
- *Changing functionality*
  - · Example: allow withdrawals to create an overdraft

**FIGURE 1.18**   Aspects of Flexibility

Techniques for obtaining flexibility are explored throughout this book, including Chapter 5, page 104.

### 1.4.5   Reusability

Engineering consists of the creation of useful products with given standards of quality at minimal cost. This usually demands mass production, or at least "multiple" production. For example, it's usually impractical to build windows by hand: Instead, we buy readymade windows. The trend in software is to reuse parts among applications, and the most convincing model for this is the Java API—a large, extensive body of widely reused classes. This book emphasizes designing for reuse and Figure 1.19 lists the main options for doing so.

*We can reuse ...*

- *Object code (or equivalent)*
    - · Example: sharing *dll's* between word processor and  spreadsheet
    - · To be covered in the Components Chapters 10–12
- *Classes — in source code form*
    - · Example: *Customer* class used by several applications
    - · Thus, we write *generic code* whenever possible
- *Assemblies of Related Classes*
    - · Example: the *java.awt* package
- *Patterns of Class Assemblies*
    - · To be covered in the Design Pattern Chapters 6–9

**FIGURE 1.19**   Types of Reuse

Reuse is revisited in Chapter 5, page 104, and throughout this book.

**KEY CONCEPT**   *Design for Flexibility and Reuse*

Good designs are more easily modified and reused.

### 1.4.6   Efficiency

Efficiency refers to the use of available machine cycles and memory: Our efficiency goals are to create designs and implementations that are as fast as required, and which make use of no more than the available memory. Efficiency is frequently at odds with other goals, requiring trade-offs between efficiency and robustness or flexibility. This subject is discussed further in Chapter 5.

### 1.4.7   Other Design Goals: Reliability and Usability

As mentioned in Section 0.5.1 of the Prologue, page 15, it is unrealistic to expect that real-world applications are 100% defect-free. An application is *reliable* if it is relatively defect-free. This sounds like a vague concept, but there are metrics that make it quite precise, such as the average time between failures. Although reliability is related to robustness, they are different. As we have seen, robustness is mostly a design issue. On the other hand, reliability is mostly a process issue that requires thorough inspection and testing. Design affects reliability in that clean designs make it easier for developers to produce error-free applications.

An application has high *usability* if users find it easy to use. Usability is attained through human-interface design, an activity that is outside the scope of this book.

## 1.5 THE NEED FOR A SOFTWARE DESIGN NOTATION

Compared with expressing software design, it appears easy enough to express the design of a bridge. This is because we can see a bridge, and we expect to be able to visualize it by means of a paper design. Functioning software, on the other hand, can be observed directly only though its interface. The interface is just the tip of the design iceberg, however, and the important question is how to express the design of the rest of an application in an effective manner.

Over the years there have been several attempts to establish a visual design notation, but none has been as successful as the Unified Modeling Language (UML), covered in Chapter 3, page 61. The UML is broad enough to describe the building blocks of applications, the manner in which applications carry out their functionality, and the manner in which they react to events occurring to them.

## CHAPTER SUMMARY

This chapter was introduced to suggest appropriate questions to the reader: The rest of this book provides many answers. We improved an initial version of the command-line calculator, but even the improvement leaves several issues unsettled, as stated in Figure 1.20.

- *Insufficient* flexibility
  - · To add subtraction, multiplication, etc.
  - · To change the nature of the project
- *Speed* efficiency *not explored*
- *Space* efficiency *not explored*
  - · Limit to number of accounts?
- Reusability *doubtful*
  - · OO not leveraged
- *No visualization of design provided*

**FIGURE 1.20**   Remaining Problems with *CommandLineCalculator*

## EXERCISES

**Exercise 1.1**   Suppose that you are building a class *Account*. Suppose that the class has a *boolean* variable *open*, as well as an *int* variable *balance* that is to be in the range –1,000 to 1,000. Suppose that you want to implement a method *add( int anAmount )* that adds *anAmount* to *balance*, and returns the new value of *balance*. Also, assume that this method is meant to be called only if the value of *open* is *true*. Write appropriate documentation to be inserted within the comments prior to *add()*.

Evaluation criteria:

- Effectiveness of your response         A = correct and complete method specification
- Clarity of documentation         A = every category present and very clearly stated

The following are errors that you should watch for in Exercise 1.1:

*Serious*:

**1.** Confusion among the preconditions / parameters etc. categories

**2.** Missing specifications

*Less than serious, more than trivial:*

**1.** Somewhat vague specifications in any category

**Exercise 1.2**    This exercise pertains to the following application:

> *This is to be a command-line address book that allows you to store a name and an address on a predetermined text file. The user can add and retrieve entries. Entries can be retrieved by name. Editing is not required. Here is a typical interaction.*

```
>> Add (a) or retrieve (r)
a
>> Name:
Eric Braude
>> Address:
2 Main St. Mytown, AZ 12345

>> Add (a) or retrieve (r)?
r
>> Name:
John Doe
>> The address is: 33 Main St. Yourtown, MN 98765
```

**Part 1.2.1** Write pseudocode and activity diagram(s) (flowcharts) for the nontrivial methods in the application. Make the application robust. You need not be concerned with the *flexibility* or *reusability* of your design and implementation. Explain your reasoning.

**Part 1.2.2** Use the code and specification standards in this chapter (or improve upon them if you can) to implement the application in a manner consistent with your activity diagram(s) and pseudocode. Your pseudocode should appear as comments in your code. Explain your reasoning. You can generate the data from scratch each time you execute the application: There is no requirement to save data between executions. Show the output for representative sample input.

**Part 1.2.3** Give at least two specific ways in which this application can be made more *flexible*. Explain your reasoning.

**Part 1.2.4** Give at least two specific ways in which parts of the design or implementation of this application can be made *reusable*. Explain your reasoning.

Evaluation criteria:

- Clarity of comments and code         A = every nontrivial code step clearly explained; comments explain very clearly
- Effectiveness of your response         A = effective and completely specific avenues for flexibility, reusability, and robustness

The following are errors that you should watch for in Exercise 1.2:

*Serious errors*:

**1.** Loops should show the arrow returning to a choice diamond.

**2.** Pseudocode is not the same as source code. Its advantage is that it is comprehensible English. A litmus test is whether it can appear, without change, as useful comments to the source.

**3.** Postconditions should not reference variables local to the method because postconditions (like preconditions) concern the method's external environment and effect.

*Less than serious errors, but more than minor:*

**1.** On choices (diamonds), state a condition on one side and "else" on the other. This is usually safer than specifying the positive and the negative conditions, which can leave gaps in conditions when an error is made. It also maps to the code more faithfully.

**2.** Pseudocode and flowcharts apply to specific methods: state clearly which ones.

**3.** The comments in the code should match those in the flowchart.

**4.** Postconditions specify state after the completion of the method. They are not intended to describe an algorithm. If you want to specify that an output sequence has taken place, you can describe this as follows. "X has been displayed, Y has been displayed …" If you need to describe the algorithm, do it separately.

**5.** Choice diamonds are set up for two-way choices. Don't use them for more than two.

**6.** Several of the questions concern "the application," such as making it more flexible. The answer to such a question should be made in terms of requirements of the application, not in terms of classes and functions. The latter are design responses to flexibility of the application.

**7.** Each pseudocode line should appear, typically, as a comment preceding each line or set of lines of code.

**8.** Use expressive names: E.g., don't waste an opportunity to be clearer by using name "hashTable"; Use *nameAutoTable* instead or perhaps *nameAutoHashTable*.

**9.** Make a clear distinction between pseudocode keywords and nonkeywords. This helps to clear up doubts about the meaning of the algorithm.

**10.** "Reusability" applies primarily to the parts of a design. A class (current or envisaged) can be reused, for example.

**11.** In giving preconditions, don't list the circumstances under which the method can be called (e.g. "retrieve button was pressed") unless *necessary* to the execution of the method. Remember that a method can be used in potentially many ways once you have written it.

**12.** When "reusing" pseudocode as comments, intersperse it with the code rather than listing it in one block at the head of the code.

*Minor errors:*

**1.** The trouble with drawing flowcharts by hand is that they are difficult to modify. As our understanding of a problem improves, we usually need to redraw parts of a diagram. Powerful tools are available for this kind of purpose, but even using Visio, or PowerPoint with the "connector" feature can save a lot of time.

**2.** Reduce tab width and font size to avoid line wraparound except in rare cases.

**Exercise 1.3**   Inspect the more robust version of the calculator application in these notes.

**Part 1.3.1** State specifically how the robustness of the implementation can be improved even more. Explain your reasoning.

**Part 1.3.2** Implement the improvements in robustness that you describe in Part 1.2.1 on page 39. Enclose each code addition or modification with the following notation. Document your code thoroughly. Show typical I/O.

```
// Begin code addition -------------------------------------------------------
// Reason for addition -------------------------------------------------------
. . . . .
// End code addition ---------------------------------------------------------
```

or

```
// Begin code modification ---------------------------------------------------
// Reason for modification ---------------------------------------------------
. . . . .
// End code modification -----------------------------------------------------
```

or

. . . . .                                                    // code added ----------------

or

. . . . .                                                    // code modified -------------

**Part 1.3.3** State specifically how this application can be made more *flexible*. You are not requested to design or code for this. Explain your reasoning.

**Part 1.3.4** State specifically how parts of the design or implementation of this application can be made *reusable*. You are not requested to design or code for this. Explain your reasoning.

Evaluation criteria:
- Clarity and specificity
- Effectiveness of your response

A = thoroughly specific answers to all questions
A = effective avenues provided for flexibility, reusability, and robustness

The following are errors that you should watch for:
*Serious*:
**1.** To make submissions clear, always show typical I/O, even when not specifically asked.

*Less than serious, but more than minor*:
**1.** On the issue of reusability (Part 1.2.4), we get reusability in terms of useful individual classes. If a class has lots of functionality, then it is more reusable. Try to avoid having that functionality depend on other classes: If you have to do so, recognize that the classes will have to be used together in other applications, which can reduce their reusability.

**2.** See error 6 in Exercise 1.2.

**Exercise 1.4** Perform the following experiment with the *Hashtable* facility of Java. Store a set of name (String) / telephone number (integer) pairs in a *Hashtable* versus a *Vector* of objects. Compare how long it takes to find the telephone number of a random individual. Explain your reasoning. Note that this is an exercise on testing for efficiency, not on the theory behind hash tables vs. linear searching.

Evaluation criteria:
- Effectiveness of your experiment

A = an experimental plan and code that clearly measure the difference

- Clarity of results

A = a presentation of your results that clearly shows the difference in performance

## APPENDIX

### NON-ROBUST CODE FOR
### CommandLineCalculator EXAMPLE

Here is the faulty code for *CommandLineCalculator* that produces the output shown in Figure 1.13 on page 29.

```
// NON-ROBUST IMPLEMENTATION: CRASHES AT MOST USER ERRORS
import java.io.*;
import java.util.*;
/**
 * Performs addition from the command line on multiple accounts.
 */
class CommandLineCalculator
```

```
{
    private int accumulatedValue = 0; // affected by arithmetic operation(s) on this
    private static Vector calculators = new Vector(); // the accounts active in this session

/**********************************************************************************************
 */
public CommandLineCalculator()
/**********************************************************************************************/
{  super();
}
/**********************************************************************************************
 * Postconditions:
 * (1) Application has obtained number of accounts from user
 * (2) Application has prompted user to add integers to any of these accounts
 * (3) Application has output to console the balance after each transaction
 */
public static void main( String[] args )
/**********************************************************************************************/
{
    solicitNumberAccounts();
    interactWithUser();
    System.out.println( "\n\t---- Application ends. ----" );
}
/**********************************************************************************************
 * Preconditions: this.accumulatedValue == 0
 *
 * Postconditions:
 * (1) The user has been prompted to add a sequence of integers or "stop" to quit
 * (2) The user has responded with a sequence of integers or "stop"
 * (3) The console has echoed each integer added and the accumulating total
 * (4) The application has ended after the user has entered "stop"
 * (5) 'accumulatedValue' contains the total of all integers entered since the application began
 * (6) The application has stated "Please enter an integer only." whenever the user has
 * entered a non-integer, and allowed re-entry.
 */
protected void executeAdditions()
/**********************************************************************************************/
{
    // Get amount to add
    System.out.println
      ( "\tPlease enter the amount you want added, or type 'stop' to stop adding for now: " );
    String userRequest = getAnInputFromUser();

    // Add the amount if valid until "stop" entered
    int amountAdded = 0;
    while( !userRequest.equals( "stop" ) )
    {
        amountAdded = ( new Integer( userRequest ) ).intValue();
      this.accumulatedValue += amountAdded;
        System.out.println
          ( "\tAdded " + amountAdded + ", getting total of " + this.accumulatedValue );
        System.out.println
          ( "\tPlease enter the amount you want added, or type 'stop' to stop adding for now: " );
        userRequest = getAnInputFromUser();
    }

    System.out.println( "\tAddition ends." );

} // end executeAdditions()

/**********************************************************************************************
 * Precondition: 'CommandLineCalculator.calculators' not null.
 * Postconditions:
 * (1) The application has prompted the user for a number of accounts
 * (2) The user has complied legitimately
 * (3) 'CommandLineCalculator.calculators' contains one 'CommandLineCalculator' object
 * for each desired account, each initialized to zero.
 */
```

```
private static void solicitNumberAccounts()
/***************************************************************************************************/
{
   int numAccounts = 0;

   // Get the number of accounts
   System.out.println( "\n=========== How many accounts do you want to open: ===========" );
   numAccounts = ( new Integer( getAnInputFromUser() ) ).intValue();
   System.out.println // echo
    ( "The application will deal with " + numAccounts + " accounts.\n" );
   // Establish the accounts
   for( int accountIndex = 0; accountIndex < numAccounts; ++accountIndex )
      CommandLineCalculator.calculators.addElement( new CommandLineCalculator() );
} // end solicitNumberAccounts()
/***************************************************************************************************
 * Postconditions: the user has been prompted for a string
 * Return: String input by user if the user provides one, otherwise one blank
 */
private static String getAnInputFromUser()
/***************************************************************************************************/
{
   try
   { BufferedReader b = new BufferedReader( new InputStreamReader( System.in ) );
      return ( b.readLine() );
   }
   catch( IOException e )
   { System.out.println( e + " Input taken to be a single blank." );
      return " ";
   }
}
/***************************************************************************************************
 */
public static void interactWithUser()
/***************************************************************************************************/
{
   // Get the account
   String userRequest = " ";

   do // as long as user does not signal desire to end the interaction
   {
      // Get the next account requested by the user
      System.out.println
       ( "\n-------- Please enter account number (starting at 1) or 'Quit application': ----------" );
      userRequest = getAnInputFromUser();
      if( userRequest.equals( "Quit application" ) )
         break;

      // Get the account and perform operations on it
      int accountNum = ( new Integer( userRequest ) ).intValue() - 1;
      CommandLineCalculator cLC =
       (CommandLineCalculator)( calculators.get( accountNum ) );
      // Report on balance
      System.out.println( "\tThe balance in this account is " + cLC.accumulatedValue + "\n");
      cLC.executeAdditions();
   }
   while( !userRequest.equals( "Quit application" ) );

} // end interactWithUser()
}
```

# OBJECT-ORIENTATION

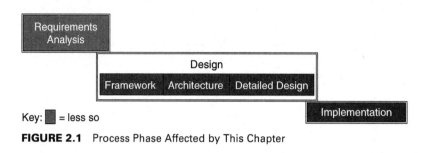

FIGURE 2.1   Process Phase Affected by This Chapter

## 2.1   THE GOALS OF OBJECT-ORIENTATION

Prior to the advent of object-orientation, code was typically organized as a collection of modules, each consisting of a collection of functions. Modules in larger applications were broken into submodules, etc. These, in turn, were decomposed into functions.

Functions implement algorithms—ways to carry out tasks. Although algorithms are important, the real world does not decompose primarily into modules and algorithms. Instead, we generally think of our world in terms of *concepts* such as automobiles and houses and in terms of concrete *entities* such as my Toyota and your desk. Because of this mismatch between functions and the way we normally think, traditional designs and code mapped poorly to the real world, as suggested by Figure 2.2.

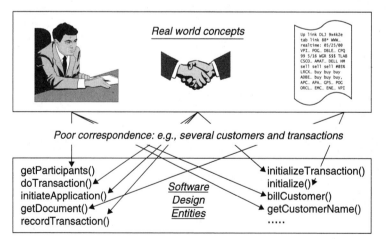

Graphics reproduced with permission from Corel.

FIGURE 2.2   *Before* Object-Orientation

To understand how object-orientation helps to remedy this mismatch between the real world and a design, we consider a mode of communication that humans find natural. One crucial such tool is language, of which the statement in Figure 2.3 is an example.

"Customers Montague and Susan entered the Ajax bank and were served by teller Andy…"

**FIGURE 2.3** How *Do* We Express Ourselves?

Of the many grammatical constructs in natural language, a good starting point is with nouns: *customer*, *Montague*, *Susan*, *Ajax*, *teller*, and *Andy*. The nouns *customer* and *teller* express concepts. The nouns *Montague* and *Susan* are instances of *customer*; *Ajax* and *Andy* are instances of *bank* and *teller* respectively. This capturing of the role of nouns is the basis of object-orientation, as suggested in Figure 2.4.

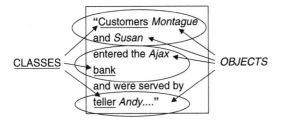

**FIGURE 2.4** Expressing Ourselves with Nouns

Figure 2.5 illustrates that object-orientation results in a far better map between the real world and the software.

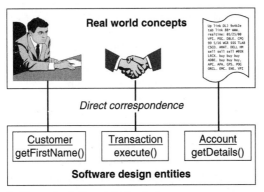

Graphics reproduced with permission from Corel.

**FIGURE 2.5** Object-Orientation

In short, *a primary goal of object-orientation is to provide a direct mapping between the real world and the units of organization used in the design*. Next, we discuss the building blocks for this mapping: classes and objects.

---

**KEY CONCEPT** *Benefits of OO*

Object-orientation provides a direct mapping between concepts and code.

---

## 2.2 CLASSES AND OBJECTS

As we have seen from the previous discussion, the principal manner in which object-orientation (OO) provides a mapping between the real world and the design is through the naming of concepts. Concepts correspond to *classes* in OO, and instances are the *objects* of those classes. For example, *"your Ford Mustang with vehicle identification number 678ABC3456GHI"* is an object of the class *FordMustang1965Model*.

OO capitalization conventions are usually the opposite of those used in English. Classes are capitalized in OO but referred to in lower case in natural language: instances such as "Andy" are capitalized in natural language but stated with lower case in OO designs.

### 2.2.1 Introducing Classes

This section discusses the process of naming a concept or idea as a class. The need to introduce a class for a concept such as *FordMustang* is fairly evident: As will be seen throughout this book, however, it is often useful to introduce classes that are less obvious. In a business application, for example, we could find that a *StockTransaction* class leads to a good design. The Java API library introduces classes for diverse concepts, including *Event* and *Color*. Figure 2.6 illustrates the introduction of some classes, and uses the UML rectangle representation.

Along with class introduction goes the issue of *allocating responsibility*: Collecting functionality within the appropriate classes. A litmus test of whether functionality belongs to a particular class is to imagine convincing other engineers to use the class in the applications they are building. If a class comes packaged with significant functionality that clearly belongs, then it is more likely to be used.

Let's take as an example an application that tracks the status of boats leaving a harbor. We can imagine the Coast Guard using such an application. One of the requirements, let's say, is a feature whereby the captain's next-of-kin is automatically notified by telephone if his excursion is more than an hour later than the scheduled time of arrival. Let's suppose that the method *notifyNextOfKin()* does the actual automated dialing. The question is: Does *notifyNextOfKin()* belong with the *CoastGuard* class, the *CrewMember* class, the *Excursion* class, or the *Boat* class? In English we might say "the Coast Guard called his next of kin": However, this refers to an action of the application as a whole, and does not necessarily mean that the *CoastGuard* class should be responsible for the actual work.

In fact, a good location for *notifyNextOfKin()* is the class *CrewMember*. Imagine convincing other developers to use the class *CrewMember*: The presence of *notifyNextOfKin()* would be a feature of *CrewMember*, making it that much more useful. The class *CoastGuard* would probably be one of the clients of *CrewMember*: Another possible client is *Excursion*. A *client* class is one whose methods call those of *Crew Member*. (See Section 2.2.4.)

The process of w*rapping* consists of introducing a class to capture something not initially object oriented. For example, wrapping a legacy application means introducing a class that represents that application. Calling a method of a "wrapper" class instance typically translates into the use of legacy functionality.

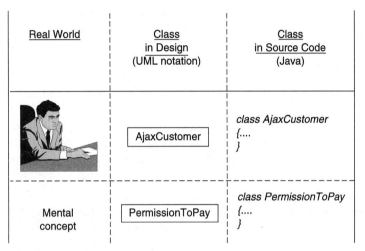

**FIGURE 2.6** Class Introduction

## 2.2.2 Instantiation

Once a class is selected to capture a concept, we typically want to create and use instances of the class. For example, if *Auto* is a class with attributes *mileage* and *identificationNumber*, then *myToyota* and *aliceBrownBMW* would be *Auto* instances.

## 2.2.3 The Members of a Class

It has long been recognized that programs consist of two basic parts: *Data* and *functions*. Classes reflect this division: The members of classes are either *variables* (also called *fields* or *attributes*) or *methods* (also called *functions* or *operations*).

*Class members* are independent of individual objects. In Java and C++ terminology, these are the *static* members. The variable *totalNumAutosMade*, for example, would be a class member. A method that increments this class variable is a *class method* in that it references only class members. On the other hand, for nonstatic variables, every object of the class has its own copy with the specified name. These are the *instance variables* of the class. For example, *mileage* and *vehicleID* in class *Automobile* are instance variables, meaning that each *Auto* instance has its own version of these variables (see Figure 2.7).

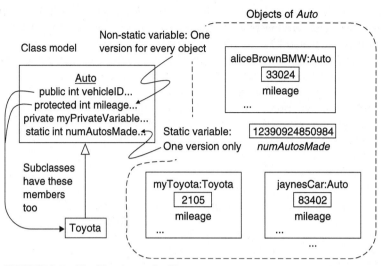

**FIGURE 2.7**   The Members of a Class

Note that some instance variables, such as *mileage* in *Auto*, vary for each instance, whereas other instance variables such as *vehicleID* do not. The latter, called "naming variables," would be *final* in Java terms. A "referential" variable implements a connection with another class. These variable types are summarized in Figure 2.8.

**KEY CONCEPT**   *Classes and Objects*

A class expresses a concept such as "Honda Civic." An object is an instance of a class such as "the Honda Civic with vehicle ID 89R783HJD894."

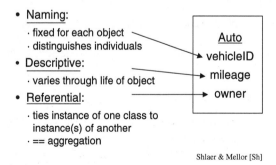

- Naming:
  · fixed for each object
  · distinguishes individuals
- Descriptive:
  · varies through life of object
- Referential:
  · ties instance of one class to instance(s) of another
  · == aggregation

Shlaer & Mellor [Sh]

**FIGURE 2.8**   Attribute Types

### 2.2.4   The "Client" Concept in Object-Orientation

Sometimes objects are useful in a stand-alone fashion: For example, the class *CommandLineCalculator* in Chapter 1 performs all of the required functionality of the application. In most applications, however, an object *o* exists to serve the needs of other objects: We call these other objects *clients* of *o*. Classes exist to "stamp out" objects that provide services to clients. Classes themselves may also service clients by means of their static methods. In either case, we often say "class *A* is a client of class *B*." We sometimes also say "class *B* is a server for class *A*." In the figure, for example, classes *AjaxAssets* and *AjaxWebsiteGenerator* are clients of the class *Customer*.

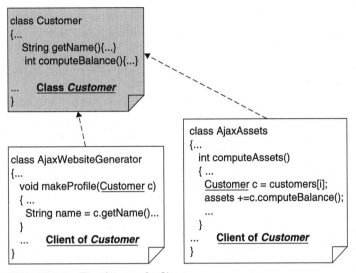

**FIGURE 2.9** The *Clients* of a Class

Note that the client/server relationship between a pair of classes in an OO application is not necessarily permanent. It may be, for example, that the class *Customer* could require services of *AjaxAssets*. We typically try to avoid such two-way dependencies, however.

Next, we list the main aspects of classes that provide their design benefits.

## 2.3 KEY FEATURES OF OBJECT-ORIENTATION

This section describes the special aspects of OO that make it useful for developing applications. These include the concepts in Figure 2.10.

Finally, we will discuss how to specify a class as it appears to clients.

- *Class Introduction*          (Section 2.2.1)
  - · basic motive of object-orientation
  - · identifying parts that correspond to the real world
- *Instantiation*          (Section 2.2.2)
  - · creating instances of encapsulated concepts
- *Inheritance*          (Section 2.3.1)
  - · capturing the way concepts occur in hierarchy
- *Polymorphism*          (Section 2.3.2)
  - · capturing use of single action word to represent different things, depending on context

**FIGURE 2.10** Aspects of OO Useful for Application Development

### 2.3.1 Inheritance

Inheritance is the term used in OO for generalization (also known as *abstraction*, *is-a*, or *a-kind-of*). Abstraction is not an academic or theoretical concept, it's fundamental to how we communicate. For example, when *Encyclopedia Britannica* wishes to explain what an "Okapi" is, it used the following description. [En]

> (species *Okapia johnstoni*), cud-chewing hoofed mammal that is placed along with the giraffe in the family Giraffidae (order Artiodactyla). . . . Its neck and legs are shorter than those of the giraffe . . .

At the beginning of this description, we are told that the *Okapi* is a mammal. In OO parlance, we say that the class *Okapi inherits* from the class *Mammal*. Indeed, it would be very difficult to communicate without this ability to abstract. The *Britannica* description for an Okapi actually uses a class, which we could call *CudChewingHoofedMammal*, between the classes *Mammal* and *Okapi* in the inheritance hierarchy. In summary, *Okapi* inherits from *CudChewingHoofedMammal*, and *CudChewingHoofedMammal* inherits from *Mammal*.

Object-orientation allows us to utilize this useful generalization facility for software design and implementation.

### 2.3.2 Polymorphism

Natural languages use the same verb in more than one sense. For example, we can "*run* to the store," "*run* a computer," "*run* a company," etc. Imagine for a minute that English did not have this ability. The verb *to run* would have to be replaced by a set of separate new verbs. We would have to "*run1* to the store," "*run2* a computer," "*run3* a company," "*run4* a baseball team," "*run5* a meeting" ("*meetingRun* a meeting"?) etc. This would be entirely impractical. Note that each of these senses of *run* is different from the others, although many share common aspects.

The idea of using the same verb whose sense depends on its context occurs in many, if not all languages, and thus seems to be fundamental. In OO, we call this phenomenon *polymorphism*, and it greatly enhances our design repertoire.

To illustrate polymorphism in action, suppose that an application must produce e-mail text for various kinds of customers in accordance with the requirements in Figures 2.11 through 2.14.

1.  **Summary:**
Produces e-mail text for various types of customers.

2.  **Detailed requirements**

2.1 The application displays choices to the console,
as shown in Figure 2.13.

2.2 For customers delinquent more than 90 days, the e-mail
message generated is the statement shown in Figure 2.12.

**FIGURE 2.11** Requirements for *e-Mail Creation* Example, 1 of 4

Output

```
Pick from one of the following:
mountain
regular
delinquent
delinquent

We regret that your account is more than 90 days delinquent.
<Record of last payment and amount inserted here>
We regret that your account has been turned over to the Friendly Collection Agency.
Please contact them at 1-800-FRIENDLY.
... lots more output specialized to delinquent customers ...
Please read the following statement of your rights.
<Statement of debtor collection rights goes here.>
```

**FIGURE 2.12**   Typical Interaction for *e-Mail Creation* Example, 2 of 4

2.3  All non-delinquent customers receive a tailored
e-mail messages as follows.

2.3.1 Mountain customers:

This month we have  a special on West Face tents.

Only $700.

... lots more output specialized to mountaineering customers

2.3.2 Regular customers:

All items are marked down 20% for this month only.

... lots more output for regular customers ...

**FIGURE 2.13**   Requirements for *e-Mail Creation* Example, 3 of 4

2.4  The e-mail is to be displayed on the console.

**3.   Future enhancements**

We anticipate that the text is likely to change frequently, and
that new kinds of customers are likely to be specified,
each with its own new set of requirements.

**FIGURE 2.14**   Requirements for *e-Mail Creation* Example, 4 of 4

A design that relies on branching would look something like the following.

```
if( customerType.equals("delinquent" )              // "delinquent" customers
{ store( "delinquent message" );
 writeToConsole( "delinquent message" );
       . . . . .
}
else
 if( customerType.equals( "mountain climbing" )     // "mountain" customers
 { store( "mountain climbing" );
 writeToConsole( "mountain climbing" );
       . . . . .
 }
 else                                               // "badminton" customers
 { store( "regular" );
 writeToConsole( "regular" );
 . . . .
```

This is a poor design for several reasons, as suggested in Figure 2.15.

- *Code for each case not cohesive*
  ("cohesive": forms a comprehensible unity)
  · All types of customers coded together in single class

*Expensive to ...*

- *... add new functionality*
  · bloat *switch* or *if-then* code
- *... remove functionality*
  · hunt for all parts that must be removed
- *... change functionality*
  · hunt for all parts that must be changed

**FIGURE 2.15**  Disadvantages of Branching

We can solve many of these design problems by using polymorphism. The next chapter discusses the Unified Modeling Language, which will enable us to visualize this solution. For now our solution will be visible at the code level only. The following polymorphic design captures the essence of customers in an abstract *Customer* class, and uses subclasses to capture the various types of customers. Each of these subclasses has its own version of the method *createMail()*. Finally, a class *CustomerMailApplication* is introduced, containing the application's *main()* method. It handles interaction with the user, and, by instantiating its *customer* instance variable with an object of the appropriate *Customer* subclass, it effectively applies the *createMail()*version corresponding to the user's request.

Branching code is limited to setting the variable *CustomerMailApplication.customer*. The real work required for generating the messages for the various types of customers is located within the respective *Customer* subclasses, where it belongs. The code for *CustomerMailApplication* is as follows:

```
import java.io.*;
import java.util.*;

/**
 * Demonstration of polymorphism: Output depends on customer type selected by user.
 */
class CustomerMailApplication
{
        private static Customer customer = new RegularCustomer(); // default <--------- LINE (a)

/*********************************************************************************************************
 */
public CustomerMailApplication()
/
*********************************************************************************************************/
{       super();
}


/
*********************************************************************************************
 * Postconditions:
 * (1) User has been prompted with type of 'customer'
```

```
 * (2) 'customer' equals an instance of the type entered if the user's input legitimate
 * (3) 'customer' equals an instance of 'Regular' if user's input not legitimate
 * (4) The message corresponding to 'customer's type has been printed to the console
 */
private static void getCustomerTypeFromUser()
/**********************************************************************************/
{
      String customerType = "regular"; // default

      // Key user input to the corresponding type of customer
      Hashtable customerTypeTable = new Hashtable();
      customerTypeTable.put( "regular", new RegularCustomer() );
      customerTypeTable.put( "delinquent", new DelinquentCustomer() );
      customerTypeTable.put( "mountain", new MountainCustomer() );

      // Get customer type from user (this avoids modification if 'customerTypeTable' is modified)

      // List available types
      System.out.println( "Pick from one of the following:" );
      for ( Enumeration enumeration = customerTypeTable.keys(); enumeration.hasMoreElements() ;)
      { System.out.println( enumeration.nextElement() );
      }

      try // pick one
      {
            BufferedReader bufReader =
             new BufferedReader( new InputStreamReader( System.in ) );
            customerType = bufReader.readLine();
      }
      catch( IOException e )
      {     System.out.println( e );
      }

      // Assign CustomerMailApplication.customer accordingly
      Customer customerTypeSelected = (Customer)customerTypeTable.get( customerType );
      if( customerTypeSelected != null )
      {     CustomerMailApplication.customer = customerTypeSelected;
      }
      else // use default if user input bad
      {
            CustomerMailApplication.customer = new RegularCustomer();
            System.out.println
             ( "Sorry: Could not understand your input: regular customer assumed." );
      }

} // end CustomerTypeFromUser()

/**********************************************************************************
 * Postconditions:
 * As stated in the requirements specificatin for the e-mail creation exercise.
 */
public static void main( String[] args )
/**********************************************************************************/
{
      getCustomerTypeFromUser();
      generateMail();
}

/**********************************************************************************
 * Postconditions: As for 'createMail()' of customer
 */
public static void generateMail()
/**********************************************************************************/
{     CustomerMailApplication.customer.createMail(); // <--------- LINE (b)
}

}
```

The line

```
private static Customer customer = new RegularCustomer(); // default <--------- LINE (a)
```

is where *CustomerMailApplication* aggregates a *Customer* object. This object is instanti-ated at runtime by the method *getCustomerTypeFromUser(),* which sets *customer* to an object of either *MountainCustomer* or *DelinquentCustomer.*

When the application is ready to create an e-mail message, it executes *generateMail()*. This method, in turn, calls *customer.createMail()* as in the statement

```
CustomerMailApplication.customer.createMail(); // <--------- LINE (b)
```

Here we gain the benefit of polymorphism because the version of *createMail()* exe-cuted is the one corresponding to the current class of *CustomerMailApplication.customer* (the *customer* attribute of *CustomerMailApplication*). For example, if *customer* is cur-rently a *MountainCustomer* object, then the *createMail()* version defined in the class *MountainCustomer* is executed, creating the e-mail tailored to customers interested in mountain gear, etc.

The code for the class *MountainCustomer* is

```
/**
 */
class MountainCustomer extends Customer
{

/******************************************************************************************
 */
public MountainCustomer()
/*****************************************************************************************/
{     super();
}

/*****************************************************************************************
 * Postcondition: A message tailored to mountaineering customers has been printed at the console
 */
protected void createMail()
/*****************************************************************************************/
{     System.out.println( "\nThis month we have a special on West Face tents. Only $700." );
      System.out.println( "... lots more output specialized to mountaineering customers ..." );
}

)
```

This design still leaves several desired properties unfulfilled, as listed in Figure 2.16.

- *We need to visualize the design*
  - · Code not an effective way to understand design
- *The design's maintainability still has flaws*
  - · As the application grows, specialized class(es) will be required to interact with the user

**FIGURE 2.16** Aspects of the *Customer* Design Needing Improvement

> ## KEY CONCEPT   *Polymorphism*
>
> The use of several versions of a method, one in each derived class. This enables *objectOfBaseClass.theMethod()* to be interpreted variously at runtime, depending on what derived class *objectOfBaseClass* belongs to.

### 2.3.3  Interfaces and Encapsulation

All objects of a class provide the same functional *interface*. Describing the interface of a class amounts to specifying the information in Figure 2.17 for each function in the interface.

- *Name of the function*
    - Example: *add*
- *Argument types(if any)*
    - Example:
        - · First parameter: *integer*
        - · Second parameter: *float*
- *Return type*
    - Example: *double,* reference type, *void*
- *Exceptions(if any)*
    - Example: *IOException*
- *More(?)*
    - · Are parameters inputs and/or outputs?
    - · Describe what the function does (natural language)

**FIGURE 2.17**  What's Needed to Specify Functionality

A class may have a hundred methods, and we may want to reuse some of these specifications for other classes that we construct in the future, but this requires a way to organize the methods. Figure 2.18 illustrates the problem.

```
class Draw
{    ...
    int setColor(String) {...}
    Pen getStandardPen() {...}
    int getLogoStyle() {...}
    void setColor(int) {...}
    void drawLogo(int, int) {...}
    void speedUpPen(int) {...}

    ...

}
```

**FIGURE 2.18**  Unorganized Lists of Methods

Function specifications are often grouped into sets to make them manageable: Each set is considered a separate *interface*. Figure 2.19 provides an example of the interfaces for a *Draw* class.

- *Functions dealing with the pen used*
  - · Pen getStandardPen()
  - · void speedUpPen(int)     } *Pen* interface
  - · ...
- *Functions dealing with the colors available*
  - · void setColor(int)
  - · int setColor(String)     } *Color* interface
  - · ...
- *Functions covering the drawing of the company's logo*
  - · void drawLogo(int, int)
  - · int getLogoStyle()     } *Logo* interface
  - · ...
- ... ...

**FIGURE 2.19**   Interface Example: a *Draw* Class

Each interface is thus a collection of function prototypes.

Note that the Java version of "interfaces" actually requires argument names. We have to write something like

```
void speedUpPen( int aSpeedUpAmount )
```

rather than just

```
void speedUpPen( int )
```

An interface can also act merely as a tag, containing no function prototypes at all. If a class implements such an interface then it can be thought of as being "marked" for a particular purpose. This idea has meaning in the context of the language that is used. For example, a Java class implements the *Cloneable* interface "to indicate to the *Object.clone()* method that it is legal for that method to make a field-for-field copy of instances of that class" (Sun [Su1]). *Cloneable* actually contains no function prototypes.

The interfaces in Figure 2.19 could be implemented as shown next, where the *Pen* interface inherits from a *DrawingDevice* interface.

```
package drawing;

/**
*/
public interface Color
{
        public void setColor( int aColorNum );
        public int setColor( String aColorName );
}

package drawing;

/**
*/
```

```
public interface DrawingDevice
{
        public void draw();
}

package drawing;

public interface Logo
{
        public void drawLogo( int aStyleNum, int aHeight );
        public int getLogoStyle();
}

package drawing;

/**
*/
public interface Pen extends DrawingDevice
{
        public Pen getStandardPen();
        public void speedUpPen( int aSpeed );
}
```

We say that the class *Draw* "encapsulates" the *Pen*, *Color*, and *Logo* interfaces. The term *encapsulation* applies when we are trying to expose functionality, hiding the manner in which that functionality is obtained (the "implementation"). We often introduce classes in order to encapsulate interfaces.

The interface provided by a *collection* of classes is no different: It is the set of functions provided by objects of classes in the collection. We will return to the topic of interfaces in Section 8.2 (page 205).

---

**KEY CONCEPT**   *Interfaces*

An interface is a set of function prototypes (each with name, parameter types, return type, exception type).

---

## 2.4   ISSUES TO BE ADDRESSED

Despite the benefits afforded by the OO concept, numerous issues remain to be addressed. Some of these are listed in Figure 2.20. The rest of this book addresses many of these issues.

- How do we visualize a set of classes?
- How can classes relate to each other?
- How *should* classes relate to each other?
- How can we describe functionality occurring among several classes?
- How do we describe the manner in which objects respond to events occurring on them?
- Are there patterns of class usage that recur?
  - So we can existing design parts

**FIGURE 2.20**   Issues to Be Addressed

# CHAPTER SUMMARY

Figure 2.21 summarizes the main points of this chapter.

- A *Class* represents a concept
  - · Example: *House*
- An *Object* is an instance of a class
  - · Example: *23 Main Street, Springfield*
- Classes can relate in several ways: Mainly...
  - · A *Client* of a class refers to that class in one of its methods
  - · *Inheritance:* "kind of" relationship
  - · *Aggregation:* "has a" relationship, explained in Chapter 3
- *Polymorphism* means "action depends on context"
  - · Executing *anObject.aMethod( )* actually executes the version of *aMethod( )* in the subclass that *anObject* belongs to

**FIGURE 2.21**   Summary of This Chapter

# EXERCISES

**Exercise 2.1**   Why would you say we use object-orientation? This is a matter of opinion, so justify your statements.

Evaluation criteria:
- Clarity of your comments          A = very clearly explained
- Backup to support your comments   A = clear examples that support opinions

**Exercise 2.2**   Which of the following are probably objects of which classes (if any)? Explain your reasoning.

*Ship, TwoMainStreet, CruiseShip, Mansion, Cruise90938, VacationTrip, House, PanamaShip89032*

**Exercise 2.3**   Consider the design of an application that controls a traffic signal, and that depends on sensors in the roadway. Classify them as *Definitely OK, No Justification* and *Maybe*.

**Part 2.3.1**  Based on this amount of knowledge, which of the following class selections can't be justified yet for this application? Explain your reasoning.

*Intersection, Automobile, Passenger, Driver, Sensor, Color*

**Part 2.3.2**  List reasonable additional class candidates for this application. Explain your reasoning.

**Exercise 2.4**   Which of the following classes inherit from which? Explain your reasoning.

*Worm, Ellipse, Animal, 2DFigure, Circle*

**Exercise 2.5**   Use polymorphism to implement the following application, to be installed in automobile showrooms. The input is the auto model (there are three to begin with). The output consists of descriptions of the model selected. For now, the descriptions can simply consist of text output to the console. Document your code thoroughly.
The figure shows typical input/output.

Output

```
Pick from one of the following:
chevy
toyota
ford
chevy
Below is a description of the auto that you requested:
.... lots and lots of header text about automobiles in general....
Here is a description of Chevys.
.... lots of material about Chevys....
```

**FIGURE 2.22**  Typical Interaction for Auto Description Exercise

Evaluation criteria:

- Effectiveness of your design
- Clarity of comments and code

- Effectiveness of your response

A = entirely appropriate classes & relationships
A = every nontrivial code step clearly explained; comments explain the code very clearly
A = effective and completely specific avenues for flexibility, reusability, and robustness

The following are errors that you should watch for in Exercise 2.5:

*Serious*:

**1.** Don't confuse postconditions with algorithms. Postconditions give the state of the environment after the application has executed. (It may be appropriate to supply an algorithm in addition, but this would not be part of the postcondition category.)

**2.** The benefit of polymorphism is that you can write code in one place that pertains to various cases. The following does not fully exploit polymorphism.

```
case( . . . . . )
{       set o to subtype 1 . . . .
        o.theMethod();
}
case( . . . . . )
{       set o to subtype 2. . . .
        o.theMethod();
}
case( . . . . . )
{       set o to subtype. . . . . .
        o.theMethod();
}
```

This should be

```
case( . . . . . )
{       set o to subtype 1. . . .
}
case( . . . . . )
{       set o to subtype 2. . . .
}
case( . . . . . )
{       set o to subtype. . . . . .
}

o.theMethod();                         // generic code
```

*Minor*:

**1.** The usual convention is to start class names with capitals.

**Exercise 2.6**  Define appropriate interfaces that the following class exhibits (or "implements" in Java terms). Assume that additional methods will be required as the application grows. Explain your reasoning.

*Hints*: The interfaces indicate what kind of transaction this is: There is a good answer with three interfaces.

```
class BankTransaction . . ..
{
void debitAccount( int anAmount ) { . . . }
String getCustomerBalance(){ . . . }
int computeDebitAmount() { . . . }
void void setTransactionTime(){ . . . }
void setLocation( Loction aLocation ){ . . . }
Customer getCustomer(){ . . . }
Account getAccount(){ . . . }
void setCoordinator( Person aPerson ) { . . . }
. . .
}
```

# *THE UNIFIED MODELING LANGUAGE*

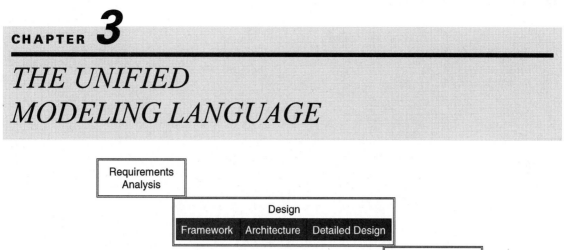

**FIGURE 3.1** Process Phases Affected by This Chapter

## 3.1 GOALS OF THE UNIFIED MODELING LANGUAGE

The Unified Modeling Language (UML) is a graphical notation for expressing object-oriented designs. It is a melding of the notations of Booch, Rumbaugh, Jacobson, Wirf-Brock, and Harel among others. The official UML standard is managed by the Object Management Group consortium of companies (www.omg.org), and requires hundreds of pages to formally specify. Most UML design expressions are called *models*.

## 3.2 CLASSES IN UML

Classes in UML are represented by rectangles containing the class name. The detailed version includes attribute and operation names, signatures, visibility, return types, etc. Figure 3.2 shows a class from the detailed design of an application that controls the flow in a chip manufacturing plant of canisters holding wafers.

Code for this class would be as follows.

```
/**
 * Describes each canister undergoing fabrication
 */
class Canister
{
     public static int numCanisters = 0;  // the number of canisters being used
     private int numWafers = 0;  // number of wafers in this canister
     private float size = 0;
     private final int TEMPORARY_RESPONSE = 0;  // placeholder for future code

     /********************************
      */
     public Canister()
     {     super();
     }
```

```
/*********************************
 * To be specified.
 */
public void display()
{       // to be completed
}

/*********************************
 * To be specified.
 */
private int getNumSlotsOpen()
{       return TEMPORARY_RESPONSE;  // to be completed
}

/*********************************
 */
public float getSize()
{       return TEMPORARY_RESPONSE;  // to be completed
}

/*********************************
 */
public void setStatus()
{       // to be completed
}
}
```

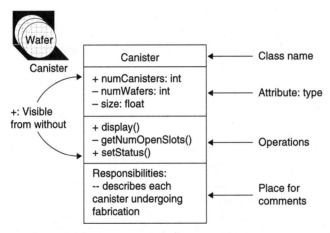

**FIGURE 3.2** Classes at Detailed Design

Notice that not all of the attributes need be specified in the class model. We show as much detail as needed but no more: Showing more detail clutters a diagram and can make it harder to understand. Some required attributes are left to the discretion of the implementers. It is also common to omit accessor functions from the class model (e.g., *getSize()* and *setSize()*), since these can be inferred from the presence of the corresponding attributes (*size*).

**KEY CONCEPT**   *Representing a Class in UML*

The UML represents a class with a rectangle containing the class name. We display additional information within the rectangle as needed: Variables, methods, etc.

# 3.3 CLASS RELATIONSHIPS IN UML

### 3.3.1 Inheritance

The Unified Modeling Language uses the term *package* for collecting design elements such as classes. "Package" also happens to be the name of collections of Java classes (only). Java packages translate into file directories; their subpackages decompose into subdirectories. UML packages can contain any materials associated with an application, including source code, designs, documentation, etc. Figure 3.3 shows an example of a package consisting of two classes. *Abstract classes*, i.e., those that cannot be instantiated into objects, are denoted with italics.

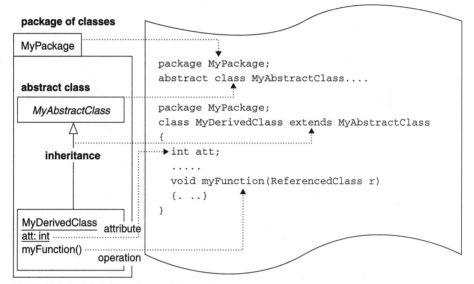

**FIGURE 3.3** UML Notation and Typical Implementation

Recall that *interfaces* are collections of method prototypes (name, parameter types, return types and exceptions thrown). Classes *realize* an interface by implementing the methods that the interface promises. The UML notation is shown in Figure 3.4. It is usual to arrange class models so that base classes are physically above derived classes. However, this positioning is not necessary in any technical sense.

> **KEY CONCEPT**  *Representing Inheritance in UML*
>
> The UML represents inheritance and interface realization with an open triangle.

### 3.3.2 Aggregation

*Aggregation*, denoted with a diamond, indicates the structural inclusion of objects of one class by another, and is usually implemented by means of a class having an attribute whose type is the included class. The aggregator can be loosely thought of as the "whole" and the class aggregated as the "part." Aggregation is shown in Figure 3.5.

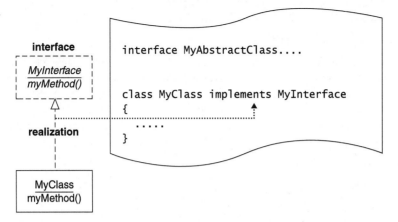

**FIGURE 3.4** Interfaces: UML Notation and Typical Java Implementation

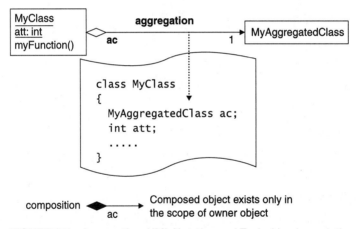

**FIGURE 3.5** Aggregation: UML Notation and Typical Implementation

The numeral at the end of an aggregation arrow denotes the number of objects aggregated. For example, the "1" at the end of the *MyClass* / *MyAggregatedClass* relationship implies that each *MyClass* object aggregates exactly one *MyAggregatedClass* object. Instead of single numerals, a range can be given, such as 3..7. The symbol "*" denotes "an undetermined number" of objects aggregated.

*Composition* is a stronger form of aggregation in which the aggregated object exists only during the lifetime (and for the benefit of) the composing object: No other object may reference the aggregated object in this case.

**KEY CONCEPT** *Representing Aggregation in UML*

Class *A* aggregates class *B* if *A* objects require *B* objects in a structural sense—typically with an instance variable. The UML symbol is an open diamond.

### 3.3.3 Dependency

*Dependency*, denoted by a dotted line arrow, means that one class depends upon another in the sense that if the class at an arrow's end were to change, this would affect the dependent class. Strictly speaking, dependency includes inheritance and aggregation. However, these relationships have their own notation, and so we usually reserve dependency to indicate that a method of one class utilizes another class. (See Figure 3.6).

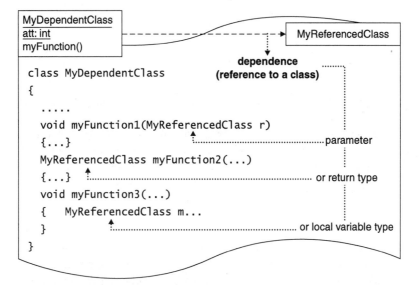

**FIGURE 3.6** Dependence: UML Notation and Typical Implementation

---

**KEY CONCEPT**     *Representing Dependency*

Class *A* depends on class *B* if *A* objects require *B* objects for their definition. In practice, this means that *B* appears in at least one method of *A*. The UML representation is a dotted arrow.

---

### 3.3.4 Association

*Association*, denoted with a solid line between two classes, commonly means that objects of each class depend on objects of the other in a structural manner. We can annotate the relationship, which may be one- or two-way, as illustrated in Figure 3.7.

One-way associations are aggregations, which we have already covered. Two-way associations are problematical because we need to be sure that both ends of the implied information are kept consistent. For example, if *joe:Employee* is employed by *ibm:Company*, then each of these classes must refer to the other in the sense shown in Figure 3.7. If *joe* changes employment, the implementation has to be changed in two places. For this reason, we often

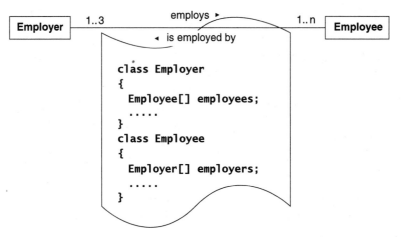

**FIGURE 3.7**   Association: UML Notation and Typical Implementation

seek ways to express an association in a different manner: In this case, a *Job* class aggregating *Employee* and *Employer* may satisfy this goal without creating the difficulties of two-way associations. Associations are useful in the early stages of building class relationships when we know a pair to be related, but are postponing the ultimate design of the relationship.

### 3.3.5   An Example

Now we will show how the UML helps us to visualize the design of applications. We return to the example in Chapter 2 of producing e-mail text for various kinds of customers. The application was used to illustrate the benefits of polymorphism. We noted that imagining the design through source code alone was unsatisfactory. The UML class model is shown in Figure 3.8.

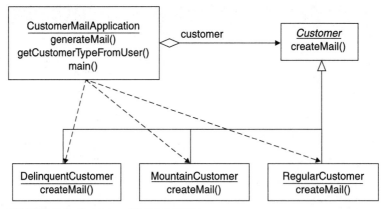

**FIGURE 3.8**   Customer Mail Application

The strength of class models is that they help us to envisage the building blocks of the application. However, they do not indicate the manner in which the application executes. In the Customer Mail Application class model, for example, there is no way to tell what method executes after *main()*. Use cases and sequence diagrams, discussed next, supply this capability.

# 3.4 USE CASES

Most applications can be executed in many ways. Despite this, Jacobson [Ja] observed that we usually think of applications through a relatively small number of typical interactions with users, such as the following:

1. User does ...
2. Application does ...
3. Application does ...
4. User does ...
5. Application does ...
6. ...

He called these *use cases*. Although use cases are often used in conjunction with object-oriented methods, they are an independent concept.

## 3.4.1 What Are Use Cases?

A use case is identified by its name, by the type of user of the application, called the *actor*, and by the interaction between the actor and the application. A use case is a kind of linear "story" detailing a common way to use an application. For example, *Retrieve a file* would be a typical use case for a word processor, with the user as actor. It could consist of the following sequence of steps.

1. *User* clicks *File* menu
2. *Application* displays file options
3. *User* clicks *open*
4. *Application* displays file window
5. *User* enters directory and file name
6. *User* hits *open* button
7. *Application* retrieves referenced file into word processor window

One person could use a system in several different ways, adopting the roles of different actors. Jacobson suggests starting requirements analysis by writing use cases, then using them to derive class selection. Use cases are particularly useful for requirements analysis (introduced in the Prologue). This application of use cases is explored fully in Chapter 13.

A use case typically requires a context. For example, a *check out* use case for on-line shopping assumes that items have been selected. The context assumptions made are expressed in preconditions in the same manner that we used preconditions in method specifications.

---

**KEY CONCEPT** *Use Cases*

A sequence of actions taken by an application and its user in which the user takes a single role.

---

### 3.4.2 Collections of Use Cases

In the UML notation, each ellipse denotes a use case. For example, Figure 3.9 shows possible use cases for a video store application.

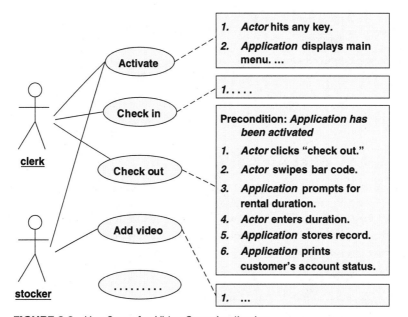

**FIGURE 3.9** Use Cases for *Video Store* Application

The actor need not be a human role: it could be another system that uses the application. For example, if the application under development is a robot control system, then the actor could be the factory automation system that needs to use the robots.

Use cases can handle limited branching, but if there is more than one level of branching, the use case should probably be decomposed into smaller ones that do not contain branching. Even a single branch in a use case leads to an awkward description. For example, the following could be a use case for a personal budgeting application.

User selects "add checks" or "reconcile account"

If "add checks" selected:

One action happens

Another action happens

...

If "reconcile account" selected:

One action happens

Another action happens

...

This would be better decomposed into "select options", "add checks" and a "reconcile account" use cases.

### 3.4.3 Combining Use Cases

Figure 3.10 shows how use cases can be dependent on other use cases. The *extends* relationship is rather like inheritance in the sense of being a specialized version. The *uses* relationship is somewhat like aggregation since it utilizes another use case as a whole.

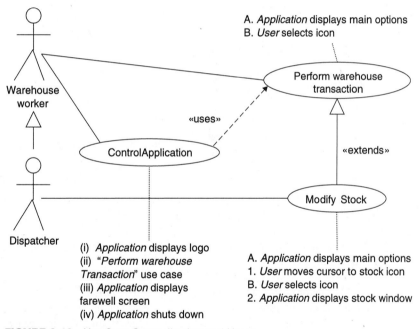

**FIGURE 3.10** Use Case Generalization and Usage

## 3.5 SEQUENCE DIAGRAMS

Use cases are a good complement to classes because they define steps through which a user and an application transition. However, they need to be developed into a more technical form. In addition, there are many sequences of actions that applications need to be designed for, but which are not use cases. *Sequence diagrams* address both of these issues. They are graphical representations of control flow and are particularly useful for describing executions that involve several classes.

### 3.5.1 The Parts of a Sequence Diagram

Sequence diagrams require us to think in terms of objects. The lifetime of each object involved is shown as a solid vertical line, with the name of the object and its class at the top. Each interaction between objects is shown by means of a horizontal arrow from the object initiating the service to the object supplying the service. The beginning of a sequence diagram for the *Checkout* use case of the video store application described in Section 3.4.2 is given in Figure 3.11.

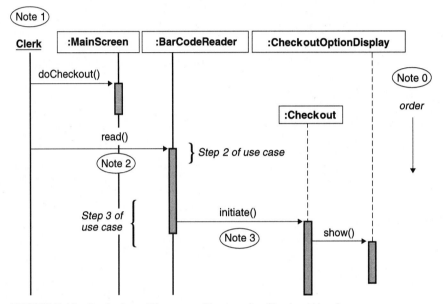

**FIGURE 3.11** Beginning of Sequence Diagram for *Checkout* Use Case

The following notes explain the corresponding features of the diagram.

**1.** Note 0: In a sequence diagram, time goes in a downward direction. In this example, *doCheckout()* occurs first, followed by *read()* and then *initiate(),* etc.

**2.** Note 1: Use cases are initiated either by the user, as this one is, or by an object. Initiation typically begins at the top left of the diagram, and a solid vertical line beneath this symbol is drawn to indicate that the entity already exists. We can supply preconditions to specify any assumptions that it makes at its inception.

**3.** Note 2: Sequence diagrams show the initiation and execution of a sequence of functions. The object at the beginning of each arrow *initiates* the work: The object at the end of the arrow *carries out* the work of the method indicated. Each elongated rectangle denotes the execution of a function of the corresponding object.

In our checkout sequence diagram, the clerk initiates the second function by swiping the bar-code reader over the video. Now we determine who or what should execute the function. Since a bar-code reader recognizes a swipe, we decide that a *BarCodeReader* class would be appropriate for dealing with actions relating to the physical reader, and that the required function of *BarCodeReader* will be named *read()*. There will be only one *BarCodeReader* object for the entire application, so the notation "*:BarCodeReader*" to represent this object is sufficient.

There is no real need to name a *BarCodeReader* object. We may even decide later to make the *read()* method of *BarCodeReader* static, in which case no actual *BarCodeReader* object would be involved. In general, the fact that no object is mentioned in a sequence diagram—just the class alone—indicates that either no object is required (e.g., using static methods), or that an object without any particular name (an "anonymous" object) suffices.

**4.** Note 3: We can capture the checkout process with a *Checkout* class. The *BarCodeReader* object then creates a *Checkout* object. We have used a factory method *initiate()* here to create and initialize the *Checkout* object. The method *initiate()* then creates a display for choosing checkout options and shows it on the console.

A complete sequence diagram for the use case is given in Figure 3.12.

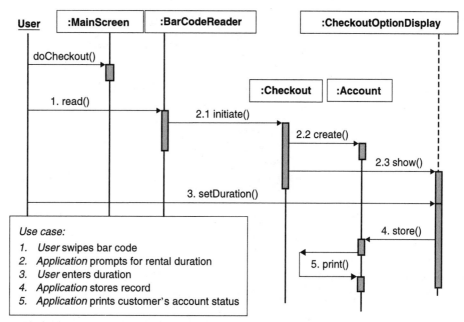

**FIGURE 3.12**  Beginning of Sequence Diagram for *Checkout* Use Case

Figures 3.13 and 3.14 summarize the steps needed to create a sequence diagram. When the initiator is the user, a simple label at the top is used rather than a rectangle. Note that the object responsible for executing the method named on the arrow is at the *end* (not the beginning) of the arrow.

**KEY CONCEPT**  *Sequence Diagrams*

Show the order in which methods of various objects execute.

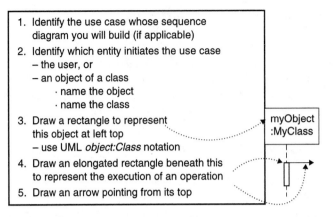

**FIGURE 3.13** Building a Sequence Diagram 1

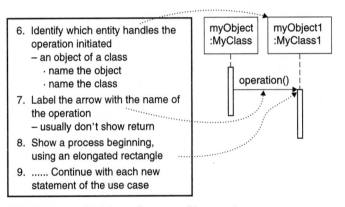

**FIGURE 3.14** Building a Sequence Diagram 2

## 3.6  STATE MODELS

### 3.6.1  The Meaning of *State*

Sometimes an application, or part thereof, is best thought of as being in one of several states. The *state* of an application is its situation or status. The idea is to divide the application into states so that the application is always in exactly one of these states. For example, it might be useful to think of an online shopper at a book site as being either in *browsing* state (looking at book information) or in *purchasing* state (providing credit card information, etc.). Formally speaking, a state of an object is defined by the values of the object's variables. For example, if an *Automobile* class has *age* and *value* attributes, we could say that an Automobile object is in *good* state when [*age* < 10 and *value* > 5000], in *scrap* state when [*age* > 15 and *value* < 500], and in *questionable* state otherwise. Each *Automobile* object is in exactly one of these states. States and substates are denoted by rounded rectangles as for an online shopper in Figure 3.15.

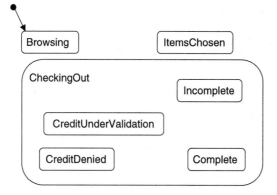

**FIGURE 3.15** States for *OnlineShopper* Class

The state *Incomplete* indicates that the shopper has signaled a readiness to check out but has not yet submitted credit card information. The black dot and arrow indicate that *OnlineShopper* objects are initially in the *Browsing* state.

### 3.6.2 Events

In the context of state models, an *event* is something whose occurrence is sensed directly by objects of the class in question. Examples of events are a button click on a *Button* object or a change in the value of an object's variable.

### 3.6.3 Transitions

An event may cause an object to *transition* from its current state to another state. We denote a transition with an arrow, labeled with the name of the event causing the transition. For example, when a *Shopper* object in *Incomplete* state submits valid credit card information, it transitions from *Incomplete* state to *CreditUnderValidation* state.

Sometimes, when an object is in a given state, and an event occurs, the object can transition to one of several states, depending on a *condition*. For example, when a shopper submits credit card information (by clicking the mouse or hitting *enter*), the resulting transition depends on whether or not the data is complete. As shown in Figure 3.16, conditions are denoted by square brackets in UML.

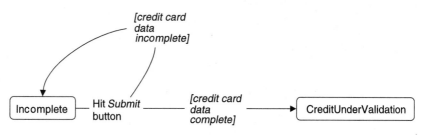

**FIGURE 3.16** Conditions on Events

### 3.6.4 State-Transition Diagrams

A *state-transition diagram* shows the states of the objects of a class, the events to which the objects are sensitive, and the resulting transitions between them. State-transition diagrams, also known as *statecharts*, are finite state machines. A complete state-transition diagram for the *OnlineShopper* is shown in Figure 3.17. Note that when the Shopper object enters the *CheckingOut* state, it automatically enters the substate *Incomplete* (more precisely, *CheckingOut.Incomplete*).

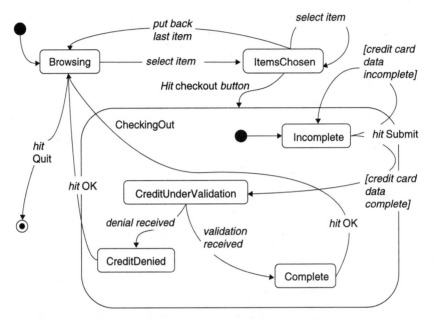

**FIGURE 3.17**  State-Transition Diagram for *OnlineShopper* Class

> **KEY CONCEPT**    *State Diagrams*
>
> Some applications or parts thereof are conveniently thought of as being in one of several possible states. UML state diagrams help us to visualize these and the events that cause transitions among them.

## 3.7  ACTIVITY DIAGRAMS

Section 1.2.3.1 on page 25 introduced UML *activity diagrams*, an updated and enhanced form of flowcharts, which include parallelism.

### 3.7.1  Activity Diagram Notation

The notation for activity diagrams is shown in Figure 3.18. This example includes parallelism, showing that *Do a Task* and *Do Another Task* operate in parallel. Control is not passed to *Do Even More* until both have completed.

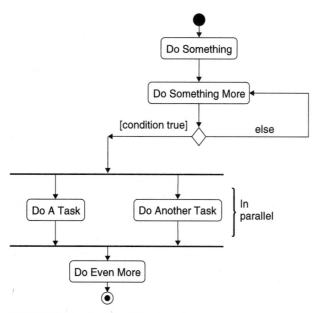

**FIGURE 3.18** Activity Chart Notation

## 3.7.2 Example Using Activity Diagrams

The following example is the "backward chaining" algorithm for expert systems, and illustrates how flowcharting can be helpful in explaining complex algorithms. *Expert systems* are usually based on knowledge in the form of rules, which take the following form:

*antecedent* AND *antecedent* AND . . . AND *antecedent* => *consequent,*

where *antecedent*s and *consequent*s are *facts.*
   For example,

*animal is mammal* AND *animal is striped* => *animal is zebra.*

Our facts will simply be strings such as "animal is mammal."
   The problem is to build a program that, given

- a list of facts, such as *A, B, Q,* and
- a list of rules, such as *A&R=>L, A&B=>C,* and *B&C=>R,*

determines whether or not a given fact, such as *L,* can be deduced.
   The answer is "yes" for this example because

*A(known)&B(known)=>C;*
*B(known)&C(just deduced)=>R;*
*A(known)&R(just deduced)=>L.*

   We will store the current list of known facts as a static *Vector* called *factList*, and the list of known rules as a static *Vector* called *ruleBase*. We will simplify the setup of these lists by hard coding the example previously given in the *Fact* and *Rule* classes. This is shown in Figure 3.19.

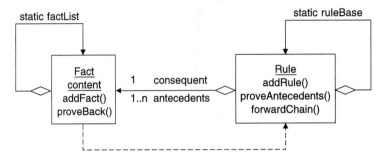

**FIGURE 3.19** A Class Model for Chaining

Our emphasis is on the harder part: the "backchaining" algorithm *proveBack()* for establishing whether or not a given fact, which we will name *soughtFact,* can be deduced from the given facts and rules. An activity diagram for this algorithm is shown in Figure 3.20. This diagram simplifies an otherwise complex algorithm. An inspection of it should uncover the fact that it fails to terminate if there is a circular chain in the rule base such as $X => Y$ and $Y => X$. Note that both *Fact* and *Rule* objects are involved.

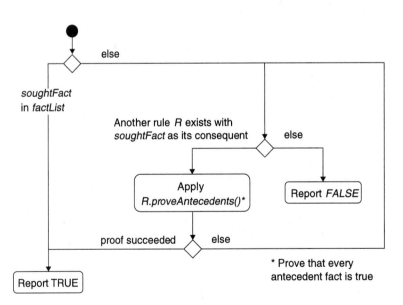

**FIGURE 3.20** Flowchart for *soughtFact.proveBack()*

## 3.8 AN EXAMPLE

As an example that illustrates several parts of the UML notation in this chapter, consider a graphics studio specializing in drawing stick people, as specified in Figure 3.21.

We will focus only on the "foot" requirements. Certainly, there is a need for *Rectangle* and *Ellipse* classes. The first question is whether we need a *Foot* class. When we drag a rectangle

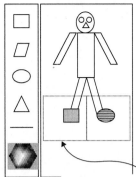

- *Facilitate drawing stick figures*
- *Drag to vicinity to auto-complete*
- *Feet can be* rectangles *or* ellipses
- *(Rest to be specified)*

Releasing dragged figure anywhere in this area causes it to appear in position at end of left leg

**FIGURE 3.21**   Specifications for Figure Drawing

near the end of a leg, the application has to know that we want it to be placed at the end of that leg in a standard position. Whereas it may well be possible to do this without the application "knowing" about legs and feet, the process is much easier to carry out if *Leg* and *Foot* classes are used (e.g., a *Leg* object would aggregate a *Foot* object).

The next question is how to relate the classes *Foot*, *Rectangle*, and *Ellipse*. Consider the possibility shown in Figure 3.22. This class model says that a *Foot* object is both an ellipse and a rectangle, which is not correct. A better option is the class model in Figure 3.23. This model is at least not incorrect as the first attempt was. It is a little clumsy, however, in that it proliferates classes (*EllipseFoot*, *RectangleFoot,* etc.). This is not tenable (do we need *ReactangleEar,* etc.?). It also uses multiple inheritance, which is problematical in general, and not available in Java.

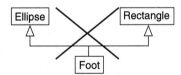

**FIGURE 3.22**   Bad Attempt: "A *Foot* is Either an *Ellipse* or a *Rectangle*"

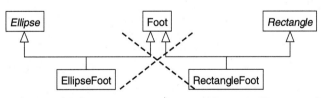

**FIGURE 3.23**   Better Attempt: "A *Foot* is Either an *Ellipse* or a *Rectangle*"

Now consider the option shown in Figure 3.24. This is a reasonable solution except for one awkward issue: it makes every *Ellipse* in our application a kind of *FootShape*, as it does for every *Rectangle*. For one thing, this limits the reusability of the *Ellipse* class. For another, it is rather strange to think of ellipses as always being *FootShapes*. Finally, if we continue with this, perhaps *Ellipse* may also have to be a *HandShape* object. One way to deal with these problems is for *FootShape* to depend only "lightly" on *Ellipse* and *Rectangle* as shown in Figure 3.25.

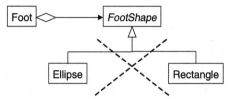

**FIGURE 3.24** Another Attempt: "A *Foot* is Either an *Ellipse* or a *Rectangle*"

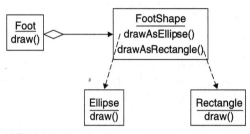

**FIGURE 3.25** Best Attempt So Far: "A *Foot* is Either an *Ellipse* or a *Rectangle*"

This class model shows that the restrictions on the shape of *Foot* objects are reflected in the methods of *FootShape*. They reference only *Ellipse* and *Rectangle* at this point, but can readily be augmented to accept other geometric shapes. We can now fill in more details of one good solution, as in Figure 3.26.

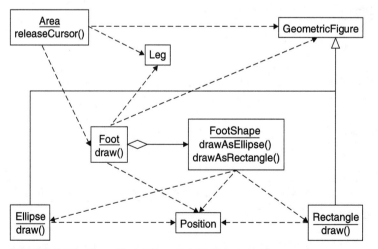

**FIGURE 3.26** Class Model Showing All Dependencies

The Area's *releaseCursor()* method handles the auto-placement (at the end of legs in the cases shown), and this information is passed along to the anatomical object (*Foot* in this case): The *draw()* of *Ellipse* and *Rectangle* are used to do actual drawing. The class *Position* could be avoided; it contains x- and y-coordinates. For example, *drawAsEllipse( Position aPosition )* in *FootShape* could have the following form.

```
void drawAsEllipse( Position aPosition )
{
        Ellipse ellipse = new Ellipse();  // the dependency shown in the class model
        ellipse.draw( aPosition );  // the actual work drawing the ellipse
        . . . .
}
```

Showing all of the dependencies in a class model can make for a complicated diagram, and for this reason dependencies are often omitted. (This is perhaps sweeping things under the rug!) The sequence diagram in Figure 3.27 specifies how the classes and methods work together, and shows details about parameters.

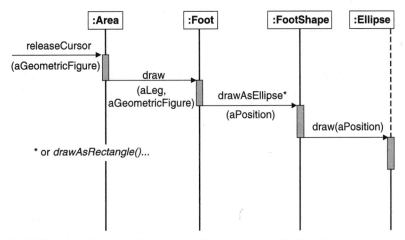

**FIGURE 3.27**   Sequence Diagram for *Figure Drawing* Application

The sequence diagram specifies that when a geometric figure is dragged to an area and the cursor is released, and the *releaseCursor()* method of *Area* executes with the *GeometricFigure* as parameter. The *Area* object knows which anatomical object is involved (*Foot* in this case), so it calls upon that object to draw itself: It also knows what geometric form is required.

Note that the *Area* class is special to this application whereas *GeometricFigure* is not. For this reason we did not have *GeometricFigure* do the drawing with an *Area* object as parameter. Section 5.2 in Chapter 5 on page 107 discusses these kinds of reusability considerations.

## CHAPTER SUMMARY

Figure 3.28 lists the UML models and diagrams covered in this chapter. Figure 3.29 summarizes the ways in which classes can relate to each other.

- Use Cases
  - Actor/application interactions
- Sequence Diagrams
  - Objects
  - Sequence of methods
    - calling methods among objects
- Class Models
- Activity Diagrams
  - Flow of control
- State Diagrams
  - States
  - Transitions among states
    - caused by events

**FIGURE 3.28**   UML Models

- **Dependency**
  - member method mentions another class
- **Association**
  - Structural
  - e.g., *sale/receipt*
  - **Aggregation**
    - common kind of association
    - e.g., *airplane/wing*
    - *one-way*
    - "has-a"
- **Inheritance**
  - "is-a"

**FIGURE 3.29**   Relationships Between Classes

# EXERCISES

**Exercise 3.1**  **Class Relationships**   Name three major relationships that could exist between classes *A* and *B*. Express each in UML and in a typical Java implementation.

**Exercise 3.2**  **Class Model from Code**   Write the class model for the following code. Explain your reasoning.

```
abstract class A {}
class B
{
        B() {}
}
class C extends A
{
        B b = new B();
}
```

**Exercise 3.3**  **Developing a Class Model for an Application**   Show a class model for an application that displays automobiles. Depending on the user's request, it displays a typical Ford, Toyota, or Chevy, together with interactive pages of information about each. We want to be able to easily add new automobile brands to the application in the future and to reuse parts of the design where possible.

Errors you should avoid:
  *Serious*:
**1.** Show *all* dependencies between classes.

**2.** Include enough to control the application.

**3.** Base classes should not depend on subclasses.

**Exercise 3.4**  **Use Cases**   Give two use cases for the shopping cart application described in Section 3.6. Explain your reasoning.

Evaluation criteria:
  ▨ Correctness of form          A = entirely correct use case concept demonstrated
  ▨ Correctness of content       A = Use cases clearly capture the essential parts of the interaction

Errors you should avoid:
  *Serious*:
**1.** Unclear partition between user and application

**2.** Key steps omitted

**3.** The ovals (UML notation for use cases) show only the titles of use cases: You were asked to provide the *substance,* which consists of the actual steps.

*Less than serious, more than minor*:

1. Use case too long (e.g., fifteen steps): Should be split into two or more use cases.

2. Use cases too short (e.g., two steps): Provide more detail, or combine your use cases.

3. Don't forget to state *preconditions*.

*Minor*:

1. Don't use the term *"actor"* in the steps of the use case: Instead, use the actual term—typically "user"—since you have more specific information about who the actor is.

**Exercise 3.5**   **Sequence Diagrams**   Give sequence diagrams for your two use cases in Exercise 3.2. Explain your reasoning.

Evaluation criteria:

▨ Correctness of UML notation        A = entirely correct usage of UML
▨ Correctness of diagram        A = effective, specific and thorough inclusion of the necessary objects and the functionalities involved

**Exercise 3.6**   **States and Transitions**   Suppose that your car has a built-in application that displays the status of the engine parts at all times. Give a state diagram for the *Starter* class that describes the automobile's starter only. Explain your reasoning.

Note that the starter is sometimes connected to and sometimes disengaged from the car's motor. The starter reacts to actions involving the car key. The key can be in one of 3 positions: vertical, 90° and 180°.

Evaluation criteria:

▨ Correctness of UML notation        A = entirely correct usage of UML
▨ Correctness of diagram        A = effective, specific and thorough coverage of the states and transitions

Errors you should avoid:

*Serious:*

1. On sequence diagrams, objects *can't call methods on human* actors.

2. On sequence diagrams, *human actors can't cause methods* to execute directly except methods of GUI objects.

3. Phrase in terms of what the user sees rather than in terms of what the application does internally. The internal sequence should be fleshed out separately.

4. State what the *role* of the actor is (*customer, game player,* etc.).

5. A state diagram corresponds to one and only *one class.* (It may affect the state diagram of other classes.)

6. Use cases do not involve steps such as "the customer walks up to the counter ... ." Use cases include only user actions directly on the application, and application actions.

*Neither serious nor minor:*

1. Objects either already exist at the beginning of the sequence, or else are created by other objects. A *human can't create objects.* Remember that a solid line denotes the existence of an object.

2. Give each use case a *name*.

3. Be careful not to combine *too many steps* in a single-use case. A typical use case has 3–6 steps. Decompose into smaller use cases.

**Exercise 3.7**   **The States of a Browser**   A web browser can be in various states that are evident to the user. Provide a state diagram showing them and their relationships. Assume that the browser cannot be interrupted while it is retrieving its initial default page. Your states should include *Retrieving Initial Page*. *Evaluation criteria* and *Errors you should avoid* are the same as for Exercise 3.6.

**Exercise 3.8**   **Activity Diagrams**   Give an activity diagram for the major functionality of the shopping cart application described in Section 3.6. Explain your reasoning.

Evaluation criteria:

▨ Correctness of UML notation        A = proper usage of UML
▨ Correctness of flowchart        A = effective and thorough description of the logic

# CHAPTER 4

# DESIGN PRINCIPLES I: CORRECTNESS AND ROBUSTNESS

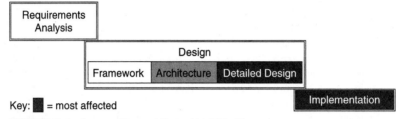

Key: ■ = most affected

**FIGURE 4.1**  Process Phase Affected by This Chapter

In Chapter 1 we gave *correctness*, *robustness*, *flexibility*, *reusability,* and *efficiency* as goals for software design. Most of this book focuses on these goals, enlisting design patterns and component technology to accomplish them. In this chapter we will elaborate on correctness and robustness. Flexibility, reusability, and efficiency are taken up in the next chapter.

In designing a software application, our goal is to accommodate the requirements, as well as a reasonable amount of change in these requirements. There is considerable variation in deciding how much change is "reasonable." At one end of the spectrum is pure *Extreme Programming*, which involves designing for the known requirements but not more. This aims for correctness and sufficiency alone. At the other end of the spectrum are flexible, reusable designs capable of accommodating many future requirements. We usually take an approach between these two extremes. Robustness is a common goal in any case.

## 4.1  CORRECTNESS AND SUFFICIENCY

The more specific a question, the more precisely we can verify the correctness of a design that answers it. For example, there is only one correct answer to the detailed question "what number adds to 3 to get 5?" But there are many sufficient answers to the less detailed question "what bridge design gets cars from point A to point B?" Thus, when we speak of the *correctness* of designs, we usually mean their *sufficiency*.

Formal approaches to correctness rely on the mathematics of logic, and periodically will be alluded to in this book.

### 4.1.1  Approaches to Correctness

How can we know that a design is correct or even sufficient? Is this just a matter of adding classes until we seem to have enough? What is the penalty (if any) for an insufficient or incorrect design? There are informal and formal approaches to these questions.

To verify a design *informally* is to be convinced that it covers the required functionality. *Formal* methods for establishing correctness involve applying mathematical logic to analyzing the way in which the variables change. Formal methods for correctness are usually applied when the design enters the detailed stage.

Recall a point made in the Prologue on testing. Testing, while essential, only establishes the *presence* of defects in an implementation. This section, however, discusses correctness, which establishes the *absence* of defects. It depends upon engineers (i.e., humans) and their ability to think through designs and implementations. Correctness is more fundamental than testing.

---

**KEY CONCEPT**   *Correctness*

Goal: That each artifact satisfies designated requirements, and that together they satisfy all of the application's requirements.

---

### 4.1.1.1   *Informal Approaches to Correctness*   Informal approaches to correctness are based on the common-sense idea that before we can proclaim a design to be correct we have to understand it completely. Thus, designs and implementations have to be *readable*. Since the human brain is severely limited in dealing with complexity, we have to *modularize* designs, that is, break them down into separate understandable parts. Figure 4.2 summarizes these points. Once we establish good modularization for a design, we proceed to specify how the modules interact.

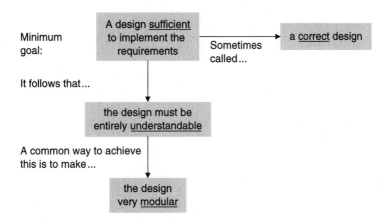

**FIGURE 4.2**   Sufficient Designs: Terminology and Rationale

There is a famous apology variously attributed to Pascal, Mark Twain and George Bernard Shaw: "I didn't have time to write a short letter, so I wrote a long one instead." One's initial designs are generally messy and complex: Attaining simplicity takes time, and the process is seldom complete. This book strives for simple designs: It generally does not include the messy attempts that may have preceded them. The astute reader will nevertheless find room for further improvement in many of the designs in this book.

**KEY CONCEPT** *Correctness by Informal Methods*

Simplify and modularize designs until they are convincing.

### 4.1.1.2 Formal Approaches to Correctness

*4.1.1.2 Formal Approaches to Correctness* Formal approaches to correctness are often based on keeping variable changes under tight control. Specifying *invariants* usually accomplishes this. Invariants are unchanging relationships among variable values such as

"*length >= 0*,"

"*length * breadth == area*," and

"*overdraft <* OVERDRAFT_MAX."

Invariants used in class-level design are called *class invariants.* For example, the statement in Figure 4.3 is a possible invariants for the class *Automobile*, with variables *mileage*, *VehicleID*, *value*, *originalPrice*, and *type.*

1) *mileage >= 0*
2) *mileage < 1000000*
3) *vehicleID* has at least 8 characters
4) *value >= –300*
   ($300 is the disposal cost of a worthless automobile)
5) *originalPrice >= 0*
6) (*type* == "REGULAR" && *value <= originalPrice*) ||
   (*type* == "VINTAGE" && *value >= originalPrice*)

**FIGURE 4.3** Invariants for Class *Automobile*

Methods of *Automobile* have to respect these invariants. This is one reason that we usually make variables private, and allow their values to change only through public accessor methods: Accessors can be coded to maintain the invariants. The following code shows how "setter" methods can be used to enforce class invariants for the *Automobile* example.

Here is a *main()* method in a client of *Automobile*.

```
package auto;
/**
 * An application using the 'Automobile' class.
 * 'Automobile' 'setter' methods enforce the 'Automobile' class invariants.
 */
public class AutoApplication
{

/******************************************************************************
 */
public AutoApplication()
{  super();
}
```

```java
/***********************************************************************
 * Demonstration of the use of invariants in 'Automobile'.
 * The 'setter' methods take effect only if parameters respect the
 * class invariants of 'Automobile'.
 */
public static void main( String[] args )
/**********************************************************************/
{
    Automobile auto = new Automobile();
    try // bad attempt to set vehicleID
    {   auto.setVehicleID( "ABCD" );
    }
    catch( AutoException e ){ System.out.println( e ); }

    try // good attempt to set vehicleID
    {   auto.setVehicleID( "ABCDEFGHI" );
    }
    catch( AutoException e ){ System.out.println( e ); }
    try // bad attempt to set mileage
    {   auto.setMileage( 20000000 );
    }
    catch( AutoException e ){ System.out.println( e ); }

    try // good attempt to set mileage
    {   auto.setMileage( 20000 );
    }
    catch( AutoException e ){ System.out.println( e ); }

    try // bad attempt to set originalPrice
    {   auto.setOriginalPrice( -3000 );
    }
    catch( AutoException e ){ System.out.println( e ); }

    try // good attempt to set originalPrice
    {   auto.setOriginalPrice( 3000 );
    }
    catch( AutoException e ){ System.out.println( e ); }

    try // bad attempt to set type
    {   auto.setType( "CLASSIC" );
    }
    catch( AutoException e ){ System.out.println( e ); }

    try // good attempt to set type
    {   auto.setType( "VINTAGE" );
    }
    catch( AutoException e ){ System.out.println( e ); }

    try // bad attempt to set value
    {   auto.setValue( 2999 );
    }
    catch( AutoException e ){ System.out.println( e ); }

    try // good attempt to set value
    {   auto.setValue( 3001 );
    }
    catch( AutoException e ){ System.out.println( e ); }
    // Final value of variables.
    System.out.println( "1.mileage = " + auto.getMileage() );
    System.out.println( "2.vehicleID = " + auto.getVehicleID() );
    System.out.println( "3.value = " + auto.getValue() );
    System.out.println( "4.originalPrice = " + auto.getOriginalPrice() );
    System.out.println( "5.type = " + auto.getType() );

} // end main()
}
```

The output for this *main()* method (Figure 4.4) shows that *Automobile*'s methods have maintained its invariants.

Output

```
auto.AutoException: Attempt to set illegal vehicleID.
auto.AutoException: Attempt to set illegal mileage.
auto.AutoException: Attempt to set negative original Automobile price.
auto.AutoException: Attempt to set illegal Automobile type.
auto.AutoException: Attempt to set inconsistently with Automobile class invariant 5.
1.   mileage = 20000
2.   vehicleID = ABCDEFGHI
3.   value = 3001
4.   originalPrice = 3000
5.   type = VINTAGE
```

**FIGURE 4.4**  Output to Exercise of *Automobile* Class Invariants

First, we will define *the AutoException* class for dealing with the exception settings to *Automobile*.

```
package auto;
/**
 * For dealing with class Automobile
 */
public class AutoException extends Exception
{

    /*******************************************************************
     */
    public AutoException()
    /******************************************************************/
    {   super();
    }
    /*******************************************************************
     */
    public AutoException( String aString )
    /******************************************************************/
    {   super( aString );
    }
}
```

The *Automobile* class is as follows. Note that the setter methods enforce the class invariants.

```
package auto;
/**
 * Class invariants:
 * 1.    mileage > 0
 * 2.    mileage < 1000000
 * 3.    vehicleID has at least 8 characters
 * 4.    value >= -300 ($300 is the disposal cost of a worthless automobile)
 * 5.    originalPrice >= 0
 * 6.    ( type == "REGULAR" && value <= originalPrice ) ||
 * ( type == "VINTAGE" && value >= originalPrice )
 */
public class Automobile
{
```

```java
   private int mileage = 0; // conforms to class invariants 2 and 2
   private String vehicleID = "not yet assigned"; // conforms to class invariant 3
   private int value = 0; // conforms to class invariant 4
   private int originalPrice = 0;
   private String type = "REGULAR"; // conforms to class invariant 5

/*****************************************************************
 */
public Automobile()
/*****************************************************************/
{  super();
}
/*****************************************************************
 */
public int getMileage()
/*****************************************************************/
{  return mileage;
}
/*****************************************************************
 */
public int getOriginalPrice()
/*****************************************************************/
{  return originalPrice;
}
/*****************************************************************
 */
public String getType()
/*****************************************************************/
{  return type;
}
/*****************************************************************
 */
public int getValue()
/*****************************************************************/
{  return value;
}
/*****************************************************************
 */
public String getVehicleID()
/*****************************************************************/
{  return vehicleID;
}
/*****************************************************************
 * Postcondition: mileage == aMileage
 *     if this honors the class invariants; otherwise exception thrown
 */
public void setMileage( int aMileage ) throws AutoException
/*****************************************************************/
{
    // Check for class invariants 1 and 2 (the only ones involving 'mileage')
    if( ( aMileage < 0 ) || ( aMileage >= 100000 ) )
        throw new AutoException( "Attempt to set illegal mileage." );
    else // OK to set as requested
        mileage = aMileage;
}
/*****************************************************************
 * Postcondition: originalPrice == anOriginalPrice
 *   . if this honors the class invariants; otherwise exception thrown
 */
public void setOriginalPrice( int anOriginalPrice ) throws AutoException
/*****************************************************************/
{
    // Check for class invariant 5 (the only one involving 'originalPrice')
    // (we can't check here for class invariant 6 because this method precedes it)
    if( anOriginalPrice < 0 )
        throw new AutoException( "Attempt to set negative original Automobile price." );
    else
        if( originalPrice != 0 ) // was already set
```

```
               throw new AutoException( "Attempt to change original Automobile price." );
        else // OK to set as requested
               originalPrice = anOriginalPrice;
}
/******************************************************************
 * Postcondition: type == aType
 *      if this honors the class invariants; otherwise exception thrown
 */
public void setType( String aType ) throws AutoException
/******************************************************************/
{
    // Check as much of class invariant 6 as we can (the only one involving 'type')
    if( aType != "REGULAR" && aType != "VINTAGE")
        throw new AutoException( "Attempt to set illegal Automobile type." );
    else // OK to set as requested
        type = aType;
}
/******************************************************************
 * Postcondition: value == aValue
 *      if this honors the class invariants; otherwise exception thrown
 */
public void setValue( int aValue ) throws AutoException
/******************************************************************/
{
    // Check for class invariant 4 (the only one involving 'value')
    if( aValue < -3000 )
        throw new AutoException( "Attempt to set value too low." );
    else // check for class invariant 6
        if( !( ( type == "REGULAR" && aValue <= originalPrice ) ||
          ( type == "VINTAGE" && aValue >= originalPrice )
                )
          )
              throw new AutoException
                ( "Attempt to set value inconsistently with Automobile class invariant 5." );
        else // OK to set as requested
              value = aValue;
}
/******************************************************************
 * Postcondition: vehicleID == aVehicleID
 *      if this honors the class invariants; otherwise exception thrown
 */
public void setVehicleID( String aVehicleID ) throws AutoException
/******************************************************************/
{
    // Check for class invariant 3 (the only one involving 'vehicleID')
    if( aVehicleID.length() < 8 )
        throw new AutoException( "Attempt to set illegal vehicleID." );
    else // OK to set as requested
        vehicleID = aVehicleID;
}
}
```

Well-chosen classes typically have a comprehensible set of invariants, which applies to the class *Automobile*. On the other hand, it is hard to find class invariants for a vague class like *Recreation*.

### 4.1.2   Interfaces to Modules

Since modularization is a key way to assess the correctness of a design, we first need to understand how client code uses modules. For our purposes, modules will be either classes or packages of classes. An *interface* is a set of function forms (or prototypes). A module's interfaces define its uses.

**4.1.2.1 *Interfaces to Classes*** When a class supports many methods, it is often beneficial to group them into several interfaces. This also allows us to reuse the interfaces. For example, consider the class *Shipment* in a transportation application, as shown in Figure 4.5.

```
Shipment
setVehicle()
perishable()
getWidth()
printRoute()
describeType()
getLength()
getDuration()
setType()
```

**FIGURE 4.5** A *Shipment* Class

Introducing the interfaces *Dimensions*, *TransportationMeans*, and *GoodsType* clarifies *Shipment*, Figure 4.6.

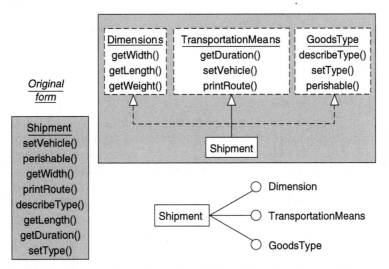

**FIGURE 4.6** Clarifying *Shipment* with Interfaces: Alternative Notations

The Java code for this is, in part, as follows.

```
interface Dimensions
{
    public double getWidth();
    public double getLength();
    public double getWeight();
}
. . . .

class Shipment implements Dimensions, TransportationMeans, GoodsType
```

```
{      . . . . .
     public double getWidth()
     {       . . . .
     }
     . . . .
}
```

We say that the class *Shipment supports* the interfaces *Dimensions, Transportation-Means*, and *GoodsType*.

### 4.1.2.2  Interfaces to Packages
The interface to a *package* has to be a little different from that of a class because a package can't be instantiated as a class can. For example, what is "the interface" to a package *purchases* consisting of the classes *Furniture, Clothing*, and *Appliances*, as shown in Figure 4.7?

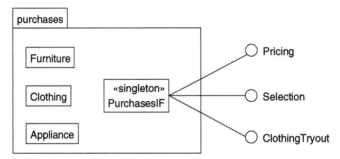

**FIGURE 4.7**  Package Interfaces

One way to get the benefits of the interface idea in the case of packages is for a designated object of a class in the package to provide the interface(s). In the figure, the class *PurchasesIF* is notated to have a single object that supports the interface. *Singleton* classes are those for which only one instance exists. This is a design pattern discussed in Chapter 7. Another alternative is for *PurchasesIF* to have exclusively static methods. The figure leaves unspecified how *PurchasesIF* uses *Furniture, Clothing*, and *Appliances* to satisfy the interfaces *Pricing, Selection*, and *ClothingTryout*.

Figure 4.8 shows a modularization for a chat application with the names of their interfaces. Because the *chatServer* package supports the *ConversationServices* interface, clients can access the methods listed in *ConversationServices*. For example, *ConversationServices* may contain the prototypes

*float computeConversationCharge(),*

*Conversation getConversation( int aConversationID )* and

*Vector durationOfCurrentConversations()*

These functions may be static members of the class *ConversationManager*. The idea of an interface to a collection of classes or objects will be exploited in the *Facade* design patterns in Chapter 8, and also in Chapter 10 on components.

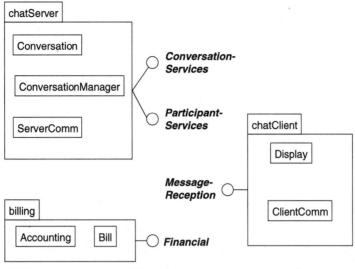

**FIGURE 4.8** Example of Package Interfaces

---

**KEY CONCEPT** *Interfaces*

Collections of function prototypes: Make designs more understandable.

---

## 4.1.3 Modularization

We have seen how interfaces can be useful once modularization has been performed, but how does one modularize in the first place? To modularize an object-oriented application, we create packages at the higher level and classes at the lower level.

***4.1.3.1 Choosing Classes*** There are two kinds of classes used in designs: *Domain* classes and *nondomain* classes. The domain classes pertain to the specific application under design. For example, the domain classes of an application simulating a bank might include classes *BankCustomer*, *BankTransaction* and *Teller*, but not *File* and *Database*. The classes *Customer* and *Transaction* may be useful classes for this application, but would not be domain classes because they are not special to this application. We generally begin class selection with the domain classes, and then add nondomain classes to satisfy design goals (as opposed to direct requirement goals). Chapters 6 through 9 indicate why and how nondomain classes arise through the employment of design patterns.

As another example of domain classes, consider an application that manages a car-buying web site. Possible domain classes include *CarBuyer*, *Car*, *CarFeature*, and *CarDeal*. The following classes could appear in the class model, but would not be domain classes: *Icon* (too general), *Customer* (not special to this application), *Site* (not special to this application), and *Feature* (too general). The nondomain classes are often needed to generalize the domain classes. The distinction between domain and nondomain classes is summarized in Figure 4.9.

- *Domain classes:* Particular to the application
  - · Examples: *BankCustomer, BankTransaction, Teller*
  - · Sufficient to classify all requirements
- *Nondomain classes:* Generic
  - · Examples: abstract classes, utility classes
  - · Arise from design and implementation considerations

**FIGURE 4.9** Domain vs. Nondomain Classes

Unless an application is primarily a graphical user interface, we try to postpone introducing Graphical User Interface (GUI) classes until the latter half of the design process. This is because GUI classes can usually be added to the core of a design. One can sometimes use only command-line interfaces for initial versions. Selecting some GUI classes early on may be inevitable for several reasons, however. One reason is that customers typically want to see some GUI's early in the project.

Typically, domain classes can be obtained from the sequence diagrams of use cases. We discuss domain classes fully in Chapter 13, and we link them to requirements analysis, use cases, and sequence diagrams.

**4.1.3.2  Choosing Packages**  Selecting packages is an essential part of choosing an application's architecture. The task is to decompose the application into a set of, typically, three to ten packages. These can then be further decomposed with the same general guidelines. There is nothing sacrosanct about the range three to ten, but people are most easily able to comprehend a set of entities of this number.

For example, suppose that we want to build an application that tracks the trajectory of an orbit-bound rocket carrying a satellite into position. Figure 4.10 gives alternative modularizations for this application. Choosing between these entails many trade-offs.

Chapter 14 thoroughly covers the subject of architecture.

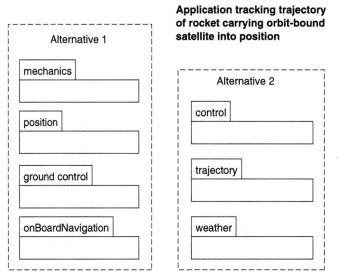

**FIGURE 4.10**  Alternative Modularizations

### 4.1.4 Refactoring for Correctness and Sufficiency

This book emphasizes ways to design flexibly using design patterns. *Extreme programming* is an alternative approach in which we first design only for the requirements given, and then revise the design and implementation when additional requirements become apparent. This process is called *refactoring*. We will list a few straightforward refactoring examples.

#### 4.1.4.1 *Refactoring: Promoting a Primitive Attribute to Class*

Class selection, introduced in Section 4.1.3.1, is the process of identifying a useful concept and defining a class for it. To accommodate increased scope, we often need to refactor by introducing a new class. For example, suppose that we already have a class *Automobile* with integer variable *mileage*.

```
class Automobile
{  Mileage mileage;
   . . . .
}
```

Additional requirements for a used car chain, however, may well reveal that the "mileage" on a used automobile is not a simple variable at all. For example, the engine may be a replacement, so that the mileage of the chassis would differ from that of the engine. In addition, let's suppose that our application has to take into account the possibility of fraud, so that the reported "mileage" would have to be modified by other attributes such as whether the car was ever stolen. For these reasons, we would consider the "promoting *mileage* to a class" refactoring. This results in the following.

```
class Mileage
{   int nominalMileageValue = 0;
    int chassisMileageValue = 0;
    int engineMileageValue = 0;
    . . . .
    public int computeEffectiveMileage(){ . . . }
}
class Automobile
{  Mileage mileage;
   . . . .
}
```

The classic reference on Refactoring is [Fo]. This book provides detailed steps to migrate an application from its original form to its refactored form.

#### 4.1.4.2 *Refactoring: Introducing Abstract Base Classes or Interface*

Object-orientation accommodates abstraction, but when should one employ abstraction? We can find an abstraction of just about any class but abstraction is not always advisable. One key indicator is whenever an application contains several classes having significant commonality. An example is the set of classes *Gymnast*, *Runner*, *FootballPlayer*: One abstraction is *Athlete* (or, *PurdueAthlete* if the application is for Purdue University). Abstraction is applied in many situations in this book, especially the design patterns section.

Note that Java abstract classes can contain every feature of a class except that objects of the class itself cannot be created. The following code does not compile.

```
abstract class MyAbstractClass
{
}
class AnotherClass
{
    MyAbstractClass m = new MyAbstractClass(); // does not compile
}
```

This is because we are trying to make an object of an abstract class. The following code is quite legal, however.

```
class AnotherClass
{    . . . .
   MyAbstractClass m; // no problem: just a declaration
    . . . .
     m = getObjectOfMyAbstractClass(); // returns obj. of non-abstract subclass
    . . . .
     m = new ConcreteSubclassOfMyAbstractClass(); // no problem
    . . . .
}
```

We often use the word "concrete" to emphasize that a class is not abstract.

Unless the base class really has useful general functionality, it should be an *interface* rather than a class. In the case of Java and C# (see Chapter 12), this does not "use up" the role of parent as a class does—whether abstract or not—and it presents fewer complications than class inheritance in any case.

## 4.2  ROBUSTNESS

Recall that one implementation of a set of requirements is more *robust* than another if it can handle more anomalous situations. Anomalous behavior includes incorrect user input, faulty data communication, and developer error. When we account for developer error we are protecting ourselves from ourselves, which is actually quite different from other anomalous behavior.

The *CommandLineCalculator* example in Section 1.4.3 of Chapter 1 on page 31 showed how an application could be made more robust in the sense of handling user error. That application could have been made even more robust against application or system errors (even crashes) by periodically saving data to a file. Even more robustness, at the expense of speed, could be obtained by sending the data to a remote repository. The example code for *CommandLineCalculator* was essentially a refactoring for robustness of the version in the appendix of Chapter 1. Figure 4.11 summarizes the sources of errors.

### 4.2.1  Verifying Input (Ensuring Environmental Robustness)

From the *CommandLineCalculator* example in Section 1.4.3 we saw ways in which we can check all input to an application for constraints before proceeding. These checks include verifying the type (e.g., integer, not just any string) and checking against preconditions and invariants (e.g., *withdrawalAmount* < *checkingBalance*). Programming systems such as Microsoft's ASP provide facilities that make it convenient for programmers to include such robustness checks.

1. *Protection from faulty Input*
   - User input
   - Input, not from user
     · Data communication
     · Function calls made by other applications
2. *Protection from developer error*
   - Faulty design
   - Faulty implementation

**FIGURE 4.11**  Improving Robustness: Sources of Errors

## 4.2.2   Initializing to Improve Robustness

It is usually good practice to initialize variables. For example,

```
int i = 0;
```

This promotes robustness because the penalty for unintentionally executing an application with an uninitialized variable is usually greater than doing so with a variable that has been given a specific initial value. When the application's bad behavior becomes evident, the initialized version is likely to yield more valuable information.

What about variables of reference type such as *MyClass c*? We could pick a default, such as the following.

```
class AnotherClass
{  . . .
   MyClass c = new MyClass( 1, 'a' );
   . . .
}
```

The problem here is that this initialization would have to be repeated wherever a class aggregates *MyClass* and requires a default object: This would cause extensive work if the default changes. A more maintainable alternative would be to supply *MyClass* with a static method that generates the standard default for that class.

```
class MyClass
{ . . .
   static MyClass getStandardMyClassInstance()
   {   return new MyClass( 1, 'a' );
   }
   . . .
}
```

We use this default as follows:

```
class AnotherClass
{ . . .
   MyClass c = MyClass.getStandardMyClassInstance();
   . . .
}
```

### 4.2.3   Parameter Passing Techniques to Improve Robustness

One important way to improve robustness is to ensure that methods are called safely. This section discusses constraints on parameters, which help to ensure safe method calling. For example, consider the parameters in the method

```
int computeArea( int aLength, int aBreadth ) { . . . } .
```

If the code for *computeArea()* is correct, then it remains only to ensure that the parameters it is called with are correct.

An ideal way to deal with parameter constraints is to introduce a class capturing the parameters and incorporating the constraints. This technique is discussed in the next section. Regardless of the technique a programmer uses to deal with violations of parameter constraints, such constraints should be clearly specified in the function comments. Figure 4.12 summarizes some key ways to improve the robustness of calling parameterized methods.

Example:
    *int computeArea(int aLength, int aBreadth) {…}*
* *Capture parameter constraints in classes if feasible*
    *int computeArea(RectangleDimension a RectangleDimension)*
* *Specify all parameter constraints in method comments*
    *aLength > 0* and
    *aBreadth > 0* and
    *aLength >= aBreadth*
* *Callers obey explicit requirements on parameters*
    · Problem is method programmers have no control over callers
* *Check constraints first within the method code*
    *if(aLength) <= 0)… …*
    · Throw exception if this is a predictable occurrence
    · Otherwise abort if possible
    · Otherwise return default if it makes sense in context
       · And generate warning or log to a file

**FIGURE 4.12**   Constraints on Parameters

There are two approaches to checking parameter values for constraint violations. One school of thought states that checking should not be performed at all if the constraints on parameters are clearly specified, and there is no reliable way to remedy a method call that should never have been made. The other is a fail-safe attitude, checking that all of the constraints are satisfied. In the author's opinion, the latter is preferable, though it should never excuse the programmer's obligation to clearly state all parameter constraints, and to always honor them in making function calls. This reflects longstanding engineering practice in which we over-design to protect ourselves from our own human imperfections. For example, to protect users from imperfections in design, fabrication, and installation, construction codes specify beam widths well in excess of their mathematically calculated minimums.

Once parameter constraints have been found violated, what are our options as programmers of the method? This depends on the nature of the application and the place of this method within it. The called method has no way of knowing what's best for the caller, and so it is usually best to throw an exception so that the calling code is forced to decide what to do. The next best action is to abort the entire application because it may be much better to have no program executing than to have one performing with entirely unanticipated data. If neither of these options is possible the method may be able to return a default result and leave a notice (on the console or a log file, for example) stating that this occurred.

**KEY CONCEPT** *Robustness*

Is promoted by verifying data values before using them.

### 4.2.3.1 *Capturing Parameters in a Class* A good way to handle recurring constraints on parameters is to "wrap" the parameters in a class instead of using them in primitive form (*int*, *float* etc.) as illustrated in Figure 4.13.

```
Replace  int computeArea(int aLength, int aBreadth)
         {..}
with     int computeArea(Rectangle aRectangle)
         {..}
--where  class Rectangle
         {...
            Rectangle(int aLength, int aBreadth)
               { if(aLength > 0) this.length=aLength;
                 else... ..
               }
         ...}
```

**FIGURE 4.13** Wrapping Parameters

The advantage of such wrapping is that the handling of erroneous lengths and breadths is performed in one place—within the *Rectangle* class. This improves design and maintenance. The disadvantages include a proliferation of classes. A good option is to make the *Rectangle* constructor private and use static "factory" methods (functions that return objects—see Section 7.2 on page 148) to obtain *Rectangle* objects, as in

```
static Rectangle getReactangleObject( . . .. );
```

As will be seen in Section 7.2, factory methods are more flexible than constructors in situations like this.

As another example, if a method *evaluate()* accepts only "car", "truck" or "bus" as parameters it might be better not to use *String* as a parameter. *String* introduces the possibility of illegal parameters. This is far less likely (perhaps impossible) if we define a class such as *SpecializedVehicle* with a private constructor, and factory functions

```
SpecializedVehicle createACar()
SpecializedVehicle createATruck(), and
SpecializedVehicle createABus().
```

The method can then take only a parameter of this type. In other words, instead of

```
evaluate( String aVehicle ) . . . // problem handling illegal strings
```

use

```
evaluate( SpecializedVehicle aVehicle ) . . . // parameter value cannot be illegal
```

When the possible parameter values are restricted but infinite, a separate class can still be valuable. For example, a person's age is an integer between 0 and 140, let's say, and so a method

```
getYearOfBirth( int anAge )
```

may have to deal with errors. The same error processing would have to be repeated for all methods taking age as a parameter. On the other hand, a class *Age* with a private constructor and a public factory method

```
Age getAge( int anAge )
```

would handle erroneous ages in a consistent manner, performed in just this one method, and combined with all of the other aspects of age. Calls such as

```
. . . getYearOfBirth( getAge( n ) ) . . .
```

would replace calls such as

```
. . . getYearOfBirth( n ) . . .
```

## 4.2.4   Enforcing Intentions

Much of the preceding sections have been concerned with threats to robustness from invalid input from users and communication devices. The section concentrates on improving robustness by protecting against design and implementation errors (the bad things we software engineers unwittingly do to ourselves).

Modern applications are enormously complex: As a result, software engineers must guard continually against being overwhelmed. When we design and implement, we are *using* the functionality of the existing design and code, as well as *providing* functionality to the rest of the application. When designing and implementing functionality, we intend it to be used in a certain manner. The converse is usually true too: We do not want the functionality to be used in a manner that we did not intend. For example, when we introduce a class that is intended to have only one instance during each execution of the application, we do not want the application to produce several instances. To make the application more robust, we then *enforce* our intentions. For example, the *Singleton* design pattern in Section 7.2 on page 148 shows how to ensure that a class has exactly one instance.

In this section we have already encountered several techniques for enforcing intentions. One is to capture parameter constraints by introducing a class of which the parameters must be an instance. This technique does not merely request callers of a method to respect constraints: It enforces obedience to those constraints.

> **KEY CONCEPT**    *Robustness*
>
> Is promoted by enforcing our intentions.

## 4.3 DESIGN DETAILS: HOW MUCH IS ENOUGH?

The most detailed designs (short of actual coding) provide class, sequence, state, and activity models: They provides a maximum of detail for each of these. For example, this would include the function prototypes for every class, the pre- and postconditions, and activity diagrams or pseudocode where appropriate. Many programmers get frustrated with this amount of design: Their desire is to "just code it—The code tells exactly what is supposed to happen." For a very simple function, this is quite true. For example, a method that does nothing more than get a variable value hardly needs a flowchart or postconditions. On the other hand, developers usually achieve far better results when designing nontrivial methods in advance. Like many programmers, the author has plunged into coding a seemingly simple method, only to discover one forgotten aspect after another: He then adds more and more code until the resulting mess has to be redesigned. In many cases, it would have been far better to have completed a method specification and design in advance, using preconditions, postconditions, and perhaps pseudocode or activity charts.

Although we aim to specify a detailed design of a method in advance of coding it, we may need to perform some coding before that design is complete due to our own human limitations in envisaging the end result. The point of departure depends on the experience of the designer and on the nature of the task. Figure 4.14 shows how these factors influence the degree of design detail that we should observe prior to writing any code. The curves refer only to the amount of design prior to *initial* coding. Complete design documentation is required eventually in any case.

Truly simple methods can be coded immediately, whether or not the developer is experienced: Complex methods should first be designed in as much detail as the designer can envisage, then implemented. This allows the developer to increase his understanding of the

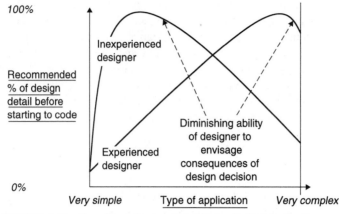

**FIGURE 4.14** How Much Design Detail Before Initial Coding?

issues involved, and inspect his designs. Experienced designer/developers are able to look much farther ahead, and are able to specify great detail before coding. Inexperienced designers, on the other hand, lack the ability to envisage the effects of designs. As a result, they may be forced to begin some experimental code sooner than the ideal time. In any case, the author has observed that programmers tend to spend too little time on design before they start coding.

## CHAPTER SUMMARY

This chapter has discussed two common design goals: *Correctness* and *Robustness*. Correctness means that the design supports the requirements. Generally speaking, there are several possible correct designs for a given set of requirements. A design is robust if it accommodates the application's execution even in the presence of errors. There are many kinds of "errors." In operating the application, the user commits some; programmers commit others during the design and coding of the application.

- *Correctness of a Design or Code*
  - · Supports the requirements
  - · In general, many correct designs exist
- *Robustness of a Design or Code*
  - · Absorbs errors
    - · —of the user
    - · —of developers

**FIGURE 4.15** Summary of This Chapter

## EXERCISES

**Exercise 4.1**  Fill in the blanks.

A *correct* design is one which _____.

A *correct implementation* is one which _____.

The first step in ensuring that a design or code correct is correct is that _____.

(Actually, preceding even this is the fact that the requirements themselves are written and clear.)

To make a design clear, we _____ it (break it down into a small number of pieces).

**Exercise 4.2**    Provide a modularization for an application that advises clients on stock picks, and enables them to transfer funds among individual stocks and savings accounts. Explain your solution. *Hint:* One reasonable solution employs four packages.

Evaluation criteria:

■ Effectiveness of your response    A = decomposition into a reasonable number of coherent packages

■ Clarity of modularization    A = very clear decomposition, very clearly explained

The following are errors that you should watch for in Exercise 4.2:

*Serious*:

1. Incoherent packaging of classes

2. Significant ambiguity as to what the packages mean.

*Neither serious nor minor*:

1. Some ambiguity as to what the packages mean.

2. Less than clear explanation of the modularization.

**Exercise 4.3**    State an invariant of the application in Exercise 4.2. Assume that no funds are transferred into or out of the application. *Hint*: One good invariant involves the quantity *TotalOfStockValues*, and consists of a single "==" equation.

Now suppose that you can transfer funds into or out of the application at runtime. Restate the invariant.

**Exercise 4.4**    In the presence of thoroughly written requirements, what does it mean for an artifact to be "correct?" A sentence or two suffices to answer this question.

**Exercise 4.5**    Why does "avoiding duplication" promote correctness?

Describe a possible duplication to avoid.

**Exercise 4.6**    Describe three appropriate interfaces for the following *Road* class in a roadway control application. *Hint*: One good solution has three interfaces.

```
class Road
{
   . . ..
   public float getLength() { . . . }
   public Surface getSurfaceType() { . . . }
   public Surface getNumVehiclesOn() { . . . }
   public Road[] listConnectingRoads (){ . . . }
   public void close() { . . . }
   public void computeCumulativeUsage() { . . . }
   public void makeOneWay( Direction aDirection ) { . . . }
   public Surface getSurfaceType() { . . . }
}
```

**Exercise 4.7**    Define "robustness." Consider an application that helps manage a fabric store. Assume that the stores sell fabrics and associated items such as buttons and ribbons. Give three to four robustness issues specific to this application. Explain your choices.

Evaluation criteria:

■ Effectiveness of your response    A = issues raised are indeed robustness issues

■ Clarity of considerations and explanations    A = very clearly explained

The following are errors that you should watch for:

*Serious*:

1. Confusing robustness with other qualities.

2. Unclear description of issues.

*Neither serious nor minor*:

1. Somewhat unclear description of issues.

**Exercise 4.8** Below is code for a method *divide()*. Make the method more robust in at least two ways.

```
public double divide( Double aNumerator, Double aDenominator )
{
    return aNumerator.doubleValue() / aDenominator.doubleValue();
}
```

**Exercise 4.9** The figure shows classes for a video store application discussed in Sections 3.4 and 3.5 of Chapter 3, which includes the following use case.

Precondition: The customer's identification has been entered.

1. Clerk clicks "check out" on main menu.

2. Clerk swipes bar code on video.

3. Application prompts for rental duration.

4. Clerk enters duration.

5. Application stores record.

6. Application prints customer's account status.

**Part 4.9.1** Are there sufficient classes for this use case in Figure 4.16? If not, explain.

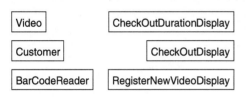

**FIGURE 4.16** Video Store Application: Sufficient Classes?

**Part 4.9.2** Generally, *String* is adequate to represent the directors of the videos (e.g., "Spielberg" for E.T.): But what requirements would cause you to rethink this? Justify your response.

**Part 4.9.3** Give a solid reason why it would *not* be adequate to design the video / customer relationship as follows.

```
class Customer
{ String[] = videosCheckOut; . . .. }
```

What are the advantages of a class *Video* instead?

**Part 4.9.4** Using UML with the class figure and possibly with additional classes, show aggregations. Justify your response.

**Part 4.9.5** Suppose that the video store is part of a chain, and that you must provide an interface so that corporate applications can use your work. Typical corporate functions are to take inventory of customers and videos. Describe that interface. Justify your response.

**Part 4.9.6** Provide a class that you could introduce to promote the robustness of this application. Justify your response.

**Part 4.9.7** In addition to your response in Part 4.9.6, explain how the *state* concept can help make this application more robust. Explain your reasoning.

Evaluation criteria:

▓ Specificity

▓ Clarity of writing and designs

▓ Effectiveness of your response

A = thoroughly specific answers to all questions

A = very clean designs with no wasted parts; every nontrivial part clearly described

A = effective avenues for flexibility, reusability, and robustness, as required

The following are errors that you should watch for in Exercise 4.9:

*Serious*:

**1.** Introducing classes whose coverage is very unclear.

**2.** Little understanding of the meaning of aggregation.

**3.** Little understanding of the meaning of interface.

**4.** Little understanding of the meaning of robustness.

**5.** No truly specific idea of how to make an application more robust.

*Less than serious, but more than minor*:

**1.** Introducing unjustified classes.

**2.** Vagueness in explaining requirements.

**3.** Inability to use *state* to promote robustness.

**4.** Failure to separate the main menu GUI from a class initiating the application.

**5.** Vague states.

**6.** Corporate applications would not require interfaces to GUI's.

**7.** GUI classes are there to provide input and output: They typically should not perform substantive work. On the other hand, internal classes perform substantive work, and typically do not do input/output from the user.

*Minor*:

**1.** Poor explanatory writing. (*Note*: Ask your professor if you may have a nonsoftware person look over your English.)

**2.** Slightly wrong drawing of UML.

# CHAPTER 5

# DESIGN PRINCIPLES II: FLEXIBILITY, REUSABILITY, AND EFFICIENCY

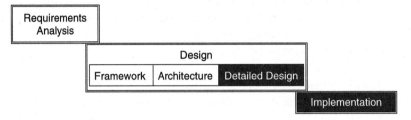

**FIGURE 5.1** Process Phases Discussed in This Chapter

This chapter completes our discussion of general software design principles. It specifies the meaning and goals of *flexible* and *reusable* designs, and provides code-level implications for these design goals. The rest of this book provides specific design patterns and component techniques that promote flexibility and reusability.

## 5.1 FLEXIBILITY

Despite efforts to freeze software requirements, they typically change even while a project is under development. For this reason, we frequently design in a way that tries to account for future changes. For example, if an application is required to track transportation stock transactions, the design may be flexible enough to track other kinds of stock transactions. It would not be reasonable, however, to expect the design to track unrelated activities such as toy purchases: "Flexibility" has limits.

### 5.1.1 The Goals of Flexibility

Figure 5.2 indicates how requirements of an application can change.

### 5.1.2 Designs for Adding *More of the Same Kind* of Functionality

Consider an application that registers members at a web site. Figure 5.3 shows a reasonable initial design.

*Anticipate*

- *adding more of the same kind* of functionality
  - *Example* (banking application): handle more kinds of accounts
    without having to change the existing design or code
- *adding different* functionality
  - *Example:* add *withdraw* function to existing *deposit* functionality
- *changing* functionality
  - *Example:* allow overdrafts

**FIGURE 5.2**   Aspects of Flexibility

**FIGURE 5.3**   Registering Website Members

The code for this would typically take the following form.

```
class Website
{
        Member[ ] members; // or maybe: Vector members;
        void register( Member aMember ) { . . . }
}
```

How do we make the design flexible enough to register new categories of members? Note that this is the *same kind* of functionality (registration). We can do this by introducing a base class. We make this base class abstract, name it *Member*, and create an inherited class, *StandardMember* to cover the situation that we started with. This design accommodates new types of member subclasses. The changes are shown in Figure 5.4.

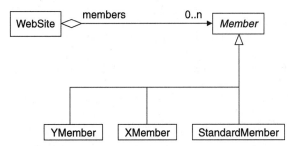

**FIGURE 5.4**   Registering Website Members Flexibly

The code above need not change: However, this new design enables us to add separate functionality to *StandardMember*, *XMember*, *YMember* etc. that distinguishes among them.

## 5.1.3   Design for Adding *Different* Functionality

Now let's consider designing an application that accommodates adding new kinds of functionality. The ability to *change* functionality is often accomplished in the same way.

Accommodating new functionality depends on its context and scope, as suggested by Figure 5.5.

Within the scope of

1. a list of related functions
   Example: add *print* to an air travel itinerary functions
2. an existing base class
   Example: add "print *road-* and *ship-* to air itinerary"
3. neither
   Example: add "print itineraries for combinations of air,
   road and ship transportation"

**FIGURE 5.5**  Adding Functionality to an Application: Alternative Situations

Case 1 can often be handled by adding the new method to an existing set of methods of a class (e.g., add the method *print()* to the class *Itinerary*). Case 3 can be designed by a number of different techniques: These are beyond the scope of this chapter, but are covered in Chapter 9.

Let's consider Case 2. The application concerns travel, and contains a *Trip* class as shown in Figure 5.6.

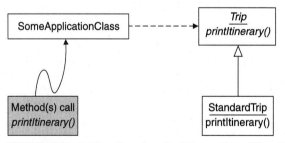

**FIGURE 5.6**  Adding Functionality When a Base Class Exists

We can accommodate new functionality by adding to the base class (Figure 5.7).

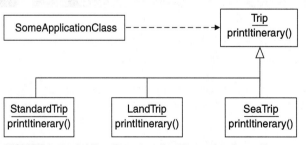

**FIGURE 5.7**  Adding Functionality Through a Base Class

This design enables the code in *SomeApplicationClass* to be generic, referring to *Trip* rather than distinguishing among different types of trips. It takes the following form.

```
. . . code concerning travel
Trip trip;
. . . interaction instantiating trip as StandardTrip or LandTrip object . . .
. . . (although none of these subclasses is actually mentioned) . . .
trip.printItinerary(); // note: this code is independent of the type of trip
. . . more code concerning travel
```

Code in *Trip* takes the following form.

```
abstract class Trip
{       . . .
        void printItinerary()
        {
                . . . code common to printing all itineraries
        }
        . . .
}
```

Each subclass can have its own version of *printItinerary()*, possibly using the inherited version. For example,

```
class SeaTrip
{       . . .
        void printItinerary()
        {       super.printItinerary (); // typically, use inherited code somehow
                . . .. // code special to sea trips
        }
        . . .
}
```

The combination of dependency / inheritance in Figure 5.7 is often referred to as *delegation*. Delegation is a form used by many design patterns (see Chapters 6 through 9).

### 5.1.4   Design for Flexibility

Figure 5.8 shows more refined flexibility requirements for designs. Designs that accommodate these requirements are covered in Chapters 7 through 11.

---

**KEY CONCEPT**   *Flexibility*

We design flexibly and introduce parts, because change and reuse are likely.

---

## 5.2   REUSABILITY

For given quality standards, the marketplace forces suppliers to create products at the lowest possible cost. One way in which suppliers obtain maximum productivity is to leverage past work: In other words, to reuse. For years, reuse has been indispensable in most areas of human endeavor: It is only recently that the software community has learned how to accomplish reuse on a significant scale. A dramatic proof of this is the widespread use of the Java API's.

| Flexibility Aspect: Ability to... | Described in... |
|---|---|
| create objects in variable configurations determined at runtime | "Creational" design patterns, Chapter 7 |
| represent variable trees of objects or other structures at runtime | "Structural" design patterns, Chapter 8 |
| change, recombine, or otherwise capture the mutual behavior of a set of objects | "Behavioral" design patterns, Chapter 9 |
| create and store a possibly complex object of a class | Component technology, Chapter 10 |
| configure objects of predefined complex classes, or sets of classes, so as to interact in many ways | Component technology, Chapter 10 |

**FIGURE 5.8**   Additional Types of Flexibility

## 5.2.1   The Goals of Reusability

Software engineers reuse at the architectural/design level, and at the implemented component level. In this section, we will be concerned with reusable functions, reusable classes, and reusable class combinations. The design pattern chapters of this book (6 through 9) cover extensive *design* reuse: The component chapters (10 through 12) cover *implementation* reuse.

## 5.2.2   Reusability of Function Design

A typical method in an object-oriented implementation is short, and so it does not appear at first that there is any point is trying to salvage individual methods for reuse. Certainly, this is true for a simple method like *getOdometerReading()* in a class *Automobile*! Implementations often involve methods with significant substance, however, and these methods may be useful for several applications. The method *computeResaleValue()* in *Automobile* could be one of these, depending on the amount of work that went into coding it. Are there pointers we should watch for in specifying and designing such a method? Figure 5.9 suggests some.

First, methods slated for reuse have to be defined completely so that reusers know what conditions these methods assume, and what they do. Section 1.2.2 on page 23 explains how to specify the assumptions and effects of a method.

The more independent a method is of its environment, the more capable it is of being reused. Static methods in particular have this quality. On the other hand, a method *computePremium()* of a class *InsurancePolicy* appears to depend heavily on the *InsurancePolicy* object that it is associated with. In other words, it depends on the instance variables of *InsurancePolicy*, and cannot be reused without the *InsurancePolicy* class. If *computePremium()* depends only on three or fewer parameters, then it might be better designed as a static method such as

```
public static float computePremium( int anAge, int anAmount, float aHealthLevel ) { . . . . }
```

- Specify completely
  - Preconditions etc. (see Section 1.2.2)
- Avoid unnecessary coupling with the enclosing class
  - Make static if feasible
  - Include parameterization
    - i.e., make the method functional
    - but limit the number of parameters
- Make the names expressive
  - Understandability promotes reusability
- Explain the algorithm
  - Reusers need to know how the algorithm works

**FIGURE 5.9**  Making a Method Reusable

The benefit of using this particular design is a method more easily reusable in other applications. The cost, on the other hand, is looser coupling with the class that contains it. The latter can make the design somewhat less coherent and less object-oriented.

A method's *name* is important if it is slated for reuse: Reusers have to be entirely comfortable that the method is just what they need, and a descriptive name helps. A programmer would reuse *computePremium()* only if he is convinced that this is the function he needs. Designers have to trade off the benefit of more explicit yet cumbersome names like *getPremiumByStandardAjaxActuarialAlgorithm1234()*. Reusers also need to know the interface (number and type of parameters etc.). In addition, they may need to know how the algorithm works because the interface specifications may not be enough to assure the level of assurance they require.

## 5.2.3  Class Selection for Reuse

Some of the qualities that tend to make a *class* more reusable are listed in Figure 5.10.

alternatives

- Describe the class completely
- Make the class name and functionality match a real world concept
- Define a useful abstraction
  - attain broad applicability
- Reduce dependencies on other classes
  - Elevate dependencies in hierarchy

**FIGURE 5.10**  Making a Class Reusable

Classes with natural names are more reusable because they fit naturally with the real world. For example, a *Molecule* class used in one application is a good candidate for use in another. Not every domain class is widely reusable: Some are too special to the application in which they are defined, such as *EmbeddedSpecialtyDevice1234*. Some nondomain classes such as *Substance* are reusable because they are abstract.

When a class *A* depends on a class *B*, no use of *A* can be made without *B,* and thus reduces the reusability of *A*. Reducing the dependence of a class on others is a challenging design issue.

As reflected in Figure 5.11, for example, a class *Piano* appears to depend on a class *Customer* because we are in the piano business in order to sell them to customers: But this limits our use of *Piano*. For example, a warehouse application needs *Piano* but not necessarily *Customer*. We could also claim that our customers depend on pianos because that's why they are our customers. Is there a way to remove these dependencies? Introducing a third class *PianoOrder* that relates the two accomplishes this goal, as illustrated in Figure 5.11.

Replace ...

with ...

**FIGURE 5.11**   Reducing Dependency Among Classes

This design has ramifications, however, that may not be acceptable in real world situations. For example, we may need to be able to access all of the orders for a given customer without the inefficiency of inspecting every *PianoOrder* object. An approach to this issue will be discussed in the *Mediator* design pattern in Section 9.4 on page 295. "Mediator" classes like *PianoOrder* reduce dependencies.

Although we try to reduce class dependencies, some dependencies at abstract levels may be acceptable. An analog in the real world is the dependency of *houses* on *entry doors*. At the abstract level just stated, this is an acceptable dependence: We don't mind committing every house to *some* entry door. On the other hand, we would not want all houses to be dependent on just one type of door such as "double French doors." In the same vein, we probably would not object to a dependence of the class *Piano* on the class *PianoManufacturer*, but would not want *Piano* to depend on *AjaxPianoCompany*.

### 5.2.4  Class Combination for Reuse

Design patterns, covered in Chapters 6 through 9, are reusable class combinations. Our goal in this section is to cover common, more elementary class combinations for reuse that are not advanced enough to be blessed with the "design pattern" title. For example, we have already seen that the delegation class combination fosters flexibility. We will look at inheritance, aggregation and dependency for reusing class combinations, which are suggested by Figure 5.12.

The code for the original version of *Customer* and each of the three alternatives is listed here:

**Original *Customer* Class**

```
package original;
/**
 * Original version of the Customer class: Re-use limited
 */
public class Customer
```

```
{
/**********************************************************
 */
public Customer()
{     super();
}
/**********************************************************
 * @return the amount owed by this customer
 */
public int computeBill()
{
      // ..... Do required computation
      return 0; // temporary
}
}
```

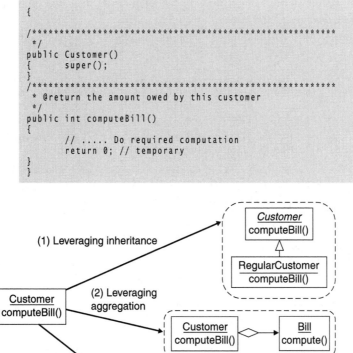

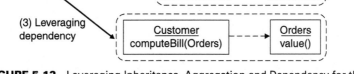

**FIGURE 5.12**   Leveraging Inheritance, Aggregation and Dependency for the Reuse of Class Combinations

### 5.2.4.1   *Leveraging Inheritance*   The base class *Customer* is:

```
package inheritance;
/**
 * All customers are of this base type.
 * This class is eligible for re-use
 */
public abstract class Customer
{
      // ----- Methods common to all customers .... ------

/**********************************************************
 */
public Customer()
{     super();
}
/**********************************************************
 * @return the amount owed by this customer
 */
public int computeBill()
{
      // Do computation required for customers of all types ....
      return 0; // temporary
}
}
```

In the derived class *RegularCustomer*, given next, we might utilize the inherited *super.computeBill()*.

```
package inheritance;
/**
 */
public class RegularCustomer extends Customer
{

/**********************************************************
 */
public RegularCustomer()
{     super();
}
/**********************************************************
 * @return the amount owed by this customer
 */
public int computeBill()
{
     int baseAmount = super.computeBill(); // perform inherited code first ...
     // ... Do required computation, possibly use baseAmount
     return 0; // temporary
}
}
```

### 5.2.4.2 Leveraging Aggregation
In this version of *Customer*, the aggregate class appears as the line

```
private Bill bill;
```

This object is utilized in the statement

```
int amount = this.bill.compute(); // delegate computation
package aggregation;
/**
 * Aggregation version of the Customer class: Reuse facilitated because
 * billing function is delegated, not embedded.
 */
public class Customer
{
     private Bill bill;

/**********************************************************
 * Customer constructor comment.
 */
public Customer()
{     super();
}
/**********************************************************
 * @return the amount owed by this customer
 */
public int computeBill()
{
     // Do required computation
     int amount = this.bill.compute(); // delegate computation
     // ... Do more work
     return 0; // temporary replacement
}
}
```

The class *Bill* can be implemented as follows.

```
package aggregation;
/**
 * Billing functionality collected here.
 */
public class Bill
{

/***********************************************************
 */
public Bill()
{     super();
}
/***********************************************************
 * Computes the value of this bill
 */
public int compute()
{
        // ... Do the required work
        return 0; // temporary
}
}
```

### 5.2.4.3  *Leveraging Dependency*
In this version, the *Customer* class has a method, *computeBill( ... )*, which takes a parameter of type *Orders*. Much of the work is then performed by this class.

```
package dependency;
/**
 * Leveraging dependency
 */
public class Customer
{

/***********************************************************
 */
public Customer()
{     super();
}
/***********************************************************
 * @return the amount owed by this customer
 */
public int computeBill( Orders someOrders )
{
        int value = someOrders.computeValue();
        // ... Do required computation using value
        return 0; // temporary replacement
}
}
```

The class *Orders* can be implemented as follows.

```
package dependency;
/**
 * Collection of orders
 */
public class Orders
{
/***********************************************************
 */
public Orders()
{     super();
```

```
    }
    /***********************************************************
     * Computes the value of these orders
     */
    public int computeValue()
    {
            //... Do required work ...
            return 0; // temporary
    }
}
```

**KEY CONCEPT**    *Design for Reuse*

Increase the reusability of a class by reducing its dependencies.

## 5.3 EFFICIENCY

Applications must execute required functionality within required time constraints. There may also be limitations on the amount of memory (RAM or disk space) that they use. This book assumes that the reader is already familiar with data structures and the relative efficiency of basic algorithms such as sorting and searching. For this reason, the discussion here of efficiency is at a high level, confined to its relationship with flexibility, reusability, robustness and correctness.

Figure 5.13 summarizes two basic approaches to designing efficiently.

- *Design for Other Criteria, Then Consider Efficiency*
  - · Design for flexibility, reusability,...
  - · At some point, identify inefficient places
  - · Make targeted changes to improve efficiency
- *Design for Efficiency From the Start*
  - · Identify key efficiency requirements up front
  - · Design for these requirements during all phases
- *Combine These Two Approaches*
  - · Make trade-offs for efficiency requirements during design
  - · Address remaining efficiency issues after initial design

**FIGURE 5.13**    Basic Approaches to Time Efficiency

It is ideal to be able to optimize a design for both time and space: In reality, however, these two goals must usually be balanced against each other. This is known as the space–time trade-off, and the reader may already be well aware of it from having studied data structures. To understand why this trade-off is common, imagine that you are planning a factory that assembles toys. Time efficiency is measured in terms of the number of toys your operation can assemble per hour (being more time efficient equals more toys per hour). Space efficiency is measured in terms of the amount of space you have to rent for your operation (being more space efficient equals less space used).

If you have very little space, it takes a long time to assemble a toy. In the extreme case, you have no place to store the parts, and so every part has to be shipped to you individually, arriving no earlier than the instant you need it. You would have to wait for most deliveries. At the other extreme you would have unlimited space, and so space would not hinder your assembly operations at all. You cannot assemble toys infinitely fast, however: Other limitations, such as the time taken to actually put the parts together, become the limiting factors on your speed. Figure 5.14 illustrates the space–time trade-off. If the requirements allow it, we generally look for a solution in the shaded area (the "knee" of the curve), where the space allocation allows us to take most advantage of the resulting speedup, but where additional space does not result in an appreciable increase in speed. This is the principle of space–time trade-offs; the rest of this section discusses how to apply it.

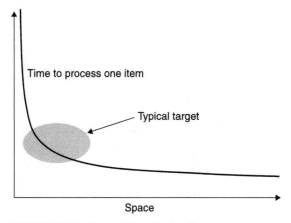

**FIGURE 5.14**   Space–Time Trade-offs

In practice, a more complex trade-off is in effect when considering designs: This trade-off also accounts for the relative ease with which a design can be implemented and maintained. "Ease" sounds indulgent towards software engineers, but can translate into money because less designer and implementer time is required when the tools and languages are easier to use. A typical three-way trade-off is shown in Figure 5.15.

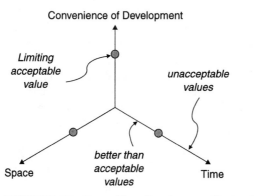

**FIGURE 5.15**   Space-Time-Development Trade-offs

As will be described in Section 5.4, there may be at least one other trade-off quantity: the size of the source code.

We are often willing to sacrifice a degree of both of time efficiency and space efficiency for the sake of more convenient, and therefore less costly, development and maintenance.

## 5.3.1  Speed Efficiency

Real-time programs are the most demanding applications in terms of speed. They require that functionality execute within a fixed time, typically measured in microseconds. Examples are airplane stability control and anti-lock braking systems. Real-time applications are beyond the scope of this book.

Even for nonreal-time applications, speed can be crucial. When an otherwise excellent application fails to complete its operations in a timely manner, users quickly lose patience. An example is an applet that loads so slowly that it annoys users: By the time it appears, users are in no mood to appreciate its features.

Ordinary single-line instructions using the primitives of the programming language do not generally cause time delays worth worrying about. A *profiler* is an application that tracks resource usage during program execution. If a profiler were available, one would run the application on it to identify slow parts. In addition, one would look for key potential speed-efficiency culprits as listed in Figure 5.16. The following sections deal with each of these speed-efficiency bottlenecks in turn.

- *Loops*
    - while, for, do
- *Remote operations*
    - Requiring a network
        - LAN
        - The Internet
- *Function calls*
    - if the function called results in the steps above
- *Object creation*

**FIGURE 5.16**   Impediments to Speed Efficiency

***5.3.1.1  Dealing with Loops***   There are numerous analyses of algorithms such as sort routines, which calculate their relative average and worst-case times. Each of these calculations requires a detailed analysis of the particular routine involved. Special focus should be devoted to nested loops. If an outer loop executes 10,000 times, for example, and it contains an inner loop that also executes 10,000 times, then the entire loop performs the inner operation(s) a staggering hundred million times (the product of the two).

***5.3.1.2  Eliminating Remote Calls***   A call to a remote process, such as over a local area network or the Internet, is liable to consume a comparatively large amount of time. There is frequently a trade-off possible between the number of times that such operations are performed, and the volume of information retrieved at each call, as shown in Figure 5.17.

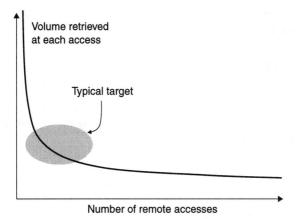

**FIGURE 5.17**   Trade-off Between Number of Remote Calls and Volume Retrieved at Each Call

An example of this trade-off is a browser application, in which a web page executes JavaScript within the client's browser: The JavaScript could cause time-consuming server-side database retrieval. A trade-off is sometimes possible between the frequency with which the JavaScript makes calls and the amount of material retrieved for each call.

Another example is the trade-off between downloading an applet—a relatively slow one-time operation—and performing servlet (server-side) processing. The latter typically downloads web pages, each occurrence of which is probably faster than applet downloading, but would probably need to occur more frequently.

Bob Schudy has pointed out to the author that it is sometimes efficient to run a background thread performing data fetches. This relies on the fact that only a fraction of a CPU's capacity is in use at one time, which often makes it worthwhile to use the "free" cycles to pre-fetch data. This may apply even if some of the data will not be used.

In Section 8.7 on page 233 we discuss the *Proxy* design pattern. Among other purposes, *Proxy* is used to avoid the unnecessary call of functions. It is often used in conjunction with calls to remote functions.

### 5.3.1.3   *Eliminating or Certifying Function Calls*   Many of the design principles and techniques detailed in this book manifest themselves in code as chains of function calls. While the organizational benefits of these principles and techniques may be high, chains of function calls reduce time efficiency. For example, a loop such as

```
for( i = 0, i < 1000; ++i )
    doFunctionCall( i )
```

looks harmless enough, but masks untold possible inner loops, depending on what *doFunctionCall()* does (and what functions *it* calls, etc.). Hunting down the entire potential spider web of functions called by *doFunctionCall()* may be necessary.

Efforts to make code efficient can frequently diminish its elegance. The same can be said of *design* and efficiency: Efficient designs are not necessarily neat, and may even be downright ugly. For example, speed efficiency induces us to reduce the number of function calls, resulting in larger methods and classes. Ugly designs are harder to extend and reuse. We'd like to have flexibility, reusability, and efficiency all at the same time, but we usually have to trade one for another to some degree.

### 5.3.2 Storage Efficiency

Applications typically require the storage of data so that it can be retrieved at a future time, either within the same execution, or via another execution. This results in a need for efficiency in utilizing the space required to store data. Figure 5.18 summarizes common issues and techniques in storing data.

- Store only the data needed
  - Trades-off *storage efficiency*
    - vs. *time to extract and reintegrate*
- Compress the data
  - Trades-off *storage efficiency*
    - vs. *time to compress and decompress*
- Store in order of relative frequency
  - Trades-off *storage efficiency*
    - vs. *time to determine location*

**FIGURE 5.18**  Attaining Storage Efficiency

There are at least three kinds of storage issues: The use of RAM (at runtime), the size of the code base itself, and the use of secondary storage (disk drives, typically) at runtime and at non-runtime.

If a profiler were available, one would run the application on it to identify space usage. Figure 5.18 summarizes common issues and techniques in storing data.

There is typically a time penalty for attaining storage efficiency because additional processing may be required. (Compression may actually improve speed as well, however, because there is less data to transfer.) This is the classical space–time trade-off already discussed.

Once again, programming convenience is a competing factor to account for. A database management system, for example, facilitates a great deal of built-in capability, thereby improving programmer convenience. On the other hand, the programmer loses some control over space and time usage by using such a system. In early days of military computing, database systems were rarely used for operational applications because of the resulting lack of control over time and space efficiency. With advances in database management systems, however, the trade-off parameters changed, allowing the use of more "off-the-shelf" tools of this kind.

## 5.4 TRADE-OFFS AMONG ROBUSTNESS, FLEXIBILITY, REUSABILITY, AND EFFICIENCY

This chapter and Chapter 4 have discussed Robustness, Flexibility, Reusability, and Efficiency. We usually can't get all of these qualities in the same design. Several of them may be in opposition to each other, and trade-offs must be made. Figure 5.19 suggests one way to go about making this trade-off.

1A.  Extreme Programming Approach
*or*       Design for sufficiency only
1B.  Flexibility-driven Approach
          Design for future requirements
            Reuse usually a by-product
2.   Ensure robustness
3.   Provide enough efficiency
          Compromise reuse etc. as necessary to
          attain efficiency requirements

**FIGURE 5.19**  Trading off Robustness, Flexibility, Efficiency, and Reusability

Note that we have not included correctness in this trade-off discussion. This is because we can't really compromise on whether or not an application satisfies its requirements: However, we can negotiate reduced scope for an application, thereby changing the requirements themselves, and this becomes part of the trade-off equation.

One must first decide whether to take a just-enough (sometimes called the "extreme programming") approach; whether to aim for a design that promotes flexibility and reusability; or to aim somewhere in between. In either case, robustness is usually pursued. Note that there is more to extreme programming than described here: It also includes extensive in-process testing, two-person programming, and the provision to refactor as requirements change. Figure 5.20 indicates some of the pro's and con's of extreme programming.

| Extreme vs. Nonextreme | |
| --- | --- |
| + Job done faster (usually) <br> + Scope clear <br> + More likely to be efficient | + Future applications more likely to use parts <br> + Accommodates changes in requirements |
| – Future applications less likely to use the work <br> – Refactoring for expanded requirements can be expensive | – Scope less clear <br> – Potential to waste effort <br> – Efficiency requires more special attention |

**FIGURE 5.20**  Pros and Cons of Extreme vs. Nonextreme Design

The meaning of "extreme programming" depends somewhat on the design skills of the participants. Less experienced designers find flexible designs to be time consuming, and often avoid them when doing extreme programming. On the other hand, it may not take experienced designers very long to include reasonable flexibility, even in an "extreme" environment.

The calculator application described in Chapter 1 was a command-line program that allowed users to add amounts to, or subtract them from multiple accounts. The implementation provided in Chapter 1 was, in effect, an "extreme" response to these requirements, since it accommodated the requirements and no more. The design was *sufficient* and *robust*: It was not at all *reusable* or *flexible*, however. To satisfy the latter, we envisage a larger scope for the application.

It is reasonable to suppose that the requirements for the calculator will grow by including a variety of operations (besides addition/subtraction), and that it will require a graphical interface rather than the present command-line requirement. Consider the design in Figure 5.21, for example.

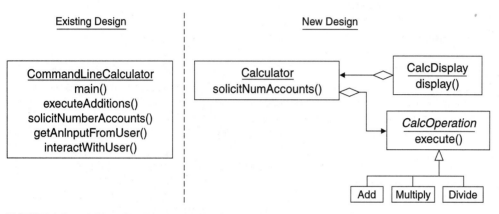

**FIGURE 5.21**  A More Flexible Design for *Calculator* Application

The new design prepares for a graphical interface with the class *CalcDisplay*. The display needs to know what it pertains to, so it aggregates *Calculator*. This is a conservative allowance for flexibility. When it comes to accommodating operations besides addition and subtraction, we have chosen to accommodate a great deal of flexibility by capturing the concept of an *operation* in a class *CalOperation* by introducing separate classes for addition, etc. This is the essence of a design pattern called "Command:" But have we gone too far? If the application later requires a multitude of special purpose operations, or if we intend to include special features when performing the operations, we have not. On the other hand, if the application remains for all time a truly simple, traditional calculator, this design flexibility may be unnecessary clutter.

Note also that the number of lines of source code in flexible designs tends to increase and, typically, so does the object code. The sheer size of the source code— called the *code base*—can sometimes be a design constraint in itself, especially for applications executing on limited devices such as PDA's. This creates a fourth axis in the trade-off shown in Figure 5.15.

# CHAPTER SUMMARY

In this chapter we discussed three desirable properties of designs that add to Correctness and Robustness covered in Chapter 4. These are Flexibility, Reusability, and Efficiency. A flexible design is one that can be easy to change. Reusability refers to the capacity for use in other applications. There are two kinds of efficiency: Time, and Space. Figure 5.22 reiterates these points.

- *Flexibility*
  - ·  ==readily changeable
- *Reusability*
  - · in other applications
- *Efficiency*
  - · in time
  - · in space

(These add to *Correctness* &
    *Robustness,* covered in Chapter 4)

**FIGURE 5.22**   Summary of This Chapter

# EXERCISES

**Exercise 5.1**   **Video Store**   Consider a design for a video store application.

**Part 5.1.1** Suppose that we use just one class *VideoStore*, which allows the entry and removal of a video name assigned to a customer, stored via a telephone number as key. What exactly is inflexible about this design?

**Part 5.1.2** Give an alternative UML class model that would accommodate the inclusion of additional operations.

**Part 5.1.3** Which of the classes you introduced are likely to be reusable in other applications?
Definitely: *Video*
Possibly: *Add, CheckIn, CheckOut*

**Part 5.1.4** How can you make more reusable the classes that reference *Video*?

**Part 5.1.5** Which classes are unlikely to be reusable in other applications in any case?
**Video Store**
Evaluation criteria:

| | |
|---|---|
| ▦ Effectiveness of your response | A = answers are effective responses to the questions asked |
| ▦ Clarity of designs | A = every nontrivial step clearly explained; prose states meaning very clearly |

The following are errors that you should watch for in Exercise 5.1:
    *Serious*:

**1.** Little evidence of understanding the term "flexible."

**2.** *VideoStore* should aggregate *Video* (or provide an equivalent design).

**3.** The possibility of easy command substitution (by abstracting *Command*, or the like) not obtained.

**4.** When asked to provide a design, use UML: That's what UML is for.

    *Less than serious, but more than minor*:

**1.** When we want a design to be flexible, we are referring to anticipated requirements, not standard ones.

**Exercise 5.2**   **Toll Booth**   Consider an automated toll application for collecting motorist tolls at unmanned booths. The minimum requirement is to store the relevant information when an automobile passes through a booth.

**Part 5.2.1** For what *purposes* could the design be made flexible? Name a specific, clear purpose not covered elsewhere in this question. Explain your answer.

**Part 5.2.2** Show the parts of a design of this application relevant to these requirements. The design should be flexible, enabling the handling of cars, trucks, trailers, and other types of vehicles yet to be determined. Justify your design: State in what way it is flexible.

**Part 5.2.3** Name a specific method within your design that has a high potential for reuse in another application if there is such a function. If there is none, explain why not. You don't have to give code for the function. Explain your reasoning.

**Part 5.2.4** Name a specific class within your design that has a high potential for reuse in another application. Explain your reasoning.

**Part 5.2.5** In what way could speed efficiency be important for this application? Explain your reasoning.

**Part 5.2.6** In what ways could space efficiency be important for this application? Name at least one. Explain.

Evaluation criteria:

| | |
|---|---|
| ▦ Specificity | A = thoroughly specific answers to all questions |
| ▦ Clarity of prose and designs | A = every nontrivial step clearly explained; prose states meaning very clearly |
| ▦ Effectiveness of your response | A = effective avenues for flexibility, reusability, and efficiency |

The following are errors that you should watch for in this Exercise:

*Serious*:

**1.** Little evidence of understanding the term "flexible."

**2.** Little evidence of understanding the term "reusability."

**3.** When asked to provide a design, use UML: That's what UML is for.

*Less than serious, but more than minor*:

**1.** When we want a design to be flexible, we are referring to anticipated requirements, not standard ones.

**2.** A class like *TollBoothApplication* is the least likely to be reused, being special to this application. This is often the case for control classes *MyApplication* in applications. A class such as *Vehicle*, on the other hand, has a much higher likelihood of being reused.

**3.** Part 5.2.1 asks about the *purposes* for increased flexibility: It should be answered in terms of *requirements, not in terms* of design or implementation elements. "Accommodate trailers" is a relevant answer to the question, but "add a class ABC" does not answer the question.

**4.** Part 5.2.6 asks about how space efficiency could be important. You need to explain the storage problem completely. (The question does not actually ask about how to solve the problem, although there is nothing wrong with suggesting solutions.)

**5.** Part 5.2.2 asks about design, and should be answered in design terms, not in terms of requirements.

**6.** Presentation methods such as printing vehicle information or displaying status are often not portable because presentation requirements tend to differ among different applications.

**7.** We typically reuse classes at the end of aggregate chains, like *Customer,* rather than at the beginning, like *Transaction*. This is because the latter involve dependencies, which may be particular to the application, whereas the former do not.

**8.** In assessing individual methods for reuse, don't include minor ones such as *getVehicleId()* because there would not be sufficient benefit even to remember where such course code is stored.

**9.** Don't use *non-standard notation* on your class models unless you explain it carefully.

**10.** Keep your *design simple* until complexity is required.

**11.** There must be a dependency from at least one class upon the classes that represent the specific vehicle types. This is because instances of these have to be identified at runtime.

*Minor*:

**1.** Poor writing.

**2.** Your examples (e.g., functions that can be reused) are not very convincing ones. Choose examples that fulfill the conditions more obviously.

**3.** One rarely reuses accessor methods (i.e., by themselves).

# CHAPTER 6

# INTRODUCTION TO DESIGN PATTERNS

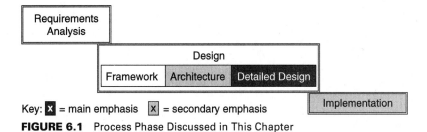

Key: ▓ = main emphasis    ▢ = secondary emphasis

**FIGURE 6.1**  Process Phase Discussed in This Chapter

This chapter is intended to familiarize the reader with the purposes and the general form of design patterns. Except for one or two examples, the chapter does not cover any pattern in depth: This is done in Chapters 7, 8, and 9.

## 6.1  RECURRING DESIGN PURPOSES

The first part of this book pointed out typical software design goals. These goals are summarized in Figure 6.2, which also outlines ways to accomplishing them.

- Reusability, Flexibility, and Maintainability
  - · *Reuse flexible designs*
  - · *Keep code at a general level*
  - · *Minimize dependency on other classes*
- Robustness
  - · *Reuse reliable designs*
  - · *Reuse robust parts*
- Sufficiency and Correctness
  - · *Modularize design*
  - · *Reuse trusted parts*

**FIGURE 6.2**  Sample Design Goals and Ways to Accomplish Them

The goals stated in Figure 6.2 are quite general. When confronted with an actual design situation, they translate into specific design purposes. For example, our design goal may be to reuse a part of a calendar application, and that might translate into a specific purpose to parameterize a set of methods so that they apply to any day, month, or year. We will start with an example design purpose, and follow it with a design pattern satisfying that purpose.

**123**

### 6.1.1 An Example of a Recurring Design Purpose

Home owners are forever contemplating the modernization of their kitchens, often using software to visualize the possibilities. Let's consider such an application, which we will call *KitchenViewer*. *KitchenViewer* enables the user to lay out the parts of a kitchen without committing to a style. The overall interface is shown in Figure 6.3.

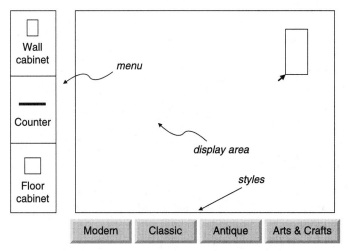

**FIGURE 6.3** *KitchenViewer* Interface

Here is a use case.

***Precondition: None***

1. *User* clicks on the "wall cabinet" icon
2. *Application* displays a wall cabinet in the center of the work area
3. *User* resizes the wall cabinet
4. *User* drags the wall cabinet to a position in the upper half of the work area
5. *User* releases the cursor
6. *Application* places the wall cabinet in the nearest conforming position
7. *User* clicks on the "floor cabinet" icon
8. *Application* displays a floor cabinet in the center of the work area
9. ...

Once the layout process is complete, the kitchen appears as in Figure 6.4.

After a kitchen has been sketched in this manner, *KitchenViewer* allows the user to try various styles for the wall cabinets, floor cabinets, and countertops. When the user selects "Antique," for example, the design appears as in Figure 6.5.

What should be our specific design purposes for *KitchenViewer*? The procedure for rendering the various styles is basically the same, regardless of the style, and we should *not* have more than one copy of this procedure in our code.

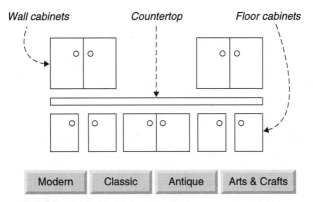

**FIGURE 6.4**   *KitchenViewer* Example

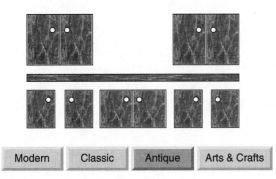

**FIGURE 6.5**   Selecting *Antique* Style

We should avoid code such as

```
Counter counter = new Counter();
draw( counter );
```

The reason is no amount of added code will enable this to draw variable types of counters at runtime—better design thinking than this is required. One approach is to design the application so as to provide a method such as *renderKitchen( myStyle )*, somehow parameterizing the rendering procedure with a required style. We would need to figure out what kind of thing *myStyle* should be, and how *renderKitchen()* uses it. This kind of design purpose recurs, and we can characterize it as follows.

> *An application must construct a family of objects at runtime: The design must enable choice among several styles.*

## 6.2   WHAT ARE DESIGN PATTERNS?

Design patterns are *class combinations and accompanying algorithms that fulfill common design purposes.* A design pattern expresses an idea rather than a fixed class combination. Accompanying algorithms express the pattern's basic operation.

To illustrate how patterns express ideas, think about how you might describe your housing preferences to a realtor. The term "ranch style," for example, denotes a useful house pattern. It conveys an idea, however, not a completely specific design.

## 6.2.1 Example Application: Without Applying Design Patterns

As an example of a software design pattern, let's return to the *KitchenViewer* example. Recall that we want to provide a method such as *renderKitchen( myStyle)*. Now we need to elaborate on what *myStyle* means.

The method *renderKitchen()* uses the classes *Kitchen*, *WallCabinet,* etc., and we will place it in a class called *Client*. If we temporarily ignore our purpose of parameterizing the style, the method *renderKitchen()* would look something like the following.

```
// VERSION IGNORING OUR DESIGN PURPOSES

// Determine the style
. . .                                    // case statement?

// Assume that the antique style was selected.

// Create the antique wall cabinets
AntiqueWallCabinet antiqueWallCabinet1 = new AntiqueWallCabinet ();
AntiqueWallCabinet antiqueWallCabinet2 = new AntiqueWallCabinet ();
. . .

// Create the antique floor cabinets
AntiqueFloorCabinet antiqueFloorCabinet1 = new AntiqueFloorCabinet ();
AntiqueFloorCabinet antiqueFloorCabinet2 = new AntiqueFloorCabinet ();
. . .

// Create the kitchen object, assuming the existence of add() methods
Kitchen antiqueKitchen = new Kitchen();
antiqueKitchen.add( antiqueWallCabinet1, . . . );    // rest of parameters specify location
antiqueKitchen.add( antiqueWallCabinet2, . . . );
. . .
antiqueKitchen.add( antiqueFloorCabinet1, . . . );
antiqueKitchen.add( antiqueFloorCabinet2, . . . );
. . .

// Render antiqueKitchen
. . .
```

This code would have to be repeated for every style! A class diagram for this would look like Figure 6.6.

This is repetitive and complicated. As a result, it is inflexible, hard to prove correct, and hard to reuse.

## 6.2.2 Example Application: Applying a Design Pattern

**DESIGN GOAL AT WORK** *Flexibility*

Our design should be flexible enough to produce any one of several kitchen styles.

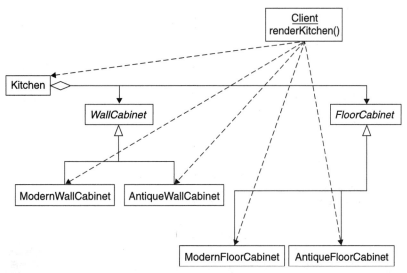

**FIGURE 6.6** *KitchenViewer* Without Design Patterns

Now let's approach our *KitchenViewer* design purpose by applying a design pattern. Here is the key: Instead of directly creating *AntiqueWallCabinet* objects, etc., our parameterized version of *renderKitchen()* delegates their creation, replacing phrases such as

```
. . . new AntiqueWallCabinet();      // applies only to antique style: Replace!
```

with versions which delegate to a style parameter:

```
. . . myStyle.getWallCabinet();      // applies to the style chosen at runtime
```

At runtime, the class of *myStyle* determines the version of *getWallCabinet()* executed, thereby producing the appropriate kind of wall cabinet. To carry out this delegation of responsibility, we introduce a new class, which we'll call *KitchenStyle*, supporting such methods as *getWallCabinet()* and *getFloorCabinet()*. *KitchenStyle* will have subclasses, which we'll name *ModernKStyle*, *AntiqueKStyle* etc., each supporting separate implementations of *getWallCabinet()*, *getFloorCabinet()* etc. This is shown in Figure 6.7.

Recall that, due to polymorphism, executing *myStyle.getFloorCabinet()* has different effects when *myStyle* is an object of *ModernKStyle* versus an object of *AntiqueKStyle*. The class model in Figure 6.8 is a more complete version of the implementation.

Notice that the client code references *Kitchen*, *KitchenStyle*, *WallCabinet*, and *FloorCabinet*, but does not reference specific wall cabinet styles or floor cabinet styles. For example, the class *AntiqueWallCabinet* does not appear in the client code. To see how this works, let's assume that at runtime, *myStyle* is an object of the class *ModernStyle*. In this case, when the method *renderKitchen()* executes a statement such as

```
WallCabinet wallCabinet7 = myStyle.getWallCabinet();
```

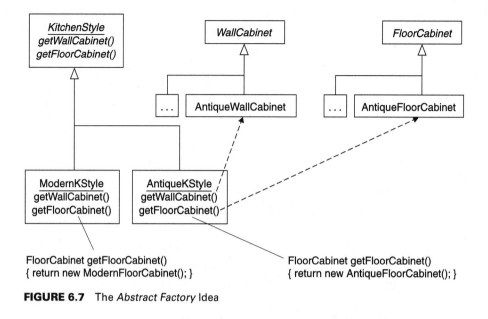

**FIGURE 6.7** The *Abstract Factory* Idea

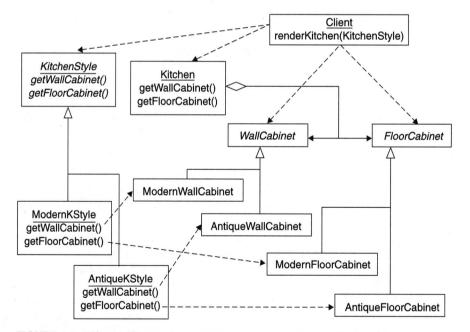

**FIGURE 6.8** *Abstract Factory* Design Pattern Applied to *KitchenViewer*

the method *getWallCabinet()* is the version defined in the class *ModernStyle*, and so it actually returns a *ModernWall* object. The method *renderKitchen( KitchenStyle myStyle )* looks like the following:

```
//VERSION ACCOUNTING FOR DESIGN PURPOSES
//Determine style by instantiating my style
// Create the wall cabinets: Type determined by the class of myStyle
WallCabinet wallCabinet1 = myStyle.getWallCabinet();
WallCabinet wallCabinet2 = myStyle.getWallCabinet();
. . .

// Create the floor cabinets: Type determined by the class of myStyle
// Create the kitchen object (in the style required)
FloorCabinet floorCabinet1 = myStyle.getFloorCabinet();
FloorCabinet floorCabinet2 = myStyle.getFloorCabinet();
. . .

Kitchen kitchen = new Kitchen();
kitchen.add( wallCabinet1, . . . );
kitchen.add( wallCabinet2, . . . );
. . .
kitchen.add( floorCabinet1, . . . );
kitchen.add( floorCabinet2, . . . );
. . .
```

This version of *renderKitchen()* is much more versatile than the previous version since it applies to all styles.

Figure 6.9 describes the *Abstract Factory* design pattern in general.

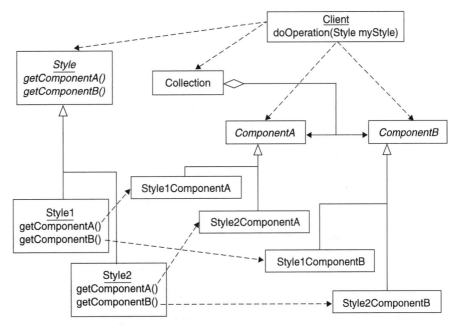

**FIGURE 6.9** *Abstract Factory* Design Pattern

The client method *doOperation( Style myStyle )* builds an instance of *Collection* in the style indicated by *myStyle* by calling *myStyle.getComponentA()* and *myStyle.getComponentB()*. If *myStyle* is a *Style1* object, for example, these two operations produce *Style1ComponentA* and *Style1ComponentB* objects respectively. The pattern thus ensures a consistent style throughout.

We have mentioned that design patterns should not be regarded in a literal manner. For example, the design in Figure 6.9 could also appear as shown in Figure 6.10.

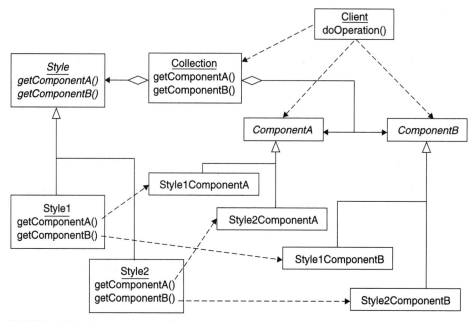

**FIGURE 6.10** *Abstract Factory* Design Pattern Alternative

In this alternative, *Collection* aggregates *Style*, *Client* does not reference *Style* directly, *doOperation()* takes no parameters, and *Collection* has methods for getting the various components. *Collection*'s aggregated *Style* object is instantiated at runtime, perhaps with separate setup code. When *doOperation()* calls *getComponentA()* in *Collection*, control is delegated to *getComponentA()* in the aggregated *Style* object. This is still the Abstract Factory *pattern*.

**KEY CONCEPT** *Design Pattern*

Class combination and algorithm fulfilling a common design purpose.

## 6.3 SUMMARY OF DESIGN PATTERNS BY TYPE: *CREATIONAL*, *STRUCTURAL*, AND *BEHAVIORAL*

Gamma et al [Ga] have classified each of the design patterns in one of three categories, depending upon whether it has to do with

- creating a collection of objects in flexible ways (*creational* patterns)
- representing a collection of related objects (*structural* patterns), or
- capturing behavior among a collection of objects (*behavioral* patterns)

We will elaborate on these three categories using example applications. In the next three chapters, we will describe each design pattern in detail.

### 6.3.1 Creational Design Patterns

Creational design patterns help us to design applications involving collections of objects: They allow the creation of several possible collections from a single block of code, but with properties such as

- Creating many *versions* of the collection at runtime
- *Constraining* the objects created: For example, ensuring that there is only instance of its class

Table 6.1 summarizes the use and nature of key creational design patterns. We will describe each of these design patterns in detail in Chapter 7.

| KEY CONCEPT | *Creational Design Patterns* |
|---|---|

Create objects in flexible or constrained ways.

### 6.3.2 Structural Design Patterns

Structural design patterns help us to arrange collections of objects in forms such as linked lists or trees. Table 6.2 summarizes the use and nature of key structural design patterns.

**TABLE 6.1**  Creational Design Patterns

| Design Pattern Name | Design Purpose Satisfied by this Pattern | Example Application Purpose Satisfied by this Pattern: *Design for the following requirements without repeating code unnecessarily. Make the design easy to change.* | Summary of the Design Pattern |
|---|---|---|---|
| Factory (see Section 7.2) | Create objects at runtime with flexibility that constructors alone cannot provide. | From a single version of control code, generate mail messages tailored to various customers. | Create desired objects by using methods that return the objects. |
| Abstract Factory (see Section 7.4) | Create coordinated families of objects at runtime, chosen from a set of styles. | Display a kitchen layout, allowing the user to select a style at runtime. | Capture each family in a class whose methods return objects in that style. |
| Prototype (see Section 7.5) | Create an aggregate object in which selected parts are essentially copies. | Display a kitchen layout, allowing the user to select at runtime a type of wall cabinet, or a type of floor cabinet etc. | Create the objects of the type by cloning a prototype. |
| Singleton (see Section 7.3) | Ensure that a class has exactly one instantiation, accessible throughout the application. | Build an application to evaluate the results of a lab experiment. Ensure that there is exactly one *Experiment* object at runtime, and ensure that it can be accessed by any method in the application. | Make the constructor private and obtain the unique object by means of a public static method that returns it. |

**TABLE 6.2** Structural Design Patterns

| Design Pattern Name | Design Purposes Satisfied by this Pattern | Example of Design Purposes Satisfied by this Pattern: *Design for the following requirements without repeating code unnecessarily. Make the design easy to change.* | Summary of the Design Pattern |
|---|---|---|---|
| Composite (see Section 8.4) | *Static purpose:* Represent a tree of objects. *Dynamic purposes:* Allow client code to access uniform functionality distributed in the subtree below any node. Allow the tree to be changed at runtime. | Represent the organization chart of a company. Allow client code to call *printOrganization()* on any *Employee* object, printing the names of the employee and all subordinates, if any. Allow the addition and removal of employees at runtime. | Have composite classes aggregate other composite classes. |
| Decorator (see Section 8.3) | *Static purpose:* Represent a list of objects. *Dynamic purpose:* Allow client code to use functionality distributed in the list. | Allow the user of an on-line clothing store to see an image of himself dressed in a variety of clothes. | Link the objects using aggregation. |
| Adapter (see Section 8.5) | Allow an application to make use of external (e.g., legacy) functionality. | Design a loan application from scratch, but allow it to use any vendor's classes that compute monthly payment calculations. | Introduce an inherited intermediary class linking the application and the class with desired functionality. |
| Façade (see Section 8.2) | Manage software architectures involving large numbers of classes. | Design the architecture of a student loan software application so that one group of developers can concentrate on the loan option database, another on the user interface (simultaneously), and a third on payment calculations. Minimize coordination problems. | For each package, introduce a singleton (see above), which is the sole access to objects within the package. |
| Flyweight (see Section 8.6) | Obtain the benefits of having a large number of individual objects without excessive runtime space requirements. | We want to be able to visualize a room with stenciling. There are five stencil patterns but thousands of potential stencil marks on the walls. This might be easy to do if each mark were a separate object, but we can't afford the memory required, and it's impractical to name all of these separate objects. | Share objects by parameterizing the methods with variables expressing the context. |
| Proxy (see Section 8.7) | Some methods are remote or require lots of resources to execute (time or space). Ensure that they are not executed more often than necessary. | Assume that rendering an image consumes a significant amount of time and space because the image data has to be read from a file, fill a buffer, and then be rendered. If the buffer is already filled by a previous invocation of the method, then invoking the function should not repeat this step. | Introduce a class standing between the requesting methods and the resource. |

**KEY CONCEPT** *Structural Design Patterns*

Represent data structures such as trees with uniform processing interfaces.

### 6.3.3 Behavioral Design Patterns

Each behavioral pattern captures a kind of behavior among a collection of objects. Let's consider the following example of mutual behavior among *Ship* and *Tugboat* objects. We want to estimate the amount of time required to bring ships into and out of a harbor and transport them to dry dock for maintenance, based on parameters such as their size. Assume that this is a complex calculation that requires a systematic simulation of the transportation process. Figure 6.11 suggests a configuration.

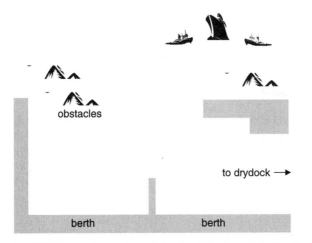

**FIGURE 6.11** Example of Behavioral Design Goal: *Port Traffic*

*Ship* and *Tugboat* are natural choices for classes, but objects of these classes play different roles, depending on whether the ship is arriving, leaving, or heading for dry dock. Since there are many potential applications in which we can use *Ship* and *Tugboat*, we do not want these classes to depend on each other, as suggested by Figure 6.12.

**DESIGN GOAL AT WORK** *Reusability*

We want to be able to use classes *Ship* and *Tugboat* separately in other applications.

We have a *behavioral* design purpose here because we want to separate the interdependent behavior of these objects from the objects themselves. The *Mediator* design pattern does this. Figure 6.13 shows the core idea of *Mediator*.

Note that the *Ship* and *Tugboat* classes do not reference each other in Figure 6.13: Instead, the *LeavingPort* class controls how objects of *Ship* and *Tugboat* behave to estimate the time for that maneuver.

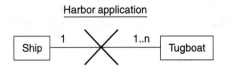

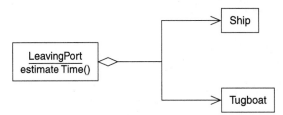

**FIGURE 6.12** Avoiding Dependencies

**FIGURE 6.13** *Mediator* Concept Applied to the Harbor Problem

The full *Mediator* pattern allows for the fact that the mediated classes may need to communicate (e.g., to respond to events on either of them). To accomplish this, the mediated classes can be made to subclass a base class that aggregates a generic mediator class (*PortMission*). This is shown in Figure 6.14.

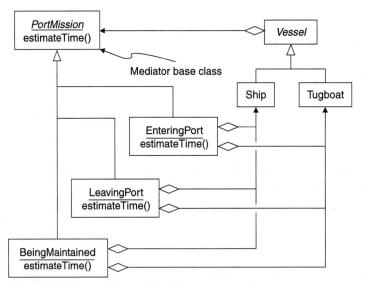

**FIGURE 6.14** Applying the *Mediator* Design Pattern to the Harbor Problem

Note that the *Ship* class does depend on the *Vessel* class, which depends on *Mission*, so we cannot use the *Ship* class without these two. These dependencies are much more

acceptable, however, than having *Ship* depend for all time on *Tugboat*. Ships are always vessels, and they usually have missions, but they are only sometimes associated with tugboats. Table 6.3 summarizes the use and nature of key behavioral design patterns.

**TABLE 6.3** Behavioral Design Patterns

| Design Pattern Name | Design Purposes Satisfied by this Pattern | Example of Design Purposes Satisfied by this Pattern:<br>*Design for the following requirements without repeating code unnecessarily. Make the design easy to change.* | Summary of the Design Pattern |
|---|---|---|---|
| Chain of Responsibility (see Section 9.7) | We want a collection of objects to exhibit functionality. At design time we want to be able to easily add or delete objects that handle all or part of the responsibility. | Design a GUI for a web application to view automobiles with requested color etc. as shown in Figure 6.15. The display is dynamic, depending on the model etc. chosen. Reuse the GUI parts among the displays. | Link objects to each other via aggregation. Each performs some of the work, and then calls on the next object in the chain to continue the work. |
| Command (see Section 9.8) | Make the execution of operations more flexible. For example, enable "undoing." | Allow users of an application to retract their last four decisions at any time (an "undo" problem) | Capture each type of command in a class of its own. |
| Interpreter (see Section 9.2) | Parse an expression. | Design an application that takes as input an order for a network of PCs, expressed in a standard syntax. The output consists of instructions for assembling the network. | Introduce a class to capture expressions, and allow expression classes to aggregate expression classes. |
| Mediator (see Section 9.4) | Capture the interaction between objects without having them reference each other (thus permitting their reuse). | Build an application that estimates the amount of time required to bring ships into and out of a harbor, and to transport them to dry dock for maintenance: But ensure that the *Ship* and *Tugboat* classes can be reused separately. | Capture each interaction in a separate class that aggregates the objects involved. |
| Observer (see Section 9.5) | A set of objects depends on the data in a single object. Design a way in which they can be updated when that single object changes attribute values. | Keep management, marketing and operations departments up to date on sales data. Each of these departments has different requirements for the data. | Capture the data source as a class. Allow it to loop through the "observer" objects, calling an *update()* method. |
| State (see Section 9.6) | At runtime, vary the effect of invoking an object's methods depends upon the object's state. | Customers fill out an order form on a web site, and then hit the "enter" button. The result must depend upon the state of the form data: *"Product Information Complete," "Personal Information Incomplete," "Credit Check In Progress"* etc. | Aggregate a class representing the state with operative method *doAction()*: Subclasses effect the required actions of substates with their own versions of *doAction()*. |
| Template (see Section 9.9) | Allow an algorithm to execute partial variants at runtime. | Organize the large number of traffic light algorithms in a city by arranging them into a few basic forms, with variants tailored to specific locations. | Have a base class contain an overall method, but with function calls where variability is needed. Have subclasses implement these function calls to capture the required variability. |

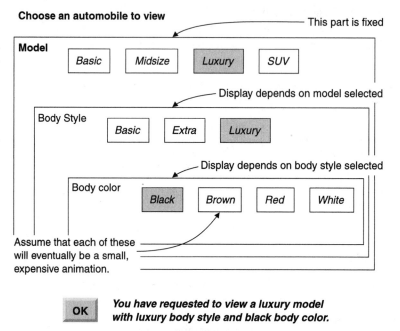

**FIGURE 6.15** A Design Problem Solvable by *Chain of Responsibility*

---

**KEY CONCEPT** *Behavioral Design Patterns*

Capture behavior among objects.

---

# 6.4 CHARACTERISTICS OF DESIGN PATTERNS: *VIEWPOINTS, ROLES,* AND *LEVELS*

Design patterns are partially described by class diagrams, but they also possess behavior: These are the *static* and *dynamic* viewpoints of the pattern respectively. This section explains these two viewpoints. It also describes the *abstract* and *concrete* (nonabstract) levels of design patterns. Finally, it covers the way in which design patterns are embedded in applications. Note that the static vs. dynamic viewpoints, abstract vs. concrete levels, and embedding issues are characteristic of many designs, and are not limited to design patterns. These characteristics are summarized in Figures 6.16 and 6.17 and explained in this section.

## 6.4.1 Two Viewpoints for Describing a Pattern: *Static* and *Dynamic*

Design patterns are illustrated with class models, showing the classes involved and their mutual relationships: This is a *static* viewpoint of the pattern. The functions of these classes execute in particular sequences, however, which class models do not illustrate: This is the *dynamic* viewpoint of the pattern, and requires appropriate means of expression.

- Viewpoints—ways to describe patterns
    1. *Static*: class model (building blocks)
    2. *Dynamic*: sequence or state diagram (operation)
- Levels—decomposition of patterns
    1. *Abstract* level describes the core of the pattern
    2. *Concrete* (=nonabstract) level describes the particulars of this case
- Roles—the "players" in pattern usage
    1. *Application* of the design pattern itself
    2. *Clients* of the design pattern application
    3. *Setup* code initalizes and controls

**FIGURE 6.16**  Characteristics of Design Patterns 1

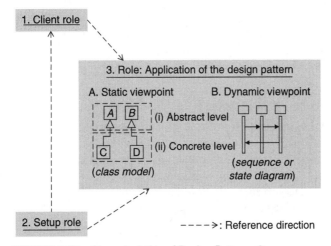

**FIGURE 6.17**  Characteristics of Design Patterns 2

We'll use the *KitchenViewer* example to illustrate the static and dynamic viewpoints. The static viewpoint was shown in Figure 6.7 on page 128. This viewpoint does not specify how the design actually works at runtime: What happens first, etc. Section 6.2 on page 125 lists the code for *getFloorCabinet()* and *getDoorCabinet()*, and although this code contributes to the dynamic viewpoint of the design pattern application, it is hard to see the whole execution picture. To express the dynamic viewpoint, we often use sequence diagrams, as illustrated in Figure 6.18. It shows the dynamic viewpoint of the *KitchenViewer* application of the *Abstract Factory* design pattern.

---

**KEY CONCEPT**  *Two Viewpoints*

We consider design patterns from the static viewpoint (what they are made from) and the dynamic viewpoint (how they function).

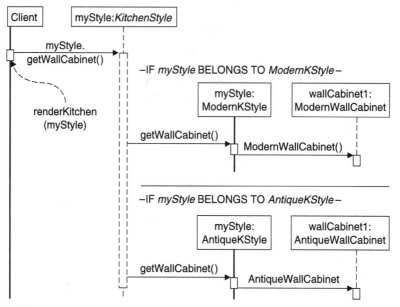

**FIGURE 6.18** *Abstract Factory Application* Sequence Diagram

## 6.4.2 Two Levels of a Pattern: *Abstract* and *Concrete*

Notice that within the *KitchenViewer Abstract Factory* pattern application some of the classes are abstract. In conformance with Gamma et al. [Ga] we will call nonabstract classes "concrete." Figure 6.19 rearranges the physical placement of classes in Figure 6.18 to emphasize the abstract/concrete groupings called *levels*.

The interface of clients with a design pattern application is often at the abstract level. This can be seen in the code for *renderKitchen()*, which is written in terms of *KitchenStyle* (and doesn't reference *ModernKStyle* or *AntiqueKStyle*) and *WallCabinet* (not *ModernWallCabinet* or *AntiqueWallCabinet*), among others.

---

**DESIGN GOAL AT WORK** *Correctness*

We want to provide an interface to a design pattern so that its functionality is clear and separate.

---

A division into abstract and concrete levels is a often a good design practice, regardless of whether design patterns are being applied, because client code can be written in terms of the more general classes of the abstract level, making it more versatile.

---

**KEY CONCEPT** *Two Levels*

Design patterns usually have an abstract level and a nonabstract ("concrete") level.

---

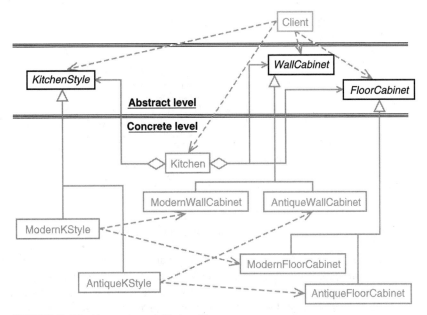

**FIGURE 6.19**   *Concrete* and *Abstract* Layers

## 6.4.3   Three Roles Involved in Pattern Usage: *Pattern Application, Client,* and *Setup*

This section explains the three parts, or *roles*, involved in the usage of a design pattern with a design. These are

- the application of the design pattern itself,
- the code that utilizes this application (the "client role"), and
- the code, if required, that initializes or changes the design pattern application (the "setup role").

---

**DESIGN GOAL AT WORK**   *Correctness*

To use design patterns effectively, we distinguish the roles involved.

---

These three roles are shown in Figure 6.20, and are explained in the following sections. The large boxes are groups of one or more classes and could be implemented as packages.

### *6.4.3.1   The* Design Pattern Application *Role*   Design patterns are themes for attaining design purposes. When we apply a design pattern, the *design pattern application* involves a specific class model. For example, *KitchenViewer*, described in this chapter, contains an application of the *Abstract Factory* design pattern. We discuss next how the design pattern application interfaces with the rest of the program in which it is embedded.

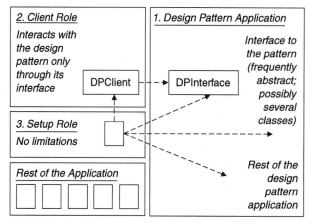

**FIGURE 6.20** The Three Roles Involved in Design Pattern Usage

**6.4.3.2  *The* Client *Role*** Many parts of a program can potentially use a design pattern application. We usually refer to these parts as *clients* of the pattern application. Each client is typically a method, but we often regard the method's class as the client. In the *KitchenViewer* design, for example, the *renderKitchen()* method is a client of the design pattern application. We will use the term *client role* for the community of clients. Typically, the client utilizes the design pattern application only through specified methods of specified classes of the design pattern application. These methods and classes constitute the interface of the pattern application. In the case of the *KitchenViewer* design, for example, the interface consists of the classes *KitchenStyle*, *Kitchen*, *WallCabinet*, and *Floor-Cabinet*: Clients may not refer to any other parts of this pattern application, and generally do not overlap the design pattern application.

**6.4.3.3  *The* Setup *Role*** The third role involved in the usage of design patterns is not terribly significant, but can get confusing if its presence isn't recognized. It consists of the code that initializes or changes the design pattern application code at runtime. You can think of this as a janitorial role. In the *KitchenViewer* design, for example, clients specifically do not reference particular styles, such as *ModernKStyle*. Recall that *renderKitchen()* takes a *KitchenStyle* object as parameter, and deliberately does not reference any subclass of *KitchenStyle*. How are these specific style objects selected and instantiated? This is the task of what we will call the *setup role*. In the *KitchenViewer* design, it is the code that responds to clicks on the "Style" buttons in Figure 6.7 by instantiating a *KitchenStyle* object and calling *renderKitchen()* with this parameter value.

Setup code needs access to many parts of the application, is normally runtime intensive, and is typically not intended for reuse. This is because it tends to be special to the application, and because it depends on too many other classes. Usually, the setup role does not overlap either the client or the design pattern application, although both are possible.

**KEY CONCEPT**  *Structural Design Patterns*

Represent data structures such as trees with uniform processing interfaces.

# 6.5   DESIGN PATTERN FORMS: *DELEGATION* AND *RECURSION*

Design patterns take a limited number of possible forms. We could say that there are patterns to the design patterns—metapatterns, if you like. In fact, most of the design patterns in [Ga] are based on the *delegation* or *recursion* forms. We describe the delegation form first.

## 6.5.1   The Origins and Meaning of *Delegation*

Delegation or "indirection" is a classical principle in computing, traceable back to machine language. A machine language operation such as *addDirect bbbbbbbb,* which adds the bit string *bbbbbbbb* to the contents of the register, has only limited usefulness. On the other hand, an operation *addIndirect bbbbbbbb*, which adds the <u>contents</u> at address *bbbbbbbb* to the register, is far more useful. The operation *addIndirect* accesses the ultimate argument by *delegating* the determination of the argument to a runtime process that places the argument in the location *bbbbbbbb*. This simple idea makes possible the introduction of variables.

Another form of delegation at the machine level is an operation such as *goThrough bbbbbbbb*, which delegates computational *control* to the address at *bbbbbbbb*. This contrasts with the direct version, *goTo bbbbbbbb*, which literally transfers control to the address *bbbbbbbb* (i.e., where the next instruction would be executed). The operation *goThrough* allows differing code to be executed, depending on runtime conditions. This delegation is found in object-oriented languages like C++ or Java in the form of polymorphism (virtual functions), discussed in Chapter 2.

## 6.5.2   The *Delegation* Design Pattern Form

To achieve flexibility, the *KitchenViewer* design replaces direct code such as

```
new AntiqueWallCabinet();       // applies only to antique style
```

with a version that delegates construction to an intermediary method

```
myStyle.getWallCabinet();       // applies to whatever style is chosen at runtime
```

The *Abstract Factory* design pattern replaces several direct method calls (constructor calls, actually) with delegated calls to separate methods, which call the desired methods in turn. The basic idea of delegation is shown in Figure 6.21.

A common way in which design patterns put delegation into practice is through a class that delegates functionality to the methods of an abstract class. When we apply *Abstract Factory* in Figure 6.7, for example, the work of creating a *WallCabinet* object is delegated to the methods of a *KitchenStyle* object.

A common form of delegation is illustrated in Figure 6.22, where an abstract class is aggregated and acts as a base class for several concrete subclasses.

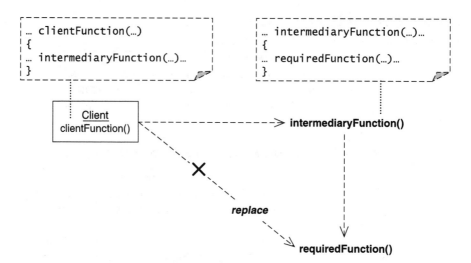

**FIGURE 6.21**  Basic Idea of *Delegation*

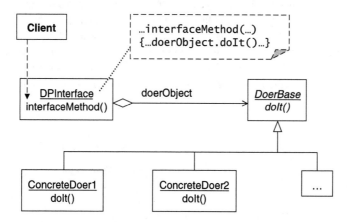

**FIGURE 6.22**  Basic Design Pattern Form #1: *Delegation*

The client calls the method *interfaceMethod()* of the interface class *DPInterface*. In turn, *interfaceMethod()* delegates the required functionality to its aggregated *DoerBase* object, *doerObject*. This is carried out by having *doerObject* execute a method that we have named *doIt()*. At runtime *doerObject* is an object of either the class *ConcreteDoer1* or *ConcreteDoer2* etc. Since the effect of *doIt()* depends on runtime conditions, so does the effect of *interfaceMethod()*. The class *DPInterface* thus has the following form.

```
class DPInterface
{       DoerBase doerObject;
        . . . . . .
        public void interfaceMethod()
        {       doerObject.doIt();
        }
}
```

Delegation, implemented using the virtual function property, is the most common form of design patterns. Another common form is *Recursion*: The use of structures to effectively reference themselves.

### 6.5.3 The *Recursion* Design Pattern Form

Several design patterns require recursion: In other words, part of the pattern essentially uses itself. For example, recursion is useful for representing a linked list of objects in which each object of a class aggregates another object of the same class. Another example is constructing graphical user interfaces that allow for windows within windows within windows .... In this case, the *Window* object aggregates itself. In a recursive pattern form, a dual inheritance/aggregation relationship exists between a base class and a subclass, as shown in Figure 6.23. Notice that the recursive form uses the delegation form: In this case the delegation doubles back on itself.

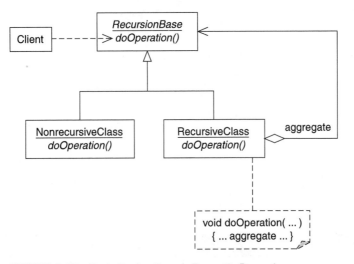

**FIGURE 6.23** Basic Design Pattern Form #2: *Recursion*

From the dynamic viewpoint, in a recursive form the client calls a method of the interface, which we'll name *doOperation()*. If the object actually belongs to the subclass *RecursiveClass*, then executing its *doOperation()* involves the object(s) of *aggregate*. These objects may once again call *doOperation()* etc.

Let's take as an example the case where *RecursionBase* is the class *Employee*, *doOperation()* is the method *printOrganization()*, and *RecursiveClass* is the class *Supervisor*. The idea is to produce a printout of all the employees of an organization. The class model is shown in Figure 6.24.

The method *printOrganization()* in *Supervisor* would be programmed to first print the supervisor's name, then call the *printOrganization()* method in each of the *Employee* objects in *aggregate*. For *Employee* objects of the class *IndividualContributor*, the method *printOrganization()* prints only the name of that employee. For *Employee* objects of the class *Supervisor*, *printOrganization()* prints that supervisor's name and the printing process repeats recursively. This recursive process eventually prints all of the names.

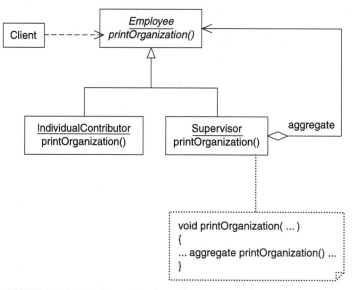

**FIGURE 6.24** The *Recursion* Form Applied to an Organization Chart

The class *Supervisor* thus has the following form.

```
class Supervisor extends Employee
{
        Vector supervisees;
        . . .
        void printOrganization( . . . )
        {           . . .
                supervisees.printOrganization();            . . .
        }
}
```

---

**KEY CONCEPT**   *Two Forms*

A design pattern's form is usually a delegation of responsibility or a class that relates to itself (recursive).

---

# CONCLUSION AND SUMMARY

This chapter introduced design patterns, which are used to satisfy recurring design purposes. A design pattern is a group of classes (the *static* viewpoint) that interact in a recognizable way (the *dynamic* viewpoint). Typically, a design pattern consists of an abstract level of classes and a nonabstract (concrete) level. Three roles (sets of code) are involved in the use of design patterns: The *application* of the design pattern itself, the code that uses it (the *client* role), and the code that initializes or changes the design pattern application (the *setup* role).

Most design patterns use *delegation*, in which calls to an interface method are handed off to another method to facilitate variation at runtime. Several design patterns also use a form of *recursion*, in which a class references either itself or a base class from which it inherits.

Design patterns can be roughly classified as *creational*, *structural* or *behavioral*. *Creational* patterns create nontrivial object ensembles in a manner determined at runtime. *Structural* patterns are used to represent collections of objects. *Behavioral* patterns deal flexibly with behavior among a set of objects. These points are summarized in Figure 6.25.

- *Design Patterns are Recurring Designs Satisfying Design Purposes*
- *Classified as* Creational, Structural, *or* Behavioral
- *Described by* Static *and* Dynamic *Viewpoints*
  - · Typically class models and sequence diagrams respectively
- *Use of a Pattern Application is a* Client *Role*
  - · Client interface carefully controlled
  - · "Setup," typically initalization, a separate role
- *Design Pattern Forms are Usually* Delegation *or* Recursion

**FIGURE 6.25**   Summary of This Chapter

# EXERCISES

**Exercise 6.1**   **Distinguishing Design Patterns**   Which of the following are design patterns? Explain your conclusion.
1. An object-oriented design

2. The ability to vary the order in which a *print()* method is applied to the elements of a *Vector*

3. Varying the order in which a *print()* method is applied to the elements of a *Vector* by introducing a class whose methods include a method like *goToNextElement()*

4. Capturing the mutual behavior of a pair of objects of two classes

5. Capturing the mutual behavior of a pair of objects of two classes by introducing a third class aggregating the two classes.

Errors you should avoid:
  *Serious*:
1. Failure to distinguish between a design purpose and a design pattern.

**Exercise 6.2**   **Categorizing Design Patterns I**   Characterize the following design purpose as *creational*, *structural* or *behavioral*. Explain your conclusion clearly.
We must build an application with 15 different screens involving various combinations of 6 user interface controls (e.g., list boxes) arranged in a simple grid. Performing a mouse action or text entry on a control (e.g., a button) in a screen affects other controls on the same screen. In all other respects the screens are not related and are not similar in appearance. The composition of these screens is very unlikely to change.

Errors you should avoid:
  *Less than serious but more than minor*:
1. Confusing the creational, structural, and behavioral categories, or failure to recognize that some problems fit more than one category.

**Exercise 6.3**   **Categorizing Design Patterns II**   Characterize the following design purpose as *creational*, *structural* or *behavioral*. Explain your conclusion clearly.
We must build a human resources application dealing with the management structure at a large company. We need to represent the organization chart within the application.

**Exercise 6.4**    **Categorizing Design Patterns III**    Characterize the following design purpose as *creational*, *structural* or *behavioral*. Explain your conclusion clearly.

We must build an application that allows a user to build and change his stock portfolio with various kinds of mutual fund picks from specified subcategories. The mutual fund categories are *technology*, *old industries*, *utilities*, *real estate*, and *mining*. The application allows users to pick categories: It then makes portfolio recommendations depending on the user's choice. For example, the user can ask for a low-risk portfolio of utilities and mining stocks, and the application describes its recommendations within these constraints.

Criteria for exercises 6.1–6.4:

- ▨ Appropriateness of your selection
- ▨ Clarity of your explanation

A = all completely and correctly justified
A = all explanations very clear; use examples when helpful in this respect

**Exercise 6.5**    **Viewpoints**    Later in this book we will study the *Observer* design pattern. Consider the following two statements.

**1.** *Observer* consists of an object of a class that reflects a data source, together with objects of classes that depend on the data source.

**2.** When the data changes value, a method with the name *update()* is called on each observing object.

Which of these two statements takes a *static* viewpoint and which a *dynamic* viewpoint?

**Exercise 6.6**    **Levels**    Figure 6.26 shows the *Observer* design pattern class model. Group the classes to show *abstract* and *concrete* levels. Group the classes to show the three *roles* described in this chapter.

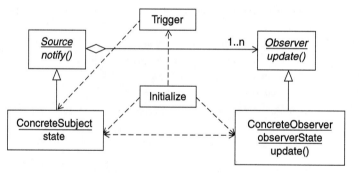

**FIGURE 6.26**    *Observer* Design Pattern

**Exercise 6.7**    **Forms**

**Part 6.7.1**    What two design pattern *forms* are described in this chapter?

**Part 6.7.2**    Which of the two forms is more likely to use virtual functions? Explain your answer and give an example.

**Part 6.7.3**    Which of the two forms is a *linked list of objects* likely to be? Explain your answer.

**Part 6.7.4**    Which of the two forms is the *Observer* pattern in Exercise 6.6?

Errors you should avoid:

     *Less than serious but more than minor:*

**1.** Confusing the two forms described in this chapter.

# CHAPTER 7

# CREATIONAL DESIGN PATTERNS

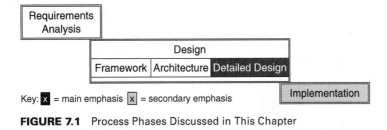

**FIGURE 7.1** Process Phases Discussed in This Chapter

## 7.1  THE PURPOSES OF CREATIONAL DESIGN

Applications typically require objects to be created at runtime. For example, the following code creates the object *myToyota*.

```
Auto myToyota = new Auto();
```

When the creation purpose is very simple, the use of a constructor alone may be adequate. However, objects often aggregate other objects or must belong to subclasses determined at runtime. For example, consider an online clothing store application in which we can view a model of ourselves dressed in selected clothing. We could use a class *Outfit* to capture the clothes selected. Let's say that *Outfit* objects consist of shirt, pants, and shoes. We would design for this by having *Outfit* aggregate *Shirt, Pants* classes, etc. Suppose that these come in various styles, which can be conveniently represented as subclasses (*FormalShirt, FormalPants,* etc.). The application would then have to continually create *Outfit* objects in many ways. The use of constructors and addition methods would limit the flexibility and reusability of the result. In particular, there is little reuse, modifiability, or flexibility in code like the following.

```
Outfit outfit = new Outfit();
outfit.add( new FormalShirt() );   // "Formal" hard coded
outfit.add( new FormalPants() );   // repeat for every kind of pants?!
```

In other words, our purposes are to create nontrivial objects such as *Outfit* in a flexible, modifiable and reusable manner. Creational design patterns attain many of these purposes.

## 7.2 FACTORY

### 7.2.1 Design Purpose of *Factory*

The purpose of *Factory* is to handle simple creational situations in which the constructor alone is inadequate. This applies when the base class of an object to be created is known but the particular subclass it belongs to is not known until runtime. For example, we may want to write code that applies to *Automobile* objects. If the code is really about autos in general, we would not write code that applies only to *Ford* objects, then repeat it for *Toyota* objects, etc. We should not know whether the *Automobile* object is a *Ford* or *Toyota* until the user provides input at runtime. The first statement in the following code—the *Automobile* constructor—would be inadequate for handling this situation.

```
Automobile automobile = new Automobile();   // <- inadequate
// can't alter the contents of automobile to make it a Ford or Toyota object!
automobile.showStats();   // . . . or something like this would go here
```

Unless *automobile* is reassigned to a different object constructed elsewhere, it can't be made a *Ford* object: But how did that "different object" get to be a *Ford* object? We still have not solved the issue of retargetable creation at runtime. The purpose and general technique of *Factory* can be described as in Figure 7.2.

Design Purpose

Create individual objects in situations where the constructor alone is inadequate.

Design Pattern Summary

Use methods to return required objects.

**FIGURE 7.2**  *Factory*

### 7.2.2 The *Factory* Interface for Clients

Let's suppose that client code needs an object of *RequiredClass*. To obtain a new instance it calls a method (usually static) of *MyClass*, as in

```
RequiredClass instanceOfRequiredClass = MyClass.getNewInstanceOfRequiredClass();
```

*RequiredClass* and *MyClass* may be one and the same: In other words, *MyClass* could have a static factory method that created instances of *MyClass*.

### 7.2.3 The *Factory* Class Model

The *Factory* design pattern is of the *delegation* form: *Factory* methods delegate creation to the constructors, as shown in Figure 7.3.

To apply the *Factory* design pattern, we equip *MyClass* with a method that returns a *RequiredClass* object. In Figure 7.3 we name this method *createObjectOfRequiredClass()*.

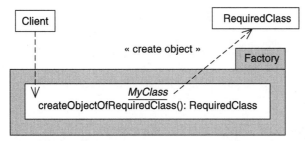

**FIGURE 7.3**  *Factory* Class Model

A common motive for using *Factory* occurs when a base class object is required but the subclass to which it belongs is not known until runtime. It is also common for the factory method of a class to create an object of the class itself, rather than of a different class. In other words, *MyClass* and *RequiredClass* in Figure 7.3 are the same. For example, client code may be written in terms of an *Automobile* class and a method *createAutomobile()* that returns *Automobile* objects: At runtime, the *Automobile* object is a *Ford* object or *Toyota* object, and *createAutomobile()* returns a new *Ford* object or *Toyota* object as the case may be.

**DESIGN GOALS AT WORK**  *Reusability and Correctness*

We want to write code about automobiles in general: Code that applies to any make.

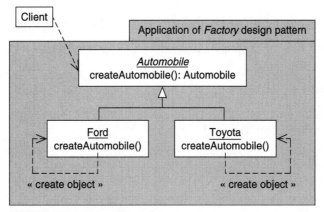

**FIGURE 7.4**  *Factory* Example

The code for *Ford* would be of the following form.

```
class Ford extends Automobile
{   . . .
    Automobile createAutomobile()
    {
        return new Ford();
    }
    . . .
}
```

Note that we can't write

```
Ford createAutomobile() {. . . }
```

because its return type is not identical with that of the *createAutomobile()* we are overriding.

### 7.2.4 Sequence Diagram for *Factory*

Figure 7.5 shows the sequence of methods for the basic *Factory* design.

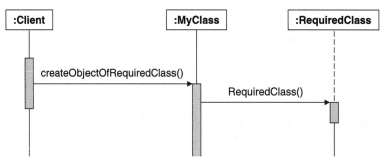

**FIGURE 7.5**   Sequence Diagram for *Factory*

### 7.2.5 Example *Factory* Application: E-Mail Generation

To illustrate *Factory* we will use a problem introduced in Chapter 6.

> *"From single version of control code, generate mail messages tailored to various customers."*

We will call this the *E-Mail Generation* application: Its requirements are described by the following use case.

**Preconditions: none**

1. *Application* asks for customer's e-mail address (not implemented)
2. *User* enters customer's e-mail address (not implemented)
3. *Application* asks what type of customer the mail message is for, listing them
4. *User* enters the intended type of customer
5. *Application* echoes the customer type to the console
6. *Application* prints the e-mail message to console, consisting of a part intended for all customers, and a part tailored to the type required
7. *Application* sends the message (not implemented)

Typical output for Steps 3-6, omitting the actual content of the e-mail, is to be as shown in Figure 7.6.

```
Please pick a type of customer from one of the following:
curious
returning
frequent
newbie
returning
This message will be sent:

Lots of material intended for all customers...
... a (possibly long) message for returning customers...
```

**FIGURE 7.6**   Typical Output of E-Mail Generation Example

**DESIGN GOALS AT WORK**   *Correctness and Reusability*

We want to separate the code common to all types of customers. We also want to separate the specialized code that generates e-mail for each type of customer. This makes it easier to check for correctness and to reuse parts.

Applying the *Factory* design pattern, we obtain a class model like that in Figure 7.7.

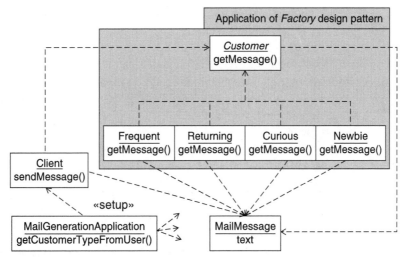

**FIGURE 7.7**   *Factory:* E-Mail Generation Example

In this case all of the factory methods generate *MailMessage* instances.

The full code listing for this is in Appendix A of this chapter.

## 7.2.6   Use of *Factory* in the Java API

The Java API makes extensive use of *Factory.* For example, the *Factory* method *getGraphics()* in the Java *Component* API class obtains a *Graphics* object that draws on the specific *Component* object to which *getGraphics()* belongs. This is illustrated in Figure 7.8.

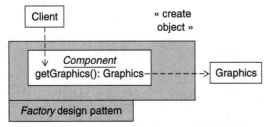

**FIGURE 7.8** *Factory* Applied to *getGraphics()* in Java

As another example, *Box* is a *Container* class allowing display in a horizontal direction or vertical direction. The API provides several factory methods in *Box,* which create particular kinds of *Box* objects such as

```
public static Box createVerticalBox()
public static Box createHorizontalBox()
```

## 7.2.7 Comments on *Factory*

■ All design patterns facilitate the addition, removal, or modification of requirements in one way or another. In the case of *Factory,* this concerns a focused area of functionality. For example, if a type of customer is added, removed or modified in the e-mail generation example of Section 7.2.5, the design is modified by the addition, removal, or modification of a *Customer* subclass representing that kind of customer.

■ *Factory* is an example of the *delegation* design pattern form (Section 6.5.2 on page 141) because every factory method delegates (passes on) the responsibility for creation to a constructor.

■ If the object to be created must be associated with an existing object, as is the case in Java when we need a *Graphics* object associated with the specific *Component* instance in question, then a nonstatic method is usually necessary. Otherwise a static *Factory* method may be sufficient.

■ Applications of *Factory* have become increasingly common in API's because they improve robustness by ensuring that objects created respect necessary constraints. For example, an *object request broker* (ORB) is a kind of "software bus" over which remote function calls can be made. To ensure that the same ORB is accessed from everywhere, the factory method *init()* is used as follows:

```
ORB orb = ORB.init( args, null );
```

The example of factory methods in Section 7.2.3 above creating instances of the class that they belong to is related to the *Prototype* design pattern discussed in Section 7.5 below. *Prototype* does not use the constructor, however, but clones an existing instance.

> **KEY CONCEPT**    Factory *Design Pattern*
>
> When a constructor alone is inadequate for creating an object: Uses a method that returns the object.

## 7.3    SINGLETON

### 7.3.1    Design Purpose of *Singleton*

Although a typical class allows the creation of many instances at runtime, we often want a class to have exactly one instance throughout the application, and no more. For example, many applications maintain a profile of the user. There would typically be no need for more than one *User* instance at runtime: In fact, the existence of more than one instance could lead to problems where one part of the application changes the user's profile in one way on one instance, and another part in another way on another instance. This leads to an incorrect implementation. We want a *guarantee* of one and only one *User* instance at runtime.

Figure 7.9 summarizes the purpose of *Singleton*.

Design Purpose

Ensure that there is exactly one instance of a class *S*. Be able to obtain the instance from anywhere in the application.

Design Pattern Summary

Make the constructor of *S* private; define a private static attribute for *S* of type *S*; define a public accessor for it.

**FIGURE 7.9**    *Singleton*

We refer to the desired unique instantiation as the *singleton* of the class, and the class as a *Singleton* class.

### 7.3.2    The *Singleton* Interface for Clients

In the example of a *User* class, client methods such as *verifyAccess()* and *sendEmailToUser()* would require a reference to the singleton of *User*. To get a reference to the singleton, they would contain a statement such as the following.

```
User user = User.getTheUser();
```

This requires that *getTheUser()* is a static method of *User.* Notice again that a statement such as

```
User user = new User();
```

would create a truly new *User* object, failing to satisfy the requirement that there be only one *User* instance.

**DESIGN GOAL AT WORK** *Correctness*

*Singleton* enforces the intention that only one *User* object exists, safeguarding the application from unanticipated *User* instance creation.

### 7.3.3 The *Singleton* Class Model

The first issue is "where do we put the single instance of our class?" We will name the class in question *S*. A good place is within *S* itself, as a static variable. So far so good, but the problem is, what's to stop another part of the application from including a statement

```
S myVeryOwnInstanceOfS = new S();
```

Well, we can prevent this by making the constructor *S()* private. The only remaining issue is a way to obtain the singleton: To do this we include in *S* a public static accessor method.

The *Singleton* design pattern is actually a special case of *Factory* in which the object returned is the one and only instance of the class with the *Factory* method. *Singleton* is thus in the *Delegation* form: The method getting the singleton delegates its creation to the constructor. The class model for *Singleton* is shown in Figure 7.10.

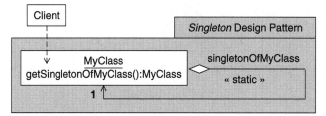

**FIGURE 7.10** *Singleton* Class Model

Let's sum up this discussion. Suppose that *S* is a class for which we require one and only one instance. The *Singleton* design pattern consists of the steps shown in Figure 7.11.

1. **Define a private static final member variable of *MyClass* of type *MyClass***

   ```
   static final MyClass singletonOfMyClass = new MyClass();
   ```

2. **Make the constructor of *MyClass* private**

   ```
   private MyClass() {/*....constructor code....*/};
   ```

3. **Define a static method to access the member**
   ```
   public static MyClass getSingletonOfMyClass()
   {
       return singletonOfMyClass;
   }
   ```

**FIGURE 7.11** *Singleton* Design Pattern Applied to a Class *MyClass*

Making the constructor of the class *MyClass* private prevents the creation of *MyClass* objects except by methods of *MyClass* itself. *MyClass* is given a static data member of type *MyClass* that will be the singleton. Let's name this object *singletonOfMyClass*. A public static factory method of *MyClass*, *getSingletonOfMyClass()*, is defined that returns *singletonOfMyClass*. Thus, to get this one and only element of *MyClass*, we merely invoke *MyClass.getSingletonOfMyClass()*.

### 7.3.4   Example *Singleton* Application: Experiment

Let's look at the following example, which was mentioned in Chapter 6 as an example of *Singleton*.

> *Prepare to build an application that evaluates the results of lab experiments. The application for this phase does no substantive evaluation, takes no input, and always prints the following message to the console:*
>    The analysis shows that the experiment was a resounding success.
> *Ensure that there is exactly one* Experiment *object at runtime. Ensure that it can be accessed by any method in the application, and verify this access by displaying the following at the console.*
>    Noting that the Experiment singleton referenced *n* times so far.
> *Your code can reference the singleton once as a demonstration.*

The output should have the appearance shown in Figure 7.12.

Output

```
Noting that the Experiment singleton referenced 1 times so far
The analysis shows that the experiment was a resounding success. ...
```

**FIGURE 7.12**   Partial Output for Singleton Experiment Example

The simple class model is shown in Figure 7.13.

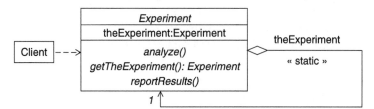

**FIGURE 7.13**   Application of *Singleton* to *Experiment* Example

A full listing for the source code is in Appendix B of this chapter.

### 7.3.5   Use of *Singleton* in the Java API

The following comment appears with the *Singleton* class *Runtime* in the IBM visual development environment: "Every Java application has a single instance of class *Runtime* that allows the application to interface with the environment in which the application is running. The current runtime can be obtained from the *getRuntime()* method."

The code for the class *Runtime* is as follows.

```
public class Runtime {
    private static Runtime currentRuntime = new Runtime();

    /**
     * Returns the runtime object associated with the current Java application.
     * Most of the methods of class <code>Runtime</code> are instance
     * methods and must be invoked with respect to the current runtime object.
     *
     */
    public static Runtime getRuntime() {
     return currentRuntime;
    }

    /** Don't let anyone else instantiate this class */
    private Runtime() {}
```

### 7.3.6  Comments on *Singleton*

▪ The form we have given for *Singleton* is simple, but it creates the singleton object even if the object is never needed. This is wasteful if the singleton is large, or if it affects limitations on time. This would apply, for example, on a Personal Digital Assistant application containing the plans (*Singleton* classes) for hundreds of house floor plans downloaded from the Web. To avoid this, we could *declare* the singleton data member and create it only when the accessor is first called (checking for *null* is a way to determine if this is the first call). In this case, we should also declare the accessor *synchronized* so that one creation process is not interrupted by another, resulting in more than one singleton.

▪ The question arises whether it is advisable to have any instance at all for a singleton class. Why do we need the object *singletonOfMyClass*? Its methods apply to one set of variables, so why not have static versions of all members of *MyClass*? The disadvantage of this approach is that it is not object-oriented, and so may fit awkwardly with the rest of an OO application. For example, if the application deals with employees, and there is a singleton *CEO* class implemented without an instance, then a method *display (Employee)* would not be able to take the *CEO* object as an argument, since there isn't one.

▪ The ideas of *Singleton* can be extended to the problem of having just two instances of a class. In this case, we would once again have a private constructor, but two factory functions such as *getFirstInstance()* and *getSecondInstance()*.

▪ Just as important as the fact that there is just one *Singleton* object is the fact that this object can be accessed from anywhere in the application. For example, if a video game application expresses the player's character by a class *PlayerCharacter*, code from many locations would probably need to reference this object. In particular, there may be a function *render()* in the class *Scene* that renders the current game situation, involving an image of the player's character. But what code in *render()* instantiates the player's character? It could *not* be

```
PlayerCharacter p = new (PlayerCharacter ;
```

because *p* is not the identical *PlayerCharacter* object referenced by the rest of the application: This would create phantom player characters in the game, resulting in chaos. A singleton of *PlayerCharacter* solves this problem. To access it, we use

```
PlayerCharacter p = PlayerCharacter.getThePlayerCharacter();
```

This guarantees that *p* is exactly the same player character object that all other parts of the application refer to.

▧ Typically, the singleton object does not change after being created, and in that case we would make it *final*.

---

**KEY CONCEPT** *Singleton Design Pattern*

When a class must have exactly one instance, make the constructor private and the instance a private static variable with a public accessor.

---

## 7.4 *ABSTRACT FACTORY*

Now we turn our attention to the creation of *families* of objects.

### 7.4.1 Design Purpose of *Abstract Factory*

Our design purpose here is to create a family of related objects, chosen at runtime from several possible families. You can often think of a "family" here as a "style" choice. We want to be able to write code that applies to these families without committing to one particular family.

As an example, consider a word processor requirement that allows the user to view a document in several styles. Modern word processors allow users to view documents in a variety of ways, for example, in outline form, showing only the headings. We will simplify this for illustration. Typical input to our primitive word processor is shown in Figure 7.14.

The application prints the document in a variety of styles. For simplicity, we will use *small* and *big* styles. In *small* style output, all headings are left justified and in lower case, and end with a colon. In *big* style they are capitalized with section numbering, etc. The title and the various subheadings also appear differently in these two styles. We can assume that more styles will be required in the future. The output for "small" and "big" styles is shown in Figure 7.15.

We want a design with a clean separation into the word manipulation part and the style choice part. We use separate classes to capture the various kinds of headings. In general, a "style" involves a family of classes. For example, *CapitalStyle* involves the classes *CapitalTitle, CapitalLevel1Heading, CapitalLevel2Heading,* etc. So the problem is to be able to change the family at runtime.

| | |
|---|---|
| ---> Enter title:<br><br>My Life<br><br><br>---> Enter Heading or "-done":<br>Birth<br><br><br>---> Enter text:<br>I was born in a small mountain<br>hut ....<br><br><br>---> Enter Heading or "-done":<br>Youth | ---> Enter text:<br><br>I grew up playing in the woods ...<br><br><br>---> Enter Heading or "-done":<br>Adulthood<br><br>....<br><br>---> Enter Heading or "-done":<br>-done<br><br><br>*(continued)* |

**FIGURE 7.14** Word Processor Interaction 1 of 2: Input

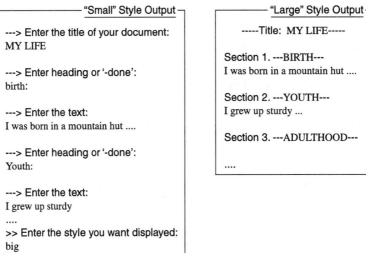

**FIGURE 7.15** Word Processor Interaction, 2 of 2: Output Options

The purpose of *Abstract Factory,* as expressed by Gamma, et al. [Ga] is as shown in Figure 7.16. The rest of this section explains the pattern that fulfills this purpose.

### 7.4.2 The *Abstract Factory* Interface For Clients

Client code has access to the entity to be constructed with the families. We will name this class *Ensemble* in general. The class *AbstractFactory* encapsulates the style of the *Ensemble* parts. The interface for the client has the appearance of Figure 7.17.

Design Purpose

"Provide an interface for creating families
of related or dependent objects without
specifying their concrete classes."*

Design Pattern Summary

Capture family creation in a class containing
a factory method for each class in the family.

*Gamma *et al.* [Ga]

**FIGURE 7.16** *Abstract Factory*

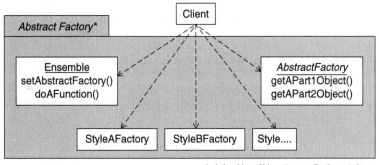

*relationships within pattern application not shown

**FIGURE 7.17** *Abstract Factory* Interface

For a discussion on a narrower interface alternative, see Section 7.4.7 on page 164.

For our word processor example, the role of *Ensemble* would be held by a class such as *Document,* which supports methods dependent upon *Style* (our *Abstract Factory*). First the client—or setup code—has to determine the required style, typically depending on user input as in the following.

```
Style currentStyle;
. . .    // interact with the user
currentStyle = new SmallStyle();
. . . or
currentStyle = new LargeStyle();
. . .
document.setStyle( currentStyle );
```

Once the style has been set, the client makes calls to *Document* such *document.display()*. A class model for this would have the appearance illustrated in Figure 7.18. But what does a "style" class look like, and how does it achieve our purposes?

## 7.4.3 The *Abstract Factory* Class Model

The *Abstract Factory* design pattern uses a class to collect coordinated factory methods in one place, one class per "style." In the standard pattern, the base class for these style classes is named *AbstractFactory*. The idea is that each *AbstractFactory* subclass interprets its factory

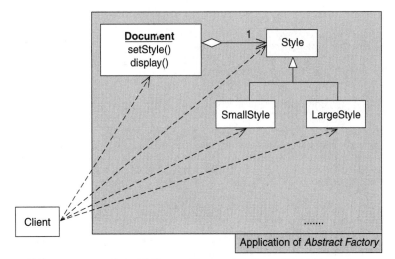

**FIGURE 7.18** Interface *of Abstract Factory* Applied to Word Processor

methods to produce objects of a single style. *Abstract Factory* is in the *delegation* form, delegating the "getters" of objects to constructors all in the desired style.

For the sake of simplicity we will begin by illustrating this with just one style. Let's call the class whose complex objects are to be constructed, *Ensemble*. Figure 7.19, a partial class

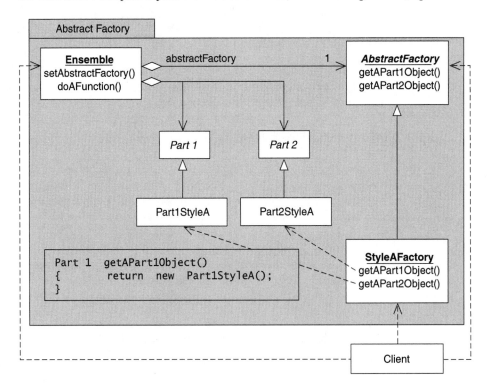

**FIGURE 7.19** The *Abstract Factory* Idea

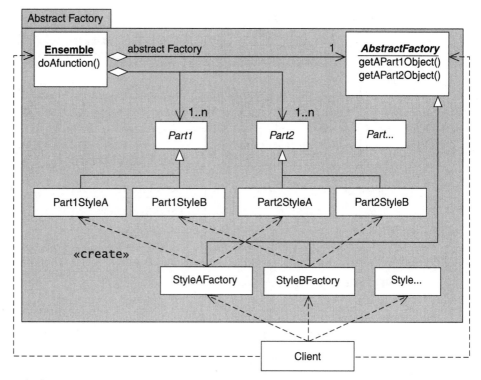

**FIGURE 7.20** *Abstract Factory*

model, shows how *Ensemble* objects are constructed in a style encapsulated as *StyleA*. *Ensemble* consists of *Part1* objects, *Part2* objects, etc. The attribute *abstractFactory* of *Ensemble* is instantiated with a *StyleAFactory* object in this case. When a *Part1* object is required, the *getAPart1Object()* method of *abstractFactory* is called. The virtual function property implies that the *getAPart1Object()* method of *StyleAFactory* is actually called, and it returns a *Part1StyleA* object. Similarly, when *getPart2Object()* of *Ensemble* is called, it returns a *Part2StyleA* object. Thus, all of the parts obtained are in the same style. The full *Abstract Factory* class model, with two styles (*AbstractFactory* subclasses), is shown in Figure 7.20. As discussed in the section on client interfaces, the client may interface with the *AbstractFactory* and *PartX* classes but specifically not with the *sub*classes of *Part1*, *Part2,* etc.

### 7.4.4 The *Abstract Factory* Sequence Diagram

A sequence diagram for *Abstract Factory*, including the setting up of the particular "style" (the *Abstract Factory* object), is as illustrated in Figure 7.21.

### 7.4.5 Example *Abstract Factory* Application: "Word Processor"

Our example will be to create a design and implementation for the word processor problem described in Section 7.4.1.

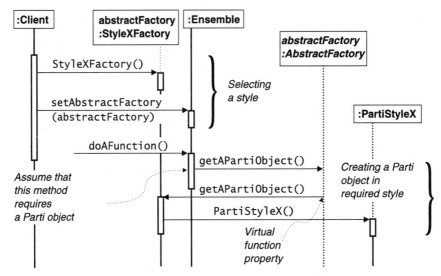

**FIGURE 7.21** Sequence Diagram for *Abstract Factory*

The following use case will remind the reader of the application.

***Preconditions: none***

1. *Application* requests the title of the document
2. *User* provides the title
3. The "Heading/Text" use case (see the following list) is executed until the user enters "done"
4. *Application* requests a style from a list
5. *User* enters a style from the list
6. *Application* outputs the document to the monitor in the style requested

The "Heading / Text" use case:

***Preconditions: user has provided the title***

1. *Application* requests a header
2. *User* provides header text
3. *Application* requests text
4. *User* provides text to fit with the header

---

**DESIGN GOALS AT WORK** *Correctness and Reusability*

We want to separate each code part that formats the document in a style. We also want to separate the common document generation code. This facilitates reusing parts and checking for correctness.

---

The class model is shown in Figure 7.22. Typical output is shown in Figure 7.23.

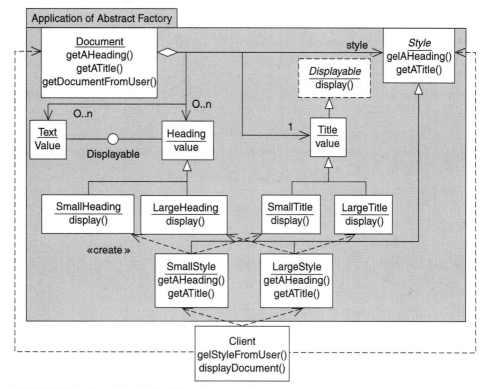

**FIGURE 7.22**   Class Model for "Word Processor"

Source code that implements this design can be found in Appendix C. Look at *main()* in *Setup*. It first gets the document content from the user (title, headings, and paragraphs), then creates a *Document* object document. It then prompts the user for the style required, and sets the *style* attribute of *document* accordingly. Finally, it activates the client to interact with the document.

## 7.4.6   Use of *Abstract Factory* in the Java API

The Java abstract class *java.awt.Toolkit* applies *Abstract Factory* to allow Java portability. GUI classes such as *Button* are developed in a manner independent of platform: The "Peer" classes *ButtonPeer, CanvasPeer,* etc. contain the platform-specific code to producing visible buttons. The class model has the appearance shown in Figure 7.24.

Platform-specific installations instantiate the appropriate concrete *ToolKit* subclass. Thus, *ToolKit* methods such as *java.awt.peer.ButtonPeer createButton( Button )* produce buttons for the platform in use when called with the appropriate *ToolKit* subclass object. For example,

```
sun.awt.SunToolkit extends java.awt.Toolkit { . . . }
```

is a *ToolKit* subclass that produces appropriate *Peer* classes for many Windows operating system versions.

```
---> Enter the title of your document:
MY LIFE
---> Enter heading or '-done':
Birth
---> Enter the text:
I was born in a mountain hut . . . .
---> Enter heading or '-done':
Youth
---> Enter the text
I grew up sturdy . . . .
---> Enter heading or '-done':
-done
---> Enter the style you want displayed ('small' or 'large'):
large



    ---- Title:  MY LIFE ----

Section 1.  ---BIRTH---
I was born in a mountain hut . . . .

Section 2.  ---YOUTH---
I grew up sturdy . . . .
```

**FIGURE 7.23**  Word Processor Interaction

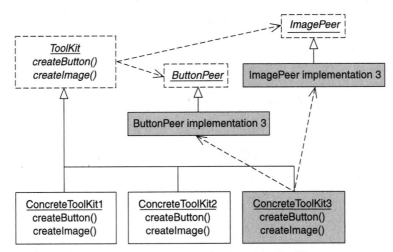

**FIGURE 7.24**  An *Abstract Factory* Application: Java *ToolKit*

## 7.4.7  Comments on *Abstract Factory*

■ In the word processor example of Section 7.4.1, suppose that changing conditions require us to add, remove, or modify a style of document presentation. In that case the design is easily modified by the addition, removal, or modification of an *Abstract Factory* class representing that style.

■ The interface to *Abstract Factory* can vary from that shown in this section.

The interface for clients shown in Figure 7.25 consists of the *Ensemble* class (the actual aggregate being constructed) and the *Style* class and its subclasses.

The interface can be made more restrictive, where *Client* references only *Ensemble*. In this case, a setup part of the application deals with instantiating the "style" (*Abstract Factory* object). This is shown in Figure 7.25.

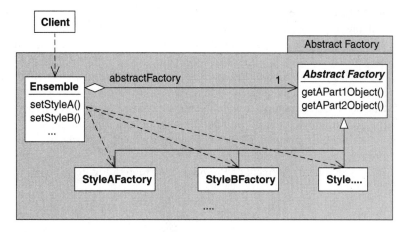

**FIGURE 7.25**   *Abstract Factory:* Narrow Interface

In this version, *Ensemble* provides the only way for clients of the pattern application to change the abstract factory setting. The code for *setStyleA()* is simply the following:

```
abstractFactory = new StyleAFactory();
```

The slight maintenance burden of this organization is that when a new style is added, the class *Ensemble* is affected. Note that the Façade design pattern, discussed in Chapter 8, also deals with narrowing interfaces to a set of classes.

At another extreme, clients could be allowed to access the *Part* classes. In any case, clients may not reference the *Part sub*classes.

*Abstract Factory* is a rather poor name for this design pattern. It is no more "abstract" than any other design pattern. The word "Factory" is satisfactory because we are using the Factory concept repeatedly. More descriptive would be "Factory Family," "Group Factory," or "Style Factory."

**KEY CONCEPT**   Abstract Factory *Design Pattern*

To design an application in which there are several possible styles for a collection of objects, capture styles as classes with coordinated factory methods.

## 7.5 PROTOTYPE

### 7.5.1 Design Purpose of *Prototype*

We have seen that by using *Abstract Factory* we can produce complex objects in one "style" or another, but we sometimes need greater flexibility to mix and match. Suppose, for example, that an application displays office suites to give customers an idea of how their furniture choices would appear. The application obeys a decorating rule that all desks are to be of the same style, color, etc., all chairs are of the same style, color texture, etc. Our purpose is to design the application so that the code displaying the offices need be written only once, and the chair, desk, etc. design sections occur in separate, maintainable parts of the design.

This is a different design purpose from that for *Abstract Factory* because we want to be able to select *any* chair style, any desk style, and any cabinet style separately rather than select an overall office style. Note that a pattern is still present here because we want to keep to a single style of chair and a single style of desk throughout.

Figures 7.26 and 7.27 show office layouts with two selections of desks, chairs, and storage. Exercise 7.1 implements this design.

The formal statement of *Prototype* is written in Figure 7.28.

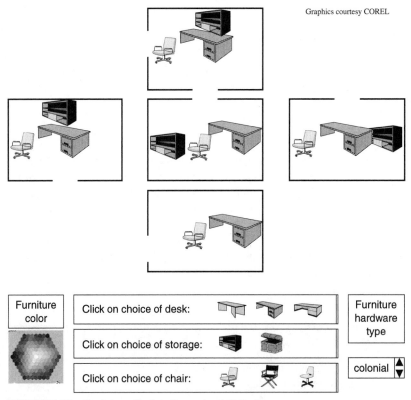

Graphics courtesy COREL

**FIGURE 7.26** *Prototype* Design Example: A Selection

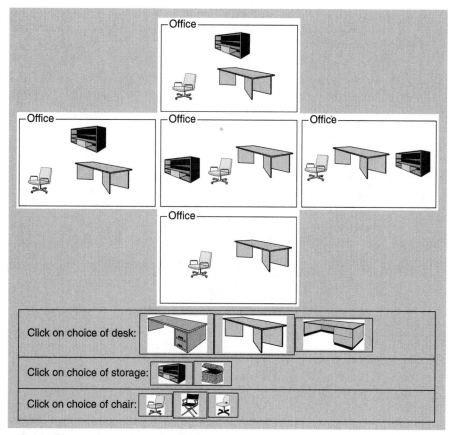

**FIGURE 7.27**  A Simplified *Prototype* Example

Design Purpose

Create a set of almost identical objects
whose type is determined at runtime.

Design Pattern

Assume that a prototype instance is known;
clone it whenever a new instance is needed.

**FIGURE 7.28**  *Prototype* Design Purpose

## 7.5.2  The *Prototype* Interface for Clients

Clients utilizing a *Prototype* design pattern application reference the aggregate object, which we will name *Ensemble*. For example, *Ensemble* could be *OfficeSuite*, and the client requires a particular office suite instance. The aggregate instance needs the prototype objects from which it is constructed. For example, the *OfficeSuite* object could be constructed with green satin Mongolian desk chairs, and so needs a prototype instance of that kind.

Clients call upon a *Prototype* application either by means of a parameterless function such as *createEnsemble()*, or by means of an interface parameterized by the variable elements in the following form.

```
createEnsemble( Element1 aPrototypeElement1, Element2 aPrototypeElement2,  . . . )
```

The latter is illustrated in Figure 7.29.

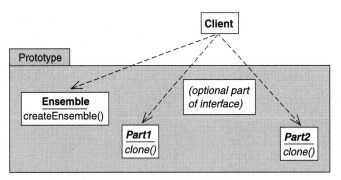

**FIGURE 7.29**  *Prototype* Interface with Clients

The *OfficeSuite* class would provide a public method such as

```
createOfficeSuite( Desk aDesk, Chair aChair,  Storage aStorageUnit )
```

The important point from the client's perspective is that the client code using the method *createOfficeSuite()* deals with *Desk, Chair,* and *Storage* in general, not with different types of desks, chairs, and storage. There should be no reference in the client code to subclasses such as *ModernDesk, ClassicChair*, etc.

In the case of a parameterless call to *createOfficeSuite()*, separate setup code determines the prototype. In the parameterized version, the setup code provides the prototype parameters that the client code uses.

Assume that setup code has instantiated the instances *myDesk* of (a subclass of) the class *Desk, myChair* of *Chair*, and *myStorage* of *Storage*. For example, *myDesk* could be a particular instance of *ModernDesk*. Here is a typical block of client code using an application of the *Prototype* design pattern.

```
. . . . .

OfficeSuite myOfficeSuite =                 // use the interface to the Prototype application
   OfficeSuite.createOfficeSuite( myDesk, myChair, myStorage );

myGUI.add( myOfficeSuite );               // now deal with the OfficeSuite objects
myOfficeSuite.setBackgroundColor( "pink" );    // for example
. . . .
```

Now we will describe how the *Prototype* design pattern attains the design purposes we've outlined.

### 7.5.3 The *Prototype* Class Model

We will start with a simplified version of the *Prototype* pattern. The idea is to clone the prototype whenever a new instance is required. *Prototype* is in the *delegation* form, with *clone()* delegating object construction to the constructor. Figure 7.30 shows the pattern class model. We are creating an instance of an object with aggregated parts. We will call the aggregating class *Ensemble* and one aggregated class *MyPart*. Each aggregate *Ensemble* object aggregates a *MyPart* object as prototype that we have named *myPartPrototype*. The method *createEnsemble()* returns a desired *Ensemble* instance: Whenever it needs a *MyPart* object, it gets one by cloning the prototype, i.e., by executing *MyPartPrototype.clone()* as in

```
MyPart anotherMyPart = MyPartPrototype.clone();
MyPart yetAnotherMyPart = MyPartPrototype.clone();
```

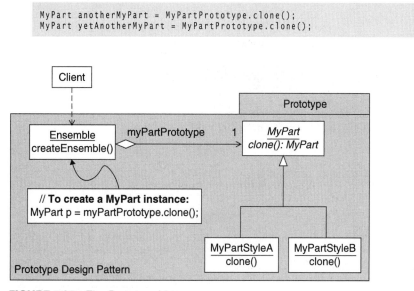

**FIGURE 7.30**  The *Prototype* Idea

Figure 7.31 shows the generic *Prototype* design pattern.

The method *createEnsemble()* constructs an *Ensemble* object made from *Part1*, *Part2*, . . . objects. Whenever a new *Part2* object is required within the code of *createEnsemble()*, we obtain it by means of *clone()* as follows.

```
Part2 part2Object = part2Prototype.clone();
```

The *clone()* method creates an entirely separate *Part2* object with the same variable values as *part2Prototype*. This usually requires a "deep" clone, discussed at the end of this section.

### 7.5.4 The *Prototype* Sequence Diagram

The sequence diagram in Figure 7.32 shows the chain of function calls when a method, *createEnsemble()* of *Ensemble* is called to create a *PartN* object. In this case, *partNPrototype* is an instance of the class *PartNStyleB*.

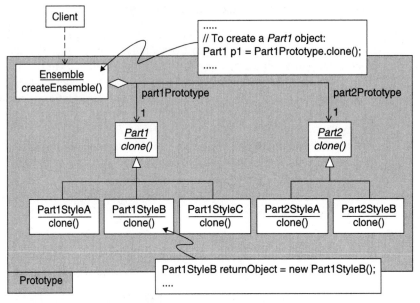

**FIGURE 7.31** *Prototype* Class Model

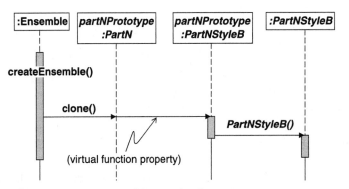

**FIGURE 7.32** Sequence Diagram for *Prototype*

## 7.5.5 Example *Prototype* Applications: Customer Information Entry

The following is an application for which *Prototype* is appropriate. Our task is to facilitate the entering of customer records into Universal Retailer's customer database. We will assume that Universal has just one database. Suppose that Universal provides discount privileges to employees of companies. In return, the companies deduct installment payments directly from employee paychecks. Universal's policy is that the company submits employee names in a single one-time batch, which is how they reduce their costs. Universal classifies customers in one of three categories, and companies must choose one category for all their employees. The categories are listed next. (The actual details are not important for the purposes of this illustration.)

■ "High volume" customers get an extra 5% discount when their annual purchases exceed $2,000, but pay 5% more if their annual purchases total less than $50.

■ "Medium volume" customers are not subjected to any additional discounts or surcharges, but are dropped if their annual purchase total falls below $30.

■ "Low volume" customers are billed a $10 annual service fee, but are not subjected to any additional discounts or restrictions.

Universal's monthly billing process operates off the database of all customers, sending billing information to the employers electronically as each customer is encountered in the database. The billing process produces a stream of messages to print invoices such as the following

```
. . .
John Doe of Universal Electric; deduct $50.00 from paycheck; . . .
Betty Don of Ultra-paramount: deduct $35.00 from paycheck; . . .
Jon Dorr of Universal Electric; deduct $15.00 from paycheck; . . .
. . .
```

The following use case describes the application's main functionality.

"Company entry" use case:

### Preconditions: none

1. The application requests the name of the company sponsoring the batch of employees
2. The user supplies the company's name
3. The application solicits extensive information about the company and the means by which customers will be billed[1]
4. The user enters the company information[1]
5. For each new customer, prompted by the user, the "Customer entry" use case applies here
6. The application outputs to the console complete information on all of the customer records created during this session. (Assume here that the application requires that all the customer objects created be available in memory.)

"Customer entry" use case:

### Precondition: The application is ready to accept an individual new customer

1. The application solicits information on the customer[1]
2. The user enters this information[1]
3. The application echoes the information
4. The application enters the customer record containing all of the company and personal information in the customer database[1]

---

[1]For this example, evidence of this process is output to the console but no actual database work is implemented.

**DESIGN GOALS AT WORK**  *Correctness and Reusability*

We want to isolate the parts pertaining to each type of customer. We also want to isolate the common customer code. This makes it easier to check the design and implementation for correctness, and to reuse the parts.

Because of Universal's policy, each time our data entry application executes, it does so for just one company and with just one type of *Customer* throughout (e.g., only *LoVolCustomer* objects). The customers selected have individual characteristics. The application identifies the customer types at runtime. Thus, one of three possible *Customer* object types is in effect at runtime. Figure 7.33 shows output from this application.

```
Enter company name
Universal Machines Inc.
Now the application would collect lots more company information....

Please pick a type of customer from one of the following (only!):
low
high
medium
medium

Client does some work.....

Client calls on the application of Prototype pattern .....
Enter customer names or '-quit'
Edith Whart
... more interaction to get information about Edith Whart... : Stored in database
Henry Jameson
... more interaction to get information about Henry Jameson... : Stored in database
Samuel Clementi
... more interaction to get information about Samuel Clementi... : Stored in database
-quit

The customer entered during this session:
Customer Edith Whart, an employee of Universal Machines Inc..  Spending category: Medium volume.  Lots more...
Customer Henry Jameson, an employee of Universal Machines Inc..  Spending category: Medium volume.  Lots more....
Customer Samuel Clementi, an employee of Universal Machines Inc.. Spending category: Medium volume.  Lots more....

Client does more work .....
```

**FIGURE 7.33**  *Customer Information Entry:* Typical Scenario

Applying *Prototype*, we design the application to create at runtime a particular static *Customer* object (the prototype) that we will name *customerPrototype*. Each subclass of *Customer* must have a *clone()* method which creates an entirely separate copy of that type of *Customer* object. A setup class initializes the application and initiates a method in *Client* which calls *doAProcess()* on *OfficeProcess*. This method creates as many *Customer* instances as requested by the user. The object model in Figure 7.34 shows this.

The code in *OfficeProcess* must not know which type of *Customer* object it is dealing with. Whenever method code in *OfficeProcess* needs a new *Customer* object, it executes

```
Customer c = customerPrototype.clone() √
```

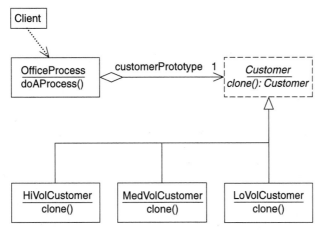

**FIGURE 7.34** *Prototype* Example Outline

instead of

```
Customer d = new Customer().
```

This ensures that a consistent type of *Customer* object is used throughout execution.

A code listing for this application can be found in Appendix D of this chapter.

### 7.5.6 *Prototype* and the Java API

Although *Prototype* may not occur explicitly in the Java API, we often use the *clone()* capability in the Java API to apply *Prototype*. Every Java class has a *clone()* method since it inherits from *Object*: However, this *clone()* is not sufficient in general. Proper cloning should make a separate copy of the object *and* all of the objects it references, directly or indirectly. Figure 7.35 shows what *clone()* is meant to do and what the code in Figure 7.36 actually accomplishes.

Given:

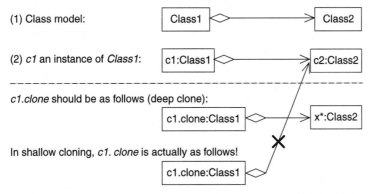

**FIGURE 7.35** Requirement for (Deep) Cloning

Figure 7.36 shows the output demonstrating this shallow clone.

```
c1.class1String: Expect 'ORIGINAL class1String value'<---->ORIGINAL class1String value
c1.class2Object,class2String: Expect 'ORIGINAL class2String value' <---->ORIGINAL class2String value

c1 has been cloned using clone() to produce c1Clone

c1.intAttribute has been changed to 'NEW class1String value'
c2.class2String has been changed to 'NEW class2String value'

c1Clone.class1String: Still expect 'ORIGINAL class1String value'<---->ORIGINAL class1String value
c1Clone.class2Object.class2String: Should still get 'ORIGINALclass2String value'
      but actually get: NEW class2String value!!!
```

**FIGURE 7.36**  Output for Demonstration of Shallow Cloning

Here is the code that fails to perform the (usually required deep) clone.
First, the *ClassUsingShallowClone* class that uses and demonstrates the cloning.

```
/**
 * Client demonstrating the cloning process.
 */
class ClassUsingShallowClone
{

/****************************************************************************************************
 */
public ClassUsingShallowClone()
/***************************************************************************************************/
{ super();
}

/****************************************************************************************************
 * Show that only shallow cloning takes place
 */
public static void main(String[] args)
/***************************************************************************************************/
{
    Class2 c2 = new Class2();
    Class1 c1 = new Class1( c2 );

    // Report on the attributes in c1:
    System.out.println
      ( "c1.class1String: Expect 'ORIGINAL class1String value'<----->" + c1.class1String );
    System.out.println
      ( "c1.class2Object.class2String: Expect 'ORIGINAL class2String value'<----->" +
      c1.class2Object.class2String );

    // Clone c1 and report on the value of c1.c2.intAttribute:
    Class1 c1Clone = (Class1)c1.clone();
    System.out.println( "\nc1 has been cloned using clone() to produce c1Clone\n" );

    // Now change c1 and c2, which should not affect c1Clone
    c1.class1String = "NEW class1String value";
    System.out.println( "c1.intAttribute has been changed to 'NEW class1String value'" );
    c2.class2String = "NEW class2String value";
    System.out.println( "c2.class2String has been changed to 'NEW class2String value'" );

    // Report on the value of c1Clone.c2.intAttribute which should not change:
    System.out.println
      ( "\nc1Clone.class1String: Still expect 'ORIGINAL class1String value'<----->" + .
```

```
      c1Clone.class1String );
      System.out.println
      ( "c1Clone.class2Object.class2String: Should still get 'ORIGINAL class2String value'" +
      "\n\t\tbut actually get: " + c1Clone.class2Object.class2String + "!!!" );
      }

}
```

Next, *Class1*, whose objects are being cloned.

```
***************************************************************************************************
 * Aggregates Class2
 */
class Class1 implements Cloneable
/
***************************************************************************************************/
{
   public String class1String = "ORIGINAL class1String value";
   Class2 class2Object = new Class2();

/***************************************************************************************************
 */
public Class1()
***************************************************************************************************/
{  super();
}


/***************************************************************************************************
 */
public Class1( Class2 aClass2Object )
/***************************************************************************************************/
{
   this();
   class2Object = aClass2Object;
}


/***************************************************************************************************
 * Uses the inherited shallow clone() of Object.
 */
public synchronized Object clone()
/***************************************************************************************************/
{
   try
   {   return (Class1)super.clone();   // use the standard clone() in Object
   }
   catch (CloneNotSupportedException e)
   {   // shouldn't happen, since this class is Cloneable
      throw new InternalError();
   }
}
}
```

Finally, *Class2*, aggregated by *Class1*.

```
/**
 */
class Class2 implements Cloneable
{
   public String class2String = "ORIGINAL class2String value";

/***************************************************************************************************
```

```
 */
public Class2()
/******************************************************************************************/
{  super();
}


/*******************************************************************************************
 * Uses the inherited shallow clone() of Object.
 */
public synchronized Object clone()
/******************************************************************************************/
{
   try
   {   return (Class2)super.clone();   // use the standard clone() in Object
   }
   catch (CloneNotSupportedException e)
   {   // shouldn't happen, since this class is Cloneable
       throw new InternalError();
   }
}

}
```

If we implement deep cloning, as in the code below for *Class1*, we obtain the desired output shown in Figure 7.37.

Output

```
cl.class1String: Expect 'ORIGINAL class1String value'<----->ORIGINAL class1String value
cl.class2Object.class2String. Expect 'ORIGINAL class2String value' <----->ORIGINAL class2String value

cl.has been cloned using clone() to produce clClone
cl.inAttribute has been changed to 'NEW class1String value'
cl.class2String has been changed to 'NEW class2String value'

clClone.class1String: Still expect 'ORIGINAL class1String value'<----->ORIGINAL class1String value
*** NOTE: clClone.class2Object.class2String: Should AND DO get
'ORIGINAL class2String value'<----->ORIGINAL class2String value
```

**FIGURE 7.37**  Output for Demonstration of Deep Cloning

The deep cloning is implemented in the following new version of the class *Class1*.

```
/*******************************************************************************************
 * Aggregates Class2
 */
class Class1 implements Cloneable
/******************************************************************************************/
{
   public String class1String = "ORIGINAL class1String value";
   Class2 class2Object = new Class2();

/*******************************************************************************************
 */
public Class1()
/******************************************************************************************/
{  super();
}


/*******************************************************************************************
 */
public Class1( Class2 aClass2Object )
/******************************************************************************************/
```

```
{
    this();
    class2Object = aClass2Object;
}

/******************************************************************************
 * Uses the inherited shallow clone() of Object.
 * BUT CLONES ITS ATTRIBUTES FIRST, resulting in a deep clone()
 */
public synchronized Object clone()
/******************************************************************************/
{
    try
    {
        Class1 returnClass1Object = (Class1)super.clone();    // clone root first
        // Now move down the aggregation tree (in general this is recursive)
        returnClass1Object.class2Object = (Class2)returnClass1Object.class2Object.clone();
        return returnClass1Object;
    }
    catch (CloneNotSupportedException e)
    {   // shouldn't happen, since this class is Cloneable
        throw new InternalError();
    }
}

}
```

The code demonstrating the use of this deep clone is in a class we'll call *ClassUsingDeepClone*, with the following source.

```
/**
 * Client demonstrating the cloning process.
 */
class ClassUsingDeepClone
{

/******************************************************************************
 */
public ClassUsingDeepClone()
/******************************************************************************/
{  super(); 
}

/******************************************************************************
 * Show that only shallow cloning takes place
 */
public static void main(String[] args)
/******************************************************************************/
{
    Class2 c2 = new Class2();
    Class1 c1 = new Class1( c2 );

    // Report on the attributes in c1:
    System.out.println
        ( "c1.class1String: Expect 'ORIGINAL class1String value'<----->" + c1.class1String );
    System.out.println
        ( "c1.class2Object.class2String: Expect 'ORIGINAL class2String value'<----->" +
        c1.class2Object.class2String );

    // Clone c1 DEEPLY THIS TIME, and report on the value of c1.c2.intAttribute:
    Class1 c1Clone = (Class1)c1.clone();
    System.out.println( "\nc1 has been cloned using clone() to produce c1Clone" );

    // Now change c1 and c2, which should not affect c1Clone
    c1.class1String = "NEW class1String value";
    System.out.println( "c1.intAttribute has been changed to 'NEW class1String value'" );
```

```
    c2.class2String = "NEW class2String value";
    System.out.println( "c1.class2String has been changed to 'NEW class2String value'" );

    // Report on the value of c1Clone.c2.intAttribute which should not change:
    System.out.println
      ( "\nc1Clone.class1String: Still expect 'ORIGINAL class1String value'<----->" +
      c1Clone.class1String );
    System.out.println
      ( "*** NOTE: c1Clone.class2Object.class2String: Should AND DO get " +
      \n'ORIGINAL class2String value'<----->" +
      c1Clone.class2Object.class2String );
  }

}
```

### 7.5.7 Comments on *Prototype*

■ If a new type of customer (currently low, medium, and high volume) is added, removed or modified in the data collection example of Section 7.5.5, the design is easily modified—mainly by the addition, removal, or modification of a *Customer* subclass representing that kind of customer.

■ One can frequently get the effect of *Prototype* by using several factory functions.

In this example, we would aggregate a *Customer* object, which we'll call *customer*, with *OfficeProcess*. We could then use a method such as *getCustomer()* in *Customer* and *HiVolCustomer*, defined in *HiVolCustomer* as

```
Customer getCustomer()
{    return new HiVolCustomer();  }
```

to get the right kind of invoice document, applying delegation/virtual functions.

The method *getCustomer()* returns a *Customer* of the same type as *customer*, but no more. It would be awkward to use this method, however, if we want new *Customer* documents to be exact copies of *customer*. *Prototype* provides this exact copy advantage. In the *Prototype* version we created a specific *Customer* object, with specific attribute values, so that when we clone it, all of this work is reproduced.

■ As with most design patterns, there is some flexibility about how and where clients interface with the application of the pattern.

In our particular *Prototype* class model (Figure 7.31), the client has a "hands-off" relationship with the pattern application, calling only on functionality of the *Ensemble* class. In particular, the client knows nothing about prototypes or about cloning. We could relax this by considering the role of *Ensemble* to be the client role: In other words, allowing the client to take the responsibility for maintaining the prototypes and cloning them when new instances are needed. We have not adopted this perspective because we have considered these responsibilities to be part of the *Prototype* pattern itself, and not part of the clients' responsibilities.

In any case, client code should not refer to the subclasses of the types being cloned (*Part1StyleA*, *Part7StyleX,* etc. in the *Prototype* class model).

■ Note that *requirements* must have some recognized pattern in order for a design pattern to apply.

For example, suppose that the office suite example consisted of placing in each office *any* style of desk, *any* style of chair, etc. in *any* position (e.g., office 1 has a modern desk and an antique chair; office 2 has a steel desk and a modern chair). In that case we would not expect the design to use a design pattern: You can't introduce a pattern when there is none at all in the requirements.

---

**KEY CONCEPT** *Prototype Pattern*

When designing for multiple instances that are the same in key respects, create them by cloning a prototype.

---

## SUMMARY

Figure 7.38 summarizes this chapter.

- Use *Creational Design Patterns* when creating complex objects

- *Factory* when creating individuals

- *Abstract Factory* when creating families

- *Prototype* to "mix and match"

- *Singleton* for exactly one, safely

**FIGURE 7.38** Summary of *Creational Patterns*

## EXERCISES

**Exercise 7.1**   **Office Layout**

**Part 7.1.1**  The source code you (may) have been given implements the office layout in Figure 7.27. It also shows 8 choice buttons at the bottom of the GUI, which are currently inoperative. The assignment is to modify this application and add appropriate design pattern classes and code so that when a button is clicked, the suite reappears with all of the relevant furniture in the model clicked. For example, if the storage chest is clicked, the shelving in the current GUI is replaced with a chest at each location. Include the following, and use numbered tabs to show where they are in your homework.

**1.** Output from four different choices of button clicks

**2.** Class model.

**3.** Sequence diagram for the most significant part of the operation

**4.** Source code, highlighting your contributions and modifications in yellow. Please arrange your classes alphabetically.

You may have to change and add to the classes selected. Keep the *client*, Prototype *application*, and *setup* roles separate.

Evaluation criteria:

- Appropriateness and correctness of your class model
- Clarity of prose and code

- Effectiveness of your response

A = thoroughly specific answers to all questions

A = every nontrivial design and code step clearly explained; prose states meaning very clearly

A = effective avenues for flexibility, reusability, and robustness

The following are errors that you should watch for in this exercise:

*Serious*:

1. Inappropriate design pattern chosen.

2. Inadequate class model.

3. Mismatch between implementation and class model.

4. Inappropriate mixing of client, setup, and Design Pattern application

*Less than serious, but more than minor*:

1. Methods not specified.

2. Fewer than specified test cases provided.

*Minor*:

1. Unkempt layout

**Exercise 7.2**   **Document Storage**   The example problem in section 7.5.5 (the *Prototype* section) concerned customers.

**Part 7.2.1**  Suggest improvements to the design or implementation besides error handling.

**Part 7.2.2**  Suppose that you are writing an application for a company that stores documents for corporations in a single big database. The application is to facilitate the entry of document text for a single corporation in a batch, all of a single type. Suppose that the possible types are *invoices*, *purchase orders* or *contracts*, and that each data entry session deals with only one type of document throughout. Each record includes the name of the corporation owning the document, the type of the document, and the title of the document. (In practice, the record would contain considerably more. Some of this would be company-specific and other parts employee-specific.) Show your class model, your output, and your source code. The process would look like the following (realistically, the application would request a lot more information).

```
Corporation name:
Universal Enterprises

Type of document that will be processed? (invoices, purchase orders or contracts):
purchase orders

Document title or "-quit" to end:
Interplanetary Supply
Document title or "-quit" to end:
Ajax Garden Service
Document title or "-quit" to end:
Acme Cleaning
Document title or "-quit" to end:
-quit

Application-->The following records will be saved
Universal Enterprises / purchase order / Interplanetary Supply
Universal Enterprises / purchase order / Ajax Garden Service
Universal Enterprises / purchase order / Acme Cleaning
```

Evaluation criteria:

- Appropriateness and correctness of your class model

A = complete and correct

▨ Clarity of prose, code, and comments      A = every nontrivial design and code step clearly explained; prose very clear

The following are errors that you should watch for in this exercise:

*Serious*:

**1.** Confusion about the roles of client and pattern application.

**2.** Part 7.2.1 asks you for improvements to the design and implementation. You cited changes in the *requirements* instead. Try to keep the difference clear.

**3.** Your output does not match the required output.

**4.** *Show all classes* in the class model.

**5.** You specified postconditions as an algorithm: Postconditions should describe a state unless users of the method also need to know the manner in which the method accomplishes the postconditions.

*Neither Serious nor Trivial*:

**1.** List classes alphabetically. Otherwise, you are imposing a significant burden on readers of your implementation that interferes with their understanding of it.

**2.** Use expressive names for methods.

**3.** This is a response to an error: Prototype is especially useful when you need copies of a particular instance. For this exercise, the data for a given company will have a significant amount that is particular to the company. Thus, we make this special Company instance and then clone it.

**Exercise 7.3**    **Word Processor Extension**    This exercise concerns the example problem in Section 7.4.5 (the *Abstract Factory* section).

**Part 7.3.1**  Suggest improvements to the design or implementation.

**Part 7.3.2**  Extend the example to include a third output format of your choosing, different from the two demonstrated. Show your class model, classes containing new source code (don't include classes unchanged from this book), and also your output for this new style.

Evaluation criteria:

▨ Appropriateness and correctness      A = complete and correct
   of your class model

▨ Clarity of prose, code, and comments      A = every nontrivial design and code step clearly explained; prose very clear

The following are errors that you should watch for in this exercise:

*Serious*:

**1.** New style addition does not leverage the existing application of Abstract Factory.

**2.** Part 7.3.1 asks you for improvements to the design and implementation. You cited changes in the *requirements* instead. Try to keep the difference clear.

*Less than serious; more than trivial*:

**1.** You did not provide suggestions for improvement. (Almost all code can be improved, even in a minor way.)

**Exercise 7.4**    **Chess**    Suppose that you are tasked to build an application that displays the progress of a game of chess. The output consists of several panels. One panel contains the state of the chessboard, another a live video of the player whose move is next, and the third panel shows the score.

**Part 7.4.1**  Suppose that the design has a *Player* class with no subclasses, and a *Score* class with a method *display()*. State clearly how you would design for the *Player* objects and how *display()* accesses them. Provide the code for *Player* and *Score*.

**Part 7.4.2**  Suppose that you use the class *ChessPiece* for this application. Suppose also that you have decided not to introduce a class for each kind of chess piece (knight, pawn, etc.). You made this decision because your application performs display only, and does not require knowledge of legal moves, etc. Thus, the pieces would be instances of *ChessPiece*. How would you design *ChessPiece* robustly to accommodate this decision? Discuss the robustness or nonrobustness of introducing a method *render( String aPiece, int row, int column )* to draw the chess piece. State how you would improve the robustness of this method. Factor for each: For example, *renderAsPawn(), renderAsKnight()* called by *render()* depending on type string and color string; *ChessPiece* retains the piece type to allow *render* to select; Allows looping through all with *render()*; Make it *render( ChessPiece aPiece, int row, int column )*.

```
private static ChessPiece whiteQueen;    // initialized in constructor type "queen" color "white"
private static ChessPiece whitePawn[] = new ChessPiece[ 8 ];  // or use prototype . . .

    public . . ..getWhiteQueen()
```

**Exercise 7.5**   **Drawing Automobiles**   You are tasked with building an application that draws automobiles for potential customers. The user is presented with the interface shown in Figure 7.39.

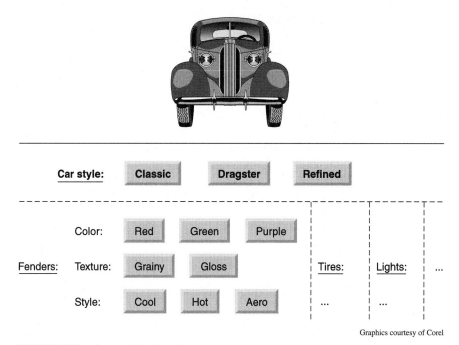

Graphics courtesy of Corel

**FIGURE 7.39**   Automobile Drawing

**Part 7.5.1**  What design pattern(s) would you use? Explain your choices.

**Part 7.5.2**  Show a class diagram for your design pattern application. Include a *Client* class and indicate how it interfaces with the pattern application(s). Include key function names on the class diagram for clarity. In words, indicate the methods and instantiations executed to render an automobile. (A sequence diagram for this is not required.) Omit setup aspects. There is no requirement to give pseudocode or code for any functions.

Criteria:
- Appropriateness of the design pattern(s) selected
- Clarity of your response

A = entirely appropriate design patterns applied; no unsuitable ones applied. Applying an inappropriate pattern loses one grade on this criterion

A = Very clear diagrams and explanations of all of the key parts

The following are errors that you should watch for in this exercise:

*Serious*:

1. Confusion about the roles of client and pattern application.

2. Inappropriate choice of design pattern.

*Less than serious, more than minor*:

1. Confusion between the client and nonclient roles.

2. Lack of explanation as to the choices made.

# APPENDIX A

## CODE LISTING FOR E-MAIL GENERATION EXAMPLE (FACTORY DESIGN PATTERN APPLICATION, SECTION 7.2)

We start with the listing for the client role, the class *Client*. Note that it interfaces with the application of *Factory* as advertised: It depends only on the class *Customer*, and not on any other classes of the pattern application.

```
/**
 * Sends messages to various customers.
 * User of the Factory design pattern application
 */
class Client
{

/***************************************************************************************************
 */
public Client()
/**************************************************************************************************/
{  super();
}

/***************************************************************************************************
 * Precondiiton" 'aCustomer != null'
 *
 * Postcondition: The e-mail message text pertaining to the type of 'aCustomer' has been output to
 *   the monitor.
 *
 * Design note: Here is where the client interfaces with an application of Factory design pattern
 */
public void sendMessage( Customer aCustomer )
/**************************************************************************************************/
{
    // Here is where the Factory design pattern application is used
    MailMessage mailMessage = aCustomer.getMessage();

    // Use the message
    System.out.println( "This message will be sent:" );
    System.out.println( mailMessage.getText() );
    // ...... more work with mailMessage .....
}

}
```

Each subclass of *Customer* has a version of *getMessage()* that returns a tailored *Message* object.

### Curious

```java
/**
 * Curious customer
 */
class Curious extends Customer
{

    /****************************************************************************************************
     */
    public Curious()
    /****************************************************************************************************/
    {  super();
    }
    /****************************************************************************************************
     * Returns: a non-null 'MailMessage' object intended for curious customers
     */
    public MailMessage getMessage()
    /****************************************************************************************************/
    {
        String curiousCustomerMessage = "... a (possibly long) message for curious customers ...";
        String messageTextForAllCustomers = ( super.getMessage() ).getText();
        return new MailMessage( "\n" + messageTextForAllCustomers + "\n" + curiousCustomerMessage );
    }

}
```

The class *Customer* is implemented as an interface as follows.

```java
/**
 * Base for customers
 */
abstract class Customer
{

    /****************************************************************************************************/
    /****************************************************************************************************
     * Returns: Non-null mail content intended for all customers
     */
    public MailMessage getMessage()
    {  return new MailMessage( "Losts of material intended for all customers ..." );
    }
    /****************************************************************************************************/

}
```

### Frequent

```java
/**
 * Customers who buy frequently
 */
class Frequent extends Customer
{

    /****************************************************************************************************
     */
    public Frequent()
    /****************************************************************************************************/

    {  super();
```

```
}
/*************************************************************************************************
 * Returns: a non-null 'MailMessage' object intended for frequent customers
 */
public MailMessage getMessage()
/************************************************************************************************/
{
   String frequentCustomerMessage = "... a (possibly long) message for frequent customers ...";
   String messageTextForAllCustomers = ( super.getMessage() ).getText();
   return new MailMessage( "\n" + messageTextForAllCustomers + "\n" + frequentCustomerMessage );
}
}
```

The setup role, consisting of the class *MailGenerationApplication*, is as follows. It initializes the client and prompts the user to identify the type of *Customer* to work with. If we were to introduce a new customer category, this is the only class we would have to alter.

```
import java.io.*;
import java.util.*;

/*
 * Demonstration of Factory design pattern
 */
class MailGenerationApplication
{
   private static Client client = new Client();

/*************************************************************************************************
 */
public MailGenerationApplication()
/************************************************************************************************/
{  super();
}

/*************************************************************************************************
 * Precondition: 'MailGenerationApplication.client' != null
 *
 * Postconditions:
 *   (1) Customer type has been solicited from user in accordance with getCustomerTypeFromUser()
 *   (2) A mail message has been output the the console for this type of customer
 */
public static void main( String[] args )
/************************************************************************************************/
{
   Customer customer = getCustomerTypeFromUser();
   MailGenerationApplication.client.sendMessage( customer );  // let the client do its job
}

/*************************************************************************************************
 * Postconditions:
 * (1) User has been prompted with type of customer
 * (2) MailGenerationApplication.customer is an instance of the type entered if the user's input
 *     legitimate
 * (3) MailGenerationApplication.customer is an instance of Newbie if user's input not legitimate
 * (4) The customer type selected has been printed to the console
 */
private static Customer getCustomerTypeFromUser()
/************************************************************************************************/
{
   String customerType = "newbie";   // default
   Hashtable customerTypeTable = new Hashtable();   // keys strings to Customer types

   // Key user input to the corresponding type of customer
```

```
        customerTypeTable.put( "frequent", new Frequent() );
        customerTypeTable.put( "returning", new Returning() );
        customerTypeTable.put( "curious", new Curious() );
        customerTypeTable.put( "newbie", new Newbie() );

        // Get customer type from user (minimizes modification whenever customerTypeTable is modified)

        System.out.println( "Please pick a type of customer from one of the following:" );
        for ( Enumeration enumeration = customerTypeTable.keys(); enumeration.hasMoreElements() ;)
        {     System.out.println( enumeration.nextElement() );
        }

        try   // pick up user's input
        {   BufferedReader bufReader =
            new BufferedReader( new InputStreamReader( System.in ) );
            customerType = bufReader.readLine();
        }
        catch( IOException e )
        {   System.out.println( e );
        }

        // Return 'Customer' instance according to user's input
        Customer customerSelected =  (Customer)customerTypeTable.get( customerType );
        if( customerSelected != null )
            return customerSelected;
        else   // use default if user input bad
        {   System.out.println( "Sorry: Could not understand your input: newbie customer assumed." );
            return new Newbie();
        }
    }   // end getCustomerTypeFromUser()

}
```

The class *MailMessage* is not part of the pattern application, the setup, or the client role. Its content is in the *String* member "text." It is as follows.

```
/**
 * e-mail for customers
 */
class MailMessage
{
    // Content of the message
    String text = "No text chosen yet";

/*********************************************************************************************
 */
public MailMessage()
/********************************************************************************************/
{   super();
}

/*********************************************************************************************
 */
public MailMessage( String aText )
/********************************************************************************************/
{
    this();
    text = aText;
}

/*********************************************************************************************
 */
public String getText()
/********************************************************************************************/
{   return text;
```

```
}
/*******************************************************************************************
 */
public void setText( String aString )
/******************************************************************************************/
{   text = aString;
}

}
```

## Newbie

```
/**
 * A new customer
 */
class Newbie extends Customer
{

/*******************************************************************************************
 */
public Newbie()
/******************************************************************************************/
{   super();
}
/*******************************************************************************************
 * Returns a non-null 'MailMessage' object intended for newbie customers
 */
public MailMessage getMessage()
/******************************************************************************************/
{
    String newCustomerMessage = "... a (possibly long) message for new customers ...";
    String messageTextForAllCustomers = ( super.getMessage() ).getText();
    return new MailMessage( "\n" + messageTextForAllCustomers + "\n" + newCustomerMessage );
}
}
```

## Returning

```
/**
 * A returning customer
 */
class Returning extends Customer
{

/*******************************************************************************************
 */
public Returning()
/******************************************************************************************/
{   super();
}
/*******************************************************************************************
 * Returns a non-null 'MailMessage' object intended for returning customers
 */
public MailMessage getMessage()
/******************************************************************************************/
{
    String returningCustomerMessage = "... a (possibly long) message for returning customers ...";
    String messageTextForAllCustomers = ( super.getMessage() ).getText();
    return new MailMessage( "\n" + messageTextForAllCustomers + "\n" + returningCustomerMessage );
}
}
```

# APPENDIX B

## CODE LISTING FOR EXPERIMENT EXAMPLE (*SINGLETON* DESIGN PATTERN APPLICATION, SECTION 7.3)

First we will look at the source code for *Client*, which is as follows.

```
/**
 * Example of a user of the 'Experiment' singleton.
 */
class Client
{

/********************************************************************************************
 */
public Client()
/********************************************************************************************/
{  super();
}

/********************************************************************************************
 * Postconditions:
 * (1) An analysis has run on the 'Experiment' singleton as per 'analyze()' in 'Experiment'
 * (2) A report has been generated on the 'Experiment' singleton in accordance with 'reportResults()'
 */
public static void main( String[] args )
/********************************************************************************************/
{
    // Here is where we use the Singleton application [can't state "new Experiment()"]
    Experiment experiment = Experiment.getTheExperiment();

    // Now work with the experiment and report the results
    experiment.analyze();
    experiment.reportResults();

}

}
```

The source code for the *Experiment* singleton class is as follows.

```
/**
 * Demonstration: Fragment of an application that evaluates the results of a lab experiment
 * Example of a Singelton design pattern.
 */
class Experiment
{
    // The singleton Experiment instance: final because it should never be assigned to another
instance
    private static final Experiment theExperiment = new Experiment();

    String result = "Experiment result not yet assigned";   // result of the experiment

    // Number of times this singleton called for within the execution
    private static int numTimesReferenced = 0;

/********************************************************************************************
 * Design Note: This is private, so that it can only be used by member methods of Experiment
 */
```

```
private Experiment()
/*******************************************************************************************/
{ super();
}


/********************************************************************************************
 * The actual work of the experiment analysis is done here
 */
public synchronized void analyze()
/*******************************************************************************************/
{
    // .... do the analysis work ....
    theExperiment.result =
    "... The analysis shows that the experiment was a resounding success. ....";
}


/********************************************************************************************
 * Here is where the client interfaces with application of Factory design pattern
 * The only way to obtain the singleton 'Experiment' object
 */
public static Experiment getTheExperiment()
/*******************************************************************************************/
{
    // Report  number of times this singleton has been accessed (for curiosity)
    ++numTimesReferenced;
    System.out.println
      ( "Noting that the Experiment singleton referenced " + numTimesReferenced + " times so far" );

    return theExperiment;
}

/********************************************************************************************
 * The results of the experiment analysis.
 */
public void reportResults()
/*******************************************************************************************/
{ System.out.println( result );
}

}
```

# APPENDIX C

## CODE LISTING FOR WORD PROCESSOR EXAMPLE (*ABSTRACT FACTORY* DESIGN PATTERN APPLICATION, SECTION 7.4)

We will first look at the *Client* code for this application, and then list the remaining classes in alphabetical order.

```
import java.io.*;

/**
 * User of 'Document' class
 * Design Note: Does not reference subtypes of 'Title' or 'Heading'.
 */
public class Client
{
    private static Document document = Document.getTheDocument();

    /********************************************************************************************
```

```
 */
public Client()
/*************************************************************************************************/
{  super();
}


/*************************************************************************************************
 * Precondition: 'aDocument' != null
 *
 * Postcondition:
 *  (1) The display form of 'aDocument' has been assembled 'buildDisplay()' of 'Document'
 *  (2) 'aDocument' has been displayed to the console in accordance with 'display()' of 'Document'
 */
public static void display( Document aDocument )
/*************************************************************************************************/
{
    aDocument.buildDisplay();
    System.out.println( "\n\n" );
    aDocument.display();
}


/*************************************************************************************************
 * Postcondition: The user has been prompted to select a style
 *
 * Returns:
 *   If the user selects a legitimate style: corresponding 'Style' subclass object
 *   Otherwise a 'SmallStyle' object
 */
public static Style getStyleFromUser()
/*************************************************************************************************/
{
    // Prepare to read from the console
    BufferedReader reader = new BufferedReader
     ( new InputStreamReader( System.in ) );

    // Get style from user: Default "small" if user enters incorrect data
    Style returnStyle = SmallStyle.getTheSmallStyle();
    try
    {
        System.out.println
        ( "---> Enter the style you want displayed ('small' or 'large')"
        + " (small if input is improper):" );
        String userInput = reader.readLine();

        if( userInput.equals( "small" ) )
                returnStyle = SmallStyle.getTheSmallStyle();

        if( userInput.equals( "large" ) )
                returnStyle =  LargeStyle.getTheLargeStyle();
    }
    catch( IOException e )
    {        System.out.println( e );
    }

    return returnStyle;
}


/*************************************************************************************************
 * Precondition: 'document' != null
 *
 * Postconditions:
 *  (1) The application has obtained the contents of the required document ('document') from the user
 *       in accordance with 'getDocumentFromUser()'
 *  (2) The application has obtained the style from the user in accordance with 'getStyleFromUser()'
 *  (3) The app. has output 'document' to the console in accordance with 'display()' of 'Document'
 */
```

```
public static void main( String[] args )
/******************************************************************************************/
{
   try
   {   document.getDocumentFromUser();
   }
   catch( Exception e )
   {   System.out.println( e );
   }

   document.setStyle( getStyleFromUser() );
   display( document );
}

}
```

The remaining classes will be listed alphabetically. The interface *Displayable* is a convenient way to group entities that are displayed on the console:

```
/**
 * Something which can be displayed at the console
 */
public interface Displayable
{
    void display();
}
```

The code for *Document* is as follows.

```
import java.util.*;
import java.io.*;

/**
 * The document being built.  Displayable in various styles.
 *
 * Class invariant: 'headings.length' == 'textSegments.length'  (I)
 *
 * Known issue: For the sake of robustness, may be better not to keep the headings and
 *   their corresponding text in separate variables.
 */

public class Document
{
    private String title;   // -- of the document as a whole

    private Vector headings = new Vector();   // text for each heading in this document
    private Vector textSegments = new Vector();   // text for each section under each heading

    // The combination of displays (the "complex object" we are constructing)
    private Vector display = new Vector();

    // The current style with which the display will be built
    private Style style;

    private static Document theDocument = new Document();   // only one

/*******************************************************************************************
 */
public Document()
/******************************************************************************************/
{  super();
}

   /*******************************************************************************************
```

```
 * Postconditions:
 * (1) The 0th element of 'display' is the 'Title' object in the style of 'style'
 *       for each heading in 'headings':
 * (2) The 1th element of 'display' is the first 'Heading' object in the style of 'style'
 * (3) The 2th element of 'display' is the 'Text' object accompanying the first heading
 *       in the style of 'style'
 * (4) The 3th element onwards of 'display' are the remaining 'Heading' and accompanying
 *       'Text' objects, in sequence
 */
public void buildDisplay()
/***************************************************************************************/
{
    // Create the vector of objects for display

    // Insert the title object
    display.addElement( getATitle( title ) );

    for( int i = 0; i < headings.size(); ++i )
    {
        // Insert the next heading
        String heading = (String)headings.elementAt(i);
        display.addElement( getAHeading( heading, i + 1 ) );

        // Insert the next text segment
        String text = (String)textSegments.elementAt(i);
        display.addElement( new Text( text ) );   // insert text
    }

}

/***************************************************************************************
 * Display on console
 */
public void display()
/***************************************************************************************/
{
    for( int i = 0; i < display.size(); ++i )
        ( (Displayable) display.elementAt(i) ).display();
}

/***************************************************************************************
 */
public Heading getAHeading( String aString, int anIndex )
/***************************************************************************************/
{  return style.getAHeading( aString, anIndex );
}

/***************************************************************************************
 */
public Title getATitle( String aString )
/***************************************************************************************/
{  return style.getATitle( aString );
}

/***************************************************************************************
 * Preconditions:
 *  (1) 'headings' != null
 *  (2) 'textSegments' != null
 *
 * Postconditions: The application has prompted the user for, and obtained the following:
 * (1) The document's title, which is set to 'title'
 * The following are solicited as many times as the user wants
 * (2) The document's next heading, which is added to 'headings'
 * (3) The text belonging to this heading, which is added to 'textSegments'
 */
public void getDocumentFromUser() throws IOException
/***************************************************************************************/
{
```

```
    // Prepare to read from the console
    BufferedReader reader = new BufferedReader(new InputStreamReader( System.in ) );
    String userInput = new String( "" );

    // Enter title
    System.out.println( "---> Enter the title of your document: " );
    title = new String( reader.readLine() );

    // Enter heading - text pairs until done
    // The fact that these are perfomed together ensures the class invariant (I) above
    while( true )  // exit with break after entering '-done'
    {
        // Enter heading
        System.out.println( "---> Enter heading or '-done': " );
        userInput = reader.readLine();
        if( userInput.equals( "-done" ) )
           break;
        headings.addElement( new String( userInput ) );

        // Enter text corresponding to the heading
        System.out.println( "---> Enter the text: " );
        userInput = reader.readLine();
        textSegments.addElement( new String( userInput ) );
    }

    // Typically, we would store the document at this point
}

/*************************************************************************************************
 */
public static Document getTheDocument()
/*************************************************************************************************/
{  return theDocument;
}

/*************************************************************************************************
 */
public void setStyle( Style aStyle )
/*************************************************************************************************/
{  style = aStyle;
}

}
```

The class *Heading*:

```
/**
 * A heading of a document (one for each section).
 */

public abstract class Heading implements Displayable
{
    protected String value = null;   // text of this heading
    protected int index = 0;   // heading number

/*************************************************************************************************
 */
public abstract void display();
/*************************************************************************************************/

/*************************************************************************************************
 */
public Heading()
/*************************************************************************************************/
{  super();
}
```

```
/***********************************************************************************************
 */
public void setValue(String aString)
/**********************************************************************************************/
{  this.value = aString;
}


/***********************************************************************************************
 */
public Heading( String aString, int aPositionInTheListOfHeadings )
/**********************************************************************************************/
{
    this();
    this.value = aString;
    this.index = aPositionInTheListOfHeadings;
}

}
```

The class *LargeHeading*:

```
/**
 * Upper case version
 */

public class LargeHeading extends Heading
{

/***********************************************************************************************
 */
public LargeHeading()
/**********************************************************************************************/
{  super();
}
/***********************************************************************************************
 */
public LargeHeading( String aString, int anIndex )
/**********************************************************************************************/
{
    super( aString, anIndex );
    index = anIndex;
}
/***********************************************************************************************
 * Precondition: 'this.value' != null
 * Postcondition: 'this.value' has been displayed at the console in upper case
 */
public void display()
/**********************************************************************************************/
{
    System.out.println
      ( "\nSection " + this.index + ". ---" + this.value.toUpperCase() + " ---" );
}

}
```

The class *LargeStyle*:

```
/**
 * Expresses "large" version of document,  Relates to all 'LargeXXX' classes
 * Design note: Application of Abstract Factory design pattern
 */
public class LargeStyle extends Style
{

private static LargeStyle theLargeStyle = new LargeStyle();    // the singleton
```

```
/*******************************************************************************
 */
private LargeStyle()
/******************************************************************************/
{  super();
}


/*******************************************************************************
 */
public Heading getAHeading( String aString, int anIndex )
/******************************************************************************/
{   return new LargeHeading( aString, anIndex );
}


/*******************************************************************************
 */
public Title getATitle( String aString )
/******************************************************************************/
{   return new LargeTitle( aString );
}


/*******************************************************************************
 */
public static Style getTheLargeStyle()
{   return theLargeStyle;
};
/******************************************************************************/

}
```

The class *LargeTitle*:

```
/**
 * Upper case version of title
 */

public class LargeTitle extends Title
{

/*******************************************************************************
 */
public LargeTitle()
/******************************************************************************/
{  super();
}


/*******************************************************************************
 */
public LargeTitle( String aString)
/******************************************************************************/
{  super( aString );
}


/*******************************************************************************
 * Precondition: 'value' != null
 * Postcondition: 'value' has been displayed at the console in upper case.
 */
public void display()
/******************************************************************************/
{
    System.out.println( "\t----- Title: " + value.toUpperCase() + " -----" );
}

}
```

The class *SmallStyle*:

```java
/**
 * Expresses "small" version of document,  Relates to all 'SmallXXX' classes
 * Design note: Application of Abstract Factory design pattern
 */
public class SmallStyle extends Style
{

private static SmallStyle theSmallStyle = new SmallStyle(); // singeleton

/************************************************************************************************
 */
private SmallStyle()
{  super();
}


/************************************************************************************************
 */
public Heading getAHeading( String aString, int anIndex )
/************************************************************************************************/
{  return new SmallHeading( aString, anIndex );
}


/************************************************************************************************
 */
public Title getATitle( String aString )
/
/************************************************************************************************/
{  return new SmallTitle( aString );
}


/************************************************************************************************
 */
public static Style getTheSmallStyle()
/************************************************************************************************/
{  return theSmallStyle;
}


}
```

The class *SmallTitle*:

```java
/**
 * Lower case version of title
 */
public class SmallTitle extends Title
{

/************************************************************************************************
 */
public SmallTitle()
/************************************************************************************************
 */
{  super();
}


/************************************************************************************************
 */
public SmallTitle( String aString)
/************************************************************************************************/
{  super( aString );
}


/************************************************************************************************
```

```
 * Precondition: 'value' != null
 * Postcondition: 'value' has been output to the console
 */
public void display()
/*****************************************************************************************/
{  System.out.println( value.toLowerCase() + ":" );
}

}
```

The class *Style*:

```
/**
 * Expresses style of document.
 * Design note: Application of Abstract Factory design pattern.  This is the base Abstract Factory
class
 */
public abstract class Style
{

/*****************************************************************************************
 */
public Style()
/*****************************************************************************************/
{  super();
}

/*****************************************************************************************
 */
public abstract Heading getAHeading( String aString, int anIndex );
/*****************************************************************************************/

/*****************************************************************************************
 */
public abstract Title getATitle( String aString );
/*****************************************************************************************/

}
```

The class *Text*:

```
/**
 * The text that follows a heading:   The content of a document.
 */

public class Text implements Displayable
{
    private String value = null;

/*****************************************************************************************
 */
public Text()
/*****************************************************************************************/
{  super();
}

/*****************************************************************************************
 */
public Text( String aString)
/*****************************************************************************************/
{
    this();
    value = aString;
}
```

```
/*******************************************************************************************
 */
public String getText()
/******************************************************************************************/
{   return value;
}


/*******************************************************************************************
 */
public void setValue( String aString )
/******************************************************************************************/
{   this.value = aString;
}


/*******************************************************************************************
 */
public void display()
/******************************************************************************************/
{   System.out.println( value );
}

}
```

The class *Title*:

```
/**
 * The title of a document (one per document.)
 */

public abstract class Title implements Displayable
{
    public String value = null;

/*******************************************************************************************
 */
public Title()
/******************************************************************************************/
{   super();
}


/*******************************************************************************************
 */
public Title( String aString)
/******************************************************************************************/
{
    this();
    value = aString;
}


/*******************************************************************************************
 */
public void setValue(String aString)
/******************************************************************************************/
{   this.value = aString;
}


/*******************************************************************************************
 */
public void display()
/******************************************************************************************/
{   System.out.println( value );
}

}
```

# APPENDIX D

## CODE LISTING FOR CUSTOMER INFORMATION ENTRY EXAMPLE (*PROTOTYPE* DESIGN PATTERN APPLICATION, SECTION 7.5)

Here is the class *Client*.

```
/**
 * A user of OfficeProcess
 */
class Client
{

/*********************************************************************************
 */
public Client()
/*********************************************************************************/
{  super();
}


/*********************************************************************************
 * Demonstration of how a client could use a Prototype pattern application.
 * Notice that this class has no references to 'Customer' or its subclasses
 *
 * Postconditions:
 * (1) This method performs unspecified work, which is represented by dummy text messages output to
 the console
 * (2) Customer information has been collected by the user as in 'doAProcess()' of 'OfficeProcess'
 */
public void DoOfficeProcess()
/*********************************************************************************/
{
    System.out.println( "\nClient does some work ....." );
    System.out.println( "\nClient calls on the application of Prototype pattern ....." );
    OfficeProcess.getOfficeProcess().getAndProcessCustomers();
    System.out.println( "\nClient does more work ....." );
}
```

Here is the class *Customer*.

```
/**
 */
abstract class Customer
{
    protected String name = "name not assigned yet";
    protected String employerName = "employerNamenot assigned yet";
    protected String type = "type not assigned yet";

/*********************************************************************************
 */
public Customer()
/*********************************************************************************/
{  employerName = "default employer name";
}


/*********************************************************************************
 */
```

```
public Customer( String anEmployerName )
/*********************************************************************************/
{   employerName = anEmployerName;
}


/*********************************************************************************
 * Require subclasses to implement clone()
 */
public abstract Object clone();
/*********************************************************************************/


/*********************************************************************************
 * Postcondition: All known details concerning this Customer have been output to the console
 */
public void describe()
/*********************************************************************************/
{
  System.out.println( "Customer " + name + ", an employee of " +
    employerName + ".  Spending category: " + getType() + ".  Lots more ...." );
}


/*********************************************************************************
 */
public abstract String getType();
/*********************************************************************************/


/*********************************************************************************
 */
public void setName( String aName )
/*********************************************************************************/
{   name = aName;
}


}
```

Here is the class *HiVolCustomer.*

```
/**
 * Customers who buy a large amount -- see requirements
 */
class HiVolCustomer extends Customer implements Cloneable
{

/*********************************************************************************
 */
public HiVolCustomer()
/*********************************************************************************/
{   super();
}


/*********************************************************************************
 */
public HiVolCustomer( String aCompanyName )
/*********************************************************************************/
{   super( aCompanyName );
}


/*********************************************************************************
 */
public Object clone()
/*********************************************************************************/
{   return new HiVolCustomer( employerName );
```

```
}
/*******************************************************************************
 */
public String getType()
/******************************************************************************/
{   return "High volume";
}

}
```

Here is the class *MedVolCustomer.*

```
/**
 * Customers who buy an average amount (see requirements)
 */
class MedVolCustomer extends Customer implements Cloneable
{

/*******************************************************************************
 */
public MedVolCustomer()
/******************************************************************************/
{   super();
}

/*******************************************************************************
 */
public MedVolCustomer( String aCompanyName )
/******************************************************************************/
{   super( aCompanyName );
}


/*******************************************************************************
 */
public Object clone()
/******************************************************************************/
{   return new MedVolCustomer( employerName );
}


/*******************************************************************************
 */
public String getType()
/******************************************************************************/
{   return "Medium volume";
}

}
```

Here is the class *OfficeProcess.*

```
import java.util.*;
import java.io.*;

/**
 * Performs processing with customers according to requirements document xx
 * Note that this class makes no reference to 'Customer' subclasses
 *
 * Demonstration of the Prototype design pattern.  Note that this class deals with
 *  'Customer' objects in general, not subtypes.
 */
```

```java
class OfficeProcess
{
    private static Customer customerPrototype;    // the prototype used to create new 'Customer'
objects
    Vector customers = new Vector();  // keep available the customers created during each execution
    private static OfficeProcess officeProcess = new OfficeProcess();    // the singleton

/****************************************************************************
 */
private OfficeProcess()
/****************************************************************************/
{ super();
}

/****************************************************************************
 * Preconditions:
 * (1) 'customerPrototype' != null
 * (2) 'customers' != null
 *
 * Postconditions:
 * (1) A list of customers has been obtained from the user via the console
 * (2) This information includes the customer's name
 * (3) The customer information is stored as 'Customer' objects in 'customers'
 * (4) A list of customers, with details, has been output to the console
 *
 * Design notes: Clones prototypes to generate instances 'Customer'  This code makes no
 *  reference to subclasses of 'Customer'
 */
public void getAndProcessCustomers()
/****************************************************************************/
{
    Customer customer;   // for temporary use
    String customerName = "not yet assigned";

    // ----- Postconditions (1) - (3)

    BufferedReader bufReader =   // prepare to read from console
        new BufferedReader( new InputStreamReader( System.in ) );

    try
    {
        System.out.println( "Enter customer names or '-quit'" );

        while( !"-quit".equals( customerName ) )   // signal to quit soliciting names
        {
                customerName = bufReader.readLine();   // get the name

                if( !"-quit".equals( customerName ) )   // a name, not a signal to stop getting names
                {
                        // KEY STEP (notice that this code does not mention subclasses of Customer)

                        customer = (Customer)OfficeProcess.customerPrototype.clone();   // make a new one

                        customer.setName( customerName );
                        System.out.println( "... more interaction to get information about "
                        + customerName + "... : Stored in database" );
                        this.customers.addElement( customer );   // keep in memory for processing
                }
        }
    }
    catch( IOException e )
    { System.out.println( e );
    }

    // ----- Postcondition (4)

    // List customers entered during this session (a reason we maintained 'customers' )
```

```
        System.out.println( "\nThe customers entered during this session: " );
        for( int customersIndex = 0; customersIndex < customers.size(); ++customersIndex )
        {
            customer = (Customer)this.customers.elementAt( customersIndex );
            customer.describe();
        }
    }

/*****************************************************************************
 */
public static Customer getCustomerPrototype()
/*****************************************************************************/
{   return customerPrototype;
}


/*****************************************************************************
 * Accessor for the singleton
 */
public static OfficeProcess getOfficeProcess()
/*****************************************************************************/
{   return officeProcess;
}

/**
 * Precondition: 'aCustomer != null'
 * Postcondition: 'customerPrototype == aCustomer'
 */
public void setCustomerPrototype( Customer aCustomer )
{   customerPrototype = aCustomer;
}
}
```

Here is the class *Setup*.

```
import java.util.*;
import java.io.*;

/**
 * Initalizes application and initiates client
 */

class Setup
{

/*****************************************************************************
 */
public Setup()
/*****************************************************************************/
{   super();
}


/*****************************************************************************
 * Postconditions
 *   (1) The application has solicited a company name
 *   (2) The user has provided a company name
 *   (3) The application has solicited the customer type for employees of this company
 *   (4) The user has provided a type for employees -- otherwise this is taken for "medium"
 *   (5) 'customerPrototype' in the 'OfficeProcess' object has been set accordingly
 *   (6) The postconditions of 'doOfficeProcess()' of 'Client' apply.
 */
public static void main( String[] args )
/*****************************************************************************/
{
    OfficeProcess officeProcess = OfficeProcess.getOfficeProcess();    // the singleton
```

```
    // Get company information (see postconditions 1 and 2)

    System.out.println( "Enter company name" );
    String companyName = "not yet selected";
    try
    {   BufferedReader bufReader =
           new BufferedReader( new InputStreamReader( System.in ) );
        companyName = bufReader.readLine();
    }
    catch( IOException e )
    {   System.out.println( e );
    }
    System.out.println( "Now the application would collect lots more company information ...." );

    // Get type of customer that the company has chosen(see postconditions 3 and 4)

    // Relate strings to prototype Customer objects
    Hashtable customerTypeHashtable = new Hashtable();
    customerTypeHashtable.put( "low", new LoVolCustomer( companyName ) );
    customerTypeHashtable.put( "medium", new MedVolCustomer( companyName ) );
    customerTypeHashtable.put( "high", new HiVolCustomer( companyName ) );

    // Solicit customer type from user
    System.out.println( "\nPlease pick a type of customer from one of the following:"
    + "('medium' will be assumed otherwise)" );
    for ( Enumeration enumeration = customerTypeHashtable.keys(); enumeration.hasMoreElements() ; )
    {      System.out.println( enumeration.nextElement() );
    }

    // Pick up user's input for customer
    String customerTypeSelected = "not yet selected";
    try
    {   BufferedReader bufReader =
          new BufferedReader( new InputStreamReader( System.in ) );
        customerTypeSelected = bufReader.readLine();
    }
    catch( IOException e )
    {   System.out.println( e );
    }

    //  Set the Customer prototype in the "Prototype" design pattern application
    officeProcess.setCustomerPrototype
      ( (Customer)customerTypeHashtable.get( customerTypeSelected ) );   // assign type to singleton
    if( officeProcess.getCustomerPrototype() == null )   // user did not enter a legitimate type
        officeProcess.setCustomerPrototype( new MedVolCustomer( companyName ) );

    Client client = new Client();
    client.doOfficeProcess();
  }

}
```

CHAPTER *8*

# *STRUCTURAL DESIGN PATTERNS*

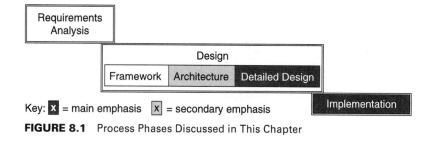

Key: ▣ = main emphasis   ▣ = secondary emphasis

**FIGURE 8.1**   Process Phases Discussed in This Chapter

## 8.1  STRUCTURAL DESIGN PURPOSES

Applications typically involve objects that aggregate other objects: Organization charts, maps, molecules, and office plans are examples. In particular, organization charts typically aggregate *Employee* objects in a tree structure. The design purposes for Structural patterns are to represent such complex objects (the *static* viewpoint) and to obtain functionality from them in a manner that utilizes their aggregated objects (the *dynamic* viewpoint).

## 8.2  *FAÇADE*: INTERFACING FOR A COLLECTION OF CLASSES

### 8.2.1  The Design Purpose of *Façade*

In building applications we parcel out sets of classes to separate developers. This requires a clear modularization of the design. Developers typically require the services of classes that others are responsible for developing, so that classes and packages often relate to each other as client and server. The client and server portions are developed relatively independently: The problem is that services are typically in various states of completion as the project progresses. Complexity is greatly reduced when there is just one object providing access to the functionality of a collection of classes.

A component acts effectively as a server when its interface is narrow. "Narrow" means that the interface (a collection of functions, described in Section 2.3.3 on page 55) contains no unnecessary parts, is collected in one place, and is clearly defined. The *Façade* design pattern establishes just such an interface to a package of classes. *Façade* regulates communication with the objects in a package by exposing only one object of the package to client code of the package, hiding all of the other classes. This helps organize development because the programmers responsible for a package can publicize the services offered by a *Façade* object and stub them while the package is under development. ("Stubbing" means temporarily substituting the real content with very simplistic content.)

Meanwhile, clients of the package have a concrete representation of the package's functionality to use during development. This advantage extends to maintenance: If maintainers can upgrade the way in which functionality is coded without disturbing the façade, they can be assured that clients of the package are not affected. The *Façade* object is a typically a singleton. Figure 8.2 summarizes the design purpose and technique of *Façade*.

**Design Purpose**

Provide an interface to a package of classes

**Design Pattern Summary**

Define a singleton which is the sole means for obtaining functionality from the package.

*Notes*: The classes need not be organized as a package; more than one class may be used for the façade.

**FIGURE 8.2** *Façade*

## 8.2.2 Interface for Clients of *Façade*

Suppose that a package contains a collection of classes and that the client code, external to the package, requires a service *myCMethod()* provided by a class *C* in the package. The client may interface only with the *Façade* object, which we will call *theFacadeObject*. Thus, the client code calls a method such as *cMethodOfFacade()* of *theFacadeObject* in order to accomplish this purpose.

## 8.2.3 The *Façade* Class Model

The *Façade* class model shows clients interfacing with a single class of a package, but no others. Actually, we could designate more than one class as a façade class. The nonfaçade classes are not accessible to code external to the package. The *Façade* structure is in the *Delegation* form (see Section 6.5.2 on page 141) since the *Façade* object delegates commands to classes internal to its package. This is illustrated in Figure 8.3.

A call that would otherwise refer to an object of a class within the package is replaced by a call to a method of the *Façade* object. This method can then reference the object in question. The sequence diagram is shown in Figure 8.4.

## 8.2.4 Example *Façade* Applications

### 8.2.4.1 Using Façade for a Video Game Architecture
The use of *Façade* in the architecture of a video game is shown in Figure 8.5. The game's classes are divided into three packages. One pertains to the characters that move about, the second contains the classes that describe the maze, and the third contains the control of the game.

Communication with game characters must occur via the single *MyGameCast* object. Reference to parts of the game's environment must occur through the *MyGameEnvironment* object, etc.

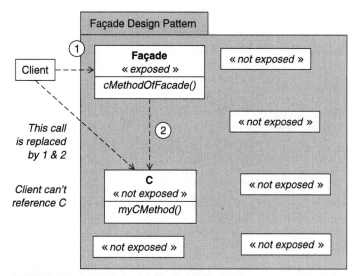

**FIGURE 8.3**  *Façade* Design Pattern Structure

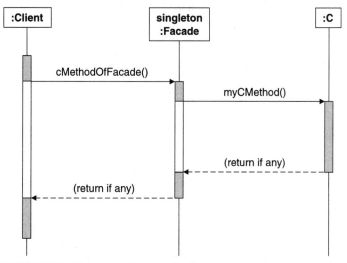

**FIGURE 8.4**  Sequence Diagram for *Façade*

***8.2.4.2  Façade* Example: Banking**  Now let's consider a simple banking example that allows users to make deposits to customer accounts and obtain balances. Suppose that we have decided to modularize the customer and accounts portion by placing them in a package, *bankCustomers*, with a façade object *BankCustomers*.

## DESIGN GOALS AT WORK    *Correctness* and *Reusability*

Collecting customer-related classes in a package with a clear interface clarifies the design, allows independent verification, and makes this part reusable.

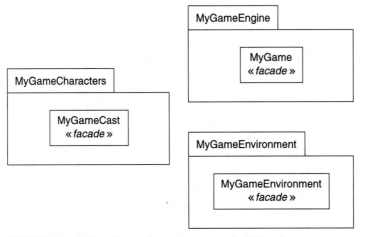

**FIGURE 8.5** Using *Façade* for Architecture of a Video Game

Section 8.2.6 explains the importance of an abstract level for the effective use of *Façade.* The class model supports a *Client* class—a user of the *Façade* pattern application—performing operations. This is shown in Figure 8.6.

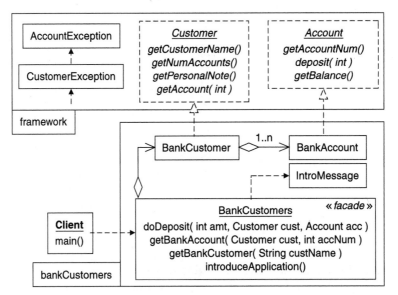

**FIGURE 8.6** Using *Façade* to Access Bank Customers

The following use case outlines the requirements.

1. The application displays an introduction. (All displays consist of console text.)

2. The application repeats the following until the user decides to quit.

   2.1. The application displays a list of customer names.

   2.2. The application prompts the user to choose a customer name.

**2.3.** The user enters a customer name.

**2.4.** The application displays some information about the customer.

**2.5.** The application prompts the user for an account number.

**2.6.** The user reports the customer's balance.

**2.7.** The application prompts the user for a deposit amount.

**2.8.** The user enters a deposit amount.

Figure 8.7 shows a scenario executing.

Output

```
Welcome to the customer / account demonstration of the Facade Design Pattern.
....          ....
   ....     ....
      ....
These are the customers to choose from.
Charles
Betty
Able
Please enter customer name:
Able
You chose Able
Gentleman and long-time customer
Please enter account number (for security, a list is not given ...1 is for testing:
1
You chose account number 1
The balance in this account is 0
Enter a positive integer if you wish to make a deposit -- 0 otherwise:
99
You chose amount 99
Deposited 99 into the account of Able
The balance in this account is 99

Enter '-quit' to end this application.
These are the customers to choose from.
Charles
Betty
Able
Please enter customer name:
-quit
You chose -quit
```

**FIGURE 8.7**   Output of *Façade* Banking Example

Note the following points.

**1.** The class *Client* references no class in the *bankCustomers* package besides *Bank-Customers*. (The rest are not public, so *Client* would be prevented at compile time from doing so anyway.)

**2.** The existence of (public) interfaces *Customer* and *Account* makes it possible for *Client* to operate in this way. This gives *Client* and the package a common set of terms which both can use to communicate.

The classes making up this application are listed in Appendix A.

### 8.2.5 Application of *Façade* in the Java API

*Enterprise Java Beans* (EJB's) are server-side Java components organized in a container. The purpose of the container is to relieve the programmer of common burdens such as managing threads, sessions with clients, and common database operations. Clients are not permitted direct access to an EJB class *MyEJBClass*: Instead, a pair of façade interfaces is supplied. One interface is used to create objects of *MyEJBClass*. The other is used to access the functionality of *MyEJBClass*. EJB's are discussed further in Chapter 14.

*Façade* is generally not applied in the Java API because it hides classes. It is in the very nature of API's that their classes are available for use, and not hidden.

### 8.2.6 Comments on *Façade*

▨ One difficulty in applying *Façade* is the prohibition against mentioning the member classes of the *Façade* object's package. For example, users of the *MyGameCharacters* package typically need to access individual game characters, but are permitted to access only the class *MGCast*: in particular, users of the *MyGameCharacters* package can't even *mention* a class "*MGCharacter*" within the package because that would contradict the principle of hiding internal classes. This is a severe restriction but it has a solution.

As demonstrated for the banking application, the presence of an abstract level deals with this issue. If a (public) framework package exists containing the class *GameCharacter*, users of *MyGameCharacters* may mention *GameCharacter*. This is usually sufficient to deal with the access problem. In particular, the *MyGameCast* Façade class could have public methods such as

```
GameCharacter getMainCharacter();
```

Client code could then contain statements such as

```
GameCharacter mainPlayerCharacter = theMyGameCastObject.getMainCharacter();
```

The *MyGameCast* Façade object controls all permissible actions affecting the main player character.

One can think of this usage of the *Façade* design pattern with the following analogy. Suppose that you call *CampaLot Corp.* with the intention of buying a tent. To do this, you need3 to know about tents in general (this is like being able to reference a *Tent* framework class), but you rely on *CampaLot*'s interface (the *CampaLot* person at the telephone) to provide access to their particular line of tents (analogous to the internal classes of the package).

▓ Using *Façade* imposes the additional design effort required to make methods available to users of the package. For example, suppose that we have a package called *Chemistry* that contains a class called *Molecule*, which, in turn, contains a useful method called *atomicWeight()*. A *Façade* class *ChemistryFaçade* would contain a public method such as *getAtomicWeight()* that passes control to *atomicWeight()*. This requires additional work and coordination in the development process. Such a price is usually worth paying, however, since the reward is increased modularization.

▓ *Web services* provide functionality at a Web site for the benefit of external software. This is the *Façade* concept. A complex array of objects and classes may be required to fulfill the functionality. Servlets are a common Java way of providing server-side *Façade* functionality.

---

**KEY CONCEPT**     *Façade* Design Pattern

Modularizes designs by hiding complexity.

---

# 8.3 *DECORATOR:* ADDING AND REMOVING RESPONSIBILITIES OF A CLASS AT RUNTIME

## 8.3.1 The Design Purpose of *Decorator*

Sometimes we want to add functionality to an object at runtime. For example, suppose that an application must track the weekly tasks performed by auto mechanics. When a mechanic begins work on a task, the application has to add a task object to his profile. This addition process is sometimes referred to as "decorating" the core object. In this example the core object is the auto mechanic profile. At the end of the week we'd like to obtain information about these tasks in a smooth manner. In an increasingly complex world, the parts of objects may not be known until runtime (e.g., an application that allows you to envision a living room furnished with items selected at a web site). In other words, we are seeking flexibility.

The term "Decorator" is used because early applications of this pattern actually decorated text with surrounding graphics such as menus and scrollbars. The design purpose and technique for *Decorator* are summarized in Figure 8.8.

**Design Purpose**

Add responsibilities to an object at runtime.

**Design Pattern Summary**

Provide for a linked list of objects,
each capturing some responsibility.

**FIGURE 8.8** *Decorator*

### 8.3.2 Interface For Clients of *Decorator*

Suppose that the core ("undecorated") object's class is *Substance*, and that the added responsibilities belong to the *Decoration* class.

Clients need to be able to add elements to or remove elements from the core object. Clients also need to be able to call on the functionality of the whole ensemble in a simple manner. An example is obtaining the total time spent by an auto mechanic where his tasks are represented as objects. To accommodate these purposes, the pattern has a base class, *Component*, and clients may interface with any *Component* object, adding objects to it, or requesting functionality from it.

### 8.3.3 The *Decorator* Class Model

*Decorator* creates an aggregated linked list of *Decoration* objects ending with the basic *Substance* object. In other words, each *Component* object that is not a *Substance* instance aggregates another *Component* object, as shown in Figure 8.9. This is in the *recursive* form described in Chapter 6.5.3 on page 143. The objects form a linked list as shown in Figure 8.10. When *doAction()* is called on any object, it performs work and calls *doAction()* on the object it aggregates. This is the dynamic viewpoint, elaborated next.

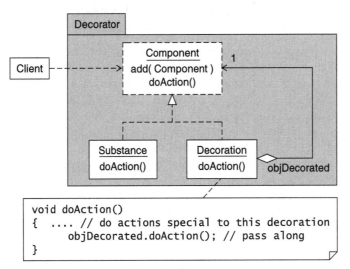

**FIGURE 8.9** *Decorator* Class Model

### 8.3.4 The *Decorator* Sequence Diagram

*Decorator's* dynamic viewpoint is its ability to carry out a command by getting each decoration to execute its version of the command, and then call the method by the same name in the *objectDecorated* that is linked to it. This delegation process ends with the *Substance* object performing its version of the method. (See Figure 8.11.)

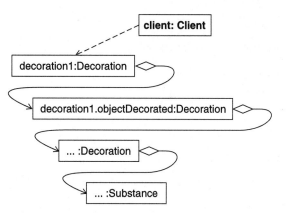

**FIGURE 8.10** Linked Objects in *Decorator*

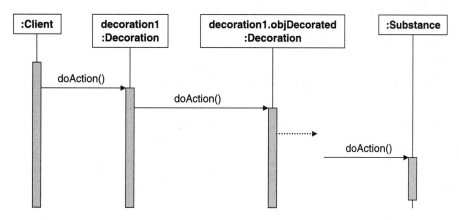

**FIGURE 8.11** Sequence Diagram for *Decorator*

## 8.3.5 Example Application of *Decorator*: Customer / Account

As an example, let's consider a customer who is permitted to open various types of accounts. The main use case is as follows.

1. The following is repeated until the client wishes to quit.

    1.1. The application lists the type of accounts available and prompts the user to choose one.

    1.2. The user enters a type of account.

2. The application lists all the details of all the accounts that the user has chosen.

A typical interaction is shown in Figure 8.12.

The *Substance* class of Figure 8.9 in this case is the class *Customer*, and the decorations are *Account* instances. The class model is shown in Figure 8.13.

Note that the interface *BankingComponent* has an *add()* method but only *Account* subclasses implement it: *Customer*'s version of *add()* does nothing except throw an

Output

```
Select an account:  Incorrect entries assume checking account.

Please select an account type from the following.
CD account
Checking account
Savings account
Please enter account type:
Checking account
You chose Checking account

Type any character if you want to add another account:  Otherwise  'quit'.
c

Please select an account type from the following.
CD account
Checking account
Savings account
Please enter account type:
Checking account
You chose Checking account

Type any character if you want to add another account:  Otherwise 'quit'.
c

Please select an account type from the following.
CD account
Checking account
Savings account
Please enter account type:
Savings account
You chose Savings account

Type any character if you want to add another account:  Otherwise 'quit'.
quit
Calling for a description of one Component:
Savings account number 1 with interest rate 4.
Check account number 2 with last check printed 12345.
Check account number 1 with last check printed 12345.
Customer decription: Jonas Smith
```

**FIGURE 8.12**  Output of *Customer/Account* Example

*AttemptToAddBadBankingComponentException* object because it should never be called. Effectively, it is *Setup*'s responsibility to see to it that *Client* is not asked to add to a *Customer* object. The source code for this example is in Appendix B.

## DESIGN GOAL AT WORK   *Flexibility*

We need to open new accounts for customers at runtime, remove them, etc.

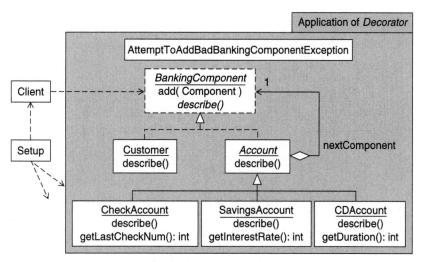

**FIGURE 8.13**  Decorator Applied to *Customer/Accounts* Example

## 8.3.6  Applications of *Decorator* in the Java API

Decorator is used in *java.io* to form input and output streams with desired properties. For example, the following statement for reading from the console appears in several of the code examples in this chapter.

```
BufferedReader bufReader = new BufferedReader( new InputStreamReader( System.in ) );
```

Recall that *System.in* is an *InputStream* object. The class model fragment from which this object comes is shown in Figure 8.14.

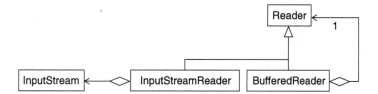

**FIGURE 8.14**  Use of *Decorator* in *java.io*

The *new* expression *InputStreamReader(System.in)* creates an *InputStream* object from *System.in*, which is an *InputStream* object. The full expression decorates this object with a *BufferedReader* object as shown in Figure 8.15.

Using *Decorator* in this way allows applications to create ways to read and write at runtime.

## 8.3.7  Comments on *Decorator*

■ As for most design patterns, there are many variants on *Decorator*. For example, the *Component* entity would be an abstract class rather than an interface if it contains useful base functionality. It is frequently necessary to distinguish among different varieties of *Decoration* classes, requiring subclasses of *Decoration*.

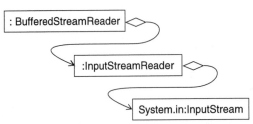

**FIGURE 8.15**   *java.io Decorator* Example

- From a static viewpoint, *Decorator* can be thought of as an object version of a linked list.

- One question that arises is: Why use *Decorator* when a simple *Vector* of *Component* objects seems to suffice? In the example, we could aggregate a *Vector* of *Account* objects with a *Customer* object.

This would make the client's interface less flexible, however. Instead of the simple interface with a single *Component* object that *Decorator* provides, the client would have to know about the subclasses *Customer* and *Account*, thereby making the client code more specialized. In particular, if other classes replaced *Customer* or *Account*, the client code would have to change: This is not the case when *Decorator* is used.

- Gamma, et al. [Ga] call the principal function of *Decorator* "adding responsibilities" dynamically. In other words, decorating adds functionality at runtime. This is more the purpose of the *Chain of Responsibility* design pattern (Section 9.7 on page 309), which the reader will find to be similar to *Decorator.* Our emphasis here has been on the structural properties of *Decorator.*

---

**KEY CONCEPT**   *Decorator* **Design Pattern**

Allows addition to and removal from objects at runtime.

---

# 8.4 *COMPOSITE*: REPRESENTING TREES OF OBJECTS

### 8.4.1   The Design Purpose of *Composite*

Suppose that we want to represent a tree of objects (e.g., the organization chart of a company). We need a class model capable of reflecting any employee hierarchy, allowing us to easily add and remove *Employee* objects, and to execute operations on all elements of the collection, such as printing their names. The design purposes and overall technique for *Composite* are shown in Figure 8.16.

### 8.4.2   Interface for Clients of *Composite*

Clients of a *Composite* application should be able to reference any of the objects in the tree, add a subordinate object, and cause the object and all of its subsidiaries to perform some action. In other words, clients should have access to the base class *Component* and should be able to call *Component* methods such as *add(Component)* and *doSomething()*.

**Design Purpose**

Represent a Tree of Objects

**Design Pattern Summary**

Use a Recursive Form in which the
tree class aggregates and inherits
from the base class for the objects.

**FIGURE 8.16**   *Composite*

## 8.4.3   The *Composite* Class Model

The heart of the pattern is to use the inherit/aggregate relationship illustrated in Figure 8.17. (We referred to this as the *recursion* form in Section 6.5.3 on page 143.)

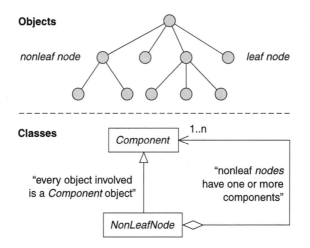

**FIGURE 8.17**   Basis for *Composite* Class Model

The idea is to show that some components (the nonleaf ones) aggregate other component(s). This is the static viewpoint of *Composite,* as fleshed out in Figure 8.18. The class model includes *LeafNode* components that do not aggregate other components.

Now let's consider the dynamic viewpoint of *Composite.* The client calls upon the *Component* object it references to execute functionality *doIt().* The *Composite* object executes *doIt()* in a manner that depends on whether it is a *LeafNode* object or a *NonLeafNode* object. Executing *doIt()* is straightforward for a *LeafNode* object. A *NonLeafNode* object calls on each of its aggregated objects (its "descendants" we can call them) to execute *doIt().* These *Component* objects continue the process down the tree structure.

Suppose, for example, that the tree is a management organizational chart, and *doIt()* is *displayEmployee().* In this case, *Component* would be more appropriately named *Employee*, and *NonLeafNode* would be better called *Supervisor. Leaf* would be named something like *IndividualContributor.* Calling *displayEmployee()* on the *Component*

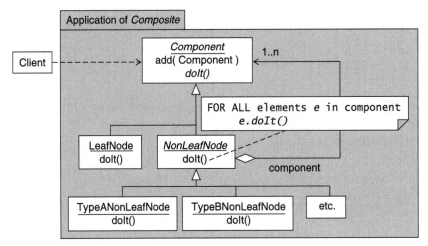

**FIGURE 8.18** *Composite* Class Model

object that represents the whole organization causes each of the objects to first execute its *displayEmployee()* method, and then call *displayEmployee()* on each of its subordinates. For vice presidents (e.g., *TypeANonLeafNode* being *SeniorVP*) the method *displayEmployee()* could have effects such as displaying a biographical press release. On the other hand, *displayEmployee()* for first-line supervisors would be more modest.

### 8.4.4 The *Composite* Sequence Diagram

A typical sequence diagram for *Composite* is shown in Figure 8.19.

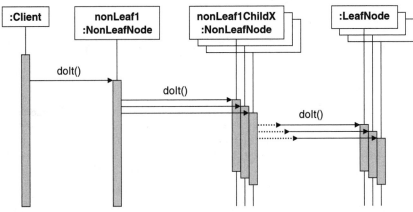

**FIGURE 8.19** Sequence Diagram for *Composite*

### 8.4.5 Example *Composite* Application: Bank / Teller

Let's suppose that we are writing a human resources application that deals with the organization of employees in a bank. Organization charts are in the form of trees, of which Figure 8.20 is an example.

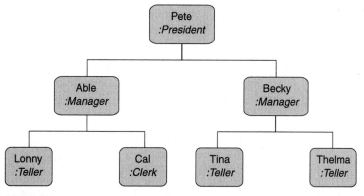

**FIGURE 8.20**  Employee Hierarchy

We want to be able to write the client code once, but be able to run it with varying configurations of the organization chart.

## DESIGN GOALS AT WORK    *Flexibility* and *Correctness*

We need to add and remove employees at runtime and execute operations on all of them.

In applying the *Composite* design pattern, we will use the *Employee* class to take the place of the *Component* class in the standard form of the pattern (Figure 8.18). *Clerk* and *Teller* are leaf nodes and *Supervisor* is a nonleaf node. There are two kinds of supervisors, *Manager* and *President*. The setup code creates the organization chart. This is shown in Figure 8.21.

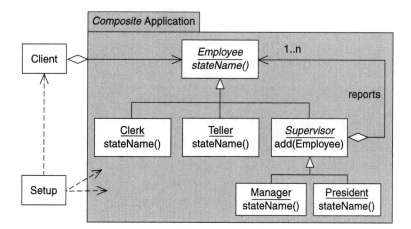

**FIGURE 8.21**  *Bank/Teller* Example

In this application of *Composite, Client* aggregates an *Employee* object. The point is that it depends on *Employee* only. The result of the following code in *Setup* is shown in Figure 8.21.

```
// Initiate client
Client.employee = pete;
Client.doClientTasks();
```

This particular example is not interactive: It does nothing more than display a list of employees to the console, including their names and job functions. Figure 8.22 shows the corresponding sequence diagram.

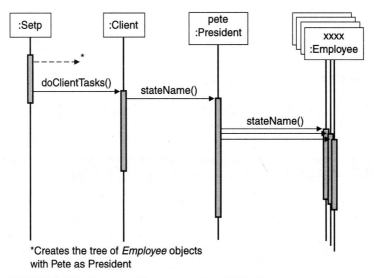

*Creates the tree of *Employee* objects
with Pete as President

**FIGURE 8.22** Sequence Diagram for *Bank/Teller* Example

The output is shown in Figure 8.23.

```
Output

President Pete
Manager Able
Teller Lonny
Clerk Cal
Manager Becky
Teller Juanita
Teller Tina
Teller Thelma
```

**FIGURE 8.23** Output of *Bank/Teller* Example

The source code for this application can be found in Appendix C.

### 8.4.6 The *Composite* Pattern in the Java API

*Composite* is at the heart of *java.awt*, enabling the nesting of windows. Nesting forms a tree structure. Figure 8.24 illustrates this.

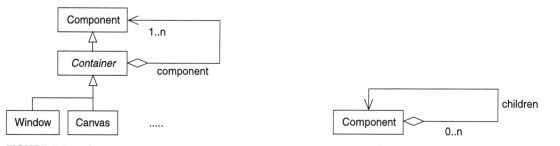

**FIGURE 8.24**  *Composite* in *java.awt*          **FIGURE 8.25**  Attempt to Simplify *Composite*

This model says that everything is a *Component* object. Containers such as *Window* objects or *Canvas* objects may aggregate other components. For example, windows can contain other windows. These, in turn, can contain still other windows, and so on.

### 8.4.7  Comments on *Composite*

▪ Eliminating leaf classes

One may be tempted to simplify *Composite* to the class model in Figure 8.25.

One could then distinguish leaf nodes by the fact that *children* has value *null*. An advantage of this approach is that leaf nodes can become nonleaf nodes at runtime by adding *children*. One disadvantage is that there is no abstract level (which has numerous benefits as explained in Section 6.4.2 on page 138). Another disadvantage is the lack of distinction between leaf and nonleaf nodes, a distinction which makes the application more robust.

▪ From the purely structural viewpoint, *Decorator* is a special case of *Composite*. However, its intention is somewhat different in that it adds responsibilities at runtime.

▪ The *dynamic* viewpoint of *Composite* concerns functionality exhibited by the nodes (such as printing the name when nodes are *Employee* objects). This has the effect of performing the operation in a particular order. When control of the order is required, the *Iterator* design pattern (Section 9.3 on page 283) may be required.

---

**KEY CONCEPT**   *Composite* Design Pattern

Used to represent trees of objects.

---

## 8.5  *ADAPTER*: INTERFACING IN A FLEXIBLE MANNER

### 8.5.1  The Design Purpose of *Adapter*

Suppose that a preexisting application, or even just a preexisting object, provides functionality that our application requires. For example, suppose that an existing application computes the principal obtained from investing a given amount for a given number of years in a special type of investment, and we want to use this functionality. In doing so, however, we want to modify our own application as little as possible. We also want to be able to easily switch to alternative implementations of the required external functionality. Figure 8.26 summarizes these purposes and the basic *Adapter* technique.

**Design Purpose**

Allow an application to use external functionality in a retargetable manner.

**Design Pattern Summary**

Write the application against an abstract version of the external class; introduce a subclass that aggregates the external class.

**FIGURE 8.26** *Adapter*

## 8.5.2 Interface for Clients of *Adapter*

The client is the application that must use the existing functionality. The client does not directly interface with the existing functionality. Instead, it interfaces with an abstract method of an appropriately named abstract class. The latter must be instantiated at runtime with an object of a concrete subclass, as explained next.

Let's call the abstract class *AbstractClass*, and its relevant method *clientNameForRequiredMethod()*. Client code would be something like the following.

```
.....
AbstractClass anAbstractClassObject;
.....     // setup code instantiates anAbstractClassObject
....
anAbstractClassObject.clientNameForRequiredMethod();    // use the external functionality
.....
```

Setup code, probably executed at initialization, must instantiate *anAbstractClassObject* at runtime in something like the following manner.

```
.....
if( . . . )   // e.g., from a setup file
{ anAbstractClassObject = new ConcreteSubclassOfAbstractClass();
  ....
```

## 8.5.3 The *Adapter* Class Model

The class model for *Adapter* is based on the *delegation* form because an *Adapter* object delegates the command to the targeted command, as shown in Figure 8.27.

## 8.5.4 The *Adapter* Sequence Diagram

*Adapter* works by handing off function calls to *clientNameForRequiredMethod()* as shown in Figure 8.28.

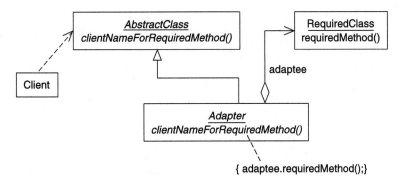

**FIGURE 8.27** *Adapter* Example

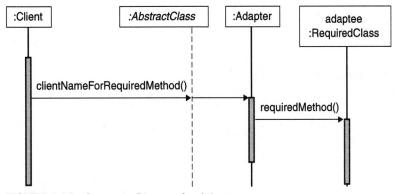

**FIGURE 8.28** Sequence Diagram for *Adapter*

## 8.5.5 Example Applications of *Adapter*

Let's consider a financial application that needs to use the method

```
computeValue( float years, float interest, float amount )
```

of a legacy class *Principal*. We want to be able to easily switch to other implementations of this functionality if necessary.

---

**DESIGN GOALS AT WORK**     *Flexibility* and *Robustness*

We want to separate the application as a whole from financial calculations that will be performed externally.

---

We write our application by giving our own names to the function of interest, and the class/object that owns the function. For example, we can name a method

```
amount( float originalAmount, float numYears, float intRate )
```

in the class *Financial*. This class is made abstract, as illustrated in Figure 8.29.

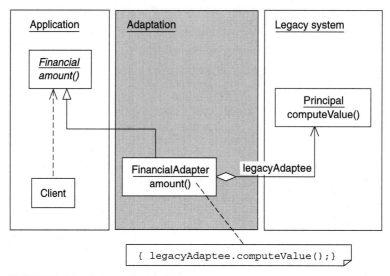

**FIGURE 8.29** *Adapter* Design Pattern

The *Adapter* design pattern in this case consists of a class, named *FinancialAdapter* here, which inherits from the application's class (*Financial* in our case), and which aggregates the legacy class *Principal*. This could be implemented as follows.

```
class FinancialAdapter extends Financial
{
    Principal legacyAdaptee = null;
    // Constructors go here . . .

    /** This method uses the legacy computeValue() method */
    float amount( float originalAmount, float numYears, float intRate )
    {
        return legacyAdaptee.computeValue
            ( originalAmount, numYears, intRate );
    }

}
```

The new application is *written* against the class *Financial*, but *executed* at runtime with a *FinancialAdapter* object. Setup code instantiates the *Financial* object as a *Financial-Adapter* instance. For example, the *Client* could be written with a method parameterizing *Financial*, such as

```
void executeFinanceApplication( Financial aFinancial );
```

It could then be executed with the following *setup* statement:

```
executeFinanceApplication( new FinancialAdapter() );
```

All calls to the *amount()* method of *Financial* are passed to the legacy method *computeValue()*.

It is easy to adapt the application to an implementation of *amount()* in a new class. We would only have to change the brief code in *FinancialAdapter*. The rest of the application would not be affected.

Being able to retarget code by making localized changes like this is valuable for development and maintenance. The alternative is having to make changes in multiple locations.

### 8.5.6   *Adapter* and the Java API

Java *Listeners* are adapters for the following reason. Suppose that we want *myMethod()* in *MyClass* to execute whenever *myButton* is pressed. To do this, we introduce a class *MyListener* that implements the *ActionListener* interface. The class model is shown in Figure 8.30.

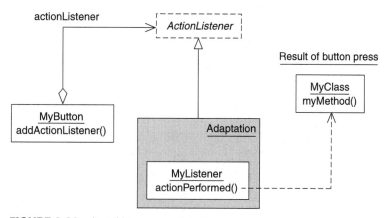

**FIGURE 8.30**   Java *Listeners* as *Adapters*

The class *MyListener* is the adapter class in this case. At runtime we can instantiate *actionListener* with an *ActionListener* subclass instance such as *MyListener*, according to the effect we require when the button is clicked. The code in *MyButton* references only *ActionListener*, not any particular subclass.

### 8.5.7   Comments on *Adapter*

▨  Instead of aggregating *RequiredClass* in Figure 8.27, we could inherit from it, as long as the language allows multiple inheritance, as shown in Figure 8.31. We may be quite satisfied to make *AbstractClass* an Interface if the language does not support multiple inheritance (e.g., Java).

▨  *Adapter* is often used when we create an application using library classes, but where we want to retain the flexibility to select alternative library classes. For example, we might use *Vector* in a Java application to store a collection, but find that it is somewhat awkward for the purpose in question. We could then design and code the application so that it uses an ideal class of our invention to store a collection (e.g., *Automobiles* with methods *storeAuto()* etc.): Then we would incorporate an adapter to fit this to *Vector*. When a more suitable collection management class appears, we could then easily retarget to it, needing to change only the adapter.

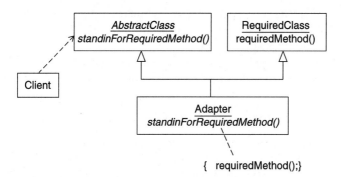

**FIGURE 8.31** *Adapter* Example: *Inheritance* Version

▨ Returning to the financial example in Section 8.5.5, to preserve the option to retarget at runtime, we could retain *FinancialAdapter*, but introduce a new *Adapter* class *FinancialAdapter2*, inheriting from *Financial*. Whenever we want to target the application to the second legacy system, we would execute the application with

```
executeFinanceApplication( new FinancialAdapter2() );
```

**KEY CONCEPT**    *Adapter* Design Pattern

To interface flexibility with external functionality.

# 8.6 *FLYWEIGHT*: MANAGING LARGE NUMBERS OF BARELY DISTINGUISHABLE OBJECTS

## 8.6.1 The Design Purpose of *Flyweight*

Some applications need to contend with a large number of almost indistinguishable objects. One example is an application that arranges text for various formats (print, browser, handheld device, etc.). To do this, it could be useful to define each character in the text as a different object, linking each to the next. It's quite easy to redisplay the linked list of objects, for example

$$M \to a \to r \to y \to \quad \to h \to a \to d \to \quad \to a \to \quad \to l \to i \to t \to t \to l \to e \to \quad \to l \to a \to m \to b,$$

when the column width for display changes from 10 characters to 5, then to 12 because, one way or another, we need to know what character follows the one we are looking at.

On the other hand, the proliferation of large numbers of separate objects can be very space-inefficient. Figure 8.32 summarizes this purpose, and the means that *Flyweight* uses to achieve it.

*Flyweight* deals with this proliferation problem by sharing objects and using context to distinguish among their use. In our text example, we would have just one object for "a", one for "b" etc. The context would be the position. The shared objects are called "flyweights."

**Design Purpose**

Manage a large number of objects
without constructing them all.

**Design Pattern Summary**

Share representatives for the objects; use
context to obtain the effect of multiple instances.

**FIGURE 8.32** *Flyweight*

## 8.6.2 Interface For Clients of *Flyweight*

Clients usually obtain the flyweights from a factory object that aggregates them all. Let's name this aggregating object *FlyweightFactory*. When we want a flyweight with a particular characteristic, which we will refer to with the variable name *characteristic* (e.g., 'a'), we call a static method such as *getFlyweight()*, as in

   *FlyweightFactory.getFlyweight( characteristic );*

Clients need to deal with each flyweight in context, and so must possess the necessary context information. For example, the "a" object in "Mary had a little lamb" occurs in four "contexts." Thus, if the client uses a flyweight *myConcreteFlyweight* to perform an action *doAction()*, the flyweight requires a context so that it behaves as if the appropriate virtual object were doing the action (e.g., the 539th "a" in a text). The call would have the form

   *myConcreteFlyweight. doAction( context );*

*context* may be a class instance. If we want to indicate that we are dealing with the 539th "a" in a text, for example, then *myFlyweight* is an "a" object, and an integer may suffice for context, as in

   *theAConcreteFlyweight.print( 529 );*

## 8.6.3 The *Flyweight* Class Model

*Flyweight* avoids making a separate object for every fine-grained entity by using a single object for the entity, and by parameterizing the flyweight's methods to indicate the context. This is roughly the *Delegation* form (see Section 6.5.2 on page 141) because the functionality of "virtually" individual objects is delegated to the flyweight. The class model is shown in Figure 8.33.

   For example, the alternative to multiple "z" (character) objects is a single z object with methods parameterized by the context in which this z object is being used. The client needs to keep track of the context. Thus, instead of

   *zObject[3493].print()* ......       // get 3493rd "z" object and print it
we would use

   // Get the single "z" object; print in context

   *theFlyweightZObject.print( chapter, paragraph, line )* ...

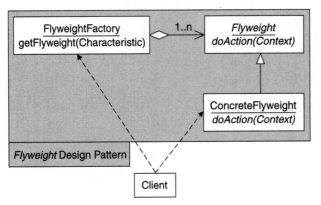

**FIGURE 8.33** *Flyweight* Class Model

where the parameters express the context. The advantage is that only one z object, *theFly-weightZObject*, has been created.

One retrieves a flyweight based on a characteristic. For example, in the text example, we could access the flyweight for "z" based on this character, as in

*ConcreteCharacterFlyweight z = FlyweightFactory.getFlyweight( 'z' );*

### 8.6.4 *Flyweight* Sequence Diagram

A sequence diagram for a *Flyweight* application has the appearance shown in Figure 8.34.

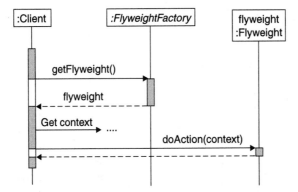

**FIGURE 8.34** Sequence Diagram for *Flyweight*

### 8.6.5 Example *Flyweight* Application: Text Magnifier

Let's consider an application that produces enlarged text for the sight-impaired. We will allow the option to color each enlarged character and to construct each one out of any individual letter, as shown in Figure 8.35.

The input is a string read from the file, together with options such as the desired color of the enlarged characters. The output is an enlargement of the string in a format

Input

---

1 ABBRA CADABBRAA ARE THE FIRST TWO OF MANY WORDS IN
  THIS FILE ...

2 Input color: RED ..... Starting character: 2 ... Ending character: 3

Output

---

```
    o        v v v      v v v
  o   o      v     v    v     v
  o   o      v     v    v     v
o       o    - R E D -  - R E D -      • • • • • •
o o o o o    v     v    v     v
o       o    v     v    v     v
o       o    v v v      v v v
```

**FIGURE 8.35**    *Flyweight* Example: Text Magnifier

determined at runtime (e.g., double spaced, or with various sizes). Because we can't show colors in this book, we will print the colors as text strings for demonstration purposes. Typically, we would want to handle capabilities such as wordwrap. If there were no space limitations, we might convert the string to a linked list, as shown in Figure 8.36.

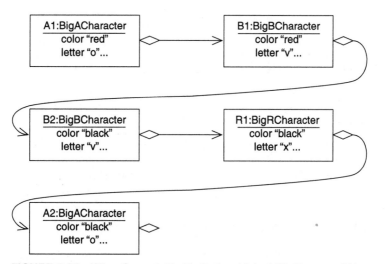

**FIGURE 8.36**    When Space is No Limitation: Linked *BigCharacter* Objects

As mentioned, an advantage of this linked list structure is the flexibility it affords in varying the text output forms.

The purpose of *Flyweight* is to eliminate the wasted storage resulting from using almost identical objects such as A1 and A2. This means that we have to maintain the state of these objects (A1 is red and points to B1, A2 is black, . . .) in some other way: i.e., without making them true separate objects. We use *context* to do this. "Context" simply refers to sufficient information to distinguish among occurrences. For example, when we use the single *BigA* object, we provide state information—the context—within the parameters used to call the methods. It should be noted that this places the burden of maintaining context on the client.

---

**DESIGN GOAL AT WORK** *Space Efficiency*

We want to avoid proliferating an object for every big character to be displayed.

---

In our Text Magnifier example, the client maintains a string "ABBRA CADABBRA.." to remember the order of characters within the text, together with a string (e.g., "blue") and a pair of integers (e.g., 24, 20) to retain color context (the characters starting at the 24th—counting from 0—through the 20th are to be blue). A realistic version of this example would involve a file containing the entire text, requiring additional context ("345th string read from file," for example), but we simplify the problem by considering only one input string.

The situation is suggested by Figure 8.37.

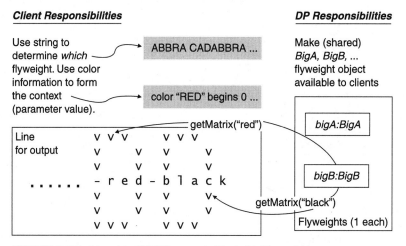

**FIGURE 8.37** Mapping "A", "B", etc. to a *BigA*, *BigB*, etc. Object

We will also allow the user to choose any letter of the alphabet with which to build the large type. For example, in Figure 8.37 the large B's were built with "v" characters.

The following is the principal use case.

1. The *application* prompts the user for a string made up of a selected list of characters.

2. The *user* enters a string at the console.

3. The *application* prompts the user to select a color.

4. The *user* enters a color, expressed in text form (e.g., "blue").

5. The *application* prompts the user to select a starting point for the coloring.

6. The *user* enters an index.

7. The *application* prompts the user to select an ending point for the coloring.

8. The *user* enters an index.

9. For each character:

   **9.1.** The *application* prompts the user to select a character that the big version is to be constructed from.

   **9.2.** The *user* enters a character.

10. The *application* displays the big version of the input string with the color name superimposed (in lieu of actual coloring).

Figure 8.38 shows typical I/O.

```
Output
```
```
Please enter string of only the following characters for enlargement:
If any other characters appear in the input, the string ABB will be assumed.
B
A
ABAABB
You chose ABAABB

You may 'color' some of the letters. Please enter any color:
red
You chose red
In what follows, if you don't type in legal entries, 1 will be assumed:
When (for first character type '1' etc.) -- do want this color to begin applying? :
2
You chose 2
When (> = your last input) do want this color to stop applying? :
4
You chose 4
What character do you want to use to build each big B?
s
You chose s.  The first character will be used.
What character do you want to use to build each big A?
t
You chose t.  The first character will be used.

    t    sss      t      t    sss    sss
   t t   s   s   t t    t t   s   s  s   s
   t t   s   s   t t    t t   s   s  s   s
  -black  -red      -red    -red  -black -black
  ttttt   s   s   ttttt  ttttt s   s  s   s
  t   t   s   s   t   t  t   t s   s  s   s
  t   t   sss     t   t  t   t sss    sss
```

**FIGURE 8.38**   Typical Output for Large Type Example

The class model for this is shown in Figure 8.39.

   The source code for this example is listed in Appendix D. In it, we obtain a line of text from the user rather than reading from a file.

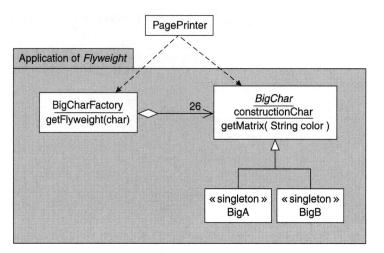

**FIGURE 8.39** *BigCharacter Flyweight* Application: Class Model

## 8.6.6 *Flyweight* in the Java API

*Enterprise JavaBeans* (EJB's) are designed to relieve the developer of common serverside tasks. One such task is the management of threads and database connections. Without EJB's, developer would have to ensure that the application does not continually create and destroy threads and database connections, thereby slowing down the application. The EJB environment uses pooling to manage this: The reuse of existing threads and database connections for new tasks. This is essentially the *Flyweight* approach.

## 8.6.7 Comments on *Flyweight*

▪ Gamma, et al. [Ga] refer to the objects that *Flyweight* deals with as "fine-grained." This means that they are too small and numerous to deserve individual "objecthood," even though we would like to treat them as such.

▪ *Flyweight* is to some extent a retreat from full object-orientation: By not treating every instance as a truly separate object, we are being "less" object-oriented, and we do thus lose some benefits. One symptom of this loss is the necessity for the client to maintain context information. Is the trade-off is worthwhile? Sometimes the answer is easy: For example, to typeset this book for various platforms, we would certainly not make every character a separate object. On the other hand, a young child's book consisting of 100 specially arranged characters might be better designed without *Flyweight*. We *would* use *Flyweight* for an application that deals with a grocery store inventory (we would not make a separate object for every bar of soap!), but we *might* make an instance of every inventory item in an exclusive jewelry store that stocks a limited number of unique jewels.

> **KEY CONCEPT** *Flyweight* Design Pattern
>
> To obtain the benefits of a large set of individual objects without efficiency penalties.

# 8.7 *PROXY*: AVOIDING UNNECESSARY OPERATIONS

## 8.7.1 The Design Purpose of *Proxy*

Suppose that a method is "expensive" to execute because it requires a time-consuming process like downloading an image from the network, accessing a large file, or drawing graphics. We can't avoid calling it because we need the method, but we certainly want to avoid having the method perform its expensive work unnecessarily. A separate but related problem is when the method requiring execution from within our application resides on a separate computer altogether: A way has to be found for our application to call that method as if it were local.

Client code should be shielded from these considerations. The main purpose and the technique of *Proxy* are summarized in Figure 8.40.

**Design Purpose**

Avoid the unnecessary execution of expensive functionality in a manner transparent to clients.

**Design Pattern Summary**

Interpose a class which is accessed in place of the one with the expensive functionality.

**FIGURE 8.40**  *Proxy*

## 8.7.2 Interface For Clients of *Proxy*

Client code is shielded from causing methods to perform unnecessary work. Instead of calling *expensiveMethod()* directly on *RealActiveClass* objects, client code is written in terms of *expensiveMethod()* of an abstract class *BaseActiveClass*. In other words, we do not write client code as follows

> *RealActiveClass realActiveObject = new RealActiveClass();    // NO*
>
> *realActiveObject.expensiveMethod();    // NO*

Instead, we write the following client code:

> *BaseActiveClass activeObject;*
>
> *. . . . .* // instantiate *activeObject* with a *Proxy* object
>
> *activeObject.expensiveMethod();    //* may not actually be expensive

### 8.7.3 The *Proxy* Class Model

Suppose again that *RealActiveClass* contains *expensiveMethod()* that we want to avoid executing unnecessarily. We introduce an abstract class *BaseActiveClass* from which *RealActiveClass* inherits. The *Proxy* design pattern calls for introducing a class, which we will call *Proxy*, also inheriting from *BaseActiveClass*. *Proxy* also contains a method called *expensiveMethod()*. It references *RealActiveClass*. This pattern is thus in the *Delegation* form (see Section 6.5.2) since *Proxy* objects delegate when the real expensive method version is needed. This is shown in Figure 8.41.

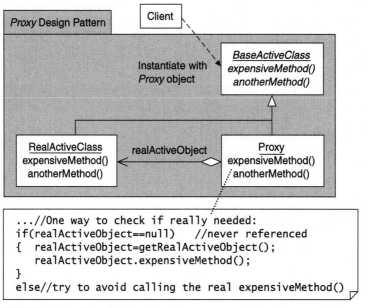

```
.../One way to check if really needed:
if(realActiveObject==null)    //never referenced
{   realActiveObject=getRealActiveObject();
    realActiveObject.expensiveMethod();
}
else//try to avoid calling the real expensiveMethod()
```

**FIGURE 8.41**   *Proxy* Design Pattern

The idea is that *Proxy*'s *expensiveMethod()* is a "fake." The client application is written in terms of *BaseActiveClass*. At runtime, the application executes with a *Proxy* object. This object effectively intercepts references that would otherwise be directly to a *RealActive-Class* object. *Proxy* does not allow *RealActiveClass* objects to be created except where necessary. In addition, *Proxy*'s version of *expensiveMethod()*, which the client calls, does not actually perform expensive parts except when necessary. As shown in the source code in Figure 8.41, when such a call is necessary, the *Proxy* object transfers the call on its *expensiveMethod()* to a call on the *expensiveMethod()* version in the *RealActiveClass* object.

### 8.7.4 *Proxy* Sequence Diagram

The sequence diagram for *Proxy* has the form shown in Figure 8.42.

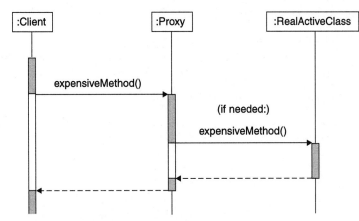

**FIGURE 8.42**  Sequence Diagram for *Proxy*

### 8.7.5  *Proxy* in the Java API

Java RMI (Remote Method Invocation) allows code residing on one platform to invoke a method of a class residing on another. Suppose that the remote functionality is an instance of a class implementing an interface *MyRemoteClass*. Running the *MyRemoteClass* file through the *rmic* translator produces the *.class* file *MyRemoteClass_stub.class*. This is a client-side proxy class that enables client-side programmers to obtain a virtual reference to the remote *MyRemoteClass* instance and invoke a method on it as if it were local. The goal here is not primarily to save unnecessary calls, but simply to enable this remote function call capability.

### 8.7.6  Example Applications of *Proxy*: *Telephone Numbers*

As one example, *RealActiveClass* could have a large disk-resident bitmap attribute. *Proxy*'s *draw()* method retrieves the bitmap only if it has not already been loaded. If *draw()* is never called, the bitmap is never retrieved from disk. Where possible, the bitmap would already be resident in memory when *draw()* is called again.

Here is an example of *Proxy* that we will follow through to code. Suppose that the application we are developing deals with telephone numbers, among other things, and that the telephone numbers are stored at a URL. Suppose that it is necessary to download all of the telephone numbers in some cases. Here is a use case that's part of the requirements.

Precondition: Telephone number information is stored at an accessible URL

1. The application prompts the user repeatedly for the options *all*, *middle*, or *quit*. (More options will be added later.)

2. Each time the user responds:

   2.1. For an "all" response, the application outputs to the console the telephone list at the fixed URL.

   2.2. For a "middle" response, the application outputs the telephone number(s) in the middle of the list (one if the list is odd in length; two otherwise). These are used for random calling.

   2.3. For a "quit" response, the application terminates.

We will add the requirements that the application. . .

   **i.** be time-efficient, and

   **ii.** outputs messages to the console describing whether or not is was necessary to retrieve records over the Internet in order to execute selected functionality.

Figure 8.43 shows typical I/O for this example.

```
Please pick a command from one of the following:
middle
all
quit
middle

= = = = = = = = = = Retrieving from the Internet = = = = = = = = = = =
9049249 John Doe      250
9049250 John Doe      251

Please pick a command from one of the following:
middle
all
quit
middle

= = = No need to retrieve from the Internet = = =
9049249 John Doe      250
9049250 John Doe      251

Please pick a command from one of the following:
middle
all
quit
all

= = = = = = = = = No need to retrieve from the Internet = = = = = = = = =
9049031 John Doe1
9049032 John Doe2
9049033 John Doe3
```

**FIGURE 8.43**  I/O of Telephone Record *Proxy* Example

Since each retrieval of the telephone list is potentially time-consuming, we want to avoid downloading it unless required to, and we generally don't want to download it more than once. The command that displays the "middle" record(s) is present to emphasize the fact that we need to have the entire list of telephone records in memory at once. The client code should be shielded from deciding whether downloading is necessary or not.

**DESIGN GOALS AT WORK**  *Efficiency* and *Reuse*

Avoid unnecessary data downloads.

The class model for this application of *Proxy* is shown in Figure 8.44.

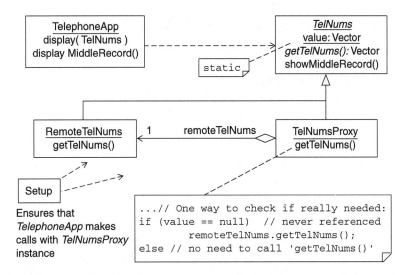

**FIGURE 8.44** *Proxy* Example

The source code for this example is given in Appendix E of this chapter.

### 8.7.7  Comments on *Proxy*

▨ *Proxy* is one of the few design patterns we'll study that promotes efficiency. It is pretty obvious that we try to avoid time-consuming operations where necessary. However, the penalties we pay for using *Proxy* can sometimes be too high. For example, if *Proxy* forces us to keep very large amounts of data in memory, and the need for this data is infrequent, we might decide instead to retrieve it every time we need it.

▨ *Proxy* promotes correctness, reusability, flexibility, and robustness. It promotes correctness by separating design and code that are independent of retrieval/efficiency from parts concerned specifically with this issue. *Proxy* promotes reusability for the same reason: Client design and code that's independent of retrieval efficiency are more likely to be reusable. Flexibility is promoted in that we can replace one module concerned with retrieval with another. (Imagine, for example, that our telephone list migrates from the Web to a disk drive on a LAN, then to a wireless-accessible medium, etc.). Robustness is promoted by the fact that *Proxy* isolates parts that check for the validity of retrieved data.

▨ As our Internet example suggests (Section 8.7.6), the growing importance of Internet-based computing increases the prevalence of *Proxy*: In fact, almost every Internet object system exploits *Proxy* because code on a platform can only be compiled with local classes, so one of those local classes is designated a proxy for remote processing.

## SUMMARY OF STRUCTURAL DESIGN PATTERNS

Figure 8.45 summarizes the design patterns discussed in this chapter.

*Structural Design Patterns* relate objects (as trees, lists etc.)

- *Façade* provides an interface to collections of objects
- *Decorator* adds to objects at runtime
- *Composite* represents trees of objects
- *Adapter* simplifies the use of external functionality
- *Flyweight* gains the advantages of using multiple instances while minimizing space penalties
- *Proxy* avoids calling expensive operations unnecessarily

**FIGURE 8.45**  Summary of Structural Patterns

# EXERCISES

**Exercise 8.1**    **Queuing Configurations**    Suppose that you are tasked to write a simulation of activities in a bank. Your purpose is to simulate bank operations with various queuing configurations. For example, Figure 8.46 shows a configuration in which customers either line up for a single teller, or join a line for a group of three tellers.

|  | **Customer being** |  |
| **Queues** | **served** | **Tellers** |
| c c c – – – – – – ▸c | | Lonny |
| | c | Juanita |
| *Key: "c"* | | |
| *== a customer* c c c c c ◂– – – – – ▸c | | Tina |
| | c | Thelma |

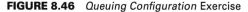

**FIGURE 8.46**  *Queuing Configuration* Exercise

The simulation code should work with any teller configuration. You are not required to design or implement the actual simulation part for this exercise.

**Part 8.1.1**  Provide a section of the class model that allows the user to create a queue configuration at runtime. When built, the simulation would then be able to execute using it.

**Part 8.1.2**  Implement the class model in Part 8.1.1, and demonstrate it with the queue configuration shown in Figure 8.46, selected at runtime.

**Part 8.1.3**  Implement functionality that prints the names of tellers (i.e., in place of what would be the simulation code). Show your output, and list your code in alphabetical order by class and method.

Evaluation criteria:

| ▩ Clarity of your class model | A = entirely clear separation of client, setup—if any required—and design pattern application |
| ▩ Clarity of your code | A = very clear code organization and documentation |

The following are errors that you should watch for in this exercise:
   *Serious*:
**1.** Incorrect design pattern.
**2.** Improper use of interface to design pattern application.

**Exercise 8.2**    **Extension of Big Characters**    This exercise concerns the *Flyweight* example in Section 8.6.

**Part 8.2.1**  Suggest improvements to the existing design and implementation aside from error checking.

**Part 8.2.2** Extend the application to handle the letters "C" and "D" on five lines of magnified characters. In other words, print words that require up to five lines of large type. Longer input should be truncated. Provide your class model and source code for classes that have been added or modified (in alphabetical order by class and method). Show sample IO.

Evaluation criteria:

| | |
|---|---|
| ▨ Clarity of your class model | A = entirely clear |
| ▨ Clarity of your code and comments | A = very clear code organization, comments and documentation |
| ▨ Effectiveness of your improvement suggestions | A = very meaningful improvements |

**Exercise 8.3**  **Inventory Subsystem**   You are responsible for designing an inventory subsystem of a large application. It is anticipated that this subsystem will eventually grow into a set of at least 10 classes. You must design the beginnings of the subsystem in a way that presents a compact, well-defined interface for the rest of the application. You can assume that the rest of the application is represented by a class *Client*. Through *main()* in *Client*, your code should execute the following use case.

1. The application displays an introduction. (All displays consist of console text.)

2. The application repeats the following until the user decides to quit.

    **2.1.** The application displays the inventory items by name and prompts the user to choose one.

    **2.2.** The user enters an item name.

    **2.3.** The application displays information about the item.

    **2.4.** The application prompts the user for a model number.

    **2.5.** The user reports the inventory of that model and item.

**Part 8.3.1** Provide a class model for this subsystem, together with the *Client* class.

**Part 8.3.2** Implement the class model and demonstrate the implementation with the use case. Show your output and your code in alphabetical order by class and method.

Evaluation criteria:

| | |
|---|---|
| ▨ Clarity of your class model | A = entirely clear separation of client, setup—if any required—and design pattern application |
| ▨ Clarity of your code | A = very clear code organization and documentation |

**Exercise 8.4**  **Construction Materials**   Consider an application that deals with the parts of planned construction. The main use case is a follows.

1. The following is repeated until the client wishes to quit.

    **1.1.** The application lists the available construction parts (windows, doors, beams) and prompts the user to choose one.

    **1.2.** The user selects a part.

2. The application displays a description of each of the construction parts that the user has chosen.

3. The application displays the price of the parts selected.

It is anticipated that these two options will expand significantly in functionality.

**Part 8.4.1** Provide a class model for this subsystem, together with the *Client* class that uses it. Design this in a way that makes it relatively easy to add new functionality to the inventory besides listing descriptions and prices.

**Part 8.4.2** Implement the class model and demonstrate the implementation with the use case. Show your output and your code in alphabetical order by class and method.

Evaluation criteria:

| | |
|---|---|
| ▨ Clarity of your class model | A = entirely clear separation of client, setup—if any required—and design pattern application |

|  |  |
|---|---|
| ▓ Clarity of your code | A = very clear code organization and documentation |

**Exercise 8.5** **Swapping Utility Classes** Implement classes *SortList1* and *SortList2* representing unrelated sorting utilities provided by different vendors. Provide each with a *Vector* attribute *list1* and *list2* respectively to represent the lists, a constructor that initializes the attribute, and a *String* key on each Vector object for sorting. Now suppose that you have a *Vector* of first names representing your friends. Design an application so that you can sort with either *SortList1* or *SortList2* as the sorting utility.

Here is a scenario:

> Enter a name or type "-stop" to complete your entries:
> Zelig (123)456-7890
> Enter a name or type "-stop" to complete your entries:
> Brad (124)656-6893
> Enter a name or type "-stop" to complete your entries:
> Vanessa (129)456-4399
> Enter a name or type "-stop" to complete your entries:
> Alec (773)436-2290
> Enter a name or type "-stop" to complete your entries:
> - stop

Select the sorting utility that you want used (enter 1 or 2):
2

> Your list, sorted by utility #2:
> Alec (773)436-2290
> Brad (124)656-6893
> Vanessa (129)456-4399
> Zelig (123)456-7890

**Part 8.5.1** Provide a class model for this sorting subsystem, together with the *Client* class that contains the names. Design this in a way that makes it relatively easy to add new functionality to the inventory besides listing alphabetically by name.

**Part 8.5.2** Implement the class model and demonstrate the implementation with the use case. Show your output and your code in alphabetical order by class and method.

Evaluation criteria:

|  |  |
|---|---|
| ▓ Clarity of your class model | A = entirely clear separation of client, setup—if any required—and design pattern application |
| ▓ Clarity of your code | A = very clear code organization and documentation |

**Exercise 8.6** **Displaying Large Images Without Wasted Time** Suppose that the application you are developing deals with displaying large images, and that each image is stored as a separate *gif* file. Suppose that we need to retrieve an image if the user selects certain functionality. Your task is to satisfy this requirement with minimal time spent retrieving images.

Here is a use case that's part of the requirements.

Precondition: Images are stored on separate *gif* files.

1. Application prompts user repeatedly for the name of an image to display.

2. For each time the user responds:

   2.1. For a "quit" response, the application terminates.

   2.2. For a non-"quit" response, the application displays the image.

   2.3. Allow for other prompts and responses to be determined in the future.

**Part 8.6.1** Provide a class model for this subsystem, together with the *Client* class that uses it.

**Part 8.6.2** Implement the class model and demonstrate the implementation with the use case. Show your output and your code in alphabetical order by class and method.

Evaluation criteria:

- Clarity of your class model    A = entirely clear separation of client, setup—if required—and design pattern application
- Clarity of your code    A = very clear code organization and documentation

**Exercise 8.7**    **Stenciled Walls**    Develop part of an application that enables you to build and visualize room interiors. It has the following features:

- Chairs and windows may be placed in the room.
- You can move your viewpoint around the room with the arrow keys: As you do, the image changes.
- For each room you can select up to 3 stencils from 30 different templates. Stencils are typically repeated many times. Figure 8.47 is an example, containing two stencils.
- You should be able to change a stencil style while you are viewing a room in perspective.

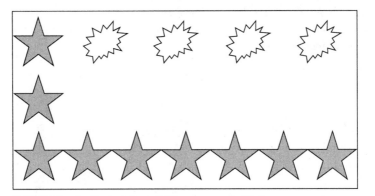

**FIGURE 8.47**    Typical Stencil Placement on a Wall

A typical perspective fragment is shown in Figure 8.48.

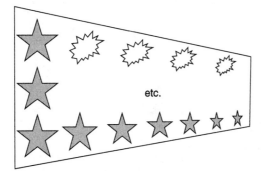

**FIGURE 8.48**    Typical Wall Perspective

**Part 8.7.1**    What design pattern(s) would you use? Explain your choices in the space provided. You are not required to include a design for the GUI enabling the user to select or place a stencil pattern. Your design should include classes *Stencil*, *Chair*, *Window* and *Room*.

**Part 8.7.2**    Show a class diagram for your design pattern application. Omit setup and client interface aspects. Include key function name(s) on the class diagram for clarity if necessary. There is *no* requirement to give pseudocode or code for any functions.

Criteria:

- Appropriateness of the design pattern(s) selected

- Clarity of your response

A = entirely appropriate design patterns applied; no unsuitable ones applied; applying an inappropriate pattern loses one grade on this criterion

A = Very clear diagrams and explanations of all of the key parts

# APPENDIX A

## SOURCE CODE FOR SECTION 8.2.4.2 "BANKING" APPLICATION (FAÇADE DESIGN PATTERN APPLICATION)

Interface *Account*:

```
package framework;

/**
 */
public interface Account
{

/*******************************************************************************************
 */
int getAccountNum();

/*******************************************************************************************
 */
int getBalance();

/*******************************************************************************************
 */
void deposit( int anAmount );
}
```

Class *AccountException*:

```
package framework;

/**
 */
public class AccountException extends Exception
{

/*******************************************************************************************
 */
public AccountException()
/******************************************************************************************/
{   super();
}

/*******************************************************************************************
 */
public AccountException( String s )
/******************************************************************************************/
{   super(s);
}

}
```

Class *BankAccount*:

```
package bankCustomers;

import framework.*;

/**
 * Simplified bank account.
 */
class BankAccount implements Account    // Note: not public
{
    private int balance = 0;
    private int number = 999;

/**********************************************************************************************
 */
public BankAccount()
/*********************************************************************************************/
{  super();
}


/**********************************************************************************************
 */
public BankAccount( int anAccountNumber )
/*********************************************************************************************/
{
  super();
  number = anAccountNumber;
}


/**********************************************************************************************
 */
public int getAccountNum()
/*********************************************************************************************/
{  return number;
}


/**********************************************************************************************
 */
public int getBalance()
/*********************************************************************************************/
{  return balance;
}


/**********************************************************************************************
 * Postcondition: 'this.balance' increased by 'aDepositAmount'
 */
public void deposit( int aDepositAmount )
/*********************************************************************************************/
{  this.balance += aDepositAmount;
}

}
```

Class *BankCustomer*:

```
package bankCustomers;

import framework.*;
import java.util.*;

/**
 */
class BankCustomer implements Customer    // Note: not public
{
```

```java
   private String name = "Not assigend yet";
   private String notes = "Nothing special known yet.";   // personalization string
   private Vector accounts = new Vector();   // the 'Account's for this object

/***********************************************************************************************
 */
public BankCustomer()
/**********************************************************************************************/
{  super();
}


/***********************************************************************************************
 */
public BankCustomer( String aName, String aNote, Vector someAccounts )
/**********************************************************************************************/
{
   this();
   name = aName;
   notes = aNote;
   accounts = someAccounts;
}


/***********************************************************************************************
 */
public String getCustomerName()
/**********************************************************************************************/
{  return name;
}


/***********************************************************************************************
 */
public String getPersonalNotes()
/**********************************************************************************************/
{  return notes;
}


/***********************************************************************************************
 * Exception: The 'Account' object returned with number 'anAccountNum' if in 'accounts',
 * otherwise throws 'AccountException'.
 */
public Account getAccount( int anAccountNum ) throws AccountException
/**********************************************************************************************/
{
   BankAccount account = null;

   // Look for an account i 'accoutns' with number 'anAccountNum'
   for( int accIndex = 0; accIndex < accounts.size(); ++accIndex )
   {
       account = (BankAccount)accounts.get( accIndex );
       if( account.getAccountNum() == anAccountNum )
             return account;
   }
   throw new AccountException( "Account not found" );   // -- if the loop terminates without return
}


/***********************************************************************************************
 */
public int getNumAccounts()
/**********************************************************************************************/
{  return accounts.size();
}

}
```

Class *BankCustomers*:

```java
package bankCustomers;

import framework.*;
import java.util.*;

/**
 * Facade for bankCustomers package.  A Singleton.
 *
 * Hard-codes the customers of this bank for demonstration purposes.
 * Each customer has an account #1 for testing.  The remaining numbers must be known to the user
 * for security: They are not output to the console at any time.
 */
public class BankCustomers    // Note "public"
{
   private static BankCustomers bankCustomers = new BankCustomers();    // singleton

   //------ Begin: Hard-coded customers for demonstration purposes

   private static Hashtable bankCustomerTable = new Hashtable();
   static   // initialize customers
   {
       // Customer Able with all of his accounts
       Vector ableAccounts = new Vector();
       ableAccounts.addElement( new BankAccount( 1 ) );    // for testing, as specified above
       ableAccounts.addElement( new BankAccount( 22 ) );
       ableAccounts.addElement( new BankAccount( 333 ) );
       bankCustomerTable.put( "Able",    // the name as key
        new BankCustomer( "Able", "Gentleman and long-time customer", ableAccounts ) );

       // Customer Betty with all of her accounts
       Vector bettyAccounts = new Vector();
       bettyAccounts.addElement( new BankAccount( 1 ) );    // for testing, as specified above
       bankCustomerTable.put( "Betty",    // the name as key
        new BankCustomer( "Betty", "Lady; new customer", bettyAccounts ) );

       // Customer Charles with all of his accounts
       Vector charlesAccounts = new Vector();
       charlesAccounts.addElement( new BankAccount( 1 ) );    // for testing, as specified above
       bankCustomerTable.put( "Charles",    // the name as key
        new BankCustomer( "Charles", "Has complained about service", charlesAccounts ) );
   }

   //------ End: Hard-code  customers for demonstration purposes

/***********************************************************************************************
 */
private BankCustomers()
/**********************************************************************************************/
{  super();
}

/***********************************************************************************************
 * Note: This returns a 'Customer' object: It can't reference any concrete subtype of 'Customer'
 * Returns/Exception: The 'Customer' object in 'customer' with name 'aName' if such a customer exists
 *                        otherwise throws a 'CustomerException'
 */
public static Customer getBankCustomer( String aName ) throws CustomerException
/**********************************************************************************************/
{
   Customer returnCustomer = (Customer)bankCustomerTable.get( aName );

   if( returnCustomer != null )    // could not find it
       return returnCustomer;
   else
       throw new CustomerException( "No customer with this name" );
}

/***********************************************************************************************
```

```java
 * To access the singleton
 */
public static BankCustomers getBankCustomers()
/***********************************************************************************************/
{   return bankCustomers;
}


/***********************************************************************************************
 * Note: This returns an 'Account 'object: It can't reference and concrete subtype of 'Account'
 * Precondition: 'aCustomer' not null
 * Returns: The 'Account' object possessed by 'aCustomer' if such an account exists
 * otherwise throws an 'AccountException'
 */
public Account getBankAccount( Customer aCustomer, int anAccountNum ) throws AccountException
/***********************************************************************************************/
{
    Account currentAccount;
    String aCustomerName = aCustomer.getCustomerName();
    String customerName = " ";

    for ( Enumeration enumeration = bankCustomerTable.keys(); enumeration.hasMoreElements(); )
        // If given customer listed
        customerName =
          ( (Customer)bankCustomerTable.get( enumeration.nextElement() ) ).getCustomerName();
        if( aCustomerName.equals( customerName ) )
            // Check if this customer has an account numbered 'anAccountNum'
            for( int j = 0; j < aCustomer.getNumAccounts(); ++j )
            {
                currentAccount = aCustomer.getAccount( j );
                if( currentAccount.getAccountNum() == anAccountNum )
                    return currentAccount;
            }

    // Could not find it
    throw new AccountException( "No customer with this name" );
}


/***********************************************************************************************
 * Postcondition: Names of customers in 'bankCustomerTable' have been printed to the console
 */
public void listCustomers()
/***********************************************************************************************/
{
    System.out.println( "These are the customers to choose from." );
    for ( Enumeration enumeration = bankCustomerTable.keys(); enumeration.hasMoreElements() ;)
    {    System.out.println( enumeration.nextElement() );
    }
}


/***********************************************************************************************
 * Postcondition: As for 'deposit( anAmount )' on 'anAccount'
 */
public void doDeposit( int anAmount, Customer aCustomer, Account anAccount )
{
    anAccount.deposit( anAmount );
    System.out.println( "Deposited " + anAmount + " into the account of " +
      aCustomer.getCustomerName() );
}


/***********************************************************************************************
 * Call to IntroMessage.display.  Demonstrates usage of class internal to the package.
 */
public static void introduceApplication()
/***********************************************************************************************/
{   IntroMessage.displayIntroductionToConsole();
}


}
```

Class *Client*: Notice again that the only class in the package *bankCustomers* that this interfaces with is *BankCustomers*.

```
import bankCustomers.*;
import java.io.*;
import framework.*;

/**
 * User of the 'bankCustomers' package via the facade.  Note that it does not (and cannot)
 * reference to any other classes in the 'bankCustomers' package.
 */
class Client
{

/*******************************************************************************************
 */
public Client()
/******************************************************************************************/
{  super();
}


/*******************************************************************************************
 * Postconditions:
 * (1) The application has asked repeatedly for a customer name from a complete list and
 *     an account number.
 * (2) The application has acknowledged each response and provided the account balance if
 *     the name and account number exist.
 * (3) The user has entered "-quit" on being asked for a customer name, and the application
 *     has terminated.
 */
public static void main( String[] args )
/******************************************************************************************/
{
    BankCustomers.introduceApplication();   // use of facade with static method

    BankCustomers bankCustomers = BankCustomers.getBankCustomers();   // the singleton
    String name = getCustomerDataFromUser();

    Customer customer = null;   // note: part of the framework, made completely accessible
    while( !name.equals( "-quit" ) )   // signal to stop this process
    {
        try
        {       // 'CustomerException' if no account
                customer = bankCustomers.getBankCustomer( name );
                // An account was found, so continue
                System.out.println( customer.getPersonalNotes() );
                // 'NumberFormatException' if not integer
                int accountNumRequested = getAccountRequestFromUser();
                // 'AccountException' if not such account
                Account account = customer.getAccount( accountNumRequested );
                System.out.println( "The balance in this account is " + account.getBalance() );
                askAboutDoingDeposit( customer, account );
                System.out.println( "The balance in this account is " + account.getBalance() );
        }
        catch( IOException e )
        {    System.out.println( "Sorry, could not read your input properly: Please retry." );
        }
        catch( CustomerException e )
        {       System.out.println( "Sorry, no such customer known: Please retry." );
        }
        catch( AccountException e )
        {       System.out.println( "Sorry, no such account known: Please retry." );
        }
        catch( NumberFormatException e )
```

```
          {         System.out.println( "Please enter an actual number: Please retry." );
          }

      System.out.println( "\nTo end this application, enter '-quit' instead of a customer name." );
      name = getCustomerDataFromUser();
   }
}
/*********************************************************************************************
 * Postconditions:
 * (1) The application has solicited a name from the user as a single string
 * (2) The application has acknowledged the input
 *
 * Return: the name as a single string
 */
public static String getCustomerDataFromUser()
/*********************************************************************************************/
{
   BankCustomers.getBankCustomers().listCustomers();   // (Note: gets the singleton again)

   BufferedReader bufReader;
   String customerName = "Unknown";   // default

   System.out.println( "Please enter customer name:" );

   try   // read the name into customerName
   {
      bufReader = new BufferedReader( new InputStreamReader( System.in ) );
      customerName = bufReader.readLine();
      System.out.println( "You chose " + customerName );
   }
   catch( IOException e )
   {   System.out.println( e ); }

   return customerName;
}

/*********************************************************************************************
 * Postconditions:  The application has ...
 * (1) ... requested an account number and mentioned 1 as a test account number
 * (2) ... obtained an acccount number -- an integer -- from the user
 * (3) ... acknowledged the input
 *
 * Return/Exception:
 * (1) The account number integer if an integer was entered
 * (2) A 'NumberFormatException' thrown if other than an integer was entered
 * (3) An 'IOException' if there was a problem with the input.
 */
public static int getAccountRequestFromUser() throws IOException, NumberFormatException
/*********************************************************************************************/
{
   BufferedReader bufReader;
   int accountNum = 0;   // default

   System.out.println
     ( "Please enter account number (for security, a list is not given ...1 is for testing:" );
   bufReader = new BufferedReader( new InputStreamReader( System.in ) );
   String accNum = bufReader.readLine();
   Integer integer = new Integer( accNum );
   System.out.println( "You chose account number " + integer.intValue() );

   return integer.intValue();
}

/*********************************************************************************************
 * Precondition: 'anAccount' is an account of 'aCustomer'
 *
```

```
 * Postconditions:
 * (1) The user has been promted for a deposit amount
 * (2) The entered amount has been added to the balance in 'anAccount' of 'aCustomer' OR
 *       The user has not supplied and integer and a 'NumberFormatException' has been thrown OR
 *       The system could not read the input and a 'IOException' was thrown
 */
public static void askAboutDoingDeposit( Customer aCustomer, Account anAccount)
 throws IOException, NumberFormatException
/*************************************************************************************************/
{
    BufferedReader bufReader;

    System.out.println "Enter a positive integer if you wish to make a deposit -- 0 otherwise:" );
    bufReader = new BufferedReader( new InputStreamReader( System.in ) );
    String amt = bufReader.readLine();
    Integer amount = new Integer( amt );
    System.out.println( "You chose amount " + amount.intValue() );

    // Make the deposit (use the singleton)
    ( BankCustomers.getBankCustomers() ).doDeposit( amount.intValue(), aCustomer, anAccount );
}

}
```

Interface *Customer*:

```
package framework;

/**
 */
public interface Customer
{

/*************************************************************************************************
 */
String getCustomerName();

/*************************************************************************************************
 * Comment about the customer to personalize the bank's service.
 */
String getPersonalNotes();

/*************************************************************************************************
 */
Account getAccount( int anAccountIndex ) throws AccountException;

/*************************************************************************************************
 */
int getNumAccounts();

}
```

Class *CustomerException*:

```
package framework;

/**
 */
public class CustomerException extends Exception
{

/*************************************************************************************************
 */
public CustomerException()
```

```
/***********************************************************************************************/
{ super();
}


/***********************************************************************************************
 */
public CustomerException(String s)
/***********************************************************************************************/
{ super(s);
}


}
```

Class *IntroMessage*:

```
package bankCustomers;

/**
 * Message introducing the application
 */
class IntroMessage
{

/***********************************************************************************************
 */
public IntroMessage()
{ super();
}


/***********************************************************************************************
 */
public static void displayIntroductionToConsole()
/***********************************************************************************************/
{
    System.out.println
      ( "Welcome the the customer / account demonstration of the Facade Design Pattern." );
    System.out.println( "....\t\t\t....\n\t....\t.... \n\t\t...." );
}

}
```

# APPENDIX B

## SOURCE CODE FOR CUSTOMER/ACCOUNT EXAMPLE IN SECTION 8.3.5 (DECORATOR DESIGN PATTERN APPLICATION)

The source code is as follows, listed alphabetically by class. The class *Account* is abstract base class for *BankingComponents* that can be added at runtime to the *Customer* object.

```
/**
 * Base class for various types of accounts
 */
public abstract class Account implements BankingComponent
{
    int accountNum = 0;
    BankingComponent nextComponent = null;  // link to next component

/*****************************************************************
 */
```

```
public Account()
/*****************************************************************************/
{  super();
}


/*****************************************************************************
 */
public void describe()
/*****************************************************************************/
{
   // First call the local describe (to be filled in for subclasses), then ...
   nextComponent.describe();
}


/*****************************************************************************
 * Make a link from this to 'aComponentToAdd'
 * Precondition: 'aComponentToAdd.nextComponent == null'
 *    (i.e., 'aComponentToAdd' not linked to a 'Component' object
 */
public void add( BankingComponent aComponentToAdd )
 throws AttemptToAddBadBankingComponentException   // we don't use this here
/*****************************************************************************/
{
   if( this.nextComponent == null )   // 'this' links to nothing
      this.nextComponent = aComponentToAdd;   // point initially to 'aComponentToAdd'
   else   // This is linked to a component.  Insert 'aComponentToAdd'
   {
      BankingComponent originalNextComponent =
       this.nextComponent;   // save component 'this' currently point to
      this.nextComponent = aComponentToAdd;   // point this to 'aComponentToAdd'
      // link 'aComponentToAdd' to prev. first component
      aComponentToAdd.add( originalNextComponent );
   }
}


/*****************************************************************************
 * For use in cloning objects in Hashtable
 */
public abstract Object clone();
/*****************************************************************************/

}
```

The class *AttemptToAddBadBankingComponentException* is as follows.

```
/**
 * Trying to add a 'Customer' object as a decoration
 */

class AttemptToAddBadBankingComponentException extends Exception
{

/*****************************************************************************
 */
public AttemptToAddBadBankingComponentException()
/*****************************************************************************/
{  super();
}

/*****************************************************************************
 */
public AttemptToAddBadBankingComponentException( String s )
/*****************************************************************************/
{  super(s);
}

}
```

Next is the *BankingComponent* interface.

```
/**
 * Base for the substance and its decorations
 */
interface BankingComponent
/******************************************************************************/
{

/******************************************************************************
 * Make a link from this to 'aBankingComponentToAdd'
 */
void add( BankingComponent aBankingComponentToAdd )
 throws AttemptToAddBadBankingComponentException;

/******************************************************************************
 * Postcondition: A description of this has been shown on the console.
 */
void describe();

}
```

The *CDAccount* class:

```
/**
 * Certificate of Deposit
 */
public class CDAccount extends Account
{
    final int DEFAULT_DURATION = 4;  // term of this CD in years
    static int numberOfCDAccountsMade = 0;   // to generate a unique account number

/******************************************************************************
 * Postcondition: 'this.accountNum' has been assigned a number unique for this execution
 */
public CDAccount()
/******************************************************************************/
{
    super();
    this.accountNum = CDAccount.numberOfCDAccountsMade;
    ++CDAccount.numberOfCDAccountsMade;   // for next new CDAccount
}

/******************************************************************************
 */
public Object clone()
/******************************************************************************/
{  return new CDAccount();
}

/******************************************************************************
 */
public int getDuration()
/******************************************************************************/
{  return DEFAULT_DURATION;
}

/******************************************************************************
 * Postcondition: The details of this CD have been output to the console
 */
public void describe()
/******************************************************************************/
{
    super.describe();
```

```
      System.out.println
        ( "CD account no. " + accountNum + " with duration " + getDuration() + "." );
}

}
```

The *CheckAccount* class:

```
/**
 */
public class CheckAccount extends Account
{
    private int lastCheckNumPrinted = 12345;   // dummy for demonstration
    static int numberOfCheckAccountsMade = 0;   // to generate a unique checking account number

    /*******************************************************************************
     * Postconditions:
     * (1) 'accountNum' == 'CheckAccount.numberOfCheckAccountsMadC'
     * (2) 'CheckAccount.numberOfCheckAccountsMade' has been incremented
     */
    public CheckAccount()
    /******************************************************************************/
    {
        super();
        accountNum = CheckAccount.numberOfCheckAccountsMade;
        ++CheckAccount.numberOfCheckAccountsMade;   // for the next new CheckAccount
    }

    /*******************************************************************************
     * Postcondition: The details of this account have been output to the console
     */
    public void describe()
    /******************************************************************************/
    { System.out.println
        ( "Check account number " + accountNum +
        " with last check printed " + lastCheckNumPrinted + "." );
        super.describe();
    }

    /*******************************************************************************
     */
    public CheckAccount( int aLastCheckNumPrinted )
    /******************************************************************************/
    {
        super();
        lastCheckNumPrinted = aLastCheckNumPrinted;
    }

    /*******************************************************************************
     */
    public Object clone()
    /******************************************************************************/
    { return new CheckAccount();
    }

}
```

The *Client* class:

```
/**
 * Note: This client interfaces with a 'BankingComponent' object within the application
 * of Decorator.
 */
class Client
```

```
{
   public BankingComponent customerWithAccounts = null;   // -- that this client uses

/********************************************************************************
 */
public Client()
/*******************************************************************************/
{  super();
}


/********************************************************************************
 * Postcondition: The particulars of 'this' have been output to the console
 */
public void describeAll()
/*******************************************************************************/
{
   System.out.println( "Calling for a description of one Component: " );
   this.customerWithAccounts.describe();
}

}
```

The *Customer* class:

```
/**
 */
class Customer implements BankingComponent
{
/********************************************************************************
 */
public Customer()
/*******************************************************************************/
{  super();
}


/********************************************************************************
 * Postcondition: The details of 'this' have been output to the console
 */
public void describe()
/*******************************************************************************/
{  System.out.println( "Customer decription: Jonas Smith" );   // dummy for demo
}


/********************************************************************************
 * Note: Should not be called because 'Customer 'objects can't add a 'Component'
 */
public void add( BankingComponent aComponentToAdd )
 throws AttemptToAddBadBankingComponentException
/*******************************************************************************/
{  throw new AttemptToAddBadBankingComponentException();
}

}
```

The *SavingsAccount* class:

```
/**
 */
public class SavingsAccount extends Account
{
   final int DEMONSTRATION_INTEREST_RATE = 4;
   static int numberOfSavingsAccountsMade = 0;

/********************************************************************************
```

```
 * Postconditions:
 *  (1) 'accountNum' == 'SavingsAccount.numberOfSavingsAccountsMade'
 *  (2)  'SavingsAccount.numberOfSavingsAccountsMade' has been incremented
 */
public SavingsAccount()
/***************************************************************************/
{
   super();
   accountNum = SavingsAccount.numberOfSavingsAccountsMade;
   ++SavingsAccount.numberOfSavingsAccountsMade;   // for the next new account
}


/***************************************************************************
 */
public int getInterestRate()
/***************************************************************************/
{  return DEMONSTRATION_INTEREST_RATE;
}


/***************************************************************************
 * Postcondition: the details of 'this' have been output to the console
 */
public void describe()
/***************************************************************************/
{  System.out.println
     ( "Savings account number " + accountNum +
     " with interest rate " + getInterestRate() + "." );
   super.describe();
}


/***************************************************************************
 */
public Object clone()
/***************************************************************************/
{  return new SavingsAccount();
}

}
```

The *Setup* class:

```
import java.io.*;
import java.util.*;

/**
 * Controls this application.
 */
class Setup
{
   // The account types available
   static Hashtable tableOfAccountTypes = new Hashtable();
   static
   {
   tableOfAccountTypes.put( "Savings account", new SavingsAccount() );
   tableOfAccountTypes.put( "Checking account", new CheckAccount() );
   tableOfAccountTypes.put( "CD account", new CDAccount() );
   }

/***************************************************************************
 */
public Setup()
/***************************************************************************/
{  super();
}

/***************************************************************************
```

```
 * Postconditions:
 * (1) The application has repeatedly requested desired account types for a standard customer
 * (2) The user has responded until typing "quit"
 * (3) The application has output to the console information on the customer and the accounts
selected
 */
public static void main( String[] args )
/****************************************************************************/
{
    // Set up the Decorator application

    Customer customer = new Customer();    // this will be the customer the client will deal with
    Account account = null;
    Account tempAccount = null;

    try
    {
        // Get and link in the first account in any case
        System.out.println( "Select an account: Incorrect entries assume checking account." );
        account = getAccountToAdd();
        account.add( customer );    // link from account to customer

        // Get as many additional accounts as desired until "quit" typed

        BufferedReader bufReader;
        bufReader = new BufferedReader( new InputStreamReader( System.in ) );
        System.out.println
          ( "Type any character if you want to add another account: Otherwise 'quit'." );
        String response = bufReader.readLine();

        while( !response.equals( "quit" ) )
        {
            tempAccount = account;   // keep to link back below
            account = getAccountToAdd();
            account.add( tempAccount );    // account linked to what was there before

            System.out.println
              ( "Type any character if you want to add another account: Otherwise 'quit'." );
            response = bufReader.readLine();
        }
    }
    catch( AttemptToAddBadBankingComponentException e )
    {   System.out.println( "Attempt to decorate with bad component" );
    }
    catch( IOException e )
    {   System.out.println( e ); }


    // Create a client and have it point to the last account linked in
    Client clientOfDecorator = new Client();
    clientOfDecorator.customerWithAccounts = account;

    clientOfDecorator.describeAll();    // now the client uses the application of Decorator
}

/****************************************************************************
 * Postcondition: The user has been presented with a list of account types
 *   in 'tableOfAccountTypes'.
 *
 * Return: If the user has selected one, this returns and object of the class
 *         otherwise it returns a 'CheckAccount' object.
 */
public static Account getAccountToAdd()
/****************************************************************************/
{
    // List available account types for user
    System.out.println( "\nPlease select an account type from the following." );
    for( Enumeration enumeration = tableOfAccountTypes.keys(); enumeration.hasMoreElements() ;)
```

```
        System.out.println( enumeration.nextElement() );

    // Get an account type

    BufferedReader bufReader;
    String accountType = "Account type not assigned yet";
    System.out.println( "Please enter account type:" );

    try
    {
        bufReader = new BufferedReader( new InputStreamReader( System.in ) );
        accountType = bufReader.readLine();
        System.out.println( "You chose " + accountType + "\n" );
    }
    catch( IOException e )
    {   System.out.println( e ); }

    // Return an Account object
    Account account = (Account)tableOfAccountTypes.get( accountType );
    if( account != null )   // user chose legitimate type
        return (Account)account.clone();
    else        // user mistyped: Default to checking
        return new CheckAccount();
}

}
```

# APPENDIX C

## *SOURCE CODE FOR BANK/TELLER EXAMPLE IN SECTION 8.4.5 (COMPOSITE DESIGN PATTERN APPLICATION)*

The class code for the Personnel example is listed next in alphabetical order. This is the class *Clerk*.

```
/**
  * Clerks: have no reports
  */
class Clerk extends Employee
{
/****************************************************************
 */
public Clerk( String aName )
/****************************************************************/
{
    this();
    name = aName;
}


/****************************************************************
 * Postcondition: as for 'Employee.stateName()'
 */
public void stateName()
/****************************************************************/
{
    // do processing special to clerk naming here .... (omitted)
    super.stateName();
}


/****************************************************************
```

```
 * Postcondition: 'title' string is "Clerk"
 */
public Clerk()
/*************************************************************/
{ title = "Clerk";
}

}
```

The following is code for *Client*. Note that it interfaces only with the class *Employee*.

```
import java.io.*;

/**
 * Class that uses the organization chart.  Aggregates an 'Employee' object , which is its interface
 * to structores of emplyees.
 */
class Client
{
    // This class relates to a specific 'Employee'
    public static Employee employee;

    /*************************************************************
     * Note: This is where the client does its work with the Employee object
     */
    public static void doClientTasks()
    /*************************************************************/
    {
        // Do work with this.employee ... (omitted)
        employee.stateName();
    }
}
```

Here is the code for the base class *Employee*. We would use an interface instead if we are willing to remove the substantive method code.

```
/**=======================================================================
 * Base class for org chart
 */
abstract class Employee
//*=====================================================================/
{
    String name = "not assigned yet";
    String title = "not assigned yet";

    /*************************************************************
     * Postcondition: 'title' and 'name' of this employee have been output to the console.
     */
    public void stateName()
    /*********************************************************/
    { System.out.println( title + " " + name );
    }

}
```

Here is code for the class *Manager*:

```
/**=======================================================================
 * Manager class has reports
 */
class Manager extends Supervisor
//*=====================================================================/
```

```
{
/*******************************************************************
 */
public Manager( String aName )
/******************************************************************/
{
    this();
    name = aName;
}


/*******************************************************************
 * Postcondition: 'title' and 'name' of this employee have been output to the console.
 */
public void stateName()
/******************************************************************/
{
    // do processing special to manager naming ...
    super.stateName();
}

/*******************************************************************
 * Postcondition: title set to "Manager"
 */
public Manager()
/******************************************************************/
{
    super();
    title = "Manager";
}

}
```

Next is the code for *President*. Note that *President* is a singleton.

```
/**
  * Presidents have reports.  This is a singleton class.
  */
class President extends Supervisor
{
    private static President president = new President();   // singleton

/*******************************************************************
 */
private President( String aName )
/******************************************************************/
{
    this();
    name = aName;
}

/*******************************************************************
 * Postcondition: 'title' and 'name' of this employee have been output to the console.
 */
public void stateName()
/******************************************************************/
{
    // Do processing special to presidential naming ...
    super.stateName();
}


/*******************************************************************
 * Postcondition: 'title' is "President"
 */
private President( )
/******************************************************************/
{
```

```
      super();
      title = "President";
}

/****************************************************************
 * Postcondition: 'name' is 'aName'
 * Returns: 'president' singleton
 */
public static President getPresident( String aName )
/***************************************************************/
{
    president.name = aName;
    return President.president;
}

}
```

Here is the *Setup* code:

```
import java.io.*;

/**
  * Sets up the org chart and intiates execution.
  */
class Setup
{

/****************************************************************
 * Postcondition: The 'title' and 'name' of the employees have been output to the console
 *      beginning with the president, then each of his or her sub-organizations recursively.
 *      The specification for this particualr organiation chart are in the notes,
 *
 * Note: This is performed by a client object whose  interface with the organization structure
 * is an 'Employee' object.
 */
public static void main( String args[] )
/***************************************************************/
{
    // Make manager Able's organization
    Teller lonny = new Teller( "Lonny" );
    Clerk cal = new Clerk( "Cal" );
    Manager able = new Manager( "Able" );
    able.add( lonny);
    able.add( cal);

    // Make manager Becky's organization
    Teller juanita = new Teller( "Juanita" );
    Teller tina = new Teller( "Tina" );
    Teller thelma = new Teller( "Thelma" );
    Manager becky = new Manager( "Becky" );
    becky.add( juanita);
    becky.add( tina );
    becky.add( thelma);

    // Create the president's direct reports
    President pete = President.getPresident( "Pete" );
    pete.add( able );
    pete.add( becky );

    // Initiate client
    Client.employee = pete;
    Client.doClientTasks();
}

}
```

This is the code for the nonleaf node class *Supervisor*:

```java
import java.util.*;

/**
 * Base class for employees with reports.
 */
abstract class Supervisor extends Employee
{
    protected Vector directReports = new Vector();   // employees reporting to this 'Supervisor'

    /***************************************************************
     * Postcondition: the title and name of all of the reports of this employee (if any)
     * have been recursively output to new lines on the console.
     */
    public void stateName()
    /***************************************************************/
    {
        super.stateName();    // print name of this employee first
        if( directReports.size() > 0 )   // be sure there are elements
            for( int i = 0; i < directReports.size(); ++i )
                ( (Employee)directReports.elementAt( i ) ).stateName();
    }

    /***************************************************************
     * Postcondition: 'anEmployee' has been added to the employees reporting
     *         to this employee ('this.directReports').
     */
    public void add( Employee anEmployee )
    /***************************************************************/
    { this.directReports.addElement( anEmployee );
    }

}
```

This is the code for *Teller*:

```java
/**
 * Tellers have no reports
 */
class  Teller extends Employee
{

    /***************************************************************
     */
    public Teller( String aName )
    /***************************************************************/
    {
        this();
        name = aName;
    }

    /***************************************************************
     * Postcondition: the title and name of this employee appear on the console.
     */
    public void stateName()
    /***************************************************************/
    {
        // do processing special to teller naming ...
        super.stateName();
    }

    /***************************************************************
     * Postcondition: title set to "Teller"
```

```
   */
public Teller()
/**********************************************************/
{  title = "Teller";
}


}
```

# APPENDIX D

## *SOURCE CODE FOR TEXT MAGNIFIER EXAMPLE IN SECTION 8.6.5 (FLYWEIGHT DESIGN PATTERN APPLICATION)*

The Class *BigA*:

```
/** ======================================================= C L A S S   BigA
 * Flyweight for large type "A" will be made with this singleton
 */
class BigA extends BigChar
{
   private static BigA bigA = new BigA( 'A' );    // Singleton: default letter to construct with

/*************************************************** C O N S T R U C T O R
 */
private BigA()
{  super();
}

/*************************************************** C O N S T R U C T O R
 */
private BigA( char aConstructionCharacter )
{  super( aConstructionCharacter );
}

/*********************************************** M E T H O D  getMatrixForm
 * Returns:
 * "matrix" filled in with a big version of "A", made from the letter 'constructionCharacter'
 * Across line 3 is superimposed "-xxxxx" where xxxxx are the first
 * 'BigChar.MAX_COLOR_CHARACTERS' letters of 'aColor'
 */
public char[][] getMatrixForm( String aColor )
{
   char c = constructionCharacter;    // for brevity

   // Fill in the actual big letter. line by line
   matrix[0][2] = c;
   matrix[1][1] = c; matrix[1][3] = c;
   matrix[2][1] = c; matrix[2][3] = c;
   matrix[3][0] = c; matrix[3][4] = c;
   matrix[4][0] = c; matrix[4][1]=c; matrix[4][2] = c; matrix[4][3] = c; matrix[4][4] = c;
   matrix[5][0] = c; matrix[5][4] = c;
   matrix[6][0] = c; matrix[6][4] = c;

   // Superimpose the color characters across the middle
   matrix[3][0] = '-';    // required to precede the color characters
   for( int i = 1; i < BigChar.MATRIX_WIDTH; ++i )    // go all the way across
      if( i <= aColor.length() )   // there is a color character to pick up
         matrix[ 3 ][ i ] = aColor.charAt( i -1 );   // fill in the next color character
      else
         matrix[ 3 ][ i ] = ' ';  // pad on right with blanks
   return matrix;
```

```
}

/***************************************************** M E T H O D  getBigA
 * Accessor of the singleton
 */
public static BigA getBigA()
{  return bigA;
}

}
```

The class *BigB*:

```
/** ========================================================= C L A S S  BigB
 * Flyweight for large type "B" will be made with this singleton
 */

class BigB extends BigChar
{
   private static BigB bigB = new BigB( 'B' );   // singleton with default construction character

/***************************************************** C O N S T R U C T O R
 */
private BigB()
{  super();
}

/***************************************************** C O N S T R U C T O R
 */
private BigB( char aConstructionCharacter )
{  super( aConstructionCharacter );
}

/***************************************************** M E T H O D  getMatrixForm
 * Returns:
 * "matrix" filled in with a big version of "B", made from the letter 'constructionCharacter'
 * Across line 3 is superimposed "-xxxxx" where xxxxx are the first
 * 'BigChar.MAX_COLOR_CHARACTERS' letters of 'aColor'
 */
public char[][] getMatrixForm( String aColor )
{
   char c = constructionCharacter;   // for brevity

   // Fill in the actual big letter. line by line
   matrix[0][0] = c; matrix[0][1] = c; matrix[0][2] = c;
   matrix[1][0] = c; matrix[1][4] = c;
   matrix[2][0] = c; matrix[2][4] = c;
   matrix[3][0] = c; matrix[3][1] = c;
   matrix[4][0] = c; matrix[4][4] = c;
   matrix[5][0] = c; matrix[5][4] = c;
   matrix[6][0] = c; matrix[6][1] = c; matrix[6][2] = c;

   // Superimpose the color characters across the middle
   matrix[3][0] = '-';   // required to precede the color characters as in "-red"
   for( int i = 1; i < BigChar.MATRIX_WIDTH; ++i )   // go all the way across
      if( i <= aColor.length() )   // there is a color character to pick up
         matrix[ 3 ][ i ] = aColor.charAt( i -1 );  // fill in the next color character
      else
         matrix[ 3 ][ i ] = ' ';  // pad on right with blanks

   return matrix;
}

/***************************************************** M E T H O D  BigB
 * Accessor for the singleton
```

```
    */
public static BigB getBigB()
{  return bigB;
}


}
```

The class *BigChar*:

```
/** ========================================================== C L A S S  BigChar
 * Base class for all large type characters
 */
abstract class BigChar
{
    // Array of characters to show the letter
    public final static int MATRIX_WIDTH = 6;   // number of columns
    public final static int MATRIX_HEIGHT = 7;   // number of rows
    protected char[][] matrix = new char[ MATRIX_HEIGHT ][ MATRIX_WIDTH ];
    {  for( int i = 0; i < MATRIX_HEIGHT; ++i )
          for( int j = 0; j < MATRIX_WIDTH; ++j )
              matrix[ i ][ j ] = ' ';
    }

    protected char constructionCharacter = 'X';   // letter that this big letter is constructed from
    protected String color = "black";   // won't actually color the letter: Superimpose a string only

/*************************************************** C O N S T R U C T O R
 */
public BigChar()
{  super();
}

/*************************************************** C O N S T R U C T O R
 * Postcondition: constructorCharacter == aConstructorCharacter;
 */
public BigChar( char aConstructionCharacter )
{
    super();
    constructionCharacter = aConstructionCharacter;
}

/*************************************************** M E T H O D  setColor
 * Postcondition:
 * color == aColor if aColor.length <= 4; otherwise color == first 4 characters of aColor
 */
public void setColor( String aColor )
{
    if( aColor.length() <= 4 )
        color = aColor;
    else
        try
        {
            color = aColor.substring( 0, 3 );
            System.out.println( "The color abbreviated because not enough space." );
        }
        catch( IndexOutOfBoundsException o )
        {
            System.out.println
              ( "IndexOutOfBoundsException in BigChar(String aColor) -- should never occur." );
            System.exit( 0 );
        }
}

/*************************************************** M E T H O D  setConstructionCharacter
 */
```

```
public void setConstructionCharacter( char aConstructionCharacter )
{  constructionCharacter = aConstructionCharacter;
}


/*************************************************** M E T H O D  getMatrixForm
 */
public abstract char[][] getMatrixForm( String aColor );


}
```

The class *BigCharFactory*:

```
/** ======================================================== C L A S S  BigCharFactory
 * Stores the flyweights and provides them on request.
 */

import java.util.*;

abstract class BigCharFactory
{
    private static Hashtable flyweights = new Hashtable();
    static   // access by correspnding character
    {   flyweights.put( "A", BigA.getBigA() );    // the singleton is the only instance
        flyweights.put( "B", BigB.getBigB() );
        /* etc. (there would be many more in reality) */
    }

/*************************************************** C O N S T R U C T O R
 */
public BigCharFactory()
{  super();
}

/*************************************************** M E T H O D  getFlyweight
 * Returns: The 'BigChar' object in 'flyweights' corresponding to 'aChar'.
 */
public static BigChar getFlyweight( char aChar )
{
    // Convert aChar to a String
    char[] aCharAsArray = { aChar };
    String aCharAsString = new String( aCharAsArray );

    // Retrieve the flyweight based on this string
    return (BigChar)BigCharFactory.flyweights.get( aCharAsString );
}

/*************************************************** M E T H O D  getFlyweights
 * Returns: 'flyweights'
 */
public static Hashtable getFlyweights()
{  return flyweights;
}

}
```

The class *PagePrinter*:

```
/** ======================================================== C L A S S  PagePrinter
 * Gets strings and prints large character form.
 * Client of the Flyweight design pattern application (Note: no separate setup required.)
 */

import java.io.*;
```

```
import java.util.*;

class PagePrinter
{
    // 2D array for constructing big characters so as to print them
    private final static int PAGE_WIDTH = 70;
    private final static int PAGE_LENGTH = 10;    // enough to allow more than one big line for now
    private static char[][] pageReadyForPrinting = new char[ PAGE_LENGTH ][ PAGE_WIDTH ];
    static   // initialize
    { for( int i = 0; i < PAGE_LENGTH; ++i )
         for( int j = 0; j < PAGE_WIDTH; ++j )
            pageReadyForPrinting[ i ][ j ] = ' ';
    }

    // Option to give "color" to the large print letters
    static String color= "black";  // color for chars. betw. startColorIndex and endColorIndex
    static int startColorIndex = 0;   // first index in input string where "color" will apply
    static int endColorIndex = 0;  // last index in input string where "color" will apply

    private static final int SPACING_BETWEEN_BIG_CHARACTERS = 2;

/*************************************************** C O N S T R U C T O R
 */
public PagePrinter()
{ super();
}

/***************************************************** M E T H O D  formPageReadyForPrinting
 * Postconditions:
 * 'formPageReadyForPrinting' conts. as many large versions of chars. as possible of 'anInputString'
 * w. 'currentColor' written across those starting at 'startColorIndex' ending at 'endColorIndex'
 * -- and "black" otherwise.  The large characters appear starting from the top right.
 */
public static void formPageReadyForPrinting( String anInputString )
{
    String currentColor = "black";    // -- of the current character

    // Form the 2D char array ("matrix") for output

    char character = 'x';
    BigChar bigChar;
    int numBigCharsOnALine =    // the number that will fit on the width of the console
     (int)( PAGE_WIDTH / ( BigChar.MATRIX_WIDTH + SPACING_BETWEEN_BIG_CHARACTERS ) );

    // Try to insert the cahracters of 'anInputString' one at a time
    for( int stringIndex = 0;
     stringIndex < Math.min( anInputString.length(), numBigCharsOnALine );   // whichever occurs first
     ++stringIndex )
    {
        // Isolate the current BigChar object
        character = anInputString.charAt( stringIndex );   // get the current character
        bigChar = BigCharFactory.getFlyweight( character );   // get the corr. large type version
        // Insert into slot for next bigChar
        if( bigChar != null)
        {
            if( ( stringIndex >= startColorIndex ) && ( stringIndex <= endColorIndex ) )
                currentColor = PagePrinter.color;   // applies within chosen range
            else
                currentColor = "black";   // default

            // Insert each big character into pageReadyForPrinting
            insert( bigChar.getMatrixForm( currentColor ), 0,
             stringIndex*( BigChar.MATRIX_WIDTH + SPACING_BETWEEN_BIG_CHARACTERS ) );
```

```
        }
        else
            System.out.println( "No big type for character " + character );
    }
}

/*********************************************** M E T H O D  getCharacterCompositionForEachBigChar
 * Each big character will be constructed with a letter of the user's choice
 *
 * Postconditions: For each character listed in 'BigCharFactory.flyweights':
 * (a) The user has been queried for a construction character (used to actually form the big letter)
 * (b) The user's response has been saved in each 'BigChar' singleton flyweight
 */
private static void getCharacterCompositionForEachBigChar()
{
    BufferedReader bufReader = new BufferedReader( new InputStreamReader( System.in ) );
    String keyToBigChar = " ";
    String input = " ";

    // Go through the list in 'BigCharFactory.flyweights'
    for( Enumeration enumeration = BigCharFactory.getFlyweights().keys();
      enumeration.hasMoreElements() ;)
    {
        // e.g., "B" for the corresponding BigChar
        keyToBigChar =  (String)enumeration.nextElement();

        System.out.println
          ( "What character do you want to use to build each big " + keyToBigChar + "?" );
        try
        {
            input = bufReader.readLine();
            System.out.println( "You chose " + input + ".  The first character will be used." );
            // Get the singelton flyweight for this choice
            BigChar bigCharSingleton =  (BigChar)BigCharFactory.getFlyweights().get( keyToBigChar );
            // set what to be built with
            bigCharSingleton.setConstructionCharacter( input.charAt( 0 ) );
        }
        catch( IOException e )
        { System.out.println( e ); }
    }
}

/*********************************************** M E T H O D  getColorRequirements
 * Postconditions:
 * (1) The user has been prompted to give start, stop and color information
 * (2) 'startColorIndex' is the index in the input string -- provided by the user
 * -- at which the color applies
 * (3) 'stopIndex' is the index in the input string -- provided by the user
 * -- at which the color no longer applies
 * (4) 'color' is the user's desired color between these two indices
 */
private static void getColorRequirements()
{
    try
    {
        BufferedReader bufReader = new BufferedReader( new InputStreamReader( System.in ) );

        // Select color
        System.out.println( "You may 'color' some of the letters.  Please enter any color:" );
        color = bufReader.readLine();
        System.out.println( "You chose " + color );

        // Select start and end points.  These are set to 0 and 0 resp. as defaults in case the user
        // fails to enter legitimate entries.
        System.out.println
```

```
                  ( "In what follows, if you don't type in legal entries, 1 will be assumed:");
            startColorIndex = 0;
            endColorIndex = 0;

            // Select start point, counting from 1
            System.out.println
              ( "When (for first character type '1' etc.) -- do want this color to begin applying? :" );
            String input = bufReader.readLine();
            System.out.println( "You chose " + input );
            startColorIndex = ( new Integer( input ) ).intValue() - 1;   // exception if not an integer

            // Select end point, counting from 1
            System.out.println
              ( "When (>= your last input) do want this color to stop applying? :" );
            input = bufReader.readLine();
            System.out.println( "You chose " + input );
            endColorIndex = ( new Integer( input ) ).intValue() - 1;   // exception if not an integer
            if( endColorIndex < startColorIndex + 1 ) // incorrect
            {
                System.out.println( "Sorry, but both indices will be set to zero." );
                endColorIndex = startColorIndex = 0;
            }

        }
    catch( IOException e )
    {   System.out.println( e ); }
    catch( NumberFormatException e )
    {   System.out.println( e ); }
}

/***************************************************** M E T H O D  getString
 * Note: In reality, the text to be translated into large type would be obtained from a text file.
 * Here we will obtain a single line from the user for demonstration.
 *
 * Returns: String typed in by user if characters are only those in' BigCharFactory.flyweights'
 *          otherwise the string "ABB"
 */
private static String getString()
{
    BufferedReader bufReader;
    String returnString = " ";

    System.out.println( "Please enter string of only the following characters for enlargement:" );
    System.out.println
      ( "If any other characters appear in the input, the string ABB will be assumed." );

    for( Enumeration enumeration = BigCharFactory.getFlyweights().keys();
      enumeration.hasMoreElements() ;)
        System.out.println( enumeration.nextElement() );

    // Get the input string
    try
    {
        bufReader = new BufferedReader( new InputStreamReader( System.in ) );
        returnString = bufReader.readLine();
        System.out.println( "You chose " + returnString + "\n" );
    }
    catch( IOException e )
    {   System.out.println( e ); }
    // Check that the string input is composed of legitimate characters: otherwise substitute "ABB"
    for( int i = 0; i < returnString.length(); ++i )
        if( BigCharFactory.getFlyweight( returnString.charAt( i ) ) == null )   // not a permissable
        {
            System.out.println
```

```
                ( "Illegal characters were input: The string 'ABB' will be used instead." );
                return "ABB";   // replace by default
        }

    return returnString;   // input was legitimate
}

/*************************************************** M E T H O D  main
 * Postconditions:  The application has ...
 * (1) ... listed the permissible characters
 * (2) ... requested a string from the user
 * (3) ... used a default string if the user has made a mistake (see 'getString()' for details)
 * (4) ... obtained from the user the color and starting place and ending place for the color
 * (5) ... obtained from the user the characters required to build the large type characters
 * (6) ... output as many characters as will fit in 'pageReadyForPrinting' of the required string
 *           using the requestedindividual characters, with the requested colors writen across them
 */
public static void main( String[] args )
{
    String inputString = getString();   // get the string to be converted

    String currentColor = "black";    // -- of the current character
    getColorRequirements();
    getCharacterCompositionForEachBigChar();   // the letter used to actually consruct large type

    // Form the 2D char array ("matrix") for output
    formPageReadyForPrinting( inputString );

    printPageToConsole();
    // end main()

/*************************************************** M E T H O D
 * Postcondition: The content of 'pageReadyForPrinting' is on the console
 */
public static void printPageToConsole()
{
    for( int i = 0; i < PAGE_LENGTH; ++i )
    {
        System.out.println();
        for( int j = 0; j < PAGE_WIDTH; ++j )
            System.out.print( pageReadyForPrinting[ i ][ j ] );
    }
}

/*************************************************** M E T H O D  insert
 * Postcondition: The chars. of 'a2DArray' have be inserted into 'pageReadyForPrinting' as follows.
 * They are placed right and down from '[aRowPlace][aColPlace]' for as long as this covers
 * 'pageReadyForPrinting'
 * -- otherwise each out-of-range character is ignored and a console message is generated.
 */
public static void insert( char[][] a2DArray, int aRowPlace, int aColPlace )
{
    for( int rowIndex = 0; rowIndex < a2DArray.length; ++rowIndex )
        for( int colIndex = 0; colIndex < a2DArray[0].length; ++colIndex )
            // Check that the element is in range of pageReadyForPrinting; insert if so
            if( aRowPlace + rowIndex < PAGE_LENGTH && aColPlace + colIndex < PAGE_WIDTH )
                pageReadyForPrinting[ aRowPlace + rowIndex ][ aColPlace + colIndex ] =
                a2DArray[ rowIndex ][ colIndex ];
            else
                System.out.println
                  ( "Insufficient space for all letters as requested. (PagePrinter.insert())" );
}

}
```

## SOURCE CODE FOR "TELEPHONE NUMBERS" EXAMPLE IN SECTION 8.7.6 (PROTOTYPE DESIGN PATTERN APPLICATION)

The classes are given in alphabetical order. The *RemoteTelNums* class:

```java
/** ========================================================= C L A S S   RemoteTelNums
 * Access to the URL containing the telephone information
 */

import java.net.*;
import java.io.*;
import java.util.*;

class RemoteTelNums extends TelNums
{
   public static final String URL_CONTAINING_THE_TEL_RECORDS =
   "http://metcs.bu.edu/~ebraude/SoftwareDesignBook/telephones.txt";   // location of the data
/*************************************************** C O N S T R U C T O R
 */
public RemoteTelNums()
{  super();
}


/**************************************************** M E T H O D  getTelNums

 * Postcondition: The 'String' objects in 'TelNums.value' consist of the records
 *  at URL 'URL_CONTAINING_THE_TEL_RECORDS' if a connection to
 * 'URL_CONTAINING_THE_TEL_RECORDS' was established.
 *
 * Design note: Data retrieved from the Internet
 */
public void getTelNums()
{
   System.out.println
   ( "=================== Retrieving from the Internet ===================" );

   BufferedReader urlReader = null;

   try
   {
      TelNums.value = new Vector();   // from now on not 'null'

      // Prepare to read from the URL
      URL url = new URL( URL_CONTAINING_THE_TEL_RECORDS );
      URLConnection urlConnection = url.openConnection();
      urlReader = new BufferedReader
      ( new InputStreamReader( urlConnection.getInputStream() ) );

      // Read the telephone records
      String lineFromURL = "";
      while( lineFromURL != null )   // read until no more lines
      {
         lineFromURL = urlReader.readLine();
         if( lineFromURL != null )   // don't keep the null read
         {
         TelNums.value.addElement( lineFromURL );   // keep the record
```

```
                    // ... Here we would normally save this data to disk ....
                }
            }
        urlReader.close();
    }
        catch( IOException e )
    {  System.out.println( e );
    }
}   // end getTelNums()

}
```

The *Setup* class:

```
/** ========================================================= C L A S S  Setup
 * Sets up the client to run with the proxy
 */

import java.util.*;
import java.io.*;

class Setup
{

/*************************************************** C O N S T R U C T O R
 */
public Setup()
{  super();
}


/*************************************************** M E T H O D  getCommandFromUser
 * Postcondition: User has been prompted to enter 'all', 'middle', or 'quit'
 *
 * Returns: "a" or "m" or "q" if user enters 'all', 'middle', or 'quit' respectively,
 *     otherwise returns "a"
 */
public static String getCommandFromUser()
{
    String command = "a";   // default
    Hashtable commandTable = new Hashtable();   // keys to user input

    // Key user input to the corresponding output
    commandTable.put( "all", "a" );
    commandTable.put( "middle", "m");
    commandTable.put( "quit", "q" );

    // Tell user what to pick from
    System.out.println( "\nPlease pick a command from one of the following:" );
    for ( Enumeration enumeration = commandTable.keys(); enumeration.hasMoreElements() ;)
    {    System.out.println( enumeration.nextElement() );
    }

    // Get command type from user
    try   // pick up user's input
    {
        BufferedReader bufReader =
        new BufferedReader( new InputStreamReader( System.in ) );
        command = bufReader.readLine();
        System.out.println();   // blank line to separate input from processing results
    }
    catch( IOException e )
    {  System.out.println( e );
    }

    // Return if legitimate -- otherwise default
    String returnCommand = (String)commandTable.get( command );
```

```
      if( returnCommand == null )    // user mistyped
      {  return "a";
      }
      else
      {  return returnCommand;
      }
}


/*********************************************** M E T H O D  main
 * Postconditions:
 * (1) The user has been repeatedly prompted as in 'getCommandFromUser()' until "q" is entered
 * (2) Each time user responded with "a", all of the telephone records have been displayed at console
 * (3) Each time the user responded with "m", the "middle" telephone records have been displayed at
 *     console as specified in 'displayMiddleRecords()'.
 * Education note: This demonstrates another need for all of the records.
 *
 * Design Notes: Using Proxy design pattern.
 * The telephone numbers are retrieved from the Internet only when necessary
 *    (taken care of in 'telephoneApp.display()' and 'telephoneApp.displayMiddleRecord()').
 */
public static void main( String[] args )
{
   TelephoneApp telephoneApp = new TelephoneApp();
   TelNumsProxy telNumsProxy = new TelNumsProxy();    // calls to 'TelNums' will be made with this

   String userRequest = "Not assigned yet";

   while( !"q".equals( userRequest ) )   // no desire to quit
   {
      userRequest = getCommandFromUser();    // get next command

      if( "a".equals( userRequest ) )    // show all
      {  telephoneApp.display( telNumsProxy );
      }
      if( "m".equals( userRequest ) )    // show middle record(s)
      {  telephoneApp.displayMiddleRecord( telNumsProxy );
      }
      // Room here for more commands ....
   }
}   // end main()

}
```

The *TelephoneApp* class:

```
/** ======================================================== C L A S S  TelephoneApp
 * Client of 'TelNums'
 * Design Note: This class is deliberately unaware of whether the needed data is
 *    remote or not.
 */

class TelephoneApp
{

/*********************************************** C O N S T R U C T O R
 */
public TelephoneApp()
{  super();
}

/*********************************************** M E T H O D  display
 * Design Note: Written in terms of 'TelNums' in general.
 * Code doesn't deal with proxies, Internet delays etc.
```

```
 *
 * Precondition: 'aTelNums' != null
 *
 * Postconditions: as for 'getTelNums()' in 'TelNums'
 */
public static void display( TelNums aTelNums )
{ aTelNums.getTelNums();
}

/********************************************** M E T H O D  displayMiddleRecord
 * Design Note: Written in terms of 'TelNums' in general.
 * Code doesn't deal with proxies, Internet delays etc.
 *
 * Precondition: 'aTelNums' != null
 *
 * Postconditions: as for 'showMiddleRecord()' in 'TelNums'
 */
public static void displayMiddleRecord( TelNums aTelNums )
{ aTelNums.showMiddleRecord();
}

}
```

The *TelNums* class:

```
/** ======================================================== C L A S S  TelephoneApp
 * Base class for the telephone information
 */

import java.util.*;

abstract class TelNums
{
   public static Vector value = null;   // records kept here; 'null' indicates not retrieved yet

/************************************************** C O N S T R U C T O R
 */
public TelNums()
{ super();
}

/************************************************** M E T H O D  displayTelNums
 * Precondition: 'value' != null
 *
 * Postcondition: the records in 'value' have been displayed to the console
 */
public void displayTelNums()
{
   for( int i = 0; i < TelNums.value.size(); ++i )
   { System.out.println( (String)TelNums.value.elementAt( i ) );
   }
}

/************************************************** M E T H O D  getTelNums
 */
public abstract void getTelNums();

/************************************************** M E T H O D  showMiddleRecord
 * Precondition: 'value' != null
 *
 * Postcondition: The middle element of 'TelNums.value' has beed displayed on the console if there is
 *    an odd number of elements in 'value': Otherwise the two middle elements have been displayed.
 *
 * Education Note: A demonstration capability to show an example of a reason why we need all of
 *     the records.
 */
```

```
public void showMiddleRecord()
{
   if( value == null )
   {  System.out.println( "showMiddleRecord() called with null 'value'" );
   }
   else
   {
       int halfValue = (int)( value.size() / 2 );   // rounds up if 'value.size()' odd
       if( 2*halfValue != value.size() )   // length of 'value' is odd
       { System.out.println( value.elementAt( halfValue ) );
       }
       else   // length is even
       { // Show the pair on either side of the middle
         System.out.println( value.elementAt( halfValue - 1) );
         System.out.println( value.elementAt( halfValue ) );
       }
   }
}

}
```

The *TelNumsProxy* class:

```
/** ========================================================= C L A S S  TelNumsProxy
 *   Handles the real time-consuming work of retrieval across the Internet
 */

class TelNumsProxy extends TelNums
{
   RemoteTelNums remoteTelNums = new RemoteTelNums();   // instantiate when needed only

/************************************************** C O N S T R U C T O R
 */
public TelNumsProxy()
{  super();
}

/************************************************** M E T H O D  getTelNums
 * Postcondition:
 * (1) 'value' has the telephone records as specified by 'getTelNums()' of 'RemoteTelNums'
 * (2) If the values have already been retrieved, a message has been displayed to the console
 *     stating that Internet access is not needed
 * (3) The telephone records have been displayed at the console as for the postconditions
 *     in 'displayTelNums()' of 'TelNums'
 *
 * Design note: Retrieves the records from the Internet only if they have not already been retrieved.
 */
public void getTelNums()
{
   if( value == null )   // check that retrieval from the Internet is necessary
   {
       remoteTelNums = new RemoteTelNums();
       remoteTelNums.getTelNums();
   }
   else   // get them from 'TelNums.value'
   {      System.out.println( "======== No need to retrieve from the Internet ========" );
   }

   super.displayTelNums();
}

/************************************************** M E T H O D  showMiddleRecord
 * Postconditions:
 * (1) -- as for 'showMiddleRecord()' in 'TelNums'
 * (2) 'TelNums.value' contains the telephone records at the Internet site specified in
'RemoteTelNums'
```

```
 * (3) If no Internet retrieval was required, a message to that effect has been displayed at the con-
sole.
 *
 * Design note: Retrieves the records from the Internet only if they have not already been retrieved.
 */
public void showMiddleRecord()
{
    if( value != null )
    {
        System.out.println( "=== No need to retrieve from the Internet ===" );
        super.showMiddleRecord();
    }
    else    // numbers not retrieved yet during this execution
    {
        remoteTelNums.getTelNums();
        super.showMiddleRecord();
    }
}

}   // end class 'TelNumsProxy'
```

# CHAPTER 9

# BEHAVIORAL DESIGN PATTERNS

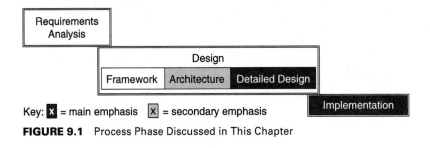

**FIGURE 9.1**  Process Phase Discussed in This Chapter

## 9.1  BEHAVIORAL DESIGN PURPOSES

Our overall design purpose in this chapter is to encapsulate behavior among objects. By doing so, we can allow multiple behavior options at runtime, reuse behavior in other applications, or simply encode behavior more effectively.

## 9.2  *INTERPRETER:* PARSING EXPRESSIONS

### 9.2.1  *Interpreter* Design Purposes and Examples

Applications must sometimes deal with *expressions* written in a *grammar*. A compiler, for example, must deal with expressions written in the grammar of a programming language. Compilers are the most common example but there are many other needs for the interpretation of grammars. The following XML, for example, is an expression and the grammar (called a *schema*, not explicitly given here) specifies the permissible form for the XML used in this context.

```
<engineer>
    <name>
            John Q. Doe
    </name>
    <task>
            Universal payroll Application
    </task>
    <task>
            Intergalactic Web Site Analyzer
    </task>
    <task>
            Financial Forecaster
    </task>
</engineer >
```

Our purpose is to design an interpreter for grammars. In the XML example, our interpreter should be able to interpret the following expression as well.

```
<engineer>
    <name>
        Sue W. Smith
    </name>
    <task>
        Friendly Server Application
    </task>
    <task>
        Intergalactic Web Site Analyzer
    </task>
    </engineer >
```

There are two parts relating to the *Interpreter* design pattern: *Parsing* and *interpreting*. Parsing is the process of converting an input, usually a string, into a tree of objects consistent with the class model. In the XML example this would include picking out individual pieces such as the engineer's name. Interpreting consists of performing useful functionality with the result of the parsing phase. The purpose and basic technique of *Interpreter* are summarized in Figure 9.2.

### Design Purpose

Interpret expressions written in a formal grammar.

### Design Pattern Summary

Represent the grammar using a
recursive design pattern form: Pass
interpretation to aggregated objects.

**FIGURE 9.2**   *Interpreter*

## 9.2.2   *Interpreter* Interfaces for Clients

Once an expression has been parsed and represented using the *Interpreter* class model, clients interface with an *AbstractExpression* object that is the root of the parse tree. The client typically calls an *interpret()* method on this object. In the above XML example, suppose that the expressions formed by parsing the two inputs are *johnDoeXML* and *sueSmithXML*. Suppose that the application is intended to convert XML to conversational prose. When the client executes *johnDoeXML.interpret()*, the following might be output.

> *Engineer John Q. Doe is working on the following three projects: Universal Payroll Application, Intergalactic Web Site Analyzer, and Financial Forecaster.*

The class model for the client / Design Pattern interface looks like Figure 9.3.

**FIGURE 9.3**   *Interpreter* Client Interface

### 9.2.3 The *Interpreter* Class Model

The *Interpreter* design pattern has the *Recursive* form because expressions can contain further expressions. The class model is shown in Figure 9.4.

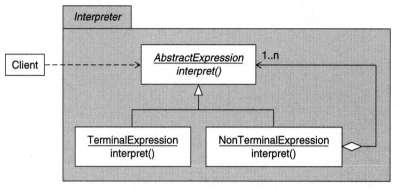

**FIGURE 9.4** The *Interpreter* Design Pattern

*AbstractExpression* objects are either *TerminalExpression* objects, on which the interpretation function is simple, or *NonTerminalExpression* objects. The latter aggregate *AbstractExpression* objects in turn. The *interpret()* function on a *NonTerminalExpression* object operates by performing required work on the object itself, then essentially commanding each of its aggregated *AbstractExpression* objects to execute its *interpret()* method. This has much in common with the dynamic viewpoint of the *Composite* design pattern described in Section 8.4.

### 9.2.4 The *Interpreter* Sequence Diagram

The sequence diagram in Figure 9.5 captures the interpretation process.

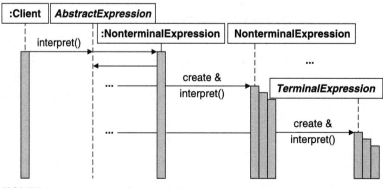

**FIGURE 9.5** *Interpreter* Sequence Diagram

## 9.2.5 Example *Interpreter* Application: Network Assembly

As an example of *Interpreter*, consider an application that handles orders from customers for networked computer systems, and generates installation instructions. For example, consider the order for a network shown in Figure 9.6. It consists of a 260Mhz system with 64MB of RAM connected to a system that consists of the following two connected computers:

a 400Mhz system with 128MB of RAM, and

a 260Mhz system with 32MB of RAM.

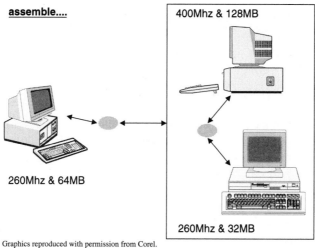

Graphics reproduced with permission from Corel.

**FIGURE 9.6**   Example of a *Virtual Machine* Problem

This order can be expressed using a notation (a grammar) as follows.

```
{(260 64)} {{(400 128)}{(260 32)}}
```

The *output* produced by the application would be instructions to the technician, describing how to perform the assembly.

The main use case for this example is as follows. All I/O is to the console.

1. The application prompts the user to enter an order.
2. The application displays the grammar to be used.
3. The application displays an example.
4. The user enters an order.
5. The application echoes the order.

Figure 9.7 specifies the grammar for the orders, and shows typical input.

The order example in Figure 9.7 is indeed a legitimate expression in the grammar specified, as the following verifies.

```
Please describe a network on one line using the following grammar for 'component.' Blank spaces are ignored.

component ::= net system | computer
net system ::= ( component ) { component } | { component }
computer ::= ( cpu ram )
cpu ::= integer
ram ::= integer

Example. {{{(400 4)}{ (900 3)} } {(600 3)} } { (750 10)}
An input with a syntactic error will be ignored without comment.

{ { {(111 11)}{ (222 22)} } {(333 33)} } { (444 44) }
You chose { { {(111 11)}{ (222 22)} } {(333 33)} } { (444 44) }
```

**FIGURE 9.7**   Input for Network Assembly Example

```
component --> net system -->
{                       component              } { component } -->
{ {           component            } { component } } { computer } -->
{ { { component } { component } } { computer } } { (cpu ram) } -->
{ { { computer } { computer } } { (cpu ram) } } { (444  44 ) } -->
{ { { (cpu ram) } { (cpu ram) } } { (333   33 )} } { (444  44 ) } -->
{ { { (111 11) } { (222 22) } } { (333  33) } } { (444  44 ) }
```

The output of the interpretation process—instructions on how to assemble this net-working order—is as shown in Figures 9.8–9.10. In this case, the user selected the example provided by the application.

```
Please describe a network on one line using the following grammar for 'component.'
Blank spaces are ignored. Inputs with syntactic errors will be ignored without comment.


component::=net system|computer
net system::={component}{component}|{component}
computer::=(cpu ram)
cpu::=integer
ram::=integer

Example:{{{(400 4){ (900 3)}}}{(600 3)}}{(750 10)}
{{{(400 4){ (900 3)}}}{(600 3)}}{(750 10)}

   .....Do some work with the order....

Assemble a network from either one or two parts as follows:

====> First Part: Assemble a network, which we will name 'component1', as follows:

Assemble a network, which we will name 'component2,' from either one or two parts as follows:
-->

Assemble a network, which we will name 'component3', from either one or two parts as follows:
-->

  Build computer component3, from the following parts:
     CPU with specifications.....400

  and
```

**FIGURE 9.8**   Output of Network Assembly Example (1 of 3)

```
      RAM with specifications.....4
second part-->

Assemble a network, which we will name component4, as follows:

Assemble a network, which we will name 'component5', from either one or two parts as follows:
-->
    Build computer component5, from the following parts:
        CPU with specifications.....900
    and
        RAM with specifications.....3

----- Now connect component3 with component4 to complete component2 -----
second part-->

Assemble a network, which we will name component6, as follows:

Assemble a network, which we will name 'component7', from either one or two parts as follows:
-->
    Build computer component7, from the following parts:
        CPU with specifications.....600
    and
        RAM with specifications.....3

----- Now connect component2 with component6 to complete component1 -----
```

**FIGURE 9.9**  Output of Network Assembly Example (2 of 3)

```
====> Second part: Now assemble a network, which we will name 'component8', as follows:

Assemble a network, which we will name 'component9', from either one or two parts as follows:
-->
  Build computer component9, from the following parts:
    CPU with specifications .....750
  and
    RAM with specifications .....10

==== Now connect component1 with component8 to get the resulting network ====

    .....Do more work with the order....
```

**FIGURE 9.10**  Output of Network Assembly Example (3 of 3)

**DESIGN GOALS AT WORK**  *Flexibility, Correctness, Reuse*

Separate the processing of each part of the network order.

Our first task is to parse the input and create the corresponding set of aggregated objects. After that, the output is generated in response to a client calling *aNetworkOrder.assemble()*. The method *assemble()* takes the place of *interpret()* in this example. The interpretation of a primitive element alone (e.g., a CPU in the example) is simple (see the CPU class in the listing). What remains is to execute an *interpret()* function when applied to a more complex expression.

Applying the *Interpreter* design pattern to the network order example, we obtain the class diagram shown in Figure 9.11.

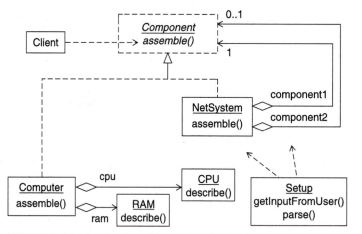

**FIGURE 9.11** Application of *Interpreter* Design Program

For simplicity, we assume that every network consists of just two components, so that each *System* object aggregates two *Component* objects. This can easily be extended to more than two. The source code for this implementation is listed in Appendix A of this chapter.

### 9.2.6 *Interpreter* in the Java API

Recall that *Container* classes in *java.awt* aggregate *Component* objects and that *Container* inherits from *Component*. Interpretation is applied in *Container* by its *validateTree()* method, which recursively descends the container tree and recomputes the layout for any subtrees.

### 9.2.7 Comments on *Interpreter*

■ Gamma et al. [Ga] point out that it is appropriate to use *Interpreter* when the grammar is small, and speed is not a significant factor.

■ *Interpreter* provides the class model describing the permissible object assemblies into which expressions are parsed; the resulting object model (combination of objects rather than classes) is then in a form that facilitates processing. For example, parsing a networking order in the previous example meant producing a set of objects that represent the order: Processing an order meant producing assembly instructions. Note that the job of parsing an expression is nontrivial. *Interpreter* does not parse for us, but it does provide a target form for parsing: The combination of objects into which we convert the input.

■ *Interpreter* has features in common with the *Composite* design pattern. They are certainly both in the *Recursive* form. *Composite* emphasizes the *representation* of a data structure (a *static* viewpoint), whereas *Interpreter* emphasizes the *functional* viewpoint (interpreting the expression).

◼ In applying *Interpreter,* it can be a challenge to produce appropriate output. The output of the Network Order example (Section 9.2.5) is still awkward: There is lots of room for clarifying the installation procedures for network installers.

◼ Section 9.2.1 discussed an XML example: The use of XML is widespread. Almost every time that XML is used, parsing and interpretation are required. One example is SOAP, the Simple Object Access Protocol, in which XML is interpreted as a function call with parameter values.

---

**KEY CONCEPT**   *Interpreter* Design Pattern

A form for parsing and a means of processing expressions.

---

## 9.3  *ITERATOR:* VISITING THE MEMBERS OF A COLLECTION

### 9.3.1  *Iterator* Design Purposes and Examples

Applications usually contain aggregates (or collections) of objects, and we often want to perform an operation on each element.   For example, we may want to send bills to all of a company's customers. This requires us to "visit" each of the elements in the same way that we use *for* loops. We may want to print the names and addresses of every customer, or transfer an image of their company logo to a file.  The process of visiting the objects of an aggregate is called *iteration*. An encapsulation of such a visiting process is called an *iterator*.

If aggregated objects must be visited in a *variety* of ways, we can use several iterators. An example is a personnel management system designed to list employees in various ways. The same operation on the set of employees can be performed alphabetically, by management seniority with the company, by number of years of service, etc. This separates the code into two parts. The first part consists of the basic control and the operations to be performed once each member is isolated—like the body of a *for* loop. The second encapsulates the order in which the aggregate is visited—like the control structure of a *for* loop.

The purposes of *Iterator* are summarized in Figures 9.12 and 9.13.

- -given a collection of objects
   e.g.,
      · the videos in a video store        Aggregate
      · a directory                        object

- -having specified ways to progress through them
   e.g.,
      · "list in alphabetical order"       iterator2
      · "list all videos currently on loan"  iterator7

- ...*encapsulate* each of these ways

**FIGURE 9.12**   Purpose of *Iterator*

**Design Purpose (Gamma et al.)**

"Provide a way to access the elements of an aggregate object sequentially without exposing its underlying representation."

**Design Pattern Summary**

Encapsulate the iteration in a class pointing (in effect) to an element of the aggregate.

**FIGURE 9.13** *Iterator*

## 9.3.2 *Iterator* Interfaces for Clients

Clients require the freedom to concentrate on the processing to be performed at each element of the aggregate, and to deal separately with how to get to the next element. To do the visiting, client code commonly takes the form of a loop, so let's walk through how we would like such a loop to appear. Whatever it is that an "Iterator" object is supposed to be, let's call it *i*. First, we want to be able to set up the situation so that the operations can be applied to the initial element. Thus, we should be able to invoke a command such as *i.setToFirst()*, which causes *i* to "point to" what it views as the "first" element of the collection. Here "point to" simply means that we can obtain the element from *i*. The client does not need to know how the iterator does this. Notice that the iterator has state—a variable or variables whose value(s) contain enough information to indicate the element that the iterator is currently pointing at.

Now we process the body of the loop, which consists of performing our desired operations on the current element. We need to get this element, and since *i* "knows" where that element is, we need a method such as *i.getCurrentElement()*. The next step in the loop is to "bump the counter." In the language of iterators, this means that we need a method on the iterator such as *i.increment()* (often named *i.next()*). The final part of the loop that we need is a test for whether or not the loop has finished: A method returning a Boolean, such as *isDone()*. An example of the resulting loop is shown in Figure 9.14.

```
To perform desiredOperation() on elements of
the aggregate according to the iteration (order) i:

*/

for ( i.setToFirst(); !i.isDone(); i.increment() )
    desiredOperation( i.getCurrentElement() );
```

**FIGURE 9.14** Using *Iterator* Functions

Thus, *Iterator* objects must support the four kinds of functionality shown in Figure 9.15.

Figure 9.16 compares the general idea of an iterator with both the well known notion of the index in an array and with iteration on a Java *Vector* object.

We can picture the effects of an iterator as shown in Figure 9.17.

// Iterator "points" to first element:
void setToFirst();
// Following returns *true* if iterator "points" past the last element:
boolean isDone();
// Cause the iterator to point to its next element:
void increment();
//Return the element pointed to by the iterator:
C getCurrentElement();

**FIGURE 9.15** Functions of *Iterator*

| | | Iterator Operations | | | |
|---|---|---|---|---|---|
| | | Set to beginning | Increment | Get current element | Check not done yet |
| **The Iterator** | Index (integer) *i* on array *myArray* | *i = 0* | *++i* | *myArray[ i ]* | *i < myArray .length* |
| | Index (integer) *j* on Vector *myVector* | *j = 0* | *++j* | *myVector .get( j )* | *j < myVector .size()* |
| | Iterator (object) *myIterator* | *myIterator .setToFirst()* | *myIterator .increment()* | *myIterator .getCurrent Element()* | *! myIterator .isDone()* |

**FIGURE 9.16** *Iterator* in Arrays, Vector, and in General

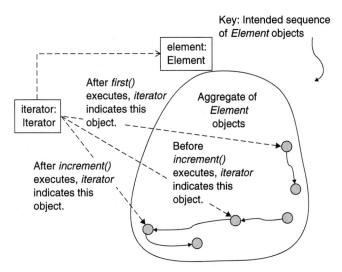

**FIGURE 9.17** Imagining *Iterator*

One can get away with fewer than the four methods listed in Figure 9.16. The iterator's constructor could set it to point to the first element automatically, eliminating the need for *setToFirst()*. A method *next()* could return the current element and cause the iterator to point to the next element. The method *next()* could even fulfill the *isDone()* role by returning *null* if the iteration is done after it has incremented the iteration.

Typical setup code for *Iterator* is shown in Figure 9.18.

```
// Suppose that we have iterators for forward and
// backward order: we can re-use print_employees()


List employees = new List();
ForwardListIterator fwd              // to go from front to back
   = new ForwardListIterator (employees);
ReverseListIterator bckwd            // to go from back to front
   = new ReverseListIterator (employees);

client.print_employees( fwd );       // print from front to back
client.print_employees( bckwd );     // print from back to front
```

**FIGURE 9.18** *Iterator* Example Setup Code

### 9.3.3 The *Iterator* Class Model

The most important feature of the *Iterator* design pattern is the fact that the *setToFirst()*, *increment()*, *isDone()*, and *getCurrentElement()* functionalities are satisfied. This is neither a *Delegation* nor a *Recursive* form, simply the encapsulation of required functionality. The class model shows a generic *Iterator* interface containing these functions.

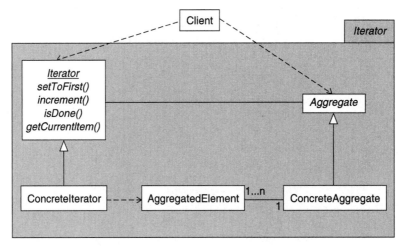

**FIGURE 9.19** *Iterator* Class Model

There are several ways to set up the iterator and the aggregate that it iterates over. For example, the *Aggregate* may have a method *getIterator()* that returns an iterator on itself.

### 9.3.4  Example *Iterator* Application: Organization Chart

Let's suppose that we build applications for a human resources department. We want an application to list the employees in the following two orders, and be designed to facilitate adding other orders:

1. by organizational seniority
2. by number of years with company

Assume that everyone reporting to a given organizational level is at the same level. For example, all direct reports to the President are Vice Presidents. There is no limit to the potential size of the organization chart.

The implementation below provides the option of iterating over either of two organizational charts, using either Iterator **1** or Iterator **2**, already described. One of the organization charts is shown in Figure 9.20.

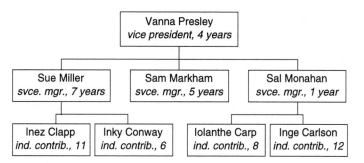

**FIGURE 9.20**   An Organizational Chart Example with Years of Service

Here is the main use case:

1. The application prompts the user for the organization over which iteration is requested: The bank of Figure 8.20 on page 219 or, alternatively, the chart of Figure 9.20.
2. The user enters a choice of organization.
3. The application prompts the user for the order in which the output is requested (organizational seniority or years of service).
4. The user enters a choice of order.
5. The application outputs to the console the members of the organization selected in the order requested.

Figure 9.21 shows the output for iterating by organizational seniority over the bank organization chart of Figure 8.20 on page 219.

Figure 9.22 shows the output when we choose to iterate by years of service over the organization chart in Figure 9.21 above.

**DESIGN GOALS AT WORK**   *Flexibility, Correctness*

Separate the "visiting" procedure from the processing of individual employees.

```
Iterate over bank ('b') or alternative organization chart (any other character)?
b
Iterate by organizational seniority ('o') or alternative (any other character)?
o
Printing names of employees acording to required order

Perform work .... with employee Buddy
... with 19 years of service.
Preform work .... with employee Lonny
... with 23 years of service.
Perform work .... with employee Tony
... with 4 years of service.
Perform work .... with employee Juanita
... with 11 years of service.
Perform work .... with employee Tina
... with 2 years of service.
Perform work .... with employee Thelma
... with 7 years of service.

Completed printing names of employees
```

**FIGURE 9.21** Iterating by Organizational Seniority Over a Bank Organization

```
Iterate over bank ('b') or alternative organization chart (any other character)?
other
Iterate by organizational seniority ('o') or alternative (any other character)?
other
Printing names of employees according to required order

Perform work .... with employee Sal Monahan
... with 1 years of service.
Perform work .... with employee Vanna Presley
... with 4 years of service.
Preform work .... with employee Sam Markham
... with 4 years of service.
Preform work .... with employee Inky Conway
... with 6 years of service.
Preform work .... with employee Sue Miller
... with 7 years of service.
Preform work .... with employee Iolanthe Carp
... with 8 years of service.
Preform work .... with employee Inez Clapp
... with 11 years of service.
Preform work .... with employee Inge Carlson
... with 12 years of service.

Completed printing names of employees
```

**FIGURE 9.22** Iterating by Years of Service Over Organization Chart in Figure 9.20

A class model for this application is shown in Figure 9.23.

The first task is to define the *representation* for our iterator *OrgChartIterator*. In other words, the means whereby it stores enough information (state) to determine what *Employee* object it refers to. Figure 9.24 shows the representation we will use by way of example: A sequence of integers interpreted in the manner specified in Figure 9.24. First, note that it is often convenient if we can introduce an element of the aggregate that is "beyond" the last one, in the sense intended by the iterator. The advantage of this is an

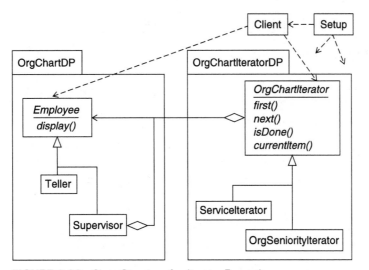

**FIGURE 9.23**   Class Structure for *Iterator* Example

easy test of whether the iteration is done or not. (A Boolean flag is usually a less desirable alternative.) We accomplish this in our example by introducing an extra node called *doneNode*, and by elevating the root of the tree to a node that we call *DeepRoot*, whose children are *doneNode* and the original root. The original tree has *root* as its root. This is shown in Figure 9.24.

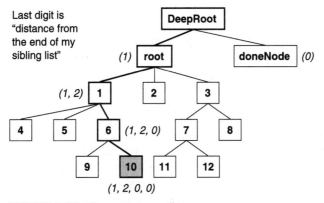

**FIGURE 9.24**   Computing *next()*

The most difficult part of defining an iterator is often the computation of *next()*. For this reason, our representation attempts to make this computation as simple as possible. As shown in Figure 9.25, our representation is a sequence of integers, each expressing the number of *remaining siblings* at each level. For example, there are two siblings remaining after node 1, which explains the presence of "2" in the representation (1,2,0,0) for node 10.

The sequence diagram for the application is shown in Figure 9.25.

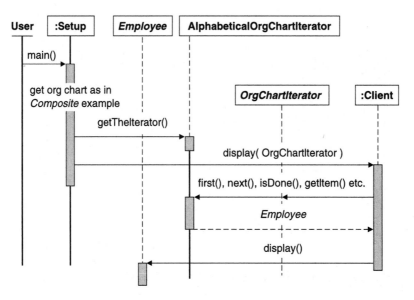

**FIGURE 9.25** *Iterator* Example Sequence Diagram

Note that the representation used in Figure 9.24 is by no means the only one possible. Another is a single integer, which is the numbering of nodes shown in the nodes themselves in this figure. With this iterator, the method *next()* is trivial—just increment the integer. It avoids the necessity of dealing with vectors: On the other hand, the computation of *getItem()* is complicated. Think about having to retrieve node 7, for example.

The retrieval process for the representation we are using in Figure 9.24 is simple, although *next()* gets quite complex. The source code for this is in Appendix B.

### 9.3.5 *Iterator* in the Java API

The *java.util* package contains an *Iterator* interface with methods *next()*, *hasNext()*, and *remove()*. The method *next()* is a combination of the *increment()* and *currentItem()* in the version of the *Iterator* pattern represented in Figure 9.15. The subinterface *ListIterator* specializes these methods to operate on *List* objects, and adds methods appropriate to *List* objects. The interface *List* has a method *listIterator()*, which returns a *ListIterator* object iterating upon it. This enables the programmer to move about and iterate on *List* objects. The class model, including some IBM-specific classes, is shown in Figure 9.26.

To illustrate the use of this API, we will implement a simple address book application with *ArrayList*. The output will be as shown in Figure 9.27.

The elements of the aggregate in this case will be *NameAddrEntry* objects (name/address entries), as shown in Figure 9.28. To iterate we create an instance of *ListIterator* using the method *listIterator()* in *AddressBook*.

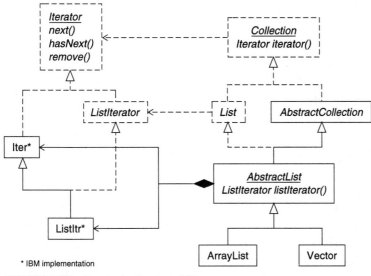

**FIGURE 9.26**   *Iterator* in the Java API

Output

```
Able
Baker
Charlie
```

**FIGURE 9.27**   Output for *Iteration* on a Java *ArrayList*

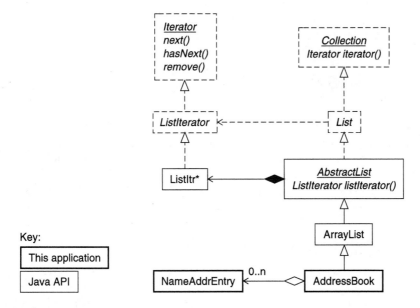

**FIGURE 9.28**   Address Book, Application Using Java *Iterator*

Here is the source code for *AddressBook*. This class contains a *main()* that adds name/address entries and then, using an iterator, prints them in the order in which they were inserted.

```java
package arraylistiteration;

/*****************************************************************************
 */
public class AddressBook extends java.util.ArrayList
{
/*****************************************************************************
 */
public AddressBook()
/****************************************************************************/
{  super();
}

/*****************************************************************************
 *   Simple demonstration of iteration on an 'ArrayList' object.
 * Postconditions:
 *      (1) Three 'NameEntry' objects have been added to an 'AddressBook' object
 *      (2) All appear on the console
 */
public static void main( String[] args )
/****************************************************************************/
{
    AddressBook addressBook = new AddressBook();

    // Add a few names: order of addition determines order in addressBook
    addressBook.add( new NameAddrEntry( "Able", "99 Main Street" ) );
    addressBook.add( new NameAddrEntry( "Baker", "66 Main Street" ) );
    addressBook.add( new NameAddrEntry( "Charlie", "44 Main Street" ) );

    // Get 'ListIterator 'object on 'addressBook' and iterate through whole address book
    java.util.ListIterator iterator =
     addressBook.listIterator();       // points to place "before" first item
    NameAddrEntry tempNameAddrEntry = new NameAddrEntry();
    for(; iterator.hasNext();)    // loop through all entries
    {
        tempNameAddrEntry = (NameAddrEntry)iterator.next();   // bump iterator and retreive entry
        System.out.println( tempNameAddrEntry.getName() );
    }
}

}
```

The following code for our *NameAddrEntry* class captures each name and address.

```java
package arraylistiteration;

/*****************************************************************************
 * Name / address entry for address book.
 */
public class NameAddrEntry
/****************************************************************************/
{
    private String name = "Name to be supplied";
    private String address = "Address to be supplied";

/*****************************************************************************
 */
public NameAddrEntry()
/****************************************************************************/
{  super();
}
```

```
/**********************************************************************************************
 */
public NameAddrEntry( String aName, String anAddress )
/*********************************************************************************************/
{
   this();
   name = aName;
   address = anAddress;
}

/*********************************************************************************************
 */
public String getName()
/*********************************************************************************************/
{  return name;
}

}
```

The *Enumeration* interface in Java is similar to *Iterator*. Its member methods are

```
boolean hasMoreElements(); -- and
Object nextElement();
```

The class *StringTokenizer* implements *Enumeration*, and is used for extracting "words" from a *String* object. For example, here is the output to a program that performs this function.

```
Please supply a short sentence. Its words will be echoed on this monitor.

Now is the winter of our discontent
Now
is
the
winter
of
our
discontent
```

**FIGURE 9.29** Output for *StringTokenizer* Example

The *source code* for this application is as follows.

```
package tokenizing;

import java.io.*;
import java.util.*;

/**
 * For manipulating words in strings
 */

public class MyTokenizer
{
/*********************************************************************************************
 */
```

```
public MyTokenizer() {
   super();
}


/*****************************************************************************************
 * Returns: string input by user; null if IO exception
 */
private static String getInputFromUser()
/****************************************************************************************/
{
   System.out.println
     ( "Please supply a short sentence.  Its words will be echoed on this monitor.\n" );
   BufferedReader b = null;

   try
   {
       b = new BufferedReader( new InputStreamReader( System.in ) );
       return ( b.readLine() );
   }
   catch( IOException e )
   {   System.out.println( e );
       return null;
   }

}


/*****************************************************************************************
 */
public static void main(String[] args)
/****************************************************************************************/
{
   // Get a string from the user and print its words on separate lines
   String string = getInputFromUser();
   printWordsIn( string );
}


/*****************************************************************************************
 * Postcondition: Each word in aString has been printed on a separate line of the console
 */
private static void printWordsIn( String aString )
/****************************************************************************************/
{
   // Make a standard iterator on this string
   StringTokenizer stringTokenizer = new StringTokenizer( aString );

   // Print each word in aString on a separate line
   String tempWord = new String();
   for( ; stringTokenizer.hasMoreElements(); )
   {
       tempWord = (String)stringTokenizer.nextElement();
       System.out.println( tempWord );
   }
}
}
```

## 9.3.6 Comments on *Iterator*

■ The question often arises as to whether the iterator should simply aggregate the element of the collection that it points to. This avoids having to *interpret* the state of the iterator: We can obtain the element directly because we have an ordinary reference to it. This is not prohibited by the *Iterator* design pattern, but it can make other parts of the processing difficult. Certainly, the *getElement()* functionality is simple to implement with this representation: However, the *increment()* functionality typically isn't, and *setToFirst()* may not be straightforward either. Perhaps a good way to think about this it to consider the classical iterator: The index on an array. Its state information is an integer: It is not a direct object reference to an element of the array.

Another problem with aggregating the element itself in the iterator is more serious. Suppose that we have an aggregate, *Company*, with *Employee* objects *Eric*, *John*, *Mary*, *Eric* and *Sue*. *Eric* appears twice in this representation because he acts as CEO and as engineer. An array *Iterator* deals with this adequately: The meaning of *employees*[4] is clearly the second *Eric*. On the other hand, if *employees* simply points to an *Employee* object, and if it aggregates *Eric*, we do not have the role of this *Eric*.

▓ Iterators are intended to leave intact the aggregate over which they iterate. For that reason, one should not "mark" or tamper with the aggregate in order to accommodate an iterator. This would be rather like noting our place in a library book with a physical mark in the book: We are not supposed to alter library books.

▓ It is not in the spirit of iterators to create new versions of the aggregate over which the iteration is taking place—for example, by presorting it and then operating from the sorted version. To gain efficiency, however, one may need to compromise on this point of elegance and modularity.

▓ The use of iterators is fundamental to the Standard Template Library, which is a set of C++ classes that promotes generic programming, programming at a highly leveraged level.

▓ Every collection must have an iterator of one kind or another: A collection in which we can't access all of its individual elements is useless. Array *a* effects iteration with *a[i]*: *Vector* effects it with *elementAt(i),* etc. Both of these are not expressed in the standard form of the *Iterator* design pattern, but we can easily do so if we need to. For example, we can define a class *ArrayIterator* which stores *i* and in which *next()* increments *i*, etc.

*Iterator* allows us to access collections of our own making, and allows us to access them in a variety of orders. Thus, even if we are using the array *a*, we may not be satisfied with the order of the standard iterator and we can use the *Iterator* design pattern to create other iterators on *a*. These would have to be written in term of the standard iterator *a[]* since this is the only way we have to access individual elements to begin with.

---

**KEY CONCEPT**   *Iterator* Design Pattern

To access the elements of a collection.

---

# 9.4   MEDIATOR

## 9.4.1   The Design Purpose of *Mediator*

Objects of classes typically interact with each other, and it is tempting to allow these interacting classes to refer to each other. The problem is that such references inhibit us from re-using each of the participating classes alone. For example, *BankCustomer* objects typically interact with *MoneyMarketFund* objects, but we do not want the *BankCustomer* class to depend on the *MoneyMarketFund* class: Otherwise, we would always have to use the *MoneyMarketFund* class whenever we used the *BankCustomer* class.

As another example, suppose that we are collecting information from various types of customers, as shown in Figure 9.30.

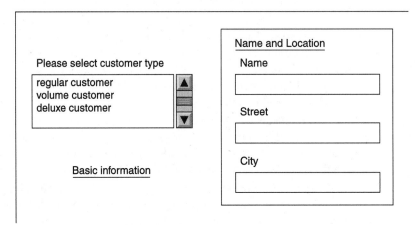

**FIGURE 9.30** Solicitation of Customer Information (1 of 2)

Suppose that the "deluxe customer" designation applies only in LA and New York (sorry, Toronto). The list box and the display therefore have dependent behavior because when either "deluxe customer" is chosen or "City" is entered, a checking process is performed to ensure consistency. On the other hand, we don't want to make the list box class and the display class depend directly on each other because we may well want to use these individual objects as part of other behavior. (Imagine, for the sake of discussion, that these two GUI elements are actually much more elaborate than those shown in Figure 9.31, requiring significant effort to develop.) The list box, for example, could also appear in the following window, in which the GUI elements have different mutual behavior, this time checking that "volume" customers have generated the required minimum amount of business.

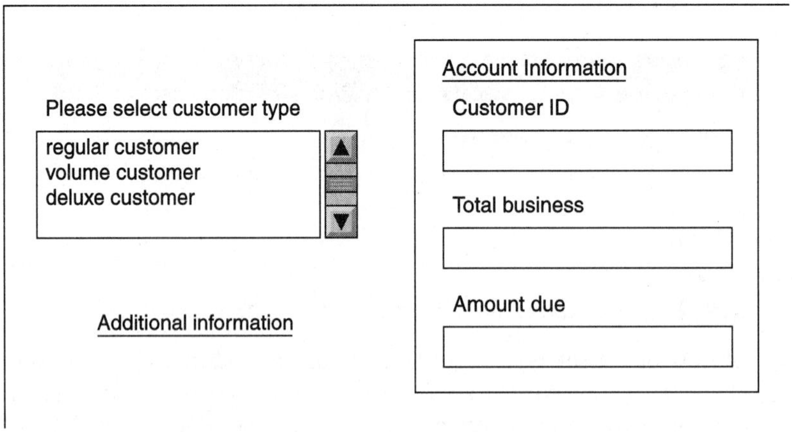

**FIGURE 9.31** Solicitation of Customer Information (2 of 2)

Another example of the interaction among objects is the "graying out" of word processor menu items when they do not apply to the text displayed. In this case, the menu item and the current display are dependent but we don't want the dependency to hinder their usage in other contexts.

The problem is how to capture behavioral relationships between objects without building knowledge about each other into those objects. This is the purpose of the *Mediator* design pattern. Its purpose and technique are summarized in Figure 9.32.

### Design Purpose

Avoid references between dependent objects.

### Design Pattern Summary

Capture mutual behavior in a separate class.

**FIGURE 9.32** *Mediator*

## 9.4.2 The *Mediator* Class Model

The heart of *Mediator* is a "third party" class that references—typically, aggregates—the interacting classes. In Figure 9.33, this is shown by the class *ConcreteMediator* aggregating *ConcreteColleague1* and *ConcreteColleague2*. This simply reflects the use of a class to capture the mutual functionality. Such aggregation alone does not solve the problem of how actions on *ConcreteColleague1* affect *ConcreteColleague2*, however. *Mediator* solves this problem by building into every interacting component a reference to a generic mediating object *Mediator* (but not a reference to any particular mediated object). This generic mediating object is instantiated as the *ConcreteMediator* object at runtime, and assumes the burden of maintaining the relationship between the objects. This is shown in Figure 9.33 ([Ga]).

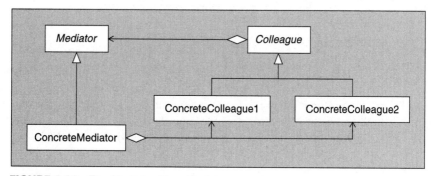

**FIGURE 9.33** The *Mediator* Class Model

The design pattern consists of a base class *Mediator*, each subclass of which encapsulates desired interaction among objects of *ConcreteColleague1*, *ConcreteColleague2*, etc. All interacting objects belong to subclasses of a base class *Colleague* that references *Mediator*. This ensures that the interacting objects need not know about each other.

There are no particular restrictions on how clients interact with applications of *Mediator*.

### 9.4.3 Sequence Diagram for *Mediator*

When we look at *Mediator* from the dynamic viewpoint, there are two possible starting points for action. In the first case, action is initiated by the *ConcreteMediator* object. It calls methods on each of the *ConcreteColleague* objects, which it aggregates. This is shown in the top part of Figure 9.34, where we have named the two methods *doPart1()* and *doPart2()*.

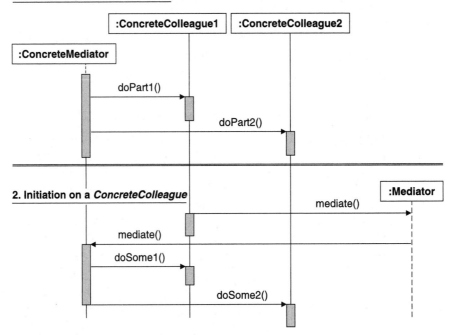

**FIGURE 9.34** *Mediator* Sequence Diagrams

The second dynamic case is when one of the *ConcreteColleagues*— *ConcreteColleague1*, for instance—initiates the action. This could be in response to a mouseclick on it if it is a GUI object, for example. We will name the method call *mediate()*. In this case, the *ConcreteColleague1* object calls on the *Mediator* object that it aggregates. (Unbeknownst to the *ConcreteColleague1* object) this is actually a *ConcreteMediator* object, where the required effect of *mediate()* has been coded, and the process continues as for the first case.

### 9.4.4 Example of *Mediator*

Let's return to the problem of constructing the GUI for soliciting customer information in Figures 9.31 and 9.32.

**DESIGN GOALS AT WORK** *Reusability* and *Robustness*

Avoid hard-coded dependencies among the game's GUI classes, enabling their use in other contexts.

Applying *Mediator*, we obtain a class model like that in Figure 9.35. This figure also shows the GUI objects to which the classes refer.

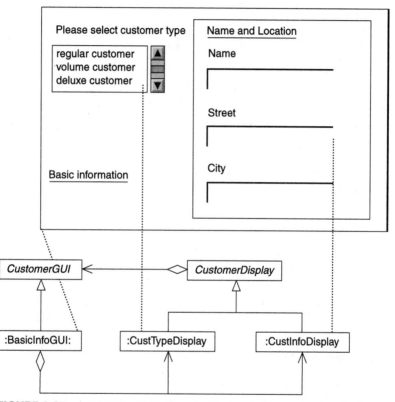

**FIGURE 9.35** Application of *Mediator* to *Customer Information* Application

At runtime, we create a *BasicInfoGUI* object *b* that aggregates the two displays. Each of the two displays aggregates a *CustomerGUI* object, and we instantiate both to *b*. This structure is sufficient to capture all mutual behavior between *CustTypeDisplay* and *CustInfoDisplay*: Neither class refers to the other, however.

### 9.4.5 *Mediator* in the Java API

One common place in the Java API that we implement a *Mediator*-like capability is the use of listeners. Suppose, for example, that we want events on a *java.awt Component* subclass

*MyComponent1* (e.g., a *JDialog* object) to affect another *Component* object, belonging to *MyComponent2*. We will name the two interacting objects *myComponent1* and *myComponent2* respectively. This is shown in Figure 9.36. We can regard *ComponentListener* as a base *Mediator* class. Defining our own *ComponentListener* class *MyEventListener*, with instance *myEventListener*, we can execute *addComponentListener(myEventListener)* on *myComponent1* to cause m*yEventListener* to react to events on *myComponent1*. By having m*yEventListener* reference *myComponent2*, we can mediate behavior between *myComponent1* and *myComponent2*.

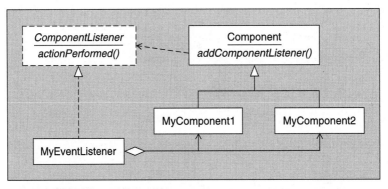

**FIGURE 9.36** The *Mediator* Class Model in the Java API

## 9.4.6 Comments on *Mediator*

■ The relationship between *ConcreteMediator*, *ConcreteColleague1*, and *Concrete-Colleague2* in the *Mediator* design pattern (Figure 9.33) can be a dependence, not necessarily aggregation.

■ We are frequently confronted in OO design by a pair of related classes such as *Customer / Account, Employer / Worker, Automobile / Driver,* etc. The situation often suggests relating these directly, but this should be done with caution because there are customers without accounts, workers without employers, and automobiles without drivers, etc. *Mediator* addresses this issue by introducing a third-party class. This third party expresses the *role* of the participants or the context of the interaction or the event involved, etc. *Mediator* classes tend to be application-specific and less reusable because they aggregate other classes.

■ Mediators provide some of the most fruitful aspects of object-oriented design. For example, introducing a *Transaction* class frequently breaks design logjams in which many classes would otherwise depend on each other. In the case of the video store example (Section 3.5.1 on page 70), we introduced the *Checkout* class, a Transaction-type class that breaks the dependence of *Customer* and *Video*. The real question is whether *Rental* would a better choice than *Checkout* etc., but this is just a matter of trading off mediator options.

■ It is unacceptable for *ConcreteColleague1* and *ConcreteColleague2* objects to reference their mutual mediator *ConcreteMediator*. That's because *ConcreteMediator* exists specifically to mediate between these two classes, and so if *ConcreteColleague1* were to reference *ConcreteMediator*, it might just as well reference *ConcreteColleague2*. On the other hand, *ConcreteColleague1* is a subclass of *Colleague*, which aggregates *Mediator*, and so *ConcreteColleague1* automatically aggregates a *Mediator* object, as we have seen. Is this bad? Not really, because *Mediator* is at an abstract level, and so the dependency price we are paying is small. To take an analogy, we would not want the class *House* to aggregate the class *AjaxFrontDoor* because not all houses are equipped with Ajax front doors: However, we probably don't mind if *House* aggregates the abstract (or, at least high-level) class *FrontDoor* even though it commits us to always using *FrontDoor* whenever we use *House*.

---

**KEY CONCEPT** *Mediator* Design Pattern

To capture mutual behavior without direct dependency.

---

## 9.5 OBSERVER

### 9.5.1 The Design Purposes of *Observer*

Software requirements and designs frequently involve a source of data, together with a number of clients that must be updated whenever the data changes.

As an example, suppose that the headquarters of International Hamburger Corporation maintains data on its server about hamburger sales throughout the country. Distributed clients for this data include Senior Management, Marketing, and Operations. The data change continually, and each of headquarters' clients needs to update its display according to their various requirements. Let's say, for example, that *Senior Management*'s bar chart must be updated after a 5% change has taken place, *Marketing* displays a new pie chart when a change of at least 1% has taken place, and *Operations* requires tables to be updated when every change takes place.

The *Observer* design pattern is intended to address these requirements. Its purposes and basic technique are summarized in Figure 9.37.

**Design Purpose**

Arrange for a set of objects to
be affected by a single object.

**Design Pattern Summary**

The single object aggregates the set, calling a
method with a fixed name on each member.

**FIGURE 9.37** *Observer*

### 9.5.2 *Observer* Interfaces for Clients

Suppose that the abstract class *Source* is aware of the data source. Whenever a client wants all observers to take notice (typically, of a change in the data), it calls a designated method of *Source*. In Figure 9.38, this method is named *notify()*. The client is shielded from the manner in which *Observer* carries out this process.

### 9.5.3  The *Observer* Class Model

The parties in the *Observer* design pattern requiring updating are known as *observers*, and are subclasses of a single abstract class, which we will call *Observer*. This pattern, shown in Figure 9.38, is in the *Delegation* form since *Source* delegates the updating process to the *Observer* objects.

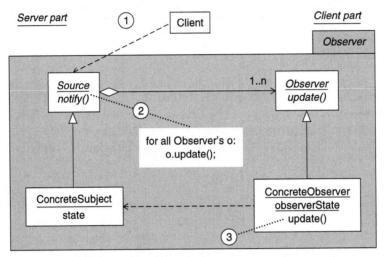

**FIGURE 9.38**  *Observer* Design Pattern

We will follow a sequence of steps to show how *Observer* operates.

1. (Step 1) The client references a known interface object, requesting that the observers be notified. For example, the client could be a process programmed to notice that the data has changed, or it could be a clock-driven task. In the model, this is shown as a *Client* object telling the *Source* object to execute its *notify()* function.

2. (Step 2) The *notify()* method calls the *update()* function on each *Observer* object that it aggregates.

3. (Step 3)The implementation of *update()* depends on the particular *ConcreteObserver* to which it belongs. Usually, *update()* compares the *ConcreteObserver* object's state (variable values) with that of the central data source, then decides whether or not to change its variable values accordingly. It typically performs other actions such as creating a new display.

### 9.5.4  Example *Observer* Applications

#### 9.5.4.1  *Hamburgers* Observer *Example*  Applying *Observer* to our International Hamburger Corporation problem, we obtain a model such as that shown in Figure 9.39.

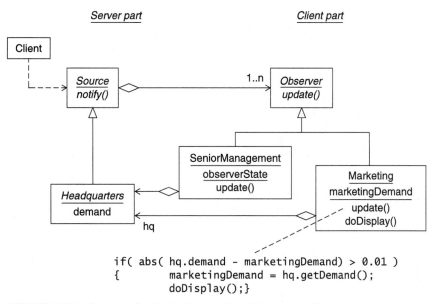

*Server part*                                    *Client part*

```
if( abs( hq.demand - marketingDemand) > 0.01 )
{         marketingDemand = hq.getDemand();
          doDisplay();}
```

**FIGURE 9.39**  *Observer* Applied to International Hamburger Co.

### 9.5.4.2  *Mutual Funds* **Observer** *Example*

Consider the updating of mutual fund portfolios as an application of *Observer.* Mutual funds invest in multiple stocks, so that when a particular stock's price changes, it affects the values of all the mutual funds that invest in it. Normally, such changes in a stock's price are transmitted electronically: In our example, we will make the change to *Awesome Inc.*'s stock through a *Client* object. The application will then display the resulting changes in the mutual funds carrying *Awesome* stock. We will use the *Observer / Observable* Java API to carry out this design and implementation. This API is described in Section 9.5.5 on page 304, but we can explore our example in the meantime.

The main use case is as follows

1. The application reports the status of mutual funds that invest in *Awesome Inc.*

2. The following repeats until the user signifies quitting.

  2.1. The application prompts the user to supply a price for *Awesome* stock.

  2.2. The user enters a price in decimal form.

  2.3. The application reports the status of mutual funds that invest in *Awesome Inc.*

Figure 9.40 shows a typical scenario.

*Observable* in the Java API allows the addition of *Observers* with *addObserver()* and removal with *deleteObserver().*

## DESIGN GOAL AT WORK  *Flexibility*

Allow mutual funds objects to easily acquire or divest stocks.

```
Note: HiGrowthMutualFund starts with 3 shares of Awesome, assumes price of 1.0, and has non-Awesome holdings totalling 400.0
Note: MedGrowthMutualFund starts with 2 shares of Awesome, assumes price of 1.0, and has non-Awesome holdings totalling 300.0
Note: LoGrowthMutualFund starts whth 1 shares of Awesome, assumes price of 1.0, and non-Awesome holdings totalling 200.0

Enter "quit": Any other input to continue.
go on
Enter the current price of Awesome Inc in decibel form
1.1
Value of Lo Growth Mutual Fund changed from 201.0 to 201.1
Value of Med Growth Mutual Fund changed from 302.0 to 302.2
Value of Hi Growth Mutual Fund changed from 403.0 to 403.3

Enter "quit": Any other input to continue.
go on
Enter the current price of Awesome Inc in decibel form.
-3.4
Value of Lo Growth Mutual Fund changed from 201.1 to 196.6
Value of Med Growth Mutual Fund changed from 302.2 to 293.2
Value of Hi Growth Mutual Fund changed from 403.3 to 389.8

Enter "quit": Any other input to continue.
```

**FIGURE 9.40** I/O Example for Mutual Fund *Observer* Example

The class model is shown in Figure 9.41.

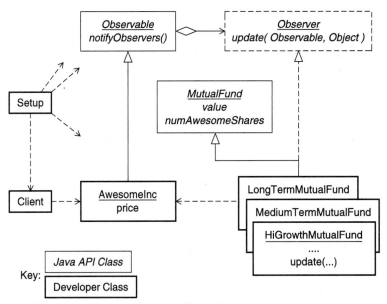

**FIGURE 9.41** Observer Example: *Mutual Funds*

This class model uses *Observer* classes in the Java API, which are discussed next. The source code is in Appendix C.

## 9.5.5 *Observer* in the Java API

Many of the design patterns discussed in this book are present in the Java API: However, one recognizes them by their form rather than by name. *Observer* is one of the few patterns explicitly called out by name in the Java API. The Java API *Observer* class model is shown in Figure 9.42.

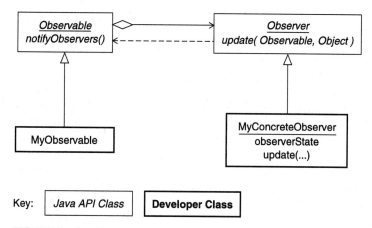

Key:   | *Java API Class* |   | **Developer Class** |

**FIGURE 9.42**   *Observer* in the Java API

The Java API uses virtually the same terms as Gamma et al. [Ga]. Notice that *update(...)* is a *callback* method because it provides *Observer* objects a reference to its source, thereby enabling them to compare their data etc. with the *Observable* object in executing *update()*. Because update is implemented as a callback, there is no need for concrete *Observer* classes to maintain references to the *Observable* object.

## 9.5.6   Comments on *Observer*

▪ *Observer* also goes by the widely used name of "Model-View-Controller" (MVC), although there are slight differences in emphasis. The "Model" in MVC is the *Source* in Figure 9.42 (the *Observable* in the Java API). The "Views" are the *Observer* objects, and the "Control" is client and possibly setup code. MVC emphasizes the fact that the model is data and the views are GUI's, whereas *Observer* is conceived with broader application.

▪ *Observer* allows the addition and removal of observers without disrupting existing observer code.

▪ *Observer* may be *dis*advantageous if very few of the observers need to react to changes (in which case the possibly frequent notifications waste resources).

▪ *Observer* is disadvantageous when updating is more naturally implemented centrally, or when update policies among observers have very little in common.

▪ *Observer* can't work if the observable cannot have a reference to all of the observers. For example, we would not use it in a client/server situation unless we were willing for the server to maintain references to all clients.

▪ In general, having the observers update themselves (as opposed to external software performing it) is good object-oriented design because it keeps related functionality together.

| **KEY CONCEPT** *Observer* Design Pattern |
| --- |

To keep a set of objects up to date with the state of a designated object.

# 9.6 STATE

## 9.6.1 The Design Purposes of *State*

Many applications are event-driven. A word processor, for example, waits for the user to click on an icon or menu item, and then reacts. Event-driven applications are often designed as state transition systems, as explained in Chapter 3.

When a system behaves by essentially transitioning among a set of *states,* the *State* design pattern can be helpful. For example, we can describe a role-playing video game at runtime in terms of the state it is in: It could transition among the *Setting-up, Waiting, Setting-characteristics,* and *Characters-interacting* states, among others. The design should capture this behavior effectively. As the game becomes better defined, the design should also be capable of gracefully absorbing new states and action handling without disrupting the existing design.

Figure 9.43 summarizes the purpose and basic technique of the *State* design pattern.

**Design Purpose**

Cause an object to behave in a
manner determined by its state.

**Design Pattern Summary**

Aggregate a *State* object
and delegate behavior to it.

**FIGURE 9.43** *State*

## 9.6.2 *State* Interfaces for Clients

To use the *State* pattern, the client simply makes a call on a specific method of a specific object. The client is shielded from the various possible effects of calling the method, which depend on the object's state.

## 9.6.3 The *State* Class Model

In general terms, suppose that we want to use a method *doRequest()* of an object *target* of class *Target,* where *doRequest()* can behaves in different ways, according to *target*'s state at the time of the call. This is solved by introducing a class, which we will call *TargetState,* and giving *Target* an attribute (we'll call it *targetState*) of type *TargetState*. We ensure that *targetState* properly represents the *Target* object's current state at all times. This is ensured by *targetState* being an object of the appropriate *TargetState* subclass. Figure 9.44 shows this. Note that the *State* design pattern is in the *Delegation* form.

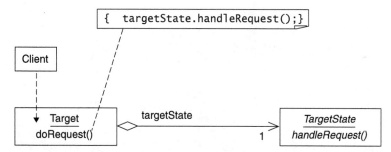

**FIGURE 9.44**  *State* Design Pattern *Basic* Structure: *doRequest()* behaves according to state of *Target*

The method *doRequest()* calls *targetState.handleRequest()*, so the call to *doRequest()* is translated by the virtual function property into the particular version of *handleRequest()* appropriate to the state of *target*. The client does not need to know the state of *target*. The full class model is shown in Figure 9.45.

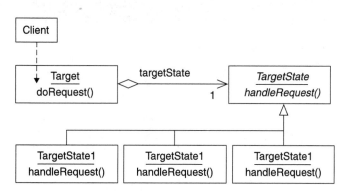

**FIGURE 9.45**  *State* Design Pattern Class Model

## 9.6.4  Example *State* Applications

A role-playing video game can typically be in a variety of states. When you start to play the game, you may have the opportunity to set your characteristics ("Setting Up" state). When you are in the midst of interacting with other characters, your state is different ("Engaging" state, perhaps). It is reasonable to expect that you can't change your characteristics in the midst of an engagement because the game would not be much fun to play in that case. If the game interface had the appearance of Figure 9.46, the effect of pressing the Set *Characteristics* button would depend on the state of the game at the time.

**DESIGN GOALS AT WORK**   *Correctness* and *Reusability*

Separate the generic code for handling button clicks from the actions that depend on the game's status at the time.

Courtesy Tom VanCourt and Corel

**FIGURE 9.46** GUI For a Role-Playing Video Game

Figure 9.47 shows how the *State* design pattern can be used to handle the states and actions of a video game.

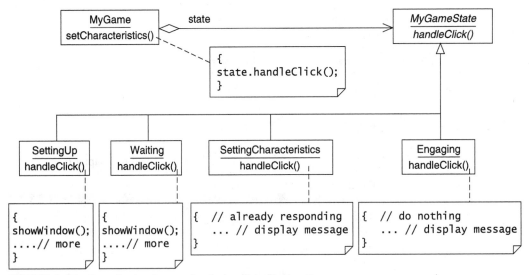

**FIGURE 9.47** *State* Design Pattern Applied to Role-Playing Game

The class *MyGame* has an attribute called *state* of type *MyGameState*. The type of the *state* object (i.e., which subclass of *MyGameState* it belongs to) determines what happens when *setCharacteristics()* is called on a *MyGame* object.

The code for *setCharacteristics()* in *MyGame* passes control to the *handleClick()* function of *state*. Each subclass of *MyGameState* implements *handleClick()* in its own manner. For example, if *MyGame* is in *Waiting* state, then the effect of clicking on the "Set Characteristics" button is that a window appears through which the player can change his characteristics. On the other hand, if *MyGame* is in *SettingQualities* state, then nothing happens on *handleClick()* execution because the user is already setting his characteristics.

### 9.6.5 *State* in the Java API

The *java.awt* class *Container* represents an aggregation of *Component* objects. It also aggregates a *LayoutManager* object that describes how the *Container* will display its *Component* objects. We can think of this *LayoutManager* object as reflecting the state of the *Component* object. When we execute *add()* on the *Container* object, for example, the effect depends on the value of the *LayoutManager* object. If the latter is a *FlowLayout* instance, then *add()* places the added component at the end of the existing ones. If the *LayoutManager* is a *BorderLayout* instance, then *add()* has a different interpretation. Note that we usually expect objects with state to change their state at runtime: However, we do not usually change the *LayoutManager* object of a *Container* at runtime.

### 9.6.6 Comments on *State*

▓ The *State* design pattern is particularly beneficial when new states are likely to be needed in the future.

▓ *State* does not handle the question of how to set up the successive state (if required) once *handleEvent()* has been performed. Although *State* does not necessarily handle the transition function, it can be a useful framework in which to implement transition. For example, *handleEvent()* can contain code that swaps in the new state. A possible companion to the *State* design pattern is a state/transition table whose entries indicate what new state the object transitions into for each "current state/event occurrence" pair.

▓ Whether or not the *State* design pattern is applied, state-oriented architectures have been used with success for many applications (see, for example, the work of Shlaer and Mellor [Sh]). Real-time applications tend to benefit especially from the *State* architecture because they often rely on a state/event perspective,

▓ The *State* design pattern is in the *Delegation* form described in Chapter 6.

| KEY CONCEPT    *State* Design Pattern |
| :--- |
| To cause an object's functions to behave according to the state it's in. |

## 9.7 CHAIN OF RESPONSIBILITY

### 9.7.1 The Design Purpose of *Chain of Responsibility*

The design purpose of *Chain of Responsibility* is to have a *collection* of objects, rather than just a single object, provide functionality. In addition, we do not want the client to have to know which objects in the collection are responsible for which part of the functionality. An example is a checker that examines prose for deficiencies. There are many possible deficiencies in prose (grammar, spelling, style, etc.) and we would like to capture each type of check separately for the sake of correctness, robustness and maintainability. The prose checking process can be seen as the collective responsibility of the individual checkers. The purpose and outline of *Chain of Responsibility* are shown in Figure 9.48.

### Design Purpose

Allow a set of objects to service a request.
Present clients with a simple interface.

### Design Pattern Summary

Link the objects in a chain via aggregation,
allowing each to perform some of the
responsibility, passing the request along.

**FIGURE 9.48**  *Chain of Responsibility*

## 9.7.2  Interface to *Chain of Responsibility* for Clients

The objects in the collection are assumed to belong to a base class—*HandlerBase,* for example. (Each object is an instance of a *HandlerBase* subclass.) We assume also that this base class has a member function named for each request honored by the collection. For example, suppose that we have a collection of GUI elements displayed on the console. These would all inherit from a base class *GUIElement,* and support a method name such as *handleDataEntry().* This is analogous to a company in which every employee, regardless of their job function, is prepared to accept a request from a customer to purchase an item.

The client must have a reference to a designated *HandlerBase* object. Let's call this *HandlerBase* object *entryHandler,* and let's suppose that the functionality required is covered by the function name *handleRequest().* The client code is simply *entryHandler.handleRequest().* In other words, the client requests functionality from a single object of the collection to perform the complete required functionality.

## 9.7.3  The *Chain of Responsibility* Class Model

The technique used by *Chain of Responsibility* is for the contacted object to decide whether it is responsible for any of the requested functionality. If so, it performs its part and then passes the request along to another object of the collection. The manner in which an object performs these decisions and actions is determined by the (sub)class that contains it. This chain process is suggested by Figure 9.49.

**FIGURE 9.49**  *Chain of Responsibility:* Object Model

The class model for *Chain of Responsibility* is in the *Recursive* form because *Handler* objects delegate to other *Handler* objects, as shown in Figure 9.50.

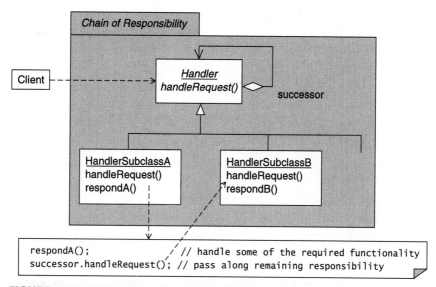

**FIGURE 9.50** *Chain of Responsibility:* Class Model

## 9.7.4 Example *Chain of Responsibility* Application: Customer Information

Suppose that we want to enable customers to update information about themselves. The input is via the GUI shown in Figure 9.51.

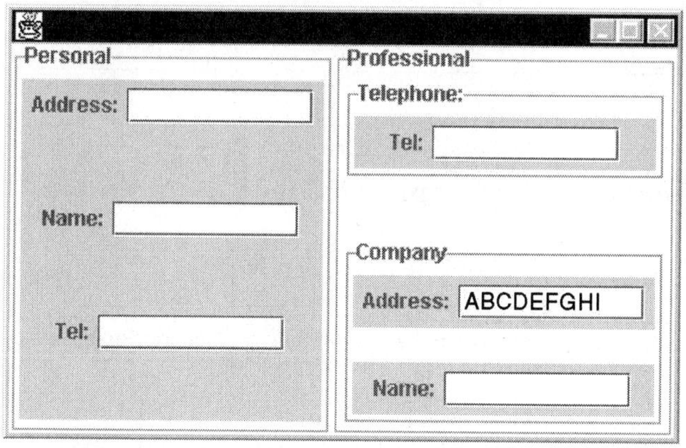

**FIGURE 9.51** GUI for *Customer Information* Application

The requirement is for update information to be generated when any text field is entered and the *Enter* button pressed. We will suppose that the update information is destined for several databases, and so it is expressed in XML.

The main use case is the following.

1. The application displays a form for entering personal and professional information.
2. The user enters this information.
3. The user hits *Enter*.
4. The application displays the corresponding XML to the console.

As an example, Figure 9.52 shows the XML generated when text is entered in the *Address* field of the *Company* panel, as in Figure 9.51, and the *Enter* key is pressed.

```
<customer>
<professionalInfo>
<company>
<address>
ABCDEFGHI
</address>
</company>
</professionalInfo>
</customer>
```

**FIGURE 9.52**  Output for *Customer Information* Application

## DESIGN GOAL AT WORK  *Flexibility*

Isolate the responsibilities of each part of the input form to generate its XML.

The class model for this could be as shown in Figure 9.53.

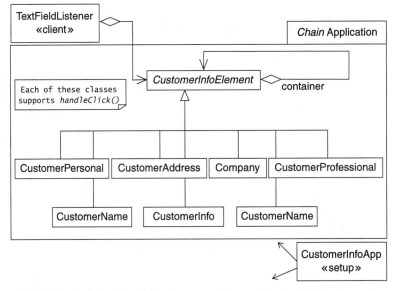

**FIGURE 9.53**  Class Model for *Customer Information* Application

The object model involving company name, for example, would be as in Figure 9.54.

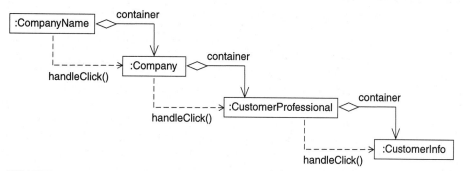

**FIGURE 9.54** Object Model Fragment for *Customer Information* Example

The code for this example is listed in Appendix D.

### 9.7.5 *Chain of Responsibility* in the Java API

When we write the command for a *java.awt.Component* object to appear on the console, we use *component.setVisible():* But for this to succeed, the container of *component* must itself be made visible, and so must its container, etc. In the IBM Visual Age implementation, *component.setVisible()* calls a method on its "parent" *Component* that calls on its parent, etc. This is a chain of responsibility for displaying. The client code of *component* is shielded from this chain of responsibility, and calls only on the method *setVisible()* of *component.*

### 9.7.6 Comments on *Chain of Responsibility*

■ The class model for *Chain of Responsibility* is very similar to *Decorator.* The difference is in the viewpoint taken. *Decorator* emphasizes the structural value of stringing objects together, primarily the static viewpoint. On the other hand, *Chain of Responsibility* emphasizes the dynamic viewpoint: Sharing functionality among a community of objects.

■ The difference between the *Chain of Responsibility* and *Decorator* class models is that the principal aggregation in *Decorator* is with the base class whereas the aggregation is with the class itself in the case of *Chain of Responsibility.* Is there any significance to this? Some. Since *Decorator* is concerned more about structure than functionality, the class model simply says that the objects strung together are from the same base class, but could otherwise be quite different. Since *Chain of Responsibility* concerns functionality, its class model emphasizes the fact that the objects in the chain all exhibit the same functionality in name.

■ *Chain of Responsibility* has flexibility in that one can easily add or remove functionality from the collective group responsibility.

---

**KEY CONCEPT** *Chain of Responsibility* Design Pattern

To distribute functional responsibility among a collection of objects.

# 9.8 *COMMAND*

### 9.8.1 The Design Purposes of *Command*

To get something done within an application, we call a method that performs the action. This approach may be too inflexible, however. For example, what if we require the action to be "undo-able?" It is difficult or impossible to unravel all the effects of a straight method call.

Another case in point is implementing the effects of menu selection. Consider, for example, the *Edit/Cut* command. For one thing, the menu item may be grayed out because a region is not selected for cutting. If a region is selected, it has to be specified for the cut method: This can be complicated if the region contains figures and tables. To better organize these factors before actually performing the *cut* action, it may be preferable to capture the command itself as an object. Figure 9.55 introduces the *Command* design pattern, which addresses these issues.

**Design Purpose**

Increase flexibility in calling for a service e.g., allow undo-able operations.

**Design Pattern Summary**

Capture operations as classes.

**FIGURE 9.55** *Command*

### 9.8.2 Interface to *Command* for Clients

Suppose that the actual work required by a command is to be performed by the *doAction()* method of class *Target1*. Here is the interface from the client's perspective when the *Command* design pattern is used: A method with a standardized name—*execute()*, let's say—of a base class with a generic name such as *Command*. The following client code would be typical.

```
  . . .
Command command = Command.getCommand( .... );    // command depends on situation
command.execute();                               // prepares for and calls the "real" method doAction()
  ...
```

### 9.8.3 The *Command* Class Model

The class model for *Command* shows the encapsulation of the command in its own class *Command,* supplied with an *execute()* method. At runtime, control is passed to the *execute()* method of a *Command* object of a nonabstract subclass. This *execute()* version has the capability to perform checking for accuracy, feasibility, or necessity before (normally) passing control to the actual work of *action()*. This is in the *Delegation* form, and is shown in Figure 9.56.

The content to *execute()* depends on many factors. Code such as the following would be typical.

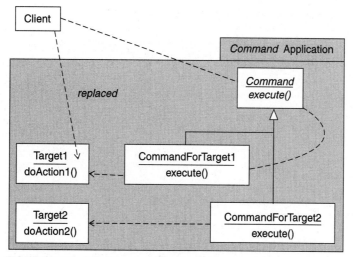

**FIGURE 9.56**   The *Command* Design Pattern

```
void execute()
{
   if( ... conditions are acceptable to carry out the requested operation ... )
      {
            this.getParameters();  // (if parameter gathering is necessary)
            getTarget1().action1();      // here is where control is passed
      }
   else
      ... respond to an operation request that can't be honored ...
}
```

## 9.8.4   Example *Command* Applications

### 9.8.4.1   *Command* Applied to a Menu Example

Let's take as an example the response to clicking on a menu item. By using *Command* we can write mouseclick response code at a generic level, as suggested by the upper level of the class model in Figure 9.57. The class *MenuItem* has the client role here, and the *MenuItem* object aggregates a *Command* object, c*ommand*. In this case, the actions are cutting and copying text.

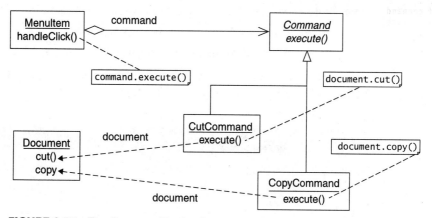

**FIGURE 9.57**   The *Command* Design Pattern: Example

The sequence diagram is shown in Figure 9.58.

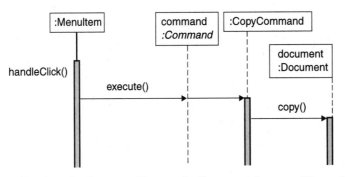

The next example also deals with editing of a document, but it emphasizes undo-ability rather than menu operation.

### 9.8.4.2 *Command* Applied to an Undo Example

Now let's examine a way to implement undo-able commands. Using *Command,* we will encapsulate each command and retain previous command objects. In the design shown below, the *WordProcessor* class takes the responsibility for retaining these objects by maintaining a stack of prior commands.

We will execute *cut, paste*, and *undo* operations for a simple command-line word processor. Our word processor can deal only with a single string of text. Here is the main use case.

The application repeatedly prompts the user to enter "paste," "cut," "undo," or "quit" until the user selects "quit."

On each selection:

1. The user enters one of commands: "paste," "cut," "undo," or "quit."
2. Depending on the user's choice, the application does one of the following.
   2.1. If the command is "quit," the application terminates.
   2.2. If the command is "undo," the last command is reversed (precondition: There was a prior command).
   2.3. If the command is "paste," the Paste use case applies.
   2.4. If the command is "cut," the Cut use case applies.
3. The application displays the result of this operation in a single line of text.

The paste and cut use cases are not stated here. Instead, Figures 9.59–9.60 are provided as an illustrative scenario for this application.

**DESIGN GOALS AT WORK** *Flexibility* and *Robustness*

Isolate the responsibilities of the Word Processor commands, making them saveable and reversible.

Pick from one of the following:
undo
paste
quit
cut

paste
Please spedcify index where the paste must start:
0
You chose 0
Please specify text to be inserted:
Mary had a little lamb.
You chose Mary had a little lamb.

    Text is now as shown between the pair of arrows.
    --> Mary had a little lamb.<--

Pick from one of the following:
undo
paste
quit
cut

cut
Please specify index where the cut must start:
5
You chose 5
Please specify number of characters to be cut:
4
You chose 4
    Text is now as shown between the pair of arrows.
    --> Mary a little lamb.<--

**FIGURE 9.59** I/O for Word Processor *Undo* Example (1 of 2)

Pick from one of the following:
undo
paste
quit
cut

undo

    Text is now as shown between the pair of arrows.
    --> Mary had a little lamb.<--

Pick from one of the following:
undo
paste
quit
cut

undo

    Text is now as shown between the pair of arrows.
    --><--

Pick from one of the following:
undo
paste
quit
cut

quit
----          TERMINATING APPLICATION          ----

**FIGURE 9.60** I/O for Word Processor *Undo* Example (2 of 2)

Figure 9.61 shows a class model for this application.

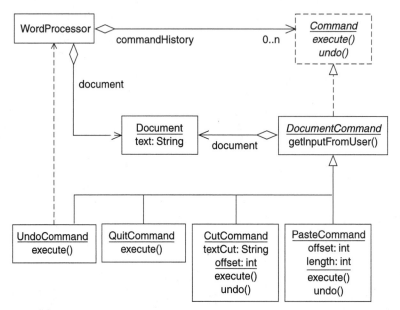

**FIGURE 9.61** *Undo* Example Class Model

This particular design captures the undo command itself as a *Command* subclass. It also captures the command to quit the application. This is not necessary, but adds elegance. The source code for this example can be found in Appendix E.

### 9.8.5 *Command* in the Java API

It is common to use *Command* in operating across the Internet. For example, suppose that client code needs to make a function call on an object of a class residing on an Internet-based server. It is not possible for the client code to make an ordinary method call on this object because the remote object can't appear in the usual compile-execute process. It is difficult to use RMI here because we often can't prepare client and server in advance, except to give the client specification of the servlet's file name. Instead, the call is made from the client by pointing the browser to the file containing the servlet. The understood procedure is for the servlet to then call its *service()* method, which has the form *service(HttpServletRequest, HttpServletResponse)*. The class *HttpServletRequest* includes all of the information that a method invocation requires, such as parameter values, obtained from "environment" variables at standardized global locations. The class *HttpServletResponse* carries the result of invoking *service()*. This technique embodies the basic idea of the *Command* design pattern.

CORBA (the Common Object Request Broker Architecture of the influential Object Management Group) has a feature similar to Servlets' *service()*, in which remote methods can be discovered at runtime. For example, it is possible to ask an *OnlineStore* object whether it has a *displaySweater()* method, then invoke that method if it does. However, we can't compile client code with a *displaySweater()* call because the compilation system will not be able to make sense of it (we *can* ask about the function using the *string* "display-

Sweater"). Once the existence of the method is established, we execute an *invoke()* method on a *Request* object associated with the actual *displaySweater()* method (here is where *Command* is being applied). CORBA packages both the request and the response in the *Request* object. Web services allow a similar runtime function discovery process.

### 9.8.6   Comments on *Command*

■ We use *Command* whenever a method call alone is not sufficient: The ability to undo a command is one reason, as is the ability to trace the course of an execution. For example, we may need to keep track of financial transactions for legal or auditing reasons.

■ *Command* affords us flexibility in dealing with operations, making it easier to modify, isolate, remove, or add operations to an application.

■ Menus often have submenus, sub-submenus or even more levels of menus. This means that there is a hierarchy of increasingly specialized commands (a paste, a special kind of paste, etc.). This hierarchy translates directly into an inheritance hierarchy of *Command* classes.

■ One downside of using *Command* is the fact that, as is common with design patterns, we are replacing what would be a single function call with multiple function calls.

■ *Command* is in the *Delegation* form because functionality is delegated to the *execute()* method of a subclass.

■ *Command* promotes modularity, and thus correctness and reusability, because it separates functionality (e.g., a cut operation) from the object to which the functionality applies (e.g., a document whose text is to be cut).

---

**KEY CONCEPT**   *Command* Design Pattern

To avoid calling a method directly (e.g., so as to record or intercept it).

---

## 9.9   TEMPLATE

### 9.9.1   The Design Purpose of *Template*

The design purpose of *Template* is to deal with multiple variations of an algorithm. Consider, for example, the problem in Figure 9.62.

There is a basic sequence of actions and outputs for this problem, but it depends on the values of the constants *a*, *b*, and *c*. Recall that the formula, for nonzero *a* and nonnegative $b^2 - 4ac$, is as follows.

$$x = [-b \pm \sqrt{(b^2 - 4ac)}]/[2a]$$

The overall procedure for solving this equation, regardless of the values of *a, b,* and *c,* looks like the four steps in Figure 9.63.

In general, the purposes and basic technique of *Template* can be described as shown in Figure 9.64.

- Required to solve equations of the form

  $ax^2 + bx + c = 0.$

- Must be able to handle all input possibilities for *a, b,* and *c.*

- This is a tutorial application that must provide full explanations to users about the solutions for all values for *a, b,* and *c.*

**FIGURE 9.62** Example of *Template* Motivation

1. Report progress
2. Display number of solutions
3. Display first solution, if any
4. Display second solution, if any

**FIGURE 9.63** A Basic Quadratic Algorithm

**Design Purpose**

Allow runtime variants on an algorithm.

**Design Pattern Summary**

Express the basic algorithm in a base class, using method calls where variation is required.

**FIGURE 9.64** *Template*

No loops are required for the basic quadratic algorithm example, but they could certainly occur for other applications.

## 9.9.2 Interface to *Template* for Clients

Clients of *Template* applications need to get work done without having to worry about which algorithm will be required to do it under varying circumstances. Client code is thus written in terms of a method – *doRequest(),* let's say – of a class, which we will name *Subject.*

## 9.9.3 The *Template* Class Model

To effect the required variability in the algorithm for *doRequest(),* the latter passes control to a method *handleRequest()* of an aggregated object, *algorithm,* of class *TemplateAlgorithm.* The method *handleRequest()* calls methods *calledMethod1(), calledMethod2(),* etc. at places where variability is required. At runtime, *algorithm* is instantiated as an object of a *TemplateAlgorithm* subclass, and the appropriate versions of *calledMethod1(), calledMethod2(),* etc. are called. This design pattern is thus in the *Delegation* form, and is shown in Figure 9.65.

## 9.9.4 Example *Template* Application: Quadratic Solutions

Let's return to the quadratic example. The main use case is as follows.

The application performs the following repeatedly until the user quits.

1. The *application* prompts the user for the 'a' value in $ax^2 + bx + c = 0.$
2. The *user* enters a value of 'a' at the console.
3. The *application* prompts the user for the 'b' value in $ax^2 + bx + c = 0.$
4. The *user* enters a value of 'b' at the console.
5. The *application* prompts the user for the 'c' value in $ax^2 + bx + c = 0.$

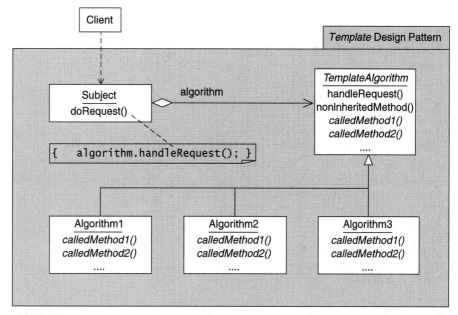

**FIGURE 9.65** Class Model for *Template*

6. The *user* enters a value of 'c' at the console.

7. The *application* states the number of solutions.

8. The *application* lists the solutions themselves.

The output we'd require is illustrated in Figures 9.66 and 9.77.

```
Please enter 'a' in the form ....m.n...:
1
Please enter 'b' in the form ....m.n...:
3
Please enter 'c' in the form ....m.n...:
2
solving the equation .....
There are two solutions to this quadratic equation.
The reason is that b**2 - 4ac is positive.
There are two solutions because b**2 > 4ac.
The first solution is obtained from the formula ( - b + Math.sqrt ( b*b - 4*a*c ) ) / 2*a )
It is -1.0
There are two solutions because b**2 > 4ac.
The second solution is obtained from the formula ( - b - Math.sqrt ( b*b - 4*a*c ) ) / 2*a )
It is -2.0

Type quit if you don't want to solve more quadratic equations, otherwise any character.
more
Please enter 'a' in the form ....m.n...:
1
Please enter 'b' in the form ....m.n...:
2
Please enter 'c' in the form ....m.n...:
3
solving the equation .....
There are no solutions to this quadratic equation.
```

**FIGURE 9.66** I/O for *Quadratic* Example (1 of 2)

```
Type quit if you don't want to solve more quadratic equations, otherwise any character.
more
Please enter 'a' in the form ....m.n...:
0
Please enter 'b' in the form ....m.n...:
3
Please enter 'c' in the form ....m.n...:
4
solving the equation .....
There is one solution to this quadratic equation.
There is one solution because a is zero and so the equation is bx + c = 0.
The solution is thus obtained from the formula - c / b.
The solution is -1.3333333333333333

Type quit if you don't want to solve more quadratic equations, otherwise any character.
more
Please enter 'a' in the form ....m.n...:
0
Please enter 'b' in the form ....m.n...:
0
Please enter 'c' in the form ....m.n...:
1
solving the equation .....
There are no solutions to this quadratic equation.
The reason is that this equation is of the form 1.0 = 0
and no value for x can make this true.

Type quit if you don't want to solve more quadratic equations, otherwise any character.
more
```

**FIGURE 9.67**  I/O for *Quadratic* Example (2 of 2)

The pseudocode for the algorithm in the base class can be expressed a shown in Figure 9.68.

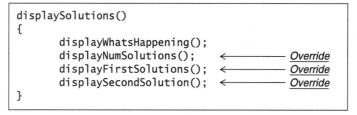

**FIGURE 9.68**  *Quadratic* Display Algorithm

## DESIGN GOALS AT WORK *Flexibility* and *Robustness*

Isolate the main algorithm for quadratic solution display. Isolate the variants that depend on the coefficients.

Figure 9.69 illustrates the class model for this example.

Note that since the methods *displayNumSolutions(), displayFirstSolution()* and *displaySecondSolution()* are abstract in *Template* (denoted by italics), they must be implemented in each of the subclasses. For example, in the class *OneSolution*, *displaySecondSolution()* does nothing. The source code for this example is in Appendix F.

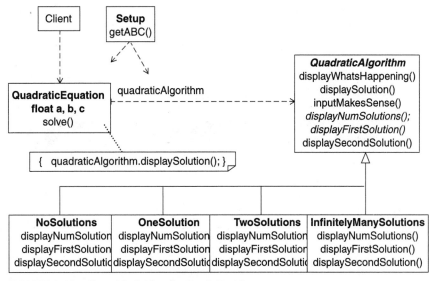

**FIGURE 9.69** Class Model for *Quadratic* Problem

## 9.9.5 Application of *Template* in the Java API

When we utilize the *Applet* class, we inherit from it and rely on the applet environment that calls *init()*, *start()*, *paint()*, and *stop()* in accordance with a standard algorithm for executing applets. This algorithm is a more or less a sequence, but it does contain some nontrivial logic. For example, *init()* is called just once, whereas *start()* is called whenever we scroll to the applet. Our applet subclass simply overrides these methods to get the particular effect we want, but the overall algorithm can't be changed. A similar *Template* algorithm controls Servlets.

## 9.9.6 Comments on *Template*

▨ *Template* promotes modularity (and thus correctness and reusability) by separating the core of a set of algorithms from its variants. You can think of it as helping us create order in an increasingly complex world. For example, doctors must submit claims to health insurance companies, but each one has a somewhat different claims procedure, leading to enormous complexity. The core of the claims process is the same, and *Template* allows us to code that process separately: We can then capture the variants for a company in its own class.

▨ *Template* is an important way to gain leverage when creating an algorithm, allowing it to apply to many separate cases.

▨ Perhaps a downside of using *Template* is the usual one with design patterns: We are introducing additional function calls, which reduces time efficiency. Another is that we are fragmenting algorithms rather than keeping each algorithm separate. This can be looked at positively for the most part, although there are negative aspects as well. For example, suppose that we are writing an algorithm to compute automobile insurance premiums using *Template*. The base template class would contain the basic overall insurance computation algorithm common to all cars: Subclasses would account for computations on the major brands (Subcompacts, Compacts, Midsize, etc.) and subclasses of those would account for particular models. This is an effective organization of algorithms. A negative factor is that the calculation algorithm for specific vehicles, 1995 Toyota Camrys, for example, is not contained in a single method. Typically, this is outweighed by our ability to maintain and change the computation algorithms.

■ By separating algorithms into a hierarchy, we promote modularity (and thus the ability to verify the design correctness), maintainability (keeping track of the various algorithms more effectively) and flexibility (allowing us to change algorithms easily).

---

**KEY CONCEPT**    *Template* Design Pattern

To capture a basic algorithm and its variants.

---

# SUMMARY

Figure 9.70 summarizes this chapter.

**Behavioral Design Patterns** Capture Behavior Among Objects

- *Interpreter* parses expressions
- *Iterator* visits members of a collection
- *Mediator* captures behavior among peer objects
- *Observer* updates objects affected by a single object
- *State* expresses behavior that depends on current status
- *Chain of Responsibility* allows a set of objects to provide functionality collectively
- *Command* captures functionality flexibly (e.g. undo-able)
- *Template* captures basic algorithms, allowing variability

**FIGURE 9.70**   Summary of *Behavioral* Patterns

# EXERCISES

**Exercise 9.1**  **Customer Information Update**   This exercise pertains to the customer information example in the section 9.7.4 concerning *Chain of Responsibility.* You are required to add a new "emergency contact" field under "personal."

**Part 9.1.1** Show your class model to solve this application, explaining the new part(s).

**Part 9.1.2** Implement the requirement, showing at least three different sample outputs.

**Part 9.1.3** List your source code, with classes arranged alphabetically.

Evaluation criteria:
- ■ Appropriate design pattern(s), correctly   A = completely appropriate and correct
  implemented
- ■ Clarity   A = very clear design, code and comments

The following are errors that you should watch for in this exercise (see also Evaluation Criteria):
  *Serious:*
1. Inappropriate design pattern.
2. Model does not separate the parts appropriately.
3. Incorrect interface with clients.

**4.** Inflexible design.

**5.** You have listed code that does not have a required counterpart in your class model, or vice versa.

*Less than serious, more than minor:*

**1.** Inadequate method documentation.

**Exercise 9.2** **XML Parser** You are required to write an XML parser, which can handle the following kinds of expressions as input. Assume that in the future the allowable input will build on this, and even possibly allow tags to repeat within tags (e.g., a <email></email> tag pair within a <body></body> tag pair). Your design should anticipate this, but you do not need to accommodate it.

```
<email>
                <author> Any-text-a </author>
                <subject> Any-text-s</subject>
                <to> Any-text-t </to>
                <cc> Any-text-c11</cc>
                ... . [possibly more cc's]
                <body>
                            Any-text-b
                                    <email> [optional]
                                            <author> Any-text-a2 </author>
                                            <subject> Any-text-s2</subject>
                                            <to> Any-text-t2 </to>
                                            <cc> Any-text-c21</cc>
                                            <cc> ... . (any number of <cc>)
                                            <body>
                                                    Any-text-b2
                                                    ... . [possibly another email]
                                            </body>
                                    </email>
                </body>
</email>
```

The output should be text readable by someone who has no knowledge of XML, as follows.

*Some text a* sent a message with the following subject: *Some text s*

The message is as follows: *Some text b*

The main recipient was *Some text t*

The message was copied to *Some text c1*, *Some text c2*, and *Some text c...*

**Part 9.2.1** State the grammar that must be parsed. If you are familiar with schemas, you may use one instead of the form provided in this chapter.

**Part 9.2.2** Show your class model.

**Part 9.2.3** List your code or pseudocode (as required by your instructor) alphabetically by class and by method within classes.

**Part 9.2.4** Show your output for at least two different samples of XML, which illustrate the requirements.

Evaluation criteria:

▨ Correctly applied design pattern to correct grammar    (A = completely appropriate and correct)

▨ Clarity    (A = very clear grammar, design, code/pseudocode where appropriate, and comments)

Points to watch for in this exercise:

*Serious:*

**1.** There is an aggregation implemented in your code that does not show up in your class model, or vice versa.

**2.** Your class model does not allow for future nesting of the body part, etc. Use *Interpreter* with suitable nonterminal (sub)classes.

**3.** Your grammar does not support multiple cc's.

**4.** Your class model does not support multiple cc's.

*Neither serious nor trivial:*

**1.** Aggregating another class limits the reusability of a class. Avoid it for classes intended for reuse unless you are prepared to use that class only in the presence of its aggregated class(es).

**2.** Don't repeat code: Elevate it to a superclass if you can.

**3.** You have not fully documented the purpose of each method. Preferably, use preconditions, etc.

**Exercise 9.3**  **Simulating Automobile Movement**  Suppose that you want to simulate the movement of automobiles in a downtown area. The problem is not difficult to design for just a single automobile traveling through the streets, but we want to handle multiple automobiles. Assume that we do not yet completely understand what happens when two automobiles get close: Similarly for automobiles and pedestrians. For this reason we want to be able to easily build and change these interactions. Give a class model *fragment* that accommodates this requirement. You are not required to build the entire simulation. Explain your reasoning thoroughly.

The output could include the following.

*The application recognizes that auto 17 has come close to auto 22, and the following results.*
   *Auto 17 slows down by 25%*
   *Auto 22 slows down by 25%*
*The application recognizes auto 1 has come close to pedestrian 3, and the following results.*
   *Auto 1 slows down by 50%*
   *Pedestrian 3 stops*

**Part 9.3.1**  Provide a class model for the fragment of requirements given here. You can regard the rest of the simulation as the client.

**Part 9.3.2**  State part of a principal use case that pertains to the auto-to-auto and auto-to-pedestrian functionality required. The sample output can be used as a guide.

**Part 9.3.3**  Implement the class model and demonstrate the implementation with the use case. List your output and code in alphabetical order by class and method.

Evaluation criteria:

| | |
|---|---|
| ▨ Clarity of your class model | A = entirely clear separation of client, setup—if any required—and design pattern application |
| ▨ Clarity of your code | A = very clear code organization and documentation |

Errors you should avoid:

*Serious:*

**1.** Inappropriate design pattern.

**2.** Model does not separate the parts appropriately.

**3.** Incorrect interface with clients.

**4.** Inflexible design.

**5.** You have listed code that does not have a required counterpart in your class model, or vice versa.

*Less than serious, more than minor:*

**1.** Inadequate method documentation.

**Exercise 9.4**  **Customer Categories**  Build a command-line application for an email-based retailer. The application accepts orders for only four items at this point: The Beatles' first album, Elvis Presley's first, Herbert von Karajan's, and Ray Matthews' first album. It is the policy of this retailer to approve customers. There is an approval process for potential customers that takes time. The application fulfils orders from approved customers only. For customers on the waiting list for approval, the application stores the order until the customer is approved. The application fulfills orders by business mail for customers with adequate credit, fulfills orders by express mail for customers with good-to-excellent credit, and adds a discount coupon for customers with excellent credit. Your design should anticipate new special offerings and deals for these and customer categories to be determined. Recognize that other applications can change the customers' credit and listing status at any time. Give a class model and explain it thoroughly.

Here is a scenario:

Welcome to *Hits of the 20th Century*. Please enter your name:
Eric J. Braude

[simulation of database search:]
User 'approved' or on 'waiting list'?
approved

[simulation of database search:]
Credit: "adequate," "good," or "excellent"
good

[simulation of mail process:]
Your order is being fulfilled by mail

**Part 9.4.1** Provide a class model for this application.

**Part 9.4.2** Implement the class model and demonstrate the implementation with the scenario provided. List your output and code in alphabetical order by class and method.

Evaluation criteria:

| | |
|---|---|
| ▩ Clarity of your class model | A = entirely clear separation of client, setup—if any required—and design pattern application |
| ▩ Clarity of your code | A = very clear code organization and documentation |

Errors you should avoid:

*Serious:*

1. Inappropriate design pattern.
2. Model does not separate the parts appropriately.
3. Incorrect interface with clients.
4. Inflexible design.
5. You have listed code that does not have a required counterpart in your class model, or vice versa.

*Less than serious, more than minor:*

1. Inadequate method documentation.

**Exercise 9.5** **Adding a 'Delete Word' Command to the Word Processor Example**  Extend the example in Section 9.8.4 (application of *Command*) to include—and undo—the following operation. "Delete word" deletes the word indicated: "1" indicates the first word, "2" the second word, etc.

**Part 9.5.1** Provide a class model.

**Part 9.5.2** Implement the class model and demonstrate the implementation with at least three dele-teundo scenarios. List your output and your code in alphabetical order by class and method.

Evaluation criteria:

| | |
|---|---|
| ▩ Clarity of your class mode | A = entirely clear separation of client, setup—if any required—and design pattern application |
| ▩ Clarity of your code | A = very clear code organization and documentation |

Errors to watch for:

*Serious:*

1. The specifications of one of the key added methods do not match its purposes.

*Less than serious, more than trivial:*

1. You have specified postconditions for a key method as an algorithm instead of describing the state precisely.

**Exercise 9.6** **Dishwasher Manuals**  Your client manufactures a line of dishwashers, and you are tasked to generate manuals that explain how to operate them. The manner of opening the dishwasher door is the same for all models. The next step is to set the "wash type" selection. For all models, short, medium, and long wash types can be selected, but each model requires a different procedure to make each of these choices. Finally, all models have the same instructions for turning the machine on once this setting has been made.

Assume that there are currently three models, and that there will be more to come in the future. Develop and design an application that generates manuals. Instead of storing the actual instructions, display substitute text to the console as shown in the following example using model 3 as your subject.

1. Display detailed instructions for opening the dishwasher door...
2. Display detailed instructions to locate the "wash type" selection dial for model.
3. Depending on the selection chosen, the following will occur, shown for model 2.

   If "short" type has been selected...

   display instructions for selecting a short wash when using model 2...

   If "medium" type has been selected...

   display instructions for selecting a medium wash when using model 2...

   If "long" type has been selected...

   display instructions for selecting a long wash when using model 2...

4. Display detailed instructions for turning on the machine...

Your design should accommodate future changes in the process, and possible voluminous details about options.

**Part 9.6.1** Provide the class model.

**Part 9.6.2** Implement the class model and demonstrate the implementation with a scenario. List your output for all models, as well as additional or changed code in alphabetical order by class and method.

Evaluation criteria:

| | |
|---|---|
| ▩ Clarity of your class model | A = entirely clear separation of client, setup—if any required—and design pattern application |
| ▩ Clarity of your code | A = very clear code organization and documentation |

The following are errors that you should watch for in this exercise:

*Serious:*

1. Inappropriate design pattern.
2. Incorrect application of a design pattern.
3. Incorrect interface with clients.
4. Inappropriate separation of design elements.
5. Your output is missing the "if" parts.

*Neither serious nor trivial:*

1. You did not take full advantage of the design pattern that you selected.

# APPENDIX A

## SOURCE CODE FOR NETWORK ASSEMBLY EXAMPLE (APPLICATION OF INTERPRETER DESIGN PATTERN)

The class *Client*:

```
import java.io.*;

/**
 * User of the Interpreter pattern application
 */
class Client
```

```
{
/*******************************************************************************
 */
public Client()
/******************************************************************************/
{  super();
}

/*******************************************************************************
 * Precondition: 'aNetworkOrder' != 'null'=*
 * Postcondition: Report to console of lots of work performed with network orders
 * Design Note: No reference to the parts being assembled.
 */
public void doProcessingWith( Component aNetworkOrder )
/******************************************************************************/
{
   System.out.println
     ( "\n\t.....Do some work with the order ...." );   // potentially lots of code here
   aNetworkOrder.assemble();   // request for assembly instructions to be printed to console
   System.out.println
     ( "\n\t.....Do more work with the order ....\n" );   // potentially lots of code here
}

}
```

The interface *Component*:

```
/**
 * Component of a computer network system
 */
interface Component
{

/********************************************************************************
 * To output assembly instructions to the console.
 */
public abstract void assemble();

/********************************************************************************
 * To output assembly instructions to the console.
 */
public abstract void assemble( String anAssemblyName );

}
```

The class *Computer*:

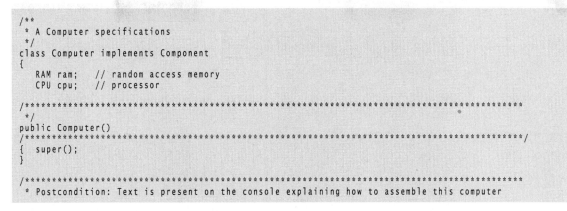

```
/**
 * A Computer specifications
 */
class Computer implements Component
{
   RAM ram;   // random access memory
   CPU cpu;   // processor

/********************************************************************************
 */
public Computer()
/******************************************************************************/
{  super();
}

/********************************************************************************
 * Postcondition: Text is present on the console explaining how to assemble this computer
```

```
   */
public void assemble()
/******************************************************************************************/
{
   System.out.println( "\tBuild a computer computer from the following parts:" );
   cpu.describe();
   System.out.println( "\tand " );
   ram.describe();
}

/******************************************************************************************
 * Postcondition: Text is present on the console explaining how to assemble this computer
 */
public void assemble( String anAssemblyName )
/******************************************************************************************/
{
   System.out.println( "\tBuild computer " + anAssemblyName + ", from the following parts:" );
   cpu.describe();
   System.out.println( "\tand " );
   ram.describe();
}

/******************************************************************************************
 */
public Computer( CPU aCPU, RAM aRAM )
/******************************************************************************************/
{
   this();
   cpu = aCPU;
   ram = aRAM;
}

}
```

The class *CPU*:

```
/**
 * Central Processing Unit for individual computers
 */
class CPU
{
   int speed = 800;   // MHz default";

   /****************************************************************************
    */
   public CPU()
   /****************************************************************************/
   { super();
   }

   /****************************************************************************
    * Postcondition: A description of this has been output to the console
    */
   public void describe()
   /****************************************************************************/
   { System.out.println( "\t\tCPU with specifications ....." + speed );
   }

   /****************************************************************************
    */
   public CPU( int aSpeed )
   /****************************************************************************/
   {
      this();
      speed = aSpeed;
   }

}
```

The class *NetSystem*:

```
/**
 * A network of networks ... of computers
 */
class NetSystem implements Component
{
   private Component component1 = null;   // there will always be one component
   private Component component2 = null;   // not always present
   static int componentNum = 0;   // for generating unique names of components

/*********************************************************************************************
 */
public NetSystem()
/*********************************************************************************************/
{  super();
}


/*********************************************************************************************
 * Network consisting of one subsystem
 */
public NetSystem( Component aComponent1 )
/*********************************************************************************************/
{
   this();
   component1 = aComponent1;
}


/*********************************************************************************************
 * Network consisting of two subsystems
 */
public NetSystem( Component aComponent1, Component aComponent2 )
/*********************************************************************************************/
{
   this();
   component1 = aComponent1;
   component2 = aComponent2;
}


/*********************************************************************************************
 * Postcondition: instructions have been output to console on how to assemble the network
 */
public void assemble()
/*********************************************************************************************/
{
   System.out.println( "\nAssemble a network from either one or two parts as follows:");

   // ====== First part of the network
   String nameOfFirstComponent = NetSystem.getNewName();
   System.out.println
     ( "\n====> First Part: Assemble a network, which we will name '" +
     nameOfFirstComponent + "', as follows: ");
   component1.assemble( nameOfFirstComponent );   // the first part

   // ====== Second part of the network -- if there is one
   if( component2 != null )   // the second part -- if there is one
   {
       String nameOfSecondComponent = NetSystem.getNewName();
       System.out.println( "\n====> Second part: Now assemble a network, which we will name '"
         + nameOfSecondComponent + "', as follows: ");
       component2.assemble( nameOfSecondComponent );
       System.out.println( "\n==== Now connect " + nameOfFirstComponent + " with " +
         nameOfSecondComponent + " to get the resulting network. ====" );
   }
}


/*********************************************************************************************
 * Precondition: component1 != null
```

```
 * Postcondition: instructions to assemble the network appear on the console.
 */
public void assemble( String anAssemblyName )
/****************************************************************************************/
{
   String nameOfFirstComponent = NetSystem.getNewName();
   System.out.println
   ( "\nAssemble a network, which we will name '" + nameOfFirstComponent +
   "', from either one or two parts as follows: ");
   System.out.println( "-->" );
   component1.assemble( nameOfFirstComponent );   // the first part

   if( component2 != null )   // the second part -- if there is one
   {
       System.out.println( "second part: -->" );
       String nameOfSecondComponent = NetSystem.getNewName();
       System.out.println( "\nAssemble a network, which we will name "
       + nameOfSecondComponent + ", as follows: ");
       component2.assemble( nameOfSecondComponent );
       System.out.println( "\n ------ Now connect " + nameOfFirstComponent + " with " +
       nameOfSecondComponent + " to complete " + anAssemblyName + " ------" );
   }
}


/****************************************************************************************
 * Returns: A unique newcomponent =name
 * Example: Returns "component123" where the previous component was "component122"
 */
private static String getNewName()
/****************************************************************************************/
{
   Integer integer = new Integer( ++ NetSystem.componentNum );
   return( "component" + integer.toString() );
}

}
```

The class *RAM*:

```
/**
 * Random Access Memory for individual computers
 */
class RAM
{
   int amount = 0;   // Gigabytes default

/****************************************************************************************
 */
public RAM()
/****************************************************************************************/
{  super();
}

/****************************************************************************************
 * Postcondition: A description of this has been output to the console
 */
public void describe()
/****************************************************************************************/
{  System.out.println( "\t\tRAM with specifications ....." + amount );
}

/****************************************************************************************
 */
public RAM( int anAmount )
/****************************************************************************************/
{
```

```
     this();
     amount = anAmount;
   }

   }
```

The class *Setup*:

```
import java.io.*;
import java.util.*;

/**
 * Gets input in the grammar and creates corresponding tree of 'Component' objects
 *
 * Implementation notes: several of these methods could be combined, making for more
 * efficiency, less code, but less clarity.
 */
class Setup
{

/*******************************************************************************************
 */
public Setup()
/******************************************************************************************/
{  super();
}

/*******************************************************************************************
 * Returns: string specifying a computer network
 */
public static String getInputFromUser()
/******************************************************************************************/
{
   System.out.println
     ( "Please describe a network on one line using the following grammar for 'component.'" );
   System.out.println
     ( "Blank spaces are ignored.  Inputs with syntactic errors will be ignored without comment.\n" );
   System.out.println( "component ::= net system | computer" );
   System.out.println( "net system ::= { component } { component } | { component }" );
   System.out.println( "computer ::= ( cpu ram )" );
   System.out.println( "cpu ::= integer" );
   System.out.println( "ram ::= integer" );

   System.out.println( "\nExample: { { {(400 4)}{ (900 3)} } {(600 3)} } { (750 10) }" );

   String returnString = "not yet assigned";
   try
   {
       BufferedReader bufReader = new BufferedReader( new InputStreamReader( System.in ) );
       returnString = bufReader.readLine();
   }
   catch( IOException e )
   {   System.out.println( e ); }

   return returnString;
}

/*******************************************************************************************
 * Preconditions:
 * (1) 0 <= aBeginIndex < aString.length
 * (2) There is at least one "{" in aString on or after index 'aBeginIndex'
 * (3) There is at least one "}" in aString on or after index 'aBeginIndex'
 *
 * Returns:
 * The index in 'aString' at which the first "{" after index 'aBeginIndex''
```

```
 * is balanced by a "}"
 *
 * Examples:
 *              indexOfBalancingBrace( "{abc), 0 ) returns 4
 *              indexOfBalancingBrace( "klm { a {bc} d }stu}", 2 ) returns 15
 */
public static int indexOfBalancingBrace( String aString, int aBeginIndex ) throws Exception
/***************************************************************************************/
{
    int returnIndex = 0;

    // Ensure aBeginIndex is within required bounds
    if( aBeginIndex < 0 || aBeginIndex >= aString.length() )
        throw new Exception
          ( "aBeginIndex out of bounds in indexOfBalancingBrace." );

    // Ensure that there is at least one "{" in aString and save the index
    int NOT_FOUND = -1;    // indicates there is no '{' in aString
    int indexOfFirstOpenBrace = NOT_FOUND;
    int stringIndex = aBeginIndex;    // begin traveling from here, looking for '{'
    for( ; stringIndex < aString.length(); ++stringIndex )
        if( aString.charAt( stringIndex ) == '{' )
        {       // Set indexOfFirstOpenBrace and stop looking
            indexOfFirstOpenBrace = stringIndex;
            break;
        }
    if( stringIndex == NOT_FOUND )   // no open brace was found
        throw new Exception( "aString in indexOfBalancingBrace contained no open brace." );

    else   // there is at least on '{'
    {
        // Find the index where the first '{' encountered on or after aBeginIndex
        // balances ( with a '}' )
        int numUnbalancedOpenBraces = 1;  // because we start right after the '{' found above
        for( int balanceIndex = indexOfFirstOpenBrace + 1;
         balanceIndex < aString.length(); // limit: break before this if balancing "}" found
         ++balanceIndex )
        {
            if( aString.charAt( balanceIndex ) == '{' )   // one more '{' to balance
                ++numUnbalancedOpenBraces;
            if( aString.charAt( balanceIndex ) == '}' )   // one more '{' closed
                --numUnbalancedOpenBraces;
            if( numUnbalancedOpenBraces == 0 )   // balance found
                return balanceIndex;   // and process stops
        }

        // No balancing '}' was found
        throw( new Exception
          ( "indexOfBalancingBrace requested to parse illegal expression " + aString ) );
    }
}


/***************************************************************************************
 * Postconditions:
 *      (1) As for 'getInputFromUser()'
 *      (2) A network order object has been created from the network input provided
 *      (3) As for 'doProcessingWith()' on the order entered (instructions output to console on
 *                  how to assemble the network).,
 */
public static void main( String[] args )
/***************************************************************************************/
{
    String input = getInputFromUser();
    Component networkOrder = new Computer( new CPU( 0 ), new RAM( 0 ) );   // default

    try
    {   networkOrder = parse( input );
    }
```

```
    catch( Exception e )
    {    System.out.println( e );
    }

    // Create the client and set it going
    Client client = new Client();
    client.doProcessingWith( networkOrder );
}

/*************************************************************************************************
 * Returns:
 * A 'Component' object, which is at the root of a tree of 'Component' objects corresponding
 * to 'anExpression', using the grammar defined in 'getInputFromUser()'
 *
 * Postcondition:The application has quit if the first non-blank in 'anExpression' is neither '('
 * nor '{'.
 *
 * Design Note: There is no attempt to discriminate among exceptions.  This is not part of the
 * Interpreter
 *              design pattern, but the latter expects a parsed object as input.
 */
public static Component parse( String anExpression ) throws Exception
/*************************************************************************************************/
{
    Component returnComponent = new NetSystem();   // default

    // (1) ----- 'anExpression' null?

    if( anExpression == null )
        throw new Exception( "parse() called with null argument" );

    // (2) ----- 'anExpression' represents a computer?

    char firstChar = firstNonBlankIn( anExpression );

    if( firstChar == '(' )  // anExpression is a computer
    {
        StringTokenizer tokens = new StringTokenizer( anExpression );

        // Get cpu
        String firstToken = tokens.nextToken();   // "(..."
        String cpuToken = null;
        if( "(".equals( firstToken ) )   // "( nnn" -- blank separator
            cpuToken = tokens.nextToken();   // pick up "nnn"
        else   // "(nnn" -- no blank separator
            cpuToken = firstToken.substring( 1, firstToken.length() );   // pick up "nnn"
        int cpu = Integer.parseInt( cpuToken );   // if not integer, exception caught by this method

        // Get ram
        String part2 = tokens.nextToken();   // ram integer but may include ')'
        if( part2.charAt( part2.length() - 1 ) == ')' )   // ends with ')'
            part2 = part2.substring( 0, part2.length() - 1 );   // remove ')'
        int ram = Integer.parseInt( part2 );   // if not integer, exception caught by this method

        returnComponent = new Computer( new CPU( cpu ), new RAM( ram ) );
    }

    // (3) ---- 'anExpression' is of the form { component } { component } or { component }

    else
    {
        if( firstChar == '{' )
        {
            // Make a Component from the first component string
            // Index of '}' closing first '{'
            int balanceIndex = indexOfBalancingBrace( anExpression, 0 );
            int indexOfFirstOpenBrace = indexOfFirstNonBlankIn( anExpression );
```

```
                    String component1String = anExpression.substring( indexOfFirstOpenBrace + 1,
                    balanceIndex );
                    Component component1 = parse( component1String );

                    // Make a Component from the second component string if there is one
                    // ... to the end of anExpression
                    String component2String = anExpression.substring( balanceIndex + 1 );
                    if( thereIsANonBlankIn( component2String ) )   // there are 2 components (not just 1)
                    {
                            Component component2 = parse( component2String );

                            // Make a network object from these two components and return it.
                            returnComponent = new NetSystem( component1, component2 );
                }
                else   // there is only one component
                        returnComponent = new NetSystem( component1 );
            }
            else   // first non-blank in expression to be parsed is neither '(' nor '{': End application
            {
                System.out.println
                    ( "first non-blank in expression given to parse() is neither '(' nor '{'---->" +
                    anExpression);
                System.exit( 1 );
            }
        }

    return returnComponent;
}

/********************************************************************************************
 * Returns: First non-blank character in 'aString' if there is one, otherwise ' '
 */
public static char firstNonBlankIn( String aString )
/********************************************************************************************/
{
    char returnChar = ' ';   // default

    if( aString != null && aString.length() != 0 )   // else skip over this
        for( int stringIndex = 0; stringIndex < aString.length(); ++stringIndex )
        {
                returnChar = aString.charAt( stringIndex );
                if( returnChar != ' ' )   // first non-blank found: stop here
                        break;
        }

    return returnChar;
}

/********************************************************************************************
 * Returns: index of first non-blank character in 'aString' if there is one,
 * Postcondition:Stops the application with message if there is no non-blank character in 'aString'
 */
public static int indexOfFirstNonBlankIn( String aString )
/********************************************************************************************/
{
    if( aString != null && aString.length() != 0 )
    {   for( int stringIndex = 0; stringIndex < aString.length(); ++stringIndex )
        {       if( aString.charAt( stringIndex ) != ' ' )   // first non-blank found: stop here
                        return stringIndex;
        }
    }
    else   // there is no non-blank character in 'aString'
    {
        System.out.println( "indexOfFirstNonBlankIn() called with blank String " + aString );
        System.exit( 0 );
    }
    return( 0 );
}
```

```
/*******************************************************************************
 * Returns: true if 'aString' contains a non-blank; false otherwise
 */
public static boolean thereIsANonBlankIn( String aString )
/******************************************************************************/
{
   if( aString != null && aString.length() != 0 )
   {  for( int stringIndex = 0; stringIndex < aString.length(); ++stringIndex )
      {      if( aString.charAt( stringIndex ) != ' ' )   // found a non-blank
                 return true;
      }
   }
   else   // there is no non-blank character in 'aString'
       return false;

   return false;
}

}
```

# APPENDIX B

## SOURCE CODE FOR "ORGANIZATION CHART" EXAMPLE (APPLICATION OF ITERATOR DESIGN PATTERN)

The class *Client*:

```
import java.io.*;

/**
 * User of iterators on the org chart
 */
class Client
{

/*****************************************************************************
 * Postcondition: Each element of the org chart referred to by 'anIterator' has been visited
 *     in the order determined by 'anIterator'.  Evidence of each visit appears on the console.
 */
public void doClientTasks( OrgChartIterator anIterator )
/*****************************************************************************/
{
   // Print the names of all employees according to order specified by anIterator
   System.out.println( "Printing names of employees according to required order\n" );

   anIterator.first();
   while( !anIterator.isDone() )
   {
       System.out.println
       ( "Perform work .... with employee " + anIterator.currentItem().getName()  );
       System.out.println
       ( "... with " + anIterator.currentItem().getYearsOfService() + " years of service." );
       anIterator.next();
   }

   System.out.println( "\nCompleted printing names of employees" );
}

}
```

The class *Employee*:

```java
import java.util.*;

/**
 * Base class for the org chart
 */
abstract class Employee
{
   String nameI = "not known";
   int yearsOfServiceI = 0;    // default

/********************************************************************************
 */
public Employee(){}

/********************************************************************************
 */
public abstract Vector getChildren();

/********************************************************************************
 */
public abstract String getName();

/********************************************************************************
 */
public abstract int getYearsOfService();

}
```

The class *IntSequence*:

```java
import java.util.*;

/**
 * A sequence of integers.  A utility class.
 */
class IntSequence extends Vector implements Cloneable
{

/********************************************************************************
 */
public IntSequence()
/*******************************************************************************/
{ super();
}

/********************************************************************************
 * Postcondition: 'anInteger' is the last element of 'this'.
 */
public void append( int anInteger )
/*******************************************************************************/
{ addElement( new Integer( anInteger ) );
}

/********************************************************************************
 * Returns: last integer in 'this'.
 */
public int getLast()
/*******************************************************************************/
{ return ( (Integer)lastElement() ).intValue();
}

/********************************************************************************
 * Returns: The integer in the sequence at index 0, 1, etc.
```

```
 */
public int getValueAt( int indexP )
/*****************************************************************************/
{ return ( (Integer)( elementAt( indexP ) ) ).intValue();
}


/*****************************************************************************
 * Precondition: there is at least one integer
 *
 * Postcondition: The last integer of 'this' is absent
 */
public void removeLast()
/*****************************************************************************/
{ removeElementAt( size() - 1 );
}


}
```

The class *OrgChartIterator*:

```
import java.util.*;

/**
 * Base class for iterators on orga charts: Interfaces with Employee.
 */
abstract class OrgChartIterator
{
   /* Position of the employee that this iterator currently points to.

   emplPositionI reflects the state of this, and denotes an element in the tree: each integer
   denotes the number of remaining sblings at that level.

   For example, the position { 0, 2, 0 } for emplPositionI has the following meaning.
   The first integer is always zero, and indicates that the root node has no more siblings.
   The "2" indicates that the node below the root has two more siblings;
   The node below that is the last of its siblings (the last 0 in the example).
   The node that this iterator is pointing to is at level 3, counting the root node's level as level 1.
    */
   IntSequence emplPositionI = new IntSequence();  // pointing to the most senior element
   Employee employeeI;   // Root of the tree of employees we intend to iterate over

/********************************************************************************
 */
public OrgChartIterator()
/******************************************************************************/
{
   super();
   emplPositionI.append( 0 );
}

/********************************************************************************
 */
public OrgChartIterator( Employee anEmployee )
/******************************************************************************/
{
   this();
   employeeI = anEmployee;
}

/********************************************************************************
 */
public abstract Employee currentItem();

/********************************************************************************
 */
```

```
public abstract void first();

/******************************************************************************
 */
abstract public boolean isDone();

/******************************************************************************
 * Effectively increments the 'OrgChartIterator'
 */
public abstract void next();

}
```

The class *OrgSeniorityIterator*:

```
import java.util.*;

/**
 * Iterates over the org chart by hierarchical seniority (i.e., by who reports to whom)
 */
class OrgSeniorityIterator extends OrgChartIterator
{

/******************************************************************************
 */
public OrgSeniorityIterator()
/*****************************************************************************/
{  super();
}
/******************************************************************************
 */
public OrgSeniorityIterator( Employee anEmployee )
/*****************************************************************************/
{
   this();
   employeeI = anEmployee;
}
/******************************************************************************
 * Make an iterator pointing to a position
 */
public OrgSeniorityIterator( Employee anEmployee, IntSequence aPosition )
/*****************************************************************************/
{
   this( anEmployee );   // iterates on same aggregate
   emplPositionI = aPosition;   // points to the given position
}
/******************************************************************************
 * Precondition: points to the original tree root or a subnode
 * (not virtual root or "done" node) so the 'size()' of 'emplPositionI' is at least one
 *
 * Returns: The 'Employee' object that 'this' points to
 */
public Employee currentItem()
/*****************************************************************************/
{
   // empl will refer to the node referred to as we go down the tree
   Employee employee = employeeI;   // start at the given root node

   for( int i = 1; i < emplPositionI.size(); ++i )
   {
      // Replace with the child number indicated by the iterator (computed first)
      int childIndex =
      ( employee.getChildren().size() ) - 1 - emplPositionI.getValueAt( i );
      employee = (Employee) ( employee.getChildren().elementAt( childIndex ) );
   }
```

```
      return employee;
   }

   /************************************************************************
    * Postcondition: 'this' points to the root.
    */
   public void first()
   /************************************************************************/
   {
      emplPositionI = new IntSequence();
      emplPositionI.append( 0 );
   }


   /************************************************************************
    * Definition:
    * The "level" of a node is the horizontal level, measured from the virtual root, which is at level 0.
    *
    * Parameters: aLevel is a level; aPosition is the position of a node in the tree,
    * represented in the manner described at the head of this class.
    *
    * Precondition: aLevel >= aPosition.size()
    *
    * Returns: Vector representation of the first element, organization-seniority-wise, in the org chart
    * at level aLevel in the sub-organization defined by aPosition if such an element; null otherwise.
    *
    * Example: for tree
    *                     Node1(0)                          level 1
    *                  Node2        Node3(0,0)              level 2
    *                Node4    Node5    Node6                level 3
    *
    * getFirstUnderThisAtLevel( 3, (0) ) = (0, 1, 1) (Node4)
    * getFirstUnderThisAtLevel( 3, (0, 0) ) = (0, 0, 0) (Node6)
    */
   public IntSequence getFirstUnderThisAtLevel( int aLevel, IntSequence aPosition )
   /************************************************************************/
   {
      // Null case: seeking at same level =====================================

      if( aLevel == aPosition.size() )   // required to seek at same level
          return aPosition;   // node is its own "descendant"

      // Non-null case: seek at lower level =====================================

      // Need an iterator on the same aggregate pointing to the parameter position
      OrgSeniorityIterator oSI = new OrgSeniorityIterator( employeeI, aPosition );

      // Get number of children of the node that oSI points at
      int numChildren = 0;
      Vector children = oSI.currentItem().getChildren();
      if( children == null ) numChildren = 0;
      else numChildren = children.size();

      // Gate 1: There are no children ----------------------------------

      // If there are no children, there is no descendant satisfying the requirement
      if( numChildren == 0 )
          return null;

      // Gate 2: A child has a descendant at the required level ---------

      IntSequence returnPosition = null;   // possible return of this method

      // For each child node, seek a descendant at the required level
      for( int childCounter = 0; childCounter < numChildren; ++childCounter )
      {
          // Point to the child
          oSI.emplPositionI.append( numChildren - childCounter - 1 );
```

```
            // See if this child has a descendant at the required level
            returnPosition = oSI.getFirstUnderThisAtLevel( aLevel, oSI.emplPositionI );
            if( returnPosition != null )
                    return returnPosition;

            // Reset the pointer for the next iteration
            oSI.emplPositionI.removeLast();
        }

    // Through gates 1 and 2: No child has required descendant ---------
    return null;
}

/*******************************************************************************
 * Returns: true if 'this' points to last element.  (Protocol for this condition: null 'emplPositionI')
 */
public boolean isDone()
/******************************************************************************/
{  return ( emplPositionI == null );
}

/*******************************************************************************
 * Precondition: the iterator is not pointing to the root.
 *
 * Returns: true if there are more children of this element's parent
 * (after the element this iterator is pointing to)
 *
 * Test status: tested on 2 data points
 */
public boolean isLastSibling()
/******************************************************************************/
{  return ( 0 == emplPositionI.getLast() );
}

/*******************************************************************************
 * Postcondition: if isDone is false, this points to the Employee object next in seniority
 */
public void next()
/******************************************************************************/
{
    IntSequence tempPosition = null;
    Integer lastInteger = null;

    int requiredLevel = emplPositionI.size(); // save current level

    if( isDone() )
    {       System.out.println( "Attempt next() in SeniorityIterator but iteration done" );
            return;
    }

    /* 4 cases: a,b,c, and d as shown in the figure.

                             given_root                        level 1

                    N               N               N               level 2

            Na  Nb          N   Nc          level 3

                             N  Nd                      level 4
    */

    //======== Case a. If this is not the last of current element's siblings, go horizontally

    if( emplPositionI.getLast() > 0 )
    {
        pointToNextSibling();
        return;
```

```
    }

    //======== Case b: this has no more siblings (and is not the root node)

    // Move up one level at a time looking for a successor at the original level

    int numSiblingsLeftM = 0;
    for( int levelCounter = requiredLevel; levelCounter > 1; --levelCounter )
    {
        emplPositionI.removeLast();   // go up one level
        numSiblingsLeftM = emplPositionI.getLast();   // num siblings left at this level

        if( ( emplPositionI.size() > 1 ) &&   // not the given root node
          numSiblingsLeftM > 0 )   // there is a next sibling at this level

                // Look for the first sibling node with a descendant at the required level
                for( int siblingCounter = numSiblingsLeftM; siblingCounter > 0; --siblingCounter )
                {
                    // Point to the next sibling
                    emplPositionI.removeLast();   // remove last element
                    emplPositionI.append( siblingCounter - 1 );   // point to the next sibling

                    // See if this now has a (first) node at the original level
                    tempPosition = getFirstUnderThisAtLevel( requiredLevel, emplPositionI );
                    if( tempPosition != null )   // an element found
                    {
                        emplPositionI = tempPosition;   // point to it
                        return;   // we are done
                    }
                }
    }


    //======== Case c. (no next was found at the same level as the starting node)

    // Point to the given root node
    emplPositionI = new IntSequence();
    emplPositionI.append( 1 );

    // Look for first node at the next level
    tempPosition = getFirstUnderThisAtLevel( requiredLevel + 1, emplPositionI );

    if( tempPosition != null )   // a node was found
    {
        emplPositionI = tempPosition;   // point to it
        return;   // we are done
    }


    //======== Case d. (no next node)

    emplPositionI = null;   // protocol for "done"
}

/****************************************************************************
 * Precondition: current node is not the last of its siblings
 *
 * Postcondition: 'this' points to the next sibling
 */
public void pointToNextSibling()
/***************************************************************************/
{
    int currentValue = emplPositionI.getLast();
    emplPositionI.setElementAt
      ( new Integer( --currentValue ), emplPositionI.size() - 1 );
}

}
```

The class *Setup*:

```java
import java.io.*;

/**
 * Set up bank structure of organization and initiate application
 */
class Setup
{

/**************************************************************************
 * Postconditions:
 *  (1) A tree of Employee objects has been chosen
 *  (2) A type of iteration (organizational or other) has been selected
 *  (3) A client object has been established which initiates the iteration specified.
 */
public static void main( String args[] )
/**************************************************************************/
{
    Supervisor supervisor= null;   // the tree of 'Employee' objects to iterate over
    OrgChartIterator orgIter= null;   // order of iteration
    String response = "not received yet";

    // Pick tree to iterate over
    System.out.println
      ( "Iterate over bank ('b') or alternative organization chart (any other character)? " );
    response = getAnInputFromUser();
    if( response.equals( "b" ) )
    {    supervisor= (Supervisor)Setup.setupBank();
    }
    else
    {    supervisor= (Supervisor)Setup.setupOrgChart();
    }

    // Pick type of iteration
    System.out.println
      ( "Iterate by organizational seniority ('o') or alternative (any other character)? " );
    response = getAnInputFromUser();
    if( response.equals( "o" ) )
    {    orgIter= new OrgSeniorityIterator( supervisor);
    }
    else
    {    orgIter= new YearsServiceIterator( supervisor);
    }

    // Establish the client and set it going
    Client client = new Client();
    client.doClientTasks( orgIter);
}

/**************************************************************************
 * Returns: Root of the tree established (the president) with Lonny etc. as employees
 *   (see the notes for the specifiations of this tree)
 */
public static Employee setupBank()
/**************************************************************************/
{
    //Bank Teller organization

    // Define the components: tellers and groups thereof
    Supervisor president = new Supervisor( "Buddy", 19 );
    Supervisor loneSupervisor = new Supervisor( "Lonny", 23 );
    Supervisor tellerSupervisor = new Supervisor( "Tony", 4 );
    Teller t1of3 = new Teller( "Juanita", 11 );
    Teller t2of3 = new Teller( "Tina", 2 );
    Teller t3of3 = new Teller( "Thelma", 7 );
    // Construct the teller structure
    president.add( loneSupervisor );
```

```
       president.add( tellerSupervisor );
       tellerSupervisor.add( t1of3 );
       tellerSupervisor.add( t2of3 );
       tellerSupervisor.add( t3of3 );

       return president;
   }

   /***********************************************************************
    * Returns: Root of the tree established -- Particular organization chart with Vanna etc.,
    *   as specified in the notes.
    */
   public static Employee setupOrgChart()
   /**********************************************************************/
   {
       // Establish the organization chart

       Supervisor vicePresident = new Supervisor( "Vanna Presley", 4 );

       // The VP's direct reports (service managers)
       Supervisor sueMiller = new Supervisor( "Sue Miller", 7 );
       vicePresident.add( sueMiller );
       Supervisor samMarkham = new Supervisor( "Sam Markham", 4 );
       vicePresident.add( samMarkham );
       Supervisor salMonahan = new Supervisor( "Sal Monahan", 1 );
       vicePresident.add( salMonahan );

       // Sue Miller's direct reports
       sueMiller.add( new Teller( "Inez Clapp", 11 ) );
       sueMiller.add( new Teller( "Inky Conway", 6 ) );

       // Sal Monahan's direct reports
       salMonahan.add( new Teller( "Iolanthe Carp", 8 ) );
       salMonahan.add( new Teller( "Inge Carlson", 12 ) );

       return vicePresident;
   }

   /***********************************************************************
    * Postconditions:
    * (1) The user has been prompted for a string
    * (2) The user has responded
    *
    * Return: String input by user if the user provides one, otherwise one blank
    */
   private static String getAnInputFromUser()
   /**********************************************************************/
   {
       try
       {
           BufferedReader b = new BufferedReader( new InputStreamReader( System.in ) );
           return ( b.readLine() );
       }
       catch( IOException e )
       {
           System.out.println( e + " Input taken to be a single blank." );
           return " ";
       }
   }

}
```

The class *Supervisor:*

```
import java.util.*;

/**
 * A component which consists of other components
```

```
 */
class Supervisor extends Employee
{
   protected Vector childrenI = new Vector();  // elements below this node

/********************************************************************************
 */
public Supervisor()
/*******************************************************************************/
{
   super();
   nameI = "A Supervisor";                                      // default
}

/********************************************************************************
 */
public Supervisor( String aName )
/*******************************************************************************/
{
   this();
   nameI = aName;
}

/********************************************************************************
 */
public Supervisor( String aName, int SomeYearsOfService )
/*******************************************************************************/
{
   this();
   nameI = aName;
   yearsOfServiceI = SomeYearsOfService;
}

/********************************************************************************
 */
public void add( Employee anEmployee )
/*******************************************************************************/
{ childrenI.addElement( anEmployee );
}

/********************************************************************************
 */
public Vector getChildren()
/*******************************************************************************/
{ return childrenI;
}

/********************************************************************************
 */
public String getName()
/*******************************************************************************/
{ return nameI;
}

/********************************************************************************
 */
public int getYearsOfService()
/*******************************************************************************/
{ return yearsOfServiceI;
}

}
```

The class *Teller*:

```
import java.util.*;

class  Teller extends Employee
```

```
{
/*******************************************************************************
 */
public Teller( String aName )
/******************************************************************************/
{ nameI = aName;
}


/*******************************************************************************
 */
public Teller( String aName, int someYearsOfService )
/******************************************************************************/
{
   nameI = aName;
   yearsOfServiceI = someYearsOfService;
}


/*******************************************************************************
 */
public Vector getChildren()
/******************************************************************************/
{ return null;   // tellers have none
}


/*******************************************************************************
 */
public String getName()
/******************************************************************************/
{ return nameI;
}


/*******************************************************************************
 */
public int getYearsOfService()
/******************************************************************************/
{ return yearsOfServiceI;
}

}
```

The class *YearsOfServiceIterator:*

```
import java.util.*;

/**
 * Iterates over the org chart by years of service.  Uses OrgChartIterator.
 *
 * Known issues:
 * (1) Could have used plain recursive interation instead of OrgChartIterator
 *     to construct this from.
 * (2) Consider saving intermediate results to make this class more efficient
 */
class YearsServiceIterator extends OrgChartIterator
{

/*******************************************************************
 */
public YearsServiceIterator()
/******************************************************************/
{  super();
}


/*******************************************************************
 */
public YearsServiceIterator( Employee anEmployee )
/******************************************************************/
{
```

```
   this();
   employeeI = anEmployee;
}

/***************************************************************************
 */
public YearsServiceIterator( Employee anEmployee, IntSequence aPosition )
/**************************************************************************/
{
   this( anEmployee );   // iterates on same aggregate
   emplPositionI = aPosition;   // points to the given positio
}

/***************************************************************************
 * Precondition: points to the original tree root or a subnode
 * so the 'size()' of 'emplPositionI' is at least one
 *
 * Returns: The 'Employee' object that 'this' points to
 */
public Employee currentItem()
/**************************************************************************/
{
   // "employee" will be the node referred to as we go down the tree
   Employee employee = employeeI;// start at the given root node

   for( int i = 1; i < emplPositionI.size(); ++i )
   {
       // Replace with the child number indicated by the iterator (computed first)
       int childIndex =
         ( employee.getChildren().size() ) - 1 - emplPositionI.getValueAt( i );
       employee = (Employee) ( employee.getChildren().elementAt( childIndex ) );
   }

   return employee;
}

/***************************************************************************
 * Postcondition: 'this' points to the employee with the fewest years of service
 */
public void first()
/**************************************************************************/
{
   // Seniority iterator starting at same place as this iterator, for use by this method
   OrgSeniorityIterator orgSenIt = new OrgSeniorityIterator( employeeI );
   orgSenIt.first();

   // The resulting employee would have less than infinity yrs of service
   int leastYearsSoFar = 1000;   // start with "infinity"
   int currentYears = 0;   // for use in while loop

   while( !orgSenIt.isDone() )    // go all the way through
   {
       // Find the first employee (in seniority sense) with fewer years' service

       currentYears = orgSenIt.currentItem().getYearsOfService();   // for convenience

       if( currentYears < leastYearsSoFar )   // found employee with lower yrs of service
       {
           leastYearsSoFar = currentYears;   // update "best value found so far"
           // Update the position of "this" iterator
           emplPositionI = (IntSequence)( (orgSenIt.emplPositionI).clone() );
       }

       orgSenIt.next();   // move one place seniority-wise
   }
}

/***************************************************************************
```

```
 * Returns: an 'IntSequence' object 'intSeqReturnM', the first element, in the sense
 * of Seniority iterator, satisfying following conditions
 * (a) 'intSeqReturnM' is reached after 'this.emplPositionI', and
 * (b) years of service of the employees at 'intSeqReturnM' and 'this.emplPositionI' are the same
 *
 *   -- if such an element exists, otherwise returns null
 */
public IntSequence getNextEqual()
/***************************************************************************/
{
    // Seniority iterator starting at same place as this iterator, for use by this method
    IntSequence emplPosition = (IntSequence)( emplPositionI.clone() );
    OrgSeniorityIterator orgSenIt = new OrgSeniorityIterator( employeeI, emplPosition );
    orgSenIt.next();   //move at least one away

    while( !orgSenIt.isDone() )   // -- or until there is a return
    {
        // If pointing to an element with the same service years as this iterator
        if( orgSenIt.currentItem().getYearsOfService() == this.currentItem().getYearsOfService() )
            return orgSenIt.emplPositionI;   // return its position

        orgSenIt.next();   //move at least one away
    }

    // null if no new element found with equal years of service
    return null;
}


/***************************************************************************
 * Precondition: this points to the last employee, seniority-wise, with the given years
 *     of service.
 *
 * Return:The first employee, seniority-wise, with more service than 'this' points to
 *     but less/equal than any other employee's service
 */
public IntSequence getNextGreater()
/***************************************************************************/
{
    IntSequence returnIntSeq = null;   // initially "none found"

    // Seniority iterator starting at same root as this iterator, for use by this method
    OrgSeniorityIterator orgSenIt = new OrgSeniorityIterator( employeeI );
    orgSenIt.first();

    // If we are going to find a "next greater", it would have to exceed this in yrs of service
    int greaterYears = 1000;   // start with "infinity"
    int currentYears = 0;   // for use in while loop

    while( !orgSenIt.isDone() )   // go all the way through
    {
        // Service time of local iterator
        currentYears = orgSenIt.currentItem().getYearsOfService();

        // If pointing to an element with more years than this YearsofServiceIterator
        if( ( currentYears > this.currentItem().getYearsOfService() ) &&
        // and this value is smaller that the best number of years found so far
          ( currentYears < greaterYears ) )
        {
            greaterYears = currentYears;   // then update "best value so far"
            // And save the position
            returnIntSeq = (IntSequence)( ( orgSenIt.emplPositionI ).clone() );
        }

        orgSenIt.next();   // move one place seniority-wise
    }

    // returnIntSeq stays done node if no element found with more years of service
    return returnIntSeq;
}
```

```
/*****************************************************************************
 * Returns: true if the current element is the last with the greatest number of years' of service
 */
public boolean isDone()
/*****************************************************************************/
{  return ( emplPositionI == null );
}


/*****************************************************************************
 * Postcondition: 'this' points to the next 'Employee' in terms of years of service
 *  If there is an 'Employee' with equal service not previously counted, it is eligible
 *  to satisfy this criterion.
 */
public void next()
/*****************************************************************************/
{
   IntSequence intSeq = getNextEqual();   // the next employee with same years of service

   if( intSeq != null )   // new employee with same years' service was found
      emplPositionI = intSeq;
   else   // get truly greater or done node
      emplPositionI = getNextGreater();
}

}
```

# APPENDIX C

## SOURCE CODE FOR MUTUAL FUNDS EXAMPLE (APPLICATION OF OBSERVER DESIGN PATTERN)

The source code is listed alphabetically.
The class *AwesomeInc* is as follows.

```
import java.util.*;

/**
 * Stock of "Awesome Inc." Singleton
 */
final class AwesomeInc extends Observable
{
   private static double price = 0.0;   // in dollars
   private static AwesomeInc theAwesomeIncStock = new AwesomeInc();   // singleton

/*****************************************************************************
 */
public AwesomeInc()
/*****************************************************************************/
{  super();
}


/*****************************************************************************
 */
public static double getPrice()
/*****************************************************************************/
{  return price;
}

/*****************************************************************************
```

```
 * Returns: The singleton theAwesomeIncStock
 */
public static AwesomeInc getTheAwesomeInc()
/**********************************************************************************/
{  return theAwesomeIncStock;
}


/*********************************************************************************
 * All observers are affected whenever the price is changed.
 *
 * Postconditions:
 * (1) 'this.price' == 'aPrice'
 * (2) 'changed' == true
 * (3) 'notifyObservers()' has been executed
 */
public void setPrice( double aPrice )
/**********************************************************************************/
{
   this.price = aPrice;
   this.setChanged();   // sets boolean 'changed'
   this.notifyObservers();
}

}
```

The class *Client* is as follows.

```
import java.util.*;

/**
 * User of the Observer design pattern
 *
 * Design note: This class references 'AwesomeInc', and not its observers.
 */
class Client
{

/**********************************************************************************
 * Client constructor comment.
 */
public Client()
/**********************************************************************************/
{  super();
}
/**********************************************************************************
 * Postcondition:
 * (1) 'anAwesomeInc' != null
 * (2) 'anAwesomeInc.price' == 'anAmount'
 * (3) As for the postconditions of 'setPrice()' of 'AwesomeInc'
 */
public void changeStockPrice( AwesomeInc anAwesomeInc, double anAmount )
/**********************************************************************************/
{      anAwesomeInc.setPrice( anAmount );
}
}
```

The class *HiGrowthMutualFund* is as follows.

```
import java.util.*;

/**
 * "Observer" of stocks (design pattern).  Can be called on to update its data about stock(s).
 */
class HiGrowthMutualFund extends MutualFund implements Observer
```

```
{
    private static HiGrowthMutualFund theHiGrowthMutualFund = new HiGrowthMutualFund();    // singleton

    private final int INITIAL_NUM_AWESOME_SHARES = 3;
    // Arbitrary starting point (until notified different)
    private final double INITIAL_ASSUMED_AWESOME_PRICE = 1.0;
    // For illustration -- we don't change this
    private final double VALUE_OF_NON_AWESOME_PORTFOLIO = 400.0;

    /***********************************************************************
     */
    public HiGrowthMutualFund()
    /**********************************************************************/
    {
        super();
        System.out.println( "Note: HiGrowthMutualFund starts with " + INITIAL_NUM_AWESOME_SHARES +
        " shares of Awesome, assumes price of " + INITIAL_ASSUMED_AWESOME_PRICE +
        ", and has non-Awesome holdings totalling " + VALUE_OF_NON_AWESOME_PORTFOLIO );
        setNumAwesomeShares( INITIAL_NUM_AWESOME_SHARES );
        setPriceOfAwesomeInc( INITIAL_ASSUMED_AWESOME_PRICE );
    }
    /***********************************************************************
     * Return: The singelton 'theHiGrowthMutualFund'
     */
    public static HiGrowthMutualFund getTheHiGrowthMutualFund()
    /**********************************************************************/
    {   return theHiGrowthMutualFund;
    }
    /***********************************************************************
     * Returns: The value of this mutual fund.
     */
    public double getValue()
    /**********************************************************************/
    {
        return VALUE_OF_NON_AWESOME_PORTFOLIO +
        ( getNumAwesomeShares()*getPriceOfAwesomeInc() );
    }
    /***********************************************************************
     * Postconditions:
     *       (1) 'this.price' is consistent with the 'price' value at the 'Awesome' object.
     *       (2) A message has been output the console reflecting the update.
     */
    public void update( Observable anObservable, Object anObject )
    /**********************************************************************/
    {
        double oldValue = getValue();    // save for future use
        setPriceOfAwesomeInc
        ( ( (AwesomeInc)anObservable ).getPrice() );    // keep up to date with price
        System.out.println    // report change
        ( "Value of Hi Growth Mutual Fund changed from " + oldValue + " to " + getValue() );
    }
}
```

The class *LoGrowthMutualFund* is as follows.

```
import java.util.*;

/**
 * "Observer" of stocks (design pattern).  Can be called on to update its data about stock(s).
 */
class LoGrowthMutualFund extends MutualFund implements Observer
{
    private static LoGrowthMutualFund theLoGrowthMutualFund = new LoGrowthMutualFund();    // singleton

    private final int INITIAL_NUM_AWESOME_SHARES = 1;
    // Arbitrary starting point (until notified different):
    private final double INITIAL_ASSUMED_AWESOME_PRICE = 1.0;
    // For illustration -- we don't change this:
    private final double VALUE_OF_NON_AWESOME_PORTFOLIO = 200.0;
```

```
/*****************************************************************************
 */
public LoGrowthMutualFund()
/*****************************************************************************/
{
   super();
   System.out.println( "Note: LoGrowthMutualFund starts with " + INITIAL_NUM_AWESOME_SHARES +
     " shares of Awesome, assumes price of " + INITIAL_ASSUMED_AWESOME_PRICE +
     ", and has non-Awesome holdings totalling " + VALUE_OF_NON_AWESOME_PORTFOLIO );
   setNumAwesomeShares( INITIAL_NUM_AWESOME_SHARES );
   setPriceOfAwesomeInc( INITIAL_ASSUMED_AWESOME_PRICE );
}
/*****************************************************************************
 * Return: The singelton 'theLoGrowthMutualFund'
 */
public static LoGrowthMutualFund getTheLoGrowthMutualFund()
/*****************************************************************************/
{  return theLoGrowthMutualFund;
}
/*****************************************************************************
 * Returns: The value of this mutual fund.
 */
public double getValue()
/*****************************************************************************/
{  return VALUE_OF_NON_AWESOME_PORTFOLIO +
   ( getNumAwesomeShares()*getPriceOfAwesomeInc() );
}
/*****************************************************************************
 * Postconditions:
 *      (1) 'this.price' is consistent with the 'price' value at the 'Awesome' object.
 *      (2) A message has been output the console reflecting the update.
 */
public void update( Observable anObservable, Object anObject )
/*****************************************************************************/
{
   double oldValue = getValue();    // save for future use
   setPriceOfAwesomeInc( ( (AwesomeInc)anObservable ).getPrice() );   // keep up to date with price
   System.out.println   // report change
     ( "Value of Lo Growth Mutual Fund changed from " + oldValue + " to " + getValue() );
}
}
```

The class *MedGrowthMutualFund* is as follows.

```
import java.util.*;

/**
 * "Observer" of stocks (design pattern).  Can be called on to update its data about stock(s).
 */
class MedGrowthMutualFund extends MutualFund implements Observer
{
   // Singleton:
   private static MedGrowthMutualFund theMedGrowthMutualFund = new MedGrowthMutualFund();

   private final int INITIAL_NUM_AWESOME_SHARES = 2;
   // Arbitrary starting point (until notified different):
   private final double INITIAL_ASSUMED_AWESOME_PRICE = 1.0;
   // For illustration -- we don't change tMeds:
   private final double VALUE_OF_NON_AWESOME_PORTFOLIO = 300.0;

/*****************************************************************************
 */
public MedGrowthMutualFund()
/*****************************************************************************/
{
   super();
   System.out.println( "Note: MedGrowthMutualFund starts with " + INITIAL_NUM_AWESOME_SHARES +
```

```
        " shares of Awesome, assumes price of " + INITIAL_ASSUMED_AWESOME_PRICE +
        ", and has non-Awesome holdings totalling " + VALUE_OF_NON_AWESOME_PORTFOLIO );
     setNumAwesomeShares( INITIAL_NUM_AWESOME_SHARES );
     setPriceOfAwesomeInc( INITIAL_ASSUMED_AWESOME_PRICE );
   }


   /*****************************************************************************
    * Return: The singelton 'theMedGrowthMutualFund'
    */
   public static MedGrowthMutualFund getTheMedGrowthMutualFund()
   /*****************************************************************************/
   {  return theMedGrowthMutualFund;
   }


   /*****************************************************************************
    * Returns: The value of this mutual fund.
    */
   public double getValue()
   /*****************************************************************************/
   {  return VALUE_OF_NON_AWESOME_PORTFOLIO +
        ( getNumAwesomeShares()*getPriceOfAwesomeInc() );
   }


   /*****************************************************************************
    * Postconditions:
    *      (1) 'this.price' is consistent with the 'price' value at the 'Awesome' object.
    *      (2) A message has been output the console reflecting the update.
    */
   public void update( Observable anObservable, Object anObject )
   /*****************************************************************************/
   {
      double oldValue = getValue();    // save for future use
      setPriceOfAwesomeInc( ( (AwesomeInc)anObservable ).getPrice() );   // keep up to date with price
      System.out.println  // report change
      ( "Value of Med Growth Mutual Fund changed from " + oldValue + " to " + getValue() );
   }

}
```

The class *MutualFund* is as follows.

```
/**
 * Base class for mutual funds.  Assumes a holding in Awesome Inc.
 */
abstract class MutualFund
{
   // Data about Awesome Inc.
   protected int numAwesomeShares = 0;
   protected double priceOfAwesomeInc = 0;

   // Data about other stocks ....

   /*****************************************************************************
    */
   public MutualFund()
   /*****************************************************************************/
   {  super();
   }


   /*****************************************************************************
    */
   protected int getNumAwesomeShares()
   /*****************************************************************************/
   {  return numAwesomeShares;
   }


   /*****************************************************************************
    */
```

```
public double getPriceOfAwesomeInc()
{   return priceOfAwesomeInc;
}


/*************************************************************************
 */
public abstract double getValue();
/*************************************************************************/


/*************************************************************************
 */
protected void setNumAwesomeShares( int aNumAwesomeShares )
/*************************************************************************/
{   numAwesomeShares = aNumAwesomeShares;
}


/*************************************************************************
 */
protected void setPriceOfAwesomeInc(double aPriceOfAwesomeInc)
/*************************************************************************/
{   priceOfAwesomeInc = aPriceOfAwesomeInc;
}


}
```

The class *Setup* is as follows.

```
import java.io.*;

/**
 * Initializes and initiates this application
 */
class Setup
{

/*******************************************************************
 */
public Setup()
/*******************************************************************/
{   super();
}
/*******************************************************************
 * Postconditions: the user has been prompted for a string
 *
 * Return: String input by user if the user provides one, otherwise one blank
 */
private static String getAnInputFromUser()
/*******************************************************************/
{
    try
    {
        BufferedReader b = new BufferedReader( new InputStreamReader( System.in ) );
        return ( b.readLine() );
    }
    catch( IOException e )
    {
        System.out.println( e + " Input taken to be a single blank." );
        return " ";
    }
}   // end getAnInputFromUser()
/*******************************************************************
 * Postconditions: The application has solicited from the user and recieved the price Awesome Inc.
 *      stock until the user has entered a decial number.
 * Returns: price of 'AwesomeInc' stock from the user
 */
private static double getPriceFromUser()
/*******************************************************************/
{
```

```
   double returnDouble = 0;

   System.out.println( "Enter the current price of Awesome Inc. in decimal form." );
   try
   {   returnDouble = ( new Double( getAnInputFromUser() ) ).doubleValue();   // repeat if not a double
   }
   catch( NumberFormatException e )
   {
       System.out.println( "Sorry, not a decimal: Try again." );
       getPriceFromUser();   // repeat solicitation
   }

   return returnDouble;

}   // end getPriceFromUser()

/***************************************************************************
 * Postconditions:
 * (1) The mutual fund singletons have been registered to observe 'AwesomeInc.theAwesomeInc'
 * (2) The user has been repetedly prompted to enter Awesome's current price -- or to quit
 * (3) The effect of each new price on all of the registered mutual funds has been reported
 *      in accordance with the postconditions of 'changeStockPrice()' in 'Client'
 */
public static void main( String[] args )
/***************************************************************************/
{
   // Register the observers
   AwesomeInc theAwesomeInc = AwesomeInc.getTheAwesomeInc();   // identify the (singleton) stock
   theAwesomeInc.addObserver( HiGrowthMutualFund.getTheHiGrowthMutualFund() );  // register observer
   theAwesomeInc.addObserver( MedGrowthMutualFund.getTheMedGrowthMutualFund() );  // register
   theAwesomeInc.addObserver( LoGrowthMutualFund.getTheLoGrowthMutualFund() );  // register

   // Set up client and instigate repeated price changes
   String userInput = "continue";
   Client client = new Client();
   System.out.println( "\nEnter 'quit': Any other input to continue." );   // allow another change
   while( !"quit".equals( getAnInputFromUser() ) )
   {
       client.changeStockPrice( theAwesomeInc, getPriceFromUser() );   // initiate client work
       System.out.println( "\nEnter 'quit': Any other input to continue." );   // allow another change
   }
}

}
```

# APPENDIX D

## SOURCE CODE FOR CUSTOMER INFORMATION EXAMPLE (APPLICATION OF CHAIN OF RESPONSIBILITY DESIGN PATTERN)

The class *Company*:

```
import javax.swing.*;

/**========================================================================
 * Company information
 */
class Company extends CustomerInfoElement
//
*========================================================================*/
```

```
{

/****************************************************************
 */
public Company()
/****************************************************************/
{  super();
}


/****************************************************************
 */
public Company( CustomerInfoElement aCustomerInfoElement )
/****************************************************************/
{  super( aCustomerInfoElement );
}


/****************************************************************
 * Postcondition: 'handleClick()' in the 'container' of this is called with
 *                'aHandedThroughString' enclosed in <company> tags
 */
public void handleClick( String aHandedThroughString )
/****************************************************************/
{
   String passAlongString =
   "<company>" + "\n" + aHandedThroughString  + "\n" + "</company>";
   container.handleClick( passAlongString );
}

}
```

The class *CompanyAddress*:

```
import javax.swing.*;

/**=============================================================================
 * Address of the company (part of professional information)
 */
class CompanyAddress extends CustomerInfoElement
//*=============================================================================/
{

/****************************************************************
 */
public CompanyAddress()
/****************************************************************/
{  super();
}


/****************************************************************
 */
public CompanyAddress( CustomerInfoElement aCustomerInfoElement )
/****************************************************************/
{
   super( aCustomerInfoElement );
}


/****************************************************************
 * Postcondition: 'handleClick()' in the 'container' of this is called with
 *                'aHandedThroughString' enclosed in <address> tags
 */
public void handleClick( String aHandedThroughString )
/****************************************************************/
{
   String passAlongString = "<address>" + "\n" + aHandedThroughString  + "\n" + "</address>";
   container.handleClick( passAlongString );
}

}
```

The class *CompanyName*:

```java
import javax.swing.*;

/**=============================================================================
  */
class CompanyName extends CustomerInfoElement
//*=============================================================================/
{

/****************************************************************
  */
public CompanyName()
/****************************************************************/
{  super();
}

/****************************************************************
  */
public CompanyName( CustomerInfoElement aCustomerInfoElement )
/****************************************************************/
{
    super( aCustomerInfoElement );
}

/****************************************************************
  * Postcondition: 'handleClick()' in the 'container' of this is called with
  *                'aHandedThroughString' enclosed in <name> tags
  */
public void handleClick( String aHandedThroughString )
/****************************************************************/
{
    String passAlongString = "<name>" + "\n" + aHandedThroughString  + "\n" + "</name>";
    container.handleClick( passAlongString );
}

}
```

The class *CompanyInfo*:

```java
import javax.swing.*;
import java.io.*;

/**=============================================================================
  * The overall information
  */
class CustomerInfo extends CustomerInfoElement
//
*=============================================================================/
{

/****************************************************************
  */
public CustomerInfo()
/****************************************************************/
{  super();
}

/****************************************************************
  */
public CustomerInfo( CustomerInfoElement aCustomerInfoElement )
/****************************************************************/
{       super( aCustomerInfoElement );
}
```

```
/****************************************************************
 * Postcondition: Following has been output to console:
 *                'aHandedThroughString' enclosed in <customer> tags
 */
public void handleClick( String aHandedThroughString )
/****************************************************************/
{
    String outputString =
      "\n\n<customer>" + "\n" + aHandedThroughString  + "\n" + "</customer>";
    System.out.println( outputString );
}

}
```

The class *CompanyInfoApp*:

```
import javax.swing.*;
import java.awt.*;
import java.io.*;
import java.awt.event.*;

/**===========================================================================
 * Sets up the application
 */
class CustomerInfoApp
//*===========================================================================/
{
    public static CustomerInfoElement customerInfo = new CustomerInfo();   // Non-GUI parts
    public static JFrame wholeGUI = new JFrame();    // to show the entire GUI

    // Tree of (non-GUI) CustomerInfo pieces containing text fields: initialized in static{}
    public static CompanyName companyName;
    public static Company company;
    public static Professional professional;
    public static ProfessionalTel professionalTel;
    public static CompanyAddress companyAddress;
    public static Personal personal;
    public static PersonalAddress personalAddress;
    public static PersonalName personalName;
    public static PersonalTel personalTel;

    static // tree of relationships corresponding to the GUI
    {
        professional = new Professional( customerInfo );
        personal = new Personal( customerInfo );
        company = new Company( professional );
        companyName = new CompanyName( company );
        companyAddress = new CompanyAddress( company );
        professionalTel = new ProfessionalTel( professional );
        personalAddress = new PersonalAddress( personal );
        personalTel = new PersonalTel( personal );
        personalName = new PersonalName( personal );
    }

/****************************************************
 */
public CustomerInfoApp()
/****************************************************/
{ super();
}

/****************************************************
 * Postcondition:
 *     (1) Whole GUI, as specified, has been displayed
 *     (2) XML has appeared on console in response to each text field entry / return.
```

```
   */
   public static void displayCustomerInfoGUI()
   /***************************************************************/
   {
      Box wholeBox = Box.createHorizontalBox(); // to fit into the entire GUI

      // ====== Create the left (personal info) part
      wholeBox.add( assemblePersonalPanel() );

      // ====== Create and assemble professional part
      wholeBox.add( assembleProfessionalPanel() );

      // ====== Add the box and display the result

      wholeGUI.getContentPane().add( wholeBox );
      wholeGUI.setSize( 400, 250 );
      wholeGUI.setVisible( true );
   }

   /***************************************************************
    * Postconditions:
    *     (1) The GUI for customer information, as specified in the notes, appears on the console.
    *         This GUI is sensitive to mouse actions as specified in the respective classes.
    *     (2) A message to hit any key to terminate appears on the console.
    */
   public static void main(String[] args)
   /***************************************************************/
   {
      CustomerInfoApp.displayCustomerInfoGUI();

      // Terminate application by entering any key
      System.out.println( "Hit enter to end application.\n" );
      try{ System.in.read(); }
      catch( IOException e ) { System.out.println( e ); }
      wholeGUI.removeNotify();
      System.exit( 0 );
   }

   /***************************************************************
    */ // Specification to be supplied
   public static JPanel assembleCompanyPanel()
   /***************************************************************/
   {
      // Define the JPanel for return
      JPanel returnCompanyPanel = new JPanel();
      returnCompanyPanel.setLayout( new BorderLayout( 10, 10 ) );
      returnCompanyPanel.setBackground( Color.white );
      returnCompanyPanel.setBorder( BorderFactory.createCompoundBorder
      (   BorderFactory.createTitledBorder( "Company" ),
          BorderFactory.createEmptyBorder( 1,1,1,1 ) )
      );

      //// Company address ---------------

      // Create the corporate address panel and add it to professionalBox
      JPanel companyAddressPanel = new JPanel();
      companyAddressPanel.add( new JLabel( "Address:" ) );

      // Create text field, add listener and add to the profesional panel
      JTextField companyAddressField = new JTextField( 10 );
      // Specify the CustomerInfoElement object that must respond
      companyAddressField.addActionListener( new TextFieldListener( companyAddress ) );
      companyAddressPanel.add( companyAddressField );

      //// Company name ---------------

      // Create the corporate name panel and add it to professionalBox
```

```
        JPanel companyNamePanel = new JPanel();
        companyNamePanel.add( new JLabel( "Name:" ) );
        // Create text field, add listener and add to the profesional panel
        JTextField companyNameField = new JTextField( 10 );
        // Specify the CustomerInfoElement object that must respond
        companyNameField.addActionListener( new TextFieldListener( companyName ) );
        companyNamePanel.add( companyNameField );

        // Assemble company information
        returnCompanyPanel.add( companyAddressPanel, "North" );
        returnCompanyPanel.add( companyNamePanel, "South" );

        return returnCompanyPanel;
    }

    /******************************************************************
     */ // Specification to be supplied
    public static JPanel assembleProfessionalPanel()
    /******************************************************************/
    {
        // ====== Create the right (professional info) panel enclosing a box

        // Define the overall panel
        JPanel returnProfessionalPanel = new JPanel();
        returnProfessionalPanel.setLayout( new BorderLayout( 10, 10 ) );
        returnProfessionalPanel.setBackground( Color.white );
        returnProfessionalPanel.setBorder( BorderFactory.createCompoundBorder
        (   BorderFactory.createTitledBorder( "Professional" ),
            BorderFactory.createEmptyBorder( 1,1,1,1) )
        );

        // Add the parts
        returnProfessionalPanel.add( assembleProfessionalTelephonePanel(), "North" );
        returnProfessionalPanel.add( assembleCompanyPanel(), "South" );

        return returnProfessionalPanel;
    }

    /******************************************************************
     */ // Specification to be supplied
    public static JPanel assembleProfessionalTelephonePanel()
    /******************************************************************/
    {
        // Define the JPanel for return
        JPanel returnTelephonePanel = new JPanel();
        returnTelephonePanel.setLayout( new BorderLayout( 10, 10 ) );
        returnTelephonePanel.setBackground( Color.white );
        returnTelephonePanel.setBorder( BorderFactory.createCompoundBorder
        (   BorderFactory.createTitledBorder( "Telephone:" ),
            BorderFactory.createEmptyBorder( 1,1,1,1) )
        );

        // Create the professional telephone panel
        JPanel telephonePanel = new JPanel();
        telephonePanel.add( new JLabel( "Tel:" ) );

        // Create text field, add listener, and add the field to the telephone panel
        JTextField telephoneField = new JTextField( 10 );
        // Specify the CustomerInfoElement object that must respond
        telephoneField.addActionListener( new TextFieldListener( professionalTel ) );
        telephonePanel.add( telephoneField );

        // Assemble telephone information
        returnTelephonePanel.add( telephonePanel );

        return returnTelephonePanel;
    }
```

```
/******************************************************************
 */ // Specification to be supplied
public static JPanel assemblePersonalPanel()
/******************************************************************/
{
   // ====== Create the left (personal info) panel enclosing a box

   // Define the overall panel
   JPanel returnPersonalPanel = new JPanel();
   returnPersonalPanel.setLayout( new BorderLayout( 1, 1 ) );
   returnPersonalPanel.setBackground( Color.white );
   returnPersonalPanel.setBorder( BorderFactory.createCompoundBorder
   (   BorderFactory.createTitledBorder( "Personal" ),
       BorderFactory.createEmptyBorder( 1,1,1,1) )
   );

   // Define the box to be inserted into the overall panel
   Box box = Box.createVerticalBox();

   //// Personal address ---------------

   // Create the personal address panel and add it to professionalBox
   JPanel personalAddressPanel = new JPanel();
   personalAddressPanel.add( new JLabel( "Address:" ) );

   // Create text field, add listener and add to the profesional panel
   JTextField personalAddressField = new JTextField( 10 );
   // Specify the CustomerInfoElement object that must respond
   personalAddressField.addActionListener( new TextFieldListener( personalAddress ) );
   personalAddressPanel.add( personalAddressField );

   //// Personal name ------------------

   // Create the personal address panel and add it to professionalBox
   JPanel personalNamePanel = new JPanel();
   personalNamePanel.add( new JLabel( "Name:" ) );

   // Create text field, add listener and add to the profesional panel
   JTextField personalNameField = new JTextField( 10 );
   // Specify the CustomerInfoElement object that must respond
   personalNameField.addActionListener( new TextFieldListener( personalName ) );
   personalNamePanel.add( personalNameField );

   //// Personal telephone -------------

   // Create the personal address panel and add it to professionalBox
   JPanel personalTelephonePanel = new JPanel();
   personalTelephonePanel.add( new JLabel( "Tel:" ) );

   // Create text field, add listener and add to the profesional panel
   JTextField personalTelephoneField = new JTextField( 10 );
   // Specify the CustomerInfoElement object that must respond
   personalTelephoneField.addActionListener( new TextFieldListener( personalTel ) );
   personalTelephonePanel.add( personalTelephoneField );

   // Add the parts to the box, then the box to the overall panel
   box.add( personalAddressPanel );
   box.add( personalNamePanel );
   box.add( personalTelephonePanel );
   returnPersonalPanel.add( box );

   return returnPersonalPanel;
}

}
```

The class *CustomerInfoElements*:

```
/**============================================================================
   * A piece of information concerning a customer
   */
abstract class CustomerInfoElement
//*=========================================================================/
{
   protected CustomerInfoElement container; // "containing" this in the GUI hierarchy

/*****************************************************************
 */
public CustomerInfoElement()
/*****************************************************************/
{  super();
}

/*****************************************************************
 */
public CustomerInfoElement( CustomerInfoElement aCustomerInfoElement )
/*****************************************************************/
{
   super();
   container = aCustomerInfoElement;
}

/*****************************************************************
 */
public abstract void handleClick( String aPassedOnString );
/*****************************************************************/

}
```

The class *Personal*:

```
import javax.swing.*;

/**============================================================================
   * "Personal" element to correspond to the "Personal" GUI part
   */
class Personal extends CustomerInfoElement
//
*=========================================================================/
{

/*****************************************************************
 */
public Personal()
/*****************************************************************/
{  super();
}

/*****************************************************************
 */
public Personal( CustomerInfoElement aCustomerInfoElement )
/*****************************************************************/
{  super( aCustomerInfoElement );
}

/*****************************************************************
 * Postcondition: the container of this is called
 * with 'aHandedThroughString' enclosed in <personalInfo> tags
 */
public void handleClick( String aHandedThroughString)
/*****************************************************************/
{
   String returnString =
```

```
          "<personalInfo>" + "\n" + aHandedThroughString  + "\n" + "</personalInfo>";
     container.handleClick( returnString );
   }

   }
```

The class *PersonalAddress:*

```
import javax.swing.*;

/**============================================================================
  * Address part of personal information
  */
class PersonalAddress extends CustomerInfoElement
//
*===========================================================================/
{

/*****************************************************************
 */
public PersonalAddress()
/*****************************************************************/
{ super();
}

/*****************************************************************
 */
public PersonalAddress( CustomerInfoElement aCustomerInfoElement )
/*****************************************************************/
{ super( aCustomerInfoElement );
}

/*****************************************************************
 * Postcondition: the container of this is called with the following parameter:
 *             'aHandedThroughString' enclosed in <address> tags
 */
public void handleClick( String aHandedThroughString )
/*****************************************************************/
{
   String passAlongString =
     "<address>" + "\n" + aHandedThroughString  + "\n" + "</address>";
   container.handleClick( passAlongString );
}

}
```

The class *PersonalName*:

```
import javax.swing.*;

/**============================================================================
  */
class PersonalName extends CustomerInfoElement
//
*===========================================================================/
{

/*****************************************************************
 */
public PersonalName()
/*****************************************************************/
{ super();
}

/*****************************************************************
```

```
 */
public PersonalName( CustomerInfoElement aCustomerInfoElement )
/**************************************************************/
{  super( aCustomerInfoElement );
}


/**************************************************************
 * Postcondition: the container of this is called with the following parameter:
 *                'aHandedThroughString' enclosed in <name> tags
 */
public void handleClick( String aHandedThroughString )
/**************************************************************/
{
   String passAlongString =
     "<name>" + "\n" + aHandedThroughString  + "\n" + "</name>";
   container.handleClick( passAlongString );
}

}
```

The class *PersonalTel*:

```
import javax.swing.*;

/**============================================================
  * Customer element to correspond to the "Personal telephone information" GUI part
  */
class PersonalTel extends CustomerInfoElement
//**===========================================================/
{

/**********************************************************
 */
public PersonalTel()
/**********************************************************/
{  super();
}


/**********************************************************
 */
public PersonalTel( CustomerInfoElement aCustomerInfoElement )
/**********************************************************/
{  super( aCustomerInfoElement );
}


/**********************************************************
 * Postcondition: 'handleClick()' in the 'container' of this is called with
 *                'aHandedThroughString' enclosed in <telephone> tags
 */
public void handleClick( String aHandedThroughString )
/**********************************************************/
{
   String passAlongString =
     "<telephone>" + "\n" + aHandedThroughString  + "\n" + "</telephone>";
   container.handleClick( passAlongString );
}

}
```

The class *Professional*:

```
import javax.swing.*;

/**============================================================
  * "Professional" element to correspond to the "professional" GUI part
  */
```

```
class Professional extends CustomerInfoElement
//
*==========================================================================/
{

/*************************************************************
 */
public Professional()
/*************************************************************/
{ super();
}


/*************************************************************
 */
public Professional( CustomerInfoElement aCustomerInfoElement )
/*************************************************************/
{ super( aCustomerInfoElement );
}


/*************************************************************
 * Postcondition: 'handleClick()' in the 'container' of this is called
 * with aHandedThroughString enclosed in <professionalInfo> tags
 */
public void handleClick( String aHandedThroughString)
/*************************************************************/
{
   String returnString =
     "<professionalInfo>" + "\n" + aHandedThroughString  + "\n" +
     "</professionalInfo>";
   container.handleClick( returnString );
}

}
```

The class *ProfessionalTel*:

```
import javax.swing.*;

/**==========================================================================
   * "Professional" element to correspond to the "Professional telephone information" GUI part
   */
class ProfessionalTel extends CustomerInfoElement
//*==========================================================================/
{

/*************************************************************
 */
public ProfessionalTel()
/*************************************************************/
{ super();
}


/*************************************************************
 */
public ProfessionalTel( CustomerInfoElement aCustomerInfoElement )
/*************************************************************/
{ super( aCustomerInfoElement );
}


/*************************************************************
 * Postcondition: 'handleClick()' in the 'container' of this is called with
 *              'aHandedThroughString' enclosed in <name> tags
 */
public void handleClick( String aHandedThroughString )
/*************************************************************/
{
   String passAlongString =
```

```
        "<telephone>" + "\n" + aHandedThroughString  + "\n" + "</telephone>";
      container.handleClick( passAlongString );
   }

}
```

The class *TestFieldListener*:

```
import java.awt.*;
import java.awt.event.*;
import javax.swing.*;

/**==========================================================================
  * Listens for entry of text fields in CustomerIntoApp GUI
  */
class TextFieldListener implements ActionListener
//*==========================================================================/
{
   // The entity that responds to the event
   CustomerInfoElement customerInfoElement = new CustomerInfo();   // default

   /*************************************************************
    * Postcondition: The 'CustomerInfo' object's 'handleClick()' has been called with the
    * text in the text field as parameter.
    */
   public void actionPerformed( ActionEvent e )
   /*************************************************************/
   {
      JTextField source = new JTextField( "not assigned yet" );
      source = (JTextField)e.getSource();  // the text filed on which this event occured
      customerInfoElement.handleClick( source.getText() );  // the element initiates the chain
   }


   /*************************************************************
    */
   public TextFieldListener()
   /*************************************************************/
   { super();
   }


   /*************************************************************
    */
   public TextFieldListener( CustomerInfoElement aCustomerInfoElement )
   /*************************************************************/
   { this();
      customerInfoElement = aCustomerInfoElement;
   }

}
```

# APPENDIX E

## *SOURCE CODE FOR UNDO EXAMPLE (APPLICATION OF* COMMAND *DESIGN PATTERN)*

The source code is listed below in alphabetical order.
Here is the source code for the class *Command*:

```
/**
 * To facilitate using prototype commands in a hashtable
 */
```

```
interface Command extends Cloneable
{
/****************************************************************/

/****************************************************************
 * Require subclasses to implement clone()
 */
public abstract Object clone();
/****************************************************************/

/****************************************************************
 * Carry out this command.
 */
public void execute( );
/****************************************************************/

/****************************************************************
 * Collect the details for the particular command entity
 */
void getDetails( );
/****************************************************************/

/****************************************************************
 * Undo all the effects of this command.
 */
void undo();
/****************************************************************/

}
```

Here is the source code for the class *CutCommand*:

```java
import java.io.*;

/**
 */
class CutCommand extends DocumentCommand
{
    private String textCut = new String( "textCut not assigned yet" );   // the text that's cut
    private int offset = 0;    // index in the string at which the cut began.
    private int lengthOfStringCut = 0;   // no restriction on size of this

/****************************************************************
 */
public CutCommand()
/****************************************************************/
{  super();
}

/****************************************************************
 * Postconditions: 'offset' == 'anOffset'; 'lengthOfStringCut' == 'aLengthOfStringCut';
 *     'document' == 'aDocument';
 */
public CutCommand( int anOffset, int aLengthOfStringCut, Document aDocument )
/****************************************************************/
{
    this();
    offset = anOffset;
    lengthOfStringCut = aLengthOfStringCut;
    document = aDocument;
}

/****************************************************************
 * Postconditions: 'document' == 'aDocument'
 */
public CutCommand( Document aDocument )
/****************************************************************/
{
```

```
   this();
   document = aDocument;
}

/*****************************************************************
 * Postconditions:
 * (1) See postconditions for 'super.execute()' (pushed onto command stack) and
 * (2) See postconditions for 'executeWithoutPush()' (cut work done, command not pushed (again))
 */
public void execute()
/****************************************************************/
{
   super.execute();
   executeWithoutPush();
}

/*****************************************************************
 * Postconditions:
 * (1) Message to console of un-honored request -- if 'document' has not been assigned content text or
 *     if 'offset' is >= document length
 * (2) (Assuming 'document' has been assigned text:) A substring has been removed from
 *     'document.getText()' as follows.
 *     Begins at index 'offset' and ends at index 'offset + lengthOfStringCut' if the latter
 *     is less that the length of the string, otherwise the entire substring beginning at 'offset'.
 * (3) (Assuming 'document' has beed assigned text:) 'textCut' is the text that was removed from
 *     'document'.
 */
public void executeWithoutPush()
/****************************************************************/
{
   final StringBuffer textOfDocument = document.getText();   // for convenience

   if( textOfDocument != null )
   {
       // Because 'offset' + 'lengthOfStringCut' may exceed length of the text:
       final int indexOfLastCharRemoved =
        Math.min( textOfDocument.length(), offset + lengthOfStringCut );
       // Cut if the offset makes sense
       if( offset <= textOfDocument.length() - 1 )
       {
           textCut = textOfDocument.substring( offset, indexOfLastCharRemoved );
           document.setText( textOfDocument.delete( offset, indexOfLastCharRemoved ) );
       }
       else
       {   System.out.println( "Request ignored to cut starting beyond end of document." );
       }
   }
   else   // textOfDocument == null
   {   System.out.println( "Request ignored to cut from document with no content." );
   }

   reportStatusOfDocumentToConsole();
}

/*****************************************************************
 * Postconditions: 'offset' and 'lengthOfStringCut' have been obtained from the user (integers);
 * Each is zero if user has entered illegal values.
 */
public void getDetails()
/****************************************************************/
{
   // Get offset
   System.out.println( "Please specify index where the cut must start: " );
   try
   {   offset = ( new Integer( getInputFromUser() ) ).intValue();
   }
   catch( Exception e )
   {
```

```
            System.out.println( "Application did not detect an integer: 0 will be assumed." );
            offset = 0;
        }

    // Get length to be cut
    System.out.println( "Please specify number of characters to be cut: " );
    try
    {   lengthOfStringCut = ( new Integer( getInputFromUser() ) ).intValue();
    }
    catch( Exception e )
    {
        System.out.println( "Application did not detect an integer: 0 will be assumed." );
        lengthOfStringCut = 0;
    }
}

/*************************************************************
 * Reverse the effect of execute
 */
public void undo()
/************************************************************/
{
    PasteCommand pasteCommand = new PasteCommand( new String( textCut ), offset, document );
    pasteCommand.executeWithoutPush();    // don't record this in ythe command stack
}

}
```

Here is the source code for the class *Document*:

```
import java.io.*;

/**
 * A document that the word processor allows the user to create
 */
class Document
{
    private StringBuffer text =
      new StringBuffer( new String( "Document text not assigned yet" ) );

    /****************************************************************
     * Postcondition: 'text' isnono-null with length zero
     */
    public Document()
    /***********************************************************/
    {
        super();
        text = new StringBuffer( new String( "" ) );
    }

    /****************************************************************
     * Postcondition: 'text' == StringBuffer( aString )
     */
    public Document( String aString )
    /***********************************************************/
    {
        this();
        text = new StringBuffer( aString );
    }

    /****************************************************************
     */
    public StringBuffer getText()
    /***********************************************************/
    {   return text;
    }
```

```
/****************************************************************
 */
public void setText( StringBuffer someText )
/****************************************************************/
{   text = someText;
}


}
```

Here is the source code for the class *DocumentCommand*:

```java
import java.io.*;

/**
 * Commands pertaining to a Document object
 */
abstract class DocumentCommand implements Command
{
    Document document = new Document("'document' contents not assigned yet");

/****************************************************************
 * DocumentCommand constructor comment.
 */
public DocumentCommand()
/****************************************************************/
{   super();
}


/****************************************************************
 */
public Object clone()
/****************************************************************/
{
    try
    {       return super.clone();
    }
    catch( Exception e )
    {
            System.out.println( "clone() in DocumentCommand threw exception (should never occur!)." );
            return null;
    }
}

/****************************************************************
 * Postcondition: 'this' is top of stack of comands in 'WordProcessor'
 */
public void execute()
/****************************************************************/
{   WordProcessor.push( this );
}

/****************************************************************
 */
public abstract void getDetails
/****************************************************************/

/****************************************************************
 * Note: Utility method for use in subclasses.
 * Returns: String entered by user at the console
 */
public static String getInputFromUser()
/****************************************************************/
{
    String returnString = Cnot yet assigned";
    try
    {
```

```
            BufferedReader bufReader = new BufferedReader( new InputStreamReader( System.in) );
            returnString = bufReader.readLine().
            System.out.prinln( "You chose" + returnString );
      }
      catch( IOException e )
      {      System.out.println( e ); }

      return returnString;
}

/*****************************************************************
 * Postcondition: 'document.text' has been output to the console between arrows
 */
protected final void reportStatusOfDocumentToConsole()
/****************************************************************/
{
      System.out.println( "\n\tText is now as shown between the pair of arrows." );
      System.out.println( "\t-->" + document.getText() + "<--\n );
}

/*****************************************************************
 * Postcondition: Stack of past commands in WordProcessor has been popped
 */
public void undo()
/****************************************************************/
{      WordProcessor.pop();
}

}
```

Here is the source code for the class *PasteCommand*:

```
import java.io.*;

/**
 */
class PasteCommand extends DocumentCommand
{
   private int offset = 0;   // index where paste begins
   private String pasteText = new String( "pasteText not assigned yet" );  // to be pasted

/*****************************************************************
 */
public PasteCommand()
/****************************************************************/
{  super();
}

/*****************************************************************
 * Postcondition: document == aDocument
 */
public PasteCommand( Document aDocument )
/****************************************************************/
{
   this();
   document = aDocument;
}

/*****************************************************************
 * Postconditions: 'pasteText' == 'aPasteText', 'offset' == 'anOffset', 'document' == 'aDocument;'
 */
public PasteCommand( String aPasteText, int anOffset, Document aDocument )
/****************************************************************/
{
   this();
   pasteText = aPasteText;
   offset = anOffset;
```

```
      document = aDocument;
   }


   /*****************************************************************
    * Postconditions: Postconditions of 'super.execute()' and 'executeWithoutPush()'
    *  (i.e., this paste command has been executed and this has been pushed onto the command stack)
    */
   public void execute()
   /****************************************************************/
   {
      super.execute();
      executeWithoutPush();
   }


   /*****************************************************************
    * Postcondition:
    * if 'offset' < length of 'document' text, 'pasteText' has been pasted into document beginning
    * at index 'offset' otherwise this method has no effects
    *
    * Known issues: It is possible to paste at an index as big or bigger than the text length
    */
   public void executeWithoutPush()
   /****************************************************************/
   {
      StringBuffer text = document.getText();   // for convenience

      if( text == null )   // never initialized
      {    document.setText( new StringBuffer( pasteText ) );   // text is now the whole insert
      }
      else   // text != null
      {    if( text.length() == 0 )   // no text to begin with
          {      document.setText( new StringBuffer( pasteText ) );   // text is now the whole insert
          }
          else
          {      if( ( offset >= 0 ) && ( offset < text.length() ) )   // 'offset' within bounds
              {    document.setText( text.insert( offset, pasteText ) );   // do the requested insert
              }
              else
              {      System.out.println( "Application error: " +
                    "Attempt to insert string at illegal offset in 'execute()' of 'Paste'." +
                    "Ignored." );
              }
          }
      }
      reportStatusOfDocumentToConsole();
   }


   /*****************************************************************
    * Postconditions: 'offset' and 'pasteText' have been sucessfully obtained from the user,
    * otherwise set to zero and null respectively.
    */
   public void getDetails()
   /****************************************************************/
   {
      // Get offset
      System.out.println( "Please specify index where the paste must start: " );
      try
      {    offset = ( new Integer( getInputFromUser() ) ).intValue();
      }
      catch( Exception e )
      {    System.out.println( "Application did not detect an integer: 0 will be assumed." );
           offset = 0;
      }

      // Get string to be pasted
      System.out.println( "Please specify text to be inserted: " );
      try
```

```
   {    pasteText = getInputFromUser();
   }
   catch( Exception e )
   {    System.out.println( "Application did not detect an integer: 0 will be assumed." );
        pasteText = null;
   }
}

/*****************************************************************
 * Postonditions: All the effects of this (command) have been undone and this has not been
 * pushed onto the command stack.
 */
public void undo()
/*****************************************************************/
{
   CutCommand cutCommand = new CutCommand( offset, pasteText.length(), document );
   cutCommand.executeWithoutPush();
}

}
```

Here is the source code for the class *QuitCommand*:

```
/**
 * to quit the entire application
 */
class QuitCommand extends DocumentCommand
{
   Document document = new Document( "Document not yet assigned" );

   /*****************************************************************
    */
   public QuitCommand()
   /*****************************************************************/
   {  super();
   }

   /*****************************************************************
    */
   public QuitCommand( Document aDocument )
   /*****************************************************************/
   {
      super();
      document = aDocument;
   }

   /*****************************************************************
    * Postconditions:
    * (1) A farewell message has been output to the console.
    * (2) The application has terminated.
    */
   public void execute()
   /*****************************************************************/
   {
      System.out.println( "\n----           TERMINATING APPLICATION        ----" );
      System.exit( 0 );
   }

   /*****************************************************************
    * Not implemented in substance
    */
   public void getDetails(){}
   public void undo() {}
   /*****************************************************************/

}
```

Here is the source code for the class *UndoCommand*:

```
/**
 * Undo the last command (top of stack in WordProcessor)
 */
class UndoCommand extends DocumentCommand
{

  /*****************************************************************
   */
  public UndoCommand()
  /****************************************************************/
  { super();
  }


  /*****************************************************************
   * Postconditions:
   * If there is a command in the command stack of 'WordProcessor':
   * (1) The last command has been undone
   * (2) The last command has been popped from 'WordProcessor'
   */
  public void execute()
  /****************************************************************/
  {
    Command command = WordProcessor.pop();   // Get the command from stack and remove it

    if( command != null )
    { command.undo();   // reverse the effcts of 'command'
    }
    else
    { System.out.println( "No command to undo." );
    }
  }


  /*****************************************************************
   * Not implemented
   */
  public void getDetails() {}
  public void undo() {}
  /****************************************************************/

}
```

Here is the source code for the class *WordProcessor*:

```
import java.util.*;
import java.io.*;

/**
 * Demonstration word processor on a Document instance
 */
final class WordProcessor
{
  private static Document document = new Document();   // -- to which this instance applies
  private static Stack commandHistory = new Stack();   // most recent commands

  /*****************************************************************
   * Postcondition: 'document' is a null instance
   */
  private WordProcessor()
  /****************************************************************/
  {
    super();
    document = new Document();
```

```
}

/******************************************************************
 * Returns: Line of text input by user at the console
 */
public static String getInputFromUser()
/*****************************************************************/
{
    String returnString = "not yet assigned";

    try
    {
        BufferedReader bufReader = new BufferedReader( new InputStreamReader( System.in ) );
        returnString = bufReader.readLine();
    }
    catch( IOException e )
    {   System.out.println( e ); }

    return returnString;
}

/******************************************************************
 * Returns: The last command that was executed on this
 * Postcondition: the stack 'commandHistory' has been popped
 */
public final static Command getLastCommand()
/*****************************************************************/
{   return( (Command)commandHistory.pop() );
}

/******************************************************************
 * Postconditions:
 * (1) The application has repeatedly prompted the user to enter "paste", "cut", "undo", or "quit"
 * (2) Each of these has called its execute() -- see individual execute() specifications.
 */
public static void main( String[] args )
/*****************************************************************/
{
    Command command = new QuitCommand();   // default

    // Key user input to the corresponding type of customer
    Hashtable commandList = new Hashtable();
    commandList.put( "paste", new PasteCommand( document ) );
    commandList.put( "cut", new CutCommand( document ) );
    commandList.put( "undo", new UndoCommand() );
    commandList.put( "quit", new QuitCommand( document) );

    while( true )   // 'quit' command terminates application
    {
        // Get customer type from user (written to avoid modification whenever hashTable is modified)
        System.out.println( "Pick from one of the following:" );
        for ( Enumeration enumeration = commandList.keys(); enumeration.hasMoreElements() ;)
        {   System.out.println( enumeration.nextElement() );
        }
        System.out.println();

        command = (Command)commandList.get( getInputFromUser() );
        if( command != null )   // -- which should always be the case, given how we built commandList
        {
            command = (Command) command.clone();   // (don't re-use the object in hash table)
            command.getDetails();
            command.execute();
        }
        else
        {
            System.out.println( "Please try again." );
        }
    }
```

```
}

/*******************************************************************
 * Returns: Command object at top of 'commandHistory' stack if latter non-empty; null otherwise
 * Postcondition: 'commandHistory' has been popped if that was possible
 */
public final static Command pop()
/*******************************************************************/
{
   Command returnCommand = null;      // default
   if( commandHistory.size() > 0 )
      returnCommand = (Command)commandHistory.pop();

   return returnCommand;
}

/*******************************************************************
 * Postcondition: 'aCommand' is top of commandHistory (stack)
 */
public final static void push( Command aCommand )
/*******************************************************************/
{  commandHistory.push( aCommand );
}

}
```

## SOURCE CODE FOR QUADRATIC SOLUTIONS EXAMPLE (APPLICATION OF TEMPLATE DESIGN PATTERN)

The class *Client*:

```
/**
 * User code of the quadratic process
 */
class Client
{

/***************************************************************************************
 */
public Client()
/***************************************************************************************/
{  super();
}

/***************************************************************************************
 */
public void doWorkInvolving( QuadraticEquation aQuadraticEquation )
/***************************************************************************************/
{
    // do work
   aQuadraticEquation.solve();   // (we'd probably prefer a 'solve()' that returns the solutions) ...
    // do more work
}

}
```

The class *NoSolutions*:

```java
/**
 * Handles quadratic equations with no solutions
 */
class NoSolutions extends QuadraticAlgorithm
{

/*******************************************************************************
 */
public NoSolutions()
/******************************************************************************/
{  super();
}

/*******************************************************************************
 */
protected void displayNumSolutions()
/******************************************************************************/
{  System.out.println( "There are no solutions to this quadratic equation." );
}

/*******************************************************************************
 */
public NoSolutions( double anAValue, double aBValue, double aCValue )
/******************************************************************************/
{  super( anAValue, aBValue, aCValue ) ;
}

}
```

The class *OneSolution*:

```java
/**
 * Solves quadratic equations with one solution
 */
class OneSolution extends QuadraticAlgorithm
{

/*******************************************************************************
 */
public OneSolution()
/******************************************************************************/
{  super();
}

/*******************************************************************************
 */
protected void displayNumSolutions()
/******************************************************************************/
{  System.out.println( "There is one solutions to this quadratic equation." );
}

/*******************************************************************************
 */
public OneSolution( double anAValue, double aBValue, double aCValue )
/******************************************************************************/
{  super( anAValue, aBValue, aCValue ) ;
}

/*******************************************************************************
 * Precondition: There is exactly one solution to ax**2 + bx + c = 0
 */
protected void displayFirstSolution()
/******************************************************************************/
{
```

```
    if( a != 0 )    // use the quadratic formula, knowing that 'b**2 == 4*a*c'
        System.out.println( "The solution is " + ( - b / 2*a ) );
    else    // 'a' == 0, so the equation is of the form 'bx + c = 0'
        System.out.println( "The solution is " + ( - c / b ) );
}

}
```

The class *QuadraticAlgorithm*:

```
import java.io.*;

/**
 * Solves ax**2 + bx + c = 0
 */
abstract class QuadraticAlgorithm
{
    // In the formula ax**2 + bx + c
    double a = 0;
    double b = 0;
    double c = 0;

/*****************************************************************************************
 */
public QuadraticAlgorithm()
/*****************************************************************************************/
{  super();
}

/*****************************************************************************************
 * Postcondition: If a solution exists to ax**2 + bx + c, it is displayed at the console.
 */
protected void displayFirstSolution()
/*****************************************************************************************/
{
}

/*****************************************************************************************
 * Postcondition: A message stating that the equation makes no sense
 *      has been displayed at the console.
 */
private void displayNoSenseMessage()
/*****************************************************************************************/
{
    System.out.println
      ( "The equation '" + a + "x**2 + " + b + "x + " + c + " = 0'  makes no sense." );
}

/*****************************************************************************************
 * Postcondition: The number of solutions to ax**2 + bx + c is displayed at the console.
 */
abstract protected void displayNumSolutions();

/*****************************************************************************************
 * Postcondition: If a second solution exists to ax**2 + bx + c, it is displayed at the console.
 */
protected void displaySecondSolution()
/*****************************************************************************************/
{
}

/*****************************************************************************************
 * Postcondition: A line indicating progress has been displayed at the console
 */
private void displayWhatsHappening()
```

```
/********************************************************************************/
{  System.out.println( "solving the equation ....." );
}


/********************************************************************************
 */
public QuadraticAlgorithm( double anAValue, double aBValue, double aCValue )
/********************************************************************************/
{
    this();
    a = anAValue;
    b = aBValue;
    c = aCValue;
}


/********************************************************************************
 * This is the Template method
 *
 * Postcondition:
 * (1) The solution(s) to ax**2 + bx + c = 0, if any exist, have been displayed
 * (2) An error message has been displayed at the console if 'aString', 'bString' or 'cString'
 *      do not represent floating point numbers.
 */
protected void displaySolutions()
/********************************************************************************/
{
    if( makesSense() )
    {
        displayWhatsHappening();
        displayNumSolutions();
        displayFirstSolution();
        displaySecondSolution();
    }
    else
        displayNoSenseMessage();
}


/********************************************************************************
 * Note: An equation of the form 'c = 0' where c is a nonzero constant (e.g., "3 = 0"),
 *       makes no sense
 *
 * Returns: true if a != 0 or b!= 0; false otherwise
 *
 * Known issues: not thought through case where 'c' is zero
 */
private boolean makesSense()
/********************************************************************************/
{  return( ( a!= 0 ) || (b != 0 ) );
}

}
```

The class *QuadraticEquation*:

```
import java.io.*;

/**
 */
class QuadraticEquation
{
    // From ax**2 + bx + c
    public double a = 0;
    public double b = 0;
    public double c = 0;

    QuadraticAlgorithm quadraticAlgorithm;    // the algorithms that will solve this
```

```
/****************************************************************************************** */
public QuadraticEquation()
/*****************************************************************************************/
{  super();
}


/******************************************************************************************
 * Postcondition: The solutions -- if any -- have been displayed to the console
 */
public void solve()
/*****************************************************************************************/
{
   if( a == 0  )   // not a quadratic equation
      quadraticAlgorithm = new OneSolution( a, b, c );
   else    // apply the quadratic formula
   {
      if( b*b - 4*a*c < 0 )
               quadraticAlgorithm = new NoSolutions( a, b, c );
      if( b*b - 4*a*c == 0 )
               quadraticAlgorithm = new OneSolution( a, b, c );
      if( b*b - 4*a*c > 0 )
               quadraticAlgorithm = new TwoSolutions( a, b, c );
   }

   quadraticAlgorithm.displaySolutions();   // now do the work
}

}
```

The class *Setup*:

```
import java.io.*;

/**
 * User code of the quadratic process
 */
class Setup
{

/**************************************************************************************
 */
public Setup()
/*****************************************************************************************/
{  super();
}


/**************************************************************************************
 * Postconditions:
 * (1) The coefficients in ax**2 + bx + c = 0 have been obtained from the user
 * (2) Whenever the user has entertered a string that does not represent a number, the application
 *      has repeated all requests from the beginning until the user has complied
 * (3) a, b, and c have been set in aQuadraticEquation as entered by the user
 */
public static void getABCFor( QuadraticEquation aQuadraticEquation )
/*****************************************************************************************/
{
   BufferedReader bufReader = new BufferedReader( new InputStreamReader( System.in ) );
   String lineOfInput = "not set yet";

   boolean aBCAllEntered = false;
   while( !aBCAllEntered )
   {
      try
      {
```

```
                  System.out.println( "Please enter 'a' in the form ....m.n...: " );
                  lineOfInput = bufReader.readLine();
                  aQuadraticEquation.a = Double.parseDouble( lineOfInput );   // exception if ill formed

                  System.out.println( "Please enter 'b' in the form ....m.n...: " );
                  lineOfInput = bufReader.readLine();
                  aQuadraticEquation.b = Double.parseDouble( lineOfInput );   // exception if ill formed

                  System.out.println( "Please enter 'c' in the form ....m.n...: " );
                  lineOfInput = bufReader.readLine();
                  aQuadraticEquation.c = Double.parseDouble( lineOfInput );   // exception if ill formed

                  aBCAllEntered = true;   // all entried in legitimate form
          }
        catch( IOException e )
        {       System.out.println( e );
        }
        catch( NumberFormatException n )
        {       System.out.println
                  ( "Entry not in correct number format: ....m.n...." +
                  "Please try again from the beginning." );
        }
    }
}
/***********************************************************************************
 * Postcondition: The user has entered as many quadratic equations that she wants,
 *                and the application has displayed the solution(s) that exist to the console.
 */
public static void main(String[] args)
/***********************************************************************************/
{
  try
  {
      String quitResponse = "Solve at least one quadratic equation.";
      BufferedReader bufReader = new BufferedReader( new InputStreamReader( System.in ) );
      QuadraticEquation quadraticEquation= new QuadraticEquation();

      while( !"quit".equals( quitResponse ) )
      {
          getABCFor( quadraticEquation );
          Client client = new Client();
          client.doWorkInvolving( quadraticEquation );
          System.out.println
            ( "\nType quit if you don't want to solve more quadratic equations," +
            "otherwise any character." );
          quitResponse = bufReader.readLine();
      }
  }
  catch( IOException e )
  {   System.out.println( e );
  }
}

}
```

The class *TwoSolutions*:

```
/**
 * Solves quadratic equations with two solutions
 */
class TwoSolutions extends QuadraticAlgorithm
{

  /***********************************************************************************
   */
```

```
public TwoSolutions()
/****************************************************************************************/
{  super();
}


/****************************************************************************************
 */
protected void displayNumSolutions()
/****************************************************************************************/
{  System.out.println( "There are two solutions to this quadratic equation." );
}


/****************************************************************************************
 */
public TwoSolutions( double anAValue, double aBValue, double aCValue )
/****************************************************************************************/
{  super( anAValue, aBValue, aCValue ) ;
}


/****************************************************************************************
 * Precondition: a != 0
 */
protected void displayFirstSolution()
/****************************************************************************************/
{
   try
   {
       System.out.println( "The first solution is " +
             ( - b + Math.sqrt( b*b - 4*a*c ) ) / 2*a );
   }
   catch( Exception e )   // Should not occur
   {
       System.out.println( "displayFirstSolution() called with zero 'a'. " );
       System.exit( 0 );   // examine source code!
   }
}


/****************************************************************************************
 * Precondition: a != 0
 */
public void displaySecondSolution()
/****************************************************************************************/
{
   try
   {
       System.out.println( "The second solution is " +
             ( - b - Math.sqrt( b*b - 4*a*c ) ) / 2*a );
   }
   catch( Exception e )   // Should not occur
   {
       System.out.println( "displayFirstSolution() called with zero 'a'. " );
       System.exit( 0 );   // examine source code!
   }
}

}
```

# CHAPTER 10

# *INTRODUCTION TO COMPONENTS*

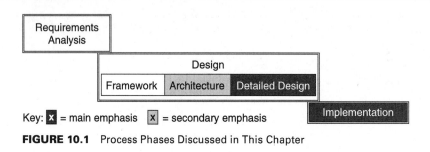

**FIGURE 10.1**   Process Phases Discussed in This Chapter

The learning goals for this chapter are shown in Figure 10.2.

Understand ...

- benefits of components
- what components consist of
- how they are developed
- how they are combined
  - with each other
  - with applications
- how components can be executed

**FIGURE 10.2**   Learning Goals for This Chapter

As emphasized throughout this book, reusing software is essential. Using an individual class (e.g., the Java library class *JPanel*) in multiple applications is a successful kind of reuse. However, reusing individual classes is not enough. We need to reuse objects of classes, collections of classes, and additional resources such as images. We also need to be able to query such assemblies at runtime in order to make optimal use of them.

## DESIGN GOAL AT WORK   *Reusability*

We want to reuse collections of software.

A straightforward kind of reuse is one in which we do not alter the element being reused. An analogy is the way builders use manufactured doors: They may paint doors and drive nails through them to connect them to buildings, but they do not alter the door model. Component technology uses this approach.

When using construction components for doors, roofs and additions, it is not necessary to rebuild a house in order to change components. On the other hand, when a house design and construction are not component-based, everything must be built integrally. For example, each window would have to be built from scratch while the wall containing it is constructed—hardly a practical construction plan. Figure 10.3 illustrates this difference.

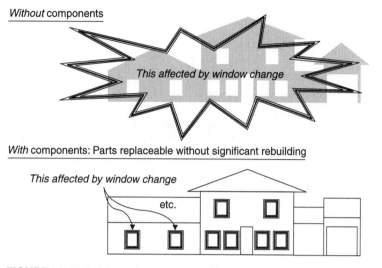

*Without* components

*This affected by window change*

*With* components: Parts replaceable without significant rebuilding

*This affected by window change*

etc.

**FIGURE 10.3**  Building With and Without Components

## 10.1  DEFINITION OF COMPONENTS

Many definitions have been put forward for "components." The definition we will use is *software usable without alteration*. Components can generate entities, typically instances, and these instances *can* be altered. Returning to our example above of a builder using a window, note that he may paint a particular window (instance): In other words, he sets the value of its "color" property. What he does not alter is the window model that he uses. What about a variation on a window model? For example, we may have a 1996 model 3ft × 4ft *WonderWindow*, succeeded by a 1997 model 3ft × 4ft *WonderWindow*. These are related in the sense that the latter is a new version of the former component.

| **KEY CONCEPT**    *What is a Component?* |
| --- |
| A software collection used without alteration. |

The Object Management Group's "Modeling Language Specification" (Revision 1.3) [Om] defines a component as "a physical, replaceable part of a system that packages implementation and provides the realization of a set of interfaces. A component represents a physical piece of a system's implementation, including software code (source, binary or executable) or equivalents, such as scripts or command files." This includes the kinds of software listed in Figure 10.4.

**Components Can Be Made of...**

- Source code
  - Classes—one or more, possibly related
- Executable code
  - Object code
  - Virtual object code
- Other files
  - Images, text, indices, etc.

**FIGURE 10.4** The Composition of Components

Although it might appear from this list that anything could be a component, note the restriction we place upon components: that they be usable without alteration. If one does alter a component, the result is considered a different component.

## 10.2 A DEMONSTRATION OF COMPONENT USE

To illustrate the use of components, we will build the application shown in Figure 10.5 from three existing components supplied by Sun as part of their *BeanBox* component environment. In particular, we will use their *Juggler* and *ExplicitButton* Beans (components) to build the application shown, in which "Duke's" manic juggling can be stopped and started with the corresponding buttons. JavaBeans are explained in the rest of this chapter and in Chapter 11.

**FIGURE 10.5** The *Controlled Juggler* Application

To follow the process of building this application, the reader may want to download and install *BeanBox* from *java.sun.com*. The website for this book may contain some tips on using *BeanBox*.

1. Bring up *BeanBox* using *run.bat* in the *BeanBox* directory. *BeanBox* consists of the three windows shown in Figure 10.6.

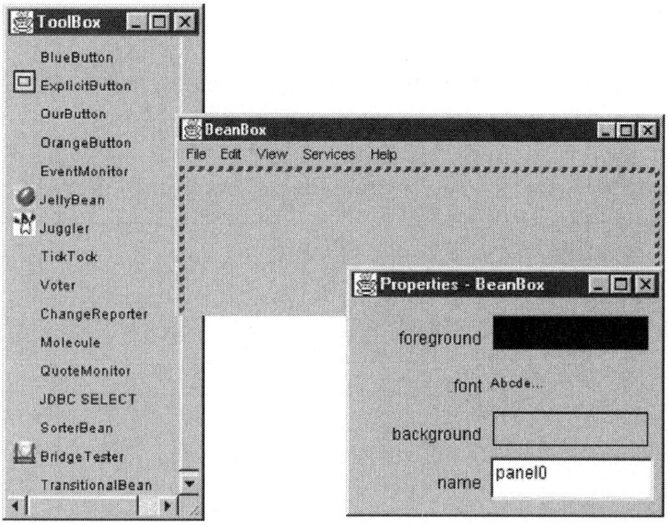

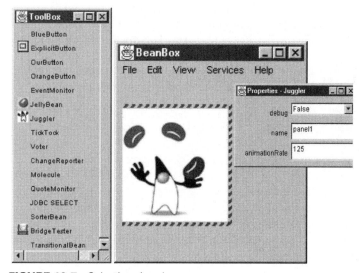

**FIGURE 10.6**    *BeanBox* Environment

2. Click on *"Juggler"* in the *ToolBox* pane. A "+" appears as cursor. Move it to the *BeanBox* pane and click. The juggler appears in the *BeanBox* pane, juggling beans, as shown in Figure 10.7. This is a visual representation of an instance of the *Juggler* component. Sometimes we say that this is "a *Juggler* Bean" for short, even though this is not strictly correct. There is only one *Juggler* Bean, and it is a Java *.class* file.

**FIGURE 10.7**    Selecting *Juggler*

The source code for *Juggler* (©Sun Inc.) is contained in the appendix for this chapter. The *BeanBox* activities described here do not alter the *Juggler* Bean. Note the *Juggler* source code information in Figure 10.8 and 10.9.

- *Juggler* is a class—actually an *Applet,* so it implements the *Serializable* interface
- We do not alter (the code for) *Juggler*
- *BeanBox* recognizes that *Juggler* is a component, and displays an image of an *instance*
- *Juggler* listens for several kinds of events
- *BeanBox* recognizes that *Juggler* implements the *Runnable* interface, and automatically executes its *run()*
- *Juggler* operates by displaying images from the array images of type *Image[]*. The key lines in *run()* are

  ```
  Image img = images[ ( loop % 4 ) + 1 ];
  ...
  g.drawImage( img, 0, 0, this );
  ```

**FIGURE 10.8**　Observations on *Juggler* Source Code 1

- *rate* is a private variable: A public method is available to set it as follows.

  ```
  public void setAnimationRate( int x )
  {   rate = x;
  }
  ```

  BeanBox recognizes *animationRate* as a property of int type, and allows it to be set.
- *Juggler* code distinguishes the behavior of the bean between "design time," "runtime," etc. For example

  ```
  /*
   * If switching to runtime, ...
   * If switching to design time and debugging is true, ....
   */
  public void setDesignTime( boolean dmode ) .....
  ```

**FIGURE 10.9**　Observations on *Juggler* Source Code 2

Sun's demonstration Beans provide a good idea of what can be done with components. In the next chapter, we will discuss Java Beans in more detail.

Now let's add a button that stops the *Juggler* instance. To do this, we click on *ExplicitButton* in the *ToolBox* pane and click in the *BeanBox* pane to make a button appear.

## DESIGN GOAL AT WORK　*Reusability*

We want to construct and reuse a *Juggler* instance connected to *Start/Stop* buttons.

We can label the button "stop" by selecting the button (so that it is surrounded by a dotted line) and setting the value of its *label* property in the *Properties* window, just by typing "stop" in the label field. (The default label value is "press.") So far, we have a *Juggler* Bean instance and the *ExplicitButton* Bean instance in *BeanBox*, but there is no relationship between them.

We want a click on the *stop* button to cause *Juggler* to cease his crazy act. To do this we select the *stop* button and press

*Edit / events / button push / actionPerformed.*

Moving the cursor outside the button causes a red "rubber band" to appear from the button to the cursor. Clicking the cursor on *Juggler* causes a window to be displayed listing *Juggler*'s methods, as shown in Figure 10.10.

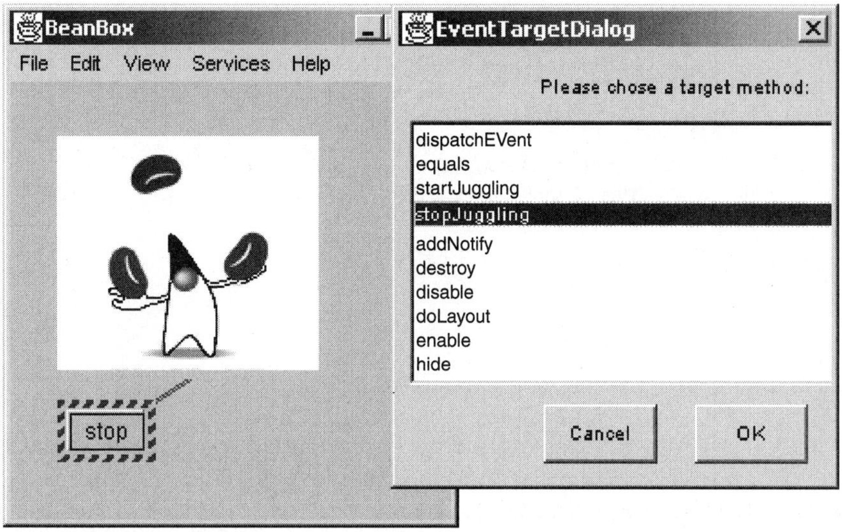

**FIGURE 10.10** Causing *ExplicitButton* Press to Call *stopJuggling()* on *Juggler*

By clicking on *stopJuggling*, we are indicating that the event on the stop button that we selected (*actionPerformed* by name, a button click in practice) calls *stopJuggling()* on *Juggler*. Try this yourself. A similar sequence of actions produces a "start" button, and the application in Figure 10.5 is obtained, running in *BeanBox*.

The resulting application can be saved. If the focus (dotted-line rectangle) is as shown in Figure 10.5, *File/Save* saves the assembled application on a file. This application is designed to run in the *BeanBox* environment, and can be retrieved with the *File/Load* command.

# 10.3  WHAT COMPONENTS CONSIST OF

## 10.3.1  Properties, Methods, Events

> **DESIGN GOAL AT WORK**  *Reusability*
>
> We want the functionality and event sensitivity of a Bean to be available in any context.

A component generally has *properties*. For example, a graphical component might have a *backgroundColor* property. Components are created to provide useful functionality for client use. This functionality is often divided into one or more *interfaces*—sets of methods. For example, a spreadsheet component might provide an interface such as *CellManipulation,* which contains a method such as *evaluateCell(int columnNum, int rowNum)*. In addition, a component may be capable of reacting to events that take place upon it: For example, a button component reacts to being clicked. Finally, it must be possible for components to answer questions about themselves: For example, *BeanBox* needs to determine whether *Juggler* is a *Component* object, what events it is responsive to, what its properties are, etc. This discussion is summarized in Figure 10.11.

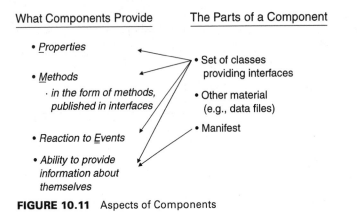

**FIGURE 10.11** Aspects of Components

Although classes have the characteristics described above, not everything having these characteristics is a class. Collections of classes have them too. The Properties/Method/Event characteristics are often referred to as "the PME model."

## 10.3.2 Manifests

Since components can consist of several parts, they are typically packaged with a list of their contents. Such a list is called a *manifest*. This is not a new term: Ship containers, for example, have an attached manifest. Component manifests contain information such as that listed in Figure 10.12.

- Identification of the component
- Authorship of the component
- List of files or classes making up this component
- Other components on which this one relies
- Encryption information
- Means of verifying that all parts of the component are present
- Version number

**FIGURE 10.12** Manifests

## 10.3.3 Introspection and Metadata

Components are usually designed to exist in an *environment*. The environment is designed to relieve the developer from having to design and code routine operations. It also facilitates visual development. *BeanBox* is an example of a component environment. Enterprise Java Beans exist in their own special environment (see Section 14.4.4 on page 500); Microsoft's .NET components provide their functionality in the .NET environment (see Chapter 12). Environments are designed to take on as many common responsibilities as possible. There is nothing new about software requiring an environment in which to operate: Even conventional programs require environments (an operating system, perhaps a Java Virtual Machine, etc.).

To be useful, component environments need to "know about" the entities using them. For example, it should be possible for the environment to find out details concerning the classes that make up each component. This information is called *metadata*, and the process of obtaining it is called *introspection*. Java in particular provides the runtime information about classes, as summarized in Figure 10.13.

| Class | Name, superclass, super-interfaces, inner classes, fields, constructors, Mmethods |
|---|---|
| Field | Name, type |
| Constructor | Parameters, exceptions |
| Method | Name, parameters, return type, exceptions |

**FIGURE 10.13**   Introspection: Runtime Java Information Classes

**KEY CONCEPT**   *The Aspects of a Component*

Properties, functionality, sensitivity to events, a manifest listing its files, and an interface providing a self description.

## 10.4   UML COMPONENT NOTATION

Figure 10.14 shows the UML notation for components and the interfaces that a component may support. The component shown consists of two sub-components and supports three interfaces. One of the interfaces is entirely supported by a sub-component.

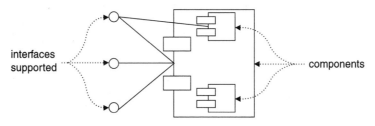

interfaces
supported

components

**FIGURE 10.14**   UML Notation for Components

## 10.5   THE PHASES OF A COMPONENT LIFETIME

Software used to be simply developed by programmers and used by users. Modern software often involves more than these two roles. Spreadsheets, for example, are originally developed by developers, then customized (e.g., to show profit-and-loss), then used for applications. "Customization" here is a kind of development.

People have several potential roles in dealing with components. At one extreme, there is a need to develop environments (containers) like BeanBox in which to do component work. Such a container can be specialized for a particular industry or purpose. Developers of containers are concerned with making the environment recognize aspects of components such as their properties and methods. This is made possible by introspection: The ability of components to provide information about themselves.

At the other end of the programming spectrum, components, being "ready-made," can be used by nonprogrammers. Typically, nonprogrammers set the properties of component instances and combine them to form useful software, as we did with *Juggler* above. This wide spectrum of roles makes component lifetimes quite varied.

As with most of software design, the first step is to decide just what software modules we need for our current application and for similar ones. This process is called "domain analysis." It consists of thinking through the required vocabulary of the applications we plan to deal with. For example, if our business consists of controlling security devices, then the words *Sensor*, *Person*, and *Security level* come to mind. These are candidates for components. Domain Analysis, similar to "Object-Oriented Analysis" or simply "Analysis," is explained further in Chapter 13.

Components need to be designed, then implemented in code. We can then use an environment to make an instance of the Bean by setting its properties (*instance creation time*). Once they have been created, Bean instances can be combined to build functionality, as we did with *Juggler* and *ExplicitButton* (*assembly time*). In some cases, this may be all the functionality that's needed. Beans can also be inserted into applications (*deployment time*), and then executed as part of an application (*execution time*). These phases are illustrated in Figure 10.15.

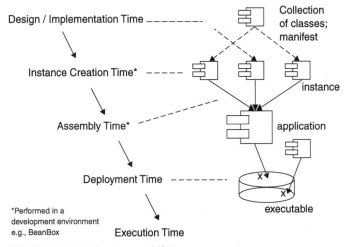

**FIGURE 10.15** Component Lifetimes

## 10.5.1 Design/Implementation Time

To design a component, we generally need to write class code. Although it is not necessary to generate components from object-oriented sources, the components in this book will be. Designing and implementing components is like writing any OO application except as outlined in Figure 10.16.

- Write source code for classes
  - · Ensure that the runtime environment contains library classes required
  - · Conform with required rules, if any (e.g., Java Beans)
- Incorporate required non-library classes
- Create a manifest listing the component's parts

**FIGURE 10.16**   Design Phase for Components

### 10.5.2   Instance Creation Time

In classical (noncomponent) OO applications, we create instances of objects with (textual) source code. The constructor is a typical way in which to do this, but we sometimes wrap constructors in creational design patterns (Chapter 7). When we want to create instances of components with a visual aspect to them, however, graphical means can be far superior to text. Instead of writing source code such as the following in order to create a textbox instance with a red background

```
....
JTextField textField = new JTextField();
TextField.setForeground( Color.red );
.....
```

we can obtain a picture of *textField* in a component development environment such as BeanBox and then click on a color palette to create the instance we need. We will call this process *Instance Creation Time*. Figure 10.17 illustrates this process.

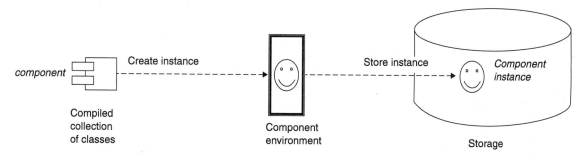

FIGURE 10.17   Instance Creation Time

### 10.5.3   Assembly Time

Components, by their very name, invite their usage in building bigger entities: We can call this phase *assembly*. For example, we assembled the *Juggler* bean instance and a pair of *ExplicitButton* instances to create the juggler *stop/start* functionality—suggestive of a useful application. Component assemblers need not be programmers in the traditional sense: It is possible for an assembler to do all of his work with a library of components, dragging, dropping, and connecting them to create new applications. Figure 10.18 illustrates this process.

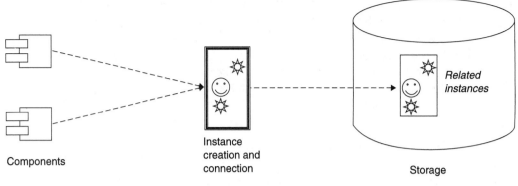

Components    Instance
creation and
connection

Related
instances

Storage

**FIGURE 10.18** Assembly Time

## 10.5.4 Deployment Time

The *Juggler* functionality that we assembled in Section 10.2 exists within BeanBox. However, we may want the assembly to operate in a different environment such as a browser. Another environment is a Java Server Page: A server-side environment into which Java Beans can be inserted to create applications. The process of placing components in operating environments is called "deployment." Figure 10.19 illustrates this.

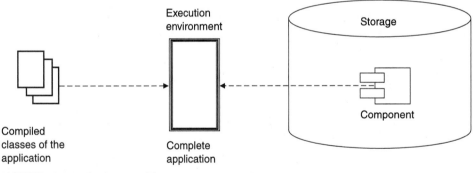

Compiled
classes of the
application

Execution
environment

Complete
application

Storage

Component

**FIGURE 10.19** Deployment Time

## 10.5.5 Execution Time

Execution time is like that of any other application. We simply have to ensure that all of the required parts are present in the environment to allow the application to execute. For example, Microsoft .NET components require the .NET environment to be present at execution time.

**KEY CONCEPT** *The Lifecycle of a Component*

Select, design, code source, instantiate, combine instances, deploy in applications, execute.

# 10.6 THE CORBA COMPONENT STANDARDS

As we have seen, components frequently require environments in which to function. An environment implies a standard that is understood by the components. We will discuss the CORBA standard in this section, the Java Beans standard in Chapter 11, and .NET in Chapter 12.

The Common Object Request Broker (CORBA) is a set of standards developed by the Object Management Group (OMG) software consortium. The OMG component standards are intended to allow components to interoperate, even when written for differing systems and platforms (Java Beans, .NET, UNIX, Windows, MAC, etc.). The CORBA component model is comprehensive: In particular, it describes not just services provided by a component, but also those used by it; not just events recognized by the component, but also those generated by it. It relies on the considerable work already in place for Object Request Brokers (ORBs), the OMG's object interoperability standard. For example, ORBs implement event services in which one object can listen for events across a network generated by another object.

A basic concept in the CORBA Component model is the "port," as indicated in Figure 10.20.

- *Facets* (functionality provided for clients)
- *Receptacles* (functionality it requires)
  Dependence on other components
- *Event sources* (that it's sensitive to)
- *Event sinks* (that it listens for on other components)
- *Attributes* (properties)

**FIGURE 10.20**  The "Ports" of CORBA Components

CORBA ports include the concepts we have discussed so far, but also event *sinks* since components can respond to events as well as produce them. This is illustrated in Figure 10.21.

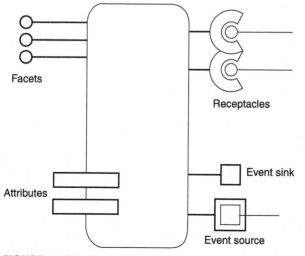

Facets

Receptacles

Event sink

Attributes

Event source

**FIGURE 10.21**  Ports

The CORBA Interface Definition Language (IDL) specifies components and the interfaces that they support. Since IDL is an interface specification language, it does not specify "action" code: For example, there are no control commands such as *while* and *for*, or any commands such as assignment. IDL specifies the collection of function prototypes in each interface, as well as the interfaces supported by a component. Figure 10.22 gives an IDL example.

```
Interface DepositTransactions { . . . };
```

*Specification of an interface (a list of function prototypes)*

Used in ...          *Specification of a component*

Component Bank supports DepositTransactions

```
{ ... Provide additional parts as desired ... };
```
**FIGURE 10.22**  CORBA Component Support Interfaces

CORBA supports a rich "naming service," which is a means of obtaining references to objects through string identifiers. The idea is to make components available to potential clients throughout a network. For example, using a path name string such as "braude/applications/bank," we utilize the naming service to obtain a reference to the *Bank* component. Once this is done, we can create an *XYBank* instance *bank*. Figure 10.23 shows CORBA code for this process.

Get reference to component *XYBank* using the
CORBA naming service. (Not covered here.)

Create instances in two steps.

(1): Use *create()* on the component
   Org.omg.Components.ComponentBase
      myXYBankInstance = XYBank.create();
(2): Cast the instance as *XYBank* object
   XYBank bank = (XYBank) myXYBankInstance;

Now use *bank* ...

**FIGURE 10.23**  Finding CORBA Components and Creating Instances

The method for obtaining the component *bank* uses the naming service and a string identifier, and is similar to obtaining Enterprise Java Beans, explained in Chapter 11.

Every CORBA component supports the *Navigation* interface, which allows one to trace the components on which a given component depends. For additional information see [Dt].

# SUMMARY OF THIS CHAPTER

Figure 10.24 shows the main points covered in this introductory chapter.
Szyperski [Sz] is a good classical reference for component technology.

Components ...
- are software elements used without alteration
- allow the reuse of compiled parts
  - Interaction via events reduces interdependence
- typically developed in a convenient container
  - e.g., for visualizing and interconnecting
- consist of classes, files, etc. and a manifest
- may be executed in a container
  - to free the developer from common tasks

**FIGURE 10.24**   Summary of Components

# EXERCISES

**Exercise 10.1**   **Family of Applications**   Give an example of a family of applications that could be built economically and conveniently with component technology.   Justify your response.

An example: A related set of applications including a calendar, "to do" lists, a phone list, bookmarks, etc., with a user interface allowing the user to create his own combination.

Evaluation criteria:
- Specificity
- Clarity of prose and code

- Effectiveness of your example

A = thoroughly specific answers to all questions
A = every nontrivial aspect clearly explained; prose states meaning very clearly
A = effective use of component technology

The following are errors that you should watch for in this exercise:

*Serious*:

**1.** Misunderstanding of the advantages of component technology.

**2.** Poor example of component application.

*Less than serious, but more than trivial*:

**1.** Unclear explanations.

**Exercise 10.2**   **Assembly in *BeanBox***   Create an assembly of the built-in beans of BeanBox consisting of at least three components. The *Juggler* bean assembly in this chapter is an example. Include at least two screen shots of your assembled component in operation.

**Exercise 10.3**   **Types of Component Activities**   State the type of each activity listed ("assembly," "deployment," etc.).

**1.** For a travel agency, Joe writes the code using JavaBeans *Vacation*, *Flight*, and *Hotel* that deal with vacations.

**2.** Joe loads each of these Beans into BeanBox and views a picture of each. The *Vacation* shows a box with "Vacation" written in it; *Flight* shows an airplane icon, and *Hotel* shows a building icon. He sets values for the *Vacation* Bean.

**3.** He connects Beans to obtain the following effects. When a user clicks on *Vacation*, both the *Hotel* and *Flight* icons are affected as follows. *Hotel* turns red and the user is prompted at the console for the name of the hotel, the city it's in, the day of arrival, and the day of departure. The *Flight* icon turns red and the user is given a choice at the console of up to three flights consistent with the hotel reservation times.

**4.** Joe saves the result in a file entitled *travelAgent*.

**5.** He writes a travel agency application in which he uses the file *travelAgent*.

**Exercise 10.4**   **Package Interface UML**   In Exercise 10.3, suppose that the classes *Vacation*, *Flight*, and *Hotel* are placed in a package, and that together they provide the following interface.

```
int getVacationId()
int getDestination()
int getDepartureTime()
double computeCost()
```

**Part 10.5.1** Show a UML diagram for this.

**Part 10.5.2** Suppose that the class *Vacation* alone is able to provide the interface described so far. Show this on your diagram.

# APPENDIX

## *SOURCE CODE FOR* JUGGLER

(Reprinted by permission of Sun Microsystems, Inc. © 2002 Sun Microsystems, Inc. All Rights Reserved.)

```
package sunw.demo.juggler;

/**
 * A simple JavaBean demonstration class that displays an animation
 * of Duke juggling a couple of coffee beans.   The Juggler class
 * is a good simple example of how to write readObject/writeObject
 * serialization methods that restore transient state.   In this case
 * the transient state is an array of images and a Thread.
 */

import java.applet.Applet;
import java.awt.*;
import java.awt.event.*;
import java.awt.image.*;
import java.net.URL;
import java.beans.*;
import java.beans.beancontext.*;
import java.beans.DesignMode.*;
import sunw.demo.methodtracer.*;

public class Juggler extends Applet implements Runnable, BeanContextProxy,
                            BeanContextServicesListener,
                            PropertyChangeListener, DesignMode {
    private transient Image[] images;
    private transient Thread animationThread;
    private int rate = 125;
    private transient int loop;
    private boolean stopped = true;
    private boolean debug = false;
    private boolean dmode = false;
    private transient MethodTracer mtService;
    private transient MethodTracer mt;

    private BeanContextChildSupport bccs = new BeanContextChildSupport() {

      protected void initializeBeanContextResources() {

        try {

        // Get method tracing service if it's available.
        BeanContextServices bcs = (BeanContextServices)bccs.getBeanContext();
        if (bcs.hasService(MethodTracer.class)) {
            mtService = (MethodTracer)bcs.getService(
                            getBeanContextProxy(), Juggler.this,
                            MethodTracer.class, null, Juggler.this);
            } else {
            bcs.addBeanContextServicesListener(Juggler.this);
            }
        }
```

```
          // Allow nesting BeanContext control design/runtime mode.
          bcs.addPropertyChangeListener("designMode", Juggler.this);

      } catch (ClassCastException ex) {
          // Nesting BeanContext is not a BeanContextServices
          // so do nothing.
      } catch (Exception e) {
          System.err.println("Error initializing BeanContext resources.");
          System.err.println(e);
      }
    }

    protected void releaseBeanContextResources() {
      if (mtService != null) { mtService = mt = null; }
        try {
          BeanContextServices bcs = (BeanContextServices)getBeanContext();
          bccs.removePropertyChangeListener("designMode", Juggler.this);
          bcs.removeBeanContextServicesListener(Juggler.this);
      } catch (Exception ex) {
      }
    }
};

public BeanContextChild getBeanContextProxy() {
   return bccs;
}

/**
 * Applet method: start the Juggler applet.
 */

public synchronized void start() {
   startJuggling();
}

/**
 * Applet method: stop the Juggler applet.
 */

public synchronized void stop() {
   stopJuggling();
}

/**
 * Initialize the Juggler applet.
 */

private void initialize() {
     // Load the image resources:
    images = new Image[5];
    for (int i = 0; i < 5; i++) {
        String imageName = "Juggler" + i + ".gif";
        images[i] = loadImage(imageName);
        if (images[i] == null) {
            System.err.println("Couldn't load image " + imageName);
            return;
        }
    }
}

/**
 * This is an internal utility method to load GIF icons.
 * It takes the name of a resource file associated with the
 * current object's class-loader and loads a GIF image
 * from that file.
 * <p>
```

```
 *  @param resourceName     A pathname relative to the DocumentBase
 *        of this applet, e.g. "wombat.gif".
 *  @return      a GIF image object.     May be null if the load failed.
 */
private java.awt.Image loadImage(String name) {
    if (mt != null) mt.traceMethod();
  try {
    java.net.URL url = getClass().getResource(name);
    return createImage((java.awt.image.ImageProducer) url.getContent());
  } catch (Exception ex) {
    return null;
  }
}

/**
 * Draw the current frame.
 */
public void paint(Graphics g) {
    if (mt != null) mt.traceMethod();
  int index = (loop%4) + 1;
    // If the animation is stopped, show the startup image.
    if (stopped) {
      index = 0;
  }
  if (images == null || index >= images.length) {
      return;
  }
  Image img = images[index];
  if (img != null) {
      g.drawImage(img, 0, 0, this);
  }
}

/**
 * If false, suspend the animation thread.
 */
public synchronized void setEnabled(boolean x) {
    if (mt != null) mt.traceMethod();
    super.setEnabled(x);
    notify();
}
/**
 * Resume the animation thread if we're enabled.
 * @see #stopJuggling
 * @see #setEnabled
 */
public synchronized void startJuggling() {
    if (mt != null) mt.traceMethod();
    if (images == null) {
      initialize();
  }
  if (animationThread == null) {
      animationThread = new Thread(this);
      animationThread.start();
  }
    stopped = false;
    notify();
}

/**
 * Suspend the animation thread if neccessary.
 * @see #startJuggling
 * @see #setEnabled
 */
```

```
public synchronized void stopJuggling() {
    if (mt != null) mt.traceMethod();
    stopped = true;
  loop = 0;
  // Draw the stopped frame.
    Graphics g = getGraphics();
  if (g == null || images == null) {
    return;
  }
  Image img = images[0];
  if (img != null) {
    g.drawImage(img, 0, 0, this);
  }
}

/**
 * An event handling method that calls startJuggling.    This method
 * can be used to connect a Button or a MenuItem to the Juggler.
 *
 */
public void startJuggling(ActionEvent x) {
    startJuggling();
}

/**
 * This method can be used to connect a Button or a MenuItem
 * to the Juggler.stopJuggling method.
 */
public void stopJuggling(ActionEvent x) {
    stopJuggling();
}

/**
 * Returns false if the Juggler is stopped, true otherwise.
 */
public boolean isJuggling() {
  return stopped;
}

public int getAnimationRate() {
    return rate;
}

public void setAnimationRate(int x) {
    rate = x;
}

public Dimension getMinimumSize() {
    return new Dimension(144, 125);
}

/**
 * @deprecated provided for backward compatibility with old layout managers.
 */
public Dimension minimumSize() {
  return getMinimumSize();
}

public Dimension getPreferredSize() {
    return minimumSize();
}

/**
 * @deprecated provided for backward compatibility with old layout managers.
 */
```

```
public Dimension preferredSize() {
  return getPreferredSize();
}

/**
 * Returns true if debugging is enabled, false if it's not.
 */
public boolean isDebug() {
    return debug;
}

/**
 * Turns debugging on, only if a MethodTracer service is available
 * and we are in design mode.
 */
public void setDebug( boolean debug) {
    if (debug) {
      if (isDesignTime() && (mtService != null)) {
        mt = mtService;
        this.debug = true;
      } else if (mtService == null) {
        System.err.println("MethodTracer service not available.");
        this.debug = false;
      } else if (!isDesignTime()) {
        System.err.println("Debugging not available during runtime.");
        this.debug = false;
      }
    } else {
        mt = null;
        this.debug = false;
    }
}

/*
 * PropertyChangeListener method.  Currently only listen for designMode.
 */
public void propertyChange( PropertyChangeEvent evt) {
    if (evt.getPropertyName().equals("designMode")) {
      boolean dmode = (boolean)((Boolean)evt.getNewValue()).booleanValue();
      setDesignTime(dmode);
    }
}
/*
 * If switching to runtime, turn off method tracing if it was enabled.
 * If switching to design time and debugging is true, then enable
 * method tracing if the service is available.
 */
public void setDesignTime(boolean dmode) {
  this.dmode = dmode;
  if (dmode) {
    if (isDebug() && (mtService != null)) {
      mt = mtService;
    }
  } else if (!dmode && (mt != null)) {
      mt = null;
  }
}

/*
 * Returns true if we're in design mode, false if in runtime mode.
 */
public boolean isDesignTime() {
  return dmode;
}

/*
 * BeanContextServicesListener methods.
```

```
  */
public void serviceRevoked( BeanContextServiceRevokedEvent bcsre) {
  System.err.println("Method Tracing service revoked.");
  setDebug( false);
  mtService = null;
}

public void serviceAvailable( BeanContextServiceAvailableEvent bcsae) {
  if (bcsae.getServiceClass() == MethodTracer.class) {
    // MethodTracer service has just become available.
    try {
        mtService = (MethodTracer)bcsae.getSourceAsBeanContextServices().
        getService( getBeanContextProxy(), this, MethodTracer.class, null, this);
    } catch ( Exception ex) {
        System.err.println(ex);
    }
  }
}

public void run() {
  if (mt != null) mt.traceMethod();
  try {
    while(true) {
      // First wait until the animation is not stopped.
      synchronized (this) {
        while (stopped || !isEnabled()) {
          wait();
        }
      }
      loop++;
      // Now draw the current frame.
      Graphics g = getGraphics();
      Image img = images[(loop % 4) + 1];
      if (g != null && img != null) {
        g.drawImage(img, 0, 0, this);
      }
      Thread.sleep(rate);
    }
  } catch (InterruptedException e) {
  }
}

}
```

# *JAVABEANS*

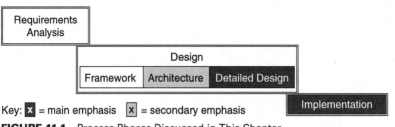

Key: x = main emphasis    x = secondary emphasis

**FIGURE 11.1**   Process Phases Discussed in This Chapter

In this chapter we introduce the Java component system: JavaBeans. Our learning goals are shown in Figure 11.2.

Understand ...

- what JavaBeans ("Beans") are
- the life cycle of a Bean
- Bean containers

Be able to ...

- create JavaBeans
- connect Beans in BeanBox
- create applications that use Beans

**FIGURE 11.2**   Learning Goals for This Chapter

## 11.1  THE GOALS OF JAVABEANS

Sun's goals for Beans are consistent with the goals for components explained in Chapter 10. Perhaps their unique aspect, especially in the context of the time at which they were introduced, is their exploitation of Java's portability. The goals are listed in Figures 11.3 and 11.4.

## 11.2  DEFINITION OF JAVABEANS

As defined in Chapter 10, a component is software used by applications, without change. "Beans" are the components of Java. They are classes or collections of classes. We also deal with Bean instances.

**DESIGN GOAL AT WORK**   *Reusability*

Facilitate the easy reuse of Java code.

- Create a component technology within Java
  - · capitalize on Java portability
- Include GUI components
  - · but not limited to GUI (e.g. server bean)
- Compete with other visual programming and component systems
  - · (which are often specific to an O.S.)
    - · usually Windows

**FIGURE 11.3** *JavaBeans* Design Goals 1

- "Light weight" for Internet applications
- Secure
  - · use Java security model
- Easy and efficient to distribute
- Provide mechanism that enables development environment ("container") to determine methods, properties, and events

**FIGURE 11.4** *Beans* Design Goals 2

## 11.2.1 An Example: Estimating Chair Production

We will use the following application as an example of applying JavaBeans.

A factory for assembling chairs is being planned. Each chair is made of four legs, one seat and one back. For simplicity, we will assume that there is only one assembly station. Chair legs arrive at the station one at a time at regular intervals; the seats arrive one at a time at regular intervals; likewise for the backs. The three interarrival times are generally different from each other. If an item arrives and is not needed it is discarded. (For example, a leg arriving when the assembly station already has four.) Assume that the factory can't control the time at which the first of each item arrives.

The application must forecast the number of chairs that the factory will produce every day, as well as the number of wasted legs, seats and backs.

We can set the rate of arrival of legs, backs and seats. We must also have a button available that produces a current report, an example of which is shown in Figure 11.5. A reset button can be introduced to start the simulation from scratch.

The diagram illustrates the situation for three example arrival frequencies.

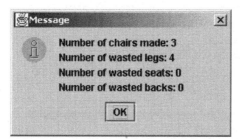

**FIGURE 11.5** Output of *ChairMaker* Bean

| Time: | 0 | 1 | 2 | 3 | 4 | 5 | 6 | 7 | 8 | 9 | 10 | 11 | 12 | 13 | 14 | 15 | 16 | 17 | 18 |
|---|---|---|---|---|---|---|---|---|---|---|---|---|---|---|---|---|---|---|---|
| Leg arrival | L | L | L | L | X | X | L | L | L | L | X | L | L | L | L | X | L | L | L |
| Seat arrival | | | | | | S | | | | | S | | | | | S | | | |
| Back arrival | B | | | | | | | B | | | | | | | B | | | | |
| Chair assembled | | | | | | C | | | | | C | | | | | C | | | |

"X" = item discarded

The results in Figure 11.5, for example, were obtained about 15 seconds after a reset. Nothing obliges us to use Beans to solve this problem, but it is convenient to think of the application in terms of components: The parts of a chair are produced by generator components, and put together at a station component. We will follow this example through the various phases of Bean development.

## 11.2.2   The Phases of a Bean

Recall the following stages in the life of a component, described in Section 10.5: Design/ implementation time, instance creation time, assembly time, deployment time, and execution time. Here we will translate these into practical phases (activities), as indicated in Figure 11.6, and show the details in Sections 11.3 through 11.5.

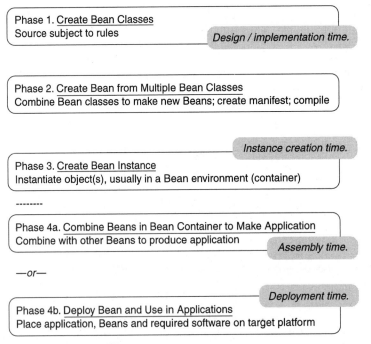

Phase 1. Create Bean Classes
Source subject to rules
*Design / implementation time.*

Phase 2. Create Bean from Multiple Bean Classes
Combine Bean classes to make new Beans; create manifest; compile

*Instance creation time.*

Phase 3. Create Bean Instance
Instantiate object(s), usually in a Bean environment (container)

--------

Phase 4a. Combine Beans in Bean Container to Make Application
Combine with other Beans to produce application   *Assembly time.*

—or—

*Deployment time.*

Phase 4b. Deploy Bean and Use in Applications
Place application, Beans and required software on target platform

**FIGURE 11.6**   Bean Phases

1. To *Create Bean Classes* we write ordinary Java code (which, after all, consists exclusively of classes). We are required to observe a few rules in creating Bean classes, however, enabling development environments to understand enough about the classes so that they can help the developer. These rules are described next. We create a manifest file indicating the Bean's ingredients, including the *java* file with the Bean class, as well as any other files that are required. (For example, *Juggler*, described in Chapter 10, requires three *.gif* files to show the juggling process.) We then *jar* all.

2. To *Create Beans from Multiple Classes* we create several classes (.java files) and combine them into one Bean by listing them in the manifest. Otherwise, the process is the same as for individual beans.

3. To *Create Bean Instances* we can use a Bean environment ("container") to set the bean's properties, obtaining real-time feedback on how the Bean appears. We can then save the Bean instances.

4. **a.** To *Combine Beans in a Bean Container to Make an Application* we use events on the Beans in order to relate them. An event occurring on one Bean causes a method in another Bean to execute.

   **b.** To *Deploy in Applications* we allow the application code to reference the Bean at compile time, and ensure that the (compiled) Bean is available at runtime. We can also create instances of Beans for use at runtime. This has the advantage that we can change the instances without recompiling the application.

---

**KEY CONCEPT**   *Ways to Use Beans*

Within environments; connected to other Beans; within applications.

---

Now we will show how to carry out each of these phases in detail.

## 11.3   PHASE 1: CREATING BEAN CLASSES

To create a Bean class, we simply write the code for a class required by Java client code (so that it needs no *main()* method). We do have to honor some naming conventions (unfortunately named "design patterns" by Sun). This enables Bean environments to recognize the Beans' parts, and thereby to provide the programmer with amenities. For example, if one of the Bean's properties is of type *Color*, *BeanBox* automatically provides a palette of colors to enable the programmer to visually set color values. Figure 11.7 lists amenities that containers may provide, some of which we have already exploited using *BeanBox*.

In order to take advantage of these amenities, Beans honor the rules in Figures 11.8 and 11.9.

- Detection of the Bean's properties
  Read only *or*
  Writeable
- Detection of listeners supported
  So events on the Bean can be handled
- Ability to easily create instances
  and display an image if an *awt* or *swing* object
  Set property values visually
- Ability to store instances

**FIGURE 11.7**  Amenities Afforded by Bean Environments

- Java source consists of Java classes
- -containing null constructor
  ... MyClass() {...}
- -implementing *Serializable* interface
- -obeying standards shown below for...
  · accessor methods
  · *Listener* registration

**FIGURE 11.8**  Required *Bean* Rules (1 of 2)

- To have property *myProp,* include methods:
  `<type> getMyProp(){ ... }`     // to access my*Prop*
  `void setMyProp( <type> p )`  // to change
- For boolean property:
  `boolean isMyProp()`
- Name for event classes to be *XXXEvent*
  · extends *Event*
- Listeners must implement *java.util.EventListener*
  · Name must end in *Listener* as in *XXXListener*
  · *added* with   public void addXXXListener(...)
  · *removed* with  public void removeXXXListener(...)

**FIGURE 11.9**  Required *Bean* Rules (2 of 2)

Let's start with our simplest Bean, *Bean0*, which has no actual functionality, but possesses an integer property. We will be able to visualize *Bean0* and its property via *BeanBox*.

```
public class Bean0
 implements java.io.Serializable   // required for Beans
{
private int myInt = 0;   // ("myInt" is not necessarily a property yet!)

public Bean0()   // Null constructor presence required for all Beans
{
}

public int getIntgr()   // Introduces property "intgr" and makes gettable
{  return myInt;
}

public void setIntgr(int anInteger)   // Makes property "intgr" settable
{  myInt = anInteger;
}

}
```

Note that this is a Bean because it implements the *Serializable* interface and has a null constructor. We want an integer property *intgr* to be readable and writeable, and so we provide the public methods *getIntgr()* and *setIntgr()* methods. (Methods named *getintgr()* and *setintgr()* have the same effect.)

Sun created *BeanBox* to demonstrate Bean environments (containers). *BeanBox* can be downloaded free from [Su2]. Although there are more capable environments than *BeanBox*, it is appropriate for learning Bean technology.

1. We first compile *Bean0* with the following DOS command (we'll allow *Bean0.class* to reside in the same directory as *Bean0.java*: See Sun's documentation for *javac* options).

   *javac Bean0.java*

2. Next, we create a manifest (text) file. This specifies the name of the class files comprising the bean, and indicates that they are indeed JavaBeans. (Other required files can also be included.) The manifest file becomes part of the JAR file. We will name it *manifest.txt*. In this case it contains just the following two lines:

```
Name: Bean0.class
Java-Bean: True
```

On Windows, include a carriage return after the last line of the manifest file.

3. Create the executable JAR file.
   Use the form of the *jar* command to include the manifest file along with the Bean1.class file as shown in Figure 11.10. (See Sun's documentation for *jar* options).

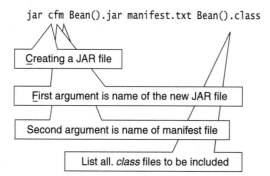

FIGURE 11.10   JAR'ing a Bean

4. Bring up the *BeanBox* window set by executing *run.bat* in the *BeanBox* directory. The set includes the three windows shown in Figure 11.11. They are explained next.

5. Apply the *File/LoadJar* menu item of the *BeanBox* window to *Bean0.jar*. The result is that *Bean0* shows up among the list of beans in the ToolBox window, as shown in Figure 11.12. (*BeanBox* does not appear to allow loading when there are blanks in the names of the path.)

Clicking on "Bean0" in ToolBox, followed by clicking in the *BeanBox* window, causes the dotted rectangle shown in Figure 11.12. *BeanBox* uses the null constructor supplied by the Bean, and looks for properties by searching for methods beginning *set. . .* or *get. . . .* If there is a pair *setX()* and *getX()*, *BeanBox* may create a graphic in the *Properties* pane to enable the user to set the value for an instance. This is the case if $X$ is a primitive data type such as *int* or *float*; it also applies if the type is a class that *BeanBox* recognizes, such as *Color*.

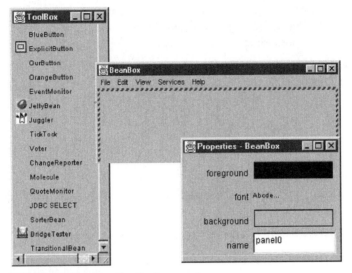

**FIGURE 11.11** *BeanBox* Environment

**FIGURE 11.12** Adding a Bean to the *BeanBox*

Now let's take a slightly more complex example, *Bean1*, which displays the decorated Hello World shown in Figure 11.13. The source for *Bean1* is as follows.

```
import java.awt.*;

public class Bean1 extends Canvas implements java.io.Serializable
{
private Color color = Color.red;   // color of interior rectangle

// Set background (color) and size properties
public Bean1()
```

```
{    setBackground(Color.green);
     setSize(80,40);
}


// Establish property "color"
public Color getColor()
{    return color;
}

public void setColor(Color aColor)
{    color = aColor;
}

// Override paint: rectangle and message within this Canvas object
// Called initially and when developer changes a property in BeanBox
public void paint (Graphics g)
{

    // Draw rectangle in "color"
    g.setColor(color);
    // Starting from top left within this: 20 pixels across, 5 down
    // draw a filled rectangle 20 across and 30 down
    g.fillRect(30,5,20,30);

    // Write "HELLO WORLD" in the foreground color
    g.setColor(getForeground());
    g.drawString("HELLO WORLD", 5, 20);
}

}
```

When loaded, *BeanBox* displays the graphics in Figure 11.13.

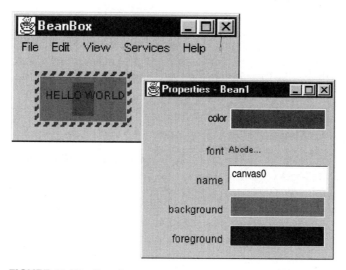

**FIGURE 11.13**   Bean1

The overall dotted line graphic is produced by *BeanBox* because *Bean1* subclasses *java.awt.Component*. Since *Component* has methods *getFont()*, *setFont()*, *getName()*, *set-Name()*, *getBackground()*, *setBackground()*, *getForeground()*, and *setForeground()*, the *Properties* window displays the corresponding properties *font, name,* etc., enabling the developer to set their values. Note that *BeanBox* is discriminating about which properties it shows. For example, *Component* (and therefore *Bean1*) possesses *setSize()* and *getSize()*, which involve the *Dimension* class: *BeanBox* is not designed to display the *size* property because it is not equipped to deal with *Dimension* properties. *BeanBox* provides a convenient way to set the value of *Color* properties, as shown in Figure 11.14.

**FIGURE 11.14**  Setting Color

When we change properties, as we did with *Bean0*, we are changing the attributes of an instance of the Bean. We are not changing the Bean (class). The *File/Save* and *File/Load* menu actions save and retrieve the current instance in a form for *BeanBox*. *File/Serialize-Component* saves the Bean instance we have created in a form that can be read by an application at runtime, as shown in the next section.

### 11.3.1  Example: Creating the *ChairMaker* Bean

*ChairMaker*, described in Section 11.2.1, is designed to respond to the arrival of chair legs, seats, and backs. For that reason, it possesses methods that can be called when these events occur. For example, we will call *receiveLeg()* to simulate the arrival of a leg at the processing station. The code for *receiveLeg()* is designed as follows. If *numLegs* is less than 4, it is incremented and *makeAChairIfPossible()* is executed. If *numLegs* equals 4, *numberOfWastedLegs* is incremented.

---

**DESIGN GOAL AT WORK**   *Reusability*

Be able to use *ChairMaker* Bean alone. Avoid having it refer to any other nonAPI class.

Here is the source code for the *ChairMaker* Bean.

```java
import javax.swing.JOptionPane;

/**
 * Simulates the assembly of chairs from parts that arrive
 */
public class ChairMaker implements java.io.Serializable
{
    // Current number delivered to this assembly station
    private int numLegs = 0;
    private boolean seatPresent = false;    // don't keep more than one
    private boolean backPresent = false;    // don't keep more than one

    private int numberOfChairsMade = 0;    // made by this object

    // Constants
    private final int NUM_LEGS_IN_CHAIR = 4;
    private final int NUM_CHAIRS_AT_REPORT_TIME = 10;   // report when multiple of this many chairs made

    // Wasted parts: data saved
    private int numberOfWastedLegs = 0;
    private int numberOfWastedSeats = 0;
    private int numberOfWastedBacks = 0;


    /** ********************************************** CONSTRUCTOR
     */
    public ChairMaker() {}

    /** ********************************************** METHOD setNumLegs
     * Postcondition: The instance variables == 0 or false
     */
    public void setNumLegs( int aNumLegs )
    {   numLegs = aNumLegs;
    }

    /** ********************************************** METHOD getNumLegs
     */
    public int getNumLegs()
    {   return numLegs;
    }

    /** ********************************************** METHOD isSeatPresent
     */
    public boolean isSeatPresent()
    {   return seatPresent;
    }

    /** ********************************************** METHOD isBackPresent
     */
    public boolean isBackPresent()
    {   return backPresent;
    }

    /** ********************************************** METHOD makeAChairIfPossible
     * Purpose: "Create" a chair if the parts are available.
     *
     * Preconditions: 'numLegs' <= NUM_LEGS_IN_CHAIR
     *
     * Postconditions:
     * If  'numLegs' == NUM_LEGS_IN_CHAIR   &&   'seatPresent' &&   'backPresent' then
     *         (1) 'numberOfChairsMade' has been incremented
     *         (2) 'numLegs' == 0;
     *         (3) 'seatPresent' == false;
     *         (4) 'backPresent' == false
     *     (5) If 'numberOfChairsMade' is a multiple of then the postconditions of 'reportStatus()' apply.
     *             NUM_CHAIRS_AT_REPORT_TIME
```

```
    */
    private void makeAChairIfPossible()
    {
        // If the resources are available to make a chair
        if( ( getNumLegs() == NUM_LEGS_IN_CHAIR ) && isSeatPresent() && isBackPresent() )
        {
            ++numberOfChairsMade; // record fact that chair made

            // Reset resources
            numLegs = 0;
            seatPresent = false;
            backPresent = false;

            // Report waste etc. when NUM_CHAIRS_AT_REPORT_TIME chairs have been made
            if( numberOfChairsMade % NUM_CHAIRS_AT_REPORT_TIME == 0 )
                reportStatus();
        }
    }

    /** ********************************************* METHOD receiveLeg
     * Postconditions:
     * If 'numLegs' >= NUM_LEGS_IN_CHAIR  then 'numberOfWastedLegs' has been incremented
     * otherwise 'numLegs' has been incremented and the postconditions of
     * 'makeAChairIfPossible()'apply
     */
    public void receiveLeg()
    {
        if( numLegs < NUM_LEGS_IN_CHAIR )   // ready to receive one more leg
        {
            ++numLegs;
            makeAChairIfPossible();
        }
        else   // have enough legs: one more wasted leg
            ++numberOfWastedLegs;
    }

    /** ********************************************* METHOD receiveBack
     * Postconditions:
     * If 'backPresent' == true then 'numberOfWastedBacks' has been incremented
     * otherwise 'backPresent' == true and the postconditions of 'makeAChairIfPossible()' apply
     */
    public void receiveBack()
    {
        if( backPresent == false )   // ready to receive back
        {
            backPresent = true;
            makeAChairIfPossible();
        }
        else   // already have back: one more wasted
            ++numberOfWastedBacks;
    }

    /** ********************************************* METHOD receiveSeat
     * Postconditions:
     * If 'seatPresent' == true then 'numberOfWastedSeats' has been incremented
     * otherwise 'seatPresent' == true the postconditions of 'makeAChairIfPossible()'apply
     */
    public void receiveSeat()
    {
        if( seatPresent == false )   // ready to receive seat
        {
            seatPresent = true;
            makeAChairIfPossible();
        }
        else   // already have seat: one more wasted
            ++numberOfWastedSeats;
    }
```

```
/** ************************************************* METHOD reportStatus
 * Postcondition: A dismissable window has popped up showing 'numberOfChairsMade',
 * 'numberOfWastedLegs', 'numberOfWastedSeats' and 'numberOfWastedBacks'
 */
public void reportStatus()
{
    String chairReportString = "Number of chairs made: " +
     Integer.toString( numberOfChairsMade );
    String legReportString = "\nNumber of wasted legs: " +
     Integer.toString( numberOfWastedLegs );
    String seatReportString = "\nNumber of wasted seats: " +
     Integer.toString( numberOfWastedSeats );
    String backReportString = "\nNumber of wasted backs: " +
     Integer.toString( numberOfWastedBacks );
    javax.swing.JOptionPane.showMessageDialog
     ( null, chairReportString + legReportString + seatReportString + backReportString );
}

/** ************************************************* METHOD reset
 * Postcondition: The instance variables == 0 or false
 */
public void reset()    // set all to zero to begin timing
{
    numLegs = numberOfChairsMade = numberOfWastedLegs = numberOfWastedSeats
     = numberOfWastedBacks = 0;
    seatPresent = backPresent = false;
}
}
```

## 11.4  PHASE 2: CREATING MULTIPLE-CLASS BEANS

If we need a Bean consisting of more than one class, we create these classes in conformance with Bean rules, declare them in the manifest, and *jar* all. The individual classes and their public members are then available from this Bean. When we *jar*, the command line has the following form.

> *jar cfm MyBean.jar manifestListingAll.txt MyBean1.class MyBean2.class . . .     MyBeanN.class*

## 11.5  PHASE 3: CREATING BEAN INSTANCES

*BeanBox* helps the user to create instances of Bean classes by allowing the user to set some properties visually. (Recall that settable properties are recognizable by the existence of public *setXXX()* and *getXXX()* methods.) In particular, *BeanBox* facilitates the setting of *Font* and *Color* values. Since the java class *Component* has public methods *getFont(Font)*, *setFont(Font)*, *setForeground(Color)* and *setBackground(Color)*, it follows that the properties of *Component* objects can be set visually. Note that when we change properties, we are not changing the Bean class—merely creating a Bean instance with the properties we want. Initially, the Properties window for *Bean0* is as shown in Figure 11.15.

Clicking on the color boxes in *Properties* allows the user to changes these colors. The default *name* property "panelX" is automatically assigned to the instance of *Bean0* highlighted by *BeanBox*. We can change this value.

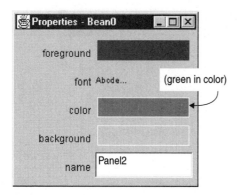

**FIGURE 11.15** Initial Form of Properties Panel

## 11.6 PHASE 4: COMBINING AND DEPLOYING BEANS

Beans can be "dropped into" many applications. Because they obey naming conventions, their hosts can determine specific aspects such as their properties. Java Server Pages (JSP's) and Enterprise JavaBeans (EJB's) are examples of specialized Bean environments (see Section 11.7.1 in this chapter, and Section 14.4.4.4 in Chapter 14, respectively).

### 11.6.1 Phase 4a: Combining Beans in a Bean Environment

In having Beans use other software, we are faced with the restriction mentioned when we defined components: They cannot be changed. When classes interact, we usually expect one of them to reference another, as in the following code example.

```
class A
{
    void aMethodOfA()
    {. . .mention class B. . .}
}

class B
{  . . .
}
```

If *A* is a Bean, then any such reference effectively makes *B* a part of the Bean *A*, which limits the reuse of *A* in multiple contexts. The solution to this issue is to apply the *Mediator* design pattern: Introduce a separate class—a *Listener*—that responds to events on one Bean and invokes methods of the other when the event is detected. The only requirement we make is ensuring that events upon them can be listened for. In the case of Beans inheriting from *Component*, this requirement is already satisfied because the *Component* class supports several *addXXListener()* methods.

Let's return to the *ChairMaker* Bean. We will use it in *BeanBox* to create the required simulation of chair factory operations. We compile and jar *ChairMaker*, load it into *BeanBox* using *File/Loadjar*. We will discuss next how *ChairMaker* is used in a simulation that produces the output shown in Figure 11.18.

**DESIGN GOAL AT WORK**   *Reusability*

Utilize *Chairmaker* with *TickTock* events. This avoids compromising either Bean.

*Chairmaker* responds to the arrival of chair parts. To simulate the regular arrival of chair parts we will use *TickTock* Beans, each of which simply generates an event at a regular interval. One of the *TickTock* beans is shown in Figure 11.16.

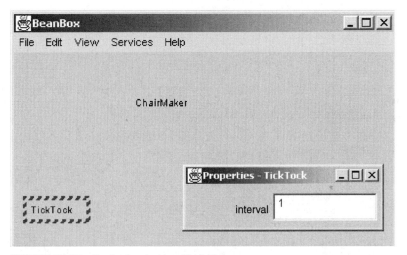

**FIGURE 11.16**   Beginning to Use *ChairMaker*

We set *TickTock*'s interval to a desired amount: In this case, we indicate that legs arrive every second by setting *TickTock*'s interval to 1. We use *Edit/propertyChange/propertyChange*, stretching the red "rubber band" to *ChairMaker* and choosing *receiveLeg()*, as shown in Figure 11.17.

We create two more *TickTock* Beans to simulate the arrival of backs and seats. A better-designed *TickTock* bean would allow us to alter the label, so that we could name them something like "Leg Source," "Back Source" and "Seat Source" instead of the nondescriptive "TickTock." We implement the automatic reporting of data every time 10 more chairs have been made, as shown in Figure 11.18. If we set the legs to arrive every second, the backs to arrive every 5 seconds and the seats every 7 seconds, the following window pops up after the first 10 chairs have been made. The numbers depend on exactly when the *TickTock* bean instances are created by the *BeanBox* user.

We are also required to implement a button that produces a report at any time. This is shown in Figure 11.19.

We have used the *BeanBox* container not merely to connect Beans, but also to create and run an application. *BeanBox* was an adequate environment for running the *ChairMaker* application.

In the next section we consider separately how to connect Beans via property changes.

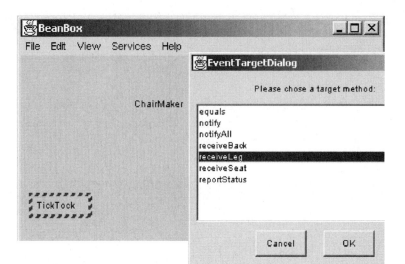

**FIGURE 11.17** Setting *ChairMaker* to Add a Chair Leg

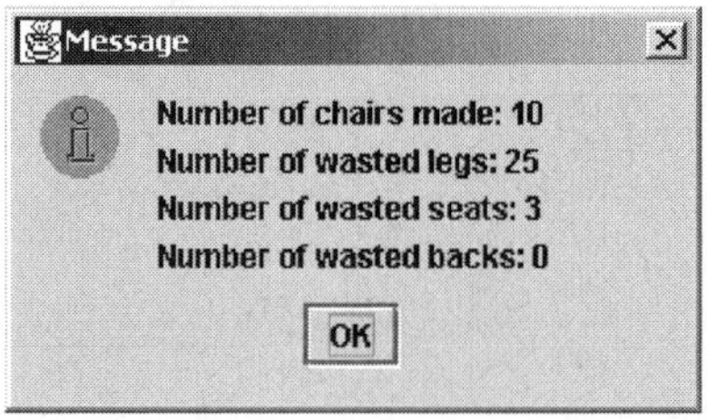

**FIGURE 11.18** An Output of *ChairMaker* Bean

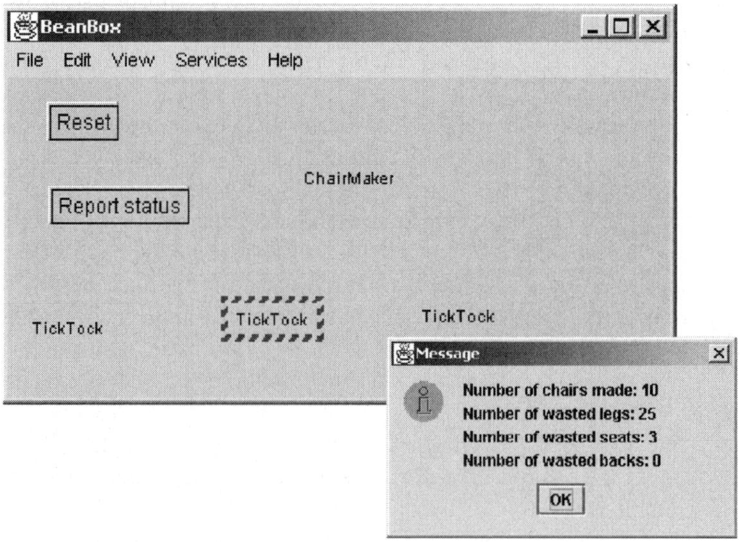

**FIGURE 11.19** Output of *ChairMaker* Bean from Button Action

### 11.6.2 Phase 4b: Using Beans in Applications

We have seen that one way to use Beans is within a Bean environment (*BeanBox*, for example—also called a "container"). This may sound cumbersome; however, most applications require an environment of some kind in which to execute: An operating system at a minimum.

Our goal is to utilize and customize software applications in safe, effective and convenient ways. The simple examples shown next illustrate that this can be done, in many cases, without going through the "add code/compile/execute" cycle *for all classes at the same time*. The idea of separate compilation is not new, and has been practiced in one form or another well before the advent of the "component" concept.

Since Beans are components, we expect that they can be used without change at runtime. As an example, we will use *Bean1* (already compiled into a.*class* file) in an ordinary application that displays *Bean1* instances in a *Frame* object. The output actually produces two frames, as shown in Figure 11.20. The black text version is generated by the application at runtime: The white text version, created previously in *BeanBox* and saved, is retrieved by the application.

**FIGURE 11.20** Using a Bean in an Application: Output

The key code for creating a Bean instance from *Bean1* (saved from a *BeanBox* session) is the following, which uses the factory method *instantiate()* of the class *Beans*.

```
Object bean1 = Beans.instantiate(null, "Bean1");
```

This allows us to load a Bean instance from any location, then use whatever knowledge we have about it or find out at runtime by probing the instance. Instead of using a constructor *new Bean1()*, which would make sense only if we had compiled *Bean1* at the same time as the application, we use the static factory method *instantiate()* of *Beans*. The first parameter of this method is the class loader—*null* if it's the System class loader, which is nominally the case. In this application, we happen to know that the instance in the file named *Bean1* is in the *Bean1* class (the name of the file gives this away!), and we cast it as such in the code. It could belong to a subclass of *Bean1*, and could include additional methods. We can ask the object about this. It could also be a new version of *Bean1*.

The *instantiate()* method looks for an instance at the given file location. If this is absent, it attempts to construct an instance of the class: It throws a *ClassNotFoundException* otherwise. This is clearly more flexible than using a constructor.

To use the existing Bean instance, stored in *Serializable* form in the file *greenWhiteBean1Instance*, the operative code is, as usual,

```
Bean1 bean2 = (Bean1)objectInputStream.readObject();
```

The source code for this application is as follows. (The code does not remove the frames at the conclusion of the execution.)

```
import java.beans.*;
import java.awt.*;
import java.io.*;

/**
 * Demonstration of using a Bean
 */
class Bean1Client
{

/**
 */
public Bean1Client()
{   super();
}

/**
 *Demonstrate the use of Bean1 by (1) instantiating a new object and
 *    (2) retrieving an old instance
 */
public static void main( String[]args )
{
    // To display Bean1 instances:
    Frame frame1 = new Frame();  // located at (0, 0)
    Frame frame2 = new Frame();
    frame2.setLocation( 100, 100 );  // shift to avoid obscuring frame1
    int frameWidth = 0;  // to be determined below
    int frameHeight = 0;

    // ------- 1 -------
    System.out.println("First instantiate a Bean1 instance");

    try
    {
        // Create an instance of Bean1.
        // First parameter of instantiate is the class loader (System Class Loader if "null")
        // Second parameter of instantiate() is the path to the Bean (in same directory in this case)
        Bean1 bean1 = (Bean1)Beans.instantiate(null, "Bean1");

        // Display bean1 in a frame of the same size
        Dimension dimensionOfBean1 = bean1.getSize();  // assumes Bean1 has property "size"
        frameWidth = (int)dimensionOfBean1.getWidth();
        frameHeight = (int)dimensionOfBean1.getHeight() + 30;  // allow for frame header space
        frame1.setSize( frameWidth, frameHeight );
        frame1.add( bean1 );  // assumes Bean1 is a Component
        frame1.setVisible( true );
    }
    catch( Exception e ) { e.printStackTrace();}
    // ------- 2 -------
    System.out.println( "Hit enter to retrieve a Bean1 instance" +
     "(which could have been created in BeanBox)");
    try{System.in.read(); }
    catch(IOException e) {System.out.println( e ); }

    try
    {
```

```
        // Get the instance of Bean1 previously saved in serialized form
        ObjectInputStream objectInputStream =
        new ObjectInputStream( new FileInputStream( "greenWhiteBean1Instance"));
        Bean1 bean2 = (Bean1)objectInputStream.readObject();

        // Display bean2 in a frame of the same size
        frame2.setSize( frameWidth, frameHeight );
        frame2.add( bean2 );
        frame2.setVisible(true);
    }
    catch( Exception e ) { e.printStackTrace(); }
}

}
```

In most applications we create instances of classes. This is a laborious task if there are numerous properties to set. For example, we may have to create particular text with particular fonts and particular colors for a GUI. The class itself is assumed here to already exist. Instead of writing the code to create the instances, is makes more sense to create them using a visual environment such as BeanBox, save the Bean instances, and then read them into applications at runtime, as shown above.

## 11.7 CONNECTING BEANS VIA PROPERTY CHANGES: "BOUND" VARIABLES

**DESIGN GOAL AT WORK**  *Reusability*

We want to associate Beans even when there is no external event such as a mouse click.

We have seen that using events to associate Beans preserves their independence, and thus reusability. One particularly useful event is the *PropertyChangeEvent*, used when a property of a Bean changes value. *PropertyChangeEvent* objects are listened for by classes implementing the *PropertyChangeListener* interface. To see ways of harnessing this kind of event, observe the following in *BeanBox*. Create a pair of *JellyBean* objects with different colors, as shown in Figure 11.21.

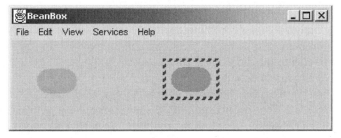

**FIGURE 11.21**  *PropertyChange* Event Demonstration 1

Because the *JellyBean* generates a *PropertyChangeEvent* object when its color changes, we can cause a change in color on the left *JellyBean* instance to affect the right *JellyBean* in the same way. Variables that generate a *PropertyChangeEvent* when their values change are said to be *bound*. This means that the setter for that property contains code like the following. The origin of *propertyChangeSupport* will be explained when the example is given in full.

```
propertyChangeSupport.firePropertyChange
(    "myProp",                          // name of the property
     oldValue,                          // old value
     aMyProp                            // new value
);
```

We encountered property change events when using the *TickTock* Bean in the *ChairMaker* example in 11.6.1. In that example we highlighted *TickTock* and hit *Edit/Event/propertyChange/propertyChange*. This had the effect of generating an event when any property of *TickTock* changed value.

To cause the color on the right *JellyBean* to change in the same way as that on the left, select the left *JellyBean* instance and click on *Edit/Bind* Property. The window shown in Figure 11.22 will pop up, listing all bound variables of *JellyBean*.

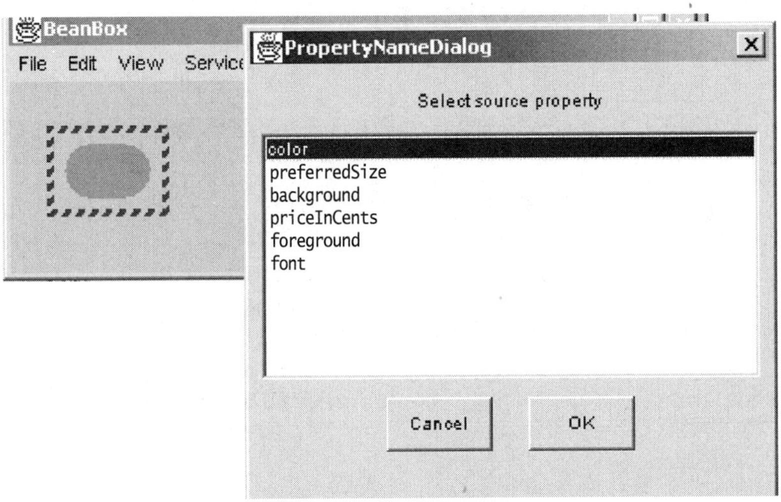

**FIGURE 11.22** *PropertyChange* Event Demonstration 2

This window is asking which property we wish to select whose value changes must generate a property change event. We select *color*, after which a "rubber band" appears, which we stretch to the second *JellyBean*. Releasing the mouse button causes a list to be displayed of all properties in the second *JellyBean* of type *Color*. By selecting the property *color* on that list, we have "bound" *color* on the right *JellyBean* to the value of *color* on the left *JellyBean*. The reader can verify that changing the *color* value on the left *JellyBean* results in the same change on the right *JellyBean* (but not vice versa). For this discussion on JellyBeans, the author is indebted to [O].

Any class implementing *PropertyChangeListener* is able to listen for *PropertyChangeEvent* notifications. *PropertyChangeListener* contains only the method *void propertyChange(PropertyChangeEvent aPropertyChangeEvent)*. The class *PropertyChangeSupport* in *java.bean*s relieves the programmer from the task of tracking the listeners to property changes. The following is source code for a Bean *PropertySourceBean* showing how to use *PropertyChangeSupport* to listen for selected property change events. Note that

- *PropertySourceBean* is a modification of *Bean0* above
- *PropertySourceBean* fires a *PropertyChangeEvent* whenever the property *myInt* is set

The key code to look for here is the following.

- In the Constructor:

```
propertyChangeSupport = new PropertyChangeSupport( this );
```

- In *setIntgr()*, which makes the property *intgr* bound:

```
propertyChangeSupport.firePropertyChange
(   "intgr",// Name of the property
    oldValue,// old value
    myInt// new value
);
```

- The methods *addPropertyChangeListener()* and *removePropertyChangeListener()* ensure that a *PropertyChangeListener* object listens to property changes.

```
// Source of a property change that can be listened for ("bound")

import java.util.*;
import java.beans.*;

public class PropertySourceBean implements java.io.Serializable
    // required for Beans
{
private int myInt = 0;   // will be bound
private PropertyChangeSupport propertyChangeSupport;   // maintains propertyChange

public PropertySourceBean()   // Null constructor required for all Beans
{   propertyChangeSupport = new PropertyChangeSupport( this );
}

// To support listening for property changes, Bean must have this method
public void addPropertyChangeListener ( PropertyChangeListener aPropertyChangeListener )
{
    // Add to the listeners unless already present
    propertyChangeSupport.addPropertyChangeListener( aPropertyChangeListener );
}

public int getIntgr()   // Introduces property "intgr" and makes gettable
{   return myInt;
}

// To support listening for property changes, Bean must have this method
public void removePropertyChangeListener( PropertyChangeListener aPropertyChangeListener )
{
    // Remove from the listeners if present
    propertyChangeSupport.removePropertyChangeListener( aPropertyChangeListener );
```

```
}
public void setIntgr( int anInteger )    // Makes property "intgr" settable
{
    int oldValue = myInt;
    myInt = anInteger;   // new value

    // This command makes the property intgr "bound"
        propertyChangeSupport.firePropertyChange
        (   "intgr",            // Name of the property
            oldValue,           // old value
            myInt               // new value
    );
}
}
```

We can now cause several kinds of consequences when *myInt* is changed. If we highlight *PropertySourceBean* in *BeanBox* and click on *Edit/Events/PropertyChange/PropertyChangeListener*, we can cause methods on other objects to be called just as with any other event. For example, we can make *Juggler* stop juggling whenever *myInt* is changed. We can also bind the *myInt* property to any other individual property by clicking on *Edit/Events/Bind Property*. For example, Figure 11.23 shows the consequences of binding *myInt* in *PropertySourceBean* to *animationRate* in *Juggler*, so that setting *myInt* sets *Juggler*'s speed automatically.

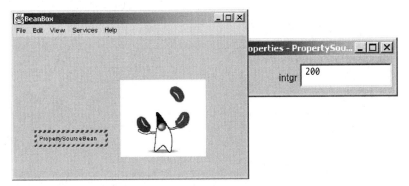

**FIGURE 11.23** *BoundProperty* Demonstration

**KEY CONCEPT** *Bound Properties*

Causes Beans to react when a property in another Bean changes value.

## 11.8 USING BEANS IN JAVA SERVER PAGES

Java Server Page (JSP) technology helps developers to implement server-side processing. A line of JSP source without special symbols is interpreted upon execution as simply sending that line to the client's browser (and is thus automatically interpreted as HTML). JSP's allow the insertion of Beans, thereby gaining processing power. The following figure shows a format for embedding a Bean just about anywhere within a JSP.

```
<jsp:useBean
    id="object name" 1
    scope="page|request|session|application" 2
    class="fully qualified classname" 3
</jsp:useBean>
```

1 Bean instance name as in MyClass myName=....
2 //Choose one; when instance is destroyed; optional;
  default is *page*
3 //e.g., *a.b.MyClass*

**FIGURE 11.24**   Embedding Beans in JSP

The "scope" options are as shown in Figure 11.25.

Because JSP's generate material intended for transmission over the Internet, they are constrained in various ways to deal with characters. One sets and gets the property values of beans from within JSPs as in Figure 11.26.

- *page*: new object created and destroyed for every page view.

- *request*: the newly created object created and bound to the request object.

- *session*: the newly created object bound to the session object. Every visitor coming to the site will have a separate session for it, so you will not have to create a new object every time for it. Able to retrieve that object later again from the session object when wanted.

- *application*: object will stay as long as the application remains loaded. E.g., you want to count page views or daily sessions for your site.

Adapted from [St].

**FIGURE 11.25**   Scope of a Bean in a JSP

```
<jsp:setProperty
        name="account17"
        property="bal"
        value="3211"
/>

<jsp:getProperty
        name="account17"
        property="bal"
/>
```

**FIGURE 11.26**   Setting and Getting a Bean Property in a JSP

We can thus think of JSP's as (among other things) special-purpose containers for JavaBeans.

# SUMMARY

Figure 11.27 summarizes the points of this chapter.

- A Java Bean is a compiled collection of Java classes and required files
  - JAR'd to reduce to a single file
- Beans are used at various phases, often in a Bean *container*
  - Creating from scratch
  - Creating instances of

**FIGURE 11.27**   Summary of This Chapter

# EXERCISES

**Exercise 11.1**    *Juggler* **Stop and Start**    Create an application in Bandbox that shows *Juggler* stopping every 5 seconds, and starting every 9 seconds. Provide a screenshot, and explain how you related the beans.

Points to watch for:
  *Serious:*
Beans should not reference other Beans if possible.

**Exercise 11.2**    **Model Railroad Layouts**    You are to build an application that plans model railroad layouts. Describe an appropriate environment using Beans. Sketch and explain its features. Don't be constrained by what BeanBox provides: Use your imagination to obtain an ideal solution. At the same time, however, be sure that your design *can* be implemented with Beans.

Evaluation criteria:

| | |
|---|---|
| ▒ Specificity | A = thoroughly specific answers to all questions |
| ▒ Clarity of prose and code | A = every nontrivial aspect clearly explained; prose states meaning very clearly |
| ▒ Effectiveness of your example | A = effective use of component technology |

Points to watch for:
  *Serious:*
1. Missing clear interface facilities that increase the effectiveness of laying out railroads.
2. Obscure mapping from the interface to the Beans.

**Exercise 11.3**    **Simulation of Painted Table Manufacture**    Use *JavaBeans* to build a simulation of a plant that manufactures painted tables. The plant consists of two stations: One for assembly, the other for painting. The assembly station receives legs and tabletops at regular (usually different) intervals. It discards items received if it does not need them at the time they are received. As soon as a table is assembled, it is sent to the painting station. If no paint is available, the painting station accumulates tables awaiting painting. The painting station receives paint cans at regular intervals and you can assume that unlimited storage is available at the station for these cans. One can is sufficient to paint five tables. Assume that no time is required to assemble a table when the required material is present, move a table between stations, or paint a table. Design your application so that it will be relatively easy in the future to add randomness in the times taken, and to a nonzero time to move tables between stations.

**Part 11.3.1** List the names of the Beans that you will use, indicating which Beans you will be writing and which are taken from *BeanBox*.

**Part 11.3.2** Provide the fully commented source code for the Beans that you are introducing.

**Part 11.3.3** Show how you connect the Beans. Explain thoroughly and provide screenshots.

**Part 11.3.4** Show representative output.

Execute with the following test case. A leg arrives every minute; a tabletop arrives every 5 minutes; a can of paint arrives every 30 minutes. The actual start of these deliveries depends on when the Beans assembler assembles the various parts.

Use your application to show the following data when 200 tables have been painted. Show the output and show BeanBox with Bean instances you created.

▒ Number of wasted legs
▒ Number of wasted tabletops
▒ Number of minutes since the run began
▒ Number of unpainted tables

Criteria:

| | |
|---|---|
| ▒ Correct and appropriate design | A = entirely suitable choice of Beans and interconnections |
| ▒ Clarity of design and code | A = Very clear design and implementation |

Points to watch for:
  *Serious:*
  **1.** Match designs to the real world whenever you can. In this problem, there are two physical stations (one for assembly and one for painting). For this reason, introduce two components with these functionalities.

  **2.** The benefit of using components is the fact that they can be combined in various ways. Associate them with events whenever you can, rather than having them reference each other. *TableAssembler* should not mention *TablePainter*, for example. We may want to use these in other contexts.

**Exercise 11.4**    **Tracking Document Movement**    You have been tasked to build an application that enables users to conveniently track the movement of documents within a company. Here is the main use case.

**1.** The user is notified by telephone that a document has left a particular desk and is en route to another.

**2.** The user clicks on the *file* menu in BeanBox and retrieves a graphic representation of the situation. This graphic shows desks colored red except for the desk that held the document, which is colored green.

**3.** The user clicks on the destination desk.

**4.** The destination desk turns green and the source desk turns red.

**5.** The times of departure and arrival are recorded by the application. Both of these are the time at which the icon was clicked.

The design, using BeanBox, has to conveniently accommodate the addition of desks. To do so, the user clicks on an appropriate item in *ToolBox,* places it in the BeanBox window, and then makes two connections.

Criteria:
▨ Appropriateness of the Bean(s) selected      A = entirely appropriate Beans applied
▨ Clarity of your response                                 A = Very clear explanations of all Beans and how
                                                                              they work together

Explain how you designed this using JavaBeans in BeanBox. You do not have to address the issue of deployment. To remind you of BeanBox's appearance, it is shown in Figure 11.28 with *BlueButton*.

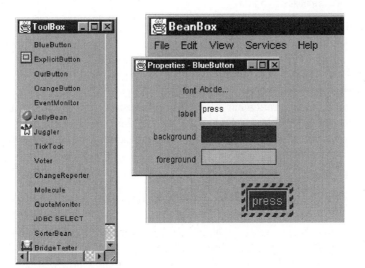

**FIGURE 11.28**    *BeanBox* with *BlueButton*

# MICROSOFT ASSEMBLIES

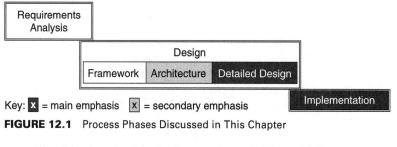

**FIGURE 12.1** Process Phases Discussed in This Chapter

The objectives for this chapter are shown in Figure 12.2.

**Understand** ...

- Microsoft's component ("assembly") architecture
- where assemblies fit in .NET
- required rudiments of C#
- the contents of .NET manifests, including:
    · Versioning
    · Attributes
- the difference between *private* and *shared* assemblies

**Be able to** ...

- create assemblies using C#

**FIGURE 12.2** Learning Goals for This Chapter

## 12.1 MICROSOFT .NET OVERVIEW

The Microsoft Corporation has a long history of using components technology through its Component Object Model (COM) architecture. This chapter outlines its .NET component framework, which succeeds COM, and is a good example of component usage.

### 12.1.1 Goals of .NET

The .NET architecture allows programmers to develop components using a number of different programming languages, including C#, C++, Eiffel, J#, and Visual Basic. The resulting components (called "assemblies" by Microsoft) can use each other, regardless of the source language used to construct each one. This is a benefit of the fact that components are essentially object code entities rather than source code entities. Assemblies execute in a common virtual runtime environment. Another goal is an improvement in the identification of components. This is especially important on the Internet, where it's more difficult to ensure that a component is exactly the one we want. The COM architecture approached this by giving each component a completely unique ID. The problem with this approach turned out to be confusion in dealing with several versions of a component: A difficulty sometimes referred to as "dll hell." COM also required that every component be registered in a fixed registry. Selected .NET goals are summarized in Figure 12.3.

- Create interoperable components
  from multiple source languages
  - · C++, Visual Basic, ... .
- Solve multiple component version clashes
  - · "dll hell": naming confusion in COM
- Define a common runtime
- Avoid registry
  - · Necessity to register components with host computer

**FIGURE 12.3**   .NET Goals and Solutions

**DESIGN GOAL AT WORK**   *Reusability*

Microsoft wanted to allow developers to create interoperable components using their choice of source language.

## 12.1.2   The Architecture of .NET

Figure 12.4 shows the major parts of .NET and their relationship. This is a layered system in which one layer depends on another. Layering in general is explored further in Chapter 14. The lowest layer, the Common Language Runtime (CLR), involves a virtual machine similar to the Java Virtual Machine. It contains the primitive types (integers, floating point numbers, etc.) used across all of .NET. It also handles chores such as dynamic memory allocation and reclamation. The .NET framework classes are built using the CLR, and they are somewhat like the Java API. Finally, various languages and programming environments depend on the framework. Frameworks in general are explored in Chapter 14.

The .NET Framework classes are compiled into an intermediate language (Microsoft's "IL"), thereby enabling their share-ability across source languages. This makes the idea of components fundamental to .NET. The CTS defines types such as integers in a universal format, allowing usage by multiple classes.

The CLR types are interoperable with corresponding type *classes* using the containerization process of *boxing*, explained below. Primitive types in the CLR are shown in Figure 12.5.

All .NET classes inherit from *System.Object*, which supports the methods shown in Figure 12.6. (Microsoft's convention is to capitalize method names.)

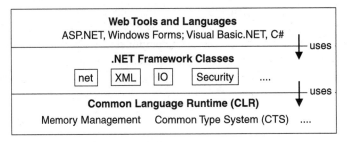

**FIGURE 12.4** The Parts of .NET

- *Boolean,*
- *DateTime*
- *Decimal:* 28 significant digits
- *Double:* 64-bit double-precision floating point
- *GUID:* unique 128-bit integer; unique identifier
- *Int16, Int32, Int64*
- *Sbyte:* 8-bit signed integer −128 to +127
- *Single:* 4-byte single-precision floating point
- *TimeSpan:* a period of time

**FIGURE 12.5** Types in the CTS

- *Boolean Equals( Object )*
- *Int32 GetHashCode()*
  - Generates an integer corresponding to the value of the object
  - Used by sorting algorithms in System.Collections
- *Type GetType()*
  - for the Reflection API
- *String ToString()*

**FIGURE 12.6** Methods of *System.Object*

.NET uses the concept of a *namespace*, a virtual region in which any declared name is recognized by every other entity named in the region at the same or lower level. This is like Java packages, except that name recognition is hierarchical: A name declared in a namespace is recognized in all subnamespaces and not vice-versa, just like variable naming in nested pairs of braces in a Java program. The .NET Class Framework is organized hierarchically, with the *System* namespace at the top, and the namespaces in Figure 12.7 subordinate, and many others subordinate to these (see [Mi1]).

- Collections
- ComponentModel
  - "to implement the runtime and designtime behavior of components"
- Data
  - To deal with databases via ADO
- Drawing
- IO
- Net
  - to interface with common network protocols
- Reflection
- Runtime
- Security
- Text
  - ASCII, Unicode etc.
- Threading
- Web
- WinForms
- XML

**FIGURE 12.7** Selected *System.XX* .NET Framework Namespaces

The compilation process within the .NET architecture is shown in Figure 12.8.

"Ancillary data" may be a component manifest, for example. There are several compilation options, including compilation all the way to native code. The most common option is assumed to be compilation into IL and just-in-time compilation into native code, making the machine code available when it's needed.

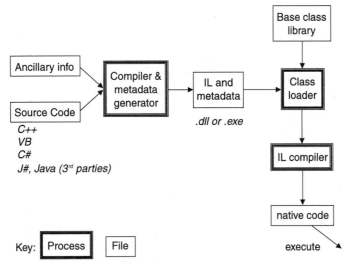

**FIGURE 12.8**   Compilation Process in .NET

### 12.1.3   .NET Assemblies (Components)

Microsoft.NET components, or "assemblies," can consist of one or more physical files. Each .NET assembly is packaged with a manifest stating the location of the parts of which it is composed. .NET assemblies in the same folder as client (using) code are available to it. Several *versions* of an assembly can coexist. For a .NET assembly to be usable by other .NET assemblies, it has to be compliant with the "Common Language Specification." .NET assemblies have *fields*, *properties*, *methods* and *events* as per the classical PME component model. They are self-describing.

A .NET assembly is constructed from a collection of files. Often the assembly itself is a single file, as suggested by Figure 12.9. However, an assembly can remain as a collection of separate files. Among other things, the manifest ensures the integrity of the assembly: i.e., that it contains the files it is supposed to. Figure 12.9 illustrates the parts involved in an assembly.

We will show a manifest "in the flesh" later in this chapter, and explain its parts as listed in Figure 12.9. First, we will describe elements of the C# language that we will use to create .NET assemblies.

The author is indebted to [Mi2] and [Mi3] for this material on metadata.

---

**KEY CONCEPT**   *A .NET Assembly*

Includes class code from multiple files, in IL form, described by a manifest.

---

## 12.2   ELEMENTS OF THE C# LANGUAGE

Microsoft introduced a new language, C#, in which assemblies can be conveniently and completely expressed. We will provide enough details of C# to enable the reader to under-

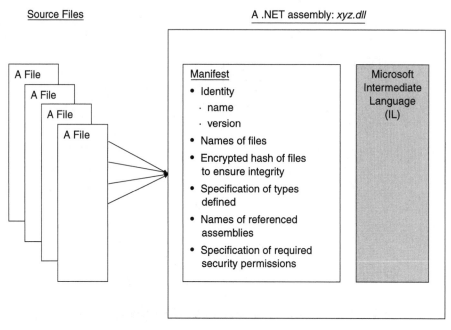

**FIGURE 12.9** The Parts of a .NET Assembly (Component)

stand the examples in this chapter. For a complete description of C# see, for example, [Mi4]. Since this book was prepared while the specifications of C# were not final, refer to the latest specifications, which may upgrade the source code. Some goals of C# are outlined in Figures 12.10 and 12.11.

- Rapid application development
  - as with JavaBeans
- Cross-platform deployment
  - generates character stream interpreted by .NET runtime.
  - as with Java Virtual Machine
- Access to platform-native resources
  - take advantage of the Windows API to run as a full-featured application on Windows 2000
- Support for the COM and .NET platforms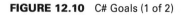

**FIGURE 12.10** C# Goals (1 of 2)

- Features of C and C++ "with the functional ease of rapid application development tools."
- Components with properties, methods and events
  - built in

**FIGURE 12.11** C# Goals (2 of 2)

Execution of a C# program begins with a designated *Main()* method of a class. By convention, C# methods begin with capital letters. The command *Console.Writeln(<string>)* writes to the "console" DOS window. Here is a "Hello World" program written in C#. The "///" comment lines are part of the XML-based document system somewhat like JavaDoc and its "/**...*/" convention.

```
using System;

namespace ConsoleApplication2    // more about namespaces later
{
        /// <summary>
        /// Simplest non-component C# application
        /// </summary>

        class MainApp
        {
                public static void Main()    // Main may also return int, have string[] parameters
                {
                        Console.WriteLine( "Hello World using C#!" );
                        Console.ReadLine();    // freeze console to inspect result
                }
        }
}
```

The output for this application is shown in Figure 12.12. Figure 12.13 lists selected features of C#.

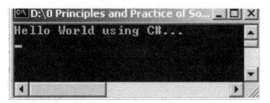

**FIGURE 12.12**  *HelloWorld* Output

- Automatic garbage collection
- Allows developers to disable garbage collection locally—
  · by marking code as "unsafe"  *Unlike Java*
  · (e.g., where real time performance required?)
- Eliminates pointers in favor of references
- Introduces *Interfaces*

**FIGURE 12.13**  Selected C# Features

Here are some of the features that C# possesses in common with C and C++, which Java does not possess.

▥ Operator overloading (defining a meaning for operators such as "+", "–" etc. among members of a class). This includes binary operators, which have two operands, and unary operators, which have a single operand.

▥ "Delegate" functions for event handling. This is the capability to parameterize methods with methods. For example, we could have a method *computeFinancialObligations()* that depends on the method chosen to compute the interest on a loan. We can execute *computeFinancialObligations()* as in the following example.

*computeFinancialObligations( FrankensteinMethod )* – or –

*computeFinancialObligations( OptimisticMethod )*, etc.

▥ An application can assign any method that matches the signature to a delegate variable. Such a variable is shown in the example.  We declare *myDelegateFunction* first as a delegate type in order to specify the kind of method required for *myFunction()*.

```
public class myClass
{
    public delegate float myDelegateFunction(int anInt);

    public void myFunction(myDelegateFunction aDelegateFunction)
    {
```

```
                    float tempFloat = aDelegateFunction(anIntVariable);
                    ...
         }
         ...
    }
```

Typically, we use delegates for event handling, as shown in the following example.

```
class SimpleForm extends Form
{
Button okButton = new Button();
Button cancelButton = new Button();

void okButton_click( Object sender, Event e )
{     System.out.println( "Clicked OK" );
}

void cancelButton_click( Object sender, Event e )
{     System.out.println( "Clicked Cancel" );
}

void initForm()
{
      okButton.setText("OK");
      okButton.addOnClick
        ( new EventHandler( this.okButton_click ) );    // takes delegate parameter
      cancelButton.setText( "Cancel" );
      cancelButton.addOnClick
        ( new EventHandler( this.cancelButton_click ) );  // takes delegate parameter
      . . . .
}

}
```

An important uses of C# is for developing *Web services*, functionality available at Internet locations. Internet searches are common examples of Web services: Effectively, we call a search function at a URL, providing it with a string, which is the parameter for the search function. The idea is to enable Web services to call other Web services without human intervention, thereby creating multi-server Web-based applications. An XML-based protocol named Simple Object Access Protocol (SOAP) is used for Web service calls.

As Szyperski [Sz1] has observed, Web services are component-like. A search function is a stand-alone function at a known location rather than a member method that's instantiated for one object among potentially many. A component is tagged as a Web service by means of an *attribute*: A meta-facility that tells about the code and is not executed. Attributes are covered in Section 12.5.4. Figure 12.13 summarizes the Web services features of C#.

- Attribute library allows wrapping of C# classes and functions as *Web services*.
  - · a hosted software module callable over the Internet typically via SOAP protocol.
  - · SOAP wraps method calls, parameters, and return values, in XML packets.
- Using appropriate attributes, programmer can turn any C# class or method into a Web service.

**FIGURE 12.14**  C# Web Features: *Web Services*

This section ends with additional features of C#.

- Boxing/unboxing: The ability to easily move to and from an object representation of primitive types as in the following code example.

```
int i = 3;
String iAsAString = i.toString();   // treat like an object
object iObject = i;   // "box" i
int j = (int)iObject;   // "unbox" iObject
```

- Properties: We defined the properties of components in Section 10.3.1 on page 389. Recall that the properties concept is more flexible that object variables.

```
class myClass
{    ...

public int myIntProp   // define a property myIntProp
{
      get
      {      return ....
      }
      set
      {      ... do whatever setting is desired
      }
}

}
...

// Use the property myIntProp

MyClass myObject = new MyClass();
myObject.myIntProp = 7;   // assign property a value as you would to a variable
int j = myObject.myIntProp;   // use the property's value as you would a variable's
```

## 12.3   A SIMPLE HELLOWORLD .NET ASSEMBLY

Let's create a .NET assembly with a function which prints "hello. . . ." Here is the source code. No special conventions are required as they are for Beans. We will follow this up by creating the (executable) assembly.

```
// A C# component with a Hello World function

using System;
using System.IO;

public class HelloComponent
{
      public HelloComponent(){}

      public void SayHelloWorld( )
      {      Console.WriteLine( "Component says: Hello World" );
      }
}
```

Suppose that this code is saved in a file "helloFile." (This name need not match the name of the class it contains.)

We'll create an assembly, which we will name "hello." Microsoft's Visual Studio.NET is a convenient environment in which to compile this into a component: However, we will use the command line shown in Figure 12.14 because it shows the required sequence of operations more clearly. We would use Visual Studio.NET to create visual instances of .NET assemblies.

We now have a component, as illustrated in Figure 12.16.

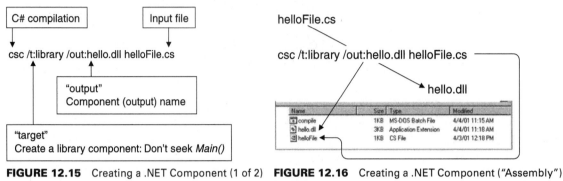

**FIGURE 12.15** Creating a .NET Component (1 of 2)   **FIGURE 12.16** Creating a .NET Component ("Assembly") (2 of 2)

Now let's write code for a class *HelloClient* that uses this component. This client announces itself, and then uses the *hello* component by calling the *SayHelloWorld()* method in *hello*'s interface. Notice in line "*a*" that *HelloClient* references the class *HelloComponent*.

```
using System;

class HelloClient
{
    public static void Main()
    {
        Console.WriteLine( "Client use of a component:" );

        // Use the component.
        HelloComponent helloComponent = new HelloComponent();    // line "a"
        helloComponent.SayHelloWorld();

        Console.ReadLine();   // freeze monitor
    }
}
```

We reference the *hello.dll* (compiled) assembly when *compiling* this *HelloClient* class, as shown in Figure 12.17.

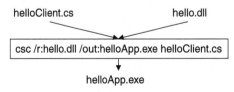

...now execute helloApp.

**FIGURE 12.17** Using a .NET Component

The key point is that we are using an already compiled component *hello* rather than compiling the classes *HelloClient* and *HelloComponent* together as we would do in classical OO programming.

## 12.4   A .NET COMPONENT CONTAINING MULTIPLE CLASSES

Recall that a component may consist of several classes. Next is an example of such a component. We enclose the classes in a common namespace "greeting." We use namespaces to create tree structures to allow distinguishing differing elements with the same local name, as we do with a file directory. We will have the following code reside on a file *HelloAuRevoirComponentSource.cs*.

```
// A C# component with multiple classes

namespace greeting
{ // begin namespace greeting
using System;
using System.IO;

// An internal class --------------------------------
internal class GreetingUtility
{
        public GreetingUtility(){}

        public static void OutputMessage( String messageP )
        {       Console.WriteLine( messageP );
        }
}


// A hello world class -------------------------------
public class HelloClass
{
        public HelloClass(){}

        public void SayHelloWorld( )
        {       GreetingUtility.OutputMessage( "Component says: Hello World" );
        }
}

// A sign-off class ----------------------------------
public class AuRevoirClass
{
        public AuRevoirClass(){}

        public void SayAuRevoirWorld( )
        {       GreetingUtility.OutputMessage( "Component says: Au Revoir World" );
        }
}
} // end namespace greeting
```

*Internal* classes in .NET, such as *GreetingUtility*, are used within a component only: They are not intended for use by clients of the component. As shown in Figure 12.18, we compile this component as before. Next, we will show client source code utilizing the component `helloAuRevoir`, and which produces the following output.

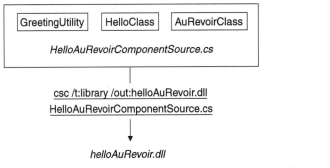

**FIGURE 12.18** Creating a .NET Component Containing Multiple Classes

**FIGURE 12.19** Output for "Multiple Class" Example

```
using System;

namespace greeting
{ // begin namespace greeting
class GreetingClient
{
    public static void Main()
    {
        Console.WriteLine( "Client use of a component containing an internal class:" );

        // Use part of the component's interface
        HelloClass helloInstance = new HelloClass();
        helloInstance.SayHelloWorld();

        // Use part of the component's interface
        AuRevoirClass auRevoirInstance = new AuRevoirClass();
        auRevoirInstance.SayAuRevoirWorld();

        // Freeze the screen
        Console.ReadLine();
    }
}
} // end namespace greeting
```

# 12.5 METADATA IN .NET ASSEMBLIES

## 12.5.1 Summary of .NET Metadata

As discussed in Chapter 10, components include metadata: Information *about* the contents of the component. One use for metadata in the .NET framework is to make components developed in different languages available to each other. Microsoft does this by means of a *Common Type System* (CTS). The CTS is a set of IL types such as *Boolean, Char* and

*Double*, into which the types of the source languages are translated. Metadata concerning each component is expressed in terms of the CTS.

Some degree of security can be checked prior to execution on the Virtual Execution System that interprets the Microsoft Intermediate Language in which components are written. This is similar to the checking of byte code by the Java Virtual Machine. The benefits of metadata in .NET are summarized in Figure 12.20, which is adapted from [Mi5]. "Unmanaged" code is designated by the programmer as not under the control of the virtual execution system. Developers can define pointers within such code, for example.

Using metadata allows the CLR to support:
- Multiple execution models
  - interpreted
  - JITted (Just-in-time)
  - native
  - legacy code (prior to .NET)
- Uniform services available to debuggers, profilers etc.
- Consistent exception handling
- Code access security
- Memory management
- Reflection
- Interoperability with existing unmanaged COM applications
- Interoperability with existing unmanaged code
- Optimization to match the particular CPU or environment

Amended from http://msdn.microsoft.com/library/default.asp

**FIGURE 12.20**  Uses for Metadata in .NET

## 12.5.2  Viewing Metadata

As an example, let's inspect the manifest for the *helloAuRevour.dll* component created above. To do this, we use the *ILDasm* Microsoft tool ("Intermediate Language Disassembler"). Figure 12.21 shows the effect of executing *ILDasm* on the file *helloAurevoir.dll*.

The component's version number is shown at the bottom of the window. This defaulted to 0:0:0:0 because we did not specify a version or use Visual Studio.NET that can automatically track versions. The namespace "greetings" is shown following a shield symbol. (We will say more about namespaces in Section 12.6: Our assembly could have involved classes from several namespaces.) The manifest describes the three classes of which the component is made (*AuRevoirClass*, *GreetingUtility*, and *HelloClass*).

The *ILDasm* utility allows users to click on parts of the manifest report in order to see more detail. If we click on "MANIFEST", the following appears.

Here is a key to some of the lines.

1. *Line 1:* This lists other assemblies (components) on which this assembly relies: In this case only *mscorlib*, which contains the .NET system classes.

2. *Lines 2-7:* These lines concern the *mscorlib* assembly (not *helloAuRevoir*).

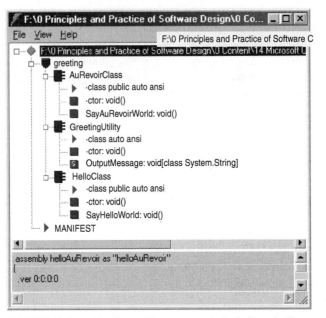

**FIGURE 12.21** Manifest of Component *helloAuRevoir.dll*

```
    MANIFEST                                                          _ □ X
1.   .assembly extern mscorlib
2.   {
3.     .originator = (03 68 91 16 D3 A4 AE 33 )                    // .h....
4.     .hash = (52 44 F8 C9 55 1F 54 3F 97 D7 AB AD E2 DF 1D E0    // RD..U.T?....
5.             F2 9D 4F BC )                                       // ..O.
6.     .ver 1:0:2204:21
7.   }
8.   .assembly helloAuRevoir as "helloAuRevoir"
9.   {
10.    // --- The following custom attribute is added automatically, do not uncomr
11.    //   .custom instance void [mscorlib]System.Diagnostics.DebuggableAttribute
12.    //
13.    .hash algorithm 0x00008004
14.    .ver 0:0:0:0
15.  }
16.  .module helloAuRevoir.dll
     // MVID: {E119ADE0-4E7E-11D5-BBBD-0050049567D7}
```

**FIGURE 12.22** Manifest Contents for *helloAuRevoir.dll* Component

3. *Line 3: originator* is a "public key" for public key encryptions, explained in Section 12.6.2.2 below.

4. *Line 4: hash* is an encrypted hash of all of the files in the *mscorlib* assembly. The .NET runtime uses this to check that hashing the *mscorlib* assembly produces the same results at load time. As explained in Section 12.6.2.2, if the content of any file in *mscorlib* becomes corrupted the resulting hash will almost certainly not match these 20 bytes. This ensures that the assembly has not been tampered with since its creation.

5. *Line 6:* This is the *mscorlib* version.

6. *Lines 8-15:* Here are details about our *helloAuRevoir* assembly itself.

7. *Line 13:* This refers to the algorithm used to generate the hash.

8. *Line 14:* Once again, this is the version of this assembly.

9. *Line 16:* This contains the name of the target file for this assembly. MVID (the Module Version Identifier) is the globally unique identifier for this assembly.

Clicking on *:sayHelloWorld* of *HelloClass* in Figure 12.21 produces the window in Figure 12.23.

```
HelloClass::SayHelloWorld : void()
1.  .method public hidebysig instance void SayHelloWorld() il managed
2.  {
3.    // Code size        11 (0xb)
4.    .maxstack  8
5.    IL_0000:  ldstr      "Component says: Hello World"
6.    IL_0005:  call       void greeting.GreetingUtility::OutputMessage(class System.String)
7.    IL_000a:  ret
8.  } // end of method HelloClass::SayHelloWorld
```

```
Recall the source:
public void SayHelloWorld()
      {    GreetingUtility.OutputMessage
           ("Component says: Hello World");
      }
```

**FIGURE 12.23**  Manifest Detail of *sayHelloWorld()* in *HelloClass*

Figure 12.23 also shows the original code side-by-side with the disassembled IL: A relatively human-readable form of IL, especially for those familiar with byte code. For example, line 5 is shorthand for *load string 'Component says: Hello World'*.

## 12.5.3  Versioning

Although a component is not supposed to change, its contents must typically be updated and extended over time. This creates potential problems for clients of the component. Version numbers help to address this problem. The *version* field of an assembly breaks down as in Figure 12.24.

- Major version
- Minor version
- Revision
- Build number

**FIGURE 12.24**  The *Version* Field of an Assembly

A version number is visible at the bottom of Figure 12.21. A client will automatically use the highest (meaning latest) compatible version of a component to the one it was compiled with unless the client specifically requests a different version to load. Microsoft defines *source-* and *object-compatibility* of versions as in Figure 12.25.

A new version is ...

- source compatible with a previous version if code that depends on the previous version can, *when recompiled,* work with the new version.

- binary compatible if code that depended on the old version can, *without recompilation,* work with the new version.

(adapted from Microsoft)

**FIGURE 12.25**  Versioning

All other things being equal, we aim for binary compatibility. This is because no modification is required of existing clients of the assembly when a new binary compatible version replaces an older version.

Versioning is an important practical issue in dealing with components. Recall the "dll hell" discussion pertaining to COM, which .NET is designed to improve upon. Versioning needs to be approached carefully, however. Microsoft supplies the following example to indicate how C# addresses versioning when a base class changes in a manner that potentially affects classes already compiled. Author *A* ships an initial version of a class *Base*. In this first version, *Base* contains no *MyFunction()* method. A component named *Derived* derives from *Base*, and introduces a *MyFunction()* method. This *Derived* class, along with the class *Base* that it depends on, is released to customers, who deploy them to numerous clients and servers. So far so good.

```
// Author A
namespace A
{
    public class Base       // version 1
    {
    }
}

// Author B
namespace B
{
    class Derived: A.Base
    {
        public virtual void MyFunction()
        { System.Console.WriteLine( "Derived. MyFunction" );
        }
    }
}
```

Suppose now that the author of *Base* produces a new version and happens to add a *MyFunction()* method (!), as follows.

```
// Author A
namespace A
{
    public class Base       // version 2
    {
        public virtual void MyFunction ()    // added in version 2
        { System.Console.WriteLine( "Base.MyFunction" );
        }
    }
}
```

This new version of *Base* should be both source- and binary-compatible with the initial version, but did *Derived* means to override *Base*'s *MyFunction()*? This seems unlikely, since when *Derived* was compiled, *Base* did not even have a *MyFunction()*. Further, if *Derived*'s *MyFunction()* does override *Base*'s *MyFunction()*, must it adhere to the contract (written intent) specified by *Base*—a contract that was not specified when *Derived* was written? In some cases, such an adherence is impossible. For example, the contract of *Base*'s *MyFunction()* might refer to derived classes. *Derived*'s *MyFunction()* could not possibly adhere to such a contract because it was written before *Base*'s *MyFunction()* appeared.

C# addresses this versioning problem by requiring developers to clearly state their intent. In the original example (without *MyFunction()* in *Base*) the code was clear since *Base* did not even have a *MyFunction()*. Clearly, *Derived*'s *MyFunction()* was intended as a new method rather than an override of a base method, since no base method named *MyFunction()* existed.

When *MyFunction()* in *Base* appears, since the intent is now unclear, the compiler produces a warning, and by default makes *Derived*'s *MyFunction()* hide *Base*'s *MyFunction()*. In other words, polymorphism would *not* operate for *MyFunction()* here. This course of action is the same as if *Derived* were not recompiled. The warning generated alerts *Derived*'s author to the presence of the *MyFunction()* method in *Base*.

If *Derived*'s *MyFunction()* is semantically unrelated to *Base*'s *MyFunction()*, then *Derived*'s author can express this intent—and, in effect, turn off the warning and accept the absence of polymorphism—by using the *new* keyword in the declaration of *MyFunction()*. He would have to perform this insertion and recompile *Derived*. The resulting code is shown next.

```
// Author A
namespace A
{
    public class Base          // version 2
    {
        public virtual void MyFunction()// added in version 2
        { System.Console.WriteLine("Base.MyFunction");
        }
    }
}

// Author B
namespace B
{
    class Derived: A.Base    // version 2a: new
    {
        new public virtual void MyFunction()
        { System.Console.WriteLine("Derived.MyFunction");
        }
    }
}
```

On the other hand, *Derived*'s author might actually decide that *Derived*'s *MyFunction() should* override *Base*'s *MyFunction()*—thus participating in polymorphism after all. He can specify this intent by inserting the *override* keyword, as shown. (For Java programmers, *override* accomplishes the relationship between base and derived methods to which they are accustomed.)

```
// Author A
namespace A
{
```

```
public class Base   // version 2
{
    public virtual void MyFunction()   // added in version 2
    { System.Console.WriteLine( "Base.MyFunction" );
    }
}
}

// Author B
namespace B
{
    class Derived: A.Base   // version 2b: override
    {
        public override void MyFunction()
        {
            base.MyFunction();
            System.Console.WriteLine( "Derived. MyFunction" );
        }
    }
}
```

This was adapted from [Mi6]. Other parts of this section were adapted from [Mi2].

## 12.5.4 Attributes

When we denote a method as *public*, we are saying something *about* the method rather than specifying what it does. In other words, we are supplying metadata. We have noted that components become particularly useful when we can query them about themselves, obtaining metadata. Imagine, for example, being able to ask a component the name of the developer who wrote the code. This is where .NET *attributes* come into the picture. C# has built-in attributes, but it also allows programmers to define their own attribute metadata, which can be accessed at runtime. Figure 12.26 summarizes these points.

- Metadata: about ...
  - variables
  - classes
  - functions
- Types of attributes:
  - built-in
  - user-defined

**FIGURE 12.26**  *Attributes* in .NET

We will first describe some of the attributes packaged with C#. We will then indicate how to attach attributes to relevant parts of the source code, and how a programmer can define his own attributes. Finally, we will explain how attributes can be accessed at runtime. This allows applications to detect properties of a component at runtime, and make decisions accordingly.

***12.5.4.1  Using Attributes***   In this section we explain how attributes are used. We don't attempt to describe all built-in C# attributes: Instead, we describe the usage of one or two by way of example.

A good example of an attribute is *conditional*, which provides capability like *#ifdef* in C++, and which is typically used with a debug switch. In general, attributes are used by means of a pair of square brackets [ ] placed just before the element (class, method, etc.) to which it is intended to apply. Here is an example.

```
#define DEBUG    // comment this line out as preferred

using System;
using System.Diagnostics; // namespace of 'Conditional' attribute

class ConditionalDemo
{
    ///
    [Conditional( "DEBUG" )]    // do this method if "DEBUG"
    public void RunTrace()
    {    Console.WriteLine( "RunTrace output ...." );
    }

    ///
    public static void Main( string[] args )
    {
        ConditionalDemo myDemo = new ConditionalDemo();
        Console.WriteLine( "Some code...." );

        myDemo.RunTrace();    // ignored if DEBUG not defined

        Console.WriteLine( "More code...." );
        Console.ReadLine();   // freeze monitor
    }
}
```

This yields the output shown, depending on whether or not the statement *#define DEBUG* is present.

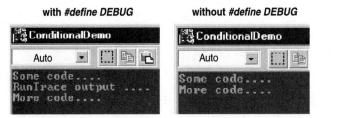

**FIGURE 12.27**   Output of *main()* in *ConditionalDemo*

Another example of attribute usage is to make assembly functionality available as Web services. For example, suppose that we want to make a monthly mortgage payment function available on the Web. We package this in an appropriate C# assembly—*FinancialServices*, let's say. We precede the relevant method with a *[WebMethod]* attribute. We can then package *FinancialServices* in an ASP.NET file, which makes it available across the Internet.

Here is an example of using a custom attribute (defined by the developer). Its purpose is to provide the authorship of a class so that the information can be used at runtime. In the next section we will show how to define an attribute like *Authorship*.

```
[Authorship("Albert Einstein")]
class Class1
{   ...
}
```

***12.5.4.2 Defining Custom Attributes*** Attributes are classes that inherit from *System.Attribute*. We have to indicate whether the attribute we are defining applies to a variable, a method, or a class. To do this, we use the built-in attribute *AttributeUsage* or *AttributeUsageAttribute* applied to the attribute we are defining (for the erudite reader, *AttributeUsage* is a meta-attribute: An attribute of attributes). This is shown in the following source code.

```
using System;

// Following attribute will apply to classes.  Another option is AttributeTargets.All etc.
[ AttributeUsage( AttributeTargets.Class) ]
public class AuthorshipAttribute: System.Attribute // must inherit from System.Attribute
{
      private string authorName;

      public AuthorshipAttribute( string aName )   // must have at least one public constructor
      {     this.authorName = aName;
      }

      public string AuthorName
      {     get{ return authorName; }
      }
}
```

The *aName* parameter of *AuthorshipAttribute* in the code is the usual kind of parameter, called a *positional* parameter. We use it as described in the previous section. We can also define *named* parameters, which allow usage in *name = value* form. This is done by defining each parameter as a property of the attribute, as shown next.

```
using System;

[ AttributeUsage( AttributeTargets.Class) ]   // this attribute will apply to classes
                                     // (AttributeTargets.All another option, etc.)
public class AuthorshipAttribute: System.Attribute   // must inherit from System.Attribute
{
      private string authorName;   // used with positional parameter
      private string date;   // used with named parameter
      private int levelTested;   // used with named parameter

      public AuthorshipAttribute( string aName )   // positional parameter
      {     this.authorName = aName;
      }

      public string AuthorName
      {     get{ return authorName; }
      }

      public string Date   // defines named parameter
      {     get{ return date; }
            set{ date = value; }
      }

      public int LevelTested   // defines named parameter
      {     get{ return levelTested; }
            set{ levelTested = value; }
      }
}
```

Most C# types can be used for named parameters. To *use* the named parameters, we precede class code with the following options.

```
[Authorship("Albert Einstein")]
```

or

```
[Authorship("Albert Einstein", Date = "3/2/01")]
```

or

```
[Authorship("Albert Einstein", LevelTested = 3)]
```

or as shown in the following small example:

```
using System;

[ AuthorshipAttribute( "Eric Braude", Date = "05/22/01", LevelTested = 0 ) ]
public class Financials
{
    /////////////////////////////////////////////////////////////////////
    // Postconditions: A message has been printed to the console
    // Return: 1 for demonstration purposes
    //
    public static int doKeyFinancialCalculation( int an Amount
    /////////////////////////////////////////////////////////////////////
    {
        Console.WriteLine( "Doing key financial calculation ..." );
        return 1;    // dummy
    }
}
```

In the preceding section, we showed how to define an attribute and how to apply it preceding a class or method. In the next section we will show how to use attributes at runtime.

### 12.5.4.3 *Accessing Attributes at Runtime*   Now let's use attributes at runtime. As an example, we will implement a method that needs a financial calculation, but only accepts those written by the famous financial wizard Peter Brucker: If the component provided is not written by Brucker, the method calls upon a default calculation. Here is output in a case where the component was indeed written by Brucker himself, and one where it was not.

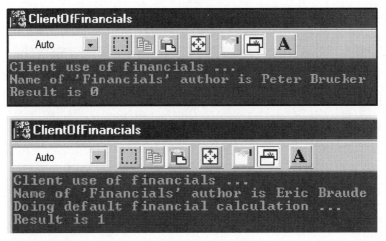

**FIGURE 12.28**   Output for Authorship Querying

To determine characteristics of a class at runtime, we can use the *Type* class as follows:

```
/*a*/  Type typeOfFinancials = typeof(Financials);
```

This returns a *Type* object with information about the class *Financials*, including the attributes of the class. To get the custom attributes of *Financial*, we execute the following.

```
/*b*/  object[] attribsOfFinancials = typeOfFinancials.GetCustomAttributes();
```

The objects in this array represent the attributes. Each object is an instance of an *Attribute* class. Hence we can access fields of any of these as in the following. In the case of our example, there is only one attribute in the array, an *AuthorAttribute* object.

```
/*c*/  string nameOfAuthor = ((AuthorshipAttribute)attribsOfFinancials[0]).AuthorName;
```

Here is the *client* code.

```
using System;
using System.Reflection;

/// Demonstration of the application of attributes

class ClientOfFinancials
{
        //////////////////////////////////////////////////////////////////////////
        // Preconditions: The only attribute of Financials is AuthorAttribute
        // Postconditons: (1) DoKeyFinancialCalculation( 60000 ) of class Financials has been
        //                    executed if the author of that component is Peter Brucker; otherwise
        //                    ClientOfFinancials.doOwnFinancialCalculation( 6000 ) is executed
        //                (2) The author of Financials has been output to the console
        //
        public static void Main()
        //////////////////////////////////////////////////////////////////////////
        {
                Console.WriteLine( "Client use of financials ..." );

                // Get object representing "Financials" class
/*a*/           Type typeOfFinancials = typeof( Financials );

                // Get the attributes of Financials
/*b*/           object[] attribsOfFinancials = typeOfFinancials.GetCustomAttributes();

                // Know there is only one attribute: Get the author's name
/*c*/           string nameOfAuthor = ( (AuthorshipAttribute)attribsOfFinancials[0] ).AuthorName;
                Console.WriteLine( "Name of 'Financials' author is " + nameOfAuthor );

                // Use the component if the author is Peter Brucker
                int calculationResult = 0;
                if( nameOfAuthor.Equals( "Peter Brucker" ) )
                        calculationResult = Financials.DoKeyFinancialCalculation( 60000 );
                else    // otherwise, perform the default calculation
                        calculationResult = ClientOfFinancials.doOwnFinancialCalculation( 60000 );

                // Report result
                Console.WriteLine( "Result is " + calculationResult );
                Console.ReadLine();   // freeze console
        }

        //////////////////////////////////////////////////////////////////////////
        // Postconditons: A message has been printed to the console
        // Return: 1 for demonstration purposes
        //
```

```
private static int doOwnFinancialCalculation( int anAmount )
///////////////////////////////////////////////////////////////////////////
{
        Console.WriteLine( "Doing default financial calculation ..." );
        return 1;    // dummy
}
}
```

To summarize, the executable application *ClientOfFinancials.exe* behaves differently, depending on the authorship of the assembly *Financials*. The reader can try this by compiling *Financials* with different authors inserted in the attribute "[ ]" section.

To remind the reader about the efficacy of components, after *ClientOfFinancials.cs* has been written and compiled with the following command:

```
csc /r:Financials.dll /r:authorshipWithNamedParameters.dll ClientOfFinancials.cs
```

(which creates *ClientOfFinancials.exe*). There is no need to recompile *ClientOfFinancials* when changing *Financials* (by altering the author). *ClientOfFinancials.exe* executes with whatever version of *Financials* is present at the time.

**KEY CONCEPT**   *A .NET Manifest*

Lists the files containing the IL-compiled classes, the .NET components on which the assembly depends, version numbers, attributes, and encrypted hash to verify no tampering in transit.

## 12.6   IDENTIFYING AN ASSEMBLY

As mentioned in Section 12.1.1, we have to be sure that when we use a component, it is the one we intend to use. Names can be deceptive. C# identifies components in two separate ways. One is through a path-oriented naming scheme similar to the way one names files in a directory system. These are called *private* assemblies, and are not intended for use by more than one user. The other kind, *shared* assemblies, are identified by the use of globally unique identifiers—identification that is guaranteed to belong to one, and only one component.

**DESIGN GOAL AT WORK**   *Reusability*

We want to reuse an assembly, confident it is the one it's supposed to be.

### 12.6.1   Private Assemblies

The identity of a private assemblies are specified by paths: For example, the assembly

```
c:\Retail\CashSales\Customer differs from c:\Wholesale\. . .\Customer:
```

The Customer files exist in different "name spaces,"

```
c:\Retail\CashSales and c:\Wholesale\. . .\
```

We will confine ourselves to private assemblies. C# allows the developer to specify the component's namespace as follows.

```
namespace MyRootNameSpace.MySubNameSpace
{
    // content intended for this namespace
}
```

For example, a component class *MyClass* defined within the braces is addressed as

```
MyRootNameSpace.MySubNameSpace.MyClass.
```

Let's take as an example an airline reservation system display with the requirement shown in Figure 12.29.

Implement applications 1 and 2. Exploit common components.

*Application 1:* List available flights in following form
    <Animated airline logo goes here>
    <Material introducing available flights here>
    From <city> to <city> departing at <time> and arriving at <time>.
    <Animated logo of the Intergalactic Reservation Service goes here>

*Application 2:* List bookings already made in following form
    <Animated logo of the Intergalactic Reservation Service goes here>
    <Material introducing instructions to the traveler goes here>
    Please arrive at <time> at <city> airport for your flight.

**FIGURE 12.29** Example Using Namespaces

In this example, the following are good candidates for components.

- Animated airline logo
- Itinerary announcement
- Intergalactic Reservation Service logo
- Instructions to the traveler

Note that the animated airline logo is used at two different locations.

Inevitably, we will need to use the same name in different contexts. For example, the *logo* component has two different meanings, depending on what package it belongs to. C# refers to these contexts as *namespaces*. Classes in a single namespace may actually be found on several different files. Figure 12.30 shows how the components could be organized.

Here is code for the three components shown on the right side of the figure. We generate one component from each of them.

| (Logical) Namespace organization | (Physical) File organization (3 files) |
|---|---|

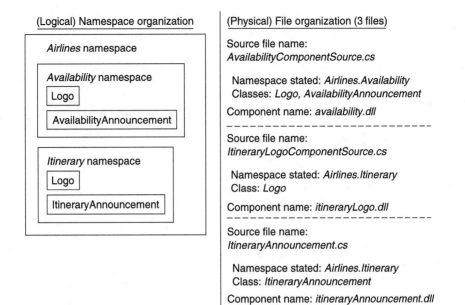

**FIGURE 12.30**   Namespaces Across Multiple Components

1. The *availability.dll* component is generated from the source
   *AvailablilityComponentSource,* which is as follows.

```
// A C# component with multiple classes

using System;
using System.IO;

namespace Airlines
{
namespace Availability
{

// Airline logo -----------------------------
public class Logo
{
    public Logo(){}

    public void PrintLogo( )
    {    Console.WriteLine( "Animated logo goes here." );
    }
}


// A sign-off class ----------------------------------
public class AvailabilityAnnouncement
{
    public AvailabilityAnnouncement(){}

    public void PrintAvailabilityAnnouncement( )
    {    Console.WriteLine
        ( "From <city> to <city> departing at <time> and arriving at <time>." );
    }
}
}
}
```

Notice that the classes are enclosed in a namespace called *Airlines* which, in turn, is enclosed in a namespace called *Availability.* This provides the context shown in Figure 12.30.

2. The source for the *itineraryLogo.dll* component is *ItineraryLogoComponentSource.cs*, as follows.

```
// A C# component with multiple classes

using System;
using System.IO;

namespace Airlines
{
namespace Itinerary
{

// Airline logo -------------------------------
public class Logo
{
    public Logo(){}

    public void PrintLogo( )
    {     Console.WriteLine( "Animated logo goes here." );
    }
}

}
}
```

3. The source for the *itineraryAnnouncement.dll* component is *ItineraryAnnouncement.cs,* as follows.

```
// A C# component with multiple classes

using System;
using System.IO;

namespace Airlines
{
namespace Itinerary
{
// A sign-off class ---------------------------------
public class ItineraryAnnouncement
{
    public ItineraryAnnouncement(){}

    public void PrintItineraryAnnouncement( )
    {     Console.WriteLine
          ( "<Material introducing instructions to the traveler here >" );
    }
}
}
}
```

Now we use these three components to create the "application" shown in Figure 12.31. The source for *airlineApp.exe, AirlineClientFile.cs,* uses assembly functionality without regard to the manner in which the assembly implements it. As we have already seen from .NET and Java components, *AirlineClientFile.cs* can be compiled independent of the referenced assemblies. .NET is willing for the code to be executed by referencing the component at execution time. *AirlineClientFile.cs* is compiled with a command such as

D:\0 Principles and Practice of Software Design\0 Content\12 Microsoft Components\C shar

```
Animated logo goes here.
<Material introducing available flights here >
From <city> to <city> departing at <time> and arriving at <time>.
Animated logo goes here.

Animated logo goes here.
<Material introducing instructions to the traveler here >
```

**FIGURE 12.31**   Airline Reservation System Display

```
csc/out:airlineApp.exe/r:availability.dll/r:itineraryAnnouncmnt.dll/
r:itineraryLogo.dll AirlineClientFile.cs
```

Its source is as follows.

```csharp
using System;

class AirlineClient
{
    public static void Main()
    {
        // Make an airline logo and print it
        (new Airlines.Availability.Logo()).PrintLogo();

        Console.WriteLine("<Material introducing available flights here >");
        Console.WriteLine
        ("From <city> to <city> departing at <time> and arriving at <time>.");

        // Make an reservation system logo and print it
        (new Airlines.Itinerary.Logo()).PrintLogo();

        Console.WriteLine("--------");

        // Make an reservation system logo and print it
        (new Airlines.Itinerary.Logo()).PrintLogo();

        // .........
        (new Airlines.Itinerary.ItineraryAnnouncement()).PrintItineraryAnnouncement();

        // Freeze console
        Console.ReadLine();
    }
}
```

## 12.6.2   Shared Assemblies

When a component is to be available to distributed clients, the requirements for naming it are much more stringent than for private assemblies. In a distributed environment, an application using *itineraryLogo.dll* created from the class *airlines.itinerary.Logo*, for example, could run into another class called *airlines.itinerary.Logo* sooner or later, creating havoc. To prevent this, "dll" names can be made unique across all systems. An assembly's *shared name* has such a guarantee of uniqueness, as well as a very high degree of protection from tampering. The latter is accomplished using *public key cryptography,* which is outlined next. Microsoft supplies utilities that create shared assemblies out of private ones. This process is performed after compilation. The default for an assembly is *private*.

Shared assemblies are placed in a standard Windows folder called the "assembly cache": *WinNT\Assembly* for Windows NT and *WINDOWS\Assembly* otherwise.

*Encryption* is a means of encoding a component. A simple encode/decode process, however, is not sufficient to allow the detection of a corrupted component, for two reasons. The first reason is that the decoding key would have to be provided to all receivers, which is not practical on the Internet. Second, the decoding key would be liable to discovery by unauthorized agents.

A common way to deal with both of these problems is to use *public key cryptography*, which provide two keys. Note the following about the pair of keys.

- Any message encoded with one key can be decoded with the other.
- One can't encrypt and decrypt a message with the same key.
- It's practically impossible to deduce one key from the other.
- It's practically impossible to decode an encoded document without knowing the decode key.

**FIGURE 12.32** Public Key Cryptography

One key is made public (available to all). The sender uses the other key (the "private" one) to encode the material. The private key is kept entirely secret. Anyone can then send an encrypted message to the owner of the private key: They simply need to encrypt the message with the public key.

To illustrate the basic manner in which .NET ensures the integrity of transmitted assemblies, we will use an extremely simple example. The example is not public key encryption at all, but it illustrates some usage of the technique. Let's assume that the decoding process is a "right rotation of the characters by 2 places." In this case 2 is the public integer key. The process works as follows: The sender transmits the intended message itself (un-encoded) together with an encoded form of the message: For example, "abcde" un-encoded together with "deabc" encoded. Receivers use the public key (in this case "left rotation by 2") to verify that the decoding of "deabc" yields the un-encoded message "abcde." If these match, receivers can be confident that the message has not been corrupted en route. This is assuming that receivers do not know the *en*coding process.

The steps in .NET required to create a shared assembly are detailed next, and are as follows.

1. Create a key pair for encryption
2. "Sign" the key pair
3. Place the assembly in the assembly cache

### 12.6.2.1 Creating a Shared Assembly I: Creating an Encryption Key Pair
Executing Microsoft's *sn.exe* produces a randomly generated pair of keys on a file specified by the user—usually with a *.snk* suffix: The command

> *sn –k myKeys.snk*

produces the file *myKeys.snk.* Executing it another time would produce a different pair of keys. The keys are effectively very long numbers.

### 12.6.2.2  *Creating a Shared Assembly II: Signing the Assembly with the Key Pair*

When compiling an assembly, one can "sign" it with a key file. The effect of this is as follows.

1. First the names and contents of the assembly are hashed—reduced via an algorithm to a small set of bits that can be used to verify their contents. Think, for example, of producing 010011 from "qjfgjfdaxsaftsxglhsa".

2. The hash is then encoded using one of the keys (the "private" one). To visualize this, suppose that the private key is $n$, and the encoding algorithm rotates bits left $n$ places. With $n = 2$, the above example would result in 001101.

3. The resulting encoded hash is included in the manifest.

4. The other key (the "public" one) is incorporated into the assembly, making it available to any user of the assembly.

The assembly includes these with the actual object code content. When an assembly is received, the content part of the assembly is hashed using the same hash algorithm. Now the public key is used to decode the received encoded hash. The two hash results are compared: They should be identical. If an assembly is corrupted in any way after construction, it is highly unlikely that the result will retain the consistency between these two hash results.

To sign an assembly with the key file generated, we edit the following line in the file *AssemblyInfo.cs* that Visual Studio.NET generates when we create a project.

```
[assembly: AssemblyKeyFile(-- insert key file name -- "myKeys.snk")]
```

We then compile the assembly. Verification can be performed by any code element that receives the assembly. The process is summarized in Figure 12.33.

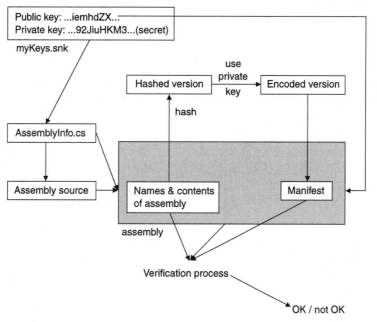

**FIGURE 12.33**  Public Key Encryption Used in .NET

**KEY CONCEPT** *Component Identity*

To ensure that the component we are using is the one intended, we use relatively or globally unique names. .NET also applies tamper-proofing via public key encryption.

# SUMMARY

The Microsoft .NET framework provides for the integration of distributed, component-based, multilingual source for Windows and Web applications. It is based on a common type system, a character-based intermediate language, and an extensive component model. The C# language provides access to the benefits of .NET. These points are summarized in Figure 12.34.

- Microsoft "assembly" == component
- Microsoft distributes computing among desktops and servers via, in part, .NET assemblies
- .NET assemblies supercede and are more versatile than (D)COM(+) objects.
    · Exist in Intermediate Language
    · Permit versioning
    · Include "attribute" feature
    · Identity technique for shared assemblies reduces "dll hell"
- C# language designed for .NET
- Assemblies constructed via C#, VB, ... are interoperable

**FIGURE 12.34** Summary

# EXERCISES

**Exercise 12.1**  Suppose that you need to use Microsoft assemblies to create a spreadsheet incorporating a financial form. Assume that you want to reuse appropriate assemblies. Describe in very general terms what would be in two of the assemblies, and which would use the other.

**Exercise 12.2**  **Part 12.2.1**  What is in a manifest?

**Part 12.2.2**  Name at least three things that could be listed in a .NET manifest.

**Part 12.2.3**  Apply the preceding answers to an assembly that provides personal calendar functionality.

Evaluation criteria:
| | |
|---|---|
| ▨ Appropriateness | A = Entirely appropriate parts to the personal calendar example |
| ▨ Clarity | A = Very clear and specific answers |

**Exercise 12.3**  The following questions require you to provide your opinions. Express these opinions clearly, and back them up.

**Part 12.3.1**  Give two benefits of Microsoft assemblies compared with Java Beans as expressed in these notes.

**Part 12.3.2**  Give two benefits of Java Beans compared with Microsoft assemblies as expressed in these notes.

Evaluation criteria:
- Appropriateness A = Entirely appropriate differences in benefits and drawbacks
- Clarity A = Very clear and specific answers

**Exercise 12.4** Provide a use for attributes in a .NET component not covered in these notes. Explain clearly.

Evaluation criteria:
- Appropriateness A = Entirely appropriate use
- Clarity A = Very clear and specific answers

**Exercise 12.5** **Part 12.5.1** How are private assemblies identified? In other words, how does a client reference one in order to use its functionality? Give an example of a situation in which a private assembly is sufficient.

**Part 12.5.2** How are shared assemblies identified and used? Give an example of a situation in which a public assembly is required

Evaluation criteria:
- Appropriateness A = Entirely appropriate answers
- Clarity A = Very clear and specific answers and examples

**Exercise 12.6** **Part 12.6.1** Create a private assembly *HealthClub* that performs the following.

**1.** Tells whether a given name (string) is a member of a health club. You can hardcode all five members of this club.

**2.** Tells how long a member has been enrolled.

**Part 12.6.2** Create a client application that uses *HealthClub* in collecting a list of names. It prompts the user for each name, noting whether or not a person named belongs to the club.

**Part 12.6.3** Create another client application that uses *HealthClub* to estimate physical fitness using the duration of club membership.

Evaluation criteria:
- Appropriateness A = Entirely appropriate assemblies
- Clarity A = Very clear and specific examples

# CHAPTER 13

# REQUIREMENTS AND DOMAIN CLASSES

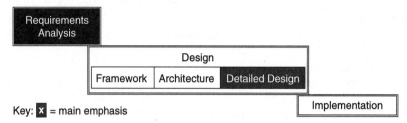

Key: ▣ = main emphasis

**FIGURE 13.1**   Process Phases Discussed in This Chapter

In this chapter and the next, we review the manner in which whole applications are built with Object-Oriented technology. Figure 13.2 outlines the learning goals for this chapter.

**Understand distinctions:**

- OO *analysis* vs. de*sign*
- Traditional application development vs. OO analysis & design
- Domain vs. nondomain classes

**Be able to...**

- determine basic use cases
- create sequence diagrams
- select domain classes
- use domain classes to organize requirements

**FIGURE 13.2**   Learning Goals for This Chapter

Although there are numerous approaches to application development, they are almost all based on the classical sequence in Figure 13.3, usually repeated several times in part or in whole. (See the Prologue for a full explanation.)

## 13.1 CHARACTERISTICS OF OBJECT-ORIENTED ANALYSIS AND DESIGN

*Object-Oriented Analysis and Design* (OOA&D) is a way of specifying and designing applications, which exploits OO technology. Its main characteristic is to approach the project using terms that occur naturally in the application. These terms are, in effect, the *ingredients*. Recall from Chapter 2 that this is the reason we use OO in general: It contrasts with non-OO

1. Gather requirements

   Specify Customer-oriented requirements specs

   Specify Developer-oriented requirements specs

2. Create design

   Select architecture

   Specify detailed design

3. Implement design

**FIGURE 13.3**  The Activities of Application Development

alternatives, which primarily approach applications through the *functionality* that they must provide. Object-Oriented Analysis and Design is characterized as shown in Figure 13.4.

- Approach is initially through the application's domain classes (its "ingredients") rather than its required functionality
  - Like starting a recipe by listing the ingredients
  - Typically obtained from introducing use cases then transforming these into sequence diagrams
- Introduces domain classes at requirements time
  - Remaining classes at design time
- Supports iterative development processes

**FIGURE 13.4**  Characteristics of OO Analysis & Design

The bullets in Figure 13.4 are explained next.

## 13.1.1  NonOOA&D Approaches to Application Development

To illustrate the difference between OOA&D and alternative approaches, let's consider the example described in Figure 13.5.

*WinHelp* shall advise novice Windows™ users on their difficulties using this operating system.

Input:    Problem description

Process:  Determine user's difficulty
             Match with solution database

Output:   Up to 3 possible solutions

**FIGURE 13.5**  *WinHelp* Example: Requirements

We have chosen a simple example to illustrate the point but this application can actually be quite demanding if we allow the user to provide imprecise input, etc. A traditional way to begin designing an application like this is with a data flow diagram such as that shown in Figure 13.6.

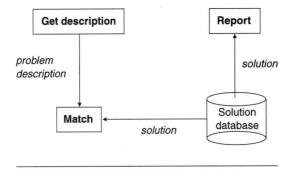

key: ⟶ = data flow │xxx│ = functional component

**FIGURE 13.6** *NonOO* Design of *WinHelp*

The organizing principle here is *functional* (verb-based): *"Get* the problem description," *"Match," "Report,"* etc. These could also be arranged hierarchically, as in Figure 13.7.

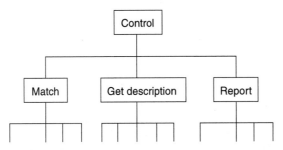

**FIGURE 13.7** *NonOO* Design of *WinHelp: Top-Down Organization*

Among other problems, the traditional, functional approach makes tracing difficult: The matching of each requirement with the corresponding place in the design and in the implementation. Typically, tracing must be performed with a *Requirements Traceability Matrix* as shown in Figure 13.8. The problem with this is that a function such as *computeBalance()* may contribute to satisfying several requirements. As a result, changes made to *computeBalance()* in order to satisfy changes in requirement 1783 can easily destroy the satisfaction of requirement 1784.

|  | Module 1 | Module 2 | Module 3 |
|---|---|---|---|
| Requirement |  |  |  |
| 1783 | showName() | computeBalance() | getInterest() |
| 1784 | showAccount() | computeBalance() | showBalance() |

**FIGURE 13.8** Requirements Traceability Matrix

When a functional approach is taken, it is usually difficult to connect real-world entities with a single, clear place in the design and code. For example, we speak naturally about *problems* that Windows™ users experience, but aspects of problems are spread out among multiple parts of the design and implementation.

Here is another problem with the functional approach. In order to use it, designers have to think from the top down at the start, and thus conceive of the application as a whole. In other kinds of engineering, this is generally a good practice but it has generally not worked the same way in software engineering. This is because software requirements change frequently, and top-down architectures are hard to redirect. For example, the functional architecture shown in Figure 13.6 would be unsuitable if the requirements are changed to "display well organized lists of common problems to novice Windows™ users." Figure 13.9 summarizes drawbacks of the functional approach.

- Whole application must be specified first
  - to do top-down design
- Usage hard to change
- Code does not match the application well
- Traceability difficult
- Reuse low

**FIGURE 13.9**   Disadvantages of Functional Methods

## 13.1.2   The Basic OOA&D Approach

Whereas pre-OO approaches to application design and development emphasized *functionality*, the OOA&D approach emphasizes *ingredients*. In other words, we first ask, "what is this application about?" The individual words (usually nouns) that answer this question are called the *domain classes* of the application, and they appear as classes in the design and implementation. We can often determine the domain classes by starting with use cases (see Section 13.3.1), converting them to sequence diagrams, and selecting the classes that appear at the top of the sequence diagrams. This is summarized in Figure 13.10.

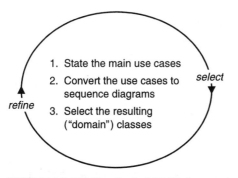

**FIGURE 13.10**   The Basic OOA&D Approach

The use cases may not be sufficient for arriving at all of the domain classes. A brainstorming process, described in Section 13.3.4.1, may be required to complete the list.

**DESIGN GOAL AT WORK**    *Reusability*

Because we want to reuse classes, we identify domain classes early in the process.

Jacobson et al. listed the difference between OO Analysis and Design. Their listing is shown in Figures 13.11 and 13.12. Item 3 about "control," "entity" stereotypes is discussed in Section 13.3.4.1.

Analysis

1. Conceptual & abstract

2. Applicable to several designs

3. « control », « entity » & « boundary » stereotypes

4. Less formal

5. Less expensive to develop

Design

1. Concrete: implementation blueprint

2. Specific for an implementation

3. No limit on class stereotypes

4. More formal

5. More expensive to develop ($\pm 5^x$)

After Jacobson et al: [Ja1]

**FIGURE 13.11**    Differences between OO Analysis and Design (1 of 2)

Analysis

6. Outlines the design

7. Emerges from conceptual thinking

8. Few layers

9. Relatively unconstrained

Design

6. Manifests the design

7. May use tools (e.g. visual, round-trip engineering)

8. Several layers

9. Constrained by the analysis & architecture

After Jacobson et al. [Ja1]

**FIGURE 13.12**    Differences between OO Analysis and Design (2 of 2)

Figure 13.13 shows a standard way to go about effecting Object-Oriented Analysis and Design. The top part summarizes the steps outlined above: The rest of this book covers the remaining steps.

This process realizes a major benefit of Object-Orientation. It creates a clean mapping from the very beginning between the real world, in the form of requirements, and the design, in the form of classes. The domain classes are key in realizing this mapping.

We will illustrate how these steps are carried out by means of several examples, including the case study that follows.

**KEY CONCEPT**    *The Object-Oriented Approach*

Begin with ingredients rather than functionality.

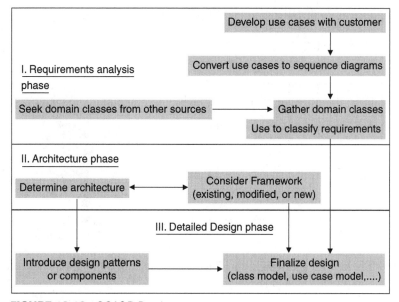

**FIGURE 13.13**   OOA&D Roadmap

## 13.2  THE *ENCOUNTER* CASE STUDY INTRODUCED

To illustrate the techniques of OO Analysis and Design, we will use the *Encounter* video game case study whose requirements are summarized in Figures 13.14 and 13.15.

- Role-playing game that simulates all or part of the lifetime of the player's character.
- Game characters not under the player's control called "foreign" characters.
- Game characters have a number of *qualities* such as *strength, speed, patience* etc.
- Each quality has a value.
- Characters engage each other when in the same area.

**FIGURE 13.14**   Case Study Summary Specification: *Encounter* (1 of 2)

- The result of an engagement depends on the area in which it takes place, and on the values of the characters' relevant qualities
- Players may reallocate the values of their qualities when the foreign character is absent
- Reallocation takes effect after a delay
- Success is measured by life points accumulated, by living as long as possible, etc.

**FIGURE 13.15**   Case Study Summary Specification: *Encounter* (2 of 2)

The configuration of the areas through which the characters travel is shown in Figure 13.16.

The image of the foreign character is shown in Figure 13.17.

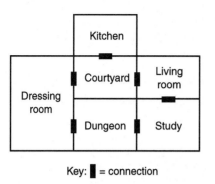

Key: ▌ = connection

**FIGURE 13.16** *Encounter* Area Configuration

**FIGURE 13.17** Foreign Character Freddie's Image

The full specification of *Encounter*, the design documents, and the Java implementation can be found in [Br].

## 13.3 OBTAINING DOMAIN CLASSES

As illustrated in our roadmap, a primary source for domain classes are the use cases and their corresponding sequence diagrams.

In the ensuing paragraphs we will illustrate the parts of this process, highlighted in Figure 13.18.

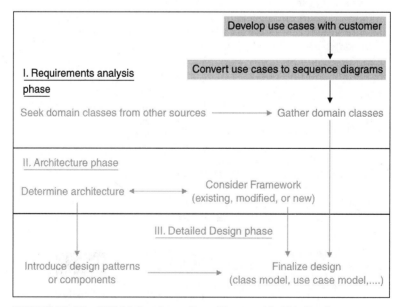

**FIGURE 13.18** OOA&D Roadmap: Parts Discussed in This Section

### 13.3.1 Use Case Requirements Description

The following are key use cases for *Encounter*. (For a detailed explanation of use cases, see Section 3.4 on page 67.)

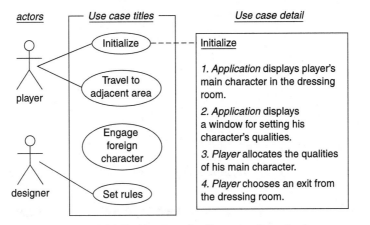

**FIGURE 13.19** *Initialize* Use Case for *Encounter* Case Study

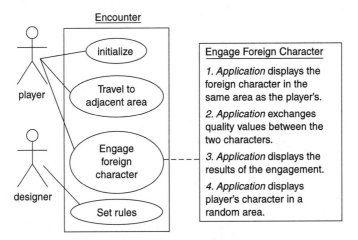

**FIGURE 13.20** *Engage Foreign Character* Use Case

In the "Engage Foreign Character" use case, step 2 could be omitted since it goes beyond the observables at the actor/application interface.

---

**KEY CONCEPT** *Use Cases*

Use cases are a beginning point for requirements and analysis.

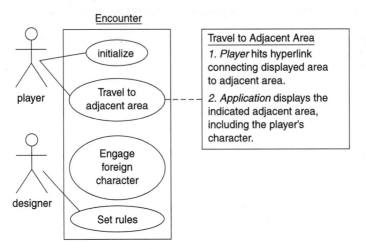

**FIGURE 13.21**   *Travel to Adjacent Area* Use Case

## 13.3.2   Converting Use Cases to Sequence Diagrams

Figures 13.22, 13.23, and 13.24 are informal sequence diagrams for each of these use cases. Notice that the user can interact directly only with GUI classes: The user cannot communicate directly with a class representing the Player Character, for example.

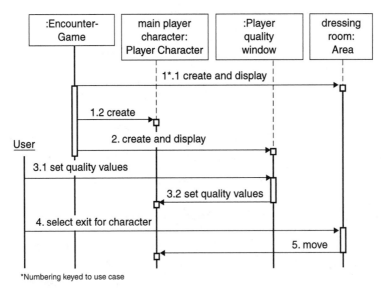

*Numbering keyed to use case

**FIGURE 13.22**   Sequence Diagram for *Initialize* Use Case

As Figure 13.23 shows, we introduce an *Engagement* class to capture the event. This applies the *Mediator* design pattern. *Engagement* computes the results of an interaction, and sets quality values resulting from it.

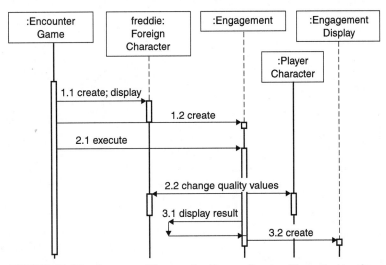

**FIGURE 13.23** Sequence Diagram for *Engage Foreign Character* Use Case

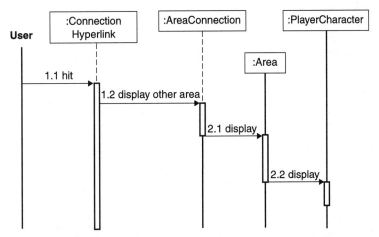

**FIGURE 13.24** Sequence Diagram for *Travel to Adjacent Area* Use Case

### 13.3.3 Harvesting Domain Classes from Sequence Diagrams

We use the sequence diagrams at this stage primarily to provide domain classes, as shown in the roadmap Figure 13.25.

The classes in Figure 13.26, for example, are harvested from the *Initialize* use case previously discussed.

Harvesting from all the sequence diagrams for the case study, we obtain the collection of classes shown in Figure 13.27.

### 13.3.4 Finding Classes from Other Sources

Sequence diagrams are not the only sources of domain classes because some requirements do not fit within use cases. For example, we can think of a few basic use cases for a word processor,

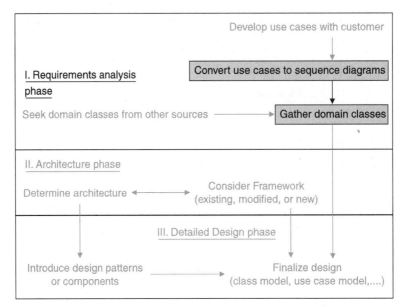

**FIGURE 13.25**   OOA&D Roadmap: Parts Discussed in This Section

*EncounterGame*
  - *a class with a single object*
*PlayerCharacter*
  - with object *mainPlayerCharacter*
*Area*
  - with object *dressingRoom*, and
*PlayerQualityWindow*
  - a GUI class included to complete the use case.

**FIGURE 13.26**   Classes in *Initialize* Sequence Diagram

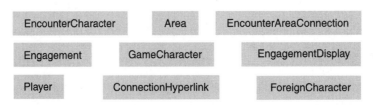

**FIGURE 13.27**   Harvesting Classes from the Sequence Diagrams

such as *Load a Document*, *Change a Document*, *Store a Document*, and *Set Toolbars*; but these do not cover all of the requirements by any means. In particular, we need to specify the allowable colors or fonts, but the domain classes *Font* and *Color* may well not appear in any use case/ sequence diagram. Figure 13.28 reminds the reader of the stage we are discussing.

An effective way to find classes from other sources is to brainstorm, collecting classes in every reasonable way, then pare these down. This is shown in Figure 13.29. We will use the following example to explain these steps.

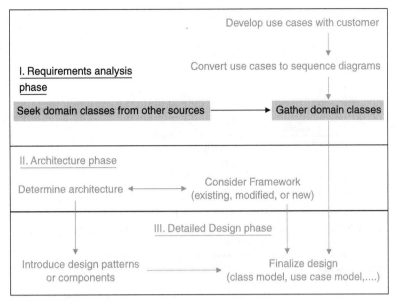

**FIGURE 13.28**   OOA&D Roadmap: Parts Discussed in This Section

Note that the use case for *PhotoComposer* does not contain explicit actions taken by the application. In addition, most of the steps are themselves use cases. (This is the *using* relationship among use cases discussed in Section 3.4.3 on page 69.)

(1) Brainstorm
  - List every reasonable class candidate.

  See checklist of potential sources.
(2) Cut
  - Pare down to a few essential classes.

  Err on the side of rejecting.
(3) Verify
  - Combine with classes from sequence diagrams.
  - Ensure class names classify all requirements.

**FIGURE 13.29**   Finding Domain Classes from Other Sources

Instead of converting this use case to a sequence diagram as we did with the videogame example in Section 13.3, we will obtain domain classes for this example using the brainstorm/cut process.

### 13.3.4.1  Brainstorming

Several authors have suggested sources for domain classes, as shown in Figure 13.31. The most important source for domain classes is the set of nouns mentioned in background documents for the application. Marketing memos are a typical of such documents. Grady Booch has classified the search for domain classes into "discovering" ideas for classes, or "inventing" them. In other words, either the concept is already a recognized one, such as *Bank* or *Molecule*, or else it has to be dreamed up for the

... a program for making compositions of photographs as illustrated ... can be used to bring together photographs of individual family members, possibly taken at different times, so that the result has the effect of a family photograph ... backgrounds can also be chosen by the user

**FIGURE 13.30** *PhotoComposer* Example

**TABLE 13.1   Preconditions:** The application has been initiated; the palette and work area appear.

| Step | Application | Actor: Composer | Note |
|---|---|---|---|
| 1 | | Retrieves existing photograph | Use case |
| 2 | | Sets photo as background | |
| 3 | | Retrieves existing photograph | Use case |
| 4 | | Masks photograph | |
| 5 | | Crops composition | Use case |
| 6 | | Prints composition | Use case |
| 7 | | Saves composition | Use case |

application in question. An example of the latter might be *Dilemmas*, for a video game that allows the player to weigh possible courses of action. The author does not recommend including abstractions here, however. Coad and Yourdon [Co1] and [Co2] list areas intended to stimulate the brainstorming process, as shown in Figure 13.31.

- Extract nouns from text

*Coad & Yourdon:*
- Structures
- Systems
- Devices
- Events
- Roles
- Sites
- Organizational units

*Booch:*
- Discovery
- Invention

**FIGURE 13.31**   Ideas for Brainstorming Domain Classes

For example, the candidate classes in Figures 13.32 and 13.33 emerge when these ideas are applied to the *PhotoComposition* example.

Figure 13.34 shows the results of this brainstorming process.

Nouns from text (existing documentation)

*Background, Frame, Composition, Display, Family,*
*Photograph, Portrait, Record, ScrollBar, User*

Invention (generalization etc.)

*Album, Ceremony, Collage, Graphic, Illustration,*
*Memento, Memorial, Souvenir, Visualization*

**FIGURE 13.32** *PhotoComposer:* Brainstorming I

Structures
    *Photo Tree*
    *Family Tree*

Systems
    *PhotoDatabase*
    *ImageManipulation*

Devices
    *Printer*
    *Monitor*

Events
    *Print*
    *Store*

Sites
    *Monitor*
    *Laboratory*

Organizational units
    *Family*
    *InLaws*

Roles
    *Composer*
    *Presenter*
    *User*

**FIGURE 13.33** *PhotoComposer:* Brainstorming II

*Album, Background, Frame, Ceremony,*
*Collage, Composer, Composition, Display,*
*Family, Graphic, Illustration, Image,*
*Laboratory, InLaws, ImageManipulation,*
*Memento, Memorial, Monitor,*
*PhotoDatabase, Photograph, PhotoTree,*
*Position, Portrait, Presenter, Print, Record,*
*ScrollBar, Souvenir, User, Visualization*

**FIGURE 13.34** *PhotoComposer:* Collected Class Candidates

### 13.3.4.2 *Paring Down*

Once candidate domain classes have been selected, they should be cut back to just the necessary ones. In fact, it is better to have too few classes at the end of this process than too many. The reason is that it's much easier to add a class when needed than to remove a class that has become embedded in a design and implementation.

Figure 13.35 shows questions to be asked of each candidate domain class. These questions ensure that each passes muster as a *domain* class. Many proposed classes are eliminated at this stage but may well reappear as useful classes later in the design process. Clearly, we don't want redundant classes, classes that are not especially needed, or classes that are not well defined. There are several warning signs that should give us pause, although they are not automatic disqualifiers by any means. These include classes that have very few apparent attributes (e.g., *Age*), operations (e.g., *Remove*), or very few actual instances (e.g., *StatueOfLiberty*). If a class is not special to the application at hand, it is suspect. For example, an abstract idea common to many similar applications such as

*BankAccount* will probably be useful as part of the eventual design, but may not be sufficiently particular to the application to be a domain class (*AjaxBankAccount,* on the other hand, would be OK).

We may also ask whether the class being considered should simply be an attribute or operation of another class. If the candidate is not a standard concept or name (e.g., *AjaxSecureReceptacle* instead of *AjaxSafeDepositBox*), it is suspect.

| Coad and Yourdon | Rumbaugh, et al. |
|---|---|
| • Redundant? | • Stay in domain |
| • Should be *attribute*? | • Needed? |
| • Should be *operation*? | • Several *attributes*? |
| • Should be left for | • Several *operations*? |
|   *design* phase? | • Several *instances*? |
| | • Standard entity? |
| | • Clear? |

**FIGURE 13.35**   Filters for Paring Domain Class Candidates

Applying these filters to the *PhotoComposer* example, we get the eliminations shown with various typefaces in Figures 13.36 through 13.38. This process leaves us with the domain classes shown in Figure 13.40. Their brief descriptions form what is sometimes called a *data dictionary*. Recall that the domain classes are obtained by combining the results of this brainstorming/paring process with those harvested from the sequence diagrams.

*Album, Background, Frame, Ceremony, Collage, Composer, Composition, Display, Family, Graphic, Illustration, Image, Laborat~~~ Inlaws, ImageManipul*~~~Generic, not special~~~*rial, Monitor, PhotoDatabase*~~~to PhotoComposer.~~~*e, Position, Portrait, Presenter, Print, Record, ScrollBar, Souvenir, User, Visualization*

——————————— Underlined: "not in domain"

**FIGURE 13.36**   *PhotoComposer* Example: Stay in Domain

*Album, Background, Frame, Ceremony, Collage, Composer, Composition, Display, Family, Graphic, Illustration, Image, Laboratory, InLaws, ImageManipulation, Memento, Mer~~~rial, Monitor, PhotoDatabase, Photograph, P*~~~e.g., not sure application has to distinguish in-laws~~~*Portrait, Presenter, Print, Recor Souvenir, User, Visualization*

**FIGURE 13.37**   *PhotoComposer:* Needed? Has Several Attributes? Has Several Operations? Has Several Instances?

*Album, Background,* **Frame,** Ceremony, *Collage, Composer, Compositio~~~* ~~~[Image]~~~ e.g., not clear e.g., not standard ImageManipula~~~n. Memento, Memorial,~~~ *Monitor, PhotoDatabase,* ~~~e.g., redundant~~~ Tree, Position, Portrait, Present~~~with Photograph~~~rollBar, Souvenir, *User,* Visualization

**FIGURE 13.38**   *PhotoComposition: Standard Entity?* Clear? [Redundant] (Should be Attribute)?

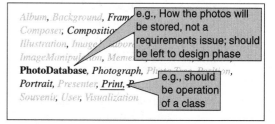

*Album, Background, Fram~~~* e.g., How the photos will be stored, not a requirements issue; should be left to design phase *Composer, Compositio~~~ Illustration, Image~~~abora~~~ ImageManipul~~~on, Meme~~~* **PhotoDatabase,** *Photograph,~~~* e.g., should be operation of a class *Portrait, Presenter, Print, P~~~ Souvenir, User, Visualization*

**FIGURE 13.39**   *PhotoComposition: Should be Operation?* Should be Left to Design Phase?

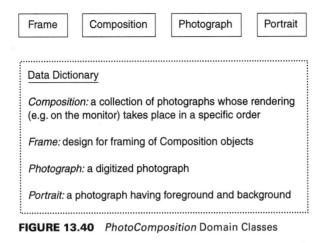

**FIGURE 13.40** *PhotoComposition* Domain Classes

Let's return to the *Encounter* video game case study. We gathered the domain classes emerging from the sequence diagrams in Section 13.3.3. The result of a brainstorming process is shown in Figure 13.41, followed by the pruning process in Figures 13.42 through 13.44. During this process, we usually do not remove the classes obtained from the sequence diagrams. The name *Area*, however, which is not particular to the game we are designing, has been changed to *EncounterArea*.

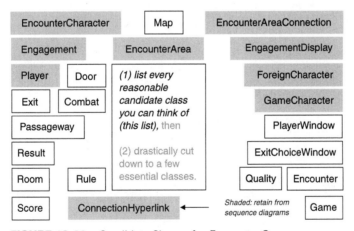

**FIGURE 13.41** Candidate Classes for *Encounter* Game

- *Encounter:* Change to *EncounterGame* to make its purpose clearer
- *Game:* Not a domain class — too general
- *GameCharacter:* Too general to be within the domain
- *Player: PlayerCharacter* is more specific to the domain, and should replace it
- *ForeignCharacter:* OK
  - act differently from the player character

**FIGURE 13.42** Filtering Candidate Domain Classes 1

- *Quality:* OMIT— try to handle as simple attribute of *GameCharacter*
- *Room:* OMIT — not sure if we need this; already have *Area*
- *Door:* OMIT— not sure we'll need it, see *Exit*
- *Exit:* Not sure if we need this: leads to neighboring area— try as simple attribute of *Area*— OMIT for now
- *Rule:* OMIT— not sure we'll need it
- *EncounterArea:* OK

**FIGURE 13.43**   Filtering Candidate Domain Classes 2

- *Engagement:* OK
- *Passageway:* Use *EncounterAreaConnection*
- *Result:* OMIT — vague
- *Combat:* OMIT — not sure we'll need it — already have *Engagement*
- *Score:* OMIT — try as attribute of other classes
- *PlayerQualityWindow:* needed for *Initialize* u.c.
- *ExitChoiceWindow:* OMIT — not needed
- *Map:* OMIT — not required yet
- *EngagementDisplay:* OK — needed by use case

**FIGURE 13.44**   Filtering Candidate Domain Classes 3

The resulting classes are shown in Figure 13.45. Note that we have included an inheritance that happens to apply among a few of the classes. However, we are not yet seeking all appropriate base classes. We will consider this process later.

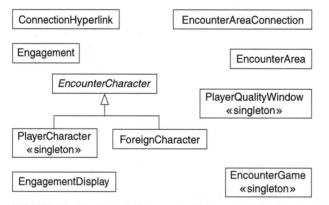

**FIGURE 13.45**   Domain Classes for *Encounter* Video Game, Showing Inheritance

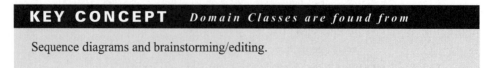

**KEY CONCEPT**   *Domain Classes are found from*

Sequence diagrams and brainstorming/editing.

# 13.4   USING DOMAIN CLASSES TO ORGANIZE REQUIREMENTS

Recall that a key advantage of the Object-Oriented paradigm is the fact that the implementation maps well to the real world. We capture this advantage when we map the requirements (the real world) to classes (the design and implementation). The classes involved in this mapping are the domain classes we have been carefully identifying. For example, we collect all requirements pertaining to customers in one section of the requirements document, headed "Customer." We use a *Customer* class in the design, which implements these particular requirements. When we do this, it is a straightforward matter to keep the requirements and the implementation consistent, even when requirements change.

We can thus verify a particular choice of domain classes by ensuring that they cover all of the application's functional requirements. As an example, we ask whether all of the functional requirements for *PhotoComposer* can be classified under sections named *Composition*, *Frame*, *Photograph*, and *Portrait*. To do this, we have to imagine writing down all of the functionality required of the *PhotoComposer* application, checking that each requirement belongs in one of these four groupings. For example, the requirement

*It shall be possible to crop photographs*

fits under the *Photograph* section. As will be seen, this will map directly to a method (probably *crop()*) in the class *Photograph*.

As another example, suppose that the *Encounter* video game were required to allow for multiple foreign characters. Since this requirement fits under the *Foreign Characters* section of the requirements document, there is no reason to change the list of domain classes. On the other hand, suppose that a requirement were added to specify "neutral" characters that enter the game: Characters not under the player's control but not the player's enemies either. In that case, we would have to add another domain class because this new requirement does not fit under any of the headings corresponding to the existing list of classes shown in Figure 13.46.

---

**DESIGN GOALS AT WORK**   *Correctness/Modularity*

We want to easily match requirements with classes.

---

Within each requirement paragraph corresponding to a domain class, the details can be organized in accordance with Figure 13.46.

Although the words "attribute", "instance", and "event" are also design terms, we are talking requirements language here: Ordinary English, where these words also happen to make sense. The requirements document should not mention design terms: In particular, the requirements document should not mention the terms "class" or "object." This organization of requirements is part of IEEE 830 [IE].

## 13.4.1   An Example Requirements Document Fragment

Let's return to the video store example. One of the domain classes is *Video*. This indicates that we should have a section in the requirements document with the title "Video." The contents of that section would be like the fragment listed below. We'll assume that this is

Section Heading (e.g., *"Customers"*)

Subsection <u>1. Attributes</u> (required properties)
    e.g., *"The application shall maintain the names of all customers."*

Subsection <u>2. Instances</u> (specific ones that must exist — if applicable)
    e.g., *"The application shall accommodate John D. Rockefeller ..."*

Subsection <u>3. Functionality</u> (the heart of the requirements spec.)
    e.g., *"The application shall be able to print customer profiles ..."*

Subsection <u>4. Events</u> (events that instances are sensitive to, if any)
    e.g., *"Whenever a customer's address is changed, ..."*

**FIGURE 13.46**  Contents of Each Requirements Paragraph

the second such section. Notice that there is no reference to OO technology: The material is written in plain English. The material in square brackets is commentary for the reader of this book: It is not content of the requirements document itself.

<u>2 Videos</u>  [Note: Introduce this topic.]

This section describes the detailed requirements pertaining to videos.

<u>2.1 Attributes Of Videos</u>  [Note: Here we tell what qualities each instance of the class is required to possess.]

<u>2.1.1 Video Name</u>  Every video shall have a unique name consisting of 1 to 15 characters. Acceptable characters shall consist of "0–9", "a–z", "A–Z" and punctuation marks.

<u>2.1.2 Video Image</u>  There shall be exactly one *gif* image to display each video on the monitor. The image shall fill an area of the monitor approximately 2 inches square.

<u>2.1.3 Video Status</u>

. . .

<u>2.2 Video Instances</u>  [Note: We specify particular videos that must exist within the application, if any. In applications, there are often many instances that arise, but they may not be called out as a specific requirement. They would not be mentioned here.]

<u>2.2.1 Gone with the Wind</u>  The application will contain an entry for the "Gone With The Wind" special edition video produced in 1998.

<u>2.2.2 Citizen Kane</u>  The application will contain an entry for the "Citizen Kane" special edition video produced in 1992.

. . .

<u>2.3 Video Functionality</u>  [Note: This is the required functionality pertaining to videos. Every functional capability of the application should belong to one of these sections.]

<u>2.3.1 Displaying Images</u>  It shall be possible to display the video image in a 2 inch square.

<u>2.3.2 Showing Delinquent Status</u>  It shall be possible to list all delinquent videos, alphabetically or by days of delinquency.

. . .

<u>2.4 Events Pertaining to Videos</u>  [Note: We separate the *events* that pertain to videos from the attributes, objects, and methods. An event is an action that occurs to the element, instigated from outside of it.]

2.4.1 Display On Becoming Delinquent    When a video becomes more than a week late, the video image shall appear on the screen with the rental information superimposed. (See the "Rental Display" section for the specifications of this information.)

2.4.2 Synopsis Printouts    [Note: This is an example of a requirement that references another part of the requirements.] When a video is rented, a synopsis is printed. (See the "Synopsis" section for details of the format.)

. . .

---

**KEY CONCEPT**    *Practical Requirements Organization*

Can be achieved by determining domain classes up front, then using them to organize requirements.

---

## SUMMARY OF THIS CHAPTER

The main points of this chapter are summarized in Figure 13.47.

- OO Analysis = Requirements analysis +
  Domain class selection
  - Product = Complete requirements document +
    Domain class model + Basic sequence diagrams
- OO Design = All other activities except coding
  - Product = Complete detailed design ready for coding
- Traditional application development: *Function-oriented*
- OO analysis & design: "Ingredients-oriented"
- Domain classes = "Ingredients"
  - Obtained via use cases –> sequence diagrams, and
  - Brainstorming/Editing process
- Use domain classes to organize requirements

**FIGURE 13.47**    Summary of This Chapter

## EXERCISES

Exercise 13.1    **Bank Simulation**    You are to build a simulation of a bank with multiple tellers. Customers form queues for individual tellers and/or groups of tellers: e.g., a single queue for three regular tellers and a separate queue for the foreign exchange teller. Assume that all customers come to the bank in order to conduct a transaction requiring a teller: The simulation will not involve any other bank employees. The application should provide statistics on customers and tellers: e.g., customer wait times, teller idle times, and the average of these.

**Part 13.1.1** Select an appropriate set of *domain* classes.

**Part 13.1.2** Explain what classes you considered and rejected, with reasons.

**Part 13.1.3** Use one of the classes as an example of how you would write a part of the detailed functional requirements.

Criteria:

| | |
|---|---|
| ▓ Completeness | A = all domain classes, or their equivalents, are present |
| ▓ Economy | A = there are no redundant or nondomain classes |
| ▓ Clarity | A = every step clear, complete and thoroughly explained |

**Exercise 13.2**  **Personal Calendar**  You are to build a personal calendar application.

**Part 13.2.1** If you were to approach this problem design in a classical, nonobject-oriented manner, describe how you would begin. Be specific and explain your steps.

**Part 13.2.2** How would you approach this problem from the object-oriented point of view? Be specific and explain your steps.

Criterion:

| | |
|---|---|
| ▓ Clarity | A = every step clear, specific, complete, and thoroughly explained |

**Exercise 13.3**  **Financial Computations**  You are to build an application that provides financial computations for homeowners, such as computing monthly mortgage payments, allocating income to a budget, and comparing options for car financing. In answering the following, explain your reasoning.

**Part 13.3.1** Provide a use case for each of the application areas described.

**Part 13.3.2** Provide a sequence diagram for each of these use cases. Explain your reasoning.

**Part 13.3.3** Are there other domain classes besides those that occur in the sequence diagrams? If so, specify them and explain how you arrived at them.

**Part 13.3.4** Give separate requirements paragraphs pertaining to mortgage calculations and to auto financing options.

Criteria:

| | |
|---|---|
| ▓ Completeness | A = all domain classes are present |
| ▓ Clarity | A = every step clear, complete and thoroughly explained: Requirements requested very well organized |

**Exercise 13.4**  **WinHelp**  Continue with the *WinHelp* example in Section 13.1.1 as follows.

**Part 13.4.1** Provide a use case and sequence diagram.

**Part 13.4.2** Are there any other domain classes? Explain your reasoning.

**Part 13.4.3** Give the functional requirements for this application.

Criteria:

| | |
|---|---|
| ▓ Completeness | A = all domain classes are present |
| ▓ Clarity | A = every step clear, complete and thoroughly explained: Requirements requested very well organized |

**Exercise 13.5**  **PhotoComposer**  Give functional requirements for the *PhotoComposer* application in Section 13.3.4.2. These should be between one and three pages long.

Criteria:

| | |
|---|---|
| ▓ Completeness | A = all requirements are present |
| ▓ Clarity | A = very well organized and clearly expressed |

# CHAPTER 14

# ARCHITECTURES AND FRAMEWORKS

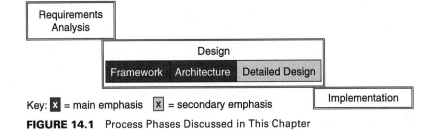

Key: ▨ = main emphasis   ▢ = secondary emphasis

**FIGURE 14.1**   Process Phases Discussed in This Chapter

The learning goals for this chapter are shown in Figure 14.2.

Understand...
- the goals of software architecture
- the meaning of "frameworks"

Be able to...
- express a software architecture
- show a full class model
- show a full state model
- show a component model
- build frameworks
- complete a detailed design

**FIGURE 14.2**   Learning Goals for This Chapter

## 14.1   THE MEANING OF SOFTWARE ARCHITECTURES

What are software architectures? One reason we think at the architectural level is the same reason we think in terms of "ranch" house architectures or "colonial" architectures: Architectures are reused again and again. In describing the architecture of a bridge, we use terms like *Suspension Bridge* or *Cable-Stay Bridge*. These terms allow us to envisage designs through an intellectually manageable number of parts (3–12 perhaps, rather than hundreds). In other words, engineering architecture is primarily a psychological concept concerning acceptability to the human intellect. Similarly, an "architecture" for a software application is its high-level design, enabling software engineers to gain understanding.

When an application is to be implemented using the object-oriented paradigm, the design is a collection of related classes. If there are only 10 classes in the entire application, we may regard this decomposition as the architecture. More often, however, there are hundreds of classes. Such a set of classes alone can no longer suffice as the architecture because it is too complex to comprehend at once. In UML, class collections are known as *packages*, and so software architecture is a decomposition into a small number of packages. Figure 14.3 shows an architecture for a video store application.

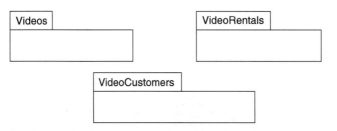

**FIGURE 14.3** An Architecture for a Video Store Application

This architecture groups all of the classes pertaining to the videos in one package. The *VideoCustomers* package contains the classes pertaining to customers, including associated GUI's. The *VideoRentals* package contains classes that relate videos and customers. Another option would be to group all displays in a package.

The requirements and domain classes help us to select an architecture. Figure 14.4 summarizes a common way in which we arrive at a class model for an application. It includes the term "framework"—a collection of classes applicable to multiple applications, described in Section 14.4.

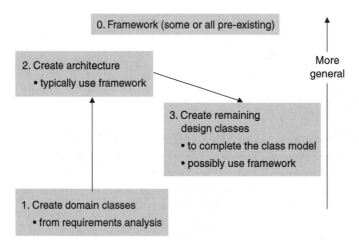

**FIGURE 14.4** A Sequence for Obtaining the Class Model

The domain classes are obtained by performing requirements analysis, as outlined in Chapter 13 (step 1). The classes in the architecture (step 2) are arrived at by stepping back, as it were, and considering how to satisfy the application's requirements as a whole. Typically, the framework classes already exist before we begin the current application, although we may add to them. Framework classes, described in Section 14.4, are obtained by collecting architecture classes for applications like the one under development. Finally the rest of the classes are added to complete the design (step 3).

# 14.2 MODELS OF OO ANALYSIS AND DESIGN

The architectural drawings of an office building comprise the front elevation, the side elevation, the electrical plan, the plumbing plan, etc. In other words, several different views are required to express a building's architecture. Similarly, several different views are required to express a software architecture. They are called *models*.

The four important models are shown in Figure 14.5 and are explained further in the succeeding sections of this chapter. We have already used these models in this book in describing the parts of a design. This organization is adapted from [Ja1].

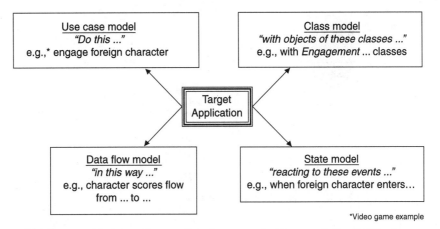

**FIGURE 14.5**   Models to Express Requirements, Architecture & Detailed Design

## 14.2.1   Use Case Model

This section describes several levels of use cases and related concepts. The *use case model* consists of the following four parts.

1. the *business use cases:* a narrative form, suitable for developer-to-customer communication, describing the required basic sequences of actions,

2. their refinement into regular *use cases* described in Section 3.4 on page 67,

3. their transformation into *sequence diagrams*, which in turn can be in two successive stages of refinement:

   3.1. with informal functionality descriptions, at first lacking all details (e.g., Figures 13.22 through 13.24),

   3.2. with specific function names and showing all details (Section 3.5.1 on page 70), and finally

4. *scenarios*: instances of use cases that contain specifics, and that can be used for testing. For example, a scenario of the use case step

*Customer chooses account*

would be something like

*John Q. Smith chooses checking account 12345.*

The use case model expresses what the application is supposed to do, and is summarized in Figure 14.6.

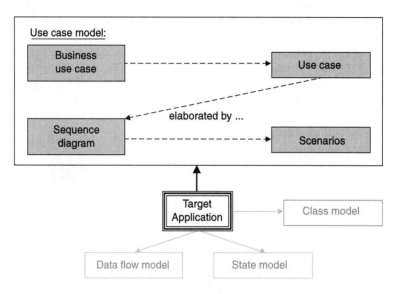

**FIGURE 14.6** Role of Use Case Models

## 14.2.2 Class Models

Classes are the building blocks—more precisely, the types of building blocks—of designs. We have been dealing with class models throughout this book, and there is little to add except to remind the reader that class models consists of packages, which decompose into smaller packages, etc., which decompose into classes, and these, in turn, decompose primarily into methods. This is shown in Figure 14.7.

## 14.2.3 Data Flow Models

The class model describes the *kinds* of objects involved: It does not show actual objects. The *data flow model*, on the other hand, shows specific objects and the types of data flowing between them. It is related to the class model because the objects involved must belong to the classes in the class model. We will now show the reader what data flow diagrams look like, and also how data flow diagrams telescope from high levels down to fine details. Figure 14.8 shows the parts of a data flow model.

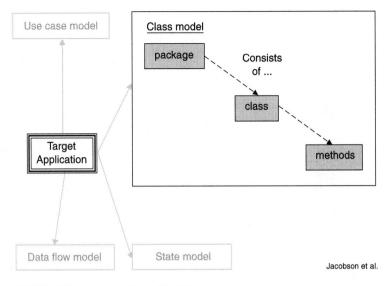

**FIGURE 14.7**   Role of Class Models

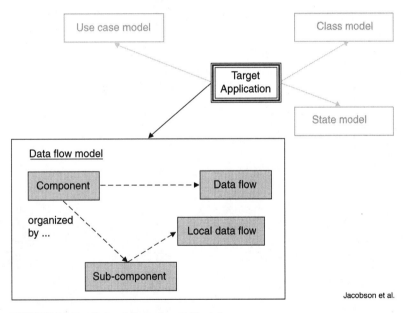

**FIGURE 14.8**   Role of Component Model

The data flow notation is shown in Figure 14.9.

Figure 14.10 shows an application of this notation to an ATM design.

Data Flow models can be telescoped, as shown in Figure 14.11. This allows us to show a high level view, followed by successive stages containing as much detail as we wish. This avoids overwhelming the viewer.

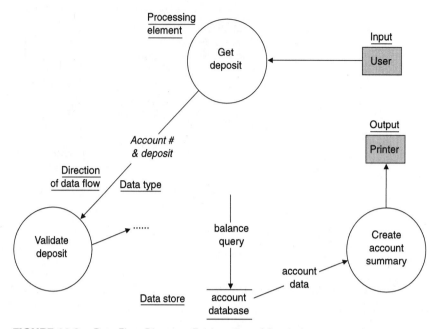

**FIGURE 14.9**   Data Flow Diagram: Explanation of Symbols

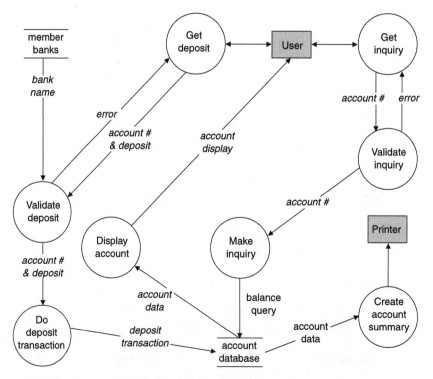

**FIGURE 14.10**   Partial Data Flow Diagram for ATM Application

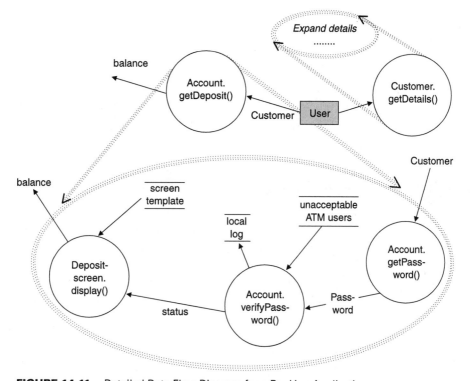

**FIGURE 14.11** Detailed Data Flow Diagram for a Banking Application

## 14.2.4 State Models

In a state model, each class has a state diagram (or "statechart"): An object of the class can be in one of the states at any instant. For example, a *Customer* class could have states *GoodCredit*, *MediumCredit*, or *BadCredit*. At any instant during runtime, a *Customer* object *johnSmith* could be in *GoodCredit* state, *Customer* object *mikeJones* could be in *OKCredit* state etc. We discussed state transition diagrams (a kind of finite state machine) in Section 3.6 on page 72.

Even though a state chart applies to just one class, the class could be representative of an entire application. For example, a rocket control application could have a *Rocket-Control* class, indirectly connected to hundreds of other classes, which indicates the status of the application as a whole. Thus, the states of a class can be indicative of the entire application: On the other hand, not every class has a useful state diagram.

Here is the state model for the *Encounter* class in the video game example. It expresses the state of the whole game: We could also have state diagrams for other classes such as *ForeignCharacter*. First, we show some of the basic states of *Encounter* and events that cause the *Encounter* object to transition among them.

Sometimes, when an object is in a state, and an event occurs, the new state of the object depends on whether some condition is true or not. For example, when the player's character in *Encounter* moves to an adjacent area, the game's new state depends on whether or not the foreign character is present. Conditional transitions are shown in Figure 14.13.

A full state model for the *Encounter* class is illustrated in Figure 14.14.

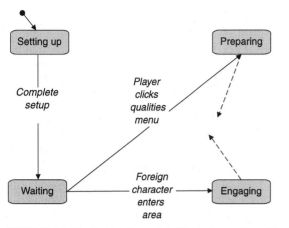

**FIGURE 14.12** Partial *Encounter* Video Game State Model

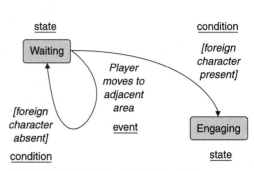

**FIGURE 14.13** Using Conditions in State-Transition Diagrams

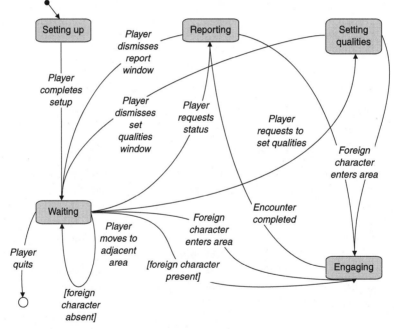

**FIGURE 14.14** *Encounter* State-Transition Diagram

State models reflect reactions to events which include mouse actions and changes in variable values. Events are not described in class models or component models, but they do occur in the use case model. Their role is shown in Figure 14.15.

**KEY CONCEPT** *To Describe an Architecture*

We need several models (views), typically Use Case, Class, Data Flow, and State models.

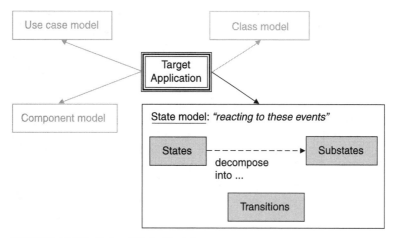

**FIGURE 14.15**   Role of State Models

# 14.3  SOFTWARE ARCHITECTURES

## 14.3.1  Goals for Architecture and Modularization

Chapters 4 and 5 describe design goals such as sufficiency, robustness, flexibility, extensibility, and efficiency. Since architecture selection is a part of the design process, these same goals apply: However, since architecture is design at a high level, we are usually more able to deal with *correctness/sufficiency* and *flexibility* than robustness and efficiency. Robustness and efficiency are usually better handled at lower levels of design. The first step in ensuring correctness is to make the architecture understandable. After all, if no one can understand an architecture besides its creator, it cannot be called correct by anyone other than the creator.

## 14.3.2  Modularization, Cohesion, and Coupling

With enough practice, it is not hard to write small programs: large applications, however, present very different problems, and are difficult to create. The principal problem of software systems is complexity—not the number of classes or lines of code *per se*, but their interrelationship. A very good weapon against complexity is decomposing the problem so that the result has the characteristics of small programs. For this reason, decomposing (or modularizing) the problem is of critical importance, and one of the most exciting design challenges. The designer should form a clear mental model of how the application will work at a high level, then develop a decomposition to match this mental model. We ask questions like, what five or six modules should we use to decompose a personal finance application? What four or five modules would neatly encompass a word processing application? After deciding this, we turn to decomposing the components. This process is sometimes called recursive design because it repeats the design process at successive scales. We start here with the goals of software decomposition itself: *cohesion* and *coupling*.

## DESIGN GOALS AT WORK   *Correctness/Modularity*

We want to decompose designs into modules, each well-knit and depending on few others.

Cohesion within a module is the degree to which communication takes place among the module's elements. Coupling describes the degree to which modules depend directly on other modules. Effective modularization is accomplished by *maximizing cohesion* and *minimizing coupling.* This principle helps to decompose complex tasks into simpler ones. Figure 14.16 suggests coupling/cohesion goals by showing an idealized architecture for a bridge, in which each of the six components has a great deal of cohesion, and where the coupling between them is low.

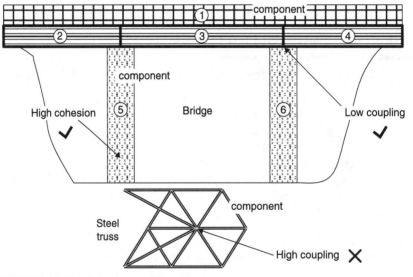

**FIGURE 14.16**   Cohesion and Coupling

The parts of each bridge component are mutually dependent (e.g., concrete with embedded metal reinforcing the columns). This is high cohesion. On the other hand, each component depends on just a few other components—two or three, in fact. This is low coupling. The "Steel truss" figure, on the other hand, shows many components depending on each other at one place. This is a high degree of coupling that we want to avoid.

Low coupling/high cohesion are particularly important for software design because of the necessity to continually modify applications. Compare the life cycle of a typical software application with that of the bridge in Figure 14.16. The likelihood that the software will require modification is many times greater. Low coupled/high cohesion architectures are far easier to modify since the effects of changes are more local compared to when these qualities are absent. Obtaining such architectures requires substantial effort.

The number of top-level packages in an architecture should be small. A range of "7 ± 2" is a useful guideline, although specific projects can vary greatly from this range for special reasons. The difference between small- and largescale projects is the amount of nesting of modules or packages. Largescale projects typically organize each top-level package into subpackages, these into sub-subpackages, etc. The "7 ± 2" guideline applies to each of these decompositions.

One possible architecture for the *Encounter* video game consists of four packages.

1. the environment in which the game takes place (areas, connections, etc.)

2. the mechanism controlling the game (encounters, reactions to events, etc.)

3. the participants in the game (player and foreign characters, etc.), and

4. the artifacts involved in the game (swords, books, shields, etc. These will appear in future releases.)

Each of these modules is quite cohesive. For example, areas are adjacent to each other. In the architecture we will use, the highest coupling among the modules is where one package that depends on all of the others. In particular, when characters encounter each other, the environment, the controlling mechanism, the participants and, ultimately, the artifacts are all involved. Since there are not many packages altogether, this relatively high coupling is not serious. The fact that two of the packages do not depend on any others reduces coupling in the architecture we will use.

As another example, consider how to decompose the design of a personal finance application. One decomposition option is as follows.

- Accounts (checking, savings, etc.)

- Bill paying (electronic, by check, etc.)

- Reports (total assets, liabilities, etc.)

- Loans (car, education, house, etc.)

- Investments (stocks, bonds, commodities, etc.)

Although this decomposition is appealing from the user point of view, it has design weaknesses. For example, there is little cohesion in the *Accounts* module since our different accounts may not interact much. There is a great deal of coupling among these five parts. For example, making a loan payment involves accounts, bill paying, loans, and possibly reports.

An alternative architecture is as follows.

- Assets (checking accounts, stocks, bonds, etc.)

- Sources (employers, rental income, etc.)

- Suppliers (landlord, loans, utilities, etc.)

- Interfaces (user interface, communications interface, reporting, etc.)

To understand which architecture options are better is an experimental and investigative activity that involves trying out alternatives, modifying them, and then retrying them. Much of this trying out has to be done at a high level because it is very expensive to retract an architecture after we have begin to build the application around it.

### 14.3.3 Using *Façade* Design Pattern

The *Façade* design pattern (see Section 8.2 on page 205) should be considered after modularization, as suggested in Figure 14.17.

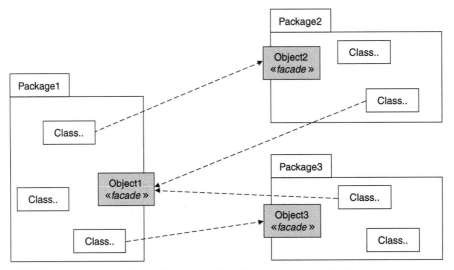

**FIGURE 14.17** Using *Façade* for Independent Components Architectures

Decompositions are suggested by looking for groupings among the domain classes we obtained from requirements analysis. For example, the domain classes of our video game case study were *Area, EncounterCharacter, EncounterGame, Engagement, Engagement-Display, ForeignCharacter, PlayerCharacter,* and *PlayerQualityWindow.* Each of these classes must fit into an application package. On thinking about this, we may obtain the architecture in Figure 14.18. It decomposes the classes into the three packages mentioned before: The game control parts, the *EncounterGame* package; the maze of areas in which the game is played, *EncounterEnvironment*; and the characters that inhabit it, *EncounterCharacters.* *Façade* objects *EncounterGame, EncounterEnvironment* and *EnconterCast* have been added, and Figure 14.18 shows relationships among them.

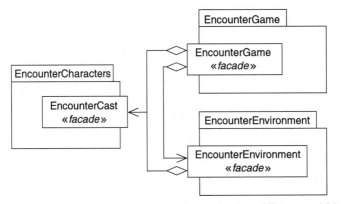

**FIGURE 14.18** Architecture and Modularization of *Encounter* Video Game

This section is summarized in Figure 14.19.

1. Develop a mental model of the application.
   · as if it were a small application, *e.g., personal finance application ...* *"works by receiving money or paying out money, in any order, controlled through a user interface"*.
2. Decompose into the required components.
   · look for high cohesion & low coupling, *e.g., personal finance application ... decomposes into* Assets, Sources, Suppliers, & Interface.
3. Repeat this process for the components.
4. Consider using *Façade* for each package.

**FIGURE 14.19**   To Select a Basic Architecture

**KEY CONCEPT**   *Modules Must*

Each have high cohesion, but be loosely coupled.

## 14.3.4   Standard Software Architectures

Garlan and Shaw [Ga1] have classified software architectures in the categories shown in Figure 14.20. We will explain each of these categories in detail, and show ways in which they can be expressed as OO models.

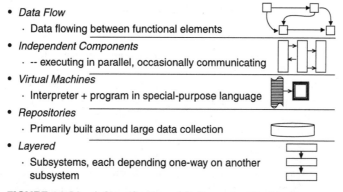

- *Data Flow*
  · Data flowing between functional elements
- *Independent Components*
  · -- executing in parallel, occasionally communicating
- *Virtual Machines*
  · Interpreter + program in special-purpose language
- *Repositories*
  · Primarily built around large data collection
- *Layered*
  · Subsystems, each depending one-way on another subsystem

**FIGURE 14.20**   A Classification of Software Architectures

**DESIGN GOAL AT WORK**   *Reusability*

We classify architectures so as to use them for several applications.

### 14.3.4.1   Data Flow Architectures in OO Form   In Chapter 13 we contrasted OO Analysis and Design with traditional data flow approaches. This is not an "either-or"

situation: At the architectural level, some applications are still best described as a data flow. For example, implementing an ATM banking system naturally involves thinking first about the flow of data from one processing station to another; only then would we start to think about classes.

This raises the question of what class model would be appropriate to implement a given data flow. A good way to do this is to *map the functional units of the data flow to methods of classes*, as shown in Figure 14.21. Before we can perform this mapping, however, we have to determine appropriate classes to which these methods would belong.

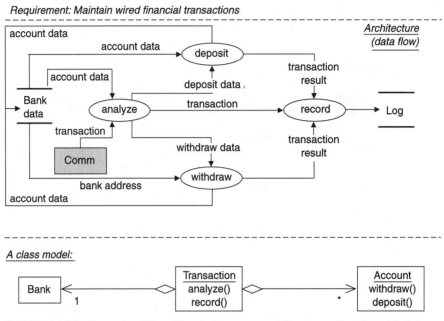

**FIGURE 14.21** Example of *Data Flow* Architecture and Corresponding Class Model

Recognizing that *deposit()*, *analyze()*, *record()*, and *withdraw()* are to be methods of classes, we ask what classes would be appropriate "homes" for them. Since we are analyzing and recording transactions, we introduce a *Transaction* class and do a similar introduction of *Account*. The data flow diagram does not dictate dependencies between these classes: We must think these through separately.

### 14.3.4.2 *Independent Component Architectures in OO Form*    Parallel communicating processes and client/server applications are examples of "Independent Component" architectures. Each independent component can frequently be collected into a separate package. The *Observer* design pattern (Section 9.5 on page 301) is of potential use in an *Independent Component* architecture: It covers one way in which observer processes can be kept up-to-date.

### 14.3.4.3 *Virtual Machine Architectures in OO Form*    Virtual machine architectures make sense when dealing with a family of applications that are all express-ible with a special-purpose high-level language. For example, suppose that we need to write a series of biochemical robotic control applications whose building blocks are the same, but which differ algorithmically. The following are examples.

*Application 1*

Place pipette in solution 6

Withdraw 4 ml of fluid

Dispense into beaker 5

*Application 2*

Repeat 15 times:

{

Place pipette in solution 2

Withdraw 6 ml of fluid

Dispense into beaker 11

}

Place pipette in solution 16

Withdraw 14 ml of fluid

Dispense into beaker 15

*Application 3*

Repeat 11 times:

{

Place pipette in solution 16

Withdraw 14 ml of fluid

Repeat 9 times:

{      Dispense 1 ml into beaker 11I

}

}


etc.

Approaching this series of applications with a *virtual machine* architecture, we would first define the grammar of the special-purpose language. The following would be such a grammar (key words are in bold).

Robotic procedure→Block

Block→Block Statement | Statement

Statement→Repeat-statement | Non-repeat-statement

Repeat-statement→**Repeat** integer **times:** {Block}

Non-repeat-statement→

   **Place pipette in solution** integer |

   **Withdraw** integer **ml of fluid** |

   **Dispense** integer **ml into beaker** integer

We would then write an interpreter that takes as input "programs" written in this language, like the previous three examples. In each of the examples, the output of the interpreter is the desired robot control. The *Interpreter* design pattern, described in Chapter 9, is useful in implementing this architecture.

### 14.3.4.4 Repository *Architectures in OO Form*

Repository architectures are used for applications consisting of relatively small processes against relatively large data stores. These are typically designed with a database management system such as Oracle. One can imagine Repository architectures as shown in Figure 14.22.

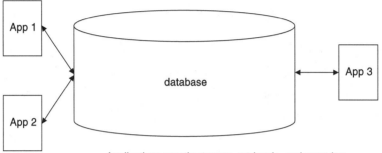

Applications mostly storage, retrievals, and querying

**FIGURE 14.22** Repository Architecture

Note that when objects need to be notified of a change in data values, the *Observer* design pattern is often useful.

### 14.3.4.5 Layered *Architectures in OO Form*

An architectural *layer* is a coherent collection of software artifacts, typically a package of classes. In general, each layer *uses* other layer(s), and *is used* by still other layer(s). Layering specifically excludes a pair of layers using each other: The relationship is one-way only. Building applications layer by layer can greatly simplify the implementation process. Some layers, such as frameworks (discussed next), are used in multiple applications just as *java.awt* is used in millions of Java applications. Figure 14.23 shows how we might organize the use of a 3D graphics engine, for example, as a layer accessible from a role-playing game layer.

**FIGURE 14.23** Layered Architecture

Figure 14.24 shows an example of a layered architecture for an "Ajax bank printing" application. In this case the usage is by aggregation.

*Requirement:* Print monthly statements

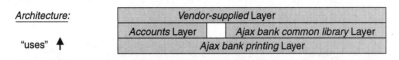

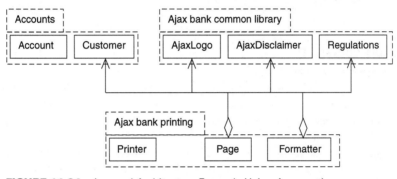

**FIGURE 14.24** Layered Architecture Example Using Aggregation

There are four layers in this architecture. *Ajax Bank Printing* concerns printing and formatting. It uses the *Accounts* and the *Ajax Bank Common Class* layers. The latter use a vendor-supplied layer, not shown, which contains general utilities such as sorting and searching. Typically, a layer is a package of classes: For example, the *Ajax common library* comprises classes that would be used throughout Ajax applications, and would include aspects such as the bank's logo, and its regulations. The "using" relationship can be inheritance, aggregation, or object reference. In the example, only aggregation is applied between layers. Coad and Yourdon [Co1] suggest that the layering in Figure 14.25 covers many applications.

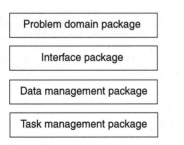

**FIGURE 14.25** Coad-Yourdon Use of *Packages*

This layering scheme places all GUI classes in a single package, which is sometimes appropriate. Another possibility is to group each GUI class with the package to which it applies (e.g., the *NurseGUI* class in package which contains the *Nurse* class).

Layered architectures have reuse benefits. The Java class library is effectively a successful system of layers. For example, the *java.applet* package (layer) relies on the *java.awt* package, which relies on the *java.lang* package, etc.

Layered architectures can operate in many ways. Sometimes the *Template* design pattern can be applied here: A layer contains a basic algorithm, and dependent layers realize the algorithm in specific ways.

---

**KEY CONCEPT**   *A Software Architectures is Essentially*

A Data Flow, a set of Independent Components, a Virtual Machine, A Repository, or Layers.

---

# 14.4 FRAMEWORKS

As we have seen, reuse is a major goal in software development. Reuse is not simply an admirable activity: If an organization can't leverage its investments in the skill of its designers and programmers by using their work several times over, competitors who do so will be faster to market with superior products. The parts of an application that are particular to it and are often not reused, are often called its *business logic*. Business classes are essentially the domain classes discussed in Section 13.3 on page 464.

We can reuse architectures, designs, and code. Garlan, Shaw, and others have shown how to identify and thus reuse architectures (see Section 14.3.4 on page 491). In Chapters 6 through 9 we showed how to apply design patterns to reuse designs. In Chapters 10 through 12 we discussed component (a kind of code) reuse. Now it is time to answer the following questions. Where do we keep the classes slated for reuse? How do we organize them? Should we build in relationships among these classes? Do they control the application or does the application control them? The computing community has learned from experience that merely making a list of available functionality does not necessarily result in much reuse. We have learned, however, that arrangements like the Java API do indeed lend themselves to highly successful reuse. The Java API's (*3D*, *2D*, *Swing*, etc.) are *frameworks*.

---

**DESIGN GOAL AT WORK**   *Reusability*

We create frameworks because we want to reuse groups of classes and algorithms among them.

---

## 14.4.1  The Meaning and Usage of Frameworks

A *framework* is a collection of software artifacts that is usable by several different applications. These artifacts are typically classes, together with the software required to utilize them. A framework is a kind of common denominator for a family of applications. Forward-looking development organizations designate selected classes as belonging to their framework. Typically, a framework begins to emerge by the time a development organization develops its second to fourth application.

Classes within a framework may be related. They may be abstract or concrete. Applications may use them by means of inheritance, aggregation or dependency: Alternatively, a framework may feel like a generic application that we customize by inserting our own parts. Framework artifacts are typically in a ready-to-use form, and are native code. Alternatively, they could be virtual machine code such as byte code or Microsoft Intermediate Language.

As an example, suppose that our organization develops imaging software for automated face recognition. Suppose that our first application is required to recognize the outline of faces in a scene, and its classes included *Face, Scene, Chin, Hair* and *Hat*. We might consider *Face, Chin* and *Hat* to be potential framework classes because we think that they will appear in many of the applications that we will be asked to develop in the future. If our second application is to identify the parts of faces, and uses *Face, Eyebrow, Mouth, Ear, Chin* and *Hair,* we might decide that the framework should contain *Face, Chin* and *Hair*. By the time we get to our third or fourth application, we are probably ready to commit to framework classes. This means that we place them in a recognized location, document them particularly well, and maintain them carefully. We take advantage of framework classes in subsequent applications, and we typically add to them over time. The Enterprise Java Bean (EJB) framework specified by Sun, for example, saves a tremendous amount of design and development time when implementing server-side applications involving databases. EJB's are explained in Section 14.4.4.4.1.

Figure 14.26 shows the relationship between framework classes, domain classes, and the remaining design classes. The complete design for an application consists of the domain classes, the design classes, and some of the framework classes. Usually, we do not use all of the framework classes in an application. The design classes consist of some required for the architecture, and some that are not. The latter are effectively the detail design classes required to complete the design.

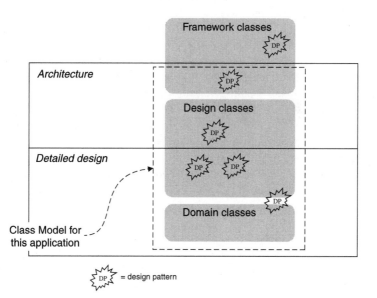

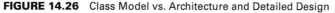

**FIGURE 14.26** Class Model vs. Architecture and Detailed Design

As noted in Figure 14.26, design patterns are sometimes applied within the framework (for example, the *Composite* pattern occurs in the *java.awt* package). They can be a significant help in creating the design classes. Typically, design patterns do not occur within the domain classes because the latter are selected in isolation. However, design patterns frequently include domain classes.

The framework classes used in the design are part of an application's architecture, as shown in Figure 14.26, although they can also be part of the detailed design. The domain classes are usually part of the detailed design since they are specific to the application and are not architectural in nature. An example from the video game case study is the domain class *PlayerCharacter*: It is not part of the architecture, as expressed in Figure 14.18. The framework class *RolePlayingGame*, however, is effectively part of the architecture because *EncounterGame* inherits from it. This will be shown next.

## 14.4.2 Framework Usages: Toolkits, Abstract Architecture, and Control

Frameworks have three possible usages. One possible framework usage is to provide a "bag of tools." In fact, some collections of classes are simply called *toolkits*. The classes in a toolkit may be related, but such relationships are not architectural in nature. The *java.math* package, for example, containing *BigInteger* and *BigDecimal*, is a toolkit. It makes no architectural assumptions. Access to toolkit classes is unrestricted (*public* in Java terms). Toolkits are sometimes not considered frameworks, although we will consider them so in this book.

Another possible usage of frameworks is when they contain architectural assumptions about the applications that use them. For example, in the *java.awt* framework (API) package, the *Container* class supports the method *add(Component)*. This is an architectural property, albeit a safe one. (Surely containers have to contain *something*.)

Access to these framework classes is again unrestricted.

In both of the two preceding framework usages, control is the responsibility of the developer: The framework classes are simply there to be used. The third possible usage of a framework is that it contains control. A simple example is the *java.applet* API. When we use *Applet* to build our own applet, we do not write a *main()* method. Instead, we must design and implement within given rules or protocols provided by the framework. In the case of applets, the rules tell us which method is called when an applet is accessed (*init()*), which is called when the applet is rendered on the monitor (*paint()*). We will see this framework usage applied in Enterprise Java Beans (Section 14.4.4.4). It is sometimes called "reverse control flow" (see [Fa]).

Figure 14.27 summarizes the three possible usages of a framework discussed.

## 14.4.3 Goals for Frameworks

Some believe that frameworks should be designed only if they will be used by a large number of applications. The Java API is one such framework. It is often sensible, however, to develop a framework layer for just a single application, even when there is no assurance that other applications will use it. Such a partial framework typically forms a generic layer from which many of the application's classes inherit. The resulting layering promotes better designs. In particular, most design patterns have an abstract and a non-

1. Toolkit
   - · A collection of useful classes
   - · Each usable in isolation
   - · (Sometimes not called a framework)
2. Common denominator of architectures
   - · An architecture in the abstract
3. A system containing control
   - · Follow the protocols to obtain your application

**FIGURE 14.27** Possible Usages of a Framework

abstract layer: The classes in the abstract layer frequently contain framework classes, and those in the concrete layer frequently contain domain classes.

One of the common goals for introducing frameworks is to manage *persistence*. The following example illustrates the problem. Suppose that we want to allow visitors to our website to depart the site at any time but return as if they had never been away. For example, they may fill their shopping cart with goods, but then leave the site temporarily: When they return to the site, we might want them to have the same goods already present in their shopping cart, or at least to provide them with this option. This can be done by having the server create an object (of a class *Visit*, for example), store the *Visit* object, and resurrect it when the customer returns. This property of having an object saved between executions is called *persistence*. Since persistence is a common requirement, a framework may support it in general, relieving the developer of repeatedly designing for it. In our example, we need to save and restore the *Visit* object: But there will be many *Visit* objects. How do we recognize the one we need? This is the problem of *object identity*. One way to approach the object identity problem is to generate a totally unique string for each and every object, saving it between executions.

Frameworks can provide numerous other useful facilities: Pooling is the last one we'll mention here. The issue, already discussed in Section 8.6 on page 226 on *Flyweight,* is that we need to share objects created at runtime. We do this to avoid the proliferation of objects (a space efficiency issue) and to avoid the constant creation and destruction of objects (a time efficiency issue). This issue arises when we access databases repeatedly.

One common requirement for servers is the creation of *connections* with databases: Means of entry into and retrieval from databases. To establish a connection is somewhat similar to connecting an application to a file, as in

```
FileReader inputReader = new FileReader("c:\Abra\Cadabra\Special\Magic");
```

Operations like this consume time, and require us to remember exact path names. This process is somewhat generic in nature, however, and it should not be necessary to create these connections repeatedly. Consequently, we look to frameworks to manage these connections: Setting them up when needed, remembering them, identifying them, pooling them, keeping them available, closing them when appropriate, etc.

Another common pooling requirement is in dealing with threads generated to handle customer interaction. Suppose, for example, that we are implementing a server-side application that handles online shopping. It is natural to create a thread for each session with a given client, since sessions consume time. We must effectively remove sessions when they are no longer needed, however; otherwise the server will soon be overwhelmed with an ever-mounting population of session objects. This continual creation/destruction cycle wastes time, however, and the solution once again is to pool sessions.

Security, the ability to verify accessors to the server, is another feature that we should not have to design for each time we build an application. Some frameworks handle security for us also.

Figure 14.28 sums up possible framework goals. We will show in Section 14.4.4.4 that Enterprise Java Beans (a framework) caters to these goals.

- *Persistence Service*
  - · Store instances between executions
- *Identity Service*
  - · Identify objects sufficiently to retrieve them across executions
- *Pooling*
  - · of objects: Reusing objects at runtime to save time and space
  - · of threads
  - · of database connections
- *Security*

**FIGURE 14.28**   Selected Framework Goals

In the next section, we identify framework classes for use via inheritance.

**KEY CONCEPT**   *We Use Frameworks*

To reuse classes, relationships among classes, or pre-programmed control.

## 14.4.4   Framework Development and Examples

### 14.4.4.1   *Seeking Framework Classes Via Inheritance*   In building frameworks, we seek generalizations (abstractions) of the classes we have selected thus far. There are two ways to find these generalizations: Bottomup and Topdown. As an example, consider the classes in the "Windows Helper" (*WinHelp*) application described in Section 13.1.1. We seek an abstraction of *WinProblem*, which captures a difficulty using with the *Windows* operating system. *Problem* is one such generalization. We use a similar process for the class *WinProcedure*, arriving at the class *Procedure*, as shown in Figure 14.29.

The reader might notice now why we made a fuss about selecting *specialized* names for domain classes such as *Win*Problem and *Win*Procedure. If we had named these classes simply *Problem* and *Procedure*, we'd be stuck at this point trying to distinguish between them and their generic base classes. As Shakespeare's Juliet finds out, the answer to "What's in a name?" is, unfortunately for her and Romeo, "a lot."

Figure 14.29 describes a bottomup process. When a framework already exists, however, we look through its classes to see whether they can be of use. For example, we might determine that the *List* and *ListIterator* classes in the Microsoft Foundation Class library

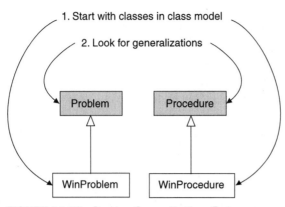

**FIGURE 14.29** Seeking Generalization: *Bottomup*

have functionality that supports the *ScheduledEvents* class in a simulation example. *ScheduledEvents* maintains a collection of simulation events. For this reason, we may have *ScheduledEvents* inherit from *List*. Actually, having *ScheduledEvents* aggregate *List* might be better, especially if multiple inheritance is not available.

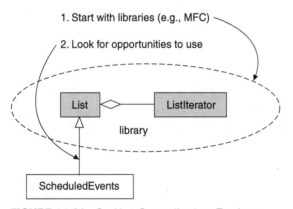

**FIGURE 14.30** Seeking Generalization: *Topdown*

**14.4.4.2  *The Java API's***  The Java Application Programming Interface (API) consists of useful framework packages: Its widespread use has shown that the development community is eager to exploit frameworks. The Java API packages are intended to serve huge ranges of applications, whereas typical development shops only need frameworks that cover their business.

**14.4.4.3  *A User Framework Example: Video Game***  As an example, let's create a framework that the *Encounter* video game case study can use (Section 13.2 on page 463). Figure 14.18 described an architecture for the *Encounter* case study. We seek a decomposition for role-playing video games in general. An application package typically uses one or more framework packages. For example, the application package *EncounterCharacters* could use a framework package *Characters,* describing the entities participating in role-playing games, as shown in Figure 14.31.

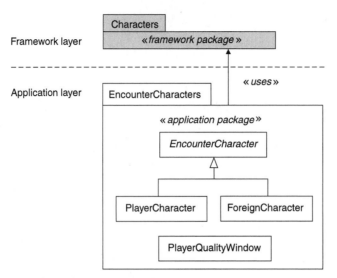

**FIGURE 14.31** RPG Video Game Layering

A simple way to identify framework package candidates is to consider each application package in turn, seeking a general version of each. This technique works well for the video game case study, because we get a clear general version of each of the application packages, as shown in Figure 14.32.

Figure 14.33 shows a version that includes the domain classes.

The *Characters* framework package involves both the characters controlled by the player, as well as those controlled by the application. The manner in which classes at the application level use the framework classes is shown in Figures 14.34 through 14.37. In particular, the details of the *EncounterEnvironment* application package and the *GameEnvironment* framework package are shown in Figure 14.34.

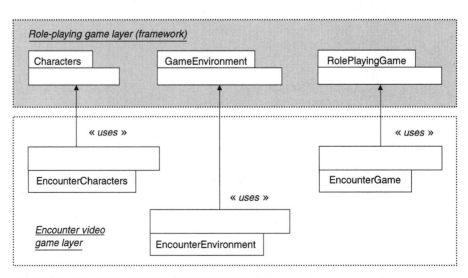

**FIGURE 14.32** Framework for *Encounter* Video Game

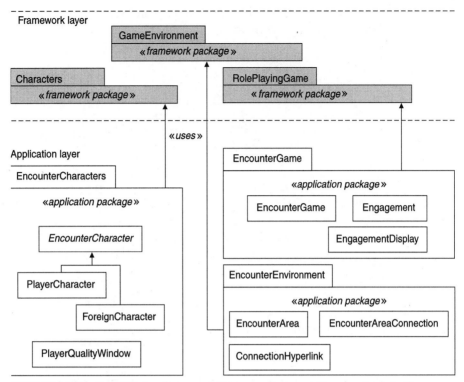

**FIGURE 14.33**  Role-Playing Game and *Encounter* Packages Showing Domain Classes

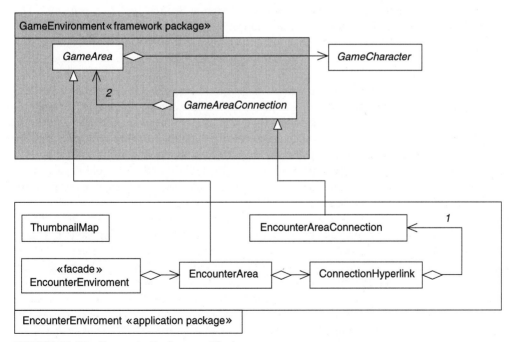

**FIGURE 14.34**  *EncounterEnvironment* Package

The details of the *EncounterCharacters* application package and the *GameCharacters* framework package are shown in Figure 14.35.

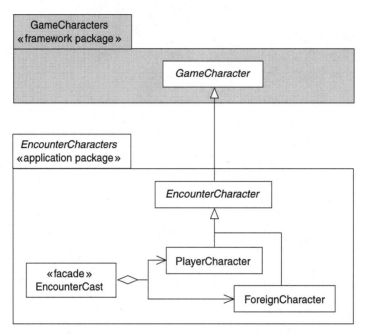

**FIGURE 14.35** Detailed Design of *EncounterCharacters* Package

We mentioned the concept of recursive design in Section 14.3.2 on page 487. The idea is to provide the highest-level decomposition, then move on to decomposing the packages of that level, etc. Let's look into the *EncounterGame* package, for example. The *EncounterGameDisplays* package is a subpackage of the *EncounterGame* package, and is as shown in Figure 14.36.

Here is an explanation of the detailed design classes in the *EncounterGameDisplays* package. It has three display classes, inheriting from *EncounterDisplayItem*. They correspond to GUI "controls" used to set and display the values of the player character's qualities. At runtime, actions on one affect another: For example, setting a quality in *QualListDispl* (a display of the player character's qualities—*strength, tact, patience,* etc.) affects what appears in the *QualValueDispl* window (the value of the quality selected). To avoid dependencies among the three subclasses, mediators *EngagementDisplay* and *SetQualityDisplay* are introduced. (See the *Mediator* design patter in Section 9.4 on page 295.)

The *EncounterGame* Package and its framework package were shown in Figure 13.37. The framework package here expresses the fact that a role-playing game has state, and is listened to for mouse events. The application package realizes the *GameState* base class with the various states illustrated in the state model in Figure 14.14. This uses the *State* design pattern (Section 9.6 on page 306). When a button action takes place, *handleEvent()* on *EncounterGame* passes control to the *handleEvent()* of its *GameState* object, and so the appropriate version of *handleEvent()* executes, depending on the state of the game. The framework in this case is architectural in usage because it contains architectural content: The use of state.

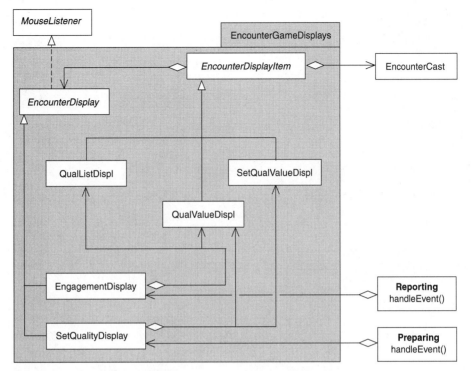

**FIGURE 14.36**   Detailed Design of *EncounterGameDisplays* Subpackage

Note that, once again, we have recursive design in that the *EncounterGame* package contains a subpackage: *EncounterGameDisplays*.

The details of the *RolePlayingGame* framework package are shown in Figure 14.38.

The framework packages relate to each other only in that *RPGame* aggregates *GameState*, as shown in Figure 14.39.

We have tried to attain high cohesion and low coupling in our *Encounter* application packages by grouping logical entities (characters, game control, and game layout). If we had grouped classes as their objects appear on a monitor (characters with areas), we would have placed *EncounterArea* and *EncounterGameCharacters* in the same package. Since there is an aggregation between them, this would bring advantages. On the other hand, coupling would have been high because we would need to be able to access the areas as well as the characters, a wide variety of entities, from outside the package.

**14.4.4.4   *A Component Framework: Enterprise Java Beans***   This section gives a summary of the *Enterprise Java Bean* (EJB) component framework. EJB's are designed to help developers create server-side applications that users can access, typically through browsers. Sun has packaged these as part of the Java "Enterprise Edition."

**DESIGN GOAL AT WORK**   *Correctness*

We want to avoid re-implementing common server-side processes.

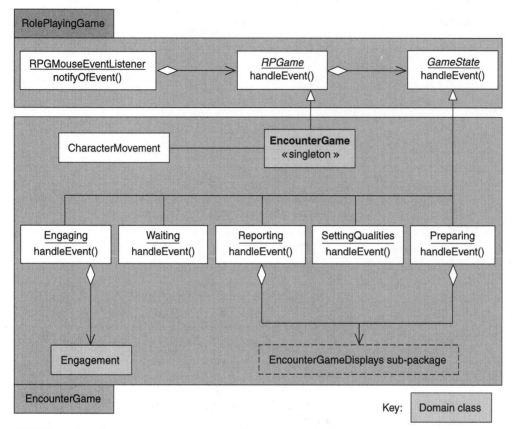

**FIGURE 14.37** Detailed Design of *EncounterGame* Package

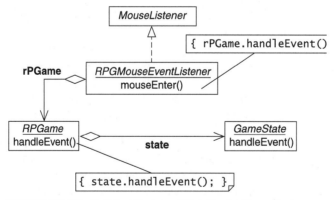

**FIGURE 14.38** Detailed Design of *RolePlayingGame* Package

**14.4.4.4.1 Motivation for EJB's** EJB's relieve the programmer of common server-side tasks such as database interaction and keeping track of sessions with multiple clients. EJB's address the framework goals of persistence, identity, and pooling, thereby helping

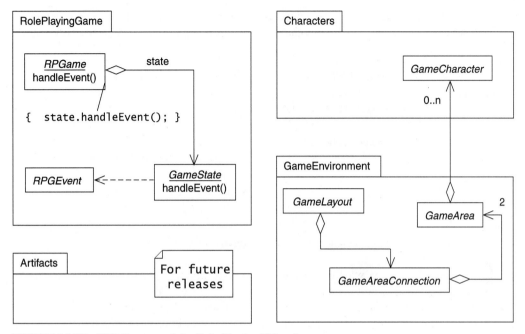

**FIGURE 14.39**  RPG Framework for Role-Playing Video Games

developers to separate out the application's business logic. For example, suppose that we want to develop a site that allows children to retrieve images of toys, and look at them from various perspectives. In that case the developer should be concerned with *Toy* instances, *View* instances, etc., but should not have to worry about the details of routine database access. Nor should the developer have to worry about tracking which client is inspecting which toy. In other words, the developer should only have to worry about the business (domain) classes, as described in Section 13.3 on page 464. These activities are necessary, of course, but they are common to just about every server-side application.

We often want frameworks to support *transactions*. A transaction is a process involving a database, in which a server provides a well-defined, short-lived service for a client. The definition is simple, but the devil is in the details. For example: What if the connection between client and server is cut during a transaction? (Has $18,000 been deducted from your savings account but never credited to your car dealer?) What if a request to write to a database pushes the server past its memory limit, etc.? Transaction support deals gracefully with both of these eventualities, allowing a rollback to the consistent previous state if necessary.

EJB's are designed to allow *portability*. In other words, it is possible to place an Enterprise JavaBean in any EJB server without modification. This is one reason they are *Beans*, not just any Java code.

EJB's are designed for *scalability*. This means that they can grow in number without disproportionate degradation in efficiency or complexity. In particular, if an application has 100 EJB's and one more EJB is added, then its speed and complexity should change linearly, by a factor of about 1/100 but not by significantly more. Non-scalable applications can grow exponentially in complexity as new objects are added.

The purpose of EJB's is summarized in Figures 14.40 and 14.41. Several protocols can be used to access EJB's—another generic capability for which developers should not be responsible.

- Server-side component architecture
- Part of Java Enterprise Edition
- Reusable, portable business components
  · no system-type code
- "Inherently transactional, distributed, portable, multi-tier, scalable and secure"
  (See [Ej])

- Customized at deployment time
- Supports
  · transactional behavior
  · security features
  · life-cycle features
  · state management of client sessions
  · persistence, etc.
- Any protocol can be utilized:
  · IIOP, JRMP, HTTP, DCOM, etc.
  Summary adapted from [Ej1]

**FIGURE 14.40**  What are EJB's? (1 of 2)

**FIGURE 14.41**  What are EJB's? (2 of 2)

Recall that one way to gain leverage from a framework is to include generic algorithms within it which developers need only customize. We do this with the *Template* design pattern. The job of developers then becomes more to describe *what* they want to happen, and less to say *how* these are to happen, since built-in algorithms are meant to handle the "how" parts. A description of "what" is a *declarative* process. Finally, EJB's do not mandate the middleware (the software medium, such as an Object Request Broker) by means of which the client communicates with the EJB container. Figure 14.42 summarizes these benefits. EJB's are used in server-side containers (environments), and to take advantage of them we must abide by a set of protocols, which are described next.

- Portable across any EJB servers and Operating Systems
- "Declarative" rather than algorithmic
  · Goal: customize, don't create from scratch
- Middleware-independent
  · independent of structure used between client and server

**FIGURE 14.42**  Benefits of EJB's

**14.4.4.4.2  Protocols for Using EJB's**  We mentioned in Section 14.4.2 on page 498 that many frameworks are used via their built-in control. This is the case for EJB's, and this section discusses the protocols for using this control.

Clients do not communicate with EJB's directly for several reasons. The most obvious reason is that the Beans are not in the same execution space as the client code. They normally reside on an entirely separate physical platform, and so client code cannot reference them directly as in a simple application. Client code addresses the EJB container through a *naming service*—effectively a table that, given a string, returns an object at the client platform through which the client can reference the EJB container. The client then provides the container with a reference to itself so that the EJB container knows how to reply to the client (step 1 in Figure 14.43). This process is called a *callback*.

The container provides a reference to an object for accessing the EJB (step 2). Further details on this part of the process are given. Figure 14.43 explains what "calling the container" means: It uses the *Façade* design pattern, in effect. EJBs can call other beans (3), or other applications (4). The client accesses the container and the EJBs by name (a string) and casts the *Object* resulting as specifically as it can. The Java Naming and Directory Service (JNDI) effectively translates the name string into a reference to the desired object.

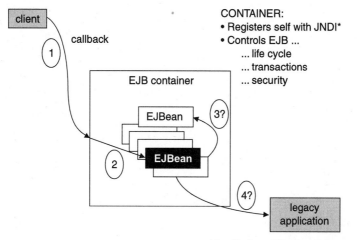

* Java Naming and Directory Interface

**FIGURE 14.43**  EJB Architecture

To make instances of an EJB and to obtain functionality from them involves a complicated-sounding protocol. With experience, the protocol is far less daunting than it first appears, and the benefits that EJBs provide make it well worthwhile. Figure 14.44 elaborates on the process. The numbering is explained next.

In step 1 of Figure 14.44 we write the *deployment descriptor* XML file which explains how our EJB, *CustomerBean,* will be positioned in the EJB container. For example, this is where we specify whether the EJB is to be a *SessionBean* or an *EntityBean,* a distinction explained later. We also provide the names of the "Home" and "Remote" interfaces for this Bean. By defining *CustomerHome* as the home interface, this designates it as the means for creating instances of *CustomerBean.*

The container creates an implementation of the *CustomerHome,* which extends the *EJBHome* interface. We will name this implementation *CustomerHomeImpl* here (step 2). The client uses JNDI (step 3) to get a proxy reference to *CustomerHomeImpl* (step 4). (Remember from Section 8.7 on page 233 that *Proxy* is a stand-in for the real class.) The proxy is not shown in Figure 14.44. The client uses *CustomerHomeImpl* to instantiate *CustomerBean* (step 5) and to get a (proxy) reference to *CustomerImpl,* which acts as a *Façade* object for creating *CustomerBean* instances (step 6). Since *Customer* is defined in the deployment descriptor as the *Remote* class, it extends the *EJBObject* interface. To obtain the services of the instance, the client makes calls on *CustomerImpl* (step 7), which exposes all of the required functionality of *CustomerBean* (step 8). In other words, *CustomerImpl* is a *Façade* for *CustomerBean.* Two *Façade* classes are in use here.

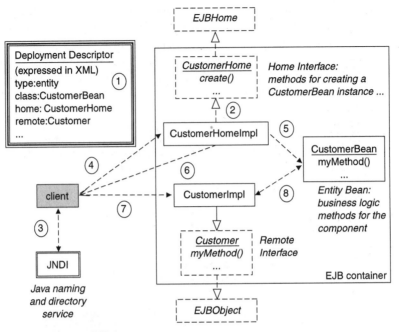

**FIGURE 14.44** EJB Access

The JNDI *naming service* is used to find and connect to a specific EJB. The procedure for using JNDI starts with obtaining the so-called *initial context* for the naming service itself, which includes the name of the file containing the JNDI data that's needed. The details of the context are first placed in a *Properties* object, which we will name *properties*.

Figure 14.45 shows the steps required for a client to obtain a proxy reference to a container's *Home* object for the EJB named *application/bank/customer*. The *narrow()* method is a *Factory* function (see Section 7.2 on page 148) that performs a cast operation. (Note this useful application of the *Factory* design pattern: Casting with a method is much more versatile that using a conventional cast.)

1. Embody location etc. of JNDI in a *Properties* object.
2. Look up the class implementing the bean's *home* interface by name using JNDI.
3. Use methods of the home interface to acquire access to an instance of the class implementing the remote interface.

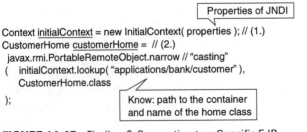

**FIGURE 14.45** Finding & Connecting to a Specific EJB

Now we can instantiate and use *Customer* beans as shown in Figure 14.46.

```
Context initialContext = new InitialContext( properties );
CustomerHome customerHome =
javax.rmi.PortableRemoteObject.narrow ( initialContext.lookup
( "applications/bank/customer" ), CustomerHome.class );


//Create bean instance and return proxy for it (3.)
Customer johnDoe = customerHome.create( "John Doe" );
johnDoe.deposit(2395);  // use the bean instance
....
```

**FIGURE 14.46**  Instantiating and Using an EJB

**14.4.4.4.3  Session and Entity EJB's**  To satisfy the goals mentioned in Section 14.4.3 on page 498 for persistence and the management of multiple clients, EJBs are classified as either *Session* Beans, used to track sessions with individual clients, or *Entity* Beans, used for dealing with data. The reason for this distinction is to inform the environment in advance so that it can manage sessions with clients. The container manages generic functionality such as threads and database access. This relieves the programmer from having to implement common functionality such as database rollback for interrupted operations.

The methods of *SessionBean* include the following.

■ *ejbActivate()* – used when the client makes contact with the container, this method retrieves the *SessionBean* object corresponding to this client

■ *ejbPassivate()* – used when the client cuts contact with the container, this method stores the *SessionBean* object corresponding to this client

■ *setSessionContext()* – called by the container when the *SessionBean* is created. In response, the container supplies a *SessionContext* object, which is associated with the *SessionBean* throughout its lifetime. *SessionContext* objects describe aspects of the *SessionBean*'s environment that it needs, such as the identity of the client.

To facilitate persistence, the methods of *EntityBean* include the following.

■ *ejbLoad()* – to retrieve the Bean's content from storage
■ *ejbStore()* – to place the Bean's content in storage

This is illustrated in Figure 14.47.

The types of EJBs are summarized in Figure 14.48.

In the example of Figure 14.44, we used an entity bean. Message Beans are not elaborated on in this book.

Figure 14.49 shows a typical configuration in which the client communicates (through a Remote interface not shown) with a Session Bean: The latter deals with entity beans, possibly retrieving them from disk or writing them to disk.

**KEY CONCEPT**  *Enterprise Java Beans*

Server-side Bean framework handling multiple client sessions, database access, persistence, etc., through control protocols.

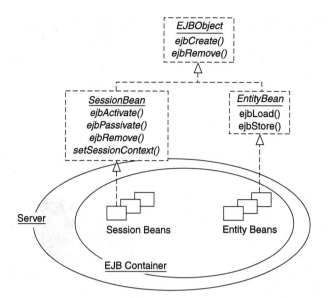

**FIGURE 14.47** The Parts of the EJB Architecture (Partial)

Entity
Bean

- specific data such as record in a relational database
- persistent

or

Session
Bean
(stateful or
stateless)

- perform sequence of tasks within the context of a transaction
- logical extension of client program
- running processes on client's behalf remotely on server

or

Message
Bean          (not covered in this book)

**FIGURE 14.48** The Types of EJBs

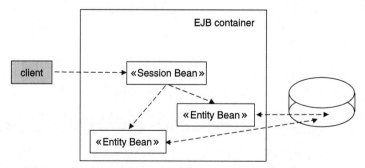

**FIGURE 14.49** Typical EJB Interaction

## 14.5  FINALIZING AN APPLICATION DESIGN

To complete an OO design, we need to fill the gap between the domain classes at one extreme and the architectural classes at the other. This process is suggested by Figure 14.50, which explains domain classes, architectures, and the remaining detailed design in terms of a civil engineering analogy. To review the process: We begin by specifying the use cases (step 1). We then extract domain classes from them (step 2) using sequence diagrams. After that, we step back and select an architecture (step 3), which introduces new classes. Next, the task of detailed design is to introduce classes and functionality so that the domain classes fit with the architecture. The use cases are then used in the form of test scenarios to validate the complete design.

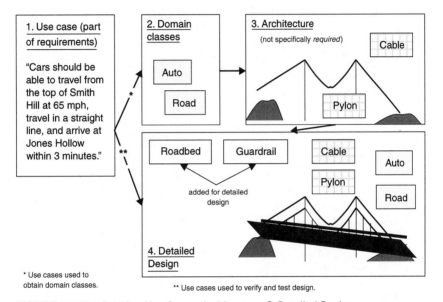

**FIGURE 14.50**  Relating Use Cases, Architecture, & Detailed Design

To develop an architecture and detailed design, we call upon as many ready-made designs as possible: These are the design patterns, covered in Chapters 6 through 9. We may also call upon component technology, described in Chapters 10 through 12.

In filling out the rest of application, we usually need to handle the issuers in Figure 14.51.

- Design the control of the application
- Design for database access
- Design interaction with outside world
- Audit relationships among classes
  - eliminate unnecessary connections
  - add required detail classes
  - clarify all classes
- Ensure all required methods implemented

**FIGURE 14.51**  Completing Detailed Design

### 14.5.1 Designing Control

Controlling an application means organizing the actions and events that it needs to progress through. We divide this into global control (i.e., of the entire application) and local control (of the parts).

***14.5.1.1 Global Control***  There are two basic means for global control—*external* and *internal*.

*Internally driven control* is associated with command-line applications: Essentially, the application determines what happens next. The user is provided with choices, but only when the application decides to offer them. A "wizard" is an example of an internally controlled application.

*Externally driven applications* shift the burden of control to the user. The application does nothing until the user—or an external device—affects it. External control is often described as "event driven," and is usually GUI-intensive. Typically, an event causes a method to execute: It's the developer's task to implement *which* method for *which* event under *which* circumstance.

These two types of global control are summarized in Figure 14.52.

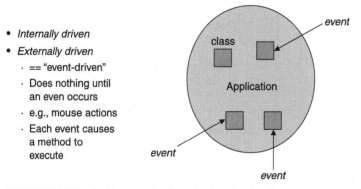

**FIGURE 14.52**  Architecture Options for Application Control

Figures 14.53 and 14.54 describe the sequence of events for internal control of the *WinHelp* example. Recall that *WinHelp* helps users with the Windows™ operating system (see Section 13.1.1 on page 459). The application creates and displays GUI artifacts one at a time, according to the sequence shown in Figure 14.53. Notice that the internal (non-GUI) classes *WinHelp*, *WinProblem* and *WinProcedure* call all the shots, and the user responds to the prompts in the windows that appear.

The corresponding sequence diagram is shown in Figure 14.54.

Now let's look at a version of *WinHelp* designed for *external* control. The order of events is shown in Figure 14.55. Notice that A GUI object is created at the beginning, and waits for user action.

The major difference here is that the GUI object creates the internal object when needed rather than vice versa, as in the case of internal control. A window specifying problems appears when the application is started. Entering a problem description on the GUI produces starts a process. The sequence diagram has the appearance shown in Figure 14.56.

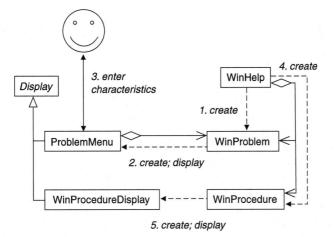

**FIGURE 14.53**   *Internal* Control

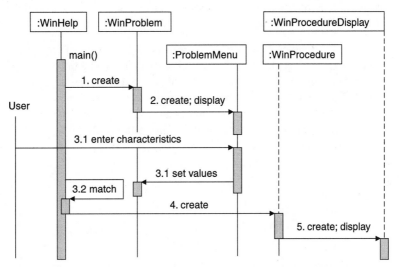

**FIGURE 14.54**   Sequence Diagram for Internal *WinHelp* Control

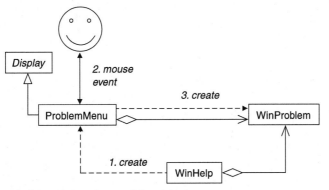

**FIGURE 14.55**   *External* Control

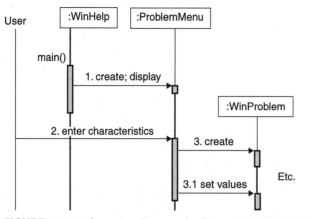

**FIGURE 14.56** Sequence Diagram for External *WinHelp* Control

There is no rigid dividing line between internal and external control, and most applications are a mix of the two. This section has focused on how to control an application as a whole. Now we will focus on local control.

**14.5.1.2 Local Control** We began our discussion of OO Analysis and Design by contrasting them with nonOO approaches, which are functionally oriented. Jacobson has pointed out that OO methods need special attention when dealing with primarily *functional* design elements. We will illustrate this with the example outlined in Figure 14.57, the theme of which was suggested by Jacobson.

There is an obvious functional design for this problem and also an obvious OO one, as shown in Figures 14.58 and 14.59.

Design a retirement information system to handle
typical transactions ...

· e.g., *open, withdraw, deposit*

on several types of accounts

· e.g., *passbook, savings, money-market funds*

**FIGURE 14.57** Example for Local Control

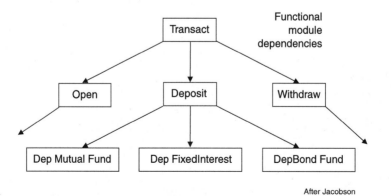

After Jacobson

**FIGURE 14.58** Functional Solution

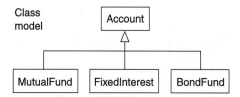

**FIGURE 14.59**  OO Solution

Following Jacobson, let's consider the impact on the design of *adding a new type of account.* The Functional design does not handle this type of change well. As shown in Figure 14.60, this requirements change impacts numerous parts of the design. The issue is not the amount of code change but its dispersal: Change in few locations is good, but change in many locations is bad. The total number of changed lines of code may well be the same in both cases.

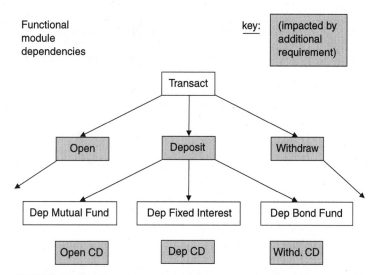

**FIGURE 14.60**  New Account Type: Impact on *Functional* Decomposition

The OO version, on the other hand, handles this very smoothly, as shown in Figure 14.61.

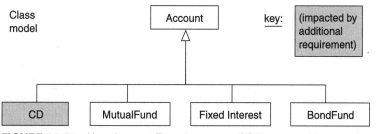

**FIGURE 14.61**  New Account Type: Impact on *OO* Decomposition

Now let's consider, as Jacobson does, a second change in requirements. This time we must *add a reporting function,* generating a report on the accounts. The nature of the report depends on which type of account is involved. The functional approach handles this change quite smoothly, as shown in Figure 14.62.

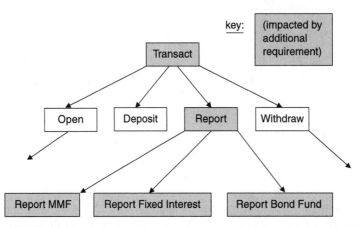

**FIGURE 14.62** Reporting Function: Impact on *Functional* Decomposition

The OO approach, on the other hand, is widely impacted by this change. Figure 14.63 shows the classes that are affected, and also shows how a client would need to interface with the resulting set of classes.

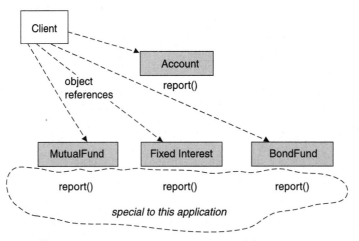

**FIGURE 14.63** Reporting Function: Impact on *OO* Approach

Since every version of reporting is different, the change affects every class. Also, the additional functional requirement is probably particular to this application: The *Bond-Fund* class, for example, might require a different version of *report()* when used in another application.

Jacobson has suggested a solution to this design issue: Introducing a separate class that captures the required control, and is associated with the base classes. The control class encapsulates functionality particular to the application under consideration. This is an application of the *Mediator* design pattern idea. Client code needs a reference to both the control class and possibly the base class in question. The base class captures the core content, and is called the "entity" class. This is illustrated in Figure 14.64.

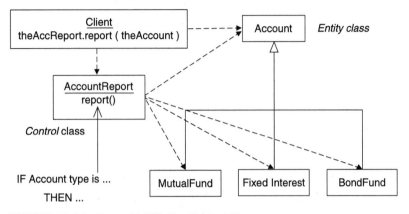

**FIGURE 14.64**   Stay with OO: Use *Control* Classes

**KEY CONCEPT**   *Control Applications*

Globally: Event-driven (externally) or internally.
Locally: May collect control in separate class.

## 14.5.2   Designing for Interfaces

This section discusses the design of classes for interfacing applications with their environments. It does not deal with human factors. The concept of "interfacing" with an application is not restricted to human users. For example, an application may be required to interface with other applications, and this is included in what we are calling "interface design" here.

There are two basic approaches to the application interface design problem: *Internally driven* and *externally driven*. These are summarized in Figure 14.65.

- *Internally driven Interface Design*
  - Class by class process
- *Externally driven Interface Design*
  - by use case
  —or—
  - by screen
  —or—
  - by user

**FIGURE 14.65**   Styles of Object-Oriented Design for Application Interface

Although this sounds similar to the discussion of internal and external control in Sections 14.5.1.1 and 14.5.1.2, we are discussing a different issue here: Not who does what first (control), but how to fit the interface classes in the class model. The internal and external interface approaches are explained next. This analysis is partially adapted from a discussion by Coad and Yourdon [Co2].

### 14.5.2.1 Internally Driven Interface Design

For *internally* driven interface design, we consider each class in turn. We ask whether it supplies data directly to or requires data directly from outside the application in order to function. This specifically excludes data that objects obtain from other internal objects. If a class does have a requirement for an external interface we supply the model with class(es) that perform this function. For example, Figure 14.66 shows the result of an internally driven analysis for the *WinHelp* example. The class *WinHelp* does *not* interact directly with the application's environment. On the other hand, *WinProblem* needs a description of the problem, and *ExampleWinProblem* provides the user with an example, so they *are* supplied with GUI classes.

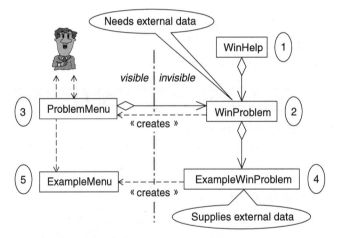

**FIGURE 14.66** *WinHelp* Internally Driven Interface Design

This internally driven analysis results in the class allocation shown in Figure 14.66. The graphical interface in this case consists of menus. The creation of the *ProblemMenu* object involves a *callback*: When the *WinProblem* object creates the *ProblemMenu* GUI object, it supplies a reference to itself so that the *ProblemMenu* object knows where to send the data it collects.

Now let's look again at the internally driven technique and the same application, this time building a more elaborate GUI to support the internal class *WinProblem*. The class *DesktopDialog* is dedicated to obtaining from the user what he sees on the monitor when the problem occurs. *ApplicationDialog* asks the user about applications active when the problem occurs. We want both of these dialogs to consist of three choice buttons and an OK button, as shown in Figure 14.67.

Figure 14.68 shows the three GUI classes we create to satisfy this requirement. The shaded classes (*Label*, *Button,* etc.) are part of the Java API. Note that internally driven design

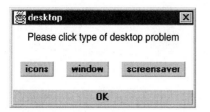

**FIGURE 14.67** GUI Fragment for Setting *WinProblem*

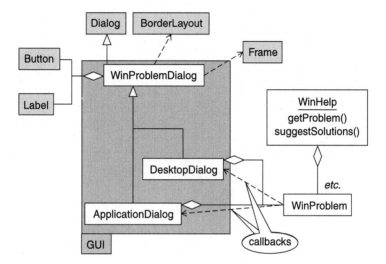

**FIGURE 14.68** Java Graphic-Based UI for *WinProblem*

focuses on design units—classes—rather than on the needs of users. When we do focus on the needs of users, we are more likely to use externally driven design, explained next.

### 14.5.2.2 Externally Driven Interface Design

To perform *externally* driven design, we consider the usage of the application, usually via use cases. For each of the latter, we design a class or collection of classes sufficient to produce the GUI. Consider as an example a warehouse application. The actors could be *Manager, Foreman,* and *Comptroller;* each being the actor is a separate use case.

We introduce a package of GUI class for each use case: For example, the *comptrollerIF* package will handle interfaces for the comptroller use case. Each of these packages (which could be complex, or as simple as a single class) depends on one or more internal classes, as shown in Figure 14.69.

As another interface design example (see Figure 14.70), suggested by Coad and Yourdon [Co3], consider the GUI for dealing with a vending machine.

Applying externally driven design, we create a collection of classes that match the required GUI shown in Figure 14.70. We can begin this design process more or less independently of the existing classes in the class model. We treat the *Add cash* function as a command whose parameter is the amount of the last coin inserted. The GUI consists of essentially two groups (*Container* objects), each having a text display (*TextComponent*

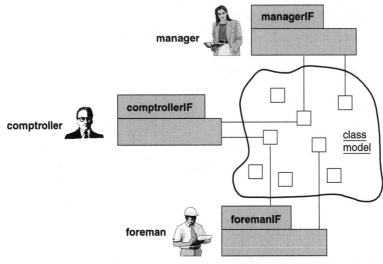

Graphics reproduced with permission from Corel.

**FIGURE 14.69** Externally Driven Design for Interfacing

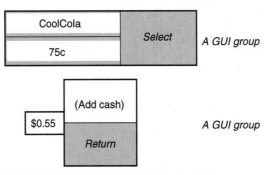

**FIGURE 14.70** A Vending Machine Interface

objects), whether constant or variable, as well as a component that causes an action (*Command* objects). The latter is performed via a button (the *Select* button) or via the addition of cash. The *Container* subclasses are called *InfoSelectContainer* for the upper one and *AddCashReturnContainer* for the lower one. Each is a singleton since there is only one realization of each. This suggests the class model shown in Figure 14.71. These classes interact with internal classes of the application, which are not shown. Our design methodology here was based entirely on the user's perspective, which is a common approach in GUI design.

Note that "interfacing" may well be with another application, rather than with humans. Figure 14.72 shows a chip-manufacturing clean-room application, which must interface with an existing factory automation system and a robotic system, in addition to a user.

**14.5.2.3  *Mixed Interface Design***  We frequently mix internal and external design, as shown in the following example. The *WinProblem* version in Figure 14.73

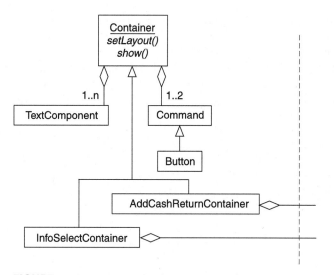

**FIGURE 14.71** Vending Machine Interface Object Model

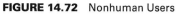

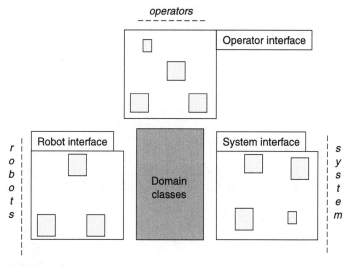

**FIGURE 14.72** Nonhuman Users

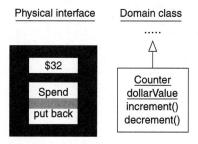

**FIGURE 14.73** UI Example: *Supermarket Counter,* 1 of 2

involved both internal and external considerations. Consider now a simple counter that one might use to keep track of the amount one has spent so far shopping at a supermarket (suggested by Coad and Yourdon [Co2]).

The class *Counter* requires data external to the application. For this reason we provide *Counter* with GUI classes. So far, this is an internally driven design process. When we start to consider what the interface for *Counter* has to look like, however, we revert to an externally driven design process. The result could be the class model shown in Figure 14.74.

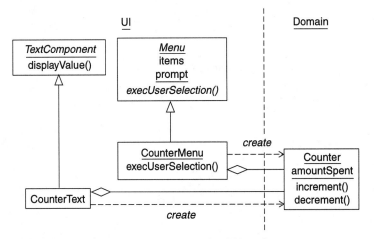

**FIGURE 14.74**   UI Example: *Supermarket Aid,* 2 of 2

The spend/put back rocker buttons can be considered a simple menu, and we inherit from a general-purpose *Menu* class. The "amount spent so far" is text, and we imagine using a general-purpose *TextComponent* class.

**KEY CONCEPT**   *Design for Interfaces*

Per use case (externally)
or
Per class (internally)

### 14.5.3  Connecting to Databases

Most applications require us to store and retrieve data. There are three issues to deal with in this regard, as shown in Figure 14.75. We consider these next.

1. Ensure class model supports collection
2. Choose centralized or distributed storage architecture
3. Store data in relational or object-oriented database

**FIGURE 14.75**   Data Access Issues

**14.5.3.1 *Ensuring Architecture for Data Collection*** First, we ensure that the architecture supports the *collection* of data. For example, when a customer deposits funds to an account, the *Customer* object, the *Teller* object, and the *Account* object each contain data but by themselves are an awkward way to save this data. In other words, an architecture that merely associates these does not necessarily support the collection of the data. What's usually needed, as in this case, is a *Mediator* class—*Transaction*, perhaps, as shown in the class model of Figure 14.76.

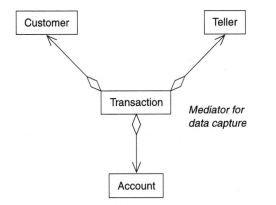

**FIGURE 14.76** Ensure Object Model Allows Data Capture

Let's consider a more involved data storage problem, involving the scoring of gymnasts by a panel of four judges. Clubs have *teams* (e.g., the senior men's team) consisting of *gymnasts* who compete in *contests* at *meets*. Contests consist of *events*. For example, the Women's uneven bars contest consists of only one event, whereas the junior women's all-around contest consists of all the junior women's events (uneven bars, floor exercise, balance beam, etc.). Figure 14.77 correctly shows the classes involved in scoring gymnasts, but makes it very difficult to coordinate *which* gymnast goes with *which* judge and *which* event.

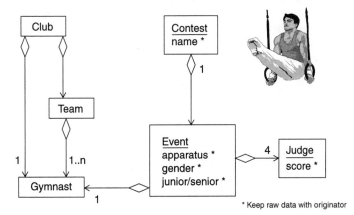

**FIGURE 14.77** Trial Data Access Example: Gymnastics

If we introduce a *Performance* class, however, which effectively aggregates these objects, then we can store them in their related form the instant each gymnast is scored after performing a routine. From the performance database, we can reconstruct whatever data we need such as meet scores and gymnast scores and ranking. The *Performance* class is shown in Figure 14.78.

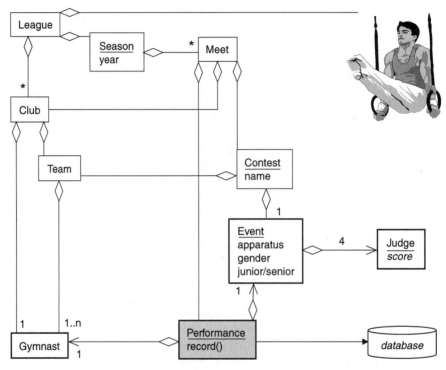

**FIGURE 14.78** Data Access Example: Gymnastics

This architecture coordinates the data in *Gymnast* and *Judge* by means of a *Performance* class. The latter obtains data from the *Gymnast* and *Judge* objects in order to record the particular gymnast performing in a particular event as scored by each particular judge. We thus call *record()* on *Performance* objects as soon as each performance has been judged. Note that we have not accounted for efficiency.

### 14.5.3.2 Choosing Distributed or Centralized Storage
There are two basic, alternative ways to store and retrieve data, as shown in Figure 14.79.

- **Distributed:** objects store themselves
- **Central:** use specialized storage classes
  - · to create instances
  - · to destroy instances
  - · to make efficient use of space
    - · e.g. garbage collection

**FIGURE 14.79** Data Management Architectures

*Distributed* storage architectures encapsulate storage methods with each object being saved (in whole or in part) as suggested by Figure 14.80.

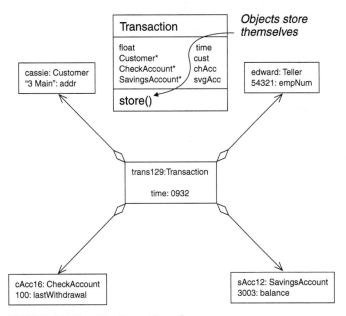

**FIGURE 14.80**  Distributed Data Storage

Distributed data storage has the advantage of packaging the storage mechanism with the class to which it pertains. Its disadvantage is that storage knowledge (e.g., concerning database management) is distributed throughout the architecture.

Figure 14.81 shows a typical *centralized* data storage architecture. An architecture may combine these data storage extremes. For example, the *store()* in *Customer* could reference a storage utility class, perhaps in the form *store(StorageUtility aStorageUtility)*.

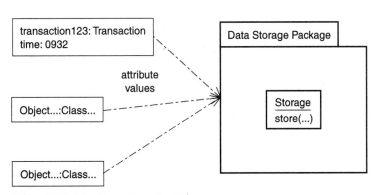

**FIGURE 14.81**  Centralized Data Storage

JDBC is the common Java facility for connecting to relational databases. After obtaining a *Connection* object to a database, one can write and read records and make queries against it. JDBC can be used for either the distributed form or the centralized form already described.

Recall from Section 14.4.4.4 that Enterprise Java Beans (EJB's) are server-side beans, used for tasks such as database access. An EJB could capture useful data such as a transaction. EJB's, like most components, exist in the context of a container. To handle the persistence of EJB's, we can use Bean-managed persistence (BMP) or container-managed persistence (CMP). CMP is a centralized form of data management, and is used where possible because the EJB container relieves the programmer of having to repeatedly implement data storage. BMP, on the other hand, requires that programmers code data storage procedures, and is generally used when CMP is not adequate. An example is storage in a data format unfamiliar to the container. BMP is a distributed data storage technique.

### 14.5.3.3 *Relational vs. Object-Oriented Databases*

When developing a system, we often use a relational database management system (RDBMS). In that case, object attributes are represented by the DBMS by rows and columns, and pointers to other objects must be mapped onto foreign keys. This assembly/disassembly process is time-consuming, error-prone and inflexible. In particular, changes in the object model cause disproportionate changes in the database schema. The manner of storing objects in an RDBMS is illustrated in Figure 14.82.

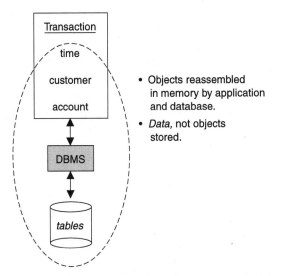

**FIGURE 14.82** Using Relational Databases with OO

It is straightforward to write a function *store(Customer c)* when the class *Customer* is as simple as:

```
class Customer {
    protected char[] name;
    protected int   age;
. . . };
```

It is straightforward to reconstruct *Customer* objects from records. It is much more of a challenge, however, to store objects as in

```
class Customer {
    Account account;
. . . };
```

This requires a reference to an *Account* database, which requires references to other tables, etc.

In OO databases, data are stored in the form of *objects*. They automatically preserve relationships among objects.  Neither assembly nor disassembly is required, and the database consists of faithful images of the state of associated objects. This is because they deal with objects *per se*, not columns and rows. The Java *writeObject()* method, for example, stores an object and all objects that it references; *readObject()* retrieves them. This is an Object-Oriented style of data storage.

OO databases are designed to keep track of unique object *identifiers* so that objects can be retrieved. For example, it is required to uniquely tag each *Transaction* object: one such object could be Joe Smith's withdrawal of $50 from his checking account; another could be Joe Smith's deposit of $1000 into his checking account, etc. This is illustrated in Figure 14.83.

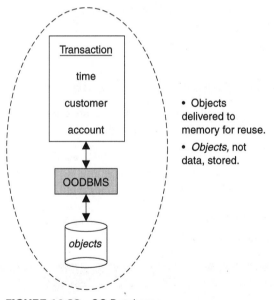

• Objects delivered to memory for reuse.

• *Objects,* not data, stored.

**FIGURE 14.83**   OO Databases

When we store a particular *Transaction* object, its references to other objects are stored as well. OO database systems also respect inheritance relationships. The syntax of OODBMS's tends to be natural to the OO style. Suppose that *db* is the internal name for a preexisting OO database of *Transaction* objects. Using the OODBMS *ObjectStore*$^{TM}$ for example, we define a persistent object *trans129*, belonging to *db* explicitly as in *Transaction trans129 = new (db) Transaction; trans129* can then be manipulated, stored and retrieved. Figure 14.84 illustrates the capture of relationships among objects.

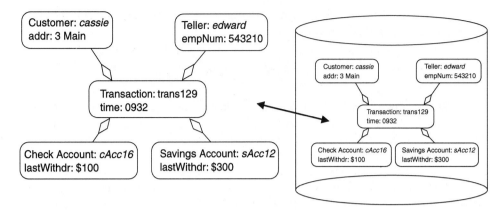

**FIGURE 14.84** OO Databases: *Relationships Maintained*

Figure 14.85 Sums up the points of this section.

- RDBMS based on a *data model*
  - · tables of rows & columns
- ODBMS based on a *programming technology* (the OO method)
  - · data model defined by the program

**FIGURE 14.85** Relational DBMS vs. OO DBMS

## 14.5.4 Putting the Finishing Touches on Class Models

In this section, we consider miscellaneous activities that are often required to complete the class model, as shown in Figure 14.86. Several of the ideas and techniques described are adapted from Coad and Yourdon [Co2].

- Replace ambiguous associations
- Expose all dependencies
- Split selected classes for improved design

**FIGURE 14.86** Completing the Design

**DESIGN GOAL AT WORK** *Reusability*

We reduce dependencies among classes to promote their reuse in other applications.

***14.5.4.1 Replacing Ambiguous Associations*** The concept of an undirected association in UML is vague because it can be interpreted in several ways. The author uses undirected associations as a kind of quick shorthand where required, meaning "these two classes are related in some way besides inheritance, and we will decide later about exactly how." The simple straight line of association can be easily drawn, but should be replaced, if possible, by the time detailed design is completed. In particular, many-to-many associations are problematical, and can often be eliminated, as described next.

Many-to-many relationships can be awkward to implement. These relationships can sometimes be simplified by introducing a third class, usually a mediator or "event remembered" (Coad and Yourdon [Co1]). The *Transaction* class in Section 14.5.3.1 above and the *Performance* class in Figure 14.78 are examples. As another example, consider a wedding gift registration system. Every *Store* (object) registers many *Couple* objects. Every couple registers with many stores. This many-to-many undirected association can be broken up by introducing a *Registration* class as shown in Figure 14.87.

**Wedding gift registration**

*may uncover a required class:* an "event-remembered" or mediator (*Registration* in this case).

**FIGURE 14.87** Examining Associations: *Many-to-Many*

The relationship with *Registration* is one-to-many for each existing class because each *Registration* object involves exactly one store and one couple. *Registration* is a mediator "event remembered." We applied the same technique to *WinHelp*, where there is a many-to-many correspondence between Windows[TM] problems and the procedures that solve them. We used the class *WinHelp* itself to break this many-to-many relationship.

When object models contain *self*-associations, a similar inspection tells whether an additional class should be introduced for clarification.

A business-to-business association, for example, could result from any number of relationships. One possibility is *JointVenture*. In other contexts, the association relationship could be *Merger*, etc. In effect, the new class captures the relationship. This is illustrated in Figure 14.88.

Business

*may uncover a required class:* frequently an "event-remembered"

| Business | 2...n | JointVenture |

| Business | 2...n | Merger |

**FIGURE 14.88** Examining Associations: *Class-to-Itself*

### 14.5.4.2 *Showing All Required Dependencies*

We investigate each chain of aggregations to make sure that they include all required possibilities: sometimes we need to introduce direct aggregations. For example, *supermarkets* consist of *shelves*, which consist grocery *items* for sale. This is reflected in Figure 14.89, which shows *Supermarket* aggregating *Shelf* and *Shelf* aggregating *Item*. However, some items are not placed on shelves, such as those stacked separately on the floor at the ends of aisles. It is thus necessary for *Supermarket* to aggregate *Item* directly as well. An additional aggregation like this was applied in the Gymnastics problem (Figure 14.78), where *Club* aggregated *Team* and *Team* aggregated *Gymnast*. Since not every gymnast in a club is part of a team at all times, *Club* aggregated *Gymnast* directly as well.

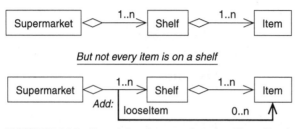

**FIGURE 14.89** Examining Aggregations for *Short Circuits*

### 14.5.4.3 *Splitting Classes*

Consider splitting potentially large classes into parts for better handling and for reuse. For example, the class *WinProcedure* is potentially too large, given that it must also support all "help" functionality. We therefore split it into at least two parts, one of which handles *WinProcedureHelp*: this also enables inheritance from a generic *Help* class. (Inheriting *all* of *WinProcedure* from *Help* would be awkward, since a *procedure* is not "a kind of" *help*.) The process of splitting classes promotes reusability since the parts are more useful in subsequent applications. This is shown in Figure 14.90.

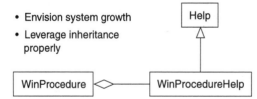

- Envision system growth
- Leverage inheritance properly

**FIGURE 14.90** Consider Splitting Classes

## 14.5.5 Completing the List of Functions

This book has mentioned several sources for the operations (methods) needed. Design patterns require methods: The four models described in Section 14.2 on page 481 are the source of many of the required methods. This is summarized in Figure 14.91.

Although we have already noted the functions that come from the sequence diagrams, several new classes will usually have been added at this point, so we revisit the sequence diagrams, obtaining their final, detailed form. This may require additional methods. The component model also requires methods, as shown in Figure 14.91. In addition,

**1.** Required by ...

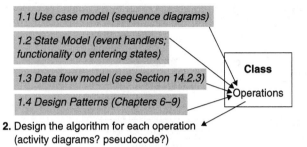

**2.** Design the algorithm for each operation
(activity diagrams? pseudocode?)

**FIGURE 14.91**  Completing Operations

we will have introduced design patterns, and they require that additional methods be added. Introducing the state model, for example, requires us to introduce additional functionality required when objects enter their various states.

As an example of the method selection process, we return to the *WinHelp* example of Section 13.1.1 on page 459. Let us follow steps 1.1, 1.2, and 1.3 to obtain operations for the *WinHelp* example.

1. *Use case model*: The operations required to execute the *WinHelp* use case outlined in Section 13.1.1 on page 459 are roughly:

   *<i> WinHelp* obtains the category of the problem from the user (*WinHelp.getProblem()* and *Problem.getCategory()*);

   *<ii> WinHelp* obtains from the user the visible parts of the problem (*Problem.getVisible()*);

   *<iii> WinHelp* recommends possible solutions (*WinHelp.match()* and *WinProcedure.describe()*), etc.

2. *State model:* For the sake of illustration, suppose that *WinHelp* allows users to begin to search for the solution to a problem, interrupt the search to modify the problem described, seek solutions to this modified problem, and then return to the original search if required. States of *WinProblem* objects such as *SeekingPrimaryProblemState* and *SeekingModifiedProblemState* would have to be used to keep track of the search status. We then ask what operations need to execute upon entry to these states: for example, the operation *savePrimaryParameters()* should execute upon entry to *SeekingModifiedProblemState*.

3. *Component model:* Figure 14.92 shows part of the *WinHelp* component model (data flow diagram): it describes the capability for the user to ask for information about problem "categories", and to obtain examples illustrating the meaning of these categories. Each functional part corresponds to an operation required by the application (e.g., *demoExample()*). These operations must then be added to appropriate classes, as shown in Figure 14.92.

After identifying the required operations, we must design their algorithms. One can perform this design using data flow diagrams, activity diagrams and/or pseudocode (see Section 1.2.3. on page 25). Doing so for the complex methods often produces better code, saves time, and provides good documentation.

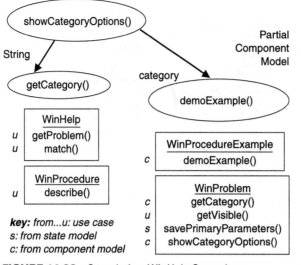

**FIGURE 14.92** Completing *WinHelp* Operations

# SUMMARY

Figure 14.93 summarizes the main points of this chapter.

1. Determine the architecture (modularization)
   · Consider standard ones
2. Use and contribute to framework
3. Apply design patterns
4. Design for data capture
5. Design control
6. Design interfaces
7. Exploit abstraction
8. Reduce many-to-many associations
9. Finalize design of associations
10. Obtain all functions from use case, state, and component models
11. Design individual functions

**FIGURE 14.93** Summary

# EXERCISES

**Exercise 14.1**     **Model Use**    Which of the four models described in Section 14.2 on page 481 would be appropriate for describing the architecture of the applications listed? Give a solid explanation of why each model is needed.

**Part 14.1.1** An application that manages online shopping.

**Part 14.1.2** A personal calendar application.

**Part 14.1.3** An application allowing the online payment of bills.

Criteria:
| | |
|---|---|
| ▦ Appropriateness | A = all appropriate models selected |
| ▦ No redundancy | A = all models selected entirely appropriate |

**Exercise 14.2**  **Online Shopping Architecture**  Here are proposed packages for an online shopping application.
*shopper, credit, goods*

**Part 14.2.1**  Is the cohesion within these packages high? Explain your reasoning.

**Part 14.2.2**  Is the coupling among these packages low? Explain your reasoning.

**Part 14.2.3**  Are these packages enough to encompass all the classes needed? Explain.

**Exercise 14.3**  **Personal Calendar Architecture**  Here are proposed packages for a personal calendar application.
*gui, calendar*

**Part 14.3.1**  Is the cohesion within these two packages high? Explain your reasoning.

**Part 14.3.2**  Is the coupling among these packages low? Explain your reasoning.

**Part 14.3.3**  What are the pro's and con's of this architecture. Explain.

**Part 14.3.4**  Suggest a better alternative to the architecture given if there is one. Explain your reasoning.

Criteria:
| | |
|---|---|
| ▦ Appropriateness | A = entirely appropriate response |
| ▦ Clarity | A = very clear explanation of your conclusions |

**Exercise 14.4**  **To Do List**  Which of the architecture(s) described by Garlan and Shaw [Ga1] would be appropriate for the following application? Explain your reasoning.

A "to do" program that enables to the user to:
- ▦ List tasks
- ▦ Precede task groups with conditions
- ▦ Allow tasks to be stated in loops.
- ▦ Allow task lists to invoke other task lists
- ▦ Generates detailed task lists from these

Here is an example.

*The input:*

```
7 am: "Clear dishwasher"
8 am: if(!holiday) "Take out trash"
3 pm: do 3 times
    {
       "File customer papers"
       "Record what's been filed"
       Do taskList11
       Wait half hour
    }
5 pm: "Go home"
```

*The output for June 11, 2002:*

```
7 am:    Clear dishwasher
8 am:    Take out trash
3 pm:    File customer papers
         Record what's been filed
         Check on status of Ajax Machine Co.
         Check that invoices sent to Big Bang Construction
         Check that the day's trades are being entered in database 892376
3:30 pm:File customer papers
         Record what's been filed
         Check on status of Ajax Machine Co.
         Check that invoices sent to Big Bang Construction
```

```
                    Check that the day's trades are being entered in database 892376
     4 pm:         File customer papers
                    Record what's been filed
                    Check on status of Ajax Machine Co.
                    Check that invoices sent to Big Bang Construction
                    Check that the day's trades are being entered in database 892376
     5 pm:         Go home
```

Criteria:
- Appropriateness
- Clarity

A = entirely appropriate response
A = very clear explanation of your conclusions

**Exercise 14.5**    **Stock Advice**    Which of the architecture(s) described by Garlan and Shaw [Ga1] would be appropriate for the following application? Explain your reasoning.

This application provides advice to stock customers. It uses a multiplatform design consisting of several websites. One website continually collects and stores prices and other information about stocks; a second site continually collects stock advice from analysts; a third recommends portfolio suggestions to users.

Criteria:
- Appropriateness
- Clarity

A = entirely appropriate response
A = very clear explanation of your conclusions

**Exercise 14.6**    **DNA**    A scientific instrument company builds equipment for analyzing molecular structures. The application you are to design analyzes the structure of DNA molecules, which are very large. What overall architecture would you use? Explain your reasoning.

Criteria:
- Appropriateness
- Clarity

A = entirely appropriate response
A = very clear explanation of your conclusions

**Exercise 14.7**    **Framework**    Your company produces software that controls a robot arm for manufacturing. Name four classes that would be appropriate members of your company's software framework. Explain your reasoning.

Criteria:
- Appropriateness
- Clarity

A = entirely appropriate classes
A = very clear explanation of your choices

**Exercise 14.8**    **EJB's**    The notes in this chapter point out favorable aspects of EJBs: But there are potential downsides to using EJBs besides the fact that Java is the only allowable source language. Name one and explain.

**Exercise 14.9**    **Control**    Say which of the following applications would best be designed with *external* vs. *internal* interface control. Explain.

**Part 14.9.1** A spreadsheet

**Part 14.9.2** A personal finance application like Quicken™ or Microsoft Money™

**Part 14.9.3** A wizard for installing an application

Criteria:
- Appropriateness
- Clarity

A = entirely appropriate response
A = very clear explanation of your conclusions

**Exercise 14.10**    **Replacing Associations**    Suppose that a class model shows a two-way association between classes *Student* and *MathClass*. How could you replace this with one or more one-way associations? Explain your reasoning.

**Exercise 14.11**    **Splitting Student Class**    Suppose that in the course of designing an application for managing student records, the class *Student* becomes unmanageably large. How can you split this class to make it more manageable? Assume that the classes *Course*, *University*, *Registration*, and *University* have already been created. Explain your reasoning.

# REFERENCES

[Be1] Bently, Jon L., *Writing Efficient Programs*, NJ: Prentice Hall, 1982.

[Br] http://wiley.com/college/bcs/0471322083/wave_i.html

[Co1] Coad, P., and E. Yourdon, *Object-Oriented Analysis*, NJ: Prentice Hall, 1990.

[Co2] Coad, P., and E. Yourdon, *Object-Oriented Design*, NJ: Prentice Hall, 1991.

[Co3] Coad, P., and J. Nicola, *Object-Oriented Programming*, NJ: Prentice Hall, 1993.

[Dt] http://ditec.um.es/cgi-bin/dl/corba-ccm-talk.pdf

[Ej] http://web2.java.sun.com/products/ejb/faq.html

[Ej1] http://web2.java.sun.com/products/ejb/faq.html

[En] Encyclopedia Britannica, www.britannica.com

[Fa] Fayad, M., *Building Application Frameworks: Object-Oriented Foundations of Framework Design*, NY: John Wiley & Sons, Inc., 1999.

[Fo] Fowler, M., *Refactoring: Improving the Design of Existing Code*, MA: Addison-Wesley Publishing Co., 1999.

[Ga] Gamma, E., R. Helm, R. Johnson, and J. Vlissides, *Design Patterns: Elements of Reusable Object-Oriented Software* (Addison-Wesley Professional Computing), MA: Addison-Wesley Publishing Co., 1999.

[Ga1] Garlan, D., and M. Shaw, *Software Architecture: Perspectives on an Emerging Discipline*, NJ: Prentice Hall, 1996.

[Hu] Humphrey, W. S., *A Discipline for Software Engineering* (SEI Series in Software Engineering), MA: Addison-Wesley Publishing, 1995.

[IE] IEEE Software Engineering Standards Collection, 1997 Edition, NJ: IEEE, 1997.

[Ja] Jacobson, I., *Object-Oriented Software Engineering: A Use Case Driven Approach* (Addison-Wesley Object Technology Series), MA: Addison-Wesley Publishing Co., 1994.

[Ja1] Jacobson, I., J. Rumbaugh, and G. Booch, *The Unified Software Development Process* (Addison-Wesley Object Technology Series), MA: Addison-Wesley Publishing Co., 1999.

[Mi1] http://msdn.microsoft.com/library/default.asp?url=/library/en-us/cpref/html/frlrfsystem.asp

[Mi2] http://msdn.Microsoft.com/library/default.asp

[Mi3] http://msdn.microsoft.com/library/default.asp?url=/library/en-us/cpguide/html/cpconinsidenetframework.asp

[Mi4] *Microsoft® C# Language Specifications*, Microsoft Corporation, Microsoft Press, 2001.

[Mi5] http://msdn.microsoft.com/library/default.asp tech overview/Overview of the Common Language Runtime

[Mi6] http://msdn.microsoft.com/library/default.asp C# specification

[O] O'Neil, J., *JavaBeans Programming From the Ground Up*, NY: McGraw-Hill, 1998.

[Om] The Object Management Group, www.omg.org

[Sh] Shlaer, S. and S. J. Mellor, *Object Lifecycles: Modeling the World in States*, NJ: Prentice Hall, 1991.

[St] http://stardeveloper.com:8080/articles/072001-1.shtml

[Su1] http://java.sun.com/j2se/1.3/docs/api/java/lang/package-summary.html

[Su2] http://java.sun.com/products/javabeans/software/

[Sz] Szyperski, C., *Component Software: Beyond Object-Oriented Programming*, MA: Addison-Wesley Publishing Co., 1998.

[Sz1] Szyperski, C., http://www.sdmagazine.com/columnists/szyperski/

# INDEX